BOLLINGEN SERIES XXX

PAPERS FROM THE ERANOS YEARBOOKS

Edited by Joseph Campbell

Selected and translated from the *Eranos-Jahrbücher*
edited by Olga Froebe-Kapteyn

VOLUME 2

The Mysteries

PAPERS FROM THE ERANOS YEARBOOKS

Julius Baum • C. G. Jung • C. Kerényi • Hans Leisegang
Paul Masson-Oursel • Fritz Meier • Jean de Menasce
Georges Nagel • Walter F. Otto • Max Pulver
Hugo Rahner • Paul Schmitt • Walter Wili

BOLLINGEN SERIES XXX · 2

PRINCETON UNIVERSITY PRESS

LCC 54-5647
ISBN 0-691-01823-5 (paperback edition)
ISBN 0-691-09734-8 (hardcover edition)

THIS IS THE SECOND VOLUME
OF PAPERS SELECTED FROM THE ERANOS YEARBOOKS.
THESE VOLUMES OF SELECTIONS CONSTITUTE NUMBER XXX
IN BOLLINGEN SERIES, SPONSORED BY BOLLINGEN FOUNDATION

These papers were originally published in French or German in
Eranos-Jahrbücher IV (1936), VII (1939), VIII (1940–41),
IX (1942), and XI (1944)
by Rhein-Verlag, Zurich, Switzerland

15   14   13   12   11   10   9   8   7   6   5

First PRINCETON/BOLLINGEN PAPERBACK printing, 1978
Fifth printing, 1990

Translated by

RALPH MANHEIM

except for the paper by C. G. Jung

which was translated by

R. F. C. HULL

NOTE OF ACKNOWLEDGMENT

Grateful acknowledgment is made to the following publishers for permission to quote as indicated: the Clarendon Press, Oxford, for passages from M. R. James, tr., *The Apocryphal New Testament;* Harvard University Press, for passages from volumes in the Loeb Classical Library (Aeschylus, Apollonius Rhodius, Clement of Alexandria, the Homeric Hymns, Julian the Apostate, Philo Judaeus, Pindar, and Virgil) and, together with Basil Blackwell, Oxford, for passages from Kathleen Freeman, *Ancilla to the Pre-Socratic Philosophers;* to Henry Holt, New York, and Aldor, London, for quotations from the Savill translation of Hesse's *Magister Ludi;* to the Modern Library, New York, and John Lane, London, for passages from Joyce's *Ulysses;* to Oxford University Press, London, for a passage from R. E. Hume, tr., *The Thirteen Principal Upanishads;* to Penguin Books, for quotation from the Graves translation of Apuleius' *The Golden Ass* and the de Selincourt translation of Herodotus; to the School of American Research, Santa Fe, for quotation from the Anderson and Dibble translation of Sahagùn; to the United Society for Christian Literature, London, for passages from E. A. Wallis Budge, *The Book of the Cave of Treasures;* to the Westminster Press, Philadelphia, and the Student Christian Movement Press of London for quotations from the Library of Christian Classics, Vol. I.

The advice and assistance of the following persons is gratefully acknowledged: Marie-Louise von Franz, Brutus Coste, Rev. Charles E. Diviney, Mircea Eliade, Laurens van der Post, N. Rambova, and Hedwig von Roques.

vi

CONTENTS

CONTENTS

LIST OF PLATES

For Hans Leisegang, "The Mystery of the Serpent"

following page 200

I. The alabaster "serpent bowl": interior
P: Courtesy of Dr. J. Hirsch.

II. The alabaster "serpent bowl": exterior details
P: Courtesy of Dr. J. Hirsch.

III. Phanes in the egg. Relief, Modena
Modena Museum. P: *Revue archéologique* (Paris), 3rd series, XL (1902), Pl. I, facing p. 432.

IV. Helios as Aeon, with the earth goddess. Mosaic, Sentinum
Facsimile in R. Engelmann, "Mosaik von Sentinum," *Archäologische Zeitung* (Berlin), XXXV (1877), Pl. III.

following page 232

V. Map of the world. Codex, Turin Library, XII century
From Konrad Miller, *Mappaemundi; die ältesten Weltkarten* (Stuttgart, 1895), Part II, Pl. 8.

VI. Tombstone of the Hecate Mysteries. Phrygia (?)
Formerly in the Istanbul Museum. From the *Bulletin de correspondance Hellénique* (Paris, 1896), Pl. XVI.

VII. Lamp with Gorgon's face. Etruscan, V century B.C.
Museum of Cortona. P: Alinari.

VIII. The Heavenly Liturgy. Eucharistic bowl, Mount Athos, *c.* XIII century
N. P. Kondakow, *Pamiatniki Khristianskago iskusstva na Afonie* (St. Petersburg, 1902), Pl. XXX.

following page 248

IX. The Pietroasa bowl. Gold, Romania
Alexander Odobesco, *Le Trésor de Pétrossa* (Paris, 1889–96), Vol. I, Pl. V.

IV*a*. The Heavenly Banquet. Catacomb of Santi Pietro e Marcellino, Rome
Facsimile in ibid., Pl. 157, 1.

IV*b*. Feast of the Dead. Tomb of Vincentius, Rome
Facsimile in ibid., Pl. 133, 1.

LIST OF TEXT FIGURES

For C. Kerényi, "The Mysteries of the Kabeiroi"

All from Paul Wolters and Gerda Bruns, eds., *Das Kabirenheiligtum bei Theben*, Vol. I (Berlin, 1940), Pls. 29, 30.

For Hans Leisegang, "The Mystery of the Serpent"

After a drawing in W. H. Roscher, "Pan als Allgott," *Festschrift für Johannes Overbeck* (Leipzig, 1893), p. 64.

After a photograph in *EJ 1939*, Pl. 6.

After an engraving from L. Lersch, ed., *Centralmuseum rheinländischer Inschriften* (Bonn), Vol. II (1840), 63, no. 90, in *EJ 1939*, Pl. 9.

EDITOR'S FOREWORD

In the Eranos meetings, which have been held near Ascona, in southern Switzerland, annually since 1933, under the direction of Olga Froebe-Kapteyn, scholars of differing points of view, but with the common purpose of allowing the truth to reveal itself, present their ideas and discuss informally the implications of their discoveries. The theme for the year, announced by Frau Froebe, usually represents an outgrowth of the leitmotivs of the earlier meetings. The topic for 1944 was "The Mysteries"; the invited speakers were historians, anthropologists, theologians, and philosophers. A radical contrast in points of view was evident in the contributions, yet equally evident was a common context of human aspiration and realization. Such a context—the "shared feast" (*eranos*) of the meeting—appears every year: expected, yet, in its precise elements, unexpected. Its development from meeting to meeting can be studied in the twenty-odd volumes of the *Eranos-Jahrbücher*, published by the Rhein-Verlag, Zurich.

The presentation in English of representative selections from the *Eranos-Jahrbücher* began in 1954 with the volume *Spirit and Nature*, which contains thirteen articles drawn from the yearbooks of the 1945 and 1946 meetings, with the addition of two from 1937. The present publication, the second of the English series, is based on the meeting of 1944, whose theme, "The Mysteries," had been anticipated—or rather, foretold—in a number of the papers presented in earlier meetings. To include several outstanding examples of these and, at the same time, to give the reader a sense of the many-threaded continuity of Eranos, the whole span of the yearbooks from 1933 to 1944 was reviewed for the selection here presented. Eight of the articles are from the meeting of 1944; but there have been added one from the meeting of 1936, two from 1939, one from 1941, and one from 1942.*

In a preface to the first volume of the present English series, Frau Froebe spoke of the primary aim of the lectures: "It has not been literary perfection

---

* The reader is referred to the Appendix for a list of the annual Eranos themes and of the papers contributed to each meeting.

nor necessarily a total treatment of the subject. Their value is *evocative*. In many cases, they carry us to the bounds of scholarly investigation and discovery, and point beyond. They touch upon unusual themes, facts, and analogies and in so doing evoke the great archetypal images."

The seventy or eighty scholars who have contributed to the Eranos meetings have been masters of their fields, capable not only of pointing beyond the limits of their own sciences but also of receiving thoughts from others and, above all, of responding to those evocative analogies that appear abundantly when the shared ideas are attentively compared. The audience in the lecture hall on the shores of Lake Maggiore participates also in this adventure; and it is hoped, now, that the reading audience for whom these selections in English are composed may likewise experience, through the suggestive juxtapositions, something of the illumination that is the "mystery" of Eranos.

I am very grateful to Frau Froebe for the sympathetic help that she has generously given to me in the task of selecting and reorganizing the materials of the *Eranos-Jahrbücher*. Also, to Mr. Ralph Manheim, translator of the majority of the articles, to Mr. R. F. C. Hull, translator of the article by C. G. Jung, and to the members of the Bollingen Series editorial staff, who have attended to all the work of editorial detail, I wish to express my sincere appreciation.

JOSEPH CAMPBELL

Colombo, Ceylon, spring, 1955

A Note on Eranos

An idea, a venture, or an enterprise that has for years been growing in a single mind, in a state of incubation, sometimes concretizes suddenly, and its inherent energy carries it over every hindrance and past all protest of the outer world. Such was the case of Eranos. The underlying pattern came to life, and it was my task to keep to the dim and fragmentary outline in the degree of my awareness.

In 1932, I set out to visit the first scholars who were to speak at the initiatory meeting of Eranos in 1933. I had the outline of the complete program with me. No one knew about it, no one had advised me, for at that time I was not in contact with a single scholar. It was a step into the unknown. I realize today that, when I rang the bell of Rudolf Otto's house, in Marburg, on a November evening in 1932, it was the signal, as in a theater, for the raising of the curtain on a stage I had for years been preparing.

On this stage, set in a garden on Lake Maggiore, all of the Eranos meetings have taken place. Against the background of ever-moving archetypal images, the actors (here speakers) move and play their parts. The scholarly form of their lectures becomes transparent, and the actual image or symbol of their respective themes seems to grip them. A scholar—or an artist or an actor—gripped by such an image becomes the channel for its energy. We see this happen here continually, and we feel the impact of the psychic force that flows through the speaker to us and in its turn grips *us*.

The conditions provided for this interchange between speaker and audience are one of the characteristics of Eranos. The result is a dynamic atmosphere in which the evocative qualities of the lectures have full play. The high intellectual and intuitional level is balanced by the kind of emotion awakened by a work of art. The relation of a speaker to his work is often that of an artist, and we are witness to the creative dialogue between the two.

The distinctly festive note of the meetings is in tune with the idea of a stage upon which a "play" of new significance is presented every year. Only one speaker at a time holds the stage, but during that period he is engaged in a fourfold relationship: first, to his own creation; second, to his fellow "actors" or speakers; third, to his audience; and, finally, to the invisible center around which the whole "play" revolves.

Eranos has developed around this creative center of its own, which is responsible for its continuity, for the archetypal and impersonal quality of the entire work, and for the integrating force that holds this nonorganized group together more securely than any outer organization.

An impersonal center is essential to any form of creative work. For creative power is not a personal attribute. The center alone can give duration and vital significance to anything men achieve.

We are greatly indebted to C. G. Jung, whose rediscovery of the archetypal world and its value for us today has from the beginning provided us with a background for the work done here in the last twenty-three years. Eranos is a cultural event; it should not be considered as a separate manifestation but as an integral part of the stream of events that expresses the culture of our times. In spite of the destruction we have passed through in two world wars, in spite of the isolating trend of all scientific research of the last hundred years, the tendency of the deeper urges within us is toward a universal humanism.

Eranos seems to be an instrument of the "sympathy" that unites and integrates all culture in our age of separation and disintegration. The development of consciousness leads to an increasing awareness of the archetypal reality in whose midst we live. This is the world that opens to deeply meditative and religious human beings, and in which all creative work is rooted. In the center all ways meet. And here the motto of Eranos may be quoted:

Krishna, speaking to Arjuna, in the *Bhagavad Gita*, says, "By whatever path a man seek me, even so do I welcome him, for the paths men take from every side are mine."

OLGA FROEBE-KAPTEYN

Ascona, March, 1955

xvi

THE MYSTERIES

Paul Masson-Oursel

1. The Indian Theories of Redemption in the Frame of the Religions of Salvation

Outside the Eranos circle, the nature of the underlying concept which gives these meetings their meaning is perhaps not fully realized. The wish to understand the Orient and an interest in psychology are uniquely combined in the personality and the work of Professor Jung. Each one of us, however, must seek to clarify what analytical psychology and the age-old experience of the Orient have in common.

As their common core we find a striving for liberation. A certain weakness must be transformed into an effective force, and this transformation must grow out of progressive insight. There is no doubt that Freud might have made this observation. But it remained for Jung to see that man can achieve liberation only by a molding of himself; Jung's Asiatic studies had shown him that, in Tantric India and Taoist China, man liberates the spirit by realizing it. Accordingly, it seems to me that our essential task in these meditations at Ascona must be to find means—every possible means—of realizing the spiritual. The investigation of mystical phenomena, whether by psychiatry or by the study of comparative religion, is perhaps the most important, but not the only basis for this endeavor. The study of artistic creation is also of great importance.

My present remarks deal with religious experience, with the genesis of that concept of salvation which awakened man's will for liberation. This event occurred at a definite moment in the Eurasian past, under conditions which varied with the environment and of which the historian today can gain no more than a bare intimation.

By religions of salvation we mean those religions which attempt to "save" some essential component of the human personality, as though it were threatened by catastrophe, as though a principle which must not die were

3

threatened with death. These religions rest on eschatological foundations. A certain state of things endangers the normal condition, the sound working of the principle in question. This gives rise to the problem of destiny. "Salvation," then, consists in restoring a normal condition, just as the physician strives to restore a sick man's health.

But we must be careful not to assume that this entity which is to be saved is a spiritual soul. Wherever it has appeared, the notion of the soul grew out of and did not precede the idea of salvation. We might add that the idea of salvation did not always lead to the idea of a soul. Anyone who turns his attention to matters of health will in all probability concern himself with the life of the body, but physical life consists of more or less subtle functions, and it is possible that the aspiration to a life after death is associated only with certain of them. Soul, or spiritual substance, on the other hand, is a metaphysical concept and does not belong to the world of religious strivings.

The most important religions of salvation are: the Osiris cults of Egypt; the Mazdaism of Zoroaster; the mysteries of Asia Minor, Syria, and Greece; the philosophical reflections of the Upanishads; Indian Jainism and Buddhism; Mithraism and Manichaeism; Christianity; and Islam. Diverse as these religious forms may be, they have in common highly significant traits to which attention would have been drawn long ago if the division of scientific labor and an awareness of their own limitations had not deterred specialists in the various historical cultures from making generalizations in this field.

I. All are techniques for achieving a favorable lot after death.

II. They stand in opposition to ritualistic cults that employ magic for earthly purposes and pursue no transcendent aims. All of them have a character of reform, which makes the cult more inward and less crassly egoistic.

III. Most of them were founded by a leader. Sometimes, older or rival religions, in order to impede the progress of the new cults, incarnated older gods, thus bringing the savior into harmony with the old religion; sometimes, conversely, saviors were elevated to the rank of gods.

IV. They are pessimistic in their judgments of natural life and everyday experience; on the other hand, they reveal a glowing optimism with regard to spiritual endeavors.

V. They build salvation on a transcendent insight that goes beyond reason: on mysteries, suprarational dogmas, revelations, intellectual intui-

4

tion outside the realm of discursive communication. Thus they prepare the way for the metaphysical systems as well as for the theories of knowledge.

This group of religions is of the utmost interest to psychology. Here we see consciousness growing, dispelling comfortable utilitarianism, and striving for a supernatural life. From the "unhappy" consciousness, to speak with Hegel, arises a beatific consciousness, a heroic clarity. The element of the irrational, attested by the need for revelation or by secret mystical initiation, is a clear indication that the saving clarity presupposes the night of the unconscious, and finds its climax in the blinding illumination of the supraconscious.

Of the greatest importance is India's contribution to the religions of redemption. Zoroaster's reform doctrine would seem to have made itself felt in India. There are historical and geographic reasons for supposing that it called forth the Jaina movement, the elder brother of Buddhism. The philosophical ideas of the Upanishads were a reaction against Brahman formalism; they point clearly to a desire for reform within the orthodox religion, doubtless inspired by the great successes of the sectarian, heretical, or non-Aryan apostles.

These are more than vague presumptions. The preachers of Jainism set themselves the task of saving the positive spiritual principles from shipwreck in the torrential stream of transmigration, and these principles have all the characteristics of the spiritual as conceived by the Iranians: they are of luminous nature and fiery essence, and man must strive to achieve them in their pure state, which has the radiance of honesty and truth. Here the release of the spiritual suffices to liberate it. And the later Sankhya philosophy held exactly the same view.

The first Buddhists did not have the same belief in the reality of the spirit. They even denied its substantial existence. But they dreaded the horrors of transmigration—not so much the necessity of dying as the need to be endlessly reborn under the curse of the accomplished deed, whether good or bad. They strove to release the individual from the eternal flux, to guide him to the "other shore," from which there is no return. What must man do to attain it? Renounce the self, negate all desires, allow himself to be extinguished, abstain from all effective action.

The oldest Upanishads (Brihadaranyaka and Chandogya) disclose a great secret: man can vanquish death and, rising up to the sun, be dissolved in the luminous substance from which a part of our self is descended; there he can find a definitive and beatific permanence, free from the danger of relapsing into the cycle of births. We have a soul, our life principle, but it is nature itself; of this we must be conscious. If we remain what we are, we shall be redeemed, for, if we achieve absolute knowledge, we shall be free in eternity.

This moving revelation gave to the heart of Asia the equivalent of what the Phrygian, Phoenician, and Egyptian mysteries, which were continued in the Orphic cults, gave to the Mediterranean world: a conception of destiny as precursor of a doctrine of being. The Punjab and Asia Minor constituted the outermost points of the Median or Persian Empire (which soon became Greek), the realm in which arose the Iranian religion of Mithras (a double of the Vedic Vritra and the Buddhist Maitreya) and later the doctrine of Mani, which spread to Europe as well as to the extreme Orient.

In India as in Greece, philosophy developed under the influence of the mysteries. The Upanishads do not contain the Platonic philosophy, as Schopenhauer and Deussen supposed, but they constitute a counterpart to it; they grew out of similar causes. The Greater Vehicle treated all the speculative problems connected with the doctrine of salvation, just as Alexandrian thought, based on the moral systems of Aristotle, Epicurus, and Zeno—the two last being the fathers of sects that correspond, again, to Indian sects—was the dogmatic climax and conclusion of Hellenism.

Even while sketching these vast parallels, we must take good care not to equate the solutions given on both sides. Both sides created the foundations of a common natural science, in the theory of the elements and in a pneumatic conception of life. But the philosophies were very different: the Occident built a theory of being seen from the standpoint of eternity, wherein knowledge contented itself with mirroring absolute reality; India, and all regions touched by Buddhism, devised a theory of the act, considered from temporal perspectives of unfathomable depth, comparable to those of Fichte, Hegel, and Novalis.

In western Asia and the Mediterranean basin the religions of salvation introduced rites of initiation which assured their adherents a place among those elected to immortality. The Indian religions of salvation knew no fear of death, but rather the fear of this life without end, this rebirth at every death. They strove either for nirvana or for eternity in the absolute, Brahmanirvanam. In birth they found a servitude from which they strove

6

to free themselves not by the practice of a cult but by the achievement of the perfect knowledge which—in the beginning at least—presupposes complete domination of the vital functions.

The first solution to this problem yielded a rather negative liberation. In Brahmanism, this solution was negation of the error, dissipation of the illusion that leads us to believe that an absolute existence corresponds to our relative life on earth. In the Buddhism of the Lesser Vehicle, it was renunciation of the nonknowledge from which selfish desires arise. The arhat liberates himself from a wretched delusion: nirvana consists in this liberation.

It was only the later Buddhism, beginning in our own era, the Buddhism of the Greater Vehicle, which sought salvation in a positive liberation, in a freedom which has to be created. From all the things that life offers us we have spun a net, a necessary course that chains and enslaves us. But we retain the possibility of undoing this Penelope's web, for we ourselves have woven it; once we have freed ourselves from the servitude into which our actions lead us, we find ourselves at the scene of our great task: possessing neither spirit nor soul, we must achieve a spiritual autonomy.

It is almost impossible to encompass the boldness of this venture. It consists in escaping from our nature by freeing ourselves from the act, though this act is what we are made of; in regaining our energies from captivity, and once more putting them to work without succumbing to egotism; it consists in strictly disciplining our vital functions and creative genius and so building worlds which do not obstruct the expansion of our self, but on the contrary enrich us with free creative force. If we succeed, we cease to be slaves and achieve full independence by fashioning it for ourselves.

It is an undertaking worthy of Jung's interest. It seems to him that those of his patients who seek their own *self* by making strange drawings, who search after new ideas in the contemplation of cloud forms or the strange shape of an ink blot, achieve an inward liberation very much in the manner of those Mahayanic or Tantric Tibetans who immerse themselves in the contemplation of mandalas. In this there is an element of illusion, for the true mandalas are as much dogmatic schemata as they are attempts at liberation. But it remains true that every striving for cure exacts creative initiative, for the impediment must, as Hegel says, be *surpassed;* we must make ourselves a new road of life, which no one else can show us, a road

7

which, as Nietzsche would have said, is situated beyond good and evil. The Buddhist without soul, who creates for himself a spiritual world, understands that freedom is not something *given* but a *task*.

2. The Doctrine of Grace in the Religious Thought of India

Our investigations and reflections thus far have shown us that the vast development of the religions of salvation that filled the last pre-Christian millennium and extended beyond it penetrated to India, but that India participated in this development in its own peculiar way: from salvation it made redemption; and it transformed redemption into a freedom that man must make for himself.

We shall now concern ourselves with a small sector of this immeasurable field. Since St. Augustine and Luther, Western men have asked themselves with trepidation whether salvation was accessible to men as such, or whether a gratuitous intervention by God was necessary. A number of German works on the religions of grace put certain Indian religions under this head. But neither in England nor in France have Indologists taken the view that there are Indian religions of grace, and the modern Hindus are not of this belief. Let us then inquire whether the Indian religions of salvation are religions of grace and, if it should transpire that the Indians knew a conception of grace, whether it is similar to the Occidental conception.

First we must establish that the ritual religions preceding the religions of salvation exclude any conception of grace. Here, it was believed that the rite could immediately and directly call forth the desired things or circumstances. To be sure, the gods were later given a spiritual interpretation, and there is no doubt that the prayer which replaces the rite contributes an element of uncertainty, for it now becomes possible that the recitation of a formula, the execution of prescribed movements, will no longer suffice to produce the desired result; it now becomes necessary to convince the god, to win him over as an indispensable intermediary. As for the gods of Brahmanism, who are almost all anthropomorphized rites, there is no danger that they will accept the rites and then refuse to hear the prayer; they can be guided by mechanical practice of the cult. They are subservient

8

if not to men in general, at least to the consecrated technicians, the Brahmans, and men cannot by any means be said to be at their mercy.

But the religious life of India prior to the religions of salvation included elements other than Brahmanism. The most characteristic and widespread of these is Yoga, which is doubtless older than the Aryan immigration. In its original form Yoga was scarcely compatible with the idea of grace. Here of course I am not speaking of the theistic Yoga of later epochs. The yogi, who is convinced that he can dominate himself and conquer the universe by his personal conduct, cannot count on the assistance of the gods; far from helping him, they might rather envy him for the power so greatly superior to theirs that he acquires by his unbending virtue, for it can become a menace to them, and they often attempt to shake his virtue.

Puja, a worship of living or dead Dravidic witches, or the cult of their images, to which fruit or garlands of flowers are offered, is a *do ut des* practice, aimed at conciliating and appeasing savage cannibal goddesses. This terrified obeisance to a principle of horror in no way resembles a hope of grace.

Let us now turn to the Indian religions of salvation. Do they or do they not know of grace? In India, strange to say, it was the great religious teachers and not the gods who first dealt out grace, in the sense that they brought men benefits to which they had not acquired any claim by the fulfillment of a rite. When the Jina or the Buddha or any of a thousand other heads of unknown sects showed their disciples the way, or preached it to the multitude, they were administering voluntary gifts. To live in a cosmic period in which a Buddha shows men how to achieve redemption is a special advantage. Is this accidental good fortune or deserved reward? Is it a blessing conferred by fate, by the Buddha, or by a god? We leave the question open.

But is the road which these masters teach imparted to them by revelation? This word has many meanings. The Vedas are looked upon as revealed; their truth was seen by those who had power to see, the rishis: but otherwise, they were not uttered or communicated by a god. Zoroaster, like Moses and Mohammed, invoked a message with which the merciful God had favored him. But the Jina Mahavira and the Buddha Shakyamuni found or understood the secret of universal suffering all by themselves; no one revealed it to them, and they contented themselves with passing it on. To share in the secret is a privilege, but it is a question here of an example to be emulated, and not of a revelation.

The mysteries of the Upanishads are closer to revelation because—at

9

least in the beginnings of this literature—they were surrounded by an impressive mystery. But even though it is transcendent, the understanding that apprehends them remains understanding. Nothing is more positive than a *yajna*, the Brahman sacrifice; and this understanding is simply an *adhiyana*. There is assuredly nothing more miraculous than that my own self, atman, should resemble the supreme Atman; but at the same time what can be simpler? Wise men, great and yet simple, have understood this without divine aid.

The divine revelation, a revelation flowing from grace (in a sense which we shall later define), appears only later. It occurs in the *Bhagavad-Gita*, but to how many errors it has given rise! Totally incompatible ideas are mingled in this text. In order to explain it meaningfully, we must study the whole Gita group before rendering judgment—for this text does not stand by itself—just as we must study a whole literary genre in order to determine the relation between form and content within it. Such an investigation yields the following conclusion: Lyrical and didactic at once, the *Gita* is a suitable form of expression for a god who reveals himself. Here we have not, as in the Upanishads, a mystery which a guru transmits and explains, but a world system and a body of ethics embodied in utterances by which the god manifests himself to his devotees. As a rule, a manifestation of the god appears, concretizing the spoken revelation. The mythological proto-type of this conception might, according to the Vedas, be *vishvarupa*, the infinite forms of Agni; the classical type, in the Hindu version, would be the infinite creative genius expressed by the dance of Shiva. To give only two examples, we may name the revelation of Krishna in the *Bhagavad-Gita* and that of Ishvara in the *Kurma-purana*, a Shivaite text. Although the revelation is here introduced as a great secret, it is actually the opposite of a mystery, for it is filled with the absolute, and our limited cognition is powerless to apprehend this absolute.

We might say then that in the heat of play, the gods—in any case the popular gods of Hinduism—wished to emulate if not outdo the great human leaders; unless we prefer to say that certain "human all too human" religions which hitherto, since they belonged to the uneducated classes, had known neither theology nor exegesis, decided to make leading personalities of their gods. Only the bhakti cults could have fathered the Gitas, for it was in these cults that the god or the human leader considered human participation in their essence as possible, for otherwise they would not have attempted to reveal their incomparable essence by manifesting themselves or communicating their doctrine. The conception of a "Sankhya-Gita" is a contra-diction in itself, akin to "son of a barren mother," for at least in its classical form the Sankhya demands an absolute, incommunicable transcendence, which can assume no natural form whatsoever.

Thus we come to the conclusion that among the Indian religions of salvation it was the bhakti religions which recognized a revelation flowing from grace, a godhead benevolently inclining toward the creature, as is the case in Krishnaism, Vaishnavism, and Shaivism. Piety is possible only when the god approaches the believer to guide him and protect him. The axis of religious life lies no longer in the karman—either in the Brahman sense of the rite or in the Buddhist sense of the accomplished act—but in the absolute; nothing exists, nothing happens, except in it. As St. Paul put it (Acts 17 : 287): *"In illo vivimus, movemur, et sumus."*

We must now seek to ascertain whether the conception of grace as con-tained in these religions is related to grace in the Occidental sense. Plato's *theia moira* is one source, the most obscure, of this "Occidental" grace. The other, more evident, is of Christian origin: the idea that it is impossible for man, with his tainted nature, with his soul in whose very substance original sin is inherent, to achieve salvation unless God comes to his help. In the Christian conception, pure spirituality is always supernatural, it can be achieved through love and grace, and all grace comes from the Holy Spirit. Now: this Spirit "bloweth where it listeth." Who can dare to lay the slightest claim to its coming? We can entreat it to lend us its grace, but we cannot hope to have deserved its aid. There is no spiritual life without the seed of God (*semen Dei*); the divine must impart itself and we must feel its presence (*pati divina*, in the Latin translation of Dionysius). When Miguel Asín Palacios finds theories of grace among the Moslems of Spain, in Ibn Arabi or Ibn Abbad de Ronda, he accounts for them on the basis of a "Chris-tianized Islam." More thorough and unbiased investigations will perhaps convince modern Catholics that there is a purely Indian theory of grace, which can be adduced in explanation of the Arabic and particularly of the Persian theories.

In India nature and non-nature are not antithetical, like the natural order and the order of grace in Leibniz or Malebranche. It is in every way a *pati divina* to arrive at that which transcends nature. For by asceticism we can dominate the vital forces and transcend the necessary course of the natural process. Since there is no original sin, there can be no manner of grace transcending nature. But piety is a form of religion which reckons with the aid of some god. Grace can be understood only in this way, as bhakti, or the possibility that the god will participate in the destiny of those who believe in him. And nothing is more normal and natural than this immanence of the absolute in the relative (nature operating as grace itself), if only the believer shuns the error of taking the relative for the absolute.

But bhakti does not exhaust the idea of grace. Prasada, a rather puzzling concept current in Krishnaism and Shaivism, expresses still other aspects of this idea. Its oldest meaning seems to have been "absence of movement," "repose" (*Maitri Up.*, VI, 20 and 34; *Bhag.-Gita*, II, 64 and 65; XVII, 16; XVIII, 37). But the meaning "radiance," "illumination," follows from *varnaprasada*, "brilliant color" (*Shvetashvatara Up.*, II, 13), *jnanaprasada*, "illumination by knowledge" (*Mundaka Up.*, III, 8), *prasannam jnanam*, "clear insight" (*Ishvara-Gita*, XI, 2). Different as these meanings may be, they all express the conviction that the appeasement of spiritual movement makes clear knowledge possible; for do the *cittavrittiniradha* of the *Yoga-Sutra* not call for the intuition of the absolute? According to the Sankhya metaphor, must nature not be tranquil as a quiet lake, in order that the purusha may be truly reflected in it?—But there are passages where the same word demands to be translated as "grace" in *Katha Up.*, II, 20; in *Shvet. Up.*, VI, 21: *devaprasada*, "divine grace"; in three texts of the *Bhag.-Gita* (XVIII, 56, 58, 62), where *matprasadat*, *tatprasadat* signify the salutary intervention of the godhead. In a fourth and later passage (ibid., 75: *Vyasaprasadac*) the term means the saving intervention of a man, though indeed of a miracle man: Vyasa. This meaning is common in the Shivaite *Gita* (V, 44; XI, 121, 138) where *prasadabhimukham*, epithet of Rudra and Mahadeva, means "inclined to benevolence" and *prasanna* means "benevolent" (I, 40; V, 7).

Apparently the word *prasada* took on the meaning of "grace" later than the two other meanings ("repose," "clarity"). These do not occur in the Shivaite *Gita* (except for the above-cited *prasannam jnanam* in XI, 2), but they do occur in the *Bhagavad-Gita*. On the other hand, the Shivaite document creates an interesting link between the gracious intervention of the god as the first step and man's participation in the divine, bhakti, as the consequence.

> bhavatprasadad amale parasmin parameshvare
> asmakam jayate bhaktis tvayy evavyabhicarini (v, 44).
> bhavatprasadad . . . jayata bhaktir (XI, 138).

We interpret this to mean that the god's benevolence permits the believer to partake in him. Expressed in European terms, this signifies the passage of grace (*gratia infusa*) from its divine source to its recipient, the creature.

It is known that the Bengalis, particularly Chaitanya, liked to interpret this participation as love, *prema;* the believer loves his god, because the god loves himself in man, but this development adds nothing new to the concept of *prasada.*

We are now in a position to examine the difference between the Indian and Western conceptions of grace. We have seen that the word which was later to signify grace of knowledge and grace of salvation first meant a definite human ascetic effort aimed at annulling the agitation of desire and thought. The appeasement and clarity which follow were looked upon as human accomplishments before they were besought as divine aids, just as the saviors were leading men before they were enrolled among the gods.

When the idea of divine grace took form, it differed from ours in being very much less arbitrary. In the bhaktas the self-willed asceticism of the wise man calls forth the Lord's assistance as certainly as the Brahman rite forces the hand of the devas in the right direction. And neither in god nor in man do the Indians juxtapose intellect and will; in this benevolence, *prasada*, there is neither capricious intervention nor supernatural miracle. No Hindu could have said *"credo quia absurdum,"* nor did a Hindu ever say that "the spirit bloweth where it listeth" or speak of a predestination of the elect. We Westerners are proud of having conceived rationalism, but we endow the human heart with more irrationality than do the Asiatics. Need I remind you that they hastened to transform the intervention of their leading men into a natural law, making the incarnations of their gods or Buddhas into avatars standing in a necessary relation to the cosmic periods?

I do not deny that the Middle Ages saw the rise of Hindu theistic systems whose problems recall the theism of Jewish, Christian, and Islamic scholasticism. In this period, but only in this period, two conceptions of grace arose: that of the young animal clinging to its mother, and that of the young animal seized and carried away by its mother. But these theories are of recent date and in part at least can be explained by Christian and Moslem influences. In so far as India remained true to its old ideals, it was far too much attached to immanent solutions to let its gods do violence to the natural order. If anyone, in Indian thinking, is entitled to this role, it can only be the ascetic.

13

Walter F. Otto

The Meaning of the Eleusinian Mysteries

In one brief lecture, it will be possible to cover only the barest essentials of the Eleusinian Mysteries. This ancient cult goes back to pre-Hellenic times; revived in the same period as the cult of Dionysus, it knew such a flowering that wherever Greeks lived its praises were sung; and a thousand years later, when Christianity put an end to the Mysteries of Eleusis, Greek life itself seemed to have sunk into the grave with them. This cult, which for centuries preserved so solemn a dignity that critique and irony scarcely dared to question it, will, more than any other—if we can raise even a little the veils of mystery surrounding it—throw light on the relation between pre-Hellenic man and the godhead.

We shall not concern ourselves with details for their own sake, but seek rather to answer two questions: What was the specific character of these mysteries? And what benefit did the believers who flocked to Eleusis from all parts of the Greek world expect from them?

The answer to the second question seems at first sight very simple. The so-called Homeric Hymn to Demeter, our oldest literary document pertaining to the Eleusinian Mysteries, tells that they were established by the goddess herself and that those who took part in them could look forward to a far better lot in the afterworld beyond the grave. "Blessed," it calls them; Pindar likewise calls them "blessed," and Sophocles "thrice blessed." These "beatitudes" run through all antiquity down to its tragic end. But this was not men's only reason for giving thanks to the Eleusinian goddess. Her unique favors included the promise of agricultural fertility, the ennoblement of human life, the cultural gifts which overcame the bestial in man. The goddess, said Isocrates at the beginning of the fourth century B.C., gave us two things when she came to Eleusis: first the fruit of the field, to which we owe our transition from an animal to a human life; and second the rites, participation in which makes us look with joyful hope upon the end of life and upon existence as a whole. And, he continues, the city of Athens (to which by then Eleusis had long been joined) communicated both of these to all others in the most magnanimous way, so that all partook in full measure of its religious and agricultural blessings. The same is attested by the most authoritative voices of later centuries. In an oration delivered in 59 B.C., Cicero, introducing a deputation from Athens, declared that it was this city in which "humanity," religion, and agriculture had originated, and from which these sublime gifts had been carried to all countries. We know that the presentation of an ear of wheat plays a central role in the mysteries. The first grain is said to have been sown and harvested on the plain of Rharus, in Eleusis. There was the threshing floor of Triptolemus, the old Eleusinian hero, to whom, as we see in many friezes, the goddesses themselves gave the first grain, bidding him to diffuse its blessing throughout the world. This agrarian element plays so large a part in the Eleusinian tradition that until recently scholars felt tempted to explain the whole Eleusinian mystery on this basis. And indeed, no interpretation can be taken seriously that does not seek to relate the mystery and the high hope it called forth to the miracle of growth. But the nature of this relation is a great question, and I do not believe that any of the answers so far given has been satisfactory.

Let us first consider the principal goddesses of the Eleusinian cult. They are, as everyone knows, Demeter and her daughter Kore, "the maiden," or Persephone. Here we can disregard the other Eleusinian deities, except for Pluto, king of the underworld, who abducted Persephone and made her his wife. Searching for her vanished daughter, Demeter came to Eleusis; there she found her, there she made her peace with the gods and gave to men the holy mysteries and agriculture. This is the narrative of the Homeric Hymn. Despite her Greek name, Demeter is indubitably descended from a pre-Hellenic culture, as we can see by many usages and conceptions connected with her religion, particularly her Arcadian cults. In Thelpusa, she was called Erinys, "the Angry One"; it was believed that, in the form of a mare, she was mounted by the stallion Poseidon, from which union she bore a daughter with a secret name and the accursed steed Areion;[1] and in Phigalia, there was a similar legend concerning Demeter Melaina, whom a wooden statue represented as a woman with the head of a horse, holding in one hand

1 Pausanias, 8, 25.

15

a dolphin, in the other a dove.[2] She was worshiped eminently as the giver of grain, but other fruits and blossoms were considered among her gifts and she was associated also with the growth of man, to whom after death she was a mother, receiving him in her womb, the womb of the earth. In Attica the dead were said to "belong to Demeter." It is easy to understand that women should have played an important part in the cult of this goddess. Persephone, who passes as her daughter, is identified as pre-Hellenic by her mere name, which also assigns her unmistakably to the realm of the dead, and Homer has indeed made her known to all as queen of the dead.

How did Demeter come by this daughter? What does the close bond between her and a daughter signify? For though every god has his father and mother, there is no other example of so close a relation between mother and daughter. Even Athene, who sprang forth from the head of Zeus, is not so much of a daughter to her father as Persephone to her mother. It seems likely she was regarded as a kind of duplication or continuation of Demeter. But the fervor of their love reminds us of those great nature goddesses who are linked with a beloved: Aphrodite with her Adonis, the Great Mother with her Attis, the Babylonian Ishtar with her Tammuz, the Egyptian Isis with her Osiris. All mourn the sudden death of their beloved; and since his death and resurrection are seen as a symbol of the death and reawakening of the earth's vegetation, the analogy to Demeter's adventure seems complete. But this comparison overlooks a difference which increases in importance the more we examine it. The *mater dolorosa* with whom Demeter has been compared mourns for her son; Aphrodite, Cybele, Ishtar, Isis, and others mourn for their beloved, their husband, their brother. But Demeter mourns for a daughter who resembles her and gives the impression of a double. The character of this relation is very different from that of the others. Despite apparent parallels, it is ultimately unique, requiring a very special explanation.

But the story of Persephone herself also represents a riddle. As she is playing in the meadow with other divine maidens, as she bends down in delight to pick the lovely narcissus, the god of the underworld bursts suddenly forth from the earth in his chariot. He seizes her and carries her down to the underworld. She becomes his wife, but subsequently he is compelled to release her for certain months of the year and send her back to the upper world. From time immemorial this story has been associated with vegeta-

2 Ibid., 8, 42.

16

tion, particularly with grain. At a relatively early date, when substances were designated in poetic diction by the names of the gods under whose protection they stood, ground wheat was called Kore and wine Dionysus.[3] But what death in nature can here be meant, and what does the marriage with the king of the dead signify? In recent times the old notion that Persephone was the seed wheat, which must die in the darkness of the earth in order to be resurrected as a seedling, has quite rightly been rejected. Ernst Haeckel expressed his indignation at the Apostle Paul for illustrating man's spiritual destiny with the remark that the seed must die before it could live. No tiller of the soil can ever have thought that he was planting seed in a grave where it must go through death. If any image was appropriate here, it was a sexual one, and many ancient peoples did indeed understand plowing and sowing in this light. Thus the myth of Persephone cannot be interpreted in this way, quite aside from the fact that her marriage with Pluto and her enduring rule over the dead would still remain unexplained. Recently, an extremely artificial explanation has been attempted. According to this version, Persephone was the threshed grain that was preserved in underground vessels, from which, in due season, the seed was taken. Since this underground supply of grain constituted the wealth of the house, it was quite understandable that Persephone should have been associated with Pluto, the god of the riches under the earth, and since he was at the same time the lord of the dead, she automatically became queen of the dead, particularly as the dead were buried in similar vessels beneath the earth; her resurrection, finally, was originally nothing other than the opening of the grain bins at the sowing season.[4] I do not believe that this explanation will find many friends.

Far more convincing is the notion that the rape of Persephone refers to the annual disappearance of vegetation, whether in the parching heat of summer or in the cold of winter. The mourning of other goddesses seems to have this significance. But here we encounter a strange circumstance which, surprisingly, has never been noted. And this leads us to the central point.

In the myths which we have compared with that of Persephone the earth loses its fertility when the god descends to the underworld. "Since Queen Ishtar went down to the underworld," says the Babylonian legend, "the bull no longer mounts the cow," etc. The goddess vanishes into the depths,

3 Eubulus and Antiphanes, in Athenaeus, III, p. 108 c, and X, p. 449 c.
4 Nilsson, after Cornford.

and fertility with her. There is a direct correspondence. But this is by no means the case in the Greek myth. Here, as the Homeric Hymn relates, Demeter wanders about for many days, seeking a trace of her vanished daughter. When finally she learns from Helios that Hades has taken her for his wife with the consent of Zeus, she is consumed with anger against the lord of Olympus. She no longer desires to live among the gods but decides to go among men. In the shape of an old woman, she comes to the palace of the king of Eleusis, where she is received with honor and offered food and drink. She remains silent and refuses all sustenance until Iambe succeeds in making her laugh with her jests. The spell is broken. The queen gives her a potion which Demeter, since her mourning prohibits wine, orders mixed of special ingredients—it is the very same as that later given to the initiates at Eleusis. Then the queen confides her youngest child to the old woman's care. The boy prospers miraculously in the hands of his divine nurse, who attempts to make him immortal, but her magic is undone by the anxious mother's curiosity. Demeter now gives herself to be recognized as a goddess and demands that a great altar and temple be built for her. No sooner is this done than she hides in her sanctuary, far from all gods, immersed in mourning for her lost daughter. Only then does she cause a terrible drought to descend on the land for a whole year. The human race would have perished, the gods would have been deprived of all offerings, if Zeus had not brought about a reconciliation based on the understanding that Persephone might spend a part of the year with her mother, but that she would remain forever the wife of Pluto. Thus the disappearance of the earth's fertility does not at all coincide with the disappearance of the goddess who supposedly personified the grain. In fact, it occurs considerably later, induced by the angry mother's vengeance. The same version prevails in the famous chorus of Euripides' *Helena* (1301ff.). Here Demeter, enraged at what has been done to her, withdraws into the mountain wastes and permits nothing to grow on earth, until at last the gods manage to appease her sorrow. In this chorus, Demeter is called the "mountain mother," that is to say, is equated with the "Great Mother," the "mother of the gods." A recently discovered Epidaurian hymn tells a similar tale concerning the "mother of the gods," except that the motif of the ravished daughter is lacking.[5] Here the "mother of the gods" dwells in the mountain solitudes and refuses to

---

5 Paul Maas, "Epidaurische Hymnen," *Königsberger Gelehrte Gesellschaft, Geisteswissen-schaftliche Klasse, Schriften* (Berlin), IX (1933), 134ff.

return to the gods unless she is given a share of the whole world, half of the heavens, half of the earth, and a third of the sea. Her demand is granted, for in the end she is called "Great Mistress Mother of Olympus." If Demeter, as we have seen, is equated with her, this is no arbitrary notion. If nothing else, the ancient image of the horse-headed Demeter Erinys in Phigalia, holding in her hands the dolphin and the dove, discloses a goddess of cosmic proportions. In Hesiod's *Theogony*, moreover, the same is said of Hecate, who seems related to Persephone by the name of her father, Perses, and who in the Eleusinian myth and cult is closely associated with Demeter (cf. the Hymn): she too has a share in heaven, earth, and sea.

Thus we recognize a primeval myth of the earth mother, or mother of the gods, in which, angry, she demands her rights. In Arcadian Thelpusa she is called Erinys, "the Angry One," sharing this name with the terrible goddesses of malediction and vengeance. Here her anger is directed primarily toward Poseidon, who has ventured too close to her.[6] Another motive for her anger is the rape of her daughter Persephone, and here as elsewhere, the gods must make a great concession to her. Kore may now spend a part of the year with her mother above the earth, but she must return regularly below and she remains forever the queen of the dead. In this she differs from all those gods who seem to symbolize the flowering and fading of nature. Clearly, her journey to the underworld cannot have reference to the grain, since growth does not cease as a result of her disappearance; rather, it is an act of vengeance on the part of the offended mother. And even more cogent proof is to be found in another circumstance, to which we shall now turn our attention.

According to the original myth, the grieving Demeter may have withered trees, grass, and flowers—but not the grain, for before the disappearance of Persephone there was no grain. The form of the myth preserved in the Hymn, which minimizes the agrarian element, has quite obscured the context in this crucial point. The most important literary and pictorial versions tell us plainly that seed and harvest were given to men only after Persephone's descent into the underworld. Accordingly, all those who regard Persephone as a symbol of the grain start from a totally false assumption. Persephone is not the grain, and she cannot be likened to the gods of dying and renascent nature. If she had any such meaning, how could she be queen of the underworld? The myth shows her picking flowers with other divine

6 Pausanias, 8, 25.

maidens on the Nysaean meadows—the Prince of the Dead seizes her and carries her off to the depths, where in future she will share his rule over the shades. What else is this but an image of the ancient and widespread belief that the divine being who rules over the dead formerly lived on earth and then vanished one day to a mysterious and remote realm, over which this being has reigned ever since?

But from the point of view of agrarian religion, we must note that this sorrowful descent of the virginal Persephone *precedes* the introduction of grain raising. Only since Persephone has been wedded to Pluto, only since she has been Queen of the Dead, has there been harvesting and sowing. Death is prerequisite to the growth of the grain.

We have already indicated that Demeter herself is not alien to the dark realm. This connection is particularly clear in the cult and myth of Demeter Chthonia in Hermione.[7] This is also shown by the epithets given to Demeter in Arcadia: Erinys, "the Angry One," and Melaina, "the Black." And it should be recalled that, according to Spartan law, mourning for the dead ends on the twelfth day with a sacrifice to Demeter. But the realm of the dead comes far closer to us in the figure of her daughter Persephone. Here we find a powerful intuition that seems extremely strange to modern thinking, while to early peoples it was as natural as if existence itself had spoken to them. And among many so-called primitive peoples, it still forms the basis of important usages and myths. The substance of this intuition is that generation and fertility, and particularly the growth of grain, are indissolubly bound up with death. Without death, there would be no procreation. The inevitability of death is not a destiny decreed by some hostile power. In birth itself, in the very act of procreation, death is at work. It is at the base of all new life. In the Bible, procreation, birth, and agriculture as well occur outside of paradise and appear only after death has been decreed for man. Certain primitive peoples of today still preserve a tradition—which is symbolically enacted at regular festivals—that a mythical woman had to die in order that the grain might spring from her dead limbs; and that only by initiation into her death can man become potent and life be renewed.[8]

This then is the core of the myth of Persephone, to which the Eleusinian Mysteries attach. Man receives the fertility which is indispensable to him

---

7 Pausanias, 2, 35, 4ff. and elsewhere.
8 Cf. A. E. Jensen and H. Niggemeyer, eds., *Hainuwele: Volkserzählungen von der Molukken-Insel Ceram* (Frankfort on the Main, 1939).

from the hand of death. He must appeal to the Queen of the Dead. And this he can do; for here in Eleusis her divine mother mourned for her, here she returned to her mother, and here the goddesses created agriculture. But they did more. They provided also for the destiny of man himself: Demeter gave them a rite and a vision through which they might gain certainty that a happy lot awaited them after their death. How Demeter takes man under her protection after his birth is shown in the story, related in the Homeric Hymn, of the Eleusinian prince who throve so prodigiously under her tutelage; her favor to man is evinced by her epithet "Kourotrophos" and many other circumstances which we need not mention here. But her daughter went down into the realm of the dead and there became queen. It is she who reigns there below. Small wonder that these goddesses should have promised superabundant grace in this world and the next to those whom they received into their mysteries!

But what was enacted in these mysteries, what befell the initiates?

"Eleusis is a shrine common to the whole earth," said Aristides in his discourse on Eleusis, in the second century A.D., "and of all the divine things that exist among men, it is both the most terrible and the most luminous. At what place in the world have more miraculous tidings been sung, where have the dromena called forth greater emotion, where has there been a greater rivalry between seeing and hearing . . . ?" And he speaks of the "ineffable visions" which, as he says, "many generations of fortunate men and women" have been privileged to behold. We have many such utterances. We must therefore take care not to belittle these mysteries, as many tend to do, by reducing them to the level of agricultural rituals, offering only a metaphoric consolation. But we must also take care not to resurrect the sad ruins of the shattered mystery cult in the image of our own religious life and lapse into the tone of certain edifying but absurd modern interpretations.

We have by far the most information concerning what interests us least: the rituals of purification and initiation preceding the supreme and crucial act. There are ample pictorial representations of this ritual, which cannot have formed part of the sacrosanct secret tradition. The preparatory acts of purification need not concern us here. And if we go into some detail about the ritual of initiation, which is known to us through the famous passage in Clement of Alexandria, it is solely because some recent writers have regarded it as a key to the authentic meaning and content of the mysteries. In this passage the mystes is quoted as testifying to the acts which he had performed: "I have fasted, I have drunk the potion, I have taken [something] from the chest, and after acting, laid [it] in the basket, then taken [it] out of the basket and [put it] into the chest." The first two points are perfectly clear. The mystes, like Demeter herself, has fasted and drunk the sacred potion, the ingredients of which are listed in the Homeric Hymn. The mystes makes himself like the goddess. This is obvious and throws no little light on the initiation into the mysteries. But the following! How many men have racked their brains over the meaning of these words! What fantastic hypotheses have been devised to explain them! What was taken from the chest we are not told, nor do we learn the nature of the activity to which the word "ἐργασάμενος" refers. The ethnologist Felix Speiser [9] has recalled the rites of primitive peoples, in which the novice, by way of initiation into farm labor, must ritually perform its essential actions. He then develops the theory that what the Eleusinian chest contained was seed wheat; the mystes tells us that he took seed from the chest and sowed it in the field. This explanation is at least more compatible with the meaning of the word than the others. However, it can be neither confirmed nor confuted; it merely shows that we know nothing. An older explanation met for a time with great approval; indeed, it seemed so convincing that writers began to take it for granted, soon forgetting that it represented not a tradition but a very daring hypothesis. The context in which Clement cites the ritual formula seemed to imply that the "action" to which the mystes refers was of an obscene character. This, to be sure, was an error in interpretation,[10] but it made it possible to associate with the Eleusinian Mysteries also a notion familiar from other contexts, the notion of mystical rebirth as a child of the godhead. Albrecht Dieterich presumed that the object taken from the chest and in some way manipulated by the mystes was a phallus. This, however, met with the objection that Demeter was after all a female deity. Alfred Körte was therefore much applauded when he announced that it must be a female sexual symbol. Now everything seemed as clear as day. By touching the "womb," as the sexual symbol was called, the mystes was reborn; and since such an act must after all have constituted the climax of the mysteries, Ludwig Noack went so far as to assume that the hierophant

9 "Die eleusinischen Mysterien als primitive Initiation," *Zeitschrift für Ethnologie* (Berlin), LX (1928), 369.
10 Cf. Ludwig Deubner, *Attische Feste* (Berlin, 1932), p. 81.

displayed this "womb" to the congregation in a blaze of light and that, beholding it, the initiates could no longer doubt their beatific lot as children of the goddess. It is difficult to report such notions without a smile. In recent years it has been soundly argued that the touching of the "womb" by the mystes, a performance which some writers have described in the crudest colors, would point rather to a marriage with the goddess than to a rebirth out of the goddess. But this "womb" is an invention, based on no evidence whatsoever. On closer examination, the traditions invoked in favor of this hypothesis fail to support it. The whole theory of rebirth in the Eleusinian Mysteries, so often and solemnly repeated, is utterly without foundation. And what is more: if it did bear the slightest semblance of truth, it would raise a great difficulty. For then the ritual to which the obscure words of Clement's formula refer would embody the highest goal of the mysteries— namely, rebirth. But if there is any point upon which all witnesses agree, it is that the climax of the Eleusinian Mysteries was not a ritual, or anything which the mystes did or physically experienced, but a *vision*.

The supreme rite is called *epopteia*. All the beatitudes refer to it and to it alone. "Happy is he who has seen it!" says the Homeric Hymn, directly relating the vision to the assurance of a favored lot in the other world. As all witnesses agree, everything was a preparation for this vision.

What can it have been, the mere display of which, even accompanied by solemn words, had power to create so deep an impression? The state of mind of the mystai beholding it has often been described. For a long while hope alternated with fear and dread, until at length the most blissful certainty flooded their hearts. The experiences of that sacred night, from whose darkness suddenly the most brilliant light burst forth, have often been evoked as a metaphor for the terrifying darkness through which the beginner in philosophy must make his way before the night of uncertainty vanishes and the sun of truth shines upon him. In his treatise *On the Soul*, Plutarch compares death and its terrors, which are suddenly transformed into the beatitude of the soul freed from suffering, with the emotion and transfiguration of the mystai who, once they have beheld the sublime vision, no longer doubt that they alone are blessed, while the others, those who have not been initiated, are damned. What can they have seen?

This we shall never know. But we can form an idea of the kind of thing that was revealed to them; and this is more important than concrete details, which would themselves require an interpretation.

No drama can have produced such an effect unless the audience had the certainty that it was no mere play, but a real event. And the truth, disclosed to the mystai by images, signs, or words, must have been something absolutely new, astonishing, inaccessible to rational cognition. This is almost self-evident. And yet it has often been forgotten. For scarcely any of the hypotheses so far conceived take it into account.

An episode in the myth of Herakles makes it clear that the certainty attained in Eleusis had reference, among other things, to man's destiny in the other world. Before descending into the underworld in search of Cerberus, Herakles has himself initiated in Eleusis.[11] In Euripides,[12] he even says, after vanquishing the hound of hell and returning from Hades: "I succeeded because I had seen the sacred actions in Eleusis." He had good fortune in the underworld. Here again, the vision is designated as the decisive experience. During the sacrosanct action the mystes is passive; he receives no teachings, but is put into a state which is not subject to natural explanation. Aristotle[13] says expressly that the mystai were not meant to learn anything, but to suffer an experience and to be moved.

Now we have a relatively trustworthy report concerning certain of the things that met the eye. The Roman bishop Hippolytus tells us that the climax of the Eleusinian Mysteries consisted in the display of an ear of wheat. We have no reason to doubt this statement; it fits in perfectly with the myth of the origin of agriculture, which is inseparable from the Eleusinian Mysteries. The ear of grain was the gift of Demeter, and from Eleusis it was transmitted, along with the principles of agriculture and the precepts of human culture, to the rest of mankind. But what does this display signify, and what effect can it have produced? "The immense life-giving power of the earth mother," we are told, "was impressed immediately upon the souls of the mystai"; "it presumably was thought to guarantee the expectation of a new life under the earth, acquired in the sacrament of divine filiation" (Körte). But what new certainty could be conferred by a sight which was as familiar to everyone as an ear of grain? And moreover, "Nature's inexhaustible generative power," symbolized, according to Noack, by the ear of wheat, did not inspire ancient man to confidence in his own fate, but rather to melancholy and resignation. Throughout ancient poetry we find the lament that the sun rises and sets, that the flowers die and reblossom, but not man. It was the Christians who first looked upon the death and

---

11 Apollodorus, 2, 122.   12 *Madness of Heracles*, 613.   13 Fr. 15.

regeneration of nature as a consolation for man.[14] And if, finally, we bear in mind that the mystery of rebirth is a modern invention, this explanation collapses entirely. Several writers have rejected it in recent years. But what remains then? Martin P. Nilsson, the Swedish historian of religion, comes to the conclusion: "The sacred ear of grain, harbinger of the future harvest, gave the epoptes the certainty of recurrence, of indestructibility not only in the vegetable kingdom, but also in the world of men"; the certainty, that is, that though man must die he will survive in his progeny. Truly a precious revelation, that communicates with such sacrosanct solemnity what every noninitiate had known since time immemorial. Such an explanation does not cast light on the mysterious, but merely negates the mystery.

Ludwig Deubner suspected that we are dealing not with any simple natural act, but with a miracle.[15] Hippolytus tells us not only that an ear was displayed but that it was cut, that it had previously been harvested "in silence" and then was shown. Both context and grammar require us to understand Hippolytus' words in this sense. And we must indeed conclude that a mysterious act, a kind of magic, was performed. Deubner believes that a magic formula (ἷε κΰε) was uttered: "And behold in this season when no grain grows"—for it is autumn—"an ear of grain has grown." He has in mind a pious fraud: a single ear of wheat has been left standing in the plain of Rharus and is now mowed to be displayed to the faithful. This idea is certainly unacceptable. But there can be no doubt of the miraculous nature of the event. The ear of wheat growing and maturing with a supernatural suddenness is just as much a part of the mysteries of Demeter as the vine growing in a few hours is part of the revels of Dionysus. And the veneration of the Mysteries by such men as Sophocles and Euripides is hardly compatible with the easy notion of a fraud practiced by the priests. We find the very same plant miracles in the nature festivals of primitive peoples. The ear of wheat suddenly grown, silently harvested and displayed to the mystai is then really a revelation and pledge of the goddess, who first gave this fruit to mankind through the Eleusinians. More than that: it is an epiphany of Persephone herself, her mythical *first* recurrence in the shape of the grain, after her descent to the realm of the dead. We need not ask what thoughts and hopes the mystes associated with an epiphany of this sort. It transported him into the realm of miracles, into the presence

14 See for example, Minucius Felix, 34, 11.   15 *Attische Feste*, p. 86.

of the great goddesses themselves in the moment when they bestowed the ear of grain upon men. And here we have the meaning of the display; this alone can account for the beatific certainty conferred on the mystes by what he saw.

The central motif of the mystery vision was doubtless Demeter's grief over the rape of her daughter and the transformation of her laments into rejoicing when Persephone reappeared. Isocrates suggests this unmistakably, though with the necessary reticence, when he speaks of the important services rendered Demeter by the Eleusinians when she came to them in search of her daughter—services concerning which "one must keep silent in the presence of the profane."[16]

We readily believe Clement of Alexandria when he assures us that Demeter and Kore had become the characters in a mystical drama, solemnizing by torchlight the wanderings of Demeter, the rape of Persephone, and the grief of the goddesses. There are still other witnesses who confirm this. We need not dwell on them, but shall cite only Lactantius, because he compares the Egyptian representations of the lament of Isis for her lost Osiris with the mysteries of Demeter and declares explicitly that Persephone was sought at night with torches and was found again in the end amid rejoicing and a blaze of light.[17] What particulars of the myth—the rape, the quest, the mourning, the reconciliation with the gods, the reunion of the goddesses, the gift of agriculture, which various witnesses associate with the mysteries—were really enacted in this sacred night, can no longer be determined with certainty. But this is of secondary importance.

There has been no end of speculation regarding the manner in which such events may have been represented. Scholars have been puzzled no little by the fact that the Telesterion's forest of pillars must have made it difficult if not impossible for the mystai sitting along the walls to follow a dramatic action. Actually we must put aside the whole idea of a drama. The proceedings were assuredly of the greatest simplicity. An indication of this is that the Eleusinian account books[18] do not, among their many items, include a single entry which could possibly refer to the production of any sort of stage play. If we can determine the true nature of what took place here, the questions of outward form will answer themselves. For lack of reliable witnesses, we shall not inquire into the part played by mimes, choruses,

16 *Panegyricus*, 28.   17 *Epitome Institutionum Divinarum*, 23.
18 Cf. L. R. Farnell, *The Cults of the Greek States* (Oxford, 1896–1909), Vol. III, p. 182.

dances, etc., or seek technical explanations for the sudden change from awesome darkness to dazzling light. We shall be quite content if we can gain some little knowledge of the general nature of what was shown and account in some measure for the profound emotion it called forth.

Let us turn to the central point. We owe our most important record of the sacred night to Apollodorus of Athens; the person of its author raises it above all suspicion. In the moment when Kore was called, he reports, the hierophant struck the so-called $\dot{\eta}\chi\epsilon\hat{\iota}o\nu$, a kind of bronze gong.[19] The context leaves no doubt that the kingdom of the dead had burst open. For immediately afterward we are told that a similar gong was struck at the death of the Spartan kings. This suggests age-old rituals which have been preserved in Eleusis and in Sparta as well. The striking of the gong recalls Oriental and particularly Chinese funeral rites.

Persephone was summoned from the depths in other Greek cults. In Megara visitors were shown a rock to which Demeter was said to have summoned up her ravished daughter, and according to Pausanias,[20] the women of Megara still performed a corresponding rite. Dionysus was also evoked at his festival. "Come, lord Dionysus . . .!" called the sixteen women of Elis. And of course he came. And in Eleusis Kore came too, in answer to the call. She rose from the dead. She appeared. This is proved, if proof is still needed, by a newly found papyrus text, in which Herakles declares that he has no need to be initiated, because he himself, in his descent to the underworld, has seen everything that the Mysteries have to offer. He speaks of the sacred night and says finally: "I have seen Kore."[21] The queen of the underworld is present. And Demeter, of course, as well. Demeter with her grief, her lament, her search and rediscovery. What other gods and spirits were there we do not know. Concerning the chief Greek shrine of Isis (that goddess who is so close to Demeter that Foucart felt obliged to derive the Eleusinian cult from Egyptian sources), Pausanias [22] tells us that once when the festival was at its climax, a frivolous intruder entered the temple and found it "all full of spirits (or gods)." And as he told his story, he fell dead.

Various other things are related more or less clearly about the Mysteries,

19 Scholiast on Theocritus, 2, 36 (Theocritus, Bion, Moschus, ed. Theophilus Kiessling, London, 1826, Vol. II, p. 41).
20 In I, 43, 2.
21 *Papiri della Reale Università di Milano*, Vol. I, ed. A. Vogliano (Milan, 1937), p. 177.
22 In X, 32, 17.

and it would be tempting to examine these reports, first, of course, as to their credibility. Asterius tells us, for example, that the hierophant went down into a subterranean chamber, where he wedded the priestess of Demeter. Clement also writes that the hierophant performed a marital act, and Tertullian speaks explicitly of an act of violence against the priestess of Demeter, in repetition of what was done to the goddess. This cohabitation can only refer to the rape of Demeter by Zeus, which is mentioned by Clement himself and in a gloss to Plato. It seems startling, however, that Zeus should suddenly enter into the Eleusinian myth, and that the mother's mourning for her ravished daughter should be disturbed by a forced union with the god. But, little as we may understand it, this does belong to the myth of Demeter. At Thelpusa in Arcadia it was related that while she was searching for her daughter, Poseidon followed her and possessed her by force and trickery; this angered her, and that is why the Arcadians called her Erinys, "the Angry One";[23] the same story is told of the "Black" Demeter in Phigalia.[24] And now Clement, in a passage on Eleusis,[25] speaks of Demeter's rage after being embraced by Zeus. According to the Arcadian myth, a divine child resulted from this rape. Hippolytus[26] tells us that the hierophant solemnly announced the birth of a ἱερὸς κοῦρος, and we might be tempted to connect this with the divine rape, as many have done. But the notion that the newborn child really represented the "reborn" mystes—see Dieterich, Körte, and Noack—is absolutely arbitrary and fantastic. In an agricultural cult there is nothing unusual about the enactment of a divine marriage. In the sun dances of American Plains Indians such an act forms an intrinsic part of the cult festival and a detailed account of this rite[27] is instructive in more than one respect. But it must be admitted that this aspect of the Mysteries raises too many imponderables; we prefer to drop the whole point. Whatever may have taken place, it assuredly did not (despite Clement's assertions) form a part of the vision. And, as we have said, it is to the vision that all the beatitudes refer. Asterius does indeed remark in very general terms that the whole congregation expected its salvation from what took place in the subterranean chamber, but to this we can attach no great significance.

We must go into all these secondary matters in order to understand the

23 Pausanias, 8, 25.   24 8, 42.   25 *Protrepticus*, II, 15–16.   26 5, 8.
27 George A. Dorsey, *The Arapaho Sun Dance* (Field Columbian Museum, 75; Anthropological Series, Vol. IV; Chicago, 1903).

meaning and effect of the supreme rite. The gods are called, the gods are present. And what gods! When the modern scholar comes to this point, he usually thinks no farther. He easily explains the amazement of the enraptured mystai on the basis of delusion and priestly artifice. But anyone who has ever witnessed a great Oriental cult rite, as for example the Chinese evocation of Confucius, knows that in this sphere our rational concepts are not adequate. The simplest settings and actions here produce an overpowering effect on all present. At the crucial moment, when the sublime spirit that has been summoned prepares to appear, when the great drum begins to beat, first slowly and solemnly, then more and more rapidly, and finally in a breath-taking rhythm—even the most enlightened observer no longer doubts the real presence of the supernatural. But here in Eleusis there was more. The privileged initiates stood in an essential relation to the event they were to witness. They had been brought closer to the goddess by the preceding ritual, the fasting, the drinking of the potion, and so on; a bond had been forged between her and them. They had been taken into the myth, as it were, and in this stupendous moment the myth became reality.

What, then, is myth?—An old story, lived by the ancestors and handed down to the descendants. But the past is only one aspect of it. The true myth is inseparably bound up with the cult. The once-upon-a-time is also a now, what was is also a living event. Only in its twofold unity of then and now does a myth fulfill its true essence. The cult is its present form, the re-enactment of an archetypal event, situated in the past but in essence eternal. And the moment when this myth is realized is the festival of the gods, the holy day, recurring at a fixed interval. On this day the whole memory of the great ancestral experience is again true and present. The gods are at hand, as they were at the beginning of time, not only as majestic figures demanding reverence, but as what they are: supreme realities of the here and now, primal phenomena of the movement of being, creating and suffering powers of the living moment which also encompasses death. Without death there can be no life; without dying, no fertility. The stupendous moment has returned, the moment when the young goddess was ravished by darkness, when the divine mother sought her, mourning and lamenting her, until she learned that she was Queen of the Dead and would remain so; but she rises up again and with her the grain, to which men owe their civilization. And the mystai are witnesses of this event, which in essence is not a play, but divine presence, realized myth. Persephone is present, for

29

mankind, for the congregation, in the great moment that time has brought to pass. And she will be present again for every single man when the moment of death has come, that terrible festival of the death night, with which the Eleusinian Mysteries have so often been compared.

It would be rash even to attempt a concrete picture of what was beheld in such a moment. And since such an attempt would be an evaluation of the Mysteries, the scholar must learn to see that it is absurd to suppose we can understand anything so great by the mere application of philological method and a little modern psychology. It is as though we were to attempt a scientific approach to the world's great works of art. No doubt those men who were familiar enough with the authentic myth to experience the moment in its eternal quality and immediate divinity experienced other and higher emotions in calling the godhead than we can conceive of today. Before we moderns pass judgment on the ancient world, we should remember the words written by Hegel in the preface to his *Phenomenology of Mind:*

> His [man's] spirit shows such poverty of nature that it seems to long for the mere pitiful feeling of the divine in the abstract, and to get refreshment from that, like a wanderer in the desert craving for the merest mouthful of water. By the little which can thus satisfy the needs of the human spirit we can measure the extent of its loss.[28]

The Eleusinian mystes lived the miracle of intimacy with the goddesses, he experienced their presence. He was received into the sphere of their acts and sufferings, into the immediate reality of their sublime being. His famous vision was no mere looking on. It was sublimation to a higher existence, a transformation of his being. What wonder then that the beholder of this vision should have been confident of a higher destiny in life, and in death, where Persephone was queen!

And is that not a rebirth? A meaningful perspective opens when we consider the ancient cult in this light. In all likelihood, the Eleusinian Mysteries were not originally secret, or at least no more so than the religious festivals of other archaic peoples and of primitive peoples today. We may regard them as a great example of that cult of the gods which goes back into prehistory and extends far beyond the Greek world; and in them we can discern that original religious spirit which we may call a spirit of rebirth, though in a sense not usually associated with that word. In the cult, the human community meets the godhead. They were taken into its sphere, just like those

28 Tr. J. B. Baillie (New York, 1931).

30

primeval ancestors who were known to have enjoyed the most beautiful intimacy with the gods[29] in the Golden Age when men still lived in paradise. Now, with the beginning of the festival, with the coming of the gods themselves, that wonderful age was back again, the myth was present and fully real; the congregation entered into the myth, became again as the primal ancestors, the "golden" race, who were said to have been happy and "beloved of the blessed gods."[30]

Here there was no need of the crude sensuality and ritual of the later mysteries. And it must be admitted that the idea of rebirth that we encounter in Eleusis is not inferior to any other. Perhaps on serious reflection, we shall find its meaning very great and its truth all the more profound in that it does not make man dependent on the favor of any single power, but links him through a higher presence with the great movements and moments of a divine cosmos.

29 Cf. Hesiod, *Theogony*, 35, fr. 82; Pausanias, 8, 24; and elsewhere.
30 Hesiod, *Works and Days*, 120.

C. Kerényi

The Mysteries of the Kabeiroi

1. The Meaning of the Term "Mysteria"

Where historical concepts have undergone profound transformations, the question of definitions becomes particularly urgent. The history of religions deals with extremely changeable elements, whether it places its initial emphasis on delineating the persons of the gods, describing their rituals, or narrating the mythologems. Consequently, the historian must never cease to ask what the transmitted names of the gods meant in any specific epoch, and must even inquire into the reality behind the traditional terms designating modes of religious action, narrative, and thought. He must inquire into the substance behind the name "Hermes" or "Helios," into the meaning of such terms as "mythology" and "gnosis"—to mention only a few subjects that have already been investigated.[1] The student is always in danger of being misled by similarities of names and of ascribing modern concepts to antiquity, and nowhere is this danger so great as in connection with the mysteries.

Here we shall not even discuss the free use of the word. ("Each man has his mysteries, dear Hyperion, his more secret thoughts," said Hölderlin.) But Christianity has sacraments, doctrines, and experiences which in Greek can be designated only as μυστήριον. These mysteries—and all the paths of initiation in the vast field known to modern men as mysticism—have a common characteristic that is much more easily and briefly grasped than the common factor in the ancient mysteries. It is encountered in the pagan philosopher Plotinus, whose mysticism was no longer that of the ancients.

[1] Kerényi, "Mythologie und Gnosis," EJ 1940–41 (and Albae Vigiliae, XIV); "Hermes der Seelenführer," EJ 1942 (and Albae Vigiliae, N.S., I); "Vater Helios," EJ 1943 (and Töchter der Sonne, Zurich, 1944); The Gods of the Greeks (London and New York, 1951). [This lecture opened the 1944 Eranos meeting and EJ 1944, where it was subtitled "An Introduction to the Study of the Ancient Mysteries." The author's preference for the more literal style of Greek transliteration has been followed.—ED.]

He was preoccupied with the "flight of the one to the one" (φυγὴ μόνου πρὸς μόνον):[2] that is, man's exit from the world in which he as an individual is "alone" (μόνος), to achieve union of his whole being with the universal "One." Regardless whether this "One" is conceived monotheistically as the supreme being, or pantheistically as a universal being, the orientation toward an essence or being *outside* the diversity of our natural existence remains characteristic. If that essence or being is interpreted as purely supernatural, as in Christianity, or if it is in some other way opposed to the manifold world of nature as in other religions of redemption, then mysticism is also a striving for redemption as a liberation of man from all natural ties.

But the original, pagan Greek usage of *mysterion* and the related word group does not lead us to these forms of Eastern or Western mysticism. For the Greek of the classical era, not even the adjective "mystic" (μυστικός) was associated with ideas pointing away from the sensory world. In the *Frogs* of Aristophanes, the "mystical aura" wafted toward those who approach the mystai, the initiates executing their dances in the hereafter, is the smell of the burning torch (δᾴδων αὔρα μυστικωτάτη). It is the atmosphere, the sensuous quality of a nocturnal festival, that this word "mystical" here evokes for the Athenian of the fifth century: his "mystical" experience is a specific festive rite. In Greek religion, the "mystical" first becomes accessible to philological interpretation as a festival, in fact, a fixed event of the calendar.

"Mysteria" was the name given to specific festivals in Athens. These festivals might equally well have been called Demetria, Koreia, or Pherephattia, after the goddesses to which they were dedicated, and perhaps they actually did bear these names. The Attic tradition speaks always of "Mysteria," in the plural—and the modern usage is to capitalize the Greek word: Μυστήρια.[3]

2 *Enneads*, VI, 9, 11; cf. Kerényi, *Der grosse Daimon des Symposion* (Albae Vigiliae, XIII), p. 27. This lecture, delivered in Basel, is a preliminary study of the ancient mysteries; the present lecture offers two additional studies, which should be considered in conjunction with the Basel lecture and with the author's treatment of the Eleusinian Mysteries in Jung and Kerényi, *Essays on a Science of Mythology* (New York, 1949) (or *Introduction to a Science*, etc., London, 1950), index, s.v.
3 In Ludwig Deubner, *Attische Feste* (Berlin, 1932), of the festivals only the Mysteria are designated as "*Mysterien,*" with the German ending, an indication of how easy it is to succumb to familiar modernizations. It has long been known that syntactically the word is used in Greek as a temporal term and proper name like the festival names. Cf. Hermann Sauppe's *Ausgewählte Schriften*, ed. C. Trieber (Berlin, 1896), p. 86; Jacob Wackernagel, *Vorlesungen über Syntax*, Vol. II (Basel, 1924), p. 149.

In Greek, the names of festivals are plural in the collective sense, embracing all the events and rites involved. Grammatically, the names are associated with an adjective signifying an identification of everything manifested in the festival with something divine, or—we might say—with the godhead, which in the festival becomes "event." In the Dionysia, the feast of Dionysos, "Dionysian things" (Διονύσια) are present, not necessarily just a single "Dionysian thing," a "Dionysion"; and it is from this plural substantive that the name of the feast is derived. Or a whole feast day may be named after a single sacred action, as in the case of the Pithoigia (Πιθοίγια), on which day the great wine vessels, the *pithoi*, were opened. The event determined the atmosphere of the day; on that day everything became, as it were, "Pithoigian." The emergence of the substantive "Pithoigia" (Πιθοιγία) for the action, indeed for the whole day, appears to be a late materialization and fixation. The original and truly festive form is the adjectival-atmospheric plural.[4]

Another small group of festival names shows an even greater similarity to "Mysteria": the Anakalypteria, Anthesteria, Kallynteria, Lampteria, Plynteria, Procharisteria, and Soteria.[5] The component elements of the last named are particularly transparent. The deity of the day is a divine savior[6] (Σωτήρ) or savioress[7] (Σώτειρα); every festive event of the day partakes of the savior, it is σωτήριος, and accordingly the festival is called "Soteria." We have, however, begun our analysis at the second step, the word for savior (Soter), which is itself secondary: the root is that of the verb for "save" (σώιζειν). And this precisely is the common element in the whole group: the verbal origin of all these feast names. They are all more ancient

4 Cf. the author's conception of the essence of the festival in his outline of ancient religion: *La Religione antica nelle sue linee fondamentali* (2nd edn., Rome, 1951); *Die antike Religion* (3rd edn., Düsseldorf, 1952), pp. 45ff.

5 To this list may be added the Therteria, mentioned in Hesychius, a festival of which no details are known, and the Stepteria, called σεπτηρία in Hesychius. Plutarch refers to the main ceremony of this latter festival as "Septerion" in discussing it in *Quaestiones Graecae*, 293 C: the relation of Σεπτήριον to Σεπτήρια is exactly the same as that of μυστήριον to Μυστήρια, according to the conception here to be discussed.

6 Zeus Soter in Aetolia: *Corpus Inscriptionum Graecarum*, Vol. II, part 1 (Berlin, 1877), no. 323, p. 147.

7 Kore Soteira in Cyzicus: here the goddess has mysteries that are designated as "great" and thus distinguished from the other, "lesser" mysteries. It is certain that this name was a later addition. Whether the feast names Koreia and Pherephattia, also recorded in connection with Cyzicus, refer to the great or lesser mysteries, no one can say. The source may be found in N. M. P. Nilsson, *Griechische Feste* (Leipzig, 1906), pp. 359ff.

than the Soteria, and it is characteristic of almost all of them that the form corresponding to the *nomen agentis* Soter is not transmitted. An exception is the god of the Lampteria, Dionysos Lampter, but a "Dionysos Anthester" as god of the Dionysian festival cycle of the Anthesteria is not known (although Dionysos as god of flowers was given the epithets Anthios and Antheus). The name of the flower festival "Anthesteria" is derived directly from the verb "to bloom" ($\dot{\alpha}\nu\vartheta\epsilon\tilde{\iota}\nu$), and a similar explanation may be presumed for the other feast names we have listed: a happening induced or suffered by the godhead—the shining and flowering of Dionysos in the Lampteria and Anthesteria, the bathing and adornment of Pallas Athene in the Plynteria and Kallynteria, the uncovering of Persephone in the Anakalypteria[8]—underlies them all.

But what of "Mysteria"? That this name also designates a festival in the sense of a time filled with sacred events and having a specific atmosphere, and does not merely signify the sacred actions, rites, and events, is shown by a classical Athenian orator, who distinguishes between the ritual event itself, the "Telete" ($\tau\epsilon\lambda\epsilon\tau\dot{\eta}$), and the Mysteria, and speaks of the "Telete of the Mysteria" as the ritual of the feast.[9] On the other hand, the term "Mysteria" is precisely limited to the time filled with the rites, otherwise Plutarch could not say: "In Eleusis, after the Mysteria, when the festive gathering was still at its height, we were regaled . . ."[10] True, Plutarch lived at a time when atmosphere had turned to object, when the festival had frozen into rite, into ceremony pure and simple. The word "Mysteria" suggests, however, that the festivals bearing this name were so designated after a distinguishing ritual. Here again we have a clear verbal origin, as in the festival names we have discussed: a ritual action that is not bound up with a cult image of the godhead, as in the case of the Kallynteria and Plynteria, but with the people who through this action become in some special way object and subject of the festival. The mystes ($\mu\dot{\upsilon}\sigma\tau\eta\varsigma$) suffers the mysteries, he becomes their object, but he also takes an active part in them.

---

8 In the Procharisteria, a festival of Pallas Athene described as "mystical," it is hard to decide whether it is the goddess for whom men prepare joy in advance ($\pi\rho\sigma\chi\alpha\rho\dot{\iota}\zeta\epsilon\tau\alpha\iota$) or whether it is men who bring her anticipated thank offerings ($\chi\alpha\rho\iota\sigma\tau\dot{\eta}\rho\iota\alpha$). Even more puzzling is the festival name Proschaireteria: cf. Deubner, p. 17.

9 Isocrates, IV, 157: $\dot{\epsilon}\nu \tau\tilde{\eta}\iota \tau\epsilon\lambda\epsilon\tau\tilde{\eta}\iota \tau\tilde{\omega}\nu \ M\upsilon\sigma\tau\eta\rho\dot{\iota}\omega\nu.$

10 *Quaestionum Convivalium*, Book II, Prob. 2: $\dot{\epsilon}\nu \ E\lambda\epsilon\upsilon\sigma\tilde{\iota}\nu\iota \ \mu\epsilon\tau\dot{\alpha} \ \tau\dot{\alpha} \ M\upsilon\sigma\tau\dot{\eta}\rho\iota\alpha \ \tau\tilde{\eta}\varsigma \ \pi\alpha\nu\eta\gamma\dot{\upsilon}\rho\epsilon\omega\varsigma \ \dot{\alpha}\kappa\mu\alpha\zeta\sigma\dot{\upsilon}\sigma\eta\varsigma \ \epsilon\dot{\iota}\sigma\tau\iota\dot{\omega}\mu\epsilon\vartheta\alpha.$

Here we shall attempt to discuss the Mysteria strictly as they appear to us in the texture of Greek life of the archaic and classical periods: as festive events fixed by the calendar. Alone of all Greek festive calendars, the Attic has come down to us in a form which though fragmentary is still relatively satisfactory.[11] It was the Attic calendar of festivals that we cited at the outset when instead of speaking generally of "mysteries" we referred particularly to the oldest Mysteria known to us. It is this basic text that we shall keep in mind in the following, which as far as possible we shall attempt to reconstitute, and on the basis of which we shall attempt to arrive at the content of the word "Mysteria." This calendar mentions two Mysteria, one in the autumnal month of Boedromion and another in the spring month of Anthesterion. Those occurring in the autumn were the "great" or "greater" Mysteria, celebrated in Eleusis, while those celebrated in Agrae in the springtime were called the "little" or "lesser" mysteries. The circumstance that the comparative and distinguishing designation is not always the same, but varies between "great" and "greater" or between "little" and "lesser," shows that for the two months the calendar recorded only Mysteria and apart from this at most the name of the place where they occurred.

What is more important—and this is the reason for our digression regarding the text of the calendar—is that there was no need to name the deity presiding over the Mysteria, just as there was no need to name the deities of the other festivals. But since these particular Mysteria were, as early as the fifth century, considered merely special instances of a type whose members were all known as mysteries,[12] various sources expressly mention Demeter and Persephone as the deities of the two festivals—the great Eleusinian festival and the lesser festival at Agrae. These statements are not sufficiently similar to allow us to identify them as quotations from the Attic calendar. The contrary is certain. In their original sites, the mysteries could be considered only as festivals of these specific deities. No matter how directly the cult action may have affected the human participants, this was a divine cult, the festival was appropriate to those goddesses and to no others, and in the eyes of the Athenians at least, this was a matter of course.

Today we tend equally as a matter of course—in accordance with Hero-

---

11 Cf. August Mommsen, *Feste der Stadt Athen* (Leipzig, 1898), a work which from the point of view of the calendar is preferable to that of Deubner.
12 Herodotus (II, 171) calls the similar secret cults of Egypt by this name as well.

dotus' usage—to take "Mysteria" to mean "secret cults" without any definite relation to specific gods. This makes it necessary for us to say a word about what was kept secret in ancient religion, before we go on to discuss the mysterious cult action which gave the Mysteria their name. "Secret" must not necessarily be taken to mean "mystery." Underneath there may indeed be a true mystery in the sense adopted by Romano Guardini, who defined a genuine mystery as one that is experienced, venerated, lived—in other words, is not kept especially secret—and yet remains forever a mystery.[13] The secret itself may be less important than the fact that it is kept secret.

In Greek religion this secrecy is not positive and intentional but rather negative and involuntary. There is no serious intention of maintaining the secrecy of the secret. The study of the religions of nature shows that in the secret cults it is a question of the same thing found, according to Goethe, in nature itself: a sacred open secret. What was concealed in the Greek cult must certainly have been known to all those who lived in the vicinity of the cult sites, but it was unutterable. It possessed this character—the character of the *arreton* (ἄρρητον)—independently of the will of those who participated in the cult. For in the profoundest sense it was ineffable: a true mystery. Only subsequently did express prohibitions make the arreton into an *aporreton* (ἀπόρρητον).

Perhaps we shall understand this ineffable character of nature's secrets— such as the mysteries pertaining to the origin of life—if we consider it on two different planes, the existential and the purely rational. On the existential plane, we act and suffer, and we ourselves are so deeply moved by our action and suffering that we find no adequate words to express them; they are simply life. On the purely conceptual plane this "life" is easily expressed in the clear, unequivocal, and unemotional concepts of biology. But is it in reality still the same "life" which moves me and concerns me, is it my "life"? The purely rational formulation encompasses only the general, detached from the individual instance; it speaks *of* my life—one might say that it merely takes my life as a point of departure—it does not express it: for this life is inexpressible. The cult representation alone can raise my experience toward the universal in such a way that it still remains my very own: my ineffable mystery that I have in common with all men.

This paradox of the public yet secret cults was also that of the Attic

13 Romano Guardini, *Zu Rainer Maria Rilkes Deutung des Daseins* (Sammlung Überlieferung und Auftrag, Reihe Probleme und Hinweise, II; Bern, 1946), p. 29.

Mysteria. They were merely particular instances of the "arretic"—as we should really say instead of the misused and misunderstood "mystic"—in Greek religion. Once uttered, its secret may well have become a commonplace: for once uttered, it simply ceased to be, it was no longer that ineffable arreton which created a special visibility and audibility, one might say an atmospheric body, out of actions and movements, darkness and light, silence and voices. Only those who gave themselves to evoking this atmosphere, who danced and enacted these mysteries, came close to uttering the unutterable. But the divine center of the Mysteria remained ineffable: their authentic great goddess who in the form of Demeter and her daughter already appeared at one remove from her original self. As *arretos Kura*, the ineffable Maiden, she dominated the festival.

The Mysteria are exemplary instances of the arretic, and yet they are merely special cases, among others no less pronounced. To cite only one classical Athenian example: the Arrephoria, a festival of Pallas Athene, which took its name from the ritual carrying back and forth of an ineffable object.[14] Arreta played a far greater part in Greek cults than is generally supposed. That which was not meant to be uttered *was* not uttered and therefore was not divulged. And the great danger in the science of "arretology," this indispensable paradoxical undertaking, without which no true picture of Greek religion is possible, is that by divulging too much it may rob the arreton of the very particular atmosphere which is its very essence. The *mystikon*, if we construe it in its original, authentic sense as the determining element in the Attic mysteries, is a special form of the arreton. To speak of it is in itself arretology. We must guard against excessive talk—a sin against the sacred atmosphere, an involuntary falsification of atmosphere. And yet we must attempt the impossible and give at least some intimation of the nature of that mystikon which the mystes suffered and participated in, and which was the central experience of the Mysteria that took their name from it.

One indication is offered by the language, another by the monuments. The source of the term "Mysteria"—as also of "mystes" and "mystikos"—consists in a verb whose ritual significance is "to initiate" ($\mu\nu\epsilon\tilde{\iota}\nu$), developed from the verb $\mu\acute{\nu}\epsilon\iota\nu$, "to close the eyes or mouth." The monuments—two replicas of a representation of the initiation of Herakles into the Mysteria[15] —show us that what we should imagine here is not a silence (closing the

14 Cf. Deubner, p. 9.
15 The Torre Nova Sarcophagus and the Lovatelli Urn, both represented in Deubner, pl. 7.

mouth) in the presence of the arreton but a ceremony of closing the eyes. Herakles is seated with his head totally covered: the Mysteria begin for the mystes when, as sufferer of the event (μνούμενος), he closes his eyes, falls back as it were into his own darkness, enters into the darkness. The Romans use the term "going-into," "*in-itia*" (in the plural), not only for this initiating action, the act of closing the eyes, the *myesis*, which is exactly rendered as *initiatio*, but for the Mysteria themselves. A festival of entering into the darkness, regardless of what issue and ascent this initiation may lead to: that is what the Mysteria were, in the original sense of the word.

Peculiar to this *initia*, this "shutting in," is its cultic character, the suprapersonal import of this very personal experience of the mystes. In his work *On the Laws*, Cicero formulated this universal meaning in rational terms, identifying the *initia* with the more philosophical-sounding *principia*:

> ... initiaque ut appellantur ita re vera principia vitae cognovimus neque solum cum laetitia vivendi rationem accepimus sed etiam cum spe meliore moriendi.

> (... and in the initia we recognized, just as the word indicates, the principles of life, and from them we obtained a basis not only for living happily but also for dying with better hope.)

But the "*principia vitae*" which Cicero found in the Attic mysteries have this philosophical sound only in Latin translation. When we read the original version in Pindar, we no longer think of "principles."

οἶδε μὲν βίου τελευτάν, οἶδεν δὲ διόσδοτον ἀρχάν.[16]

> (Happy is he who, having beheld these things, descends beneath the earth: he knows the end of life and he knows the Zeus-given beginning.)

The Mysteria took the initiate back to the very beginning of life, its natural genesis, and not to any philosophical "principle"—though this too is called ἀρχή. And it is not by accident that they were enacted at night.

The nocturnal element was not limited to the covering of the mystes in the first moment of initiation. The Mysteria were so essentially nocturnal that in them every aspect of the night was experienced, even that power residing solely in the night, the power to engender the light as it were, to help it come forth. They were not merely a nocturnal festival, they actually —or at least it seems so—solemnized the feeling of being shut in by the night,

16 Fr. 137 a; the passage in Cicero: *De legibus*, II, cap. 14, par. 36.

culminating in a sudden great radiance. Surely it is no accident that the Mysteria took place at the waning of the moon. The preparations were made at full moon. But the atmosphere of the waning moon already prevailed on the sixteenth of Boedromion, when the mystai who had assembled on the fifteenth took the purifying sea bath, which was still a part of the preliminaries. Only on the nineteenth did they start on the road to Eleusis, and the sacred nights began with the eve of the twentieth, on which they were to arrive. It may be assumed[17] that the little Mysteria in the month of Anthesterion were held in approximately the same lunar nights. The Mysteria, as a feast of shutting in and *initia*, thus formed a kind of contrast to the festival of the month's naming, the Anthesteria, which opened the phase of the full moon in the period from the eleventh to the thirteenth. The "flowering" which gives this festival its name meant a general opening: not only of the flowers and the moonlight but also of wine jars and even of graves. While, on the other hand, the same verb ($\mu\acute{v}\epsilon\iota\nu$) applies to the closing of the flowers and of the eyes.[18]

"Mysteria" as a festival name has yet another complementary antithesis, which from a linguistic point of view is quite clear and certain: the feast of the Anakalypteria. The veiling in the Mysteria and the uncovering ($\dot{a}\nu\alpha\kappa\alpha\lambda\acute{v}\pi\tau\epsilon\iota\nu$) in the Anakalypteria fall together within a higher unity that is known to us as a sacred action in high mythology and in its human repetitions. The name "Anakalypteria" has come down to us from the cult of the very same goddess with whom the Mysteria are associated: Persephone. It has reference to her marriage, which was also solemnized under the name of "Theogamia," "marriage of gods."[19] Both names were current in Sicily, but the divine event they evoke can only be that which constituted the mythological content of the Attic Mysteria. The marriage of Persephone and Hades was also a prototype of human marriage. In antiquity, when the bride was given over to her betrothed, she was covered like the departed, destined to the underworld at the moment of being given over to death—and so it is with the mystes. But for neither human mystes nor human bride has this symbol and instrument of descent into the night such profound meaning as for the goddess whose betrothal was death and surrender to the god of the underworld. Prerequisite for the nuptial unveiling

17 The reasons for this in Mommsen, pp. 406ff.
18 Nicander of Colophon, fr. 74, 56: $\kappa\rho\acute{o}\kappa os\ \epsilon\emph{i}\alpha\rho\iota\ \mu\acute{v}\omega\nu$.
19 Nilsson, p. 358.

40

and uncovering was *this* betrothal: the descent of Persephone into the subterranean night of the killing and fructifying bridegroom. Re-enacted as festival, this is called "Mysteria."

It is in threefold darkness—the darkness of the veiling, that of the sacred nights in Agrae and Eleusis, and his own inner darkness—that the mystes, man as well as woman, finds his way back to his own suffering and conceiving motherliness. And at the same time he is filled with wonder at the eternal and common element in his life's beginning, the archetypal in that unique conjugal union which was *his* origin, as he sees it in the persons and destinies of the gods: an arreton which was already impossible in late antiquity. By mythological images the Attic mysteries still easily led man back to the natural roots of his existence. No special miraculous instrumentality was needed to open access to the realm in which those roots lay; it was a realm whose power had not yet been exhausted, and he who was rooted in it stood firm as a god; the festival with its natural, atmospheric wonders, and man's continuity with his history back to the profoundest sources of his life, back to the world of his ancestors; these were enough. The presence of what had gone before, which the soul harbors as its most intimate treasure, was efficacious and powerful. Christianity consciously passed beyond this whole realm of roots and sources, with a deep and not unfounded distrust toward the forces that the Mysteria (in the second part of our study we shall learn something of this) knew in their own way how to tame and restrain. The "Mysteria" of Christianity, above all its sacraments, were conceived as new and more powerful instrumentalities by which man might be helped to take root in a wholly different, supernatural realm.

With the growth in importance of miraculous instrumentalities—magical among the pagans, sacramental among Christians—the "Mysterion" (in the singular) comes more and more into the foreground. Just as the Phylakterion (from φυλάττειν, "to protect") is a means of protection, so, by grammatical analogy, *mysterion* should signify a "means of veiling, of keeping secret." But it actually means that which is kept secret, the secret, indeed the whole secret cult (at a late date to be sure[20]), the content of the Mysteria. And this is logical, if we consider the Mysteria as a festival and exemplary

20 Scholiast on Aristophanes, *Lysistrata*, 645. Also in late inscriptions: *Monumenta Asiae Minoris Antiqua*, Vol. IV (Publications of the American Society for Archaeological Research in Asia Minor, IV; Manchester, England, 1933), no. 281, p. 105.

41

secret cult: everything they embraced was a Mysterion, a means of enacting the festival and at the same time, like the whole festival, something veiled, kept secret. But fundamentally all this was purely a means of attaining to a realm that surpassed all the tangible trappings, objects, actions, and words of the cult. Of the ear of wheat, silently manifested at the climax of the ceremony, or of the so simple words ὕε κύε, "Rain, bring fruit," the Christian writers say ironically, "That is the great and ineffable Eleusinian mystery."[21] They outdo themselves in listing the unworthy, common objects which are supposed to constitute the Mysterion. And thus they prove that for ‚them the pagan arreton has ceased to exist. Their mysteries are fundamentally different from the pagan Mysteria.

2. The Legend of the Foundation of the Shrine of the Kabeiroi near Thebes

An analysis of the word "Mysterion" and of its older use in the plural, "Mysteria," had to precede any general investigation of the ancient mysteries and particularly any special study of the mysteries of the Kabeiroi. We shall now turn to these latter, though we shall not attempt to give any exhaustive account of the puzzling mythological creatures called "Kabeiroi" (Κάβειροι)—or in the Boeotian dialect form, as they were called in their shrine near Thebes, "Kabiroi" (Κάβιροι)—and shall not attempt to describe the secret cult that Herodotus already designated as the "mysteria" of the Kabeiroi. (This is actually the oldest mention of Greek "mysteria" in literature, apart from the references to the great Eleusinian festival in inscriptions.)[1] Herodotus used the term in that more general sense which moderns also usually have in mind when they speak of ancient "mysteries." But in addition to an analysis of the word, a scientific study of the mysteries requires an analysis of certain traditions connected with the Kabeiroi. In the following we shall therefore discuss a legend that has come down to us in connection with the Theban shrine of the Kabeiroi.

21 Hippolytus, *Refutatio omnium haeresum*, V, 7, 34: τοῦτο . . . ἐστὶ τὸ μέγα καὶ ἄρρητον Ἐλευσινίων μυστήριον· ὕε κύε. V, 8, 39: ἐπιδεικνύντες τοῖς ἐποπτεύουσι τὸ μέγα καὶ θαυμαστὸν καὶ τελειότατον ἐποπτικὸν ἐκεῖ μυστήριον ἐν σιωπῆι· τεθερισμένον στάχυν. The unusual position of ἐν σιωπῆι is explained by Hippolytus' ironical emphasis.

1 II, 51; cf. O. Kern, "Mysterien," in Pauly-Wissowa, XVI, 1209ff.

Though we now return to the more customary usage and speak no longer of "Mysteria" but more loosely of "mysteries," we should not entirely forget the festive context in which they disclosed their original, ancient content. This context was a marriage, mythologically represented and experienced, the primeval marriage of a divine bride and a divine bridegroom, of which human marriages are an imitation and copy. The veiling was the phase preliminary to the unveiling, the Anakalypteria: we must look upon it as a special preparatory act. Through this act marriage itself becomes no less natural. The Greek view that the nuptial union was the fulfillment and culmination of an initiation ($\tau\acute{\epsilon}\lambda os$ $\acute{o}$ $\gamma\acute{a}\mu os$)[2] was based on the conception that mystery festival and marriage festival were variations of the same underlying theme—a theme that concerned ancient man primarily as procreator of his family and race.

But precisely the cultic enactment of this entirely natural process, whether as open family festival or as a secret cult of Greek clans, not to mention its most grandiose and sublime enactment in the Eleusinian Mysteries— precisely this cultic action, molded out of the raw substance of life, shows the animal and natural elevated to a higher plane. On this higher plane, both human and natural, the animal element of the nuptial union attained to almost metaphysical depths, touching on the roots from which sprang the life of the individual. Even in its periodic recurrence, animal life has about it something momentary; in all its acts it emerges only as it were *hic et nunc*, without conscious connection with past or future. The *conscious* periodic repetitions of cultic actions, their consciously fixed, recurring ritual form, the form of all marriages down through the successive generations, restores that connection with the ancestral world, the roots, or however one may wish to designate the past that is present in the soul.

And in this natural event turned cult, the preparatory phase of nuptial fulfillment, the act of veiling, seems most particularly to point beyond the purely animal. The flight of the bride, her capture and subjugation, all the phases of her abduction, correspond like a mirrored reflection to moments in the love play of certain animals preparatory to mating. But the cloaking in *darkness* has a prototype only in the heavens, where sun and moon vanish in darkness at the time of their conjunction. To this corresponds the vanishing of the veiled man in his own darkness. This event, however, is no mere

2 See, in answer to H. Bolkenstein's unfounded criticism, Kerényi, *Hermes der Seelenführer* (Albae Vigiliae edn.), p. 80, 4.

43

imitation but is an actual introversion, with a meaning and psychological reality of its own. This preparatory event gave the mysteries their name and is in both its aspects the original mystical element, the characteristic of the mysteries of antiquity: on the one hand as preparation and introduction, on the other hand as a transcending, in the sense both of an elevation and of a profounder rooting. And now as we attempt to analyze an interesting tradition regarding the cult of the Kabeiroi, we must not forget this specific character of the ancient mysteries.

The mysteries of the Kabeiroi were considered by the Greeks as age-old. Their principal site, the northern Greek island of Samothrace, off the Thracian coast, and the neighboring islands of the Thracian Sea, was so far removed from the Hellenic sphere dominated by the classical Homeric religion that the long survival of archaic cults there need not surprise us. This geographical situation also explains why the records of the archaic traits characteristic of the religion of this island date from a relatively late era, beginning with the age of Hellenism, when Samothrace already belonged to the inner circle of the Hellenized world around the Aegean Sea. Indeed, excavations systematically carried down to virgin rock by Karl Lehmann[3] have not brought to light anything in the shrine earlier than, at the very earliest, the eighth century B.C. The rock altars, however, which surely were dedicated to the Great Mother, like similar ones in Phrygia, are the monuments of an extremely archaic cult. In addition, we should like to mention other archaic elements. First, there are two traditions from Samothrace, which, though of late date, do provide immediate testimony of the antiquity of the cult. The one is to be found in the Greek historian Diodorus, who tells us that the natives of the island—whether at the time of Diodorus or of his source is immaterial: at all events, in the Hellenistic period[4]—possessed their own peculiar language and made much use of it in their cult. Inscriptions in this language have been found in the course of the excavations. It appears best to follow M. Terentius Varro, who visited Samothrace in the first century B.C. and who was an initiate, and call it the language of the Sai:[5] this was the name of the earliest inhabitants of the island, and the priests of the mysteries were also Sai.

---

3 In *Hesperia*, XIX (1950), 8. [The author has revised the rest of this paragraph, 1955.— ED.]
4 Diodorus lived in the 1st cent. B.C.
5 Kerényi, *Studi in onore di Gino Fumaioli* (Rome, 1955), p. 158.

The other tradition is a historical anecdote in two different variants and linked to two different persons.[6] According to one, the Spartan general Antalcidas wished to be initiated into the mysteries of Samothrace. The priest asked him what he had done in his life that was more terrible than any common crime.[7] To which the Spartan, demonstrating a truly Hellenic attitude, replied: "If I have committed any such deed, the gods themselves must know of it!" In the other version, it is another well-known Spartan, Lysander, who goes to Samothrace to consult the oracle. This in itself tends to discredit the source, because no reliable source speaks of an oracle on Samothrace. The essential here and in the other, scarcely more authentic variant is the question asked in Samothrace, which to a Hellene seemed so unworthy and so sacrilegious that Lysander answered with the counter question: "Who desires to know this, you or the gods?" And when the priest replied, "The gods!" he sent him off with the words: "Then begone, for if *they* wish to know, I will tell *them!*"

In this version the wording of the question itself is extremely significant: the priest asks Lysander, "What is the greatest crime against divine justice you have committed in your lifetime?"[8] This question—startling enough in Greek eyes to inspire anecdotes—is something more specific than a general summons to confess one's sins. The novice had to prove that he had offended against the divine order, in order that the *Sai* might purge him of his guilt. But he *had to* be an offender, because the original initiates of Samothrace, the Kabeiroi themselves, the prototypes of all subsequent initiates, had been criminals. Here two other stories might briefly be mentioned. A tradition of Thessalonica, the large city on the coast opposite Samothrace, tells of two Kabeiroi who killed a third and hid his head in a blood-red cloth. And on Imbros, an island in the same region, the names of the Titans, the original criminals of Greek mythology, were listed in an invocation of the Kabeiroi.[9]

The significance of these two characteristics—the use of a pre-Greek, barbarian language in the ritual, and the presupposition of a great crime in the life of the novice—is revealed by comparison with the Eleusinian Mysteries.

6 In the *Apophthegmata Laconica*, attributed to Plutarch, 217 D and 229 D; cf. the analysis in Pettazzoni, pp. 164ff.
7 Τί δεινότερον δέδρακεν ἐν τῶι βίωι.
8 Ὅ τι ἀνομώτατον ἔργον αὐτῶι ἐν τῶι βίωι πέπρακται.
9 Cf. Kern, "Kabeiros und Kabeiroi," in Pauly-Wissowa; *Inscriptions græcæ*, XII, 8, 1909, n. 74.

There the two indispensable requirements for admission to the secret events of the great festival were Hellenic language and freedom from all blood guilt. The lesser mysteries purified the mystes—in case it was necessary—from any blood guilt. But a general purification does not imply insistence on past crime. Any such emphasis is lacking in Eleusis, as is also the memory of a pre-Greek past. Not that an un-Greek past is unthinkable. The express exclusion of people of barbarian language, stated in the priest's *prorrhesis*, or prologue, leads us rather to conclude that if so much effort was spent in making the great Eleusinian festival appear as a pure Hellenic institution, it was because the festival had been erected with conscious art on other foundations. As opposed to this emphasis on the Hellenic and on the purity of the novices in Eleusis, remnants of barbaric language and a religious preoccupation with the impure attest the archaic and pre-Greek character of the mysteries of the Kabeiroi, even though the records concerning them are of more recent date.

Here we have established merely an order of archaic traits and no actual chronology: at any time accessible to us, the mysteries of the Kabeiroi appear more archaic than the Eleusinian Mysteries. They represent an earlier phase than the Eleusinian Mysteries, as can be seen from the characteristics already noted. Thus it is a welcome confirmation when Herodotus, the first writer to speak of the "mysteries of Samothrace," ascribes them to the aboriginal population that he, in line with a tradition widespread in ancient Greece, calls "Pelasgians." At an earlier time, he tells us, these Pelasgians had lived also in Attica. According to another historian,[10] they had come from Boeotia, from the region of Thebes. It seems to us that such statements by ancient historians cannot be confuted in their essentials: the task of science is to interpret them. In the main, however, we shall restrict our interpretations to the religious documents and monuments connected with a Theban shrine of the Kabeiroi. This site was excavated as far back as 1888–89, but the remains were not made fully available until 1940.[11]

When we leave Thebes in a northerly direction on the road leading to Livadia (the ancient city of Lebadeia) in order to visit the nearby shrine

<hr/>

10 Ephorus in Strabo, IX, 401; cf. the still instructive account of K. O. Müller: *Prolegomena zu einer wissenschaftlichen Mythologie* (Göttingen, 1825), pp. 146ff.
11 By Paul H. A. Wolters and Gerda Bruns, *Das Kabirenheiligtum bei Theben*, I (Archäologisches Institut des Deutschen Reiches, Berlin, 1940). Cited in the following as *Kabirenheiligtum*. [The excavations by Lehmann on Samothrace in 1938–39 and 1948–54 still await systematic publication.—C. K. (1955).]

of the Kabeiroi, we come first to the plain which in ancient times was called the "Aonian" ('Αόνιον πεδίον).[12] Whether we translate this geographical name as "plain of dawn" or "plain of the people of dawn," in either case it derives from *Eos*, the morning light.[13] This is of interest because the isle of Samothrace was known by two similar names: Leukania, "island of the white dawn,"[14] and Isle of Elektra, a goddess of light.[15] Thus we see that also at Thebes the approach through the open plain to the darker mountain fastness where the mysteries of the Kabeiroi were celebrated was sacred to the dawning light. And now, taking as our guide and mentor Pausanias, whose topographical indications have been exactly confirmed by archaeological findings,[16] we leave the Aonian plain in a westerly direction.

Where the path turns off to the rediscovered and excavated shrine of the Kabeiroi, there was in ancient times a sacred grove of Demeter Kabeiria and her daughter. "Only he who has been initiated may enter," Pausanias adds. "Some seven stadia from this grove lies the shrine of the Kabeiroi. As to the Kabeiroi, who they are and what the rites sacred to them and the mother are, on this I will keep silent: may those who would like to hear of these things forgive me. But nothing prevents me from revealing to all what the Thebans relate concerning the origin of these rites." Once we branch off the path in the grove of Demeter, we have entered the sphere of that which is kept secret. To this sphere belong not only such sites as the grove itself, and not only the sacred rites, which here have the same names as the rites of Demeter and Persephone: *dromena, telete, orgia.* (The last word, ὄργια, as applied to the mysteries, is taken in its basic meaning, as "action" pure and simple, yet, like ἔργον, "deed" or "work" used in the same connection, with a particular overtone suggesting the bloody deed of sacrifice.) Not only the cult itself is kept secret, but also the very nature of the Kabeiroi and the whole mythology in which this nature is expressed. Pausanias is permitted merely to relate a bit of pseudo history, the legend of the founding of the mysteries of the Kabeiroi.

Though we wish at this point merely to analyze and interpret the legend of the founding of the shrine and its variants, it is necessary to indicate here

12 Strabo, IX, 412.
13 W. Borgeaud, *Les Illyriens en Grèce et en Italie* (thesis, Geneva, 1943), p. 134.
14 Source and literature in Borgeaud, p. 136.
15 Apollonius Rhodius, *Argonautica*, I, 916: "Elektra," like Elektrone the daughter of Helios, derives from ἠλέκτωρ, a word for "sun."
16 Pausanias, 9, 25, cited and interpreted in *Kabirenheiligtum*, pp. 7ff.

47

certain characteristics of the Kabeiroi, which are confirmed by the tradition as a whole. The first of these is that they are deities who are secret and must be kept secret. The fact that mariners in danger at sea invoke their help doubtless gives some indication of their nature. But we are not justified in regarding them as helper deities pure and simple, because they were called upon for help. They are precisely—and this is the only characterization that the tradition permits—mystery deities "pure and simple." Their name in Greek is a foreign word. It was formerly held to be a Hellenized form of the Semitic *"kabirim,"* "the Great," since the Greeks also called the Kabeiroi "the great gods" ($\mu\epsilon\gamma\acute{a}\lambda o\iota\ \vartheta\epsilon o\acute{\iota}$). But this is a general term applied to gods of the mysteries, even when it has no linguistic basis in the particular names of the gods and cannot have arisen as a translation. Actually it is not known what the word "Kabeiroi" originally meant, and we must merely assume that, like the invocation "Great Gods," it is appropriate to mystery gods. The meaning of the name is unknown to us, but neither the form "Kabeiria" nor the variant "Kaeira" or "Kapheira"[17] suggest a Semitic religion, but, like the crude rock altars, point rather to the sphere of archaic Mediterranean cults that have been partly preserved in the religions of Asia Minor. The name "Kabeiros" is associated with a mountain or a mountain region in Phrygia known to have been held sacred to the Great Mother of the gods, who was known in this region as Berekyntia.[18] Aside from the fact that they were mystery gods, the most noteworthy feature of the general tradition regarding the Kabeiroi is that it places them among the wider group of distinctly male deities (Kuretes, Korybantes, Idaioi, Daktyloi), who made up the retinue of the Great Mother.[19] In Asia Minor these phallic demons were known also as Berekyndai, a name closely related to Berekyntia, and were looked upon as the spirits of the most primitive secret cult utensil known to anthropology, the bull-roarer.[20] We may envisage this host of

17 This goddess must be included in the group because of her connection with the Telchines, figures related to the Kabeiroi. Cf. Kerényi, *The Gods of the Greeks*, p. 184.
18 Demetrios of Skepsis in Strabo, X, 472, and Strabo, XII, 556.
19 This fundamental insight (and its sources) occurs already in C. A. Lobeck, *Aglaophamus* (Königsberg, 1829), Vol. II, pp. 1105ff.
20 The use of bull-roarers in Greek secret cults ($\tau\epsilon\lambda\epsilon\tau a\acute{\iota}$) is expressly attested by the Pythagorean Archytas: Diels, fr. 1 (Freeman, *Ancilla*, p. 79). They are called $\acute{\rho}\acute{o}\mu\beta o\iota$ and $\acute{\rho}\acute{v}\mu\beta o\iota$; cf. in particular Clement of Alexandria, *Protrepticus* (ed. Potter), p. 15 (Migne, *PG*, VIII, 7); Hesychius and *Etymologicon Magnum*, s.v. For their identity with the Berekyndai, Hesychius, s.v. Β$\epsilon\rho\epsilon\kappa\acute{v}\nu\delta a\iota$. The importance of these passages was recognized by Pettazzoni, *I Misteri* (Storia della religione, 7; Bologna, 1923), pp. 3ff.

petty gods that appear under different names in the retinue of the Great Mother Goddess of Asia Minor as ghostlike phallic demons, not essentially different from the Kabeiroi.

We have seen that they were also criminals: their fratricide is no less Titanic than the murder of Dionysos by the Titans. And in the legend of the founding of the shrine, we shall see that the relation of Prometheus to the Kabirian men is similar to his relation to the Titans in the classic mythology. For an understanding of the legend, we must note that the "men" whom it speaks of in a pseudo-historical form intended for the profane are essentially such secret mythological figures, who in their spectral outlines seem to us now Titanic, now dwarflike and spiritlike, but always distinctly masculine.

At the site of the Kabirian shrine, we read in Pausanias' version of the legend, there was once a city, and the people who lived in it were named Kabeiroi. The goddess Demeter came to Prometheus, one of these Kabirian men (Καβειραῖοι), and to his son Aitnaios. She brought something which she entrusted to them, but what it was and what was done with it Pausanias does not feel permitted to divulge. Suffice it to say that the secret cult—the *telete*—was a gift of Demeter to these Kabirian men. It need scarcely be pointed out how superficially the Kabeiroi have here been transformed into Kabirian men. Aitnaios, the "Etnean," is a transparent disguise for Hephaistos, the god of fire and blacksmiths, whose association with the Kabeiroi is also expressed by the fact that they were sometimes called "Hephaistoi" (Ἥφαιστοι).[21] The essential point that the legend seeks to establish was apparent also from the situation of the shrines. Legend and topography both aim to show Demeter—in her association with the Kabeiroi called Kabeiria or simply "The Mother"—to have been the founder of the Kabirian mysteries.[22]

The other version of the same legend is told in Pausanias as though it constituted a later event in the history of the Kabirian city or—after the city was abandoned—of the region. When the Kabirians fled from the Argive conquerors, his story continues, the secret cult died out for a time. It was Pelarge, daughter of Potnieus and her husband Isthmiades, who reestablished the secret cult, but at a different place, called Alexiarus. But since Pelarge consecrated the shrine outside of the former boundaries, the cult,

---

21 Cf. Preller-Robert, pp. 850f.
22 Regarding the mythological relation of Demeter to the Kabiri (also in the form of three "Kabirian nymphs") see Kerényi, *Hermes*, pp. 90f.

after the return of the remnant of the Kabirian race (γένος Καβειριτῶν), had to be moved back to their soil.[23] On the advice of an oracle from Dodona, the cult elevated Pelarge to the rank of a goddess and sacrificed a gravid beast to her. Here the founder of the mysteries is again a goddess, and there can be no doubt as to what goddess is intended under the name Pelarge. It is certain that the daughter of the "man from Potniai" (Ποτνιεύς) was associated with the cult of Demeter in Potniai.[24] Potniai was a city in Boeotia, dedicated to Demeter as Potnia, the mistress, from whom it took its name. Just as the name Aitnaios indicates Hephaistos, so "Isthmiades" suggests the great god of the Isthmus, Poseidon: as Posi-das, he was the "husband of Demeter." And a gravid beast—a sow—was sacrificed to no other goddess than Demeter.

Such stories are *légendes à clef* which were transparent to the initiate. The question inevitably arises: What does it signify that Demeter, "The Mother," should have initiated the mysteries of the Kabeiroi? But before we can proceed to answer, we must ask: Is this association of a goddess with a secret cult otherwise characterized exclusively by male gods old enough to carry any profounder meaning? Is this or that motif in the founding legends old enough, we might say fundamental enough, to justify us in drawing conclusions as to the antiquity of the link between the Kabeiroi and Demeter? Here our attention is drawn to an element in the legend that we have not explained above, the one name that is not transparent: "Pelarge." We can definitely recognize the goddess concealed beneath this name but not through the name itself. Was this name more intelligible to the initiate than to us? What memories and ideas did it arouse in them?

"Pelarge" is the feminine form of *pelargos*, "stork." If we did not wish to limit ourselves strictly to those conceptions which can be proved to have played a role in the religion of antiquity, we might be tempted to point to a widespread popular explanation of birth. There is a mythology of the stork, and traces of it would not surprise us in a secret cult connected with the source of life. We have, however, no need to evoke psychologically relevant

23 From here on the text of Pausanias (IX, 25, 6) has come down to us in a rather corrupt form. "Potnieus" has the form "Potneus," perhaps by an intentional distortion. The ending of "Alexiarus" is presumably erroneous: "Alexiares" would no doubt be more correct. But perhaps only the accusative Ἀλεξιάρουν is corrupt for Ἀλεξιαροῦντα, and the topographical name Ἀλεξιαροῦς derives from the plant ἀλεξιάρη. Cf. Nicander, *Theriaca*, 861 and schol.

24 Cf. N. M. P. Nilsson, *Geschichte der Griechischen Religion*, Vol. I (Handbuch der Altertumswissenschaft, V, 2; Munich, 1941), p. 140.

images (the stork as mythological bringer of babies would be such an image), since the traditions that have come down to us from Greece itself are far richer than the interpreters of myth—whether romantic or psychological—have ever suspected. Here we must consider the possibilities offered by the very mobile Greek language, which sometimes intentionally mixes dialect forms. Thus "Pelarge" might well be a translation of "Pelasge" into another dialect, and it might also be connected with the word "Pelasgos," or Pelasgian. According to phonetic law, the combination rg corresponds to an older sg[25] and the change is not so great as to prevent an evocation—the evocation of the Pelasgians by the name Pelarge.

We know of one tradition that connects Demeter as founder of mysteries with Pelasgos, who gave his name to that mysterious aboriginal race.[26] The tradition of Argos associated the founding of the mysteries of Demeter as a whole with the region between Argos and Lerna, a well-known mystery site. According to this tradition, it was not to the king of Eleusis but to an aboriginal inhabitant of this region that Demeter appealed in her search for her ravished daughter, and it was here that she established her mysteries. Demeter's host, upon whom she bestowed the secret cult, bore, according to one tradition, the name of Pelasgos.[27] He is said to have built the temple outside the city of Argos, where she was worshiped as Demeter Pelasgis. Thus the goddess who founded the mysteries was also looked upon as a Pelasgian, but in this quality she was called "Pelasgis" and not "Pelarge." This latter name, even if it was merely a cover name of the Pelasgian, evokes the "stork."

But here another possibility must be considered. From a purely linguistic point of view, "Pelargos," "the stork," might be a later form of "Pelasgos," a word which might originally have referred not to men but to birds. It would be quite in keeping with the character of primitive secret cults, if in the ritual all the men of a tribe had been identified with animals—in this case, since the rites were established by a stork goddess, with storks. And this identification could have been preserved in the name. Then the "Pelasgoi," wherever they appear in the legendary prehistory of Greece, whether in Argos, in Attica, in Boeotia, or in Samothrace, to mention only those

25 Cf. Eduard Schwyzer, *Griechische Grammatik*, Vol. I (Handbuch der Altertumswissenschaft, II, 1; Munich, 1939), p. 218.
26 Pausanias, 1, 14, 2; 2, 22, 1.
27 According to another tradition his name was Mysios, a suitable name for the first mystes; cf. Preller-Robert, p. 751, n.

mystery sites we have touched on, would be the adepts of primordial secret cults, and perhaps also members of the men's societies that ethnological studies show to have played a part in the secret cults. The tribal name would then have broken away from the animal name "Pelargos," originally differing from it only in dialect, and would have lost its original meaning. But we have not set out to discuss the still very problematic question of the Pelasgians; we wish rather to describe and interpret what the Greeks erected on a foundation that the ethnologist can reconstruct with a considerable measure of likelihood, but only in broad outlines. The crowning of this edifice, the purest Greek form of the secret cult, was no doubt the Eleusinian Mysteries. It is all the more noteworthy that the figure of the priest in Eleusis has also preserved some trace of an earlier identification with a bird.

The initiating priests and priestesses, the hierophants and hierophantides of Eleusis, belonged to the race of the first mystery priest Eumolpos and were looked upon as his descendants: Eumolpidae. But more accurately speaking, they were all "Eumolpoi" like their mythical ancestor.[28] For "Eumolpos" was a name of office; the Eumolpides lost their own names the moment they entered upon the office of the Eumolpos.[29] The word "Eumolpos," however, does not designate the bearer of the office as the "priest"— who in Eleusis is called "hierophant"—but as the "good singer." This meaning is clear, but in reference to the Eleusinian priesthood it does not seem particularly appropriate. The role of the hierophant was for the most part visual and not auditory. This is shown by his name: "he who discloses that which is sacred (and kept secret)". His fine voice may have rung out when he called the mystai together or proclaimed the birth of the divine child. But on the basis of all that we know of the mystery ritual, we have difficulty in imagining him as a "singer."

And yet the name "Eumolpos" surely expresses something of the character of the first priest of the Mysteries. On a famous vase painting of the fifth century, Eumolpos—shown in the company of the Eleusinian gods in a scene representing the mission of Triptolemos—has beside him a swan as attribute,[30] and the swan, although supposedly he sang only in his last hour, was regarded by the Greeks as one of the best singers among the birds. And the swan seems most appropriate to the whole mythological tale of the

28 Cf. Johannes Toepffer, *Attische Genealogie* (Berlin, 1889), p. 25.
29 Lucian, *Lexiphanes*, 10; Toepffer, p. 52.
30 Skyphos of Hiero, reproduced in Nilsson, pl. 43, 1.

lineage of the first priest, whom later mythographers split up into several Eumolpoi.[31] He is said to have come to Eleusis from Thrace: ordinarily, this would have been a stumbling block, since the Thracians were barbarians and the barbarians were excluded from the Mysteries. But the Greeks looked on Thrace, and particularly on the mouth of the Strymon, as the home of the swans. Even in historic times there were people living there who took their name from the swans, as Pelasgos from the stork. Famous Athenians claimed kinship with a Thracian king, Oloros—the swan.[32] The mother of the mythical Eumolpos was named Chione, the "snow white"; she was a daughter of Boreas, the Thracian north wind, and of Oreithyia, whom he had ravished at the scene of the mysteries of Agrai by the Ilissus.[33] The Thracian companions of Eumolpos were said to have been drowned while bathing in the lake of Eschatiotis—i.e., the water at the extreme end of the world.[34] According to certain Eleusinian funeral verses, the lay name of the priest or priestess likewise vanished in the waters:[35] they emerged from the water as new, holy beings with no other name than that of the swan, the good singer.

The father of the "good singer," the husband of the snow-white Chione, was the god venerated in Eleusis as "the father"[36] and considered the husband of Demeter: Poseidon. In a theriomorphic figuration of the rape-marriage which constituted the mythological foundation of the Demeter mysteries, Poseidon as a stallion played the role of the bridegroom.[37] In another theriomorphic version of the same marriage, the bridegroom takes the form of a swan, the bride that of a goose. In the poetic elaboration of this mythological marriage scene, he is called Zeus and she Nemesis.[38] The original element seems to have been the scene itself, which was raised to the sphere of epic mythology only through the names of Zeus and Nemesis. In the mythology of the mysteries, it was presumably Demeter's daughter

31 Toepffer, pp. 26ff.
32 He was the father-in-law of Miltiades, the victor of Marathon; the father of Thucydides likewise bore the name of Oloros; regarding his kinship with Miltiades, cf. Toepffer, pp. 282ff. The corresponding word in Latin (olor) has the meaning of "swan."
33 Plato, Phaedrus, 229 b; Pausanias, 1, 38, 2.
34 Etymologicon Magnum, s.v. This lake is said to be south of Eleusis "behind the Isthmus," hence in the realm of Poseidon.
35 The poems in Toepffer, pp. 52 and 62.
36 Pausanias, 1, 38, 6; Toepffer, p. 30.
37 Pausanias, 8, 25, 4. Kerényi in Jung and Kerényi, Science of Mythology, pp. 170ff.
38 In the cyclic poem Kypria, in Athenaios, Deipnosophistae, 334 B; Kerényi, Mnemosyne (1939), pp. 162ff.; Kerényi, Die Geburt der Helena (Zurich, 1945), pp. 9ff.

herself who played the role of bride in the marriage of the swan. In Eleusis only the priests and priestesses were looked upon as descendants of dwellers in the air and water, gods of the winds and the sea, and particularly of the swanlike "good singer": the primeval swamp-bird scenery of the whole event has otherwise vanished. In Boeotia, a memory of it was retained in connection with Persephone herself; there it was related that she was playing with a goose in a cave near Lebadeia[39] and that there—as in so many other places—she was ravished. Corresponding with this form of the mythologem, a vase from nearby the Kabirion—the Theban shrine of the Kabeiroi —shows water birds accompanying the goddesses Demeter and the winged Hekate Angelos—in their search for the ravished Persephone.[40]

The swan, the goose, and surely the duck, which is so often represented on Greek vases, form a group of water birds, out of which—as out of a homogeneous substance, in which the particularities of the species are unimportant—the mythology of the divine mother and her daughter, expressing the destiny of woman, of the soul, and of all human beings, was molded in archaic times. The designation—transparent no doubt to the initiate—of the same mother goddess, the founder of the Kabirian mysteries of Thebes, as a "stork woman" is no less archaic and suggests the existence of a long-legged group in addition to the short-legged group we have listed. Stork, heron, and crane form a group parallel to that of swan, goose, and duck, and in vase paintings they are seldom accurately differentiated. There are actually half-way creatures between the two groups, and on the basis of the material now available to us no one can say whether the differentiation of the two birds—the one by long, the other by short legs—in the vase painting from the Theban Kabirion is accidental or intentional.

It still remains for us to cast at least a passing glance at the results of the excavations of the Kabirian shrine at Thebes, in order to answer the question raised above: What does it signify that Demeter should have founded this cult? The preliminary question of the age of Demeter's connection with the cult may be regarded as already answered. The designation of the founder of the cult as Pelarge suggests the most archaic implications. And these are reflected in the archaeological findings, which carry us back at least

39 Pausanias, 9, 39, 2.
40 *Kabirenheiligtum*, pl. 26, figs. 9 and 10. The identification of the winged goddess with Iris is false: Hekate and not Iris plays the role of messenger in the Persephone mythologem, and she also has an association with the Kabeiroi who purify her; cf. Preller-Robert, pp. 324ff.

to the classical age. The oldest of the temples to have been excavated was built in the sixth or at least the fifth century B.C.[41] On the basis of Pausanias' text, however, we may assume that there once existed an older shrine, called "Alexiarus," which was surely not yet built of stone, outside the confines of the historical stone temple. A second stone temple was built in the fifth century in place of the first, which was destroyed by the Persians; a third temple was built at the end of the fourth century, after the second had been laid waste by the Macedonians. The findings that chiefly interest us here are the vases, with their characteristic figures. Characteristic are both the themes and the stylized manner, which, where it is not actually grotesque, borders on the grotesque. The most typical group dates at the latest from the second half of the fifth century; the iconography of the vases is certainly older: the water birds—both short- and long-legged—carry on an archaic tradition.[42]

Like the texts, the vase paintings reflect the content of the secret cult in two different ways. There are direct mythological representations of the theme of the mysteries, and there are also *narratives à clef*, which were

Fig. 1. *Kabiros with his son Pais and others*

transparent to the initiate but to the outsider appeared as mere fairy tales or as purely human genre paintings. The Pelarge legend and the water-bird scenes on the Kabirion vase paintings may be considered on the same plane. Mythological texts belonging to the first group were, to be sure, kept as secret as possible, and this circumstance enhances the value of a mythological scene, with inscriptions, which has been preserved in a few now-famous

41 *Kabirenheiligtum*, pp. 10ff.
42 One of the oldest examples is the geometric amphora from Thebes with the representation of the "queen of the beasts," published by Wolters in pls. 8–9 in the *Ephemeris Archeiologike* for 1892 (Athens, 1893) and reproduced in Nilsson, pl. 30, 1.

55

shards.[43] It has often been discussed.[44] The giant figure of the god (assimilated to the archaic Dionysos type), which in this painting bears the name "Kabiros," shows that the male principle in the function of a divine father—for this is the god Kabiros with his son the Pais—was elevated to the highest conceivable rank in this secret cult founded by a goddess. True, the life emanating from him, the source, passes through the Pais into a grotesque being, the Kabirian primeval man, a spirit still in process of birth: "Pratolaos." But the bride of the likewise grotesque, unkempt primeval bridegroom "Mitos" ("the seed"), the woman who will bear life drawn from the mixing bowl of her father Kabiros, is distinguished by beauty and the characteristic name "Krateia" ("the strong one").

Fig. 2. *Kabirian pygmies with cranes*

To a second group of vase paintings belong the representations of the legendary Kabirian people of the pygmies, accompanied by cranes.[45] The absurd, phallic dwarfs, or pygmies, and the noble, powerful birds of heaven, the cranes, indicate the contrast between the initiating female and the male requiring initiation—a contrast which seems characteristic of these mysteries. In secret cults all over the world, the novice is placed in painful and oppressive situations, tormented and ridiculed. He resists; but when he surrenders, his defeat is only apparent, for a resurrection follows. This seems to have been the situation of those who were to be initiated in the Kabirian mysteries. We see here something of the essential quality of the Kabeiroi:

43 *Kabirenheiligtum*, pl. 5; our fig. 1.
44 Kerényi, *Das Agäische Fest* (3rd edn., Wiesbaden), pp. 63 and 72; *Der grosse Daimon des Symposion* (see above, p. 43, n. 2); and *Hermes*, p. 88.
45 *Kabirenheiligtum*, pl. 29, figs. 3 and 4; our fig. 2. The Kabirian mystai are quite pygmylike in the vase paintings. Regarding their relation to the Kabiri themselves, cf. Kerényi, *Das Ägäische Fest*, p. 61.

they represented the antithesis to the paternal dignity of the source of life, they stand for the absurd unrestraint, and yet helplessness, of the phallic element. It is something grotesque and savage which can prove fatal; it is manifested, for example, in the wild voracity of the pygmies devouring the beautiful birds they have killed. Contrasted with such creatures, the celestial nature of the birds is all the more striking. The water birds in the Kabirion vases do not at all suggest inert matter, a lower sphere which is transcended by the male principle; it seems rather to be the dwarflike and earthy, the wild and crude male principle, which is elevated into higher spheres by a winged femininity.[46]

And here we can at least suggest a provisional answer to the question of Demeter's role in founding the Kabirian mysteries. The interpretation of one particular group of mythological genre paintings—the initiation scenes, which seem to render the comical rather than the sacred—must be reserved for a later monograph. Here, however, we may say briefly that in these grotesque dwarf scenes the marriage motif is not lacking: a heavily veiled bride bears on her head a wreath and beside it two little branches, a special cultic symbol.[47] In another picture, the bridegroom in a Dionysian mystery marriage—enacted, however, in the same atmosphere, hence certainly in the Kabirian temple—is characterized by two similar branches.[48] A branch of this sort is called in Greek *"bakchos"* and is more correctly translated as "shoot" or "scion," including the sense of the tender, almost plantlike creature resulting from the marriage. And for this reason Dionysos, the tender, premature divine child, is also Bakchos.[49]

Among all the symbolic objects that the initiates carry in the Kabirion vase paintings, this branch is the only one that is also represented by itself: for the most part with two aquatic birds, in a continuous, repetitive decora-

---

46 Highly as the author prizes the genius of Bachofen, he must point out nevertheless, in order to avoid a superficial generalization, that the present interpretation differs from that of Bachofen both in principle and in conclusions. Cf. Kerényi, *Bachofen und die Zukunft des Humanismus* (Zurich, 1945), pp. 22f.; *Neue Schweizer Rundschau*, XIX (1952), 676ff. That in the scenes of pygmies and cranes the birds, the "celestial creatures," represent the female element is confirmed by two stories in Ovid's *Metamorphoses*, VI, 90–97: the transformation of the pygmy woman Gerana (feminine form of γέρανος, "crane": Eustathius, 1322, 50) into that species of bird, after which the cranes waged war on the pygmies; and the story of Antigone, the daughter of Laomedon, who was turned into a stork.
47 *Kabirenheiligtum*, pl. 33, fig. 3.
48 Ibid., pl. 33, fig. 1.
49 Hesychius: βάκχος· κλάδος ὁ ἐν ταῖς τελεταῖς.

tion, but also composed into a kind of legendary scene.[50] On a bowl, the other side of which reveals only a runner of myrtle, this scene—the branch, between two water birds—is flanked by two strange fabulous beasts. These are cocks, stylized to resemble griffins, those miraculous creatures of archaic Greek art whose origin suggests the Orient. As cocks and griffins they express the matutinal aspect of sprouting growth that may be said to enjoy the supervision and protection of the two birds; they serve as a mythological designation of place, similar in meaning to "Leukania" and "Isle of Electra" for Samothrace, and the "Aonian," the "dawning" plain for the approach to the Theban shrine of the Kabiri.

Fig. 3. *Branch, with water birds and monsters*

And thus this picture-narrative discloses the meaning of the founding legend: for those initiated in it, the secret cult was the creation of primeval woman in the stork goddess, whose maternal care was devoted to budding life, to the scion, the sun rising in the human body. Masculinity, particularly in its uncouth, youthful stage, reveals a surface of destructive aggression: it is only beneath the surface that man also is fruitful. The fertility of woman, however, is evident on both planes, in visible, tangible actions, and as a profound, mysterious inner process. To open the path to those depths, to the source of life, to the almost metaphysical roots of our being, was, so it seems, the mission of woman. Women elevated the warlike,

50 The picture we are about to discuss: *Kabirenheiligtum*, pl. 30, fig. 3, our fig. 3. Reverse of the vessel: *Kabirenheiligtum*, pl. 53, fig. 4: *Archäologischer Anzeiger*, Appendix to *Jahrbuch des Archäologischen Instituts*, 1895, Vol. I, p. 36, no. 31 (Inv. 3285); Georg Weicker, *Der Seelenvogel in der alten Litteratur und Kunst* (Leipzig, 1902), pp. 148f.; *Kabirenheiligtum*, p. 111. A similar independent representation, without the miraculous cocks at the sides, on a *lebes* in Heidelberg: Inv. VI, 77, *Kabirenheiligtum*, pl. 55, fig. 1. The same scene as repetitive frieze on a *lebes* in Paris: *Kabirenheiligtum*, p. 36, fig. 1 and 2. A shard, pl. 55, fig. 6, shows half of the scene.

death-dealing men to the function, the dignity, the consciousness of the source of life. Perhaps there is an indication of this in the name of the sacred site of Pelarge: "Alexiarus." The composite of *alexi-* and *-ar-* means "he who dispels the war-god." Like all warriors, the Kabeiroi, who are primeval men in need of initiation, had something murderous about them, something calling for atonement. Yet at the same time they were spirits of life, who in their most archaic form whirred[51] in the bull-roarers, the *rhomboi*, and, in later language, blew as soul-nourishing winds,[52] bringing fertility to women. To transform men into *true* sources of life in the service of that most fragile living thing, the embryo, "man in the germ"; to lead them, perhaps to the earliest, assuredly to the simplest form of humaneness: this, according to the founding legend as we have analyzed it, may be taken as the function of the Kabirian mysteries.[53]

51 The verb ῥέμβειν connected with ῥόμβος is applied also to the soul, freely moving outside of the body: Plutarch, *De sera numinis vindicta*, 22.
52 Cf. The Orphic hymn to the armed Kuretes (38, 21): ἐν Σαμοθρήικηι ἄνακτες . . . πνοιαὶ ἀέναοι, ψυχοτρόφοι, ἠεροειδεῖς.
53 The present two essays are merely prolegomena to the exposition of the great Greek mysteries, particularly those of Samothrace and Eleusis. The Dionysian element that is abundantly present in the Theban Kabirion—it is no accident that the Dionysian krater in the center of the Kabiros-Pais-Krateia-Mitos scene (fig. 1) serves as the mixing bowl whence men arise—has been reserved for special treatment. In the author's opinion Orphism, a related form, constitutes—like the Gnosis—a particular genus, the scientific treatment of which requires especially sharp distinctions. As a preliminary to this, see Kerényi, *Pythagoras und Orpheus* (3rd edn., Albae Vigiliae, N.S., IX; Zurich, 1950).

APPENDIX

The Castello of Tegna

A Parallel to Pausanias, IX, 39

The remarkable remains of the so-called Castello of Tegna[1] have been described in the reports of excavation published in *Urschweiz*, 1942, no. 2, and 1943, no. 4. The traveler to the Val Maggia and the Centovalli will find them very much worth visiting. Standing on the mountain crest beneath which the two valleys meet, the Castello dominates the countryside in all directions. Whether, during the period from which the principal structure dates, it was really a Roman *castellum* is more than questionable. For this, in the opinion of experts, the walls of the great square building (which alone will be discussed here) are not strong enough. It seems, then, most plausible to regard it as a temple. If it was a temple, it must, to judge by its situation and dimensions, have had sufficient religious importance to protect itself and the region immediately surrounding it. And it must have been the site of a pre-Roman cult that lasted into the Roman period. In the first century A.D., to which the excavated structure belongs, Roman temples did not have this square ground plan, nor the puzzling parallel and diagonal walls of the enclosure. These walls seem to have supported a complicated passageway around the square central portion of the temple.

The remarkable part of the building is this central part. It rested on a cellarlike substructure, which three arches, placed side by side, divided into two rooms; as a whole it is so imposing an edifice for a small mountain settlement such as this must have been that its central importance for the cult to which the temple was dedicated cannot remain in doubt. For a time it was believed that this substructure might be a cistern underneath the actual temple. But this theory became untenable when an excellent spring was discovered nearby. The idea of a cistern, however, is typical and frequently crops up in attempts to interpret unusual religious structures. To

---

1 [A Swiss village a few miles west of Locarno and northwest of Ascona; therefore a short distance from the site of the Eranos conferences. Professor Kerényi conducted a party from the 1944 conference on a visit to the Castello.—ED.]

cite a seemingly remote parallel, the cistern theory was put forward in connection with the mountain sanctuary of Apollo Ptoös, a highly archaic oracle site in Boeotia, consisting of a rectangular building with several rooms, although this site was characterized by a special abundance of natural water. Precisely because of the natural abundance of water, such ruins often develop spontaneously into "cisterns," as R. Ganszyniec quite soundly observed in speaking of the Ptoön.[2]

Geographically, this Greek region is rather far removed from Switzerland. But recent philological studies have shown that in the ethnic composition of Boeotia an important part was played by a pre-Greek though not pre-Indo-Germanic people, whose ramifications can be traced as far as southwestern Europe. Linguistic remnants, preserved chiefly in place names and names of peoples, cannot but be ascribed to a common ethnic stratum extending westward, southward, and even in some part northward of the Danube: a stratum which may be characterized as Indo-Germanized rather than Indo-Germanic, and whose best known representatives were the Illyrians, predecessors of the historical Greeks in the southeast, and in the southwest the Ligurians, who preceded the Celts. So common are the place names belonging to this ethnic stratum in the southern valleys of the Alps that evidently what Celtization did take place was extremely superficial and short-lived.[3]

Seen against this background, the temple of Tegna takes on special significance as a parallel to a Boeotian temple that, so far, is unique in its kind. Even if there were no possibility of showing a common prehistoric basis, the parallel would indeed be striking enough. Beneath the cult site, the valley of the Maggia assumes the character of a gorge, and similarly, the visitor to the temple of Trophonios, near the Boeotian city of Lebadeia, first passes into the gorge of the Hercyna, which seems almost to flow underground as it passes beneath the sacred mountain. In that almost subterranean valley there is a sacred grotto, whence arose one of the sources of the Hercyna; in it stood two statues with staff and serpent; one might have taken them for Asclepius and Hygeia. But they were, so Pausanias our guide informs us, far more probably the oracle god Trophonios—a god

---

2 *Archiv für die Geschichte der Medizin*, XV (1923), 37.
3 With regard to the far broader, almost generally European significance of this Illyrian-Ligurian stratum, the readiest source of information is the introduction to W. Borgeaud's dissertation, *Les Illyriens en Grèce et en Italie* (Geneva, 1943).

whose name is not characteristically Greek, but rather "Illyrian"[4]—and the river goddess Hercyna. In any event a Greek, because of his views on the distribution of the gods, would have expected to find a god of so strongly subterranean a character as Trophonios in precisely such a grotto and such a valley.

It is all the more surprising, precisely from a Greek point of view, that to reach the subterranean cult site of this god, his actual shrine, one had to climb a mountain. For those who wished to visit Trophonios and obtain from him an oracle for their whole lives, this climb was a path of initiation. Above, on the mountain crest, where today stand the ruins of a medieval castle, there stood in ancient times, as Pausanias wrote in the second century A.D., a circular wall of white marble approximately one yard in height, surrounding a kind of threshing floor, though indeed a very small one. The wall was surmounted by a fence and had doors though which one could enter the threshing floor, which in turn merely formed a passage around a structure two yards in breadth and four yards in depth. This structure was built into an artificial cleft in the rock and looked like a baking oven. Ovens of this shape, comparable to a gigantic half egg, are, as Frazer remarks in his commentary, seen beside Greek peasant huts. The visitor was given a ladder and climbed through the extremely low aperture in the "oven," into the subterranean shrine, there to experience something never to be forgotten.

The site of this shrine is no doubt to be sought beneath the ruins of the medieval castle. An early Byzantine notation suggests the church of St. Christopher as the site, and about one hundred years ago the archaeologist and traveler Stephani believed that he had rediscovered the ancient shrine under a little church in the castle. In the floor of this church, he reported, there were two quadrilateral holes, through which one could look down into an artificial cave that had perfectly regular walls and pillars, but was in part filled with water. Since then the church has fallen more and more into

---

4 This is not the place to illustrate the philological connections with examples. We may be allowed to point out, however, that the name Trophonios (older Boeotian form: Trephonios) corresponds phonetically to the Latin Trebonius. In this it reveals its non-Greek but Indo-Germanic character. The Greeks may have felt that their verb *trephein*, "to nourish," was present in the root. It is at all events present in the place name Trebenishte, a place where pre-Greek antiquities, claimed for the Illyrians, have been found. The ending *-onios* (in Greek not characteristic for names of gods and places) occurs in such place names as Mosogno, Comologno, Sonogno (the last village in the nearby Val Verzasca), not to mention the characteristic "Ligurian" ending *-asc* of Bignasco in the Val Maggia itself.

ruins, and I do not know if any excavating has ever been done there. Frazer found a larger hole than Stephani and remarked contemptuously: "It is most probably a cistern." So far the shrine of Trophonios has not been really rediscovered, but its idea has perhaps been rediscovered—in the Castello of Tegna.

Here, in an architectural sphere different from that of Boeotia, this idea is expressed in angular form, just as for example the idea of the labyrinth could be expressed in angular as well as spherical form. The negative element common to both structures, the absence of stairs both in the subterranean room of the Castello of Tegna and in the shrine of Trophonios in Lebadeia, seems not without significance. Pausanias tells us how the visitor to the shrine of Trophonios, when he had penetrated as far as his knees into the aperture of the "oven" and hovered, as it were, in a dark abyss, was overcome by dizziness. Nor was the ovenlike element lacking in the temple of Tegna: it was indeed doubly present, in the shape of the two arches which divided the lower room in two. Where the opening—or perhaps two openings, since there were two rooms—was situated, is to my knowledge not known. Into the outer room an entrance leads from the east, and there is also an opening on the west side. The dividing line between the underground rooms also shows an east-west orientation. Among all possible interpretations, the most likely seems to be that this cult was related to that deity who could be seen descending over the still higher mountains and in whose destiny, on certain festive occasions, the devotees wished to participate.

However, we wish merely to call attention to the architectural idea, for in the present state of research it seems best to let the visitor apprehend the religious idea for himself.

Walter Wili

The Orphic Mysteries and the Greek Spirit

1. The Orphic Mysteries

I

Owing to the influence of Greek fifth-century sculpture, our conception of Greek religion has in a way remained Herodotean. The father of historiography wrote in a famous passage (II, 53): "It is they—Hesiod and Homer—who created the Greek theogony, who gave the gods their epithets, distributed honors and aptitudes among them, and gave substance to their figures."

The gods of the Homeric world were shaped like men, though they were far more powerful, larger, more beautiful, and more vital than men. Aristotle called them "immortal men." They "lived lightly," entered into amorous relations with mortals, and took delight in mortal offspring.

The attitude of Homeric man toward his gods was in keeping with his anthropomorphic conception of them. He had no terror of them, since their dimensions after all were human. As hero he was descended from them and as warrior he took this fine though dangerous relationship for granted. He might fear the actions of the "immortal men," but he felt no horror, because their divine workings remained outside the sphere of the numinous. Indeed the incursion of the numinous was to be the decisive event in the history of Mediterranean culture. In the Ionian corner of Asia Minor, man can be said, with a clear eye to reality and a sound sense of the origin of the princely type, to have drawn the godhead down to himself: the world was still twofold, divine and human, but there was no transcendent being. There was no ethical, no metaphysical, and above all no genealogical distinction between god and man. Only immortality separated them; but this immortality served more to legitimize the lineage of the hero than to establish the god as essentially different from man. True, the gods are ever present in the Homeric epic; though not, as a number of scholars have recently declared,

64

because they were required by the epic apparatus and the free narrative technique of the epic poet, but because man, in this prerational stage, did not yet feel himself to be the originator of his own decisions. The primary function of the gods, wheresoever they appear, is to help; they make man free and brave, as in the case of Athene and Odysseus. And when they are angry, obstructive, or hostile, Homeric man accepts this as fate. Where he suspects that he himself has been at fault, he conciliates the godhead—as, in the first book of the *Iliad*, Agamemnon propitiates Apollo after the god has sent down pestilence. Death, darkness, and terror exist, but no more than the souls of the dead can they interfere with life in this utterly immediate world, or deflect it from its even keel.

In everything, the gods, these immortal men, show that they derive this nature of theirs from the heroic epic and not from the cult.[1] Their existence is a unique song of triumph of the Ionian rhapsodists, precursors of the Ionian natural philosophers, over the dark powers of the utterly different pre-Homeric gods. These rhapsodists preserved but one traditional motif, their estimate of Moira, fate. Fate governs both gods and men. And it is this primordial acceptance of fate which gives Homeric religion, with all its affirmation of this world and of human existence, its peculiar realistic pessimism. Yet, even in awareness of the bitterest fate, Homeric man never demands a reversal of nature nor expects rivers to flow uphill. His natural and vital existence, to which the numinous and the miraculous are alien and hostile, called forth gods in its own image.

From the sixth century on—after an entirely different orientation in the eighth and seventh centuries—the Greek sculptors strove to represent the Homeric god. And for this god the architects built suitable abodes, thus creating that sacral architecture which seems to have appeared all at once in Greece, Sicily, and southern Italy. Significantly, the basic proportions both of statue and of temple are the same as those of man, abstracted into the geometric forms of the pentagram, as the Swiss writer Lucie Wolfer-Sulzer, working with the theories of the American mathematician Jay Hambidge, has recently shown with great ingenuity.[2]

1 Recently stressed by Bruno Snell in *Das neue Bild Der Antike*, ed. Helmut Berve (Leipzig, 1942), Vol. I, pp. 122ff.
2 Lucie Wolfer-Sulzer, *Urbild und Abbild der griechischen Form* (Zurich, 1941), pp. 18ff. Something similar is attempted by Ernst Fiechter, "Raumgeometrie und Flächenproportionen," in *Concinnitas, Beiträge zum Problem des Klassischen*, Festschrift for Heinrich Wölfflin (Basel, 1944), pp. 64ff.

Hesiod was indeed far removed from this conception of the god as warrior and victor. And yet he retained the Homeric gods and fitted them into his metropolitan Greek mythology. He thus offers evidence that, returning to the Greek mainland from the coast of Asia Minor, the gods of the Homeric epics conquered the Greeks. Yet something new is manifested in Hesiod: his narrative of the gods, which is almost exclusively genealogy, not only creates a cosmos, but is also a "form of revelation expressing the essence of the cosmos."[3] And a second significant and un-Homeric element appears: the gospel of justice, Dike as companion of Zeus, Dike who from then on presided over the homely custom of ordering daily life by petitions to the gods. Thus Hesiod, drawing on the irrational resources of archaic man, combines the Homeric vision of the gods with that of metropolitan Greece.

These two basic forms of religious life, the Homeric and the Hesiodic, were in force in the seventh century when first metropolitan Greece and then the other spheres of Greek culture were surprised by a religious revolution. Probably at the end of the eighth century, the god Dionysus had set out from his original Thracian home;[4] first to Thessaly and Thebes, then to Attica, he had brought wild ecstasy, dark terror, the ideas of guilt and atonement, condemnation and election—forces and concepts which have usually been regarded as un-Greek and anti-Greek. Such was the god's might that he even carried his ecstatic prophecy to the shrine of Apollo at Delphi.[5]

First to Thebes and Thessaly, then to the rest of the Mediterranean world, Dionysus brought the orgiastic cult of the Bacchantes—an accomplishment celebrated with striking frequency by the Greek tragic poets beginning with Aeschylus, and later by the Roman poets. Become milder, he brought to Attica the Orphic mysteries and the drama. The march of Dionysus in the seventh and sixth centuries was an astounding triumph. In contrast to the widely accepted view that this Dionysian revolution was un-Greek, it can be understood only if we assume that the god found in his path a kindred extra-Homeric, pre-Homeric religious substance, amenable to the doctrine of sin and atonement, stain and purification. The truth is that the Dionysian

3 This somewhat exaggerated formulation is used by Paula Philippson in her *Untersuchungen über den griechischen Mythos* (Zurich, 1944), p. 40. The work is dedicated to Hesiod.
4 Otto Kern, *Die Religion der Griechen* (Berlin, 1926–38), Vol. I, p. 229, presumes that Dionysus was revered in Thrace as early as the second millennium B.C.
5 Recently placed in doubt by Martin Nilsson, *Geschichte der griechischen Religion*, Vol. I (Munich, 1941), pp. 536f., whose arguments, however, do not seem conclusive.

revolution had revived an archaic Greek sentiment that had lain dormant in the motherland.[6]

One of the most essential expressions of the Dionysian is to be found in the Orphic mysteries. These were named after the mythical figure of Orpheus, and as early as the end of the archaic period he was regarded as the actual founder of all the Dionysian mysteries. Otto Kern, the leading authority on Orphism, who devoted his life work to this study and in his publication of the fragments has accomplished no less than did Franz Cumont in his studies of the Mithraic mysteries, believed Orpheus to have been a creation of an early sixth-century cult group.[7] However, scholars of the rank of Nilsson and Peterich hold what seems to be the sounder view that Orpheus was an early religious figure who had been elevated to the sphere of myth.[8] Here we shall not go into Eisler's brilliant speculations concerning the name of Orpheus, which he derives from the name of a fish, giving it the meaning of "fisherman."[9]

By the beginning of the sixth century, Orpheus was definitely a myth: the singer whose song has power to tame all creatures, to gather wild animals and trees around him, who moves stones and cliffs and even abrogates the laws of Hades.[10] His magical power is exerted through music. Orpheus stands extremely close—whether from the very outset cannot be shown—to his god Dionysus; like him he originated in Thrace and had close ties with Phrygia in Asia Minor; as Dionysus-Zagreus is torn to pieces by the Titans, so is Orpheus rent by the wild women of Thrace. Dionysus is mysteriously devoted to the Muses at the foot of Olympus in Pieria, and so likewise is Orpheus, son of the Muse Calliope. Both were held to be the true bringers of culture, a theme that the classic Greek dramatists and Augustan poets never wearied of celebrating. Dionysus journeyed to Hades, and on one occasion Orpheus bested Hades. And yet, despite all these ties, despite his similarity to the god, the man Orpheus shows through.[11]

6 The chief exponent of this view is Eckart Peterich, who construed the pre-Hellenic as archaic Greek in his highly controversial yet significant book *Die Theologie der Hellenen* (Leipzig, 1938), passim.

7 Otto Kern, *Orpheus* (Berlin, 1920), pp. 16ff.

8 Nilsson, p. 644; and, more emphatically, Peterich, pp. 26off.

9 Robert Eisler, *Orpheus the Fisher* (London, 1921), pp. 6ff.

10 Konrat Ziegler, in Pauly-Wissowa [hereafter PW], XVIII, 1248, rightly stresses the frequency of the motif of the gathering of beasts and trees by song.

11 Peterich (pp. 26off.) takes the sound view in opposition to the often attempted mythicization of Orpheus. Plato, the most reliable ancient authority, sees Orpheus primarily as a man.

Three legends particularly distinguish the founder of the mysteries and indicate the essence of his myth:

1. *The legend of his birth.* While his father, Oeagrus, almost fully preserves his Thracian origin, thus proving that he belongs to the oldest Orpheus legend, a father was very early disclaimed for Orpheus, and he retained only his mother, Calliope. As early as the seventh century, this identification of Orpheus with music gave him this Muse as mother, while his father was forgotten.[12]

2. *The quest of his wife Eurydice.* So greatly did Orpheus love her that he undertook the journey to the underworld; he obtained her release from Hades with his singing, and for a time it was held that he actually saved her.[13] But soon the un-Greek conception that a human being could really escape death was overlaid, and the original myth, though strangely transformed, was restored: In this myth, Orpheus gains power over Eurydice, "the widely judging one" (thus probably herself a goddess of the underworld), by his song, but he does not succeed in redeeming her from the underworld, because he breaks the magic spell by looking back. Humanized, indeed raised from the primal religious element into the sphere of the purest humanity, but not entirely removed from the realm of magic, this version appears in the magnificent Naples relief—the best copy of an Attic original of the late fifth century—which has a musical counterpart worthy of Orpheus in Gluck's aria "J'ai perdu mon Eurydice." In the relief the primordial myth of the queen of the underworld is combined with the sublimely human song of the hero who undertakes the journey to Hades; in both cases the song of Orpheus achieves its supreme triumph. The same world appears on those southern Italian vases where Orpheus gains the release of Eurydice by singing and playing the cithara before the king and queen of the underworld.[14] Plato ventured a magnificent variation on this in the *Phaedo* (68 a),

---

12 Kern, *Religion*, p. 133, regards the myth that Orpheus is the fatherless son of the Muse as the older version and sees in it a deposit of archaic Greek religious thinking, in which "a far greater part is ascribed to the mother than the father." This view is scarcely tenable, though it cannot be rejected as sharply as is done by Konrat Ziegler, in PW, XVIII, 1219, who moreover does not interpret the important metamorphosis of the myth. Cf. Kern, *Orphicorum fragmenta* (Berlin, 1922) (henceforth referred to as *OF*), testimonia 22–26.

13 This version occurs in the oldest authorities, Isocrates, XI, 8, and Plato, *Symposium*, 179 d.

14 Ziegler's sharp rejection (PW, XVIII, 1277) of Kern's thesis (PW, VI, 1323) is based on the fallacy, which has so often proved catastrophic, that a myth growing over hundreds of years permits of a simple interpretation; it is as though a forester were to

where he declares, half in jest, half in earnest, that some, in order to see again those whom they loved, had undertaken the journey to Hades; with how much greater joy must we then start out for Hades in order to obtain wisdom and be with it.

3. The most original is perhaps the third legend: *Orpheus is torn to pieces by the Thracian women.* Aeschylus made this the subject of his tragedy the *Bassarae.* The angry Dionysus sends out the Bacchantes, who are dedicated to him, against Orpheus, because Orpheus had abandoned his god and turned to Apollo-Helios. The Muses gather up the scattered limbs of Orpheus and bury him. Interpreted from the point of view of the history of myths, this seems to be the vengeance of Dionysus against Orpheus for renouncing the maenadic element and softening the Dionysian mysteries in an Apollonian sense. But first and foremost, this myth calls for an intrinsic interpretation that was seen even in antiquity:[15] the prophet suffers the same fate as his god, Dionysus-Zagreus. We may speak of the rending to pieces as sacramental. Thus the tragedy of Aeschylus has two meanings: Orpheus suffers the fate of his god, and he is assimilated to Apollo and the Muses. This assimilation to Apollo was transferred to the god and finds its highest expression in the culture-bringer Dionysus and in the "Dionysation" of Delphi.[16]

Thus the essential elements in the legend of Orpheus are sacred song, the other world, and the ennobling of man by song and transcendence, by the mysteries and the divine suffering of their founder. This legend was firmly established in the sixth century. It retains the supreme characteristics of Orpheus as the founder of a religion. Yet the far older figure of a historical personality seems to shine through the legend.

---

say that the 25th and the 50th annual rings of a fir tree *are* the fir tree. See *Berlin Papyrus* 44 (= *OF*, fr. 49).

15 The important testimony of Proclus on Plato (commentary on *Republic*, ed. W. Kroll, Leipzig, 1899, Vol. I, p. 174; *OF*, test. 119, with *OF*, test. 113, the most important testimony in this matter).

16 This was clearly the view of Aeschylus in his Lycurgia trilogy. It was also the view of Sophocles that Apollo approached the Dionysian sphere (*Trachiniae*, 205ff., and *Oedipus Rex*, 1098ff.). This fact should be borne in mind by those scholars who regard Orpheus the Apollonian singer as the older figure and who are of the opinion that Orphism took over the Apollonian figure for its own purposes. This thesis is put forward by W. K. C. Guthrie, *Orpheus and Greek Religion* (London, 1935), pp. 45ff., and Ziegler seeks to establish it in PW, XVIII, 1304f. The Guthrie-Ziegler view is controverted by what has been said above, by the important fragment *OF*, fr. 209 (Plotinus-Olympiodorus), and also by the identification of Dionysus with Helios in *OF*, fr. 212, which again impresses upon us that a god of light (Phanes?) was at the source of the Orphic doctrine.

II

We now turn to the mysteries that were named after Orpheus. They are a cult of Dionysus. From Thrace they were brought to Thessaly and Boeotia, and in the middle of the sixth century spread rapidly in Attica under the Pisistratids (560–524). In their first appearance, they exerted an influence on the Eleusinian Mysteries, of which we shall have more to say later. They swept southern Italy and Sicily so rapidly that the route by which they traveled can no longer be ascertained. Before the middle of the sixth century the impact of the Orphic doctrines was felt by the Ionian philosophers—first of all Anaximander, later followed, in a spiritual development whose importance can scarcely be overestimated, by Pythagoras and the Pythagoreans in southern Italy, by Pindar and the tragic poets of Attica. The rapid spread of the Orphic mysteries contrasts strikingly with the mysteries of Eleusis and of the Cabiri. It is explained only in part by the fact that the Orphic mysteries were not, like the others, bound up with any place, since they required no temples but were enacted in dwellings. The song, or more accurately the epic hymn, soon came to be more important than the sacred action; and the central theme of the song was the narrative of the theogony, created at an early time and then adorned and transformed over a period of eight centuries. Set in writing, these sacred tales, these ἱεροὶ λόγοι, gained great authority with the Orphic believers, although like all "Orphic writings they remained in a fluid state."[17] They were finally fixed in twenty-four books, the number concurring with that of the Homeric poems. One of these works was known to Plato, who already looked upon it as "old story" (*Laws*, IV, 715 e). They have been called the "Orphic Bible,"[18] with a certain justification in so far as the collection of rhapsodies was the only sacred book in pre-Christian literature deserving of this name, but fallaciously in so far as neither they, nor the similar theogonies that have come down to us under various names,[19] enjoyed dogmatic authority, since they were in a process of constant change.

17 Nilsson, Vol. I, p. 646, rightly gives strong emphasis to this characteristic of Orphic poetry.
18 Kern, *Religion* (1935), Vol. II, p. 150.
19 Ziegler (PW, XVIII [1942], 1341–1417) gives a sound orientation on the philological problems connected with the Orphic writings, astutely summing up the work of his predecessors. Unfortunately, he gives little or no attention to the two most important modern attempts to treat the Orphic theogony as a whole, those of Kern, *Religion*, Vols. II (passim) and III; and of Nilsson, Vol. I, pp. 644ff.

Any attempt to reconstitute the content of the theogony from the fragments, to interpret and evaluate the theogonic cosmos, is venturesome. And yet it is a venture that must be undertaken, because the Orphic myth of the genesis of the gods, of man, of the world, is the most important guide to the Orphic mysteries themselves. In recent times, two significant attempts have been made: that of Kern who, following Rohde's *Psyche*, represents the theogonic cosmos of Orphism according to the six ages of the cosmos; and that of Nilsson, who bases his picture of the old Orphic world exclusively on records of the sixth to the fourth century.[20] Here I shall submit to you a narrative of the threefold Dionysus and the six ages of the world such as may well have been read by the aged Plato, fully aware that its basic elements belonged to an "old *logos*."

In the beginning time created the silver egg of the cosmos.[21] Out of this egg burst Phanes-Dionysus. His name of Phanes unmistakably reveals the root φαν (φαίνειν, "to bring light"; φαίνεσθαι, "to shine"), and later the Orphics disputed as to whether the god should be considered in the middle voice, as "the Glittering One," or in the active voice, as "the bringer of light"; he was in any case a god of light.[22] For them he was the first god to appear, the firstborn, whence he early became known as Protogonos. He was bisexual and bore within him the seeds of all gods and men. He was also the creator of heaven and earth, of the sun, the stars, and the dwelling of the gods.[23] The sixth Orphic hymn, dated to be sure in the Christian era but preserving old elements, represented him in epic hexameters:

> O mighty first-begotten, hear my prayer,
> Twofold, egg-born, and wandering through the air;
> Bull-roarer, glorying in thy golden wings,
> From whom the race of Gods and mortals springs.
> Ericapaeus, celebrated power,
> Ineffable, occult, all-shining flower.
> 'Tis thine from darksome mists to purge the sight,
> All-spreading splendor, pure and holy light;
> Hence, Phanes, called the glory of the sky,
> On waving pinions through the world you fly.[24]

---

20 Explicitly stressed by Nilsson, p. 660. Rohde's work tr. W. B. Hillis (London, 1925).
21 *OF*, fr. 54, 68, 70, 75.
22 Rightly stressed by K. Preisendanz, PW, XIX (1938), 1769, on the basis of *OF*, fr. 109 and 86.
23 *OF*, fr. 85, 108, 89.
24 *OF*, fr. 87 (tr. Thomas Taylor [1824], *The Mystical Hymns of Orpheus*, London, 1896).

The hymn suggests a strange hybrid: Phanes has golden wings and the head of a bull; the reference to his solar power could not be more forceful. In view of the penchant for the daemonic revealed by the Greek sculptors of the seventh century, his plastic representation might well have been of that "Greek" type which elaborated elements originating in Asia Minor.[25]

The myth of Phanes must have been in existence by the end of the archaic period.[26] Soon Phanes acquired many names, the self-explanatory Protogonos and the unexplained Ericapaeus, the revealing name Eros—an identification which was known to Aristophanes;[27] and finally, Dionysus and Metis.

Thus Phanes bears within himself infinite time, whose child he is, and Eros, the all-creating; he embodies the omnipresence of the human generations, and all the souls of future generations.

Phanes first created his daughter Nyx, the Night; in his bisexual quality, he was her father and mother at once. With Nyx, who alone was privileged to behold him, Phanes at vast intervals of time begot Gaea, Uranus, and Cronus, who after Uranus became lord of the world.

In the "holy legends," Zeus was the great-grandchild of Phanes and ruler of the fifth period of the world, succeeding the ages of Phanes, Nyx, Uranus, and Cronus.[28] Here the Orphic theogony ventured a significant amalgamation. Enriching upon the Hesiodic theogony after which it is modeled, it knew six ages of the world; but its myth reduced the six to three, each of

25 Cf. the Gorgon and the Lion of Corfu in sculpture; the griffins' heads and gorgoneum from Olympia in toreutics; the fabulous beings on 7th-cent. vases. As to the significance of the new excavations in Olympia, which in good part belong to the 7th cent., an excellent orientation is given by Ernst Langlotz in *Das neue Bild der Antike*, Vol. I, pp. 163ff. As to the site of the encounter between the Orphic Cronus and the Mithraic Zrvan (and also presumably of Phanes with Mithras) Robert Eisler, writing in 1921 (*Orpheus the Fisher*, p. 7), presumed it to be Asia Minor. When? Perhaps a new light is shed on this question by the investigations of Heinz Mode, *Indische Frühkulturen und ihre Beziehungen zum Westen* (Basel, 1944), p. 149, pp. 69ff.

26 Aristophanes, *Birds*, 690ff. (= *OF*, fr. 1), presupposed a similar Orphic theogony. Cf. *OF*, fr. 54, which is rightly regarded by Kern and by Diels (Orpheus B 13, in *Fragmente der Vorsokratiker*, 5th edn., ed. W. Kranz, Vol. I, Berlin, 1934, p. 11 [Freeman, *Ancilla*, p. 3]) as a document of ancient Orphism. The name Phanes can only be attested for the post-classical period; but to suppose with K. Seeliger (Roscher, *Lexikon*, VI, col. 492) that Phanes entered into Orphism only in Hellenistic times is to build too heavily on the silence of tradition. The opposing view is excellently presented by Guthrie, pp. 90ff.

27 That Phanes = Eros in Aristophanes, *Birds*, 697, has been brilliantly demonstrated by Preisendanz, in PW, XIX, 1765ff.

28 Cf. *OF*, fr. 101 (a decisive fragment, along with Proclus on Plato, *Timaeus*, proem E (ed. Diehl, Vol. III, Leipzig, 1906, p. 168, li. 15 [= *OF*, fr. 107]) and fr. 109 and 135.

which is governed by Dionysus. Phanes-Eros-Dionysus thus became the lord of the first Orphic age of the world.

Zeus could enter into his domination of the world only by devouring the primal god Phanes.[29] By this act he assimilated and embodied the whole previous world. The world of Zeus was thus a rebirth. It was the world of Phanes enriched by the action of Zeus himself; it was the presence of all souls and all things, as the profound Neoplatonist Proclus recognized, saying: "After he had devoured Phanes, the essential forms of the universe became manifest in Zeus."[30]

This devouring did not, as has often been maintained, reflect barbaric thinking but was actually based on Hesiod. In the Hesiodic theogony Zeus swallowed his first wife Metis and brought forth her child Athene from his head.

In view of all this we can understand how in Orphic thinking Zeus should have been the most powerful of gods, as he is revealed to be in an Orphic hymn which was recognized as such by Plato.

> Zeus was first and Zeus last, he with the glittering lightning; Zeus is the head, Zeus is the middle, all things are accomplished out of Zeus. Zeus is the foundation of earth and of the starry heavens. Zeus became a man, Zeus became an immortal woman. Zeus is the breath of all things, Zeus is the impulse of the unwearying fire. Zeus is the root of the sea, Zeus is the sun and moon. Zeus is king, Zeus is the ruler of all things, he with the gleaming lightning.[31]

It has long and repeatedly been pointed out that these words form a prototype of the famous formula for eternity, which recurs in numerous variations in the epic poetry of the ancients and in the early Christian texts, and which in the second hymn of Synesius achieves the stature of mystical prophecy.

But even though the Orphic mystic held Zeus to be the greatest god of his age, i.e., the second Orphic age, and the fifth king of the universe, he was not the favorite god. This distinction falls to the second Dionysus, Dionysus-Zagreus, whom Zeus begot upon his daughter Persephone.[32] This was the second divine incest in the life of the Orphic Dionysus. Obviously,

---

29 *OF*, fr. 164–68.
30 Proclus on Plato, *Tim.*, 28 c (ed. Diehl, Vol. I, 1903, p. 312, li. 26 [= *OF*, fr. 167]).
31 *OF*, fr. 21 and 21 a; 168.   32 Ibid., fr. 58, 153, 195, 210.

the son of Persephone is a ruler of the dead. While he was still a child Zeus bequeathed to him the rule over the world and the underworld, and as symbolic expression of this, the boy Dionysus plays with the apples of the Hesperides.[33] This astonishing rise to power aroused the envy of the Titans. As the boy Dionysus was looking at himself in the mirror, thus exposing himself to the danger of the Dionysian self-encounter, they tore him to pieces and devoured him. Enraged, Zeus destroyed the Titans with his thunderbolt and burned them. From their ashes rose the human race, not that of the age of Phanes, nor of the age of Cronus, but the third human race of the Zeus period. This human race, which still lives, is by nature Titanic and terrible.[34] It is easy to see that the Orphics took a negative view of the Titanic nature, in strange contrast to the previous Greek view, which finds its expression in the *Prometheus* of Aeschylus, in the fifth century. The Orphics were not able to impose this negative attitude on their myth, for even the late Orphic hymns do not entirely preserve it. The Titans retained for the Greeks a remnant of their original nature as sun gods.

All the richer was the ethical evaluation of the Titan myth. For in the Orphic view, when man rose from the ashes of the Titans, it was not only the evil Titanic nature that he inherited. The Titans had eaten the boy Dionysus; thus the ashes, and hence man as well, contained a divine, Dionysian part. The evaluation of man as a good and evil creature of Titanic and Dionysian origin is essential to Orphism and occurs here for the first time in Greece. Only recently a writer has called it the most original and farreaching creation of the Greeks and spoken of the Titanic nature as the Orphic original sin. Rightly, in so far as this basic view led the Orphics to devaluate human life and brought them the conviction that man must redeem himself by fleeing the Titanic and saving the Dionysian in himself. The divine soul must strive to return to its source. The body becomes the tomb and prison of the soul, which seeks flight into transcendence: the myth of the Titanic-Dionysian origin of man created the belief that the body was the tomb of the soul, the σῶμα-σῆμα dogma. This is the center of the Orphic Mysteries. It epitomizes the Orphic and un-Greek flight from the world. I should like to give every possible stress—contrary to certain hypercriti-

33 Fr. 34, 208.
34 Fr. 140. The myth of the rending of Dionysus by the Titans is attested for the 6th century (Onomacritus). *OF*, test. 194 and fr. 210. The notion of the Titanic and terrible human race is taken as old and proverbial by Plato, *Laws*, III, 701 b. The trivializing interpretation of Thomas, *Epekeina*, pp. 44, 138 (see n. 35, below) is impossible.

74

cal modern writers—to the fact that beginning with Philolaus and Plato all ancient thinkers regarded this doctrine as Orphic and that consequently, in their view, the Pythagoreans had taken over the soma-sema dogma from the Orphics.[35]

The third Dionysus, the bringer of redemption to the soul languishing in prison, is Dionysus-Lyseus.[36] Athene had succeeded in saving the heart of Dionysus-Zagreus and bringing it to her father Zeus. Zeus ate it and thus preserved in himself the nature of his father-child Dionysus. Moreover, he now begot upon Semele—an old Thracian-Phrygian earth goddess—the third Dionysus. The myth in itself indicates to what a degree the child partakes of the nature of Zeus: for it is the father who carries the child in his thigh.

Dionysus-Lyseus thus becomes the sixth king of the old theogony, the ruler of the third Orphic age of the world, the redeemer and healer of the soul.

In the myth of the threefold Dionysus, who is devoured as Phanes and Zagreus and yet rules as primal creator and re-creator of the world, we have a prerational expression of the notion that in periodic change the one is split into many, that the many become one again, and that universe, god, and man are governed by this primal rhythm.

The Orphic myth of the genesis of the cosmos, the gods, and man offers a unique expression of the eternity of the soul, of the "one and all,"[37] of life arising from the force and spirit of Dionysus, of redemption and the return of the soul to its divine place; and moreover the central figure of the three-fold Dionysus foreshadows the last essential element in the Orphic mysteries: the doctrine of transmigration. This is the doctrine according to which the soul lives its life in different bodies before returning, purified and cleansed,

---

35 The testimony of Plato (*Cratylus*, 400 c; *Gorgias*, 493 a; *Phaedo*, 70 c) is clear; and that, furthermore, Philolaus, in fr. 14 (Freeman, p. 76), has the Orphics and no one else in mind, can be denied only by inveterate negativists. An example of how hypercriticism can paint a picture more fantastic than even the most uncritical crackpots is provided by Hans Werner Thomas in *Epekeina, Untersuchungen über das Überlieferungsgut in den Jenseitsmythen Platons* (Würzburg, 1938), particularly pp. 5off. Nilsson, Vol. I, p. 661, now believes that the soma-sema doctrine is the primary idea of the older Orphism.

36 *OF*, fr. 232, 218.

37 This fundamental idea is clearly expressed by Proclus among the Neoplatonists (*OF*, fr. 215, 216) and—in a variant that is an anticipation of Nietzsche's basic ideas—by Olympiodorus on Plato's *Phaedo* 67 c (= *OF*, fr. 211). The myth itself proves that this periodic flux between the one and all is Orphic wisdom and cannot be Neoplatonic speculation; this is also shown by *OF*, fr. 165.

to its divine home. While the threefold Dionysus, by being metaphysically torn and devoured, suffers these changes without repentance and atonement, the human soul experiences them in order to atone for past injustices and to be purified. Just as the threefold human race corresponds to the threefold Dionysus,[38] so does the transmigration of the soul correspond to the transformations of the myth. Thus, seen from the point of view of the myth, the doctrine of transmigration must originally have been Orphic.[39]

A strong sense of justice, far greater than in previous Greek thinking, is manifested in the Orphic mysteries. In the doctrine of transmigration, which naturally posits the immortality of the individual soul and its existence prior to birth, the soma-sema myth is combined with the new ideas of justice and retribution. We now understand the pronounced severity of the Orphic rites of purification. These—in contrast to the mysteries of Eleusis and Samothrace—were demanded not only in times of festival, but throughout life. The Orphics also abstained from all meat—an astounding notion for the Homeric Greeks, who so eagerly held forth their hands for the tasty roasted morsels. They were not permitted to kill animals, for this would have been to kill their "brothers" and interfere with the migration of souls;[40] and moreover, it would have meant a concession to their Titanic nature. They were not even allowed to eat eggs, since in the Orphic view Dionysus-Phanes was born from an egg and the egg was the principle of life. These commandments and prohibitions, early taken over by the Pythagoreans, thus enjoyed currency in the most spiritual order of the classical era.

Their belief in retributive justice, in purification and atonement, caused the Orphics to form a particular view of the hereafter. For the impure and the evildoers they created a hereafter of muck and torment—we might call it hell. They were the Greek "discoverers" of hell. They created the judges of the dead. With them, death ceased to be a copy of life on earth—as it was for Homer, for the Ionians, and even for Pindar as a young man—but was divided according to the good and just and their opposites: beginning with the Orphics, there was an isle of the blessed and a Tartarus.

38 Surely this is the conception underlying *OF*, fr. 140.
39 Recently Nilsson, Vol. I, p. 664, has on a purely historical basis come to the same conclusion, namely that the Orphics were the first Greeks to sustain the doctrine of transmigration.
40 Vegetarianism is expressly imputed to the person of Orpheus in the oldest sources, Euripides, Aristophanes, and Plato. For details, PW, XVIII, 1267.

III

These then were the substance of the Orphic mysteries: the story of the threefold Dionysus; the story of the genesis of the gods, the cosmos, and men; punishment and retribution in the hereafter; and the transmigration of souls.

But here we come to the crucial question. What was the nature of their ceremonies? What sacred action was represented in them? What were the *dromena*—the things that were *done*? Or were the Orphic "mysteries" no mysteries at all, but mere speculations? They must have been authentic mysteries, for in the records of the ancients, the words τελεταί (completed actions), ὄργια (works), μυστήρια, occur too frequently to allow of any other interpretation.[41] But we know even less about this sacred action than about that of Eleusis, and scarcely more than we know about the mysteries of Samothrace.

It is not only because of the nature of mysteries which are and should remain a holy secret that we know so little about the actual dromena, but because the Orphics in particular had no fixed sites hallowed by tradition. Nowhere has the existence of an Orphic temple been proved, and this applies most particularly, regrettable as it is, to the Villa Item at Pompeii, which was recently designated by an Italian archaeologist as an "Orphic basilica." True, the mysteries were performed in "sacred houses." But since the Orphics do not seem to have had sedentary custodians of their *teletai*, and since their priests were itinerant missionaries, the necessary local traditions were lacking; though indeed their vast tradition of mythical poetry did much to compensate for this lack.

It would seem to be definitely established, at all events, that the mystai were painted with lime and plaster:[42] this was intended to symbolize the Titanic in them, since according to the myth the Titans smeared themselves with "plaster" in order to approach the infant Dionysus unrecognized. The mystai, then, were first reminded of their Titanic nature; we may presume accordingly that the first part of the mysteries represented the Titanic "original sin." But the center of the mysteries must have been the sufferings of the threefold Dionysus and the related redemption of man.

---

41 With regard to the whole question, see primarily *OF*, test. 173–219. Kern himself exploited these sources and expatiated on them in PW, XVI (1935), 1279ff.
42 The supporting proofs of this are best assembled by Kern, PW, XVI, 1281f.

And according to the record of the activities of Onomacritus, this would seem to apply to so early a time as the age of the Pisistratids. Did the dromena end with an epiphany of Phanes?[43]

Surveying the substance, scope, and greatness of the Orphic mysteries, we readily understand how it came to be the universal opinion of antiquity that—to cite Jacob Burckhardt—Orpheus "was the father of all rites and of all mysticism in general"; and how he ultimately became the great fisher of souls and was assimilated to Christ.[44]

And we come to understand various other things of importance for the history of Greek thought:

First: Retribution and the hereafter prevent a fusion of the Orphic mysteries with the ecstatic Bacchic cults. But although they make for a "narrow" path, the world which we find encompassed in the religious symbols of Orphism remains immensely broad and heterogeneous. This is due to the myth of the threefold Dionysus; it embraces experience of the world and of the gods, brute worldly action as well as the transformation and preservation of man; and it also embraces the culture of the word, the act, the gesture. The unity of word, song, and dance is as inherent in the Orphic mysteries as in those of Eleusis and—though in a very different way—as in Greek tragedy.

Second: Orphism had its noble and its vulgar followers; accordingly, we find rude elements side by side with subtle myths. Lofty intellects were moved by Orphism, though repelled by its excrescences. Plato, who knew both aspects of Orphism, offers the best proof of this.

Third: Despite the imagination of the Orphic theologians, the "basic agreement of early 'Orphicism' with that of late antiquity"[45] is conspicuous. The rich variations had little effect on the central substance of the myths. This tradition, in which poetic adornment, rich as it is, is secondary, again reveals the power of the Orphic-religious element.

Fourth: The Orphic heritage has been transmitted to us mainly by the Neoplatonists. The last really significant thinker of antiquity aside from Boethius—the Neoplatonist Proclus—presents every guarantee of a historically disciplined philosophical speculation. Consequently, with all his

43 Cf. Seeliger, in Roscher, *Lexikon*, VI, 489ff.
44 Regarding the extraordinary transformation and significance of Orphic symbols in early Christian art, see Robert Eisler in his eccentric book *Orpheus the Fisher*, pp. 51ff.
45 Nilsson, Vol. I, p. 649—I have cited the passage because of its importance in spite of the hideous word Orphicism [*Orphizismus*].

creative reinterpretation of Orphism, he always preserves some trace of the sacred blood of the Orphic myth and mysteries. This insight also belongs to the study of the mysteries.

2. Orphism and the Greek Spirit

I

How did the Greek spirit react to the powerful reality of the Orphic mysteries? This is a complex question and we shall approach it with all caution. Scholars have generally agreed—in so far as agreement is possible—that purification, atonement, sense of guilt, and belief in immortality are un-Homeric if not un-Greek conceptions; that the idea of justice, which emerged in Hesiod, was intensified by the Orphics in a manner not typically Greek; that, in particular, punishment in the hereafter and the transmigration of souls are un-Greek conceptions; and moreover, that the syncretism that enveloped the threefold Dionysus as early as the sixth century was alien to the Greeks.

For this reason, most students of Greek antiquity have represented Orphism as a body alien to Greek culture. With Burckhardt they have carried their distrust to the point of belittling Orphic influence; or they have worked themselves up into such irritation as led a scholar of the stature of Wilamowitz to make insufferably superficial statements, as in his *Der Glaube der Hellenen*,[1] where he characterizes everything which was or might have been Orphic as Pythagorean or nonexistent. On the other hand, scholars open to the irrational, like Bachofen and Rohde, have taken a particular interest in Orphism.

The word "un-Greek" is ambivalent, to say the least. Was Orphism un-Greek because it was of un-Greek origin, or did the Hellenic spirit reject it as alien to its nature? Or are both interpretations applicable?

At last a certain light has been cast on the obscure question of origin. Scholars had long, without real proof, imputed the doctrine of immortality and the consequent devaluation of earthly existence to Oriental influence. But everything that we know of Orpheus and Orphism points, as we have

---

1 Ulrich von Wilamowitz-Moellendorff, *Der Glaube der Hellenen* (Berlin, 1931–32), Vol. II, p. 199.

shown, to Thrace. Recently it has rightly been stressed that the radical "metaphysical pessimism"—manifested in the Orphic devaluation of this world—was a characteristic of that people among whom the cult of Dionysus had its earliest home, namely the Thracians, the "greatest nation on earth after the Indian," as Herodotus called them. Indeed, one of the Thracian tribes, the Thrausians, looked upon life as suffering and upon death as *"eudaimonia,"* wherefore, as Herodotus reports,[2] it was their interesting custom to mourn the newborn and bury the dead "amid joy and merry-making." The belief in immortality and the hereafter had developed in the primordial, chthonian Dionysus cult of the Thracians, and from the Thracian-Phrygian home of Dionysus-Zagreus it came to Greece. Once we are aware of this, we have to cease inquiring whether transmigration came to Greece from India or Asia. A significant contact between Orphism and the Orient would have been possible only on the coast of Asia Minor, chiefly via the Babylonized cult of Mithras. But at so early a date?[3]

The second question can be answered with far greater certainty. How did the Greek spirit react to the Orphic revolution, which—quite contrary to the views of Homer and Hesiod—dematerialized the soul, devaluated earthly life, and subordinated even the gods in heaven to a simple ethos? I have already noted the most representative answers. But despite the illustrious names of their authors, I should like to venture a new answer to this central question. First of all, the question itself is multiple and so accordingly are the answers. For Greece as a cultural cosmos was never homogeneous. On the contrary, this aggregate of small communities succeeded, in the course of a thousand years, in producing successive miniature cultural spheres: the archaic metropolitan, the Homeric-Aeolian, the Hesiodic, the Ionian, the Pythagorean-Italian, the Sicilian-Empedoclean, and the Attic. In the change from one to another and in their rich interrelations lies the secret of the greatness and duration of Greek culture, whose Hellenistic age, long after the death of the city-states, continued to draw strength from those cultural spheres, their variations and mixtures. Contrary to the belief of those scholars we have mentioned, the answer to the question of how the Greek spirit reacted to the Orphic revolution must therefore be manifold. Let us attempt to approach the matter historically.

2 Herodotus, Book V, 3f.
3 I.e., in the 7th century. Cf. my n. 25, above, and my study of Mithras, *EJ 1943*, pp. 149ff.

II

The first demonstrable reaction to the Orphic incursion into Attica falls in the middle of the sixth century—hence later than in Ionia! At this time Onomacritus of Athens, the theological adviser of the Pisistratids, paraphrased and enlarged on the Orphic songs in free epic style, and the ruling house was influenced by this work. At the same time, the Pisistratids, as has been shown by the most recent archaeological findings in Eleusis, built the great Eleusinian temple. Since the god Iacchus, strangely resembling Dionysus, played an important part in the Eleusinian Mysteries, it was long presumed that Onomacritus had made a bold attempt to draw them into Orphic mysticism.[4] In order to understand such an attempt and weigh its historical likelihood, it is necessary to call up before the mind's eye a picture of the ritual and content of these mysteries.

These most Greek of mysteries were dedicated to two primeval earth goddesses, who were known simply as "the two goddesses"; they were mother and daughter, Demeter and Kore. In performance of the rite, the devotees formed an immense procession from Athens to Eleusis. The rite began after a threefold sacral purification: a bath first in the sea, then on the road to Eleusis in the salt lakes, the *rheitoi*, and finally within the sacred confines of Eleusis. Catharsis by water thus played an important role. The image of Iacchus, a god early assimilated to Dionysus, was solemnly borne over the sacred highway from Athens to Eleusis, a distance of nearly fourteen miles. Then the mystery rites were performed in and around the temple. The holy actions, in which the essence and meaning of the Mysteries were expressed, were as follows:[5]

1. The rape of Kore by Hades and the loving wanderings of her mother Demeter.

2. In the sacred night, the climax of the Mysteries, the divine birth, in which Demeter bears the boy Pluto, symbol of wealth and abundance. This event was enacted amid an abrupt change from veiled darkness to full light, and to vision attained through the purifying power of light and fire. The mystes, who "has his eyes closed and veiled," becomes the epopt, the seer.

4 Kern, *Die Religion der Griechen*, Vol. II, p. 164, in conjunction with the work of his student, Adolf Krueger, *Quaestiones Orphicae* (Halle, 1934).
5 The sources are now competently collected in PW, XVI, 1236ff., and in Victor Magnien, *Les Mystères d'Eleusis* (Paris, 1929), pp. 198ff.

3. The sending out of Triptolemus, who brings men wheat, the earth's greatest blessing, from Eleusis. A spike of wheat, symbol of mother earth's eternal fertility, was displayed amid the cry "Let the rain come! Conceive!"—the former word being addressed to the heavens, the latter to the earth.

The irrational, religious core of these sacred actions, the highest arcanum, consisted in the effigy of a womb, which the devotee had to touch. By this act, to which everything preceding and following was attuned, he would be born to new life. The holy symbols—water, torch, fire, spike, and *cista*—predominate in these mysteries; through them and the enacted myth the devotee experiences atonement and purification, elevation and beatitude.

The Eleusinian Mysteries solemnized the initiation of fertility; they celebrated the return from the underworld, the fertility of the earth, and the loving gift of Demeter to mankind, and also the procreation of man and his hallowed rebirth. The beauty and grandeur of these sacred games opened the reticent mouths of the greatest of Greek poets, Aeschylus and Pindar; as early as the middle of the seventh century they wrung these words from the author of the Hymn to Demeter, the narrator of Persephone's abduction, a poet grown strong in the purifying power of the Eleusinian fire:

> Happy is he among men upon earth who has seen these mysteries; but he who is uninitiate and who has no part in them never has lot of like good things once he is dead, down in the darkness and gloom.[6]

The points of contact between the Eleusinian and the Orphic mysteries are apparent:

1. The assimilation of the young god Iacchus to Dionysus, and specifically to that Dionysus who is the son of Persephone. And this is why the rape of Persephone plays so prominent a part in Orphic poetry.[7]

2. The development of both mysteries under the Pisistratids.

3. The influence of both rites on the development of Attic tragedy, which up to Euripides retained its sacral character. Without the two mysteries, the conception of tragic "catharsis" would scarcely have come into being.

4. The center of both mysteries is purification, fertility, rebirth; they both, though in greatly varying degree, strive toward a luminous "other world."

6 *Hymn to Demeter*, 480ff. (tr. Hugh G. Evelyn-White, *Hesiod, the Homeric Hymns, and Homerica*, LCL, 1920, p. 323).
7 *OF*, fr. 47–53.

The similarities are striking; and yet up to now it has been impossible to prove that Orphism exerted a significant influence on the Eleusinian Mysteries. Did the similarities result merely from the general religious revival of the seventh and sixth centuries? Were both mysteries spontaneous discoveries of the religious soul? This would seem to be the case; for particularly in the Eleusinian Mysteries, fertility, the blessings of the earth and the body, rebirth through the grace of the godhead, and the joys of the hereafter are all attained and preserved through the "goddesses." In all this the powerful undercurrent of a very ancient Demeter cult is evident. In Eleusis we would seem to find a quality peculiarly Greek, an attitude of caution against excessive admixture of alien elements, a tendency to preserve a purely Greek religious life. And if this is so, we must come to the important conclusion that the "most Greek of all mysteries" were oriented toward rebirth and transcendence—two phenomena which Burckhardt and so many scholars after him have rejected as un-Greek.

III

Let us now turn to another cultural sphere: it seems surprising that precisely where rational thought was pursued with the passion of the first discoverers, namely among the earliest thinkers of Ionian Asia Minor, a distinct Orphic note is audible. Even the ancients discerned it in the most important fragment of Anaximander, which runs: "The Non-Limited is the original material of existing things; further, the source from which existing things derive their existence is also that to which they return at their destruction, according to necessity; for they give justice and make reparation to one another for their injustice, according to the arrangement of Time."[8] Here the idea of retribution seems only recently to have left the religious sphere in order to govern the natural universe, and the Orphic god Cronus seems to have just cast off his mythical cloak. Anaximander's Cronus, repentance, and retribution appear in part to be Orphic figures newly recast in conceptual form.

But most noteworthy of all was the influence of the Orphic doctrine on Pythagoras and on the order founded by him in Crotona, which for two generations governed the intellectual life of southern Italy. Scholarship has long endeavored to distinguish between Pythagorean and Orphic ele-

8 Diels, fr. 3 (tr. Freeman, *Ancilla*, p. 19) and *OF*, fr. 23 and 158. The relation to Orphism is most clearly seen by Guthrie, pp. 222ff.

ments in the doctrines attributed to both movements. Common to both sects were the doctrines of transmigration and retribution in the hereafter, purification, and the prohibition of meat; their myths, symbols, and mysticism were similar. In so far as the question has meaning in the present state of historical research, it can be established that the basic Orphic myth and the main elements of the new Orphic ethos must have preceded their Pythagorean repetition and variation by one to three generations.[9] And a recent writer presumes that Pythagoras, in accordance with the Mediterranean

9 The following considerations argue the priority of archaic Orphism over Pythagoras:
  (a) According to all ancient tradition, Orpheus came from Thrace. And so likewise did Orphism. The route of its journey, beginning in the 7th century, was the route of Dionysus. Thus presumably:

$$\text{Thrace} \rightarrow \text{Thessaly and Boeotia} \rightarrow \text{Attica}$$
$$\text{Thrace} \rightarrow \text{Phrygia} \rightarrow \text{Attica}$$
$$\rightarrow \text{Western Mediterranean}$$

An itinerary as precise as our knowledge would allow is much to be desired. Unless all indications are misleading, Attica was influenced earlier and more strongly than the West. Eduard Meyer, *Geschichte des Altertums*, Vol. III (Stuttgart, 1937), p. 691, almost literally following Erwin Rohde, writes of the Orphic doctrine: ". . . its true home is Attica!" Archaic Orphism in Boeotia in particular (O. Gruppe's chief thesis) is in need of further investigation, though Ziegler is justified in rejecting Gruppe's theory as such in PW, XVIII, 1238.
  (b) The ancient tradition, including Plato, regards Orpheus and his hymns, but not Pythagoras, as very ancient (*OF*, test. 10 and 220). According to the ancient genealogies (*OF*, test. 7-9), Orpheus lived seven to nine generations before Homer—a notion recently taken "rather" seriously by Franz Dornseiff, "Altorientalisches in Hesiods Theogonie," *Antiquité classique* (Brussels), VI (1937), 236ff. Antiquity regarded Pherecydes, the important 6th-century Orphic, as the teacher of Pythagoras (PW, XIX [1938], 2025ff.).
  (c) The doctrine of transmigration is ascribed by the crown witness Plato (see above, p. 76, and *Laws*, VI, 782) to the Orphics and not to the Pythagoreans. Our first record of the Pythagorean doctrine of transmigration occurs in the 1st century B.C.—G. Rathmann, "Quaestiones Pythagoreae, Orphicae, Empedocleae" (diss., Halle, 1933), pp. 32ff.
  (d) The soma-sema doctrine is Orphic and not Pythagorean (see above, p. 75, and PW, XVIII, 1379ff.).
  (e) Vegetarianism is attributed primarily to Orphism (see above, p. 76).
  (f) A considered treatment of this question of priority (avoiding the fantasies and hypercriticism so favored in this particular field) is now to be found in Guthrie, pp. 216ff.; Ziegler, PW, XVIII, 1383ff.; Nilsson, pp. 640-95. Among earlier writers, in Meyer, *Geschichte des Altertums*, III, 2 (1937), pp. 681ff. and 757ff.
  (g) On the positive side, it may be presumed that Pythagoras, a figure naturally open to the mystery and the mystical, received strong impressions from Orphism in Greece and carried them to the West, thus establishing the most important variation of Orphism, to which he gave a mathematical-astronomical form. In this light it becomes understandable that according to ancient tradition the Pythagoreans liked to be known as disciples of Orpheus.

psyche, transformed Orphic metempsychosis into a doctrine of the immortal aristocratic soul, thus setting up an entirely new theory of transmigration.[10]

It was precisely Empedocles, the sage of Sicily (the most westerly West) and disciple of Pythagoras, who, turning back to ancient Orphism, made this doctrine of the immortal aristocratic man and his soul the foundation of a general conception of life. Standing spiritually between Orpheus and Pythagoras, he took an Orphic view of rational thought, regarding it as a downfall from the realm of piety; and he looked on man as an ephemeral creature. He began his doctrine of nature with this plea to the Muse:

> Convey (to me) such knowledge as divine law allows us creatures of a day to hear, driving the well-harnessed car from (the realm of) Piety![11]

His proximity to Orphism is revealed in the very title of his second great work, the *Katharmoi* (Purifications). Retribution, transmigration, atonement are all present in the words:

> There is an oracle of Necessity, an ancient decree of the gods, eternal, sealed fast with broad oaths, that when one of the divine spirits whose portion is long life sinfully stains his own limbs with bloodshed, and following Hate has sworn a false oath—these must wander for thrice ten thousand seasons far from the company of the blessed, being born throughout the period into all kinds of mortal shapes, which exchange one hard way of life for another.[12]

Thus the culture of southern Italy and Sicily in the late sixth and the fifth century can be regarded essentially as a Mediterranean and secular variation of Orphism. The power of this influence extended even to Pindar, a Greek from the mother country who at first glance seems firmly rooted in this world.

Pindar is known to us as the singer of the Greek aristocratic ethos, whose proponents unite veneration of the gods with courage, discipline, and devotion to the just, the true, and the seemly. It has often been pointed out that the secret of his influence on the youthful victors in the Olympic, Pythian, Nemean, and Isthmian games lay in his "mature religiosity." But this very quality carries an unmistakable Orphic imprint. Pindar keeps the image of his gods free from unworthy traits and quite un-Homerically endows his Olympians with omniscience and omnipotence, purity and

10 C. Kerényi, *Pythagoras und Orpheus, Aufsätze zur Geschichte der Antike und des Christentums* (Berlin, 1937), pp. 16–49.

11 Diels, fr. 3 (tr. Freeman, p. 51).   12 Diels, fr. 115 (tr. Freeman, p. 65).

sanctity. True, this might be derived from Hesiod. But like the Orphics he praised Cronus as the "father of all things," and Nomos, law, as "the king of all."[13]

He speaks specifically of transmigration, and it is interesting to note that this occurs most unmistakably in the Ode for Theron, lord of Acragas in Sicily, the home of Empedocles and apparently an Orphic settlement. Speaking of retribution, the poet begins:

> But if, in very deed, when he hath that wealth, he knoweth of the future, that immediately after death, on earth, it is the lawless spirits that suffer punishment—and the sins committed in this realm of Zeus are judged by One who passeth sentence stern and inevitable....[14]

Transmigration and the "Islands of the Blest" were known to him; indeed, he gives us the oldest known description of the isles as a place of sojourn of the "pure."

> But whosoever, while dwelling in either world, have thrice been courageous in keeping their souls pure from all deed of wrong, pass by the highway of Zeus unto the tower of Cronus, where the ocean breezes blow around the Islands of the Blest, and flowers of gold are blazing, some on the shore from radiant trees, while others the water fostereth; and with chaplets thereof they entwine their hands, and with crowns, according to the righteous counsels of Rhadamanthus....[15]

In one important fragment we encounter transmigration of the southern Italian, Sicilian tinge—the wanderings of the great soul:

> But, as for those from whom Persephone shall exact the penalty of their pristine woe, in the ninth year she once more restoreth their souls to the upper sunlight; and from these come into being august monarchs, and men who are swift in strength and supreme in wisdom, and for all future time men call them sainted heroes.[16]

13 Documentation in Wilhelm Nestle, *Vom Mythos zum Logos* (Stuttgart, 1940), pp. 163ff.
14 *Olympian*, II, 102ff. (Schroeder). (Tr. Sir John Sandys, *The Odes of Pindar*, LCL, 1915, p. 23.) The ode deals with Theron's victory in the year 476 and was presumably written shortly thereafter. Empedocles was then about 18 years old.
15 *Olympian*, II, 123ff. (tr. Sandys, p. 25). Cf. Erwin Rohde, *Psyche* (tr. W. B. Hillis, London, 1925), pp. 416–17: "It is rather the substance of what he believes himself and has achieved by his own struggles that in a solemn hour he [Pindar] reveals for a moment to like-minded friends." An observation far sounder than the statistical elaboration of archaeological data to be found in Wilhelm Schmid and Otto Stählin, *Geschichte der griechischen Literatur*, Vol. I (Munich, 1929), pp. 582f.
16 Fr. 133 (tr. Sandys, p. 591).

These to be sure, are sparse, isolated strains in the work of Pindar. Yet this fact itself is often misinterpreted: for it must not be forgotten that barely a quarter of Pindar's work has come down to us, including none of his dithyrambics or processional and funeral hymns, in which other-worldly preoccupations would be most likely to find expression. In the four fragments of the *Threnoi* we find, indeed, more references to the transcendent than in all the triumphal odes taken together.[17] What little we possess of Pindar's poetry indicates that Orphism awakened and intensified old, essentially Greek impulses, and it is certain that the whole of his work would more than bear out this impression. Master of an aristocratic ethos based on traditional values, precursor of the rationalistic Ionian metaphysic, adept of Orphic piety, Pindar speaks of three different worlds, and it is certain that he did not reject the Orphic, ostensibly un-Greek one.

IV

Now that we have gained some idea what to listen for, we may perhaps approach that thinker who realized Attic thought and art in their purest form, that thinker without whom there would be no European culture, and to whose thinking all subsequent thinking is related as vast variations to a basic theme: I am referring to Plato. What was his reaction to Orphism?

Plato's writings are a union of two essentially different and antithetical forms of expression, namely, *logos* and *mythos:* by logos we mean faithful representation of reality, inquiring discourse as the instrument of Ionian ratio; while for Plato mythos—originally the word denoted legend, fairy tale, fable—meant at first everything contrary to logos, but subsequently everything that could no longer be apprehended or expressed by the logos, hence, unlike the early Platonic myth, embracing essential elements of the logos. The Platonic myth thus became predominantly an exposition of elements that could no longer be encompassed by pure thought, though they presupposed it; the expression of inner, intrinsically extrarational experiences.

In his first period Plato makes the logos, the discourse which seeks out and examines the truth, culminate in such myths: this he does in the *Apology*, in the *Crito, Gorgias, Phaedo,* and *Republic.* According to its literary form, I have called this myth *"Endmythos."*[18] The specific function of this

17 Fr. 129–31, 133.
18 See my *Versuch einer Grundlegung der Platonischen Mythopoiie* (diss., Zurich, 1925), pp. 65ff. Hans Leisegang, in his *Die Platondeutung der Gegenwart* (Karlsruhe, 1929), pp. 141–51, gave an able exposition and sound critical appraisal of my findings.

myth is to represent life in the other world. Now, in Plato's early works, the *Apology* and *Crito*, the other world is still seen in archaic and un-Orphic terms, as a reflection of this world; in the *Gorgias*, however, the dialogue which reveals Plato's intellectual turning point, the birth of his theory of ideas, a very different picture of Hades suddenly makes its appearance. Here the souls, naked and removed from the body, are judged according to the virtue and piety of their lives (*Gorgias*, 523 c). Here for the first time Plato seized upon the Orphic principle of retribution, making it hinge on justice and injustice. Retribution, philosophically apprehended and justified, is the central phenomenon of the *Gorgias* myth—born at the very moment when Plato was discovering the "idea"!—and from then on it remained the central motif of his end myths. In the *Phaedo*, that hymn to the immortality of the soul, Plato made use of an impressive Orphic conception, philosophically purified: each soul is led to judgment in Hades by its daemon, which is its guide and guardian angel, and thence to its appropriate place of retribution (*Phaedo*, 107 d). In assigning the souls to their various sites of punishment, the philosopher produces an astonishing cosmography: the earth, spherical in shape, hangs free in the center of the cosmos. But men, who think they are living on earth, actually live in misty hollows (Orphic note), while the true earth, the "earth of ideas," exists in the pure ether and sends only a feeble glimmer of its perfect beauty down into the hollows. The holes themselves are surrounded by rivers, whose home seems to be the inside of the earth. Most prominent are the four chthonian (and Orphic) rivers: Oceanus, Acheron, Pyriphlegethon, Styx. The ideal earth in all its glory is juxtaposed to the human earth (109 e ff.). In this cosmos the souls are judged and assigned to five categories: the most wicked, the murderers and temple robbers, atone forever in Tartarus; the curable sinners are driven each year from Tartarus into the Acherusian Lake; the third, those who have lived well-ordered lives, achieve atonement and purification in the Acherusian Lake; the fourth, who have lived piously, dwell, liberated from those earthly sites "as from prisons,"[19] in a place of purity on the ideal earth. And finally, the fifth category, those who have been sufficiently purified by philosophy, live disembodied and eternal in a place even more beautiful than the abode of the category before them—a place which defies all description.

19 ἀπαλλατόμενοι ὥσπερ δεσμωτηρίων (*Phaedo*, 114 b); the Orphic ring of the words requires no further elucidation.

88

We pause in amazement. The "Orphic" myth has been subordinated to a metaphysical pure substance, the idea. In this myth the supreme purification, the catharsis attained in the Mysteries, has indeed ceased to be Orphic, and yet the style of this ultimate thinking remains Orphic, and the injunction to purification continues to ring through. The concept of retribution is metaphysically transfigured by the idea.

It might seem as though this thinking could achieve no higher form. Yet it does so in that work which is the alpha and omega of Greek and Platonic political thought, the *Republic*. This work is crowned by a myth which is related by Er the Pamphylian (hence originating on the southern coast of Asia Minor). According to the legend, this man fell in battle but came back to life eleven days later just as he was about to be burned. Having been appointed "messenger to the world of men," he was able to describe the other world (*Republic*, X, 614 b – 621 d). The souls were judged and divided in accordance with pure justice; the good, rewarded tenfold for their deeds, wandered through heaven; the wicked, punished tenfold for their misdeeds, through the underworld. After this wandering, which continued for a thousand years, all the souls—with the exception of the tyrants eternally banished to Tartarus—gathered in the meadow of souls and prepared for a new incarnation. From the meadow of souls they journeyed to the Milky Way and from there to the spindle of Ananke, Necessity (=celestial axis). Here amid the music of the spheres, the soul, led by the Fate Lachesis, chose its new incarnation, which, once chosen, was unalterable. Freely, but on the basis of its earlier life, the soul elected the life of a man or animal. And Lachesis gave to each soul the daemon appropriate to its choice, as the "guardian of their lives and the fulfiller of the choice" (620 d, e). Since the new life was marked out by fate and guided by the daemon, the path of the soul was irrevocably "predestined." The souls chose in all manner of ways. The stupidest among them chose the life of a tyrant; Orpheus chose the life of a swan, since women had done him to death and he did not wish to be born of woman again (620 a); Odysseus, finally, the shrewdest of all the Greeks, made the best choice, "the life of a private man who had no cares" (620 c). The souls now passed on to the River Lethe, where they took varying draughts of forgetfulness and then as they slept were hurled amid thunder and lightning to earth for a new embodiment.

There is no doubt that in this myth Plato arrived at the doctrine of predestination. Fundamental to this doctrine is the axiom that all thought

89

is remembrance (=anamnesis), recollection of what was known in the pure state of the soul. In the *Meno*, Plato had developed the notion of anamnesis on the basis of pure thought. But in the myth of Er, he derived predestination from Orphic elements: from retribution and judgment, from the immortality of the soul, which for him as for the Orphics was necessarily post-existent and pre-existent, and from the doctrine of transmigration, in which, cautiously as he expressed himself, he indubitably believed.

Thus, in a process of reciprocal sublimation, Orphic experience was purified in pure thought, and pure thought, through Orphic experience, attained to the spheres which can no longer be encompassed in logical discourse. It is safe to say that without Orphism and its Pythagorean variations Plato would not have arrived at anamnesis and pure ideas. And this may shed new light on Plato's so crucial statement of a truth which he experienced at the time of the *Gorgias*, which he intimated in his myths and openly professed in the seventh *Letter* (341 d), saying that the highest in philosophy cannot be stated, but after laborious thought arises suddenly as a fire in the soul, and then feeds on itself.

Strange to say, Eros, a force that like the ideas and anamnesis is central to Plato, underwent a similar transformation through the Orphic experience. This is the theme of a second form of Platonic myth, which I designated years ago as a "metaphoric myth"[20] because its prototype is the celebrated metaphor of the cave (*Republic*, VII, 514ff.), and because Eros himself might almost have become a metaphor for the philosopher, if Plato had not been Plato and Eros had not been Eros.

In the *Symposium* Socrates, after the others have delivered their speeches on Eros, declares that Eros is not a god but a striving for what one lacks (*Symposium*, 199–202). It is the great intermediary—between god and man, between beautiful and ugly, between knowledge and ignorance. Hence its most peculiar characteristics are desire and vision. Precisely vision is the good for which Eros by nature strives. For through vision he seeks the possessor of the beautiful and becomes his lover, guiding the beloved in vision and knowledge. The road in common, leading and being led, the duality of the erotic existence, is an essential characteristic of the Platonic Eros.

The Platonic Eros includes three basic irrational forces: the desire for the beautiful, sensory vision, and the common striving of those who love. These three basic forces might still belong to the best Attic conception of Eros,

20 *Mythopoiie*, pp. 75ff.

but Plato sublimates them in his passionate thought. For, inextricably intertwined, they become for him the impulsion, immanent in man, to gain pure vision and thought, to travel the road of knowledge and wisdom. Eros apprehends the beauty of a body, then the beauty of many bodies, then the beauty of concrete things, then the beauty of categories of knowledge, and finally beauty as such, beauty as transcendent substance.

This is the holy ascent of philosophical knowledge; the road of Eros has become the road of pure thought. Why am I telling you all this? Because Alcibiades revealingly designated this Eros as the "sacrament of philosophical madness and frenzy," before which the profane should "close up the doors of their ears."[21] And because Plato represents this same ascent in the parable of the cave in the *Republic* (VII, 514ff.). Here man is represented as a prisoner in a cave lighted by a fire, who first sees only the shadows of things, then having gained his freedom of movement is able to perceive the things themselves and finally the fire; who then emerges to the surface of the earth and, at first blinded, can see only the shadows and reflections of things in the world, but then is able to perceive the things themselves and finally, his eyesight strengthened, the sun. Just as the man in the cave is blinded to the free world and the sun, so is the thinker blinded to the luminous world of ideas. Both the prisoners and the thinkers need a "release from their chains and a cure from nonthinking" (*Republic*, 515 c). These words are a direct extension of the Orphic dogma that the body is the tomb of the soul, that dogma which we find announced in the end myth of the *Phaedo* and to an even greater degree in the composition of the *Phaedo* as a whole.[22] In the parable of the cave, the cave is primarily a prison. Now, all at once, it becomes evident that the parable of the cave was made possible by the soma-sema dogma of Orphism, and we see how a very ancient Orphic experience reappeared in the pure thought of the metaphysician Plato—as a sudden fire—and with the power of Eros forces its way from the tomb to the sun. The road of Eros and of Orphism are one and the same. It is the road from the mystes, who has closed his eyes, to the epopt, the seer, "whose eyes have been opened"; it is the road from the *mysteria* to the Anakalypteria.

In the myth, the second plane of his life and his art, the wisest among

---

21 *Symposium*, 218 b. The Orphic coloration of this important passage (= *OF*, fr. 245) has long been recognized.
22 See above, pp. 68f.

Greeks confesses that his Orphic religious experience is not only the beginning of his metaphysical experience but actually "releases" it as by the
power of a catalyst. This can be seen and "proved" for anamnesis, for the
immortality of the soul, for the theory of ideas, and for Eros. This Platonic
confession strikes us as a great *mysterion*.[23] But it also makes it understandable that the Platonic Eros and anamnesis bear within them the power of
supreme religious symbols.

23 Thus we find partial confirmation in an entirely new sense of the Neoplatonist Olympiodorus' much despised remark on *Phaedo* 70 c, to the effect that "Plato everywhere
varies the doctrine of Orpheus" (= *OF*, fr. 224). What has been said above automatically corrects the formulation of so serious a student as Leisegang, p. 143, which
I should nonetheless like to quote here because of its importance: "The Orphic element used by Plato was for the most part detached from its original meaning and
context and removed to a new context essentially determined by his philosophical
and metaphysical ideas, so that, from this time on, the philosophers at least and many
poets dependent on them saw Orphic things through Platonic eyes, and there remained
in Greek literature only a Platonic Orphism."

Paul Schmitt

The Ancient Mysteries in the Society of Their Time, Their Transformation and Most Recent Echoes

1. Eleusis: The Local Cult and Early Christianity

The ancient—that is, Greek and Hellenistic-Roman—mysteries constitute a part of the religious life of their time, and like all religion they are an expression of men's feeling for something mightier than the human, an expression of the *"sensus numinis,"* as Count Zinzendorf called it: "All men have a feeling for something above them."[1] If we consider all that we know about the words μυστήρια and μυστήριον, we must say with Otto Kern: "From the word μυστήριον no inference can be drawn with regard to the origin and meaning of the mysteries; its derivation still remains entirely doubtful."[2] Despite masterly philological analysis of the words, this conclusion seems fully justified when we consider, for example, that in an Athenian legal code the word μυστήριον refers to the Eleusinian Mysteries, in Herodotus to those of Samothrace, in Heraclitus to the mysteries of the "night ramblers, magicians, bacchants, maenads, mystics,"[3] while in the writings of the physicians it signifies cough medicine, and in the Septuagint, the famous Greek translation of the Old Testament, it means "the secret plan of the king." It is certain, however, that in the sphere of Greek and Hellenistic-Roman religion the word *mysteria* (the plural is more frequent than the singular) means not simply a cult but a "secret," "hidden" cult, which is not manifested to all, but accessible only to the "initiate"; it is also certain that *initium*, the Latin term for a secret divine service, has the same meaning as

---

1 Quoted from Rudolf Otto, *Das Gefühl des Überweltlichen (Sensus numinis)*, (Munich, 1932), p. 6.
2 Pauly-Wissowa (1935), Vol. XVI, 1209.
3 Freeman, *Ancilla*, p. 25, fr. 14.

μυστήριον and that *initiare* also means to "inspire" and to "initiate." This contributes nothing to an etymological explanation of the word "mystery," but it does tell us that in the Latin usage a partial aspect of the mysteries, the initiation into the mysterious cult action, served as a designation for the whole.

Concerning the mysteries celebrated in Rome and Italy, I shall merely say here that they seem to have been imported from the eastern Mediterranean region, and that they all led to the universalistic theology of the sun emperors and to the development of the state mystery of Mithras, the Sol Invictus. (Here it should be noted that, though the derivation of the substantive *mysterion* from the verb μύειν, which would make μυστήριον mean "that which is or must be kept silent," accords with the customary liturgical German translation by "*Geheimnis*," it is certain that "secrecy," the "closing of the mouth," the "closing of the eyes," or the "closing of the senses in general" is not the main element in the mysteries; the main element is the hidden, concealed content of the divine, "numinous" event designated as *mysterion*.)

When we seek to visualize the most typical characteristics of the ancient mystery cults, it is always those of the cult of Eleusis that come to mind; this has been true of the scholars who have studied the mysteries of the Cabiri and of the Orphics; and it was true of that Ptolemaic king of the third century B.C. who, wishing to found a solemn Greek-Egyptian cult in Alexandria, sent for a scion of the high priests of Eleusis. Though it is hard to tell the reason, this Attic cult strikes the observer as an archetype of the ancient cults, although the cult of the Cabiri is presumably a good deal older. With this in mind, let us piece together our incomplete knowledge of the ancient mysteries.

After purification (*catharsis*) and other preliminary rites, a rite of initiation (*myesis*) leads the neophyte into the circle of the initiates (*mystai*); he enters into a bond with them and with the numen of the cult; degrees or stages of initiation or knowledge lead him upwards; he becomes a seer (*epoptes*). The mystes or epopt keeps his insight or vision entirely or partially secret from outsiders or from those who have not yet attained to the same stage. A line is drawn between the esoteric and the exoteric. The degrees of insight are transmitted by δρώμενα and λεγόμενα (ritual actions and words). *Dromena* and *legomena* are enacted and spoken by priests and mystai.

94

(The term ὄργια, related by its root to ἔργα, "work," also occurs.) The τελετή ("completion," from τέλος) designate the final stage of "knowledge" and consecration.[4] The *telos* (ultimate aim) consists in the attainment of a beatific immortality, of a desirable state after death. Symbolically, man enters the underworld, he "dies" in a dromenon, or is "wedded," and he is always symbolically reborn; then he lives no longer in "death" but in "life."[5] The uninitiate and hence unconsecrated remains "in death." Accordingly in the dromenon, symbolic night alternates with symbolic light. Only he who, in a suitable state of spiritual readiness, cleansed of guilt, participates in the dromenon, the sacral mime, becomes "blessed" (μακάριος).

It seems likely that the dromenon of death most particularly purified, fortified, and exalted the receptive soul, and specialists have pointed out to me that death appears as a central motif in the "mysteries" (that is, the secret cults) of primitive peoples. This is noteworthy, for the discursive intelligence has still another formulation of the relation between life and death. According to this formulation, widespread in antiquity, the earth (γῆ) or matter (ὕλη) in its simplest form—e.g., as *cinis*, ashes of the dead— is immortal, is God: not every free Greek or Roman considered it necessary to be initiated. And it may further be presumed that perhaps one of the reasons for keeping secret a cult concerned with such profound psychic currents lay in the early realization that certain spiritual experiences are not communicable to all but only to kindred souls, that, as the poet said,

4 That "immortality" was achieved in the Eleusinian Mysteries was no secret, but was generally known; only the sacred "actions and words" of a certain part of the cult were kept secret.
It should be obvious that the term "knowledge" or "insight" as used above, implies no "scientific" insight; and it is evident that in the Hellenistic mysteries no *mathesis* (learnable knowledge) and (at least in the beginning) no *gnosis* (insight in the later Hellenistic sense) is acquired; what the mystes achieves in the successive stages of the dromenon is a spiritual experience, a *"pathein,"* as a passage in Synesius (*Dion*, p. 48 [Petavius]: Migne, *PG*, LXVI, 1155) quotes Aristotle as saying, an *aisthesis ton theon* (a perception of divine efficacy). Another passage in Synesius (*De providentia*, II, 124: Migne, ibid., 1272) speaks, in connection with the mystery rites of the ἀγνωσία σεμνότης ἐπὶ τελετῶν καὶ νύξ, the unknowable solemnity that lies over the rites and the night. The essential consisted in sense perceptions. We know from Plutarch (*De defectu, oraculorum*, 422) that no "intellectual" process accompanied the sacred words and actions of the mysteries, but that these were a *"mythologein."* This makes it clear that I have above used the word "knowledge" in the sense of a "perception or experience or suffering of the divine," and this because I am convinced that Hellenistic Gnosis was preformed in the Hellenic mysteries, for in their great explorations of the soul, the Gnostics developed such mystery elements as "life," "death," "sacred marriage," etc.
Cf. Heraclitus, frs. 20 and 62 (Freeman, pp. 26, 29).

"one man's wisdom is another man's folly." And in the following we shall consider some other possibilities.[6]

The Christian usage of the word *mysterion* emphasizes a particular meaning, namely that of a divine action or essence which is by its very nature "ineffable" (ἄρρητον). Here we may mention the use of the words *mysterion, mysteria*, in the Gospels, particularly in Luke 8 : 10, Matthew 13 : 11, and Mark 4 : 11, where we find almost identical formulations: "To you [i.e., the disciples] it is given to know the mystery of the kingdom of heaven [or of God]." And the passage in Luke continues: "But to the rest [the mystery is given] in parables, that seeing they may not see and hearing may not understand. Now the parable is this: The seed is the word of God [ὁ σπόρος ἐστὶν ὁ λόγος τοῦ θεοῦ]." This clearly is the style of a Hellene of the first century A.D., the language of a trained theologian who is thoroughly familiar with the Gnostics and Heraclitus and the Stoics (e.g., their λόγοι σπερματικοί) and the Pauline Epistles—one of those theologians who, in combating the heresy of Marcion (expelled from the Roman congregation in A.D. 144), established the definitive text of the Scriptures, an inspired man who wrote down the divine word in the terms of his day. The New Testament canon was established approximately in its present form after A.D. 100 and before 200. And the Septuagint was given its present form by Christians, namely Origen (A.D. 185–254) and the martyrs Lucian and Hesychius (both of whom met their death in 311 in the persecution of Maximin).[7] But in the Pauline Epistles a man of the first century speaks to us directly in his original, peculiarly impassioned language. And of all the New Testament authors it is he who uses the word "mystery" by far the most frequently. It is therefore incumbent on the historian (though apparently not on the theologian) to inquire in what sense St. Paul used the word μυστήριον. Doubtless the word was familiar to the apostle in its paled Septuagint sense, but it must have been even more familiar to him in the current usage of his time, when mysteries were celebrated throughout the Mediterranean regions he had

6 It is to be noted that almost all mystery festivals involved public games, whether of a gymnastic or musical type, and public processions, for the mysteries, as we have said, were merely an aspect of more general cults. Only certain parts of the mystery festivals were solemnized in secret.

7 All this indicates that the Pauline Epistles are the earliest source and the primary historical document for the Christian use of the word *mysterion*, inasmuch as the Septuagint and the Gospels exist only in recensions—of translations—from the 4th and 2nd cents. A.D. respectively. Of course this estimate of the order of the sources presupposes the historical existence of Paul in the 1st cent. A.D., but if this is assumed no other appraisal of the sources seems possible.

visited. Near Athens, where he delivered his famous sermon suggested by the inscription to the *Agnostos Theos* (Unknown God), lay Eleusis; in Alexandria, in Rome, in Asia Minor, mysteries were solemnized; the apostle who taught the mystery of Christ was thoroughly familiar with the "pre-Christian" usage of the word *mysterion*. Let us now consider that highly significant passage, that statement of Christian gnosis, in the Epistle to the Ephesians (1 : 9–12), and see how the apostle used the word *mysterion:* "That he might make known unto us the mystery of his will"; and (Eph. 3 : 2–9): "How that, according to revelation, the mystery has been made known to me," that mystery of Christ "which in other generations was not known to the sons of men, as it is now revealed to his holy apostles and prophets in the Spirit; that the Gentiles should be fellow heirs and of the same body, and co-partners of his promise in Christ Jesus, by the gospel of which I am made a minister, according to the gift of the grace of God. . . . To me, the least of all the saints, is given this grace, to preach among the Gentiles the unsearchable riches of Christ [πλοῦτος τοῦ Χριστοῦ]"—no longer the riches promised by the mysteries of the Hellenes and barbarians (for example, the cult of Eleusis or that of Ephesus; hence, no doubt, the Epistle to the Ephesians) but the riches conferred upon the "saints" (ἄγιοι) by the fellowship of the mystery "which hath been hidden from eternity in God who created all things [τὰ πάντα]." Here Paul clearly juxtaposes to other mysteries the *mysterion tou Christou* as that of the all-creating God; and of course the "principalities and powers in heavenly places" (the well-known ἀρχαὶ καὶ αἱ ἐξουσίαι ἐν τοῖς ἐπουρανίοις) "now"[7a] (νῦν, i.e., after the epiphany of Christ) are to see the now-manifested "manifold wisdom of God . . . according to the eternal purpose which he made in Christ Jesus our Lord" (Eph. 3 : 10–11). If I correctly understand the apostle in this passage he furthermore juxtaposes the "saint" (*hagios*) of the new Christian *gnosis* and *pistis* to the "initiate" (*mystes*) of the old mysteries. And later the Gnostic treatise that has become known under the name of *Pistis Sophia*, referring to those very passages in the Gospel, uses the word *mysterion* in the same sense as St. Paul does.

Subsequent Christian writers refer to such implications of redemption as

7a [The word νῦν, "now," is not translated in Eph. 3 : 10 according to the Douay Version (which is cited for the Biblical passages in this lecture because of the author's communion): "That the manifold wisdom of God may be made known to the principalities and powers in heavenly places through the church." Cf. the Knox tr.: "The principalities and powers of heaven are to see, now, made manifest in the Church, the subtlety of God's wisdom."—ED.]

baptism and the Eucharist as *"mysteria,"* and the oldest Latin Bible translations, as well as Tertullian, render *mysterion* as *sacramentum*, a term suggesting one element of the "secret," namely the initiation.

The question has often been asked: Why are certain cults celebrated in secret, why have men resolved to hide their mysteries from the light of the sun, to assemble at night for their sacred action, to withdraw to closed and hence exclusive temples and caves? A common answer is that this concealment is a historical reminiscence, a memory of days when an old cult was oppressed and persecuted by rulers adhering to another religion. This is the opinion of Otto Kern.[8] A masterly poetic picture of a repressed religion of this sort is given us by Goethe in his poem "Erste Walpurgisnacht," in which he speaks of the Druid religion oppressed by Christian rulers; in this nocturnal festival hidden from the enemy, there bursts forth a yearning for the day:

> But it is day
> As soon as we
> Can offer thee a pure heart.

And the Druids gathered round the fire pray:

> The flame is purified of smoke:
> So purify our faith.[9]

Thus we may imagine a cult hiding from the enemy and purifying itself in concealment. And it may have been thus in Eleusis. But this explanation does not seem too plausible. For the question remains: Why, in Eleusis for example, after the cult had gained strong state support, were parts of the festival celebrated publicly and with positively triumphal splendor, and parts amid secrecy and nocturnal darkness—while Christianity quickly abandoned its catacombs once the persecutions had ceased, though, to be

---

8 In *Die griechischen Mysterien der klassischen Zeit* (Berlin, 1927).

9
> Doch ist es Tag,
> Sobald man mag
> Ein reines Herz dir bringen.
>
> Die Flamme reinigt sich vom Rauch:
> So reinige unsern Glauben!

This poem of Goethe epitomizes the growth in refinement and inwardness of traditional cults; it points at once to the remote origins of "faith" and to its development toward a "purification" of the heart. In a civilization, the cults can travel either this path of "purification of faith" or the opposite path involving the most terrible "sacrifices."

sure, certain rites continued to be performed at night? And why should the latest pagan mystery, celebrated by soldiers who ruled the world, the Mithraic mystery, have been solemnized in caves and in the strictest seclusion?

The presumable answer is that historical reminiscence may in part account for the cult form, but that both in its public and in its mysterious, nocturnal aspects, it is principally molded by profound psychic forces. The cult of Eleusis, for example, is devoted to one of the primordial forms from the soul's abysses, to a form suggesting the darkness before birth as well as the darkness after death, to Mother Earth as represented by Demeter and her daughter Kore. Here forces originating in the earth and returning to the earth are worshiped, and Kore's husband Pluto (interpreted as Plutodotes, the giver of riches) suggests "the wealth of grain which the earth gives year after year." The darkness of night and the darkness of the cave may be taken as a symbolic expression of a religious feeling bound up with the "earth," and indeed in all primordial cults the "mysteries" of birth, death, and rebirth, rising from and returning to the darkness of the earth, are shrouded in darkness.[10] The cult of the Earth Mother Demeter "bears all the traits of a firmly rooted family cult, of a cult attached to a particular soil. There were few subsidiaries of the Eleusinian shrine. Only in the sacred bay itself could a man receive the supreme initiations, at the hands of the representatives of the old priest families resident in Eleusis. (The best known of these are the Eumolpides, one of whom always filled the office of the hierophant, and the Keryces, who performed the office of herald.) New gods were not admitted. Iacchus, the divine child, who bore the torches in advance of the mystai, was considered entirely as a guest; his cult image had its home in a special temple in Athens and was carried each year in solemn procession from Athens to Eleusis and from Eleusis to Athens."[11]

Nocturnal cults, and particularly those of a primordial mother, almost always bear a demonstrable relation to the moon. The investigations of August Mommsen[12] show that the Athenians celebrated their great mysteries in the month of Boedromion (roughly our September) "in the sign of Libra" (according to the fifth Oration of Julian the Apostate), hence in the period of the autumnal equinox, and the lesser mysteries in the month of Anthesterion (approximately our April) "when the sun is in the sign of

10 Cf. W. F. Otto, "The Meaning of the Eleusinian Mysteries," pp. 14ff. of this volume.
11 Kern, pp. 6ff.
12 *Feste der Stadt Athen im Altertum* (Leipzig, 1898), pp. 205ff.

Aries," hence in the period of the vernal equinox. "The Attic months followed the course of the moon. . . . [But] the Athenians celebrated their
festivals according to numbered calendar days. . . . The festival was celebrated on the day of the month bearing the determined number, even if
the calendar was a little wrong. How else could Selene have complained of
neglect?"[13] From this complaint attributed to the moon (Selene) it can be
seen that at one time at least the cult was related to the moon; and it is
well known that difficulties arise in any attempt to make a lunar accord
with a solar calendar. The Emperor Julian's precise dating presupposes
Julius Caesar's solar reform of the calendar and perhaps even a distinct
"reform" of the Eleusinian Mysteries themselves in line with the imperial
cult of sun worship, for beginning in the fourth century a priest of Mithras
filled the office of hierophant at Eleusis.[14] Thus the imperial Helios had
vanquished the Earth Mother of the Greeks in the calendar as well as
the Mysteries. True, the Athenians of the fifth century calculated certain
dates according to phases of the fixed stars, as, for example, the Proarcturia,
indicated by the matutinal phase of Arcturus in mid September; it was at
this time that grain quotas were due to be delivered in Athens, and the
occasion was celebrated with a small sacrifice called Proērosia. "Then
followed the great mysteries. After them, it is presumed, the pilgrims left
Eleusis confident that they had adequately provided for their native agriculture. In the planting month of Pyanepsion [our October] they were back
home again, tilling their fields."[15]

This aspect of the great festival of the Earth Mother may seem rather
matter-of-fact to the city dweller, nevertheless it is essential for an understanding of the role of the mysteries in ancient society; those familiar with
the religious festivals of predominantly agricultural peoples will find countless analogies. And here let us recall the agrarian women's festival of the
Haloa (ἀλῷα from ἅλως, "threshing floor"). It was celebrated in the
month of Pyanepsion (in our October, or perhaps early November). This
festival was devoted to the mysteries of Demeter and Kore. A scholium to
Lucian's *Dialogues of the Hetairai* (7, 4) related, Mommsen states, that "in
the Haloa the officials [archons] must set up tables and serve all good things
of land and sea. According to the scholium, only those foods forbidden to
the mystai were excluded, such as pomegranates, apples, poultry, eggs,
certain types of fish, and crabs. Wine was served in abundance, and with it

13 Ibid., p. 206.　　　　14 Kern, p. 2.　　　　15 Mommsen, p. 195.

pastries in phallic and ctenic [animal] shapes. After the officials had set the tables, they withdrew and turned the room over to the women. It is clear from the scholium that the banquet took place in a closed room, but it is never designated as a house or temple. Men were not admitted. The women behaved with great freedom, manipulated phalluses and toy animals, made lewd speeches, or listened to the priestesses who whispered about secret love. . . . We know also of related usages among men, who prepared clay phalluses and set them up. . . . The Haloa also included an *agon*, known as *patrios* [the paternal]."[16] This name speaks for itself.

The famous procession along the "sacred road" (ὁδὸς ἱερά), leading from Athens to Eleusis, on the nineteenth of Boedromion, must have been a popular festival. If Herodotus (8 : 65) spoke the truth, "three myriads" participated in the procession, the dust could be seen far and wide, and the celebrants cried out *"Iakch', o Iakche!"*; the image of the divine child Iacchus and *"ta hiera"* of Eleusis (of which we have no precise description) were borne in the procession; from time to time a halt was made and, according to Plutarch (*Alcibiades*, 34), "sacrifices and dances were held and other customary usages were carried out." An imperial inscription[17] mentions "sacrifices, libations, and paeans."

A few days earlier, the festival had officially begun with an address of the *archon basileus*, and on the sixteenth of Boedromion the call had gone out: *"ἅλαδε μύσται"*—"To the sea, O mystai!" This was the great day of purification and atonement on which the mystai cleansed themselves of all stain in the vast sea, a ceremony rich in symbolism flowing from the primordial depths of the soul.[18]

---

16 Ibid., pp. 359ff. As an ancient philologist tells us, Taurus and Luna coincide at the festival of the "honey-sweet" earth goddess.

17 *Corpus inscriptionum Atticarum* (Berlin, 1878), Vol. III, no. 5; after Mommsen, p. 225.

18 "Without water there is no salvation!" sing the Sirens, calling on man to betake himself to the sea. But the poet might equally well have made them say *"Halade,"* "to the Aegean Sea," for here as in the Eleusinian Mysteries, what is meant is *thalatta*, the "sea that was before the gods, the ungodly sea," and not Pontus, the sea as an avenue of navigation and trade. — Purifications (ἡ κάθαρσις, "purification, atonement") are connected with nearly all chthonic cults: the man who becomes earth is at first κόπρος, dirt, mud, dung, but is in the end manifested as "unmingled, pure" earth (γῆ), from which a new form arises, which is καθαρός, i.e., "unmingled, pure, genuine, untainted, immaculate." (καθαρὸς θάνατος in Homer is a clean, honorable death, ὁ καθαρὸς στρατός in Herodotus is the healthy, sound part of an army; in the *Odyssey* Telemachus washes his hands in the sea before praying to Athene; in the *Iliad* the army throws everything that is polluted into the sea at the end of the plague, and sacrifices to Apollo.) Here Heraclitus' sea water is meant (Diels, fr. B, 61: Free-

On the twentieth of Boedromion, "the high festival began in the dark night; on this day the moon does not appear until several hours after sunset. We know from the *Frogs* of Aristophanes that the procession following the image of Iacchus became a *lampadephoria*, a torchlight dance: Iacchus himself is said to wave the torch and inaugurate the dance; he is the bright star of the nocturnal feast in which the fields gleam in the firelight. Those who say this are the initiate (οἱ μεμνημένοι),[19] and it is of the initiate that the procession consists. In the *Ion*, Euripides speaks of the festive *lampas* of this sleepless night, in which the dance revolves around the Eleusinian Kallichoron, 'the well of the beautiful dance'; even the stars of heaven and the daughters of Nereus in the waves accompany the dance.[20] According to Euripides, χορεύει δὲ Σελάνα—the moon, Selene herself, joins in the dance." The theological or dogmatic or mythological basis, or however one may call it, of this lampadephoria is that Demeter carried torches when she wandered through the world looking for her child. Whether this torchlight dance was actually thought to recall the πλάνη, the wanderings of Demeter, is not known for certain, but it seems likely.

---

man, p. 29): *Thalatta hydor katharotaton kai miarotaton* . . . ("sea water is the purest and most polluted: for fish it is drinkable and lifegiving; for men not drinkable and destructive"). And it would seem as though Heraclitus wished to express a doubt in the purificatory effect of *thalatta hydor* on "men." In another fragment (Diels, B, 14: Freeman, p. 25), he doubts the purifying, sanctifying efficacy of the usual mysteries: τὰ γὰρ νομιζόμενα κατ' ἀνθρώπους μυστήρια ἀνιερωστὶ μυεῦνται "the rites accepted by mankind in the mysteries are an unholy performance." From this as well as other utterances, we may judge Heraclitus to have been the first philosopher who observed the mysteries not only in the cultic sense as an outward action, but as a sacred rite (ἱερόν) enacted within the soul: for him the ψυχή is the sea and into that sea Socrates, like a "Delian diver," thought it necessary to plunge in order to understand the former basileus of Ephesus, for (fr. B, 45: Freeman, p. 27): "You could not in your going find the ends of the soul, though you traveled the whole way." — In the preliminaries to the Eleusinian festival, however, the sea, to which the celebrants are summoned, has a purifying effect. *Thalatta* is here a companion, psychic aspect of *ge*. In the Eleusinian catharsis we see two forms of the generative element, but essentially all "elements" have a purifying power, as is shown by a notation from late antiquity: In a comment on Virgil's *Georgics* (II, 388) dealing with the ancient mysteries, Servius says: *Omnis purgatio per aquas, aut per ignem fit aut per aerem* ("All purifications are effected by water or fire or air"). Life arose in the watery deep, in the eternal Protean waters; the eternally changing waves are propitious to life, says Goethe, the masterly re-creator of ancient conceptions. But these waters with their eternal nuptials are also forever devouring the created, the dead and the unfinished.—With this reference to the "Klassische Walpurgisnacht" (*Faust*) we draw attention for the first time to a late echo of the ancient cults.

19 Aristophanes, *Frogs*, 318.   20 Euripides, *Ion*, 1074.

Our knowledge of the telete, the principal rite, is meager, for the silence solemnly imposed on the novices by the *hierokeryx* was observed by pre-Christian writers, and the notes of Christian writers are too polemical in intention to be very reliable. But there are a few observations which give us some knowledge or intimation of the telete. For example, we are told that the sacred mime, the dromena and legomena, was performed by priests with the attributes and often the masks of the gods. And Otto Kern points to another important observation:[21] In a melodious voice ($\epsilon\dot{v}\varphi\omega\nu\acute{\iota}\alpha$, after Philostratus), the hierophant pronounced the words, known also to the Christian liturgy, proclaiming the birth of the sacred boy: "$\iota\epsilon\rho\grave{o}\nu$ $\check{\epsilon}\tau\epsilon\kappa\epsilon$ $\pi\acute{o}\tau\nu\iota\alpha$ $\kappa o\tilde{v}\rho o\nu$ $B\rho\iota\mu\grave{\omega}$ $B\rho\iota\mu\acute{o}\nu$."[22]—"The sublime one has borne a sacred boy, Brimo has given birth to Brimos." On the basis of various considerations, Kern comes to the conclusion that Brimo (Terrible One) refers in all probability to Kore, and that Brimos is "the divine boy Pluto whom according to the Homeric Hymn the goddesses of Eleusis dispatched to the temple and who expresses the same divine power as Pluto the bestower of riches, the husband of Kore."

In the Pauline epistle, this divine power of Pluto, conferred by the "two goddesses" of Eleusis in the mystery of their cult, becomes, as we have seen, the *ploutos tou Christou*, the "unsearchable riches of Christ" in the *oikonomia tou mysteriou*—"the dispensation of the mystery which hath been hidden from eternity in God who created all things." It cannot be doubted that Paul, "the least of all the saints," not only wished to carry the happy tidings ($\epsilon\dot{v}\alpha\gamma\gamma\epsilon\lambda\acute{\iota}\sigma\alpha\sigma\vartheta\alpha\iota$) of the mystery of the God who rules the world to "the Gentiles" ($\tau o\tilde{\iota}s$ $\check{\epsilon}\vartheta\nu\epsilon\sigma\iota\nu$) and "to enlighten all men" ($\kappa\alpha\grave{\iota}$ $\varphi\omega\tau\acute{\iota}\sigma\alpha\iota$ $\tau\iota s$), but is also attacking the ancient mysteries "of the Gentiles."

Here we have touched on the religious history of the eastern Mediterranean basin over a period of roughly seven hundred years. We have elsewhere[23] described the development of astrological-cosmogonic religion in approximately the same period and saw that it found its most intransigent adversary in the apostle; there we noted the strange phrase: "the weak and needy

21 Kern, p. 11.
22 Hippolytus, *Refutatio omnium haeresum*, V, 8, 40 (*Werke*, Vol. III, ed. P. Wendland, Leipzig, 1916, p. 97, li. 18).
23 "Sol Invictus: Betrachtungen zu spätrömischer Religion und Politik [Reflections on Late Roman Religion and Politics]," *EJ 1943*, pp. 190–91.

elements"[24] which are "the elements of the world" (Col. 2 : 8); whereas in Christ lies "all the fullness of the Godhead corporeally"; he is "the head of all principality and power" (Col. 2 : 10), that is, of the astrologically conceived cosmos. Instead of these "weak and needy elements," to which the philosophy of the apostle relegates Mother Earth, Demeter, and her Pluto, he promises the *ploutos tou Christou*, the "unsearchable riches of Christ" (Eph. 3 : 8). In addition to these dogmatic (consciously didactic) passages, the epistles we have quoted embody an important sociological element: a new, universal *mysterion* is distinguished from a *mysterion* and cult bound up with a locality and soil, with firmly rooted priestly families; the apostle had abjured "the" people, his own people, and the Jewish aristocracy of the high priests, and now he abjures the mysteries and cults of the Gentiles with their earthbound priesthoods: he no longer, to use his own terms, teaches "the" people, but "the peoples." Marcion, the great "one-sided Biblicist" as Adolf von Harnack called him, later exaggerated to such a degree this tendency to disengage the New Testament theology from "the" people that the Church classified him among the arch-heretics.

2. Serapis: The Universal Mystery Religion

The Christian apostle was not without precursors in his striving for universality. In the years following the death of Alexander the Great in 323 B.C., various factors combined to introduce a strong universalizing trend into religious life. These circumstances were partly of a sociological, partly of a religious and philosophical nature. For one thing, all cults were not epichorian (i.e., bound up with the locality), nor were all priesthoods hereditary (ἱερεῖς διὰ γένους) as in Eleusis, where the hierophant was one of the Eumolpides, while the *daduchos*, the *keryx*, and the altar priest were Keryces, and in Jerusalem, where both high and low priesthood were hereditary.[1]

24 [Gal. 4 : 9.—Ed.]

1 Like Chinese and Japanese religions of today, ancient religion had a strong leaning toward the paternal, the hereditary, which however stood in no contradiction to the veneration of the maternal. The power of the gods was handed down through the fathers. For this reason the nobles—*eupatridai, gennetai*—were more closely related to the gods than the common citizens who worshiped the ἱερὰ πατρῷα (paternally sacred) in the cults of Zeus Herkeios and of Apollo Patroös; after Solon, participation in these religious services became the touchstone of the true citizen. Sometimes the

There were also priests and priestesses who were chosen by popular election, oracles, or lots, who were appointed by rulers, or who purchased their offices. All this tended to break down the traditional cults. The corporations of eunuch priests of the cults of Asia Minor also contributed to the process, but this is a chapter in itself (particularly in its bearing on the increasing orientalization of the eastern part of the Roman Empire) which cannot be treated here. Nor can the financial basis of the priesthoods—an important factor—here be discussed in detail; but various inscriptions and literary notations throw light on this matter, and, all things carefully considered, it would seem that particularly at the time of the Caesars, the priesthood was often a financial burden on its incumbents rather than an advantage. We have mentioned elsewhere[2] the grave economic difficulties standing in the way of the Emperor Julian's attempted repristinization; and we might also point to the discussion of Symmachus with Bishop Ambrose of Milan regarding the means of subsistence of the (Roman) vestal virgins.

The trend to universality in pre-Christian religion was first and most significantly represented by the Orphics. They possessed no holy site or city that those in quest of knowledge or redemption must visit, and no cult temple hallowed by local tradition; their "dromena" were performed in scattered "sacred houses." "They were indeed Europe's first itinerant preachers. Their activity in Hellas began at latest in the seventh century and extended through all antiquity, deep into the Christian period. There was an Orphic literature down to the end of paganism." These "Orphic" doctrines and mysteries, originating in Thrace, revolve around the concept of immortality. "They preach an orthodoxy. And indeed this word seems

---

candidate for the priesthood, in addition to the usual requirements of physical beauty and perfection, was expected to be of patrician descent; e.g., the priestess of Artemis in Halicarnassus was required to show "aristocratic descent on both sides down to the third generation." The ancient religions retained to the very end this trait, which strikes us modern individualists as astonishingly conservative, and as late a writer as Galerius defends this *mos maiorum*, "paternal usage," against the Christians and Manichaeans. But the ancient religions also had a revolutionary trend, as can be seen for example from Professor Wili's remarks on the Orphics [in the present volume], and it is characteristic that the Pisistratids, those "enlightened despots" who replaced the old Athenian form of government with their "tyrannis," supported the "revolutionary" Orphics against the "paternal" cult of the nobility who supported the traditional government. Cf. Paul Stengel, *Die griechischen Kultusaltertümer* (Munich, 1898–1920); Georg Busolt, *Griechische Staatskunde* (2 vols., Munich, 1920–26); and August Böckh, *Die Staatshaushaltung der Athener* (2 vols., Berlin, 1817), passim; Plato, *Euthydemus*, 302 B.

2 ["Sol Invictus," cited above.—Ed.]

to have first been coined among the Orphics."[3] Preachers, missionaries of a religion of salvation, wandering from city to city, must always be convinced that they represent the "right," in fact the only "right" doctrine, in short, an orthodoxy, and that they celebrate the mysteries appropriate to it. It is understandable that the Christians of late antiquity should have compared Dionysus, the god of the Orpheotelestai, and Orpheus himself with Christ.[4]

> Happy is he among men upon earth who has seen these mysteries; but he who is uninitiate and who has no part in them, never has lot of like good things once he is dead, down in the darkness and gloom.[5]

This dogmatic, almost medieval hymn, beginning with a beatification (perhaps the first in the Western world), is assuredly a complete expression of faith in a liberation from a "dead life" through a sacrament, a mystery, a dromenon (opere operato) effected by a priest. Those possessed of such faith cannot be shaken by any philosophizing religion. But with the increasing differentiation of ancient civilization and the consequent advancing clarity of consciousness, philosophizing religion gained supporters among other sections of the Mediterranean population. Here I shall not enter into the welter of assertions and counterassertions regarding the supposedly disintegrating effects of the great Greek philosophers upon Greek religion. I permit facts such as the following to speak for themselves: Though Alcibiades, the fanatical aristocrat and enthusiast for philosophy, was lacking in respect for Eleusis and imitated the hierophant for the amusement of his drinking companions, on another occasion he found it politically expedient to provide armed support for the festive procession to Eleusis. Religion, then, cannot have been greatly weakened by philosophy. And it is incontestable that long after the Ionian philosophers (e.g., the definitely "anticlerical" Heraclitus), after the great Sophists, and after Plato and Aristotle, the ancient mystery cults not only continued to be celebrated, but moreover new mystery cults were established, some of which survived for centuries. Here it is primarily the cult of Serapis or Sarapis that comes to mind. (The Egyptian form of Σάραπις is Osiris-Apis, a fact significant for the

---

3 Kern, p. 49.
4 F. J. Dölger, Antike und Christentum (Münster, 1929ff.), passim.
5 Hymn to Demeter, 480 (tr. Hugh G. Evelyn-White, in Hesiod, the Homeric Hymns and Homerica, LCL, 1920, p. 323).

theology of this cult.) The cult of Serapis was founded in the bright light of history; a king, the first of the Ptolemies, gave it to the important seaport city of Alexandria, in approximately 300 B.C.; in A.D. 361 it was still in existence, and the Emperor Julian still concerned himself with the theology of Serapis. In A.D. 100 the cult was thriving, as we know from Tacitus and Philostratus (*Vita Apollonii*). The remarks of Tacitus[6] show that the cult was established in accordance with the advice of a Eumolpid from Eleusis. Tacitus tells us how the cult of Serapis was designed in accordance with the prescriptions of the Egyptian priesthood and other advisers; his account reveals an astonishing mixture of gods. A statue of Juppiter Dis, brother of Proserpina, was brought from Sinope. This was Serapis. His temple was erected in a spot where a *sacellum* of Serapis and Isis had long stood. But Serapis also came from Syrian Seleucia and Egyptian Memphis; he was Aesculapius the healer, and he was also Osiris and Jupiter *omnipotens* and Pater Dis. His cult was so familiar among the Romans in the second and third centuries that Minucius Felix[7] says that he and the related Isis had formerly been Egyptian, but were now Roman deities. The image of Serapis was worn around the neck, and in the seaport of Ostia people kissed the hands of his statue. His theology—it goes without saying—was universalistic: πάντα νικᾷ ὁ Σάραπις, "Serapis conquers all things," runs the inscription on a gem, and according to Origen, "Serapis embraces the whole world of life." According to Macrobius,[8] a Cypriot inquiring about Serapis received the answer: "My head is the heavens, my belly the sea, my feet the earth, my ears extend into the ether, my eye is the sunshine visible far and wide." He is the cosmos with all its elements. And in his apostrophe to Helios, Julian the Apostate declares: "By Hades we understand Sarapis, the *invisible*, thinking God." According to other sources, he is also Sarapis-Jao, the "gnostic" god. And so universal had the god become that a Kore or Proserpina or Isis-Proserpina was often connected with him.

At first the rise of Serapis encountered difficulties. According to Macrobius,[9] he was accepted by the Alexandrian population only "under the pressure of the Ptolemaic *tyrannis*"; according to Suetonius and other historians,[10] the first Augustus ridiculed Serapis as an "ox"; Caligula (A.D.

---

6 *Histories*, IV, 81, 84, 85.   7 *Octavius*, 22, 2.
8 Origen, *Corpus inscriptionum Graecarium* (Berlin, 1856), Vol. IV, no. 7044 (p. 49); *Contra Celsum* V, 38 (Migne, *PG*, II, 1241). Macrobius, *Satires*, XX, 17.
9 Macrobius, *Satires*, I, 7.
10 Suetonius, *Octavius*, 93; Cassius Dio, LI, 16; Zonaras, X, 31.

37–41), Vespasian (A.D. 69–79), and Titus (A.D. 79–81) were more favorably disposed toward the cult of Serapis, no doubt because its influence in the politically important city of Alexandria had increased. With regard to the political importance of Alexandria, it need only be mentioned that much of the grain essential to Italy was shipped from there. Tacitus reports[11] that, following the advice of Serapis, Vespasian undertook to heal a blind man in Alexandria by spitting upon the sufferer and to cure a diseased hand by treading on the afflicted person. Both operations were successful. But the cautious Vespasian had previously asked the physicians about the prospects of such miraculous cures, and they had told him that a cure was possible if the organ in question was not destroyed but merely impaired, and that if the "obstructions were removed," the cure would be successful. Thus we find in this mystery cult "magical" miracles vying with psychotherapy; the cult also inspired dreams, visions, and prophecies of coming events (particularly of a political nature) and it purged men of their guilt: Cassius Dio[12] tells us how Caracalla consecrated to the god the sword with which he had slain his brother Geta in the arms of his mother.

The temple of the cult, the Serapeion, was oriented according to astrological principles. For the nocturnal rite it was oriented toward the star Regulus in Leo, belonging to Helios (for Serapis is not only Zeus, Hades, Dionysus-Osiris, but also Helios), and for the celebration of the founding of the cult toward the sun: at a certain hour the beams of the sun fell upon the lips of the statue of Serapis. The ancient planet worship, which no doubt lay at the source of certain local cults, the sites of which were in some specific way related to the rising sun, moon, or other heavenly body, found its place in the cosmic dromenon of the eclectic cult of Serapis. The Church Fathers, Ambrose and Augustine, for example, thought it necessary to detach natural science from religion (with which Mani had once again identified it), to relegate the courses of the sun and moon "to the school," and to insist that the phenomena of weather, rain, and drought were independent of religion.[13] In the prayers for rain and fine weather, however, the Catholic Church was compelled to relinquish the rationalism of the great Latin Fathers and make a place in the cult for the consideration of natural phenomena.

On this occasion we shall not be able to discuss the cult and mysteries of Isis, which theologically are closely related to those of Serapis. Nevertheless I should like to cite a significant passage from the *Metamorphoses* of Apuleius,

11 *Histories*, IV, 81.   12 LXXXVII, 23.   13 "Sol Invictus," p. 236.

in which he describes a procession of the devotees of Isis to the sea and makes clear their social composition:

> Then followed a great crowd of the Goddess's initiates, men and women of all classes and every age [*viri feminaeque omnis dignitatis et omnis aetatis*], their pure white linen clothes shining brightly. . . . The Goddess's bright earthly stars, they carried rattles of brass, silver, and even gold, which kept up a shrill and ceaseless tinkling.[14]

The passage is plain: all social classes meriting the consideration of an educated Roman of the time were initiated in the cult of Isis (those possessing the above-mentioned *dignitas*), i.e., the slaves and the very poor were absent, for the various initiations (*teletae*, as Apuleius calls them[15]) involved equipment and other expenses which, as he expressly states, even an advocate found burdensome. We may conclude that in the first centuries of the Christian era Isis was the form of the Great Mother worshiped by the "respectable bourgeoisie." Compare the bitter mockery with which Apuleius[16] treats the mutilated priests of another form of the Great Mother, "the almighty and all-creative" Syrian goddess, the wretched, mendicant *clerus minor* of the Dea Syria. Apuleius was an adherent of the state religion; for him Osiris was the "Invictus,"[17] and the grandiloquent title which, in taking leave of the reader, he gives to this god in whose mysteries (after those of Isis) he was initiated, sounds as solemn as that of the Emperor Aurelianus: "*Deus Deum magnorum potior et maiorum summus et summorum maximus et maximorum regnator Osiris.*"—"Most powerful of all gods, the highest among the greatest, the greatest among the highest, the ruler of the greatest, Osiris."[18]

This title has presumably a dogmatic significance: *Deus Deum* may well be interpreted as placing Osiris, the *regnator maximorum*, on a level with or above Cybele, the *Magna Mater Deum*, but on tombs also called *Maxima Mater*.[19] Apuleius' formula epitomizes in its way this late Hellenistic, late

14 *Metamorphoses*, XI, 10 (tr. Robert Graves, *The Golden Ass*, London, 1950, p. 276).
15 Ibid., XI, 27 (Graves, p. 291).
16 Ibid., VIII (Graves, p. 199).
17 Ibid., XI, 27 (Graves, p. 290: "invincible").
18 Ibid., XI, 30 (Graves, p. 293).
19 Cf. on this point Franz Cumont's remarks (*Les Religions orientales dans le paganisme romain*, Paris, 4th edn., 1929, p. 62): "Only the men, in the West at least, were permitted to take part in the secret ceremonies of the Persian [Mithraic] cult; therefore this cult had to be complemented by other mysteries to which women were admitted.

Roman religious system encompassing the highest and the lowest. Like the wisdom of other, more recent ages, as the Irish poet put it with mingled irony and admiration, ancient "wisdom hath built herself a house, this vast majestic longstablished vault, the crystal palace of the Creator all in applepie order, a penny for him who finds the pea."[20] This Alexandrian, late Hellenistic, late Roman theosophy (as we may well call this kind of wisdom or *sophia*) embraced—and so annulled—all things: a mystical philosophy had gradually become the content of the mysteries.

And here we must refer to the efforts of the house of Severus (A.D. 193–235) to fuse the eastern and western religions of the empire. In his *Vita Apollonii*, Philostratus espoused this tendency with considerable philosophical and theological ability. He reveres the local cults, but treats them relatively, and this applies even to the mystery cult of Eleusis with its local and aristocratic ties. Philostratus relates that once Apollonius was in Athens during the Eleusinian festivals and that "many thought it more important to converse with Apollonius than to participate in the Mysteries." To this the hierophant reacted with angry words; Apollonius replied that he knew more about the rites than the hierophant himself, and finally, as we might expect, the hierophant, persuaded by the "emperor's friend," renounced his objection.[21] This account shows distinctly that about A.D. 200 when the mysteries were widespread and when even Christianity half cloaked itself in "mystery" (consider, for example, the iconostasis which concealed the *mysterion*), the intellectual upper classes took a very relative attitude toward the traditional cult forms: those trained in philosophy no longer believed that man could be "saved" *only* in Eleusis, or *only* through a dromenon in the temple of Isis, but that all cults and rites drew their efficacy from a single divine force. (This was the view of so late a writer as Symmachus in his *Relationes*.)[22]

Those of Cybele took in the wives and daughters of the Mithraists. As impassioned worshipers of the fecund, nourishing mother, they were drawn by the pathos of this cult, and entered both its sisterhoods and its priesthood." And here we find a recurrence of an ancient motif in this originally Persian, though much adapted, cult: "In the ancient religion of the Achaemenids, Mithras, the genius of light, formed a pair with Anâhita, the goddess of the fertilizing waters."

20 [James Joyce, *Ulysses*, London, 1949, p. 376; New York, Modern Library edn., p. 388. —ED.]

21 *Vita Apollonii*, III, 24. See my remarks in "Sol Invictus," pp. 213ff.

22 See "Sol Invictus," p. 248. At a much later date the Church Father Augustine (A.D. 354–430) was still concerned with the problem of local or national cults: "Indeed there was no other people [but Israelites] properly called the people of God, but they cannot

In the same period the Hermetic tract bearing the name of Apuleius (Pseudo-Apuleius) makes an astounding declaration. "In the presence of Ammon and Thoth, Asclepius" announced to Hermes Trismegistus "the end of the old religions."[23]

If a historian is permitted to express himself in allegorical-mythical terms, we might say that Thoth, the Egyptian god of books, who is actually Hermes Trismegistus, was then entering upon his hidden realm which endures down to our days: the *hermetica*, the *mysteria*, the secrets, are set down in books and nevertheless they remain inaccessible to those "of closed mind"; astrologers, alchemists, natural philosophers, and poets—and in our times also psychologists—are their guardians, the Christian hierarchs and theologians are their—sometimes stern, sometimes mild—adversaries.

Mystical literature, "book mysticism," was widely disseminated in the Roman Empire from the second century on. In the *Pistis Sophia*, a Gnostic treatise (of Coptic, i.e., Egyptian, origin), Jesus lectures the disciples on the structure of the universe. Here the term *mysterion* is used to mean a kind of cosmic power station, charged with divine force. There are twenty-four of these stations, and they control other stations such as the aeons, archons, and daemons, the spheres and chaos, which includes "outer darkness," so sustaining the eternal motion of the firmament. Persephone is demoted to the rank of ruler of chaos, who punishes murderers;[24] while ἡ παρθένος, Virgo, the celestial virgin, another of the soul's archetypes, has become the cosmic judge; it is she who dispatches the souls to light, to darkness, or to rebirth.[25] And similarly in the teachings of the Persian Mani (according to

---

deny that some particular men lived in this world and in other nations that were belonging to the heavenly hierarchy."—*De civitate Dei*, 18,47 (tr. John Healey, in R.V.G. Tasker, ed., *The City of God*, Everyman's Library, 1945, Vol. II, p. 222). By this theological formulation he succeeds in characterizing the "old" as well as the "new" faith as subordinate to a unified principle and so showing both Old and New Testament thought to be universal or ecumenical.

23 According to Martin Schanz, *Geschichte der Römischen Literatur* (Munich, 1896), Part III, it was written in the 2nd cent. A.D.
24 *Pistis Sophia*, tr. from the Coptic by Carl Schmidt (Leipzig, 1929), p. 279, li. 35–36.
25 Cf. Goethe's conception (in *Faust*, Part II, Act I, "Hall of the Knights" scene) of the Mothers—instead of *Virgo caelestis*—who send the *"Lebens-Bilder"* (forms of life) to life or death:

> Around you weave
> The forms of life, which move but do not live.
> What once existed in full glow and flame,
> It still moves there, eternity its aim.
> And you, omnipotent Powers, apportion it
> To the tent of day or to the vault of night.

Augustine),[26] the zodiac is the path of souls, and Christ is the sun moving—
as in the *Pistis Sophia* he moves through the twenty-four mysteries—
"through the heavens, gathering in the segments of God with his rays."
And he moves *per discursum solis et lunae*, "through the circuits of sun and
moon."[27] And as the firmament revolves, the constellations move like twelve
buckets on a bucket wheel, carrying the souls downward to matter or upward to the realm of light. Saved, i.e., liberated from the inexorability of the
stars, from Heimarmene or Fortuna (as Apuleius says[28]), are those who have
"found the mystery of light," whether like Apuleius' Lucius through Isis,
or like the Manichaeans through Christ, or in the manner described in the
Pistis Sophia.[29] Goethe, who by his study of the Neoplatonists, Gnostics,
and alchemists penetrated deep into the thinking of late antiquity, gave
these ideas a perfect poetic expression in his verses on the "sign of the
Macrocosm":

> Into one Whole how all things blend,
> Function and live within each other!
> Passing gold buckets to each other
> How heavenly powers ascend, descend!
> The odor of grace upon their wings,
> They thrust from heaven through earthly things
> And as all sing so *the* All sings!

> What a fine show! Aye, but only a show![30]

(Tr. Louis MacNeice, New York and London, 1952, pp. 185f., from: "Euer Haupt
umschweben / Des Lebens Bilder, regsam, ohne Leben, / Was einmal war, in allem
Glanz und Schein, / Es regt sich dort, denn es will ewig sein. / Und ihr verteilt es,
allgewaltige Mächte, / Zum Zelt des Tages, zum Gewölb der Nächte")

26 *Contra Faustum*, XXI, 8 (Migne, *PL*, XLII, 392f.).

27 Augustine, *De natura boni*, c. 44 (Migne, ibid., 567).

28 *Metamorphoses*, XI (Graves, p. 288).

29 *Pistis Sophia* (Schmidt), p. 284, li. 34–35.

30 *Faust*, Part I, Act I, opening scene, tr. MacNeice, pp. 21f., from:

> Wie alles sich zum Ganzen webt,
> Eins in dem andern wirkt und lebt!
> Wie Himmelskräfte auf und nieder steigen
> Und sich die goldnen Eimer reichen!
> Mit segenduftenden Schwingen
> Vom Himmel durch die Erde dringen,
> Harmonisch all das All durchklingen!

> Welch Schauspiel! aber ach! ein Schauspiel nur!

The house which wisdom, *sophia*, has built itself, the crystal palace of systematically, harmoniously ordered ideas and conceptions, is only a play.

Infinite Nature, where can I tap thy veins?
Where are thy breasts, those well-springs of all life . . .?[31]

This same question was asked by the man of the ancient Mediterranean world, and that was why he prayed to the many-breasted Ephesian Artemis (cf. Goethe's "Gross ist die Diana der Epheser"), and that is why both men and women sought in their epitaphs to convince themselves that they were ashes—*cinis*—but that ashes were *terra*, earth, and that the earth was the godhead, *dea*, and that consequently they would not be dead, but would survive in and through the godhead:

Cinis sum, cinis terra est, terra dea est,
Ergo ego mortua non sum.[32]

(I am ashes, ashes are earth, earth is the goddess,
Therefore I am not dead.)

So wrote a woman; and a man says almost literally the same words in a Greek epigram:

εἰμὶ νεκρός, νεκρὸς δὲ κόπρος, γῆ δ' ἡ κόπρος ἐστίν
εἰ δέ τε γῆ θεός ἐστ' οὐ νεκρὸς ἀλλά θεός.[33]

(I am a corpse, a corpse is dust, earth is dust;
Since the earth is god I am not dust but god.)

Terra and γῆ—*dea* and θεός—ashes and corpse—and all this so much alive! Such was the ancient faith in the animation of the earth, in hylozoism, whose latest offshoot is modern materialism.[34]

---

31 Ibid., p. 22, from:

Wo fass' ich dich, unendliche Natur?
Euch Brüste, wo? Ihr Quellen alles Lebens . . .?

32 *Corpus inscriptionum Latinarum*, Vol. VI, pt. 4 (Berlin, 1894), no. 29609, p. 2867.
33 Ernst Diehl, *Anthologia lyrica graeca* (Leipzig, 1925), Vol. I, p. 64.
34 Behind the image of man's ashes as living dust, we find in modern poets as in ancient poets and artists, the idea of "generation," in the form of the primordial woman, and mother awaiting the marriage bed, often directly associated with the fertile earth furrow and the fertility of animals: in the *Walpurgisnacht* episode of Thomas Mann's *Magic Mountain* the "philosophical" idler thinks of "drawing little pigs"; and the colonial Hollander to whom Mann gave the monumental features of a pagan priest calls "life," which is also "death," a "sprawled-out woman" (*The Magic Mountain*, Ch. V and VII). — The Irish poet, of whom we shall have more to say, makes his learned young philosopher, contemplating the world's decay, address the primordial

A process of spiritual elevation enabled the Latin- and Greek-speaking world in which divergent psychic attitudes lived side by side to produce the lovely "Prayer to the Earth Mother" which I have commented on elsewhere.[35] And further spiritual development is shown by those "sarcophagi showing the seasons, in which winter is represented by Attis. One of them, in which the busts of the dead are surrounded by the signs of the zodiac, reveals belief in an astral immortality."[36] And this brings us back to the astrological conception of the cosmos.

I hope that I have convinced you of the likelihood of my thesis at the start, that the ancient mystery cults were a part of the ancient religions as a whole, and that, essentially, psychic substrata and archetypes formed the cults both in their public and in their mysterious nocturnal aspects. We may say that the cults underwent a development from a so-called "primitive" stage presenting comparisons and analogies with the ethnology of "primitive peoples"; that at the high level of civilization achieved by the Greeks and Romans they assumed the qualities of great religion—for example, with the call for bloodless sacrifices put forward by the devotee of Serapis, Apollonius of Tyana, in the service of a "secret, ineffable love";[37] and that the "secret" of the dromenon withdrew more and more to the realms of philosophy and mystical speculation (i.e., books and poetry), or to new cults.

There is a mystical saying to the effect that forsaken Eleusis celebrates itself. I believe we may be justified in interpreting this freely to mean that if ever the essential depths of the human soul were manifested in Eleusis— and this seems to have been the case, for in Eleusis two archetypes, the earth mother and the divine son, were carried to the surface from those depths—

---

mother as follows: "Spouse and helpmate of Adam Kadmon: Heva, naked Eve. She had no navel. Gaze. Belly without blemish, bulging big, a buckler of taut vellum, no, whiteheaped corn, orient and immortal . . ." (Joyce, *Ulysses*, London edn., p. 29. N.Y. edn., p. 39).

35 "Precatio Terra Matris," in "Sol Invictus," p. 182. [Reading:

"Forever faithfully thou givest the food of life,
And when the soul departeth we take refuge in thee;
Whatsoever thou givest, all things return to thee.
Deservedly art thou called Great Mother of the Gods."
—Trans.]

36 Cumont, p. 226, n. 50; and his "Un Fragment de sarcophage Judéo-Païen," *Revue archéologique*, 5th series, IV (Paris, 1916), 6ff.

37 Philostratus, *Vita Ap.* VII and I, 7.

the mystery will, *in changing forms*, forever be solemnized: for "the quietly busy" forces of the great genetrix fear none of the powers that be, political or otherwise, and mighty as such powers may seem, they are constantly undergoing transformation in the stream of human development.[38]

3. Mysteries in Poetry

The dromenon, the *orgia*, the sacred mime, the legomena, and above all the *teletai* (the fulfillments) have become the dromenon of man, the "event" in his self, his soul, and his spirit. Man passes through a psychic-spiritual world of beginnings, though a world of inner images, and through the world of his "education." Let him see to it that his dromenon has a cathartic, purifying efficacy and leads him to the *telos*, to perfection.

Among the *philosophoi* (the philosophers in the ancient sense), the dromenon was early detached from priestly families and earth cults.[1]

"You have gained fellowship in the madness and the Bacchic frenzy of the philosopher." So spoke Alcibiades—who bore Eros with the thunderbolts on his shield and whom Hadrian centuries later still celebrated as a great Hellene—in his speech praising the philosophy of Socrates.

There is a faint anticipation here of the "fellowship" of that mystery which Paul juxtaposed to the pre-Christian mysteries.

The dromenon has traveled inward.

Joyce quotes Maeterlinck:

> If Socrates leave his house today, he will find the sage seated on his doorsteps. If Judas go forth tonight it is to Judas his steps will tend.

And continues:

> Every life is many days, day after day. We walk through ourselves, meeting robbers, ghosts, giants, old men, young men, wives, widows, brothers-in-love. But always meeting ourselves.[2]

Or: On a perfectly commonplace occasion, a conversation about childbirth in a modern hospital, an intimation of the mysteries (mingled with

38 Cf. *Faust*, II, Act II.

1 Plato, *Symposium* 33, 218, *Laws*, X, 908, etc. And Heraclitus, Diels fr. B 5, 14, 15 (Freeman, p. 25).

2 Joyce, *Ulysses*, p. 201 (N.Y. edn., p. 210).

Aristotelo-Thomism) arises like an anamnesis, a recollection of primordial experience.

> The adiaphane in the noon of life is an Egypt's plague which in the nights of prenativity and postmortemity is their most proper *ubi* and *quomodo*. . . . The aged sisters draw us into life. . . over us dead they bend. First saved from water of old Nile, among bulrushes, a bed of fasciated wattles: at last the cavity of a mountain, an occulted sepulchre amid the conclamation of the hillcat and the ossifrage. And as no man knows the ubicity of his tumulus nor to what processes we shall thereby be ushered nor whether to Tophet or to Edenville in the like way is all hidden when we would backward see from what region of remoteness the whatness of our whoness hath fetched his whenceness.[3]

Or: A simple Dubliner, of Eastern origin, thinks of his dead son, and through his mind and heart pass gigantic visions running from Chaldaic star religion down to the astrological cosmology of the *Pistis Sophia:*

> On the highway of the clouds they come, muttering thunder of rebellion, the ghosts of beasts. . . . Elk and yak, the bulls of Bashan and of Babylon, mammoth and mastodon, they come trooping to the sunken sea, *Lacus Mortis*. Ominous, revengeful zodiacal host! They moan passing upon the clouds, horned and capricorned, the trumpeted with the tusked, the lionmaned the giantantlered, snouter and crawler, rodent, ruminant and pachyderm, all their moving multitude, murderers of the sun.
>
> Onward to the dead sea they tramp to drink, unslaked and with horrible gulpings, the salt somnolent inexhaustible flood. And the equine portent grows again, magnified in the deserted heavens, nay to heaven's own magnitude till it looms, vast, over the house of Virgo . . . the everlasting bride, harbinger of the daystar, the bride, ever virgin. . . . It floats, it flows about her starborn flesh and loose it streams emerald, sapphire, mauve and heliotrope, sustained on currents of cold interstellar wind, winding, coiling, simply swirling, writhing in the skies, a mysterious writing till after a myriad metamorphoses of symbol, it blazes, Alpha, a ruby and triangled sign upon the forehead of Taurus.[4]

Or: The same man dreams of the highest worldly dignity, he becomes emperor of the earth, and, behold, Selene comes and weds him. And the representative of the new world-priest approaches him and anoints him with the words *"habemus carnificem"*: we have the hangman of the world.—Thus James Joyce.[5]

3 Ibid., p. 376 (N.Y. edn., pp. 387f.).　　4 Ibid., p. 396 (N.Y. edn., p. 407).
5 Ibid., p. 462 (N.Y. edn., p. 473).

Or: In a curious tale, another great poet speaks of the secret of secrets. The circle of the "Travelers to the Orient" possesses it. And each member possesses it. It must not be revealed, a vow of silence is imposed on the neophyte. But it cannot be disclosed in any case, for any one who leaves the "circle" loses this soul treasure automatically, he "forgets" it. But sometimes, like a "golden path" the secret reappears, and he who has suffered long to win it finds his way back to the "circle," and in an inward room of the soul the master and the members gather together, and like the music of Mozart's *Magic Flute*, a hierarchy of soul and spirit is composed, and the humblest and simplest mounts the degrees to become highest of the high, and then he speaks of the suffering that purifies and of endless yearning.

This inwardly enacted dromenon comes from Hermann Hesse.[6] And in a night scene which he situates in the beginning of civilization, he gives an intimation of the genesis of the mysteries.

> The rising in the night, the adventure of being led through the dark silent wood full of danger and mystery, the sojourn on the rock plateau high up in the morning cold, the appearance of the thin, ghostly moon, the sparse words of the wise man and the solitude with his master at that extraordinary hour—all this was experienced and preserved by Knecht as a feast and a mystery, as the mystery of initiation and as his acceptance into a bond and cult, into a menial but honorable relationship with the unnameable, the cosmic mystery.[7]

Magister Ludi Knecht, master of a noble game (*das Glasperlenspiel*, the game of the glass beads) established in opposition to a world of blood and horror, a game whose purpose it is to "make the boundless, the tempestuous, life itself, crystallize into clear metaphors," experiences the scene related above in a vision at the beginning of civilization. But like Goethe, Hesse knows that permanence is impossible in the world of becoming, and accordingly Magister Ludi, master of the perfect game and of the game of perfection, frees himself and leaves the crystal palace of wisdom; and the poem "Stufen" (Steps), also titled "Transzendieren" (Transcendence), which interprets the musical form of irresistible progression as a "metaphor," "as an admonition and call to life," serves him as a maxim for life and death:

6 Hermann Hesse, *Die Morgenlandfahrt* (1933).
7 *Magister Ludi*, tr. Mervyn Savill (London, and New York, 1949), p. 411 (from *Das Glasperlenspiel*, Zurich, 1943).

As every blossom fades and all youth sinks
into old age, so every life's design,
each flower of wisdom, every good, attains
its prime and cannot last forever.
At life's each call the heart must be prepared
to take its leave and to commence afresh,
courageously and with no hint of grief
submit itself to other, newer ties.
A magic dwells in each beginning and
protecting us it tells us how to live.

High-purposed we must traverse realm on realm
cleaving to none as to a home. The world
of spirit wishes not to fetter us
but raise us higher, further, step by step.
Scarce in some safe accustomed sphere of life
have we established house, than we grow lax;
he only who is ready to inspan
and journey forth can throw old habits off.

Maybe death's hour too will send us out
new-born toward undreamed-of lands, maybe
life's call to us will never find an end . . .
Courage, my heart, take leave and fare thee well![8]

8 Ibid., p. 396.

Georges Nagel

The "Mysteries" of Osiris in Ancient Egypt

Before speaking of the "mysteries" of Osiris, we must ask: what is known of this god? what legends were told of him by the Egyptians? We all of us know something about him, but for the sake of clarity we must briefly consider these questions before examining the ceremonies of the Egyptian cult that have sometimes been designated as mysteries.

Strange as it may seem, it is not the Egyptian texts that give us the most coherent accounts of the legend of Osiris, but Greek literature and most particularly Plutarch's famous treatise *On Isis and Osiris*.[1] Of course, the Greek writers add their own interpretations, which we shall not consider here, since they are of greater interest for the history of the Greek mind than for the study of Egyptian religion. In any case it is the work of these authors that enables us to fit into their place the numerous details of this legend that we find in the most diverse Egyptian texts dating from all epochs.

In certain of his aspects, Osiris is an agrarian god, god of the vegetation that is reborn each year and of the flood that, year after year, brings the country its fertility and prosperity. But the legend of Osiris has more to do with another aspect: with the god as king of the earth.

In the beginning, as we all know, it was Ra the sun god and creator of the universe who reigned over the earth. Weary of men, who had rebelled against him, he withdrew to heaven[2] and left his place to his son Shu, god of the atmosphere, then to his grandson Geb. The legend leaves these two sovereigns somewhat in the shadow. Then followed the reign of Osiris, son of Geb, the earth god, and Nut, the goddess of heaven; his reign was distinguished by great advances in civilization. It was Osiris who gathered men

1 In *Moralia*, with tr. by Frank Cole Babbitt and others (LCL, 1927ff.), Vol. V, pp. 6–191.

2 Cf. my "Le Culte du Soleil dans l'ancienne Égypte," *EJ 1943*, esp. pp. 38ff.

into organized societies and taught them the rules of agriculture. He abolished cannibalism and taught men to make use of wheat and to weave clothing. It was also he, it is said, who instituted the cult of the gods. Isis, his sister and wife, helped him in this work; she founded the family and the marriage tie. All these traits of his activity characterize Osiris clearly as a king who was a benefactor to his people.

But not content with assuring the happiness of Egypt, he wishes to spread his benefits afar, and sets forth to conquer the world, reducing men to submission by suasion and gentleness. During his absence Isis rules with a firm hand.

Osiris has a brother, Seth, whom the Greeks called Typhon; Seth is his direct counterpart. In contrast to the fertile, beneficent earth, he is the barren, burning desert; he is tempest and war; and he is barbarism as opposed to civilization.[3] Jealous of his brother, he seeks to supplant him; through her vigilance, Isis prevents this during her husband's absence. But Seth nevertheless attains his ends: by means of a stratagem he shuts up Osiris in a wooden chest, which he throws into the river. The Nile carries it down to the sea, some say as far as the coasts of Phoenicia, to the holy city of Byblos. Without further opposition, Seth occupies the throne of Osiris.

Now only a few remain faithful to Isis, particularly Thoth and Anubis the jackal god. She sets out in search of her husband's corpse, and hides in the marshes of the Delta. After many wanderings she finds the corpse. According to other legends, Seth, in order to be sure that his brother is dead, cuts his body in pieces which he scatters to the four winds of heaven. Isis is compelled to seek them one by one, and she finds them all excepting the phallus, which has been devoured by an oxyrhynchus fish. But it is not enough for her to have the pieces of his corpse; she wants her husband again, yet in spite of all her magic she does not succeed in restoring earthly life to the pieces she has assembled; the best she can do is to make a mummy capable only of an other-worldly half-life. She manages, however, to become impregnated by her husband's corpse and gives birth to Horus, his father's avenger and successor.[4] The funeral rites that Isis, aided by Anubis and

3 He also represents the relation between Lower Egypt, where civilization developed earlier, and Upper Egypt, which remained much longer in a barbaric state.
4 Elsewhere it is related that after the murder of her husband Isis flees with her young son Horus, whom she hides carefully in the marshes of the Delta to save him from the persecutions of Seth.

Thoth, performs over the body of Osiris make him first of the dead. After having been king of the living he quite naturally becomes king of the dead. During his reign he had transformed the earth; now he transforms his new kingdom, which becomes a fertile, well-cultivated country. Here the dead, provided that, like Osiris, they have been given the prescribed funeral rites, enjoy perfect happiness in the midst of a magnificent nature.

Grown to manhood, Horus prepares for the battle against the usurper. Followed by those faithful to him, he attacks his uncle. A bitter struggle ensues; victories alternate with defeats; the two adversaries inflict upon one another terrible wounds that Thoth, god of wisdom and magic, dresses.[5] Just as Horus is about to kill Seth, Isis intervenes in Seth's favor and saves him; furious, Horus cuts off his mother's head, and Thoth can replace the lost head only with the head of a cow. The battle might have gone on forever, but Thoth intervenes as arbiter and divides the kingdom into two halves, giving Lower Egypt to Horus and Upper Egypt to Seth.[6]

This legend does not give us a story coherent in all its details; many divergent notations have merely been juxtaposed without the slightest attempt at unification. In the Egyptian texts the incoherence is greater and is further increased by the fact that, as a rule, no text gives us more than a small part of the legend. We have already said that Osiris is a god of vegetation and at the same time king of the earth. His opposition to Seth preserves the memory of prehistoric rivalries between the north and the south of Egypt just as the battles of Horus and Seth are a living echo of the struggles a little later in prehistory between Upper and Lower Egypt for the hegemony of the Nile Valley. These battles, which ended in the victory of Horus— that is, the victory of Lower Egypt over Upper Egypt—are anterior to Menes, the first king, for then Upper Egypt was victorious and imposed its domination on the Delta.[7]

To give some idea of what the clearest and most accessible Egyptian texts tell us of this legend, I shall cite two of them. The first is a fragment of a

5 Cf. my "Le Dieu Thoth d'après les textes égyptiens," *EJ 1942*, esp. pp. 117ff.
6 In other forms of the legend the contest is settled by a long trial, characterized, of course, by numerous ups and downs, before the supreme god Ra. It is only because of the ruses of his mother Isis, the skillful magician, that Horus ends by triumphing over Seth, despite the help given to Seth by Ra the sun god himself. Cf. Papyrus Chester Beatty no. 1, The Combats of Horus and Set (Alfred Chester Beatty Collection, Dublin).
7 Cf., among other works, Kurt Sethe, *Urgeschichte und älteste Religion der Ägypter* (Abhandlungen für die Kunde des Morgenlandes, XVIII, 4; Leipzig, 1930).

hymn to Osiris from the Middle Kingdom. Among the few allusions to his legend, I have chosen those concerning Isis:

> His sister protected him,
> It is she who expelled his enemies and averted misfortune,
> Who repulsed the adversary by the magic formulas of her mouth,
> Whose tongue is crafty,
> Whose mouth is never lacking in words,
> Who wields authority well,
> It is she, Isis, the just, who protects her brother,
> Who seeks him without wearying,
> Who in mourning traverses the whole land without respite before
>   finding him,
> Who gives shade with her feathers,
> And wind with her wings.[8]
> It is she who praises her brother,
> Who relieves the weakness of him who is tired.[9]
> Who receives his seed and gives birth to his heir,
> Who nurtures the child in solitude,
> Without anyone's knowing where she is.[10]

The second text is from the New Kingdom. It is the story of the struggle between Seth and Horus as it appears in a calendar of lucky and unlucky days, for the twentieth day of Thoth, which corresponds approximately to the sixth of October:

> Utterly luckless day. Undertake nothing on this day. It is the day when Horus battled against Seth. They smote one another. Then they lay down on their sides, both having turned themselves into hippopotamuses at the gate of . . . of Kheraha. Thus they spent three days and three nights. Then Isis cast her harpoon[11] at them, it fell on the face of Horus. Then he cried in a loud voice: "I am thy son Horus." Then Isis said to the harpoon: "Depart from my son

---

8 Isis is sometimes represented as a falcon. She appears in this form among others in one of the vignettes of Ch. XVII of the Book of the Dead; here the two falcons to the left and right of Osiris' catafalque are Isis and her sister Nephthys.
9 I.e., who is dead.
10 Paris Stele, formerly in the Bibliothèque nationale (no. 20), now in the Louvre (C. 286). Cf. F. J. Chabas, "Un hymne à Osiris traduit et expliqué," in his *Oeuvres diverses* (Bibliothèque égyptologique, IX; Paris, 1899), pp. 95ff., Pl. II; and Charles Boreux, *Musée nationale du Louvre, Département des antiquités égyptiennes: Guide-catalogue sommaire* (Paris, 1932), Vol. I, pp. 156–57. A complete [German] tr. of the text is in Günther Roeder, ed., *Urkunden zur Religion des alten Ägypten* (Jena, 1923), pp. 22–26.
11 The weapon commonly used for hippopotamus hunting.

Horus." Then she cast a second harpoon, and it fell on the face of her brother Seth. Then he cried out in a loud voice and lamented. Then she said to the harpoon: "Hold fast." Then he cried out several times: "Dost thou hate thy mother's son?" Then her heart was grieved. And she said to the harpoon: "Set him free! He is my mother's son." Then the harpoon set him free. Then they arose and turned against one another, and the majesty of Horus was angered against his mother Isis like a panther of Upper Egypt. Then he cut off the head of Isis. Thoth then turned himself into the god of magic [Heka], and mended her with a cow's head. On this day an offering is made to her name and to the name of Thoth.[12]

I have intentionally chosen texts of very diverse periods and types, in order to give an idea of the wide range of our Egyptian sources. In a more or less official hymn we cannot expect to find the same picturesque details as in a consistent narrative, where the divine legend is humanized and romanticized. It would have been easy to cite much more ancient texts, but the numerous allusions that we find in the Pyramid Texts would have made them much harder to understand and necessitated considerable explanation. But in connection with all these texts, I should like to stress one point. The various episodes of the legend are not attested in the same way and with the same frequency. The texts often speak of the battles of Horus and Seth for the heritage of Osiris, and often they mention the laments of Isis over her husband's death. But with regard to the actual death and resurrection of Osiris they are always quite reticent and usually give us no more than brief allusions.

What I have told of the legend of Osiris is very much schematized; but, even so, one can see how very human this legend is, how close to human preoccupations, to the fate of every man. It does not merely recount the adventures of a king of olden time; it is the story of every man who must die and who, if he cannot continue his little life here below, wishes at least to know the joys of the life beyond the grave. In other words, this is a legend that will not remain on a theoretical plane, that is not merely a beautiful tale, pleasant to hear. It is a legend that will become a part of men's

12 British Museum Papyrus Sallier IV, 2/6ʳff. Cf. Chabas, *Le Calendrier des jours fastes et néfastes de l'année égyptienne* (Chalon-sur-Saône, 1875?), pp. 28ff. We find the same story, but in a more developed form, in the text of The Combats of Horus and Set (Pap. C. Beatty no. 1), 8–9ff. As we have seen above, Plutarch, in *On Isis and Osiris*, ch. 19, has preserved a very similar version of the same legend.

lives, a source of hope and of faith. And moreover, the various episodes of this legend so full of life lend themselves admirably to dramatization. It may well have seemed almost natural that in the cult of this god the diverse scenes of his life should have been enacted by priests representing the gods of the Osiris cycle. These dramatizations in a rather simple form seem to have been a frequent feature of the temple rituals, and while this is not peculiar to the cult of Osiris, his legend offered broader scope for dramatization than did that of the other gods.

The oldest and most precise record of this cult dates from the Middle Kingdom. It is a stele originating in Abydos and now in the Berlin Museum.[13] From it we learn that at Abydos, the great Upper Egyptian center of the cult of Osiris, there were special ceremonies recalling the great moments in the life of the god. A personage named Ikhernofret, bearing numerous titles, particularly that of head treasurer, tells us of the works he has executed at Abydos on the order of Sesostris III (XIIth dynasty) in the nineteenth year of his reign, in 1868 B.C.[14] These works consisted in repairing all the sacred furnishings of the temple of Osiris, in beautifying and enriching the statues of the principal god and his companions, in repairing the sacred barge that the god used in his solemn processions, and in organizing or reorganizing the holy ceremonies. "I caused the priests," he himself tells us, "to take their duties seriously, and I taught them the ceremonies."[15]

After these indications of the works accomplished in the sanctuary of Osiris, he speaks, too briefly for our liking, of the ceremonies that he performed in the temple. As representative of the king, he undertook the ritual dressing of the divine statue. Then he tells us:

13 Berlin, Stele no. 1204. It has been published and studied by, among others, Heinrich Schaefer, in *Die Mysterien des Osiris in Abydos* (Untersuchungen zur Geschichte und Altertumskunde Ägyptens, IV, 2; Leipzig, 1904).

14 The exact date is not given in the Berlin monument but in a Geneva stele (D. 50). Cf. E. H. Naville, *Mélanges de la Société auxiliaire du Musée* (1922), pp. 45ff. Here we find this brief text: "Privy councillor Sasesit says: I came to Abydos with head treasurer Ikhernofret to make the image of Osiris, the First of the dwellers in the West, the Lord of Abydos, in the days when the King of Upper and Lower Egypt Sesostris III, who lives forever, set out on a campaign to destroy the miserable Kush [Ethiopia], in the year 19." Since Sesostris reigned from 1887 to 1850, this places us in 1868.

15 At the beginning of the New Kingdom, under the reign of Thutmosis I (1539–1520), we learn that the royal treasurer, also on mission to Abydos, charged with restoring the holy statues and barges, received similar orders. "I ordered the priests to be informed of their duties," the king tells us; "to him who did not know, I taught what he did not know, I did more than the old kings who lived before me had done." Sethe, *Urkunden der 18. Dynastie*, Sec. I, Vol. I (Leipzig, 1906), p. 102, li. 5ff.

I organized the solemn departure of the god Ophoïs[16] when he goes to the rescue of his father, I repulsed those who had rebelled against the barge Neshemet,[17] and I slew the enemies of Osiris. I organized the great procession, I followed the god on his march. I sailed the god's barge, while Thoth protected its voyage. I installed a cabin in the barge of the Lord of Abydos called "He appears in truth" [i.e., as a conqueror], I decked it out with fine ornaments for the journey to Peker,[18] I avenged Unennofer [Osiris] on this day of great battles, and I slew his enemies on the waters of Nedit. I caused him to enter the ship that bore his beauty. I rejoiced the hearts of the dwellers in the East, and I filled with joy the dwellers in the West when they saw the beauties of the barge Neshemet, which approached Abydos and brought back to his palace Osiris, the First of the dwellers in the West, the Lord of Abydos. I followed the god into his house and I accomplished its purification. . . .[19]

In this all too brief text we have an indication of certain ceremonies which, on some special occasion, were performed in the temple of Abydos, ceremonies recalling and without doubt re-enacting the events of the god's earthly life. We see the god Ophoïs going forth as the advance guard of Osiris, who sails like a king in his sacred barge. Thoth is there, presumably in advance of the barge, to destroy any enemies who may appear. It is at this point in the story that we would expect to hear of the god's death, of his wife's lamentations as she goes out in search of his corpse, of the finding of the corpse and the ceremonies for the god's resurrection. But the text says nothing of all this.[20] We are only told that Osiris is taken to his tomb at Peker, that his enemies are subsequently defeated, and that he returns triumphant to his sanctuary, where he reigns in peace until next year's festival. The absence of certain elements is somewhat disconcerting, but nevertheless we do seem to be dealing with a sacred drama, a "mystery of the passion of Osiris," as enacted, according to the Greek writers, in various Egyptian sanctuaries. For the present, I shall defer the question of whether these are mysteries in the strict sense of the word.

16 Upuaut (opener of the roads), the jackal god of Abydos, who is presented to us here as the son of Osiris.
17 The sacred barge of Osiris, which he employed in processions.
18 One of the holy sites of Abydos.
19 These are the ceremonies which conclude the festival. The last line is mutilated, though not much is missing.
20 It is possible that these ceremonies were performed in the seclusion of the sanctuaries, behind closed doors.

I should like to mention here another element in the "mystery of Osiris," attested by Greek travelers and by the Egyptian texts. Herodotus writes: At Papremis [in the Delta] there is a special ceremony in addition to the ordinary rites and sacrifices as practiced elsewhere. As the sun draws toward setting, only a few of the priests continue to employ themselves about the image of the god, while the majority, armed with wooden clubs, take their stand at the entrance of the temple; opposite these is another crowd of men, more than a thousand strong, also armed with clubs and consisting of men who have vows to perform. The image of the god, in a little wooden gold-plated shrine, is conveyed to another sacred building on the day before the ceremony. The few priests who are left to attend to it put it, together with the shrine which contains it, in a four-wheeled cart, which they drag along toward the temple. The others, waiting at the temple gate, try to prevent it from coming in, while the votaries take the god's side and set upon them with their clubs. The assault is resisted, and a vigorous tussle ensues in which heads are broken and not a few actually die of the wounds they receive. That, at least, is what I believe, though the Egyptians told me that nobody is ever killed.[21]

Here we assuredly have to do with a liturgical ceremony, since the god is represented by his statue, but on the other hand the participants play a role that is hardly very symbolic, since they expose themselves to blows and merrily crack one another's skulls in the name of their god. A similar ceremony is represented in a Theban tomb dating from the reign of Amenhotep III (1405–1370).[22] At the top of the scene, we see the king followed by the queen and several princesses; he is raising the great sacred pillar, the Djed, symbol of Osiris, by means of ropes. We shall return directly to this part of the ceremony. Below, on several different planes, various persons (smaller than the king, as is fitting) participate in the festival. Some

21 Herodotus, II, 63 (tr. Aubrey de Selincourt, Penguin Books, Harmondsworth and Baltimore, 1954, p. 126). In ch. 61, speaking of the festivals of Isis at Saïs, he also tells us: "It is here that everybody—tens of thousands of men and women—when the sacrifice is over, beat their breasts: in whose honor, however, I do not feel it is proper for me to say" (ibid.). This is the prudent formula he employs in speaking of the mysteries of Osiris.
22 Tomb of Kheriuf (no. 192). The part of the tomb in which this scene is situated is inaccessible today and we know it only through a sketch by J. P. A. Erman, published in H. K. Brugsch, *Thesaurus inscriptionum aegyptiacarum* (Leipzig, 1883–91), pp. 1190ff. It is reproduced in Alexandre Moret, *Mystères égyptiens* (Paris, 1922), fig. 3, p. 15, and elsewhere.

carry cult objects, others are performing ritual dances, still others are striking one another with sticks. Contrary to the report of Herodotus, this does not appear to be a disorderly turmoil, but rather a simulated combat regulated by the liturgy, with much brandishing of sticks and with heavy blows that injure none of the participants. In the lower part of the scene we see groups of animals, cows and asses, being herded "around the city"; most probably they would later be sacrificed. The combatants seem to be the partisans of Osiris and of Seth.[23] They are battling in support of their god, and their games represent the struggles between the supporters of the two rivals.

The pillar of Djed, which the king is raising with ropes, is the fetish of Osiris, it is Osiris himself.[24] When the pillar is on the ground, Osiris is dead; when it is raised, he comes back to life. In certain of the temple ceremonies this pillar is treated like a real statue, eyes are drawn upon it, arms holding scepters are attached to it, it is dressed, and a crown is placed on top of it, just as if it were really a statue of the god. This ceremony of the pillar is also found in the famous text known as the "Dramatic Papyrus of the Rameseum."[25] This is a kind of libretto for the benefit of the priest who directs these ceremonies on the occasion of the coronation or funeral of a king of the Middle Empire, but its sources are much more ancient. Each scene begins with a statement of the liturgical action involved and its mystical significance. Then we have the names of the actors and a summary indication of the words they are to exchange. There follow brief notations evoking a character or a gesture that must not be lost sight of, and finally, we have a vignette commenting on the scene. Here is a sample of this text with its somewhat random notes, seeming here even more disjointed than in their original arrangement, which helped in understanding them.

23 The brief inscriptions do not tell us much. However, we have one group which is described as "the people of Pe and of Dep," the sacred quarters of Busiris, the city of Osiris in the Delta.

24 We do not know exactly what it represents; it is probably the stylized image of a branchless tree trunk.

25 Kurt Sethe, ed., *Dramatische Texte zu alt-ägyptischen Mysterienspielen* (Untersuchungen zur Geschichte und Altertumskunde Ägyptens, X; Leipzig, 1928), Vol. II, pp. 83ff. The few scenes of which we shall speak here bear the nos. xiii–xv, pp. 153ff. They are also studied in Étienne Drioton, "Ce que l'on sait du théâtre égyptien," *Édition de la Revue du Caire* (1938), p. 11. Drioton's tr. is used here [Englished].

SCENE XIII

It happens that an offering of a calf's and a goose's head is made to the sacred pillar. It is Horus who has become powerful and his commands are obeyed.

Give me my diadem!

Geb to Thoth: Give him his head.

The head of Seth.

Two offerings. Cereals.

Offer a calf's head and a goose's head. Gilded chamber.

SCENE XIV

It happens that the sacred pillar is set up by the royal Parents. It is Horus who has ordered his children to place Seth under Osiris.

Horus to the Children of Horus: See to it that he remain under him.

Isis and Nephthys to the Children of Horus: Push him under him who has fallen!

Seth under Osiris the lamented.

The Children of Horus.

Raise the sacred pillar.

The royal Parents.

The Great Priest of Heliopolis.

SCENE XV

It happens that a rope is placed around the sacred pillar. It is Seth immolated, as Horus has ordered his children.

Horus to the Children of Horus: Put him on his feet, bound!

Seth bound.

Incline the sacred pillar.

What strikes us at first glance in this strange text [remarks Drioton] is the difference between the sequence of the ritual actions, which are perfectly clear and logically related (an offering is made to the sacred pillar, the sacred pillar is raised, a rope is passed around the sacred pillar), and the detail of the dialogue and scenic indications, which is not only obscure but sometimes frankly disconcerting.[26]

But we must not look upon these ceremonies with our own eyes or habits of thought. With the eyes of the flesh, the Egyptian believer who attended a ceremony of this sort saw just what we see, what for example is represented

26 Drioton, p. 17.

in the above-mentioned tomb of the epoch of Amenhotep III, and what we also see in certain paintings on the walls of the Egyptian temples: the priests or the king raise a pillar by means of ropes while various personages bustle about.

> But with the eyes of faith, the Egyptians saw something quite different. For them, the king was really Horus, the sacred pillar was Osiris, the butcher was the god Thoth, the slain calf was the god Seth, the goats his accomplices; when the sacred pillar was raised, this was Osiris, standing in triumph on the back of Seth his murderer. One detail shows how little this symbolism was connected with visible objects or persons, and how dependent it was on the action, taken in the absolute and not in its material conditions. In the moment when the sacred pillar was girded with the rope, it suddenly ceased to be Osiris and became Seth, his bound enemy. Such changes were familiar to the Egyptian mysteries: they were, it should be added, evoked rather than expressed by mysterious words spoken in the course of the rites.[27]

These texts enable us to put our finger on the element of mystery in these ceremonies performed in the temples or funeral chapels. The curious Greek traveler who attended them saw only strange objects and gestures, but if an obliging priest explained and commented on the scenes, how could he have helped feeling that he was being initiated not only into profound mysteries but really into a "mystery," unknown to the profane and truly understood only by priests versed in wisdom and piety? Such must have been the reaction of the Greek traveler curious in matters of orientalism, but the Egyptian believer raised in this atmosphere passed without difficulty from the plane of pure visual perception to the plane of faith. Behind the gestures he immediately grasped the idea or image which these gestures were intended to evoke.

The temple ritual, made uniform under the New Kingdom, makes frequent allusions to the legend of Osiris, and we might have multiplied our examples. However, it is in the funeral cult that this legend is most consistently dramatized. The reason for this is simple: was Osiris not the first dead man who, thanks to the enlightened care of his sister Isis and her acolytes, recovered a certain life after death? It was not the life he had known on earth, but it was nevertheless a life worthy of the name, in the kingdom whose first king he had been. In this kingdom he received all those

27 Pp. 13, 14.

who had been given the rites that had proved so effective in his case, whose corpses had been ritually embalmed amid the magic formulas that turned the deceased into a new Osiris. He was now no longer Amenhotep or Pashed, but Osiris Amenhotep or Osiris Pashed. Obviously it was not Isis, or Horus, or Thoth, or Anubis in person who officiated, it was not they who performed the prescribed rites;[28] priests took the place of the gods, sometimes wearing identifying masks.[29] In the tombs, for example, we often see representations of the deceased in his mummy wrappings, lying on a great mortuary bed similar to those found in the tomb of Tutankhamen. Under the same canopy, the god Anubis or the priest who plays his role bends over the mummy and performs the last rites that are needed to assure his perfect resurrection.

It was not only at the time of the embalming that formulas identifying the deceased with Osiris were spoken,[30] but also during the funeral, when similar rites were performed over the mummy itself, often in its coffin, and over the statues of the deceased, in order to make them fully Osiris. The purpose was to give them back the full use of their limbs and faculties and thus enable them to enjoy their Osirian life to the full in the other world. These ceremonies were called "the opening of the mouth" from the name of the most characteristic rite. In the tombs both of kings and others, we find numerous more or less detailed representations of the rites performed on this occasion. The main priest is assimilated to Horus, the son of Osiris, performing his most sacred duties toward his father. I shall not discuss these rites in detail but will merely quote one of the scenes to give an idea of this type of text. It is an "opening of the mouth" in the strict sense.

> The "servant" (one of the mortuary priests) leads the "son" before the statue of the deceased and says: "O statue of Osiris N., I have come, I have brought thy son who loves thee in order that he may part thy lips and open thine eyes." The "officiating priest" says: "Son whom he loves, open the mouth and the eyes of the deceased, first with the iron chisel, then with the scarlet finger." The son

28 These rites were originally designed only for the kings, and they preserved something of this royal character even after they had been fully democratized. Some of the ceremonies derive from the royal ritual of the prehistoric period.
29 Certain museums, that of Hildesheim, for example, possess masks in the form of a jackal's head, worn on the priest's head.
30 For an embalming ritual of the late period, see G. C. C. Maspero, "Mémoire sur quelques papyrus du Louvre," *Notices et extraits des manuscrits* (Académie des inscriptions et belles-lettres, Paris), XXIV (1883), 14ff.

takes the chisel, raises it in his two hands and respectfully touches the mouth and the eyes with the edge. During this time the officiating priest recites the formula: "O statue of Osiris N., I have pressed thy mouth. I have put pressure upon thy mouth, O statue of Osiris N., in thy name of Sokaris;[31] O statue of Osiris N., Horus has pressed thy mouth, he has opened thine eyes and they shall be solid henceforth. O statue of Osiris N., thy mouth was stopped, I have restored it as well as thy teeth, I have opened thy mouth. Horus has opened thy mouth, O statue of Osiris N., Horus has opened thy mouth and thine eyes."[32]

And the speeches, accompanied by the gestures of the priests, continue in this way, with much monotony.

The numerous ceremonies that were performed at this moment were of very diverse origin, and many have not yet received satisfactory explanations. Some that seem to have fallen into disuse in the course of the New Kingdom, such as the one that has sometimes been called "rebirth by the skin," are more mysterious in character.[33] It would be quite simple to describe these scenes, but there would be little interest in doing so; an attempt to explain them would carry us too far, for it would involve too many hypotheses that could not be verified. I prefer merely to note them in passing rather than complicate our discussion with abstract speculations.

I might also cite clearer texts such as the "Lamentations of Isis and of Nephthys," dirges sung by the two goddesses for their brother Osiris.[34] These texts are of interest even if they do not reveal any great poetic or mystical inspiration. But they would bring us little that is new.

Now that we have passed in review the texts that have seemed to me most characteristic, it is time to utilize them. In conclusion, that is, we must raise the question of principle which it would have been useless to take up at the beginning of our study. The Greek authors tell us that the

31 One of the gods identified with Osiris.
32 Cf. Maspero, "Le Rituel du sacrifice funéraire," in his *Études de mythologie et d'archéologie égyptiennes*, Vol. I (Paris, 1893), pp. 283–324. The text quoted is on pp. 310ff.
33 Cf. Moret, *Mystères égyptiens*, pp. 41ff., but I am far from sharing the author's view on this point.
34 Of these we have several texts. The best known is Berlin Papyrus no. 1425, pub. long ago by P. J. F. de Horrack. Cf. his *Oeuvres diverses* (Bibliothèque égyptologique, XVII; Paris, 1907), pp. 35–53. We also have some of them in a more developed form in the Bremner-Rhind Papyrus (Brit. Museum no. 10188). Cf. R. O. Faulkner's edn. of the text (Bibliotheca Aegyptiaca, III, 2 parts; Brussels, 1932–33) and his tr. in *Journal of Egyptian Archaeology* (London), XXII–XXIV (1936–38).

Egyptians had "mysteries" in their religion and that these mysteries formed the basis of those celebrated in Greece. Were they right? "Hippocrates says yes and Galen says no," and the historians of religions are no more unanimous in their statements than the physicians.

Herodotus speaks unmistakably of mysteries devoted to two gods: Osiris[35] and Isis. Here is the most explicit passage:

> It is on this lake [before the temple of Athene, at Saïs, in the Delta] that the Egyptians act by night in what they call their Mysteries the Passion of that being whose name I will not speak. All the details of these performances are known to me, but—I will say no more. Similarly I propose to hold my tongue about the mysterious rites of Demeter, which the Greeks call Thesmophoria, though in this case there are one or two points which may be mentioned without impiety. I may say, for instance, that it was the daughters of Danäus who brought this ceremony from Egypt and instructed the Pelasgian women in it.[36]

The Ionian historian, as we see, is quite explicit, and on this point he is supported by all the ancient authors, the profane historians as well as the Church Fathers. Diodorus Siculus,[37] Plutarch,[38] Clement of Alexandria,[39] and Origen[40] all support him in this point and give further details that are of no interest for the present study.

Today we are better informed than these writers as to what the Greeks consciously borrowed from Oriental civilizations and from Egypt in particular. Should the mysteries really be considered in this category? Since in the eyes of the Greeks the Egyptians were the most religious of men, it would seem perfectly reasonable to find numerous elements of Egyptian origin in the Greek mysteries, and particularly in those of Eleusis. But if we turn to the Egyptian texts, we are obliged to recognize that the ceremonies that have been called "mysteries" fail to meet the requirements of this term used in its proper sense. Mysteries must have their *mystai*, that is, initiates. They also demand the religious silence of which Herodotus speaks, and their ceremonies are performed only before the initiate. But we find nothing of the sort in the Egyptian rites that we have studied. We have no

---

35 He is always designated by a prudent circumlocution, but we are certain that he can be no one but Osiris.
36 Herodotus, II, 171 (tr. Selincourt, p. 169).
37 Diodorus, I, 20, 21, 22, 23, 29.   38 *On Isis and Osiris*, ch. 35, 68.
39 *Stromateis*, V, 7; I, 15.   40 *Contra Celsum*, I, 12 and 20; III, 17.

proofs or even indications that these ceremonies were reserved for a small number of the initiate. These supposed "mysteries" were held in broad daylight, sometimes in the presence of the entire populace, sometimes of a more limited number of persons;[41] but there is no reason whatsoever for supposing that these persons were initiates. Nor is there anything in the structure of the temples to suggest that mysteries may have been celebrated in them.[42] The mortuary cult included many strange ceremonies, but it was open to all ever since these texts, at first reserved to the kings, were made accessible to the general public. In this cult we do not see living men being initiated into the "mysteries" of Osiris in order to benefit by them after their death. They are ceremonies performed over the dead and for their benefit. Nowhere do we see any ceremony which suggests the initiation of a living man[43] into the mysteries of a god, and yet Herodotus glories in having been so initiated. If there are no initiates, there can be no mystery in the true sense of the term;[44] the Greek authors have led us astray on this point, and the moderns who followed them have been mistaken.[45]

We can easily understand how, in the presence of certain ceremonies performed in the temples, the Greeks came to speak of "mysteries." In connection with the raising of the pillar of Djed, we have seen all the symbolism underlying a ritual of this sort, all the meaning that the eye of faith discerned

41 We know from the representations and texts of the Ptolemaic and Roman temples that certain ceremonies were performed in small chapels situated on the roof of the temple, hence far from the crowd of the faithful, but they no more than the others bear a character of "mystery." Cf. Hermann Junker, *Die Stundenwachen in den Osiris-mysterien* (Denkschriften der Kaiserlichen Akademie der Wissenschaften in Wien, Phil.-hist. Klasse, LIV; 1910), and the interpretations of Moret, who upholds the mystery theory, in *Mystères égyptiens*, pp. 22ff.

42 This is one of the arguments advanced by Camille Sourdille against the existence of mysteries in Egypt: *Hérodote et la religion de l'Égypte* (Paris, 1910), pp. 302ff.

43 Some writers speak of a text which allegedly mentions the initiation of the Persian king Cambyses into the cult of Neith at Saïs, but the text says nothing of the sort. Cf. G. Posener, *La Prèmière Domination perse en Égypte* (Institut français d'archéologie orientale, Bibliothèque d'étude, XI; Cairo, 1936), p. 14.

44 It should be noted in passing that the word "mystery" has sometimes been used in an entirely different sense in connection with Egypt, applying to a dramatic performance, as in the Middle Ages. Cf. among others, Schaefer, *Die Mysterien des Osiris in Abydos*, p. 20, n. 5 (cf. n. 13 above). This use of the term "mystery" would be less incorrect than the interpretation discussed above, but it would still be misleading, for in these mysteries the dramatic element is certainly not predominant. Essentially we are dealing with rites in which several persons sometimes participate and exchange words. This constitutes a kind of drama, but the ritual interest is always paramount.

45 On this point, see the highly pertinent remarks of Gustave Jéquier, *Drames, mystères, rituels dans l'ancienne Égypte* (Mélanges Niedermann; Neuchâtel, 1944), pp. 37ff.

behind very simple gestures. At the sight of these Egyptian cult ceremonies, Herodotus must have been just as disconcerted as a modern Buddhist, Moslem, or even Protestant might be while attending a solemn Mass for the first time. The most touching gestures would leave him indifferent because he would fail to see their meaning. But Herodotus, enlightened by obliging priests, understood that these strange and baffling gestures had a profound meaning that he would not have understood by himself. Thus instructed, how could he have helped feeling that he had been initiated into mysteries? The Egyptian priests knew how to flatter the foreigners who did them the honor of taking an interest in their cult and their faith. They took pleasure in showing these astonished travelers that profound truths were hidden beneath simple or strange gestures.

It becomes evident that ancient Egypt had no true mysteries. It is true that certain elements of the Egyptian religion exerted a profound influence on the Greek mysteries or, let us say, on certain Greek mysteries. But the reverse became true in the Ptolemaic period, when the mysteries of Osiris and above all of Isis were instituted under the influence of the Greeks and with the Greek religious mentality. These mysteries attained an immense vogue; they spread through the whole Roman Empire and brought a little of the mystical spirit of ancient Egypt to the Hellenistic and Roman world.

Jean de Menasce

The Mysteries and the Religion of Iran

A quarter of a century ago it was quite common to seek in Iran, if not quite a prototype of the Christian religion, at least the main elements of a religion of salvation. Moving from the Greek scholars' notion of a mystery religion to that of a soteriological mystery such as appears in the thinking of St. Paul,[1] scholars sought, and actually went so far as to reconstruct, an "Iranian mystery" of the soul's return to its divine origin through an initiation both gnostic and ritual, and this they alleged to have been widely disseminated in the Mediterranean world, precisely at the dawn of the Christian era. If the following remarks served no other aim than to demolish this construction, I should regard them as superfluous today: most specialists in the field have abandoned Richard Reitzenstein's thesis, including many who worked with him. But I believe that my remarks may cast a certain light on a far broader question of religious typology, for in speaking of an Iranian mystery we are dealing with two unknowns, or at least with two elements known very inadequately. And consequently, I feel that I must preface my remarks with certain essential distinctions concerning mysteries.

It is most important, it seems to me, to retain this notion of mystery in the science of religions, and yet to purify it of the coloration it assumes in any particular context, while considering the various colorations as so many individual varieties. Whatever may be the etymology of the basic Greek word, what a religious man understands by a mystery is, very generally speaking, something which is both hidden and revealed: revealed because, being essentially hidden, it requires, in order to manifest itself to mind, a new act that enables man to apprehend it by either independent quest, initiation by a teacher, or divine gift, or most frequently by all three.

1 [A most thorough and acute re-examination of that problem has now been published by Professor Arthur D. Nock: "Hellenistic Mysteries and Christian Sacraments," *Mnemosyne* (Leiden), series 4, V (1952), 117–213.—J. DE M. (1955).]

Its hiddenness is indeed a property inherent in this reality, and expresses its eminence, its transcendence. A something that is only factually hidden remains essentially discoverable, within our reach. The truly hidden is only that which is sacred and which, even when revealed, retains the nature of the inaccessible that can be manifested only in symbols. Thus we can give the name of mystery to the reality itself, which is essentially mystery, to the symbol or sign that communicates it, and to the action in which this communication, this presence, is accomplished; but the last two elements are mysteries only by participation.

It goes without saying that this natural order may be accidentally reversed: the mystery of a magic word, of an initiatory rite, sometimes conceals the revelation of very commonplace realities. A poem, for example, may be hermetic only in form. Normally, however, the content of the revelation transcends all cognition, and this reality is given to our love as well as to our intelligence. It speaks to us through what is most sublime and profound, most speculative, most practical within us, encompassing us and transforming us entirely, so that it matters little whether the revelation is effected through didactic doctrine or through ritual initiation, since in any event it implies a transcendence that becomes immanent for us in our whole self: all wisdom overflows into action and every act reflects a knowledge. Accordingly we believe that it is a mistake to specialize the meaning of the word *mystery* by applying it exclusively either to a higher instruction or to a ritual initiation. It is for the historian of religions or for the ethnologist to determine the relative importance of the speculative and the practical in any particular instance of revelation.

The social repercussions of the mystery can be understood only in the light of what we have just said. Access to the mystery traces a new and specific line of demarcation among men. The group of initiates may sometimes coincide with a given social category, determined by sex, age, race, condition, but this remains merely a convenient coincidence: only certain men can be initiates, and moreover, they must *become* so, for it is in the process that they come to constitute a new group, of which the first group marked only the greatest possible field of extension. But the essential is the principle of distinction: even where it coincides practically with a pre-existent social division, the community of the initiate is characterized by its participation in this essential mystery, according to a pattern assigned either by the free spontaneity of man or by the social institution. On what-

136

ever basis a man enters into the society of the initiate, there remains an element of choice, and the principle of this choice is itself a sort of mystery, but a secondary, derived mystery, an institutional rather than an ontological mystery, though closely dependent on the latter. This explains why it is eminently in its social manifestations that the religious mystery strikes us and interests us. The phenomenon of a religious society may arise in different ways: sometimes the sacred sanction will serve simply to reinforce a structure that is, strictly speaking, human and temporal; sometimes the religious tie will give rise to a social formation that may occasionally forget its original motive and change in essential orientation; sometimes the process will remain equivocal, and then it is the despair of the religious historian in search of a rigorous typology by which to distinguish between a temporal society with sacred rites and a sacred society imperceptibly laicized. But from the point of view of religious psychology, what matters is this sentiment of exclusive belonging, of selection and consequently of election, defined with reference to the sacred content in which the initiate has made himself a participant.

This content itself calls for distinctions. On the basis of an observation developed here[2] by Professor Kerényi, I should like to speak of natural mysteries and of supernatural mysteries, the former immanent in the visible tissue of individual and social human life, the latter rooted in the nature and intervention of the godhead. In the natural mysteries: these irreducible accidents, these banalities forever new—life, death, birth, sickness, fertility, culture (language, the arts), the origins (of the cosmos and of every reality), initiatives, transitions. In the supernatural: the divine life and the divine plan, not merely as explanation of the world, as crowning of the system, but in their intrinsic reality, participation in which is purely gratuituous. The natural mysteries are the domain of the explicative myth (the speculative point of view), giving rise to a moral norm, calling man to a festive commemoration and suggesting a corresponding activity that is its realization: supplication (verbal prayer) or mime (not necessarily magical). All this reflects the world of man's struggles: it is the favored domain of the ethnologist who moves amid this intermingling of the sacred and the temporal and seeks to disentangle them. These are realities of daily life, to be sure, but apprehended, lived in their profoundest aspect, in their renewable spontaneity, and above all in their relation to something else, to this

2 [At the 1944 Eranos meeting. See Dr. Kerényi's lecture in the present volume.—Ed.]

transcendent, sacred element which, if it does not interest us for itself, nevertheless underlies these realities, and whose discreet presence enables us to distinguish religion from poetry, mystery from drama, devotion from wonder.

If the mystery of natural fertility (vegetable or animal according to the types of civilization) leads more than any other to secret organization, it would seem to be not only because of the mysterious and irreducible aspect of fertility, but also no doubt because of the sense of shame which surrounds things sexual and which, like the ultramodesty of polite society, induces by compensation a whole organization of license. The ethnologists seek the origin of these secret associations in agrarian, matriarchal societies; but there is not necessarily an indissoluble link between the two.

The use of the terms "mystery" and "mystery religions" can very well be restricted to manifestations of this kind. I do not believe, however, that we can thus escape asking why other aspects of social life, having no immediate relation to fertility, are enveloped in secret rituals. The mystery, it seems to me, goes beyond the social organization of any stage in civilization and implies a reference to a reality that is essentially religious, hence transcendent and in itself mysterious.

The supernatural mystery, on the other hand, is the mystery of God himself. But so poor is our knowledge of God that we are constantly tempted, apart from revelation, to load it with myths, that is to say, with images primarily expressing practical and temporal realities, surreptitiously detached from their context and enjoying a kind of new, apparently independent existence, but in truth entirely impregnated with their earthly origins. We think we are concerned only with the life and act of God, but the human weighs down the divine and makes it unrecognizable. Similarly, the problem of the immortality of the soul, of survival after death, can be formulated in terms of individual salvation, of a new life, filled, as it were, with new and utterly divine objects; or quite the opposite, as a continuation of this earthly life for itself, or as a highly effective collaboration in the most urgent social functions of the living (agricultural prosperity). If there is sometimes a development from one to the other, this does not mean that between the two conceptions there is any strict order of succession, any rectilinear and fated evolution. It is for the historian, the psychologist, to say in what measure, *hic et nunc*, the symbol is transcended and taken as a metaphor, in what measure a reference to pure transcendence is manifested in the myth. We need only recall the singularly persistent character of mythologies and rituals in order to understand that historians must not make things too easy for themselves and that to seek too high or too low for the spiritual dominant of a religious fact is to be guilty of literalism and simplism.

Finally we must accord a proper place to the phenomena of linguistic attraction: the spiritual can be expressed only by recourse to analogy with some inferior reality that concretizes it. In the Upanishads, the unity of the knower and the known is frequently expressed in terms of digestive absorption. In Aristotle, this same process is described, in connection with the vegetative life, by the word "assimilation," which derives from the vocabulary of the life of sensibility and the intellect. Accordingly, we must learn to distinguish the moment when a people has consciously restored a worn-out myth by interpreting it, as a prefiguration of a more refined notion: this is the case with all syncretisms and all henotheisms. These restorations of myths may serve a propagandist purpose, as in the case of the first Christian Apologists, preaching the gospel in the language of the mysteries and of mythology; or their function may be purely ornamental— all liturgies (because they are conservative) are full of dubious elements that merely evoke images and leave the dogma intact. Whenever, for example, a cult becomes too interior, too exclusive, too angelic, it tends to divest the gesture of all literal meaning: lustrations replace bloody sacrifice, the pilgrimage to Mecca is enacted in a room.

Where then shall we seek a Christian mystery? For a Christian the mystery is essentially that of God himself, not only transcendent, not only living and intervening in a world which is entirely His work, but living a life inconceivable to any created intelligence as such: the life of the Holy Trinity, which the Son alone reveals to us. This life is diffused as love in those souls which God calls to His society. It illumines them, kindles them, transforms them, and this love is itself a mystery. For God gives himself to whom He pleases, to whom He elects to love Him with a love of our own choosing: and this election carries mystery into the heart of humanity. This is no longer a purely human and practical demarcation, a "secondary," borrowed mystery, it is a divinity in which we share, it is, as the theologians say, "essentially supernatural."

On the other hand, there is nothing in Christian revelation that is not public, "proclaimed from the housetops," to use the words of the Gospel.

There is no esotericism. The arcanum is here ornamental, secondary, a passing reflection of the Hellenistic milieu, playing a far smaller part in the Christian cult than does the solemn and festive liturgy of the synagogue. In the Christian ritual everything is open to the infinite appeal of love. Even the initiation, the baptism, like the faith which it represents and sanctions, is for all: only he who excludes himself is excluded; this election is essentially catholic. But at the beginning stands the mystery of God's own life, and finally there remains a true human mystery: what we call the secret of the heart, the authentic response of the human will to the divine summons. For no man knows whether he merits praise or blame. Christian life does not rest upon any certainty as to our own state of grace, and surely we cannot discern the state of our neighbor's soul.

All the rest is visible, and in its perpetual visibility more baffling to our complex souls than the "artistic" chiaroscuro of any human drama. The Christian mystery is more mysterious than any other: it is the very mystery of God, reflected in the secret of conscience. Otherwise, all is clarity. As Barrès once said of El Greco, it is a mystery in broad daylight.

With regard to the Iranian material, some highly original studies[3] have appeared in the last few years, and a number of ready-made ideas have been discredited. Nonetheless many regrettable gaps remain to be filled. Two tasks in particular demand our attention. The first is a more careful analysis of the Mazdean sacrificial liturgy. Since Darmesteter's commentary, which makes his French translation of the Avesta so valuable,[4] it can be said that nothing has been done to clarify the origins and development of the Yasna liturgy. We have a few scant pages by Victor Henry serving as an appendix to the magnificent monograph on the Indian *Agnistoma* which he wrote in collaboration with Caland.[5] The Iranian scholar must envy the Indologist who has at his disposal a vast liturgical material enabling him to clarify his

---

3 I refer the reader once and for all to the work of E. Benveniste, *The Persian Religion According to the Chief Greek Texts* (Paris, 1929); H. S. Nyberg, "Questions de cosmogonie et de cosmologie mazdéennes," *Journal asiatique* (Paris), CCXIV (1929), 193ff., CCXIX (1931), 1ff., 193ff.; idem, *Die Religionen des alten Iran*, tr. H. H. Schaeder (Leipzig, 1938); Geo Widengren, *Hochgottglaube im alten Iran* (Uppsala, 1938); M. S. Wikander, *Der arische Männerbund* (Lund, 1938); and idem, *Vayu* (Uppsala, 1941).

4 James Darmesteter, tr. and ed., *Le Zend-Avesta*, new tr. with historical and philological commentary (Annales du Musée Guimet, 21, 22, 24; Paris, 1892–94).

5 Willem Caland and Victor Henry, *L'Agnistoma* (Paris, 1906–7).

researches in the light of comparative ethnology: we need only consider, for example, the benefit that Father Koppers was able to draw from Dumont's work on the *ashvamedha*, or horse sacrifice. With regard to the sacrifice of the bull, it is Mr. Lommel who has made the soundest remarks.[6]

Second, the Middle Iranian texts have not been exploited systematically enough. I am convinced that they might contribute greatly to our knowledge of the Avesta itself. And primarily, it would be profitable to restore those quotations of the lost Avesta that have been preserved in Pahlavi translation in a number of Mazdean works, and whose style definitely shows them to be extremely literal—indeed, a phrase-by-phrase translation, of the same type as the interlinear translation that accompanies our manuscripts of the Avesta. An exact, exhaustive study of the methods followed in those translations of which we possess the original would provide us with a key by which to decipher the quotations from the lost Avesta and to translate them back into the original tongue. The very absurdities of the Mazdean translators would reveal forms that they no longer understood and that comparative philology now enables us to understand. It is by a similar process that the study of the Greek of certain passages in the Septuagint leads us back to a Hebrew original that we are better able to understand than either the Hellenists or the Masoretes; it is through the use of this method that we are able without difficulty to translate back from Syriac to Greek certain Patristic works the originals of which have been lost, and from Tibetan or Chinese certain works that had been lost from the Sanskrit or Pali canon. The number of these passages that were certainly translated is considerable: and, if we set aside the glosses (generally introduced by the particle *ku*), the meter can also prove most helpful as a criterion for restoring the originals.

It is particularly in connection with the legend of Zarathustra that these restorations might prove of interest, for the whole tone of the Mazdean religion depends on him, and we shall see how far we are from agreement on this point.

What do the documents of the Mazdean religion have to say of mysteries? Prima facie, only the mysteries of Mithras seem to enter into consideration.

---

6 Wilhelm Koppers, *Pferdeopfer und Pferdekult der Indogermanen* (Wiener Beiträge zur Kulturgeschichte und Linguistik, IV; Vienna, 1936); Paul Emile Dumont, *L'Aśvamedha* (Paris, 1927); Herman Lommel, "Yasna 32," *Wörter und Sachen* (Heidelberg), N.S., XIX (1938).

But it must be recalled that very little is known to us about these mysteries at the present time.[7]

On the one hand we have a monumental tradition revealed by archaeology (the documents have been magnificently assembled by Cumont[8]). But it should be noted that the episodes of the life of Mithras represented in the monuments do not lend themselves to any clear interpretation. We are reduced to conjectures. The same is true of the ritual of initiation and sacrifice. The trials of endurance have for the first time been definitely revealed to us by the paintings of the Mithraeum in Capua, and the sacrifice of the bull is attested by the texts; but as for the holy meal, is it a banquet of initiation, a love feast, or a eucharistic office?

On the other hand, we know the god Mithras from the Avestan texts. His character as a great celestial god appears to us more and more clearly since the work of Nyberg and Widengren: an ambiguous god, both beneficent and terrible, just and arbitrary. Certain of his attributes seem to have gone over to secondary deities, a part of his favorable aspect to Srosh, of his violent aspect to Ešm.[9] It was among the devotees of this god, among what he calls the Mithraic community (*Mithrasgemeinde*) that Zarathustra, according to Mr. Nyberg and his school, found his first converts. But it is also from Mithras that those brotherhoods of young men are descended, those two-legged wolves, so severely judged by the Avestan code, whose sinister cults seem to have involved the slaying of a bull and a ritual in caves sheltered from the light of day.[10] All this is possible, but what evades us completely is the continuity between these ancient, condemned esoteric cults and the Mithraea of the Roman Empire. For in the latter, the central rite is the slaying of a bull (by the initiates), in commemoration of Mithras' own slaying of the bull, which seems to be interpreted not as an act of violence proper to this god but rather as an act to which he gave himself reluctantly

7 This is too often forgotten. I share the skepticism of Franz Cumont as to Albrecht Dieterich's *Mithrasliturgie* (Leipzig, 1910); but cf. Professor Wili's article in *EJ 1943*.
8 [Since 1945, excavation and research have greatly increased our knowledge of Mithraism. Many new Mithras temples have come to light; see, for instance, G. Becatti's excellent publication *Scavi di Ostia*, Vol. II: *I Mitrei* (Rome, 1954) and M. J. Vermaseren's comprehensive work *De Mithrasdienst in Rome* (Nijmegen, 1951). Vermaseren is preparing a full corpus of the monuments of Mithras to appear under the auspices of the Flemish section of the Belgian Royal Academy. On the literary evidence, see S. Wikander's re-examination of the main texts: *Études sur les Mystères de Mithras*, Vol. I (Lund, 1950).—J. DE M. (1955).]
9 Widengren, pp. 312, 350.
10 Wikander; and Przyluski, in *Revue de l'Histoire des Religions* (Paris), 1940.

and whose aim was probably to insure the fertility of nature. It is the liturgy of a cosmic "sacrifice," and we understand very little of its relation to the Mithras of the Avesta. Another trait which brings Mithraism close to the brotherhoods is the hierarchy and names of its dignitaries, who in certain frescoes appear masked.

We have said that the continuity between the cults whose late form we have just interpreted and the religion of the Avesta is scarcely apparent to us. In the Avesta, the fertility rites seem to involve solely the *fravartis*— the souls of the dead or of people yet to be born, the shades of ancestors who in some way participate in the increase of the population and their cattle. The festival of the *fravartis* fulfills the function that we should expect to see performed by the feast of the god Mithras.[11]

It is no explanation of this discontinuity to say with Widengren that a distinction must be made between an Eastern and a Western tradition. Scholars agree that the Western tradition profoundly affected the traits of this god and of his cult: but this in itself requires explanation. Perhaps we should take into account Mithras' pre-Avestan past, as recorded in the Indian tradition. Here it is worth our while to consult the fine work of Georges Dumézil,[12] in which he adduces a little-exploited text from the famous Indian ritual, the Shatapatha Brahmana, disclosing Mitra's reluctance to immolate the bull, an attitude so characteristic of Roman statuary.[13]

If Mithras plays a part in the final ekpyrosis, is it because he is a savior god? and because one can speak of a *mystery of salvation* in connection with him, of a spiritual role involving the elevation of the soul to a celestial world outside of the world of corruption? This raises the famous question of an Iranian mystery. Its solution depends entirely, in my opinion, on our conception of the nature of the spirit and of the destiny of the soul in Mazdaism.

The type of doctrine of salvation symbolized by the phrase *soma-sema*, which seems characteristic of all gnostic theories and most particularly of

11 See the judicious remarks of M. Meuli, *Schweizer Masken* (Basel, 1944).
12 *Mitra-Varuna* (2nd edn., Paris, 1948). [This has been followed by a long succession of books and articles that offer undoubtedly a most valuable contribution to the study of Indo-Iranian religion; see in particular *Naissance d'Archanges* (Paris, 1945), *Tarpeia* (Paris, 1947), and *Les Dieux des Indo-européens* (Paris, 1952).—J. DE M. (1955).]
13 Shatapatha Brahmana, IV, 1, 4, 8: At the time of the pressing of the soma, the soma is mixed with milk. Soma was Virtra; the gods kill him and call on Mitra to do the same. He refuses, for Mitra is the Friend. Thereupon, the gods wish to exclude him from the sacrifice. At this he too sacrifices; the cattle turn away from him and he is without flocks. Then the gods provide him with the milk to mix with the soma. That is why the milk of the mixture belongs to Mitra and the soma to Varuna.

Manichaeism, is certainly absent from Mazdaism.[14] According to this pattern, the material principle and everything that emanates from it is essentially evil. The soul, divine in itself, a fragment of the good and luminous godhead, is imprisoned in the body and its salvation consists in escaping to rejoin its principle and regain its essence. The soul is connatural with its savior to the point of identity: the savior saves himself, the gnosis is an awakening in which the soul achieves consciousness of its own true nature (and not only of its end, of its destiny).

Mazdaism presents a striking contrast to this dualist pattern. True, it also knows two worlds, *menok*, transcendent, ideal, and for the moment invisible, and *getih*, realized and implicated in the history and accidents of existence. But *menok*, unlike the world of Platonic ideas, embraces all realizable realities, including those of a material nature. On the other hand, it is not exclusively good: Ahriman is also *menok*. Finally, and this is crucial, the distinction between Ormazd the creator and his creatures is everywhere affirmed. Their return will set things to rights; at the end of the world *getih* will return to *menok*, but it will not merge with its author and principle. This becomes still more evident when we consider the theory of "mixture." When the creatures of darkness attack the world of light, Ormazd projects and creates the realization of the world that is to serve as battlefield and as trap for the demon: far from granting him his own substance or emanations to feed on, as though something had to be lost, Ormazd assigns to the demon a relative period of triumph and the moment of his final expulsion. It is evil that will be repulsed, not the good that will withdraw, just as it was evil that had invaded the world of the good, not the good which had been held captive in the nets of evil. In this manner of conceiving evil as a parasite upon the create good (but without access to the Principle), there is a mitigation of the initial dualism of Mazdaism, a kind of vindication of truth. Manichaeism, on the contrary, is, like all gnosis, more consistent in its dualism: God is without defense against evil and can only surrender to it. His emanations from the very outset bear a character of defeat. The creatures of Ormazd are provided with defenses; they are the army of God, not his scapegoats. For Mazdaism preserves from its Gathic origins a far more

14 On all this, permit me to refer to my edition of the Pahlavi text *Shkand-Gumāṇīk Vicār* ("the decisive solution of doubts") (Fribourg, 1945); in the introduction to Ch. XVI, I have studied the Mazdaist criticism of Manichaeism on the basis of all the relevant texts.

moral and psychological conception of evil: it would seem that in the Gathas the demons become what they are through free choice. The late Avesta and, even more so, the Sassanid theology lend a cosmological orientation to this view; but one need only consider the Mazdean criticism of the Manichaean practice of confession to perceive the exact shading. Indeed, it is because the good creatures can be corrupted (partially) that they can also repent and purge themselves by repentance. If evil were merely a fact of *nature*, the evil man could not repent, the good man could in no way be the agent of evil, there would be in man two souls neither of which could be susceptible of conversion, the one because it could only be innocent, the other because it would be naturally impenitent.

Thus any attempt to interpret the Mazdean soteriology in the light of Manichaeism proves vain and erroneous; nor does Mandaeism furnish greater light, for its pattern coincides with the Manichaean and Gnostic schema, and this is even more characteristic than the indubitable Manichaean infiltration in its literature. The confrontation of Manichaeism and Mazdaism is interesting precisely in so far as it provides a living example of how Gnosis transforms and distorts the themes of the religions to which it parasitically attaches itself. The theme of Mazdean dualism was "Manichaeanized"; and later, when Manichaeism expanded into central Asia and China, Buddhist and Taoist themes underwent similar accommodations. Of this the Iranian and Chinese texts of Turfan present striking proof.

The inquiry may be continued with a study of the notion of the savior. The Mazdean savior is neither a messianic king nor a holy prophet nor a docetic avatar—he is, in the Gathas, a king or a protector and patron, a leader, military perhaps, who puts the secular arm at the service of the Church and the Faith; he is far closer to a caliph than to a Mahdi. That the three Saoshyants of the late Avesta are considered as scions of Zarathustra changes nothing in this: this is the effect of another speculation: the history of the world is organized into symmetrical periods of the same type, and to each is assigned a leader at once spiritual and temporal, endowed with the features of the Reformer.

Can we at least find in Zarathustra the representative of an esoteric cult, of a form of religious life which brings him close to the mysteries? This is the point of view of Nyberg, who looks upon him as a shaman. We can have nothing but admiration for Mr. Nyberg's book: to have undertaken an almost complete translation of the Gathas, to have retraced from these obscure poems the development of the prophet, his milieu, his adversaries, his methods of adaptation, shows a boldness which commands our respect. And yet I believe that it is precisely on the subject of Zarathustra that his book is most questionable.[15]

His point of departure is the meaning that he imputes to the Gathic *maga-*, which is ordinarily translated as "gift," "wealth," "benefit"; all translators agree that it implies a reality of a religious nature.[16] In the late Avesta, the word designates the lustration holes in the enclosure reserved for ritual purifications, or the enclosure itself, indicated by furrows traced in the ground. For Nyberg the two meanings, the Gathic and the more recent, coincide. The Zarathustrian *magha* is the place where the shaman communes with the spirits and conducts his séances. I do not know why Nyberg calls these séances an ordeal. An ordeal is a trial to which a person is subjected with a view to determining a hidden fact. The ordeal was known among the Iranians, but it is not a rite characteristic of shamanism, and, furthermore, it is hard to see how an ordeal ritual can be the determining factor in constituting a group, a community. It seems to me, moreover, that Nyberg's notion of the "Magaschar" or "Ordalschar" contradicts Zarathustra's rather solitary nature, a circumstance the importance of which a poet like Nietzsche has grasped better than a good many philologists. Though the Gathas, like the legend of Buddha, speak of new converts, there is an immense contrast between Buddha journeying with his troop of *bhikkhus* whom the tradition numbers by tens of thousands, and the austere, solitary wanderer of the Gathas. It is true that this, too, is a characteristic of the shaman. Though he is reared in a tradition, in a milieu of shamans, he acts alone, or almost so; but in this case we must choose between the system of Zarathustra-shaman and the system of the *Ordalgemeinde*. If we decide for the latter, in any case, we must note that what Zarathustra teaches, the content of his message, is not a technique of inspiration or of divination, but a view of the world, with at its center a wise, omniscient

15 [At the time this paper was first published (1945), scholars had not yet delivered an opinion on Nyberg's thesis. Since then E. Herzfeld's *Zoroaster and His World* (Princeton, 1947) offered a severe criticism of it and put forward an altogether different but still less tenable opinion on the personality and activity of Zoroaster. Both views have been re-examined and rejected by W. B. Henning in his *Zoroaster, Politician or Witch-Doctor?* (Oxford, 1951).—J. DE M. (1955).]

16 See particularly E. Benveniste, *Les Mages dans l'ancien Iran* (Paris, 1938), and the reviews by Giuseppe Messina, *Orientalia* (Rome), N.S., VIII (1939), 204ff., and H. H. Schaeder, *Orientalistische Literaturzeitung* (Berlin), XLIII (1940), 145ff.

God, acting in the lives of men (Nyberg's pages on this theme are excellent, even if he makes too much of the notion of a *deus otiosus* opposed by the Zarathustrian Ormazd), with a moral choice at the beginning of the life of spiritual beings, a moral judgment at the end of existence, and finally a theological view of cosmic realities dependent on a supreme creator or on the deities (or should these already be considered as aspects of the one God?) called the Amesha-Spentas, which represent, as Nyberg has very well said, not only categories of nature but also social realities, human activities. And not only does the prophet give us a "system" infinitely more coherent than we should expect to find in a shaman, but his psychological attitude itself seems quite opposite from that of shamanism. If there is shamanism here,[17] it can only be of the type that is conventionally called grand shamanism, the shamanism of the rather spectacular séances in which the shaman achieves a state of ecstasy by violent methods, the lesser shamanism being that which is confined to the field of healing and the quest of lost objects. Observers who have described the shamans of northern Asia agree in stressing their neuropathic character. How different from the cold, almost didactic passion of the author of the Gathas! Where in the Gathas do we find a trace of an artificially induced ecstasy? Nyberg builds a whole system around a rare and obscure word and persists in seeking here the practice of "steam huts" characteristic of American shamanism and attested for the Scythians by Herodotus.[18] The story of Artā Vīrāf, the legend of Vishtaspa, provide us with instances of sleep induced by drugs (or perhaps in the case of Vishtaspa by a magic potion) as a means of entering into communication with the spirits. But the legend of Vishtaspa is only an episode in the legend of Zarathustra, and of Zarathustra it is merely said that he converses with the gods by means of questions and answers, which is the Middle Iranian manner of explaining the interrogative or dialogue form of the great Avestan texts. No more than it attests the existence of a community based on the ordeal (though it gives us ample information on the authentic rites of the ordeal), does this legend provide us with any definite facts regarding the shamanism of the prophet.

What does appear clearly in the Gathas is the singularly spiritual and

17 Cf. Å. Ohlmarks, "Arktischer Schamanismus und altnordischer Seidr," *Archiv für Religionswissenschaft*, XXXVI (1939), 171ff.; and Wilhelm Koppers, "Probleme der indischen Religionsgeschichte," *Anthropos* (Freiburg i. B.), XXXV–XXXVI (1940–41), 761–814.
18 Nyberg, *Religionen*, pp. 175ff.

sober character of the message. As to the reaction found in them to the orgiastic cults associated with the sacrifice of the bull, Nyberg has shown himself well aware that this is not a protest of the agricultural proletariat against the depredations of the warrior caste, even though there may have been economic reasons for the Indo-Iranian prohibition of the slaughter of cattle.[19]

Thus, nothing in Mazdean soteriology can justifiably be identified with the Gnostic type, and there is nothing in the Mazdean tradition of revelation to suggest a selective and occult initiation. So open is the Mazdean preaching that it provides an appropriate basis for the holy war waged in the name of the faith by defenders well-armed with the temporal sword. Moreover, the Mazdeans frequently attack other religions for propagating themselves in a fashion that is secret, hidden, and hence shameful.

Nor do we find anything in the nature of a ritual bestowal of immortality or grace, for the victory of the good is bound up with a period established by Ormazd at the time of his retort to the Spirit of Darkness.

It is idle to seek in Iran a prehistory of Christianity; but if it is permissible to note certain points of contact between Mazdaism and Christianity, it is not in the field of the "mystery" that they are to be found. Neither the ritual "mysteries" nor the "mysteries" of salvation coincide. The similarity between the two religions consists rather in a common orientation toward "light," considered primarily God. And in both religions men will enjoy this light at the end of a life which continues to be a struggle, but a struggle which is foreseen and sanctioned, not an exile which takes God himself by surprise.

19 For arguments to the contrary, see the fine pages of A. Meillet in his *Trois Conférences sur les Gatha de l'Avesta* (Paris, 1925).

Fritz Meier

The Mystery of the Ka'ba: Symbol and Reality in Islamic Mysticism

The title of this lecture[1] will perhaps lead one to expect a historical study of a localized symbol. But Islam lends itself not only to historical study; we may also conceive of a moral approach, in which Islamic culture is tested for its extratemporal, biological truth. In line with this second approach, the following is not derived from a "geographical" exploration of the historical field; our aim has been rather to take moral, essentially human, knowledge as a starting point and tap the tradition "geologically," in search of its substance. Thus, to speak with Mephistopheles, we shall have to embark on a journey to "the Mothers."

When we examine the cultural accomplishments of the past, we find that some ages and peoples have certain specific characteristics that are more or less absent in other ages and peoples. The sum of these characteristics impresses the observer as a kind of spiritual inner form existing in that people or that time, which the people or time cannot intentionally or arbitrarily assume or cast off—if they could, the form would no longer be a specific quality but a caprice, and arbitrariness would then be the specific quality of the people or time in question. No, the form we speak of must rather be a something that is impressed on the heart of the people "from above." And if we find that the same conformities and deformities of the inner being pass beyond times and peoples (though in forms adapted to the different peoples and ages), we give them names, we discern causes and

1 Dedication: "To Professor Rudolf Tschudi on his sixtieth birthday." First read on February 8, 1944, in the Akademische Vorträge series in Basel. [In translating Persian material into German, Professor Meier used Latin for quotations in Arabic (i.e., the "classical" language), and this convention has been followed in the English translation. The abbreviation A.H. follows a date in the Mohammedan calendar, which reckons from the year of the hegira, A.D. 622.—ED.]

effects in them, and we construe the causes as forces with which man stands in a never-ending struggle. A few great individuals will then seem exceptions, who have overcome these forces and thus for a certain time imposed a new trend upon the spirit of their fellow men.

For the Islamic nations of the Middle Ages, particularly the Arabs and Persians, I have always found characteristic an attitude that can, perhaps in a general way, be designated as intellectualism. The principal achievements of Islamic intellectual life are not so much to be sought in the ideas and insights growing out of inner vision as in logical analyses. Proof of this may be found in the numerous works that break down language, traditions, nature, and art into their atoms and define the character of the whole on the basis of its composition. The virtuosity with which the parts have been detached from the whole, with which such rational categories as likeness and unlikeness, trunk and ramification, cause and effect, etc. (though less in name than in substance) have been applied and exploited, can be regarded as the characteristic style of Islamic culture, whereas that superior artistic knowledge that never expresses itself directly, but which gives depth and plasticity to what has been said, can scarcely be said to have condensed into valid wisdom except in the circles that will concern us here. Astrology would surely assign the Islamic Orient to the province of the planet Mercury.

This mercurial aspect of the Islamic Orient is also visibly dominant in the field of religion. Moslems look on Mohammed as the last of God's messengers, the "seal of the prophets,"[2] after whom there could be no prophecy, so that nothing remained but to comment and elaborate on his words; and moreover Mohammed taught and the Moslems believed that God himself is little more than a rational abstraction for the sum of all those forces outside or opposed to human will and power. (In the present discussion we need not consider the role of Satan in this connection.) The foundations of Islamic doctrine were not accepted without proofs and arguments; and the attention that was given to questions of religious tradition in Islam may be taken as an indication that the believer did not at first assimilate the actual religious content of his religion, but allied himself only with the knowledge and ideas contained in the tradition. His concern was with knowledge rather than conscience; religion remained external, man accepted it only as an attitude, and it left untouched all those forces that were

2 Koran 33 : 40.

capable of transcending a mere attitude and activating a higher order of inner life. Reason is blind to the depths in which the events of the cosmos and of our own lives are rooted, and the criteria of reason are not an adequate guidance in life. The laws which the higher insight of the prophets had laid down for men were observed, but reason denied that man can become so great as to impose these laws on himself, that is to say, that he can transcend himself from within, and denied it rightly as long as reason sought this transcendence in itself. The attitude of reason toward religion can be twofold: either it can study the history and dogma of a religion inductively on the basis of the documents and hold only such religious ideas as could be justified by historical accounts or, conversely, it may search the sacred writings for confirmation of theses that it had formulated in advance, reinterpreting the official doctrine accordingly. As long as these two trends combat one another and no basis is found on which the truth of both can exist side by side, i.e., as long as orthodoxy and heterodoxy do not combine in a higher synthesis, men have not attained to that area which is both end and source of religion.

With reference to Koran exegesis, the eleventh-century Persian thinker Nasir Khusrau[3] recognized both of these irreligious attitudes and looked on their causes as still living forces. He says that there are men who believe that the Antichrist is not yet alive but will come only at the end of days. But this, he declares, is not true, the truth being that there are two Antichrists. The one, the left-eyed Antichrist, teaches exclusively an outward understanding of the Koran and the law. The other, the right-eyed Antichrist, represents the inner, symbolic understanding as the only true understanding.[4]

3 This is the Persian pronunciation (without *Iḍāfat*). Lived 394–481 A.H./A.D. 1004–1088.
4 *Wajh-i dīn* (Berlin, 1343 A.H./A.D. 1924), 280, 2 – 281, 14 : "Koran 7 : 99: Were they therefore secure from the stratagem of God? But none will think himself secure from the stratagem of God, except the people who perish. God sayeth: Do not think yourselves secure from God's temptation, for from God's temptation only evildoers think themselves secure. This verse is addressed to the conscience of those who believe that there is no Antichrist [*dajjāl*] today but that he will only appear in the end. But the tradition of the prophet says: Beware of that one-eyed man, the Antichrist; if the right eye is taken to signify the inner meaning, the left eye the outward meaning of the Koran and the religious law . . . then the one-eyed Antichrist has this meaning: The one-eyed Antichrist is he who directs men to the outward, i.e., the left side. This Antichrist, who is blind in the right eye, is accursed; for we have the tradition that the prophet said: He who is blind in the right eye is assuredly cursed. By which he meant the orthodox [*zāhiri*], who annulled the inward. The other one-eyed Antichrist is he who summons men to inner understanding. . . . He is blind in the left

And here we come to the point where genius breaks through the barriers of convention and transcends the usages and forms of life in which man is imprisoned, a prey to the two Antichrists. And in his growth toward inner maturity man must reach this point before the battle can be joined against the Antichrists, and indeed before he can even recognize them. This point is the subject of the self-consciousness, it is the I. If man succeeds in separating all predicates (seeing, walking, sleeping, love, poverty) from this I and nevertheless in experiencing a quality in himself, he has established a bridgehead from which he can counter the assaults of his enemies and gain that free will which will permit him to disregard heritage and convention, rules and caprices, and enable him to carry on an existence which will realize virtue in the form suitable to the moment. Here he finds himself beyond the *ratio;* to reason the I is no more than a colorless focus with no other quality than that of being, and only in these deeper strata beyond

---

eye, and there is a tradition that the prophet said: He who is blind in the left eye is accursed. By which he meant the heterodox [*bātinī*] who annuls the outward sense of religious dogma. In saying that each group had its Antichrist, he meant that the Antichrist of the orthodox was he who annulled the inward and the Antichrist of the heterodox was he who annulled the outward. Neither of these two Antichrists has religion, their followers are far removed from the doctrine of religion, and both Antichrists along with their followers are in hell fire. . . . Both groups are enemies of God and the prophet, for God said, Koran 6 : 112: Thus have we appointed unto every prophet an enemy; the devils of men and of genii; who privately suggest the one to the other specious discourses to deceive. . . . The devils of men are the orthodox and the heterodox are the devils of genii; both practice lies and deception in order that men should remain without religion. The true religion is advocated [only] by him who soundly perceives both outward and inward at once and through both [?] obeys and worships God." In this text the Antichrist is used sometimes for the superhuman power and sometimes for the men who are misled by it; *dēvān*, "demons," occur in a similar sense in the Pahlavi Zoroastrian writings (Jean de Menasce, *Shkand-Gumānīk Vicār*, Fribourg, 1945, p. 15) and likewise *djinn* is generally taken in both meanings in the Islamic world (Nuri Pasha, in Theodor Menzel, "Ein Beitrag zur Kenntnis der Jeziden," in Hugo Grothe's *Vorderasienexpedition*, Vol. I, Leipzig, 1911, p. clxxviii). Cf. Nasir Khusrau, *Zād al-musāfirīn* (Berlin, 1341 A.H./A.D. 1922), 420, 14 – 424, 8. Consonant with the fundamental attitude of Nasir Khusrau (and directly related to Zād al-musāfirīn, 416, 15 – 419, 13, and other passages), the translated passage has also another aspect which we cannot enter into here. 'Attār (12th cent. A.D.), *Ilāhīnāma*, ed. by H. Ritter (Bibliotheca Islamica, XII; Istanbul, 1940), 91, 10, distinguishes three Antichrists: the demon deceiver, the spirit of this world, and the tyrannizing soul, the last two of which clearly correspond to those of Nasir and the first of which seems to encompass the other two. Regarding the one-eyedness of the Devil, in the sense that he saw only the outward in Adam, cf. Najm ad-dīn ad-Dāya, *Mirṣād al-ʾibād* (Teheran, 620 A.H./A.D. 1223), 1312/52, 183 ult. A folkloristic interpretation of the one-eyed Antichrist in Julius Wellhausen, *Reste arabischen Heidentums* (2nd edn., Berlin, 1897), p. 204.

abstraction, in new experience, does it gain that luminous power which enables man to lead a truly personal, metaphysically personal and therefore sacramental life, counter to the forces of custom and mere instinct. The area upon which man then enters is that of the "heart"; it is the realm of an imagination which speaks truth and acts with virtue, which combines thought and feeling, being the root of both, and in relation to which the intellect is no more than a dutiful scribe. This *sacrificium intellectus*, which is a transcending and not a rejection of the intellect, was interpreted by Islamic mystics sometimes as a rebirth and sometimes as a resurrection, because in it man died to his previous existence and awakened to a new life:

> "*Qui non bis nascitur, in regnum caelorum non ascendit.*"[5] This means: He who is born from the womb sees only this world, only he who is born out of himself sees the other world.[6]
>
> O friend, he who knows the forms of things, has *vita externa* and is in the *resurrectio minor* [i.e., has behind him only the resurrection from the grave of the womb through natural birth, he is a child]. He who knows the natures of things has *vita intestina* and is in the *resurrectio media* [i.e., has developed his normal thinking, is an adult]. [But] he who knows the substances of things, has the *vita bona* and is in the *resurrectio grandior*.
>
> And he who knows the realities[7] of things has the *vita vera* and is in the *resurrectio maxima*.[8]

If mysticism is an experience and perception occurring when the senses are closed (μύειν in Proclus[9]), the discovery of resurrection and true life within oneself is a mystical process; considered from this standpoint, the Islamic mystics were primarily a fellowship of those Moslems who were desirous and capable of transposing their life from the reason to the heart.

---

5 "He who is not twice born will not ascend to the kingdom of Heaven." [See n. 1, above.]

6 'Ayn al-quḍāt al-Hamadhānī (d. 525 A.H./A.D. 1131), "Tamhīdāt," no. 1 (Basel University Library, MS. M III 45), 6a, 13–15. It was known in Islam that the underlying saying originated with Christ (John 3 : 3). 'Azīz-i Nasafī (still living after 680 A.H./A.D. 1281), "Kashf ul-ḥaqā'iq," MS. Nuru Osmaniye (Istanbul) 4899, 304b, 13–14.

7 The alchemistic *veritas*. See C. G. Jung, *Psychology and Alchemy* (New York and London, 1953), p. 256.

8 Nasafī, "Tanzīl ul-arwāḥ," MS. Shehit Ali Pasha (Istanbul) 1363, 130a, 6–9. And his "Kashf," 306a, 10 – 306b, 19 (6th risāla); also 264a, 15 – 264b, 1 (2nd ris.); other variants, 311b, 21 – 312b, 6 (7th ris.).

9 F. A. G. Tholuck, *Blüthensammlung aus der morgenländischen Mystik* (Berlin, 1825), 6/16.

The "men of the heart" (as they were called) were those who to the development of reason based on the senses added the development of a higher spiritual life; who to normal, natural maturity added a second, inner growth. Accordingly it was said:

> The time for traveling [the mystical path] extends over twenty years, from the twentieth to the fortieth year of life. During these twenty years, a man must not march in slovenly fashion and weary of his aim, for if he does so, all his trouble and his life are lost and he goes astray. The first twenty years [of life] are the time in which the body grows to maturity and in which a man acquires the knowledge connected with the external. The second twenty years are the time in which the spirit matures and he acquires inner knowledge. He who matures in these forty years is mature; he who does not mature in these forty years, will never be mature.[10]

It is evident that this second maturity brings with it or presupposes a transformation as important for man as the first, but with the difference that it is not a gift which all may expect to inherit from nature but one which some gain by labor and prayer while others neglect it or perhaps even fail to perceive it.[11] The profound nature of this transformation can be seen from the autobiographical notes of the two most fruitful mystics of Islam:

10 Nasafī, "Tanzīl," 146b, 8 – 13. Similarly, his "Kashf," 273a, 15 – 273b, 22. Mawlānā Jalāl ud-dīn ar-Rūmī (d. 672 A.H./A.D. 1273), *Fīhi mā fīh* (lith., Azamgarh, A.D. 1929) 64, 11 – 12: "And so he who sees only the outward is also a mineral and has no access to the spirit. He is a child and immature, even though he may outwardly be an old man and a hundred years old."

11 Nasafī, "Kashf," 273b, 9 – 20: "Know that when a child leaves his mother's womb and enters into existence he has nothing to do but eat, sleep, and play, up to his fifth year. But once he has passed the fifth year, he must be sent to school [*dabīrān*=Arab. *kuttāb;* see R. P. A. Dozy, *Supplément aux Dictionnaires Arabes,* Leiden, 1881, s.v.] and instructed in the book that represents the authority and guide of the community in question; the child should learn its words by heart, acquire the letters of his language, and learn to read and write. This up to the age of ten. Once he has reached this age, he must learn a trade in order to earn his daily bread and sustenance. Up to the age of fifteen. Past the age of fifteen [eighteen in the text] he must learn religious doctrine and ritual and contract law prescribing individual duty. Up to the age of twenty. So far, O dervish, all children are alike, and he who does not cause his child to attain his twentieth year in this manner is not to be reckoned among men, excepting when distress prevents him, when he is without means, when he lives in disordered circumstances and lacks the opportunity. But after the twentieth year is passed, each man turns to a particular occupation and task. One to commerce, one to agriculture, the third to theology, this is common duty [concerning common duty and individual duty, see Th. W. Juynboll, *Handbuch des islamischen Gesetzes,* Leiden, 1910, p. 60], the fourth to philosophy and the natural sciences, the fifth to spiritual struggle and the purification of the heart, etc."

154

Ghazzālī (A.D. 1058–1111) and Ibn 'Arabī (A.D. 1165–1240). The first, Ghazzālī, was a Persian who for four years taught canon law in Baghdad, but at the age of thirty-seven renounced this calling and became a wandering dervish. By an enormous intellectual effort, through the experience of the heart and his own supra-intellectual spiritual life, he gained a fresh approach to theology, and succeeded in revivifying it through the incorporation of mysticism. The crises accompanying his transformation, which even affected him physically so that for a time he could neither speak nor eat, are too well known to require comment here.[12]

So far no record has been found of the event which turned Ibn 'Arabī from a Saul to a Paul—this must have occurred at a far earlier age than Ghazzālī's conversion—but the inner encounter which began the great period of his life has been preserved in the artfully stylized preamble to his mystical handbook *Meccan Revelations*.[13] This preamble has thus far neither been translated nor commented upon. It has all the characteristics which might lead a critical philologist to set it down as a biographically worthless invention: instead of a sober record which an attentive intelligence might follow, it contains several visions, accompanied by fantastic discourses and responses, so interwoven with hidden references that from the text itself the reader can derive no conclusion or meaning. Since, moreover, the preamble culminates in the assertion that the content of the 560 chapters constituting the *Meccan Revelations* was taken from a celestial book that had been divulged to the author, the critic is tempted to let the matter rest there and to concentrate on seeking a possible literary source for the preamble. It may, however, be said that if the irrational, the life of the heart, is to be put into words, the words are bound to be alien to the understanding and seemingly irrational.

Ibn 'Arabī, like Ghazzālī a mystic with a knowledge of the tradition and the law, journeyed in the year 1201/2 from his native Spain to Mecca and there, while walking round the Ka'ba, the famous cubical temple, had the crucial experience of his life. As he passed the Black Stone in the eastern corner of the Ka'ba, he found, as he tells us, "the eagle stone of the youth zealous in devotion, of the silent speaker who neither lives nor dies, the

---

12 Hellmut Ritter, *Al Ghasali, das Elixir der Glückseligkeit* (Jena, 1923), pp. 5–14.
13 *Al-futūḥāt al-Makkiyya* (written 598–629 A.H./A.D. 1201–1231; pub. Cairo, 1293 A.H./A.D. 1875), Vol. I, pp. 59–64. Neither the commentary of 'Abdalkarīm al-Kīlānī (Carl Brockelmann, *Geschichte der arabischen Litteratur*, Suppl. I, Leiden, 1937, p. 792) nor Ibn 'Arabī's book *Tāj ar-rasā'il* (ibid., p. 797) has been available to me.

encompassed encompasser" (59, 15–16), "who is eloquent and does not
speak, who inquires concerning what he knows" (61, 23). We are reminded
of alchemy by the "eagle stone" and to an even greater degree by the
paradoxes that are supposed to explain it. First of these is the "youth zealous
in devotion." If only we are sufficiently familiar with the philosophical
content of alchemy to acknowledge the foundation of its seeming contradictions, we shall be able with Ibn ʿArabī to "know the youth's rank and his
situation beyond When and Where" (60, 3); we shall know that this youth
signifies and intimates more than all the eloquence of the world (60, 6–7).
For when Ibn ʿArabī cries out, "Behold him who yearns to sit with thee and
strives to enjoy thy friendship!" (60, 4–5), he is thrust back upon himself,
he recognizes the secret communication existing between himself and the
youth, but sees no way of attaining to him. But the realization that he confronts his own wholeness, from which he has fallen through his temporal
consciousness, takes root in him, and when he resolves to encourage the
apparition and strives to learn more about him, he is admonished: "Behold
the articulation of my nature and the order of my structure and form, and
there thou wilt find delineated the answer to thy question. For I am no
speaker and no partner in conversation [but thine own trans-subjective
being]. My knowledge extends only to myself, and my essence is no different
from my name" (60, 14–16). And then the youth, citing the so-called
Theology of Aristotle[14] (a Neoplatonic work preserved only in Arabic), makes
his crucial statement: "I am knowledge, the known and the knower; I am
wisdom, the wise man and his wiseness" (60, 16). In the *Theology of Aristotle*
these words are spoken by the mystic who has freed himself from his body
and entered into his spiritual essence. Here they are spoken by this spiritual
essence itself, appearing to the mystic in a vision. And thus we have proof
that Ibn ʿArabī met none other than himself at the Kaʿba, that he met his
alter ego, his transcendent self, the "true I," as a fourteenth-century mystic
puts it,[15] the self which is related to its form in this life as the thing in itself
is related to its manifestation. To Ibn ʿArabī the self, at once the subject

14 Ed. F. Dieterici (Leipzig, 1882), 8, 6–7; tr. F. Dieterici (Leipzig, 1883), 9, 1–2. The work
   is a paraphrastic translation of Porphyry's commentary on Plotinus' *Enneads 4–6*,
   written by Ibn Naʿīma and revised by Kindī (both 9th cent. A.D.; Brockelmann,
   Suppl. I, p. 364ff.).
15 ʿAlāʾ ad-dawla as-Simnānī (d. 736 A.H./A.D. 1336), "Tafsīr," Basel University
   Library, MS. M II 14, 70a, 1 (in the commentary to Sura 114): "O thou who fleest
   from the evil of thy soul [I-self] and strivest toward thy true [self] [*anāniyyata ḥaqqika*,
   lit., I-ness of the (= thy) true thou]."

and sought-for object of normal consciousness, was revealed, in its substantial depth, as a starting point of a far more comprehensive entity, an entity transcending space and time.[16]

A glance at other ages and other cultures may make it clearer in what sphere this depth lies and what the meaning of this encounter is. In the Upanishads we read:

> Those who, verily, depart from this world—to the moon, in truth, they all go. During the earlier half it thrives on their breathing spirits; with the latter half it causes them to be reproduced. This, verily, is the door of the heavenly world—that is, the moon. Whoever answers it, him it lets go further. But whoever answers it not, him, having become rain, it rains down here.[17] Either as a worm, or as a moth, or as a fish, or as a bird, or as a lion, or as a wild boar, or as a snake, or as a tiger, or as a person, or as some other in this or that condition, he is born again here according to his deeds, according to his knowledge. When he comes thither it [the moon] asks him: "Who are you?" He should reply: . . . "I am you." It lets him go further [i.e., pass beyond it].[18]

We find a similar motif in the Egyptian Book of the Dead[19] and the same encounter occurs in Novalis' *Heinrich von Ofterdingen:*[20] here Ginnistan (Fantasy), hastens with Eros to the moon her father:

> Love passed through desert spaces
> And through the land of the clouds
> And entered the court of the moon,
> Holding his daughter[21] by the hand.

16 Maḥmūd-i Shabistarī, "Gulshan i-rāz" (written 717 A.H./A.D. 1317), Basel University Library, MS. M III 45, 167b, 6–10:
"Why makest thou a guide of thy reason?
Dost thou not know that thou art only a part of thyself?
Go, dear Lord, and gain sound knowledge of thyself;
For to be fat is not the same as to be [merely] swollen.
I and thou are higher than soul and body,
For those two are only parts of me.
Is not the whole man meant by the word I,
That thou sayest the soul is meant?
Rise above thy bondage to time and place,
Leave the world and leap into thy self!"
17 Cf. Louis Massignon, "Die Auferstehung im Islam," *EJ 1939*, p. 16.
18 Kaushitaki Upanishad, I, 2 (tr. R. E. Hume, *The Thirteen Principal Upanishads,* London, 1921, p. 303).
19 Cf. C. Fries, *Mythologisches in den Gesta Romanorum und der Legenda Aurea* (Mythologische Bibliothek, VIII, 4; Leipzig, 1916), Appendix, 51–52.
20 Novalis, *Werke,* ed. Rudolf Bach (Leipzig, 1942), pp. 239ff.   21 Fantasy.

He was sitting on his silver throne,
Alone with his grief;
He heard the voice of his child
And fell into her arms.[22]

Thus the Pegasus upon which Ibn 'Arabī was carried away was imaginative illumination.[23] It carried him to the uppermost limit of the "sublunar" consciousness and disclosed to him that it was none other than himself, his own transcendent person, which awaited him beyond night and day. "Therefore," says Ibn 'Arabī (60, 27–29), "I shall return in the end to the beginning, just as in describing a circle the leg of the compass returns to the beginning when it reaches the end. Thus is the end of life bound up with its beginning and its prenatal eternity fuses with the eternity after death.[24] Existence is only transient [our present life on earth], but there is a lasting, enduring vision" (i.e., an eternal life in the spirit which is only obscured by our earthly existence). Thus man is dualized by the limits of his consciousness, he consists of an earthly and a transcendent mode of being,[25] and it is the eternal, supralunar aspect of this twofold unity which, according to the religions, survives a man's death; for the most part we remain unconscious

22 Die Liebe ging durch Wüstenein
Und durch der Wolken Land,
Trat in den Hof des Mondes ein,
Die Tochter an der Hand.

Er sass auf seinem Silberthron,
Allein mit seinem Harm;
Da hört er seines Kindes Ton
Und sank in ihren Arm.

23 A theory of the imagination in connection with Mohammed is to be found in Ibn 'Arabī's *Fuṣūṣ al-ḥikam*, with commentary by Bālī Effendi (Istanbul, 1309 A.H./A.D. 1891), pp. 151–53.
24 Shabistarī, "Gulshan," 168a, 6–9:
"And thou askedst further: Who is a traveler on the [mystical] path?
One who has gained knowledge of the beginning of things.
His striding, know, is an apocalyptic journey out of the [world of the mere] possibility [of being]
To necessary [being], leaving behind the blemish of imperfection.
A traveler is he who quickly
Is cleansed of himself as fire from smoke,
Who in the direction opposite to that of the first journey [into birth]
Advances station by station until he becomes a Perfect Man."
Ibid., 168b, 13:
"When the end becomes the beginning,
In that place there is room neither for an angel nor for a messenger of God."
25 Carl du Prel, *Die Philosophie der Mystik* (Leipzig, 1885), Preface.

158

or barely conscious of this transcendent aspect, and often it therefore seems nonexistent to us, although the mystics have experienced its reality time and time again and have gained awareness of it as the cause of spirit in themselves.[26]

With the discovery of this new reality transcending ordinary existence, with the entrance of this other world into experience, earthly life loses its claim to exclusive reality; sublunar existence turns out to be a torso whose head is situated beyond death, beyond the three-dimensional world of the common man; the hieroglyphs of life begin to yield their meaning to a growing insight. What seemed to be mere surface gains an inner depth; things which were only outwardly discernible become transparent, they lose something of their absoluteness and assume a certain character of illusoriness, of *maya*. In short, they no longer represent the whole, but become a part.

At this stage, both of Nasir Khusrau's Antichrists are exposed. The left-eyed Antichrist who fixed man's interest upon things and said, Things are the whole, and the right-eyed Antichrist who detached man's libido from things and said, Only the province of the soul matters—both are recognized

26 Skr. *purusha* : Av. *daēnā* (Gathic) and *fravashay;* Arab. *sirr* in the formula *quddisa sirruhū* or *rūḥ* in similar locutions. For the orthodox view of the destiny of the *rūḥ* after death, see Pseudo-Ibn al-ʿIrrīf in M. Asín Palacios, *Mahasin al-Madjalis d'Ibn al-ʿArif* (Paris, 1933), Text 101, no. 23ff. (tr., 66, no. 23ff.). The supralunar home of the spiritual man was a familiar conception to the esoteric thinkers of Islam through their knowledge of the classical tradition. See Najm ad-dīn ad-Dāya, *Mirṣād al-ʿibād,* passim. The word for "sublunar" is *suflī*, for "supralunar" or "astral," *ʿulwī.* Nasafī, "Kashf," 291a, 1–10: "Although the rational soul is a luminous and pure substance it turns one face to this sublunar [*suflī*] world, since it is connected with the body, and for this reason it can take on reprehensible qualities and undesirable traits of character. Since it is an emanation of the celestial soul, it turns its other face toward the other world, and for this reason it can take on praiseworthy qualities and desirable traits of character. If thou has understood this, then know that if this rational soul has achieved its perfection in this body, it returns after separation from the body to its home, i.e., the supralunar [*ʿulwī*] world. Perfection in this soul means assimilation to the world of its home, and this assimilation lies in the possession of praiseworthy qualities and desirable traits of character, of knowledge and piety. But if it has not achieved its perfection in this body, it cannot return home after its separation from the body but remains below the sphere of the moon in this world of growth and decay." In the Persian poets the soul that survives death is the "bird that travels supralunar paths" (*murgh-i ʿulwikhīram*)—Niẓāmī, *Iqbālnāma* (Teheran, 1317 A.H./A.D. 1899), 278, 5 (Death of Socrates); the "bird that flies through the supralunar sphere and whose nest is the heavenly Jerusalem"—ʿImād ad-dīn-ī Faqīh, in *Wiener Zeitschrift für die Kunde des Morgenlandes,* XLIX (1942), v. 8, etc. (the tr. given there might be improved). In this context we should also mention the passage in Maqqarī, "Nafḥ aṭ-ṭib," in *Futūḥāt,* I, 8, 22–28, where Ibn ʿArabī weds the star in a dream, which is said to mean that the *ʿulwī* sciences will be disclosed to him.

FRITZ MEIER

as liars and adversaries of that spirit which man has recognized his self and which grows forever mightier in his heart. This spirit is one which fuses the disparate purposes of the soul into a creative self-certainty and enables man to lead a poetic life in the truest sense. Every commission and omission, every event and phenomenon, everything he perceives in life and the world, appears to him as a *pars pro toto*, vehicle of a meaning and an idea, an allusion to a secret which can be found by inner contemplation.[27] We call such vehicles of meaning, which all things now become,[28] symbols, from the Greek σύμβολον, which designated the visible part of a whole, whose other half was invisible or absent. (We need not concern ourselves with the etymology of the word.)[29]

Since it is common for the contemplative mind to take the first object at hand as the occasion for its turn inward in quest of the secret, it need not surprise us that Ibn 'Arabī should have found the most impressive interrelations and experienced the boldest certainties in the symbolism of the *circumambulatio* of the Ka'ba. Ibn 'Arabī did not find self-sufficiency in the content of his normal consciousness, but discovered his pleroma beyond sense perception and logical abstraction in the form of the youth, and similarly the essence of the Ka'ba round which he circles is no longer ex-

27 Cf. the Babi Mīrzā Jānī, *Nuqṭat al-Kāf* (written A.D. 1850–52), ed. E. G. Browne (Gibb Memorial Series XV, London, 1910). Text 12, 15–24: "As for the circumstance that the sayings of the prophet as transmitted by the recognized religious leaders are also quoted here, this is done in order to set aside the scruples of the weak; for they have no minds, that is, they stand before barriers. Even though in their thinking [*wijdān*] they sometimes understand something correctly, they nevertheless love, since they remain imperfect in their souls, to hear confirmation from the mouth of the infallible prophet. Now since there are two kinds of reason, the native [= natural, a priori] reason, a thinking [*wijdān*] out of the mere soul, or argumentation *ab intra*, and beside it, the 'acquired' [= historical, a posteriori] reason, which heeds the word of the outward argument, an accord between the two modes of reason is desirable in the interest of the imperfect souls. It is for this reason that I cite canonical utterances of Mohammed. When, however, the soul achieves perfection and dissolves in its beloved, all its perceptions are revelations of God." The exact meanings of *wijdān* are to be found in Muṣṭafā al-Ghalāyīnī, *Naẓarāt fī'l-lugha wa'l-adab* (Beirut, 1927), pp. 108–11; the meaning of the word *wijdān* underwent a development parallel to that of *'uthūr*. Here "thinking" seems to be the correct translation.
28 Ibn 'Arabī, *Fuṣūṣ al-ḥikam*, 296, 9–10: "When the prophet said, Men are asleep, and when they die, they awaken, he wished to suggest that everything that a man sees during this earthly life represents nothing other than dream images and illusion, which themselves require interpretation."
29 Paul Deussen, *The Philosophy of the Upanishads*, tr. A. S. Geden (Edinburgh, 1906), p. 99.

160

hausted in its draped walls. He hears the call: "Behold the secret building before it is too late, and thou wilt see how it takes on life through those who circle round it and walk round its stones, and how it looks out at them from behind its veils and cloaks! And then I saw it take on life, as he [the caller] had said" (59, 25–26). And Ibn 'Arabī recites the following poem (59, 28–60, 1):

> I see the building animated by those who circle round it.
> And there is no self-animation, except through a physician with effective power.[30]
> But this is rigid matter which neither feels nor sees,
> Which is without understanding or hearing!
> A lord spake: This[31] is our duty
> Imposed on us all our lives by religious dogma.[32]
> I answered him: That is what thou sayest. But hear
> The discourse of him to whom science has been revealed by the rite!
> Thou seest only solid mineral, without life of its own,
> Harboring neither benefit nor harm.
> But for the *eye of the heart* it contains visibilities
> If the eye have no weakness or flaw.
> To this eye it is so sublime when it reveals its essence,
> That no creature can withstand it . . .

Up to this time the relation of Ibn 'Arabī to the Ka'ba was that of his body to the mass of the building and that of his reason to the abstract concept Ka'ba; but now that the abstract concept man has been transfigured through the experience of the meaning he embodies, there descends upon the Ka'ba the Pentecostal fire of the meaning which it represents. Its dead form—"And astonishing is a dead man round whom a living man revolves!" says Ibn 'Arabī (59, 21)—becomes, through its relation to the faithful who

---

30 This refers to Ibn 'Arabī himself, through whom the Ka'ba is animated. This "science" (*ḥikma*, v. 8) has been restored to him by the rite. The passage might also be translated "except by a wise man with creative power," which would mean God (*aṣ-ṣāni' al-ḥakīm*); but then we should have to translate *ḥikma* by "wisdom" rather than "science."
31 The *circumambulatio* of the Ka'ba.
32 As a component of the Great Pilgrimage to 'Arafa the *circumambulatio* of the Ka'ba is the individual duty of every Moslem; see *Encyclopedia of Islam*, ed. M. Th. Houtsma et al. (Leiden and London, 1913–38), s.v. "Ḥadjdj." Although this is an allusion to the Great Pilgrimage, which is made only once a year, at the beginning of the month of Dhu'l-ḥijjah, I do not regard it as certain that Ibn 'Arabī had his experience at the time of the Great Pilgrimage. This unfortunately makes it impossible to date the event with certainty between the end of August and the beginning of September, A.D. 1202.

circle round it, the vehicle of a spiritual content,[33] which like the mystic youth cannot be derived by logic but is accessible only to the heightened perception of the mystic. A voice tells Ibn 'Arabī that in kissing the Black Stone he is kissing God's right hand (62, 19);[34] for the Ka'ba signifies the essence of God, and the seven prescribed circuits mean the seven attributes of God (62, 20).[35] Thus the symbolism of the Ka'ba and the *circumambulatio* may be represented graphically by a circle, the center of which represents God's essence and the circumference his attributes.

Formula 1

But one thing that does not quite convince the reader in this symbolism is the interpretation of the seven circuits as the attributes of God; for then the role of the mystical youth who performs the seven circuits would seem to be overlooked. But since Ibn 'Arabī's encounter with his self was brought about by the Black Stone, which is a part of the Ka'ba, his self might appropriately be a spark of the Ka'ba's life, i.e., part of a greater self, which would be symbolized by the Ka'ba, and this must be so if we bear in mind that by God nothing other is meant than the self of the cosmos, in which all phenomena and hence also the existence of man are contained, and without

33 *Futūḥāt*, 1, 880, 15–16:
"Nothing exalts this house above others
But thou alone my servant by turning toward it.
Illumined is the Ka'ba by thy walking round it,
While the other houses of men remain in darkness."
34 *Futūḥāt*, 1, 882, 21ff.; 884, 28. Alleged saying of the prophet: Ibn Baṭṭūṭa (d. 779 A.H./ A.D. 1377), *Tuḥfat an-nuẓẓār*, ed. and tr. C. Defrémery and B. R. Sanguinetti (Paris, 1853–58), Vol. I, p. 314.—Cf. 'Aṭṭār, *Manṭiq aṭ-ṭayr* (Aligarh, n.d.), 15, 4 from below. 'Abd al-Ghanī an-Nābulusī (d. 1143 A.H./A.D. 1731), *Dīwān al-ḥaqā'iq* (Cairo, 1306 A.H./A.D. 1888), 95, 20.
35 Life, speech, power, will, knowledge, hearing, sight; H. S. Nyberg, *Kleinere Schriften des Ibn al-'Arabi* (Leiden, 1919), p. 73, n. 1; Arab. text, 28; 'Abdalkarīm al-Jīlī (d. 832 A.H./A.D. 1428), *Al-insān al-kāmil* (Cairo, 1316 A.H./A.D. 1878), 2, 89, 8.

162

which the cosmos could no more exist than could the individual man without the idea of his person.[36] And now we begin to understand the discrepancy. Since not the Black Stone but Ibn 'Arabī himself is the outward sign of his transcendent witness, the youth, not the Ka'ba but the cosmos as a whole would have to be a symbol of God. Just as Ibn 'Arabī's transcendent companion departs from the Black Stone and circles round the building with him, so after his illumination concerning the Ka'ba, the self of the cosmos departs from its particular abode, the Ka'ba, and the Ka'ba becomes a more special symbol, one namely of God's throne.

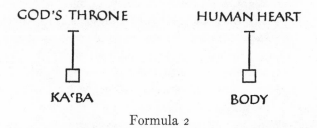

GOD'S THRONE   HUMAN HEART

KA'BA   BODY

Formula 2

This to be sure offers a possibility of a correspondence between man and the Ka'ba, and Ibn 'Arabī hears the words, "Thy body is ranked below thine integral[37] heart, and so likewise is the Ka'ba ranked below the encompassing throne" (63, 11–12; Formula 2). I.e., just as the Ka'ba is an allusion to God's throne, so is the human body the sign of a transcendent essence, of the integral heart. Both vehicles are to their meaning as the outward to the inward. But on closer inspection, this formula can be fully experienced no more than the preceding one. For since, as we have seen, the road to God leads through the heart, and since, if the *circumambulatio* of human bodies round the Ka'ba is to be taken as representative of this road, it can only refer to the centering of man's being on the heart (63, 10–11); there is no place left in this symbolism of the *circumambulatio* for the conception of the Ka'ba as the throne of God.[38] Thus the symbolism must

36 Jīlī, 2, 89, 2: "The Ka'ba signifies the essence [of God], the Black Stone the human spiritual essence [*Laṭīfa*]."
37 Integral [*basīṭ*] means here approximately "incorporeal" or "supra-corporeal."
38 Cf. to the contrary *Futūḥāt*, 1, 879, 3 – 2 from below: "And he [who is circling round the Ka'ba] should appear to himself during this rite like the [angels] circling round the throne of God." According to one version, Adam, after his expulsion from Paradise, was given the Ka'ba to circle round as a substitute for God's throne: Ṭabarī, *Annales* (Leiden, 1879–81), Vol. I, 122, 9–17.

undergo a third transformation which will restore the link between the
circumambulatio and this concept of the Ka'ba.

And this third transformation occurs. Prepared for this step by the assertion that the Ka'ba is the heart of existence (63, 8) and thus has "heartness"
in common with the human heart (63, 13), Ibn 'Arabī enters the Ka'ba
with his transcendent companion,[39] who speaks to him as follows: "I am
the seventh at the stage where spiritual growth and the secrets of existence,
of the individual, and of the Where are encompassed" (64, 5-6). And the
Ka'ba "is the house that is elevated above cloaks and veils. It is the entrance
of those having insight, and in it is the repose of those who circle round"
(64, 4-5). Thus only when the *circumambulatio* ceases is its meaning revealed: the seven leftward circuits round the Ka'ba signify the acquisition
of the seven divine attributes[40] during the ascent of the consciousness to
the sphere of the self;[41] in the Ka'ba Ibn 'Arabī converses with the self at
its highest degree, and the limit of consciousness which dualizes his being
is thrust back so far that he is enabled to view his individuality in its entire
range.[42] Thus the Ka'ba, the "entrance of those having insight," is a symbol
for the point at which the human self touches upon the cosmic self, at
which the psychic principle, the Ātman, becomes identical with the cosmic
principle, the Brahman, and the human spirit takes root in the spirit of the
cosmos: a symbol of the "attribute of communion," as Ibn 'Arabī says
(63, 22). This divergence and identity of the human self and the cosmic
self at the point symbolized by the Ka'ba[43] might be graphically represented by two concentric circles, the greater of which symbolizes the cosmic

39 The Ka'ba was opened every Monday and Friday, and in the month of Rajab every
day: Ibn Jubayr, *Riḥla*, ed. Wm. Wright and M. J. de Goeje (Gibb Memorial Series V,
London, 1907), 93, 4-5. (This refers to the autumn of 579 A.H./A.D. 1183.)
40 Jīlī, 2, 89, 9-11. Fr. Buhl's comment in *Encyclopedia of Islam*, s.v. "Tawāf," that
those circling the Ka'ba have it "on the right," is erroneous, and was perhaps suggested
by J. Wellhausen, *Reste arab. Heidentums*, p. 74.
41 The Arabic verb *ṭāfa*, from which the term for the *circumambulatio* of the Ka'ba is
derived, can actually have the meaning "To attain to the summit of a thing by spiral-
ing round it"; thus in the Persian *Bayān*, according to E. G. Browne, in his edn. of
the *Kitāb-i Nuqṭatu'l-Kāf* of Ḥājji Mīrzā Jānī, 1850-52 (Gibb Memorial Series XV,
Leiden and London, 1910), p. *la*, 12-14.
42 Jīlī, 2, 89, 7; "The *circumambulatio* signifies that we must attain to our selfhood,
origin, root, point of union."
43 Cf., on the one hand, *Futūḥāt*, 1, 880, 10: "God's Ka'ba is nothing other than our essence;" on the other hand, Mawlānā, *Fīhi mā fīh*, 108, 10-11: "Among those men who
cling to the external, the Sacrosanct Mosque is the Ka'ba, but among the loving and
the elect, it is the attainment to God."

self and the lesser the human self, having as their common center or navel the Ka'ba in which the lesser and the greater self coincide.

Indian as this seems, it refers to the same relationship as that between Father and Son in Christianity and, in the eyes of the esoteric thinkers of Islam, between God and the so-called Spirit of Mohammed.[44] In the ensuing words Ibn 'Arabī tells us God's message to him in the matter: "I am comprehended only by you [men], and I have revealed myself in no form of perfection[45] other than your spirituality [ma'nākum]. Know then the value of the high nobility I have given you; henceforward, I am the Great, the Sublime, limited by no limit, known neither by master nor servant. Hallowed is the godhead and removed, so that it cannot be comprehended, and

Formula 3

so that it can be ranked with nothing. Thou art the I! And I am I! [I.e., thou art thine I, thy self, and I too am I, but not thou.[46]] Seek me not in thyself for thou wilt only gain weariness! [I.e., I am not in what thou already possessest as thyself.] And not outside thyself, for thou wilt not gain happiness. But cease not to seek me, or thou wilt be unhappy. Seek me until thou findest me, then thou wilt be exalted!" "But . . . distinguish between me and thee; for thou seest not me but only thine own nature.[47] Remain then in the quality of communion. If not, be [rather] a servant and say, The inability to attain to comprehension is precisely comprehension" (63, 17–23).[48]

44 Also called "reality of Mohammed," "perfect man," "the God in the Creature," etc.: *Fuṣūṣ al-ḥikam*, 38, ult.
45 Entelechy?
46 Elucidated in detail in *Fuṣūṣ*, 128–39, where *rabb*, "Lord," sometimes means the divine I of man and sometimes God, i.e., the sole substance of the I's.
47 Elucidated in *Fuṣūṣ*, 32.
48 A maxim several times quoted by Ibn 'Arabī, *Fuṣūṣ*, 51, 18 – 19; 'Uqlat al-mustawfiz (in Nyberg), 96, 17. Also taken up by Shabistarī, "Gulshan," 163a: "What other relation has the dust to the pure world [= the world of the spirit] than this, that its understanding is inability to arrive at understanding?" Also cited by Nasafī, "Kashf," 271b, 14.

FRITZ MEIER

Now the question arises, If Ibn 'Arabī, as he maintains, really read the 560 chapters of the *Meccan Revelations* after his *circumambulatio*, in a supernatural book that was set before him in the Ka'ba at this stage, how can the rite symbolize the preparations for this work? Is his ascent to his metaphysical individuality not reality? The answer to this question is indeed evident from the foregoing exposition, but perhaps it can be made even clearer by the following consideration: Since, as we have shown, every symbol is a fraction of a whole, and as nothing can be a fraction before its whole exists, the Ka'ba can become a symbol of the mystical communion between Brahman and Ātman only after this communion is perceived or believed. Thus the symbol does not exclude the reality but presupposes it as the part presupposes the whole. And it is evident that Ibn 'Arabī did not fabricate the other half of the reality, the spiritual self of the rite, or derive it from some ancient tradition through a rational process, but experienced it through a transmutation of his consciousness (even though the words in which he expressed it may be borrowed). This is clear from the obscurity behind which the abstraction, as we have rendered it, is concealed in the preamble, from the fact that such an encounter with the self as that experienced by Ibn 'Arabī is in itself an initiation, and from the esoteric content of the *Meccan Revelations* themselves. Thus there is no uncertainty as to whether Ibn 'Arabī traveled the mystical path that is symbolized by the *circumambulatio*, but only as to whether he did so in A.D. 1201–2 at the Ka'ba. For since Ibn 'Arabī was a mystic before his departure from Spain, and since in the course of his long subsequent sojourn in Mecca he often visited the Ka'ba,[49] it is conceivable that he had only a part of his experience at this time—the vision of the youth, for example, which, it may be said in passing, recalls a purported vision of Mohammed—and later transposed the remaining elements to make a continuous narrative.

We have no basis for an answer to this question, but in no case would an answer reflect on the author's concern for truth. In giving an account of his experiences, Ibn 'Arabī is not striving to date his conversion but to explain the foundation of his mysticism. Elsewhere he attacks the philosophers[50]

49 *Futūḥāt*, 1, 88off.
50 *Futūḥāt*, 2, 689, 17–24; *Fuṣūṣ*, 224. Cf. *Futūḥāt*, 1, 38; *Fuṣūṣ*, 77; Martin Schreiner, "Beiträge zur Geschichte der theologischen Bewegung im Islam: III, Der Sûfismus und seine Ursprünge," *Zeitschrift der deutschen morgenländischen Gesellschaft* (Leipzig), LII (1898), 518; M. Asín Palacios, *La Psicología según Mohidin Abenarabi* (Actes du 14e Congrès international des orientalistes, Algiers, 1905; Vol. III, Paris, 1907), p. 93; Ignaz Goldziher, *Vorlesungen über den Islam* (Heidelberg, 1925), p. 172.

who believed that they could deduce the nature of the transcendent by abstract reasoning from the experiences of the sensory world (though he makes an exception of the "divine Plato," who did not yet "think," but "experienced"). And indeed the narrative of the preamble may be regarded as a kind of methodology, intended to show that the mystical insights expounded in the following four volumes were arrived at not by a dialectical process but by an elevation of consciousness to a higher plane, and that they are to be judged only from that plane. This places Ibn 'Arabī, like Ghazzālī, among those thinkers who argue that beyond a certain limit the problems of existence and even questions of dogma cannot be approached through a philosophical apparatus, nor by a regression to the world of feeling, but that the contradictions involved in these matters can be solved only by an inner growth into the realm from which prophecy itself springs.[51] The mysticism advocated by these men is not, to be sure, directed against the intellect[52] but against the intellectualism which forgets that only a limited sector of reality can be seen from any one vantage point and that the intellect is only one such vantage point.[53] With regard to dogma, this means that the interpretations of a religious doctrine can never be final and exclusive, since the spiritual attitude which proclaims them is never exclusive. Thus, if the rite of the *circumambulatio* has received an interpretation in the course of Ibn 'Arabī's *sacrificium intellectus* and attainment to a mystical life of the spirit, even the researches of modern historians of religion will be powerless to deny its validity.[54]

Image and meaning are a unit like existence and being, phenomenon and thing-in-itself. But only the two together, image and meaning, symbol and what it symbolizes, constitute the reality which we seek to grasp. All things in the world and their totality are only a fragment of a still greater whole, σύμβολον of an inner world, and the rite takes on life only through the

51 *Futūḥāt*, 1, 39, 4 from below; Mawlānā, *Fīhi mā fīh*, 67, 4–5: ". . . That thou [God] mayest lead us from this prison of the dark world into the luminous world of the prophets." See my book, *Vom Wesen der islamischen Mystik* (Basel, 1943), n. 44 (Dhākir; it seems worth mentioning that this Dhākir has been found to be identical with 'Alā' ad-dawla as-Simnānī; see above, n. 15).

52 *Futūḥāt*, 1, 39, 5 from below ff.; *Fuṣūṣ*, 30, 7 from below ff.

53 *Fuṣūṣ*, 215, 8 – 9: "For reason is a fetter and subsumes the matter in a single qualificative, while reality declines to be subsumed." (Nasir Khusrau, *Zād al-musāfirīn* 217, 21 – 218, 2: "No one has ever fully read this divine script [i.e., Creation], and the meanings which lie in this script are infinite. Every prophet has read a little of the script, according to the grace accorded him.")

54 For the opinion of scholars, see *Encyclopedia of Islam*, s.v. "Ḥadjdj"; Carl Clemen, "Der ursprüngliche Sinn des ḥaǧǧ," *Der Islam* (Strasbourg), X (1920), 161–77.

167

participation of the spirit.[55] Since nothing holds image and meaning so firmly together as the rite, or so compellingly evokes the intrusion of the irrational into the rational, it is understandable that Ibn 'Arabī's overwhelming experience of the self should have taken place at the Ka'ba. Through Ibn 'Arabī this ceremony, which even then struck the reason as an empty formula, and which today's materialistic thinkers must frankly regard as an error, regained something of the original *magic* meaning which presided over its founding by the Arabs of the pagan era.

55 For this reason 'Alā' ad-dawla as-Simnānī ("Ṣawfat al-'urwa," ch. 6, MS. Laleli Jami, Istanbul, 1432, 105b, 15; 107a, 2), represents the Sufis as those representatives of the middle "who combine outward and inward" [al-jam' bayn aẓ-ẓāhir wal-bāṭin]; Ibn 'Arabī's remarks (*Fuṣūṣ*, 67–88; Comm., 97, 15–25) would seem to have been influenced by this passage in Simnānī.

Max Pulver

Jesus' Round Dance and Crucifixion According to the Acts of St. John

I

A strange religious painting, a kind of fresco, takes form as we ponder chapters 94 to 102 of the Acts of St. John.[1] Here and there a bit of the surface has crumbled away, the whole is a little faded, and yet it is very much alive; it is remote and yet singularly near to us. In it we perceive a fragment of the empyrean, but at the same time a fragment of life, mysterious as life itself, a question calling as it were for solution and release. It is a strange space, a strange world—unlike ours—a world above the world that opens before us when we enter into the round dance of the disciples, led by Christ.

The dance is described by John, the very same John who was believed to have written the fourth Gospel, the book of Revelation, and the three epistles of John, and concerning whom the other disciples whispered: "This disciple shall not die" (John 21 : 23). And indeed he did not die. He lived on—it is related—in Patmos and in Ephesus, and he also journeyed to the legendary kingdom of Prester John. Still more than Peter, Paul, Andrew, or Philip he passed into myth. Even in the gospels, a breath of mystery surrounds him. There it is said that Jesus loved him and that he leaned on His bosom at the Last Supper (John 13 : 25).

1 [The author left the bibliographical apparatus somewhat less than complete, and the attempt has been made to finish and order it according to his indications. Dr. Pulver tr. the passage of the Acts of St. John from the Greek text of the *Acta apostolorum apocrypha*, ed. R. A. Lipsius and M. Bonnet (2 vols.; Leipzig, 1891–98), Vol. II. For reasons which he explains in the lecture, he did not use the German tr. of Edgar Hennecke, in *Neutestamentliche Apokryphen* (2nd edn., Tübingen, 1924), therefore its analogue, the English tr. of M. R. James, in *The Apocryphal New Testament* (Oxford, 1924), has not been cited, and Dr. Pulver's German version has been directly translated. The author cited the N.T. in Greek as well as in German; these refs. are here given only in English (AV).—ED.]

He is the initiate among the disciples; he is the witness, the "other disciple" in the episode of Peter's threefold denial of the Lord (John 18 : 15) in the courtyard of the high priest's palace; and lastly, it was he who followed the risen Jesus at his last appearance (John 21 : 21–23). Peter saw this and asked, "Lord, what shall this man do?" and Jesus answered, "If I will that he tarry till I come, what is that to thee?"

Biblical criticism distinguishes three or four individuals named John. Yet even in the Gospel, John has something mythical about him and cannot be pinned down historically. The critics are agreed that the Gospel of St. John and the first Epistle of John had the same author, who, however, is not identical with the disciple. The second Epistle of John is thought to be by another author, and the third by still another, while the Book of Revelation is held to be a Christian recension of a late Jewish apocalypse, written under a pseudonym.[2]

The preference and love Jesus felt for him lent the Apostle John an aura from the very outset, and the stories of his deeds, the *praxeis Ioannou*, with their atmosphere of supernatural virtue and miraculous powers, are spiritually related to the canonical books of John. They are known as *praxeis Ioannou* in the same way that the canonical accounts of the apostles are known as *praxeis apostolon*.

And such accounts—Acts of the Apostles or *actus* (e.g., the *actus Vercellenses* in the Acts of St. Peter)—were at first intended as stories of the life and works of these holy men, that is, as popular accounts, and only in the course of time did these *actus* become *acta*, i.e., did stories become history.

The Acts of St. John are regarded as the earliest among the apocryphal Christian Acts, because evident use has been made of them in the others—for example, in the Acts of St. Peter, with their reference to the hidden mystery of the Cross,[3] and in the Acts of St. Andrew. In both cases, chapter 97 of the Acts of St. John seems to have served as the point of departure. We are likely to misunderstand the special atmosphere of this book, however, if we draw for comparison only on Christian sources, whether canonical or apocryphal.

The literature and stylistic form of *praxeis*—Acts—begins among the Greeks with Xenophon's *Cyropaedia*,[4] relating the acts of Cyrus, and with

---

2 Cf. Carl Clemen, *Die Entstehung des Neuen Testaments* (Göschen, 1906), pp. 113, 125, 133, 135.

3 *Actus Vercellenses*, ch. 37 (8). (Cf. James, p. 304.)   4 I, 2, 16.

the works of the school of Isocrates. Not much later, Callisthenes related the "Acts" of Alexander the Great, and soon the literary world abounded with the "Acts" of gods, demigods, and heroes. Furthermore, ancient shrines kept their *aretalogoi*, recounting the miraculous deeds and cures of their own particular gods. All these books are full of the miraculous virtues (*aretai*= most nearly, Ital., *virtù*) and powers (*dynameis*) of their heroes, whether historical or mythical. At their center stands an individual charged with magical power, with mana; and that is their aretalogical motif.[5]

It was a fusion of this Hellenistic form with Christian legend that gave rise to the *praxeis* of the most important apostles, fragments of which have come down to us. Some two thirds of the Acts of St. John seems to have been preserved; its original length is estimated at 2500 lines. The *praxeis* were sometimes called *periodoi*, travels or accounts of travels. The apostles journey on earth; mystically speaking, they journey in ecstasy; and after death, they journey through the celestial spheres.

In this conception, too, the Christians drew upon the Greeks and other peoples; one need only think of Hesiod's *Theogony* (lines 411–52), with its hymn to Hecate, of the *Odyssey*, and finally of the Hellenistic tales of the miracles and wanderings of Alexander of Abunoteichos, of Apollonius of Tyana, of Peregrinus Proteus, and of Pythagoras. I hope at a later date to take up the connection between these legends and Christianity in a work to be entitled "On the History of a Rumor."[6]

Although for various reasons that we shall not go into here we regard the Acts of St. John as the oldest of the apocryphal Acts, still it is difficult to determine the date at which they were written. Here again, in all probability, legend has been added to legend; for example, our hymn in chapters 94 and 95 is no doubt earlier than the prose commentary that follows it (ch. 95–102). But both hymn and prose text are Gnostic: in the version that has come down to us they represent a Gnostic recension of the Christian legend or a Christian recension of the Gnostic legend. I should like to leave the question open as to whether the Gnostic element is older than the Christian, for later we shall find that certain passages are strikingly close to the *Corpus Hermeticum* and that certain of the formulas used in these Acts are older than the version of the *Poimandres* (*Corpus Hermeticum*, Book I) that has come down to us.

5 Hennecke, p. 164.
6 [So far as is known, Dr. Pulver (d. 1952) never produced this work.—ED.]

Of course, the literary references to the Acts of St. John and particularly to the hymn of praise have been studied. What Clement of Alexandria[7] says in his "Sketches" on I John 1 : 1, of the "traditions" in regard to the pseudobody of Christ, shows points of contact with chapters 89 and 93 of the Acts of St. John. Clement died in 215 at the latest. The Acts of St. John contain no such thoroughgoing encratistic (ascetic) ethic as we find in the Acts of St. Paul and St. Andrew and in the Manichaean Acts of St. Thomas. This too argues for their greater age, and so likewise does their Gnostic core. For it is at the beginning of the third century that Christianity was most permeated with Gnosticism. And so-called Scriptural proofs, or one might better say references, from both Old and New Testaments, are rare in the Acts of St. John, and, where they do occur, are very unconvincing. Perhaps we do well to place the extant version of the Acts of St. John in the third century, but it cannot be regarded as the original version. Bousset identifies a certain Leucius (= Lucius) as their author (or at least their compiler and editor),[8] but this may remain an open question. Late but still important testimony concerning their influence as well as their existence is provided by St. Augustine in his letters. In chapter 2 of his letter to Ceretius, which cannot be dated with precision, he mentions the hymn of praise which we find in chapter 95 of the Acts of St. John. "The hymn of praise which they [the Priscillianists] impute to our Lord Jesus Christ," writes St. Augustine, ". . . is found, to be sure, in the apocryphal books, yet these are not peculiar to the Priscillianists, but are also used by members of various other sects with infamous vanity."[9] It runs, essentially:

> Salvare volo et salvari volo;
> Solvere volo et solvi volo;
> Ornare volo et ornari volo;
> Generari volo (nasci volo et gignere volo);
> Cantare volo, saltate cuncti;
> Plangere volo, tundite vos omnes;
> Lucerna sum tibi, ille qui me vides;
> Janua sum tibi, quicumque me pulsas;
> Qui vides quod ago, tace opera mea;
> Verbo illusi cuncta et non sum illusus in totum.[10]

7 Hennecke, p. 132, par. 8.
8 Wilhelm Bousset, "Manichäisches in den Thomasakten," *Zeitschrift für Neutestamentliche Wissenschaft und die Kunde des Urchristentums* (Giessen), XVIII (1917–18), 37ff.
9 Letters, No. 237 (Migne, *PL*, XXXIII, 1034ff.). [Here and below, tr. from the German tr. of Alfred Hoffmann (Bibliothek der Kirchenväter; Munich, 1917), p. 332.]
10 [For a partial tr., see Part II, below. This text is not, however, precisely paralleled.—ED.]

In their introduction to the *Acta apostolorum*, Lipsius and Bonnet refer to this hymn as *"Versiculi quidam in latinum conversi"*—"a few lines translated into Latin."

Augustine continues: "Greatly as their opinions otherwise differ . . . they have these books in common; and much use is made of them particularly by those who do not recognize the old Law and the canonical Prophets." And he goes on to polemicize against Marcion, against the Manichaeans (in this case *en connaissance de cause*), and against the Montanists and the Priscillianists, to whom he ascribes the following exhortation to perjury: *"Jura, perjura, secretum prodere noli."* ("Swear, swear falsely, disclose not the secret.")

The Priscillianists, says Augustine, refer to the hymn of praise as "The Lord's hymn which he secretly imparted to the holy apostles, his disciples, and of which it is written in the Gospel: 'And when they had sung an hymn, they went out into the mount of Olives' (Matthew 26 : 30; Mark 14 : 26). They say that it does not stand in the canonical books because of those who think according to their own mind and not according to the spirit and truth of God, wherefore too it is written: 'It is good to keep close the secret of a king, but it is honorable to reveal the works of God' (Tobit 12 : 7)."

Augustine's polemic proves to the Priscillianists that the canonical books are no part of the king's secret, that they were not written for initiates, Gnostics, or pneumatics, and that if therefore one interpreted this secret hymn according to the canonical Gospels, one could not be an initiate. Thus, as late as the fourth century the hymn from the Acts of St. John was still regarded as a ritual of initiation; here Christ is a mystagogue, his disciples are mystai who are to become, as it were, the *symmystai* of Christ. That is, Christ was held to have delivered a secret initiation and to have left a secret tradition to his disciples, and above all to John. This belief, which was widespread outside the orthodox church, accounts for the bitterness with which the second council of Nicaea attacked the Acts of St. John. Chapters 93 to mid 95 and chapters 97 and 98 were read aloud and strongly condemned.

To anticipate the essentials of our subject matter: the hymn of praise and other important passages from the Acts of St. John are Gnostic. The hymn of praise is a λογική θυσία, a spiritual (or inward) sacrifice, in the exact sense given the term in the *Poimandres*: "Receive the spiritual sacrifices consecrated by the soul and the heart that are uplifted toward thee, O thou Unnamed, Unspoken one, Thou who art addressed by silence alone."[11] And in another passage: "Thy logos sings Thee through me; receive then through me, oh Thou who art all spiritual, the spiritual sacrifice."[12]

Over and over again the early Apologists, Origen for example, mention the immaterial character of the Christian sacrifices. But they speak of it negatively by way of disparaging the material sacrifices of the heathen and the Jews, whereas the *logike thysia* of the *Corpus Hermeticum* and the Acts of St. John signifies a positive spiritual act, a substantial offering. In the Acts of St. John the hymn of praise is at the same time the fulfillment of the Lord's Supper. The giving of thanks *is* the Eucharist. And in still other passages of these Acts, as in the *consummatio Joannis* (ch. 106–110), "the Eucharist is celebrated as a feast of thanksgiving and praise."[13]

Similarly in the *Apology* of Justin Martyr,[14] though the cup of water and wine appears in addition to the bread, the accent is again on the praise of the Father through the name of the Son and the Holy Ghost. In the Acts of St. John the whole essence of the Eucharist is praise and thanksgiving, and the sacrificial supper is minimized: the inward or spiritual sacrifice consists in the thanksgiving (the Eucharist).

Here we still have no set formulas, no finished ritual, no epiklesis: clearly there is no interest in the idea of sacrifice, but only in the rich and varied prayers of thanks. In the end, John administers communion to himself with the words: "May I too partake with you! and peace be with you, dearly beloved" (ch. 110). And in the Acts of St. John, John assumes the position of the Prophet in the *Didache* (11 : 7): "And ye shall neither try nor judge those prophets who speak in the Spirit." The absence of ritual in this Eucharist is an indication of its authenticity and popular character, and not, as some have supposed, of its literary origin.

In our text (ch. 94–102) the hymn of praise is sung in conjunction with a kind of round dance. Christ stands in the middle, and the apostles, presumably conceived as twelve in number, walk round him in a circle. This

11 *Corpus Hermeticum*, I, 31: δέξαι λογικὰς θυσίας ἀγνὰς ἀπὸ ψυχῆς καὶ καρδίας, πρὸς σὲ ἀνατεταμένης, ἀνεκλάλητε, ἄρρητε, σιωπῇ φωνούμενε. [Here tr. from the German of Gustav Parthey's edn. (Berlin, 1854), p. 18, quoted by Dr. Pulver. The Hermetic passages are also located in the edn. of Walter Scott, *Hermetica* (Oxford, 1924–36), Vol. I, in this case p. 31.—ED.]
12 Ibid., XIII, 18–19: ὁ σὸς Λόγος δι' ἐμοῦ ὑμνεῖ σε, δι' ἐμοῦ δέξαι τὸ πᾶν Λόγῳ, λογικὴν θυσίαν. (Cf. Scott, pp. 251–53.)
13 Leonhard Fendt, *Gnostische Mysterien* (Munich, 1922).
14 *Apology I*, ch. 65–66 (Migne, *PG*, VI, 428).

strange *chorea mystica*, this ecstatic cult dance, in which the apostles respond with the Hebrew *Amen* (="verily," "so be it") is as ancient as the form of the dance mystery itself. In the Mimaut Papyrus we read: "Come to me, Thou who art greatest in heaven [in this case, Helios], to whom heaven was given for a dancing ground."[15] Enraptured by hymn and dance, the mystai circle through the gates of initiation. Such rituals were common throughout antiquity, and they continued to reappear among Christians outside of the orthodox church.

This kind of round dance occurs in the first book of Jehu: "And he spake to them, to the twelve: All stand round me! and they stood round him. And he spake to them: Respond to me and praise God with me, that I may praise my father for the emanation [$\mathring{a}\pi\acute{o}\rho\rho o\iota a$] of all treasures. And he began to intone the hymn of praise, praising his father and saying: . . ."[16] Then begins a hymn which appears to be meaningless, a speaking in tongues, a glossolalia, perhaps containing magical formulas, as in the Magic Papyri. Such sounds exert a magical force upon the god, with whom the initiate thus achieves a union, a ἔνωσις. The hymn is magic, an enchantment as well as an incantation. Even such gods as Osiris and Isis may not rise up from earth to the primal god before offering up a secret hymn of praise to him.[17] The hymn redeems the spirit from the earthly body.[18]

The hymn is the sacrifice that is pleasing to God. This was already so in the Hermetic mysteries, and it is so in the Acts of St. John, where the ancient mysteries are presented with a Christian coating. We have here a Hermetic—but also a Gnostic—initiation. According to the hymn in the Gnostic *Pistis Sophia*,[19] Pistis Sophia is saved by Jesus. Whereupon she "entered into the midst of the invisible ones and there praised me [Jesus]."[20] The mystical Mechthild of Magdeburg cries out: "And there will be a glorious dance of praise!" And in her poem *Der Minne Weg* (the Way of Love): "Maiden, dance as deftly as my elect have danced before thee," and the Virgin replies:

15 Col. V, 130, in Karl Preisendanz, *Papyri Graecae Magicae*, I (Leipzig and Berlin, 1928), pp. 38f.
16 Carl Schmidt, *Koptisch-Gnostische Schriften*, Vol. I (Die griechischen Christlichen Schriftsteller der ersten drei Jahrhunderte; Leipzig, 1905), p. 297.
17 Richard Reitzenstein, *Poimandres* (Leipzig, 1904), p. 218.
18 *Corpus Hermeticum*, XIII, 15: καλῶς σπεύδεις λῦσαι τὸ σκῆνος (as is fitting thou strivest for release from the body [the corpse]). (Cf. Scott, p. 249.)
19 Schmidt, p. 346. [Page ref. apparently in error.—Ed.]
20 Ibid., p. 115.

I would not dance, Lord, unless thou leadest me.
Wouldst thou that I spring mightily,
Then must thou sing for me.
Thus will I leap into love,
From love into knowledge,
From knowledge into joy,
From joy beyond all human senses. . .[21]

Here then we have a Eucharist without sacrifice. This we have called Gnostic or Hermetic, because the spiritual or inner sacrifice, the *logike thysia* leads to union with God. God here is above all the One, whereas the God of the eucharistic sacrifice is above all the Just. Where there is an authentic sacrifice, there are also sinners and righteous men, and there God is primarily just. Christ, according to Mark 10 : 45, is λύτρον ἀντὶ πολλῶν, "ransom for many": "For even the Son of man came not to be ministered unto, but to minister, and to give his life a ransom for many."

For the Gnostic the disciple is seen in terms of the cult; the μαθητής is a student, one who would gather experience. For the orthodox Christian the core of the Lord's Supper is the idea of sacrifice, of Christ's atonement and martyrdom, and the martyr is his model. The early Christian Ignatius of Antioch held that martyrdom, because it is a suffering in atonement, makes Christ-like. In his Epistle to the Romans (4 : 1) he describes his impending martyrdom in terms taken from the Lord's Supper: "I am the wheat of God, and by the teeth of wild beasts am I milled, that I may be found to be the true bread of Christ."[22] Here deification occurs in real suffering, which alone enables one to become a disciple, to learn and gain experience. For Ignatius, the believer must repeat the destiny of his God, he must become an imitator of God, μιμητὴς τοῦ θεοῦ. For this he must

---

21   Ich mag nicht tanzen, Herre, du leitest mich denn.
                Willst du, dass ich sehre springe,
                So musst du selber vorsingen.
                So springe ich in die Minne,
                Von der Minne in die Erkenntnus,
                Von Erkenntnus in Genuss,
                Von Genuss über alle menschlichen Sinne. . .

     —Friedrich Schulze-Maizier, ed., *Mystische Dichtung aus sieben Jahrhunderten* (Leipzig, n.d.), p. 78.
22 σῖτός εἰμι θεοῦ, καὶ δι' ὀδόντων θηρίων ἀλήθομαι, ἵνα καθαρὸς ἄρτος εὑρεθῶ τοῦ Χριστοῦ.—Cf. H. W. Bartsch, *Gnostisches Gut und Gemeindetradition bei Ignatius von Antiochien* (Gütersloh, 1940).

also have knowledge of the secret name of God and of certain formulas, such as the recurrent though much varied "Thou art I and I am thou."[23]

But in Gnosticism and also in the Acts of St. John, the suffering of the Redeemer implies not his real death, but his descent into the hyle (matter) and the gathering of the spermata in the hyle. Here the Eucharist is a hymn of praise and hence understood as in the mysteries, that is to say, in the significance that a sacrament had for the mystery community. Each mystery has a corresponding myth that is repeated in the mystery action of the faithful—outside of sensuous reality. The ancient Christian's view of the Eucharist, on the other hand, is sacramental, that is, it endows *magically* with a power of life and immortality. The sacrament is a sacred substance that is communicated to the believer. With his conception of the sacrifice in the Lord's Supper and in martyrdom, Ignatius of Antioch stands between the tradition of the Christian congregation and the Gnostic-Hermetic tradition. In chapter 100 of the Acts of St. John the death of Christ is mere illusion. It is a seeming death for the multitude, and according to this conception, the story related in the Gospels is valid for the multitude. The death of Christ, however, is not a case of sham death [*Scheintod*, "asphyxia"], as Hennecke rather unfortunately formulated it. Docetism, as this conception is called (from δοκεῖν, "to seem," "to appear as if"), means the "as-if" death of the Redeemer, his seeming death as a model, a prototype. Through this seeming death Christ says to man, *Tua res agitur*.

What places the Acts of St. John in the Johannine group is its characteristic adaptation to Christian purposes of such Gnostic terms as *pneuma* and *logos*. This may be the result of a later editing, but what may be regarded as a fundamentally Gnostic motif of the Acts is the idea expressed in chapter 96 that the Logos, the spoken word, is less than the creative silence of the primal Father: "When thou seest what I do, keep my mysteries silent." At that time, presumably the beginning of the third century, the Logos meant not only the creative word, but also the inwardness, the Spirit. Thus the Logos, interpreted as inwardness, can also encompass σιγή, silence. It should also be pointed out that, according to Valentinian Gnosis and the Hermetic writings, an emanation stands between God and the Logos. For Ignatius, for example, this emanation of God, and not the Logos, is Christ.

This perhaps will clarify a passage in the hymn. Christ brings the knowledge of God; he is taken not as a revealer but as a mystery God, to whom

23 σὺ γὰρ εἶ ἐγὼ καὶ ἐγὼ σύ.—Preisendanz, II (Leipzig, 1931), p. 123, li. 795.

177

the devotee raises himself in mystical silence.[24] A pseudo passion and pseudo
death of Christ were also tenets of the contemporary Mandaeans;[25] Christ
descends into the hyle and gathers the spermata.

This whole manner of thinking, for which the essence of God is $\sigma\iota\gamma\dot{\eta}$ or
$\dot{\eta}\sigma\upsilon\chi\dot{\eta}$, silence or quietness, this manner of thinking which Reitzenstein[26]
identifies with the "prayer language of the Poimandres" is at least very
closely related to the attitude underlying the Acts of St. John. This attitude
is not eschatological; it is the thinking of the mystery cults. As Bartsch
puts it, "the resurrection which the believer experiences in the cult is his
mystical resurrection in the cult."[27]

In the following, I offer a new version of the passage—Acts of St. John,
chapters 94-102—according to Bonnet's classic edition of the Greek text.[28]
This proved to be necessary because the most reliable of previous translations into German, that of Hennecke,[29] discloses a number of slight devia-
tions, resulting perhaps from the translator's theological position. I have
undertaken

1. to render the meaning as faithfully as possible.
2. to preserve the idiosyncrasies of the language.
3. to render the special rhythms of the hymn and of the prose.

The reader is invited to compare the numerous extant translations with
the original text and with this translation.

II

The Acts of St. John, Chapters 94–102

[94]   And before he was taken by the Jews outside the law, whose law
comes from a serpent outside the law, he gathered us all together and
said: Before I give myself over to them, let us praise the Father in a
hymn of praise, and so let us go to meet what is to come. Then he
bade us form a circle; we stood with folded hands, and he was in the

24 Bartsch, ch. 71.
25 *Ginzā: Der Schatz oder das Grosse Buch der Mandäer*, tr. Mark Lidzbarski (Quellen
     der Religionsgeschichte, Group 4, Vol. 13; Göttingen and Leipzig, 1925), p. 199.
26 *Poimandres*, p. 264, n. 3.
27 Bartsch, p. 118.
28 In *Acta apostolorum apocrypha*, ed. Lipsius and Bonnet, Vol. II, pp. 197ff. [See n. 1,
     above.—ED.]
29 In *Neutestamentliche Apokryphen*, pp. 175 ff. [In James, pp. 253ff. See n. 5, above.—ED.]

middle. And then he said: Answer me with Amen. Then he began to intone a hymn of praise and to say:

Praise be to thee, Father.

And we all circled round him and responded to him: Amen.

Praise be to thee, Logos.
Praise be to thee, Grace, Amen.
Praise be to thee, Divine Spirit (Pneuma).
Praise be to thee, Holy One.
Praise be to thee, Transfiguration, Amen.

We praise thee, Father.
We give thanks to thee, Light, wherein there is no darkness, Amen.
[95] And wherefore we give thanks, that will I utter:
I will be saved and I will save, Amen.
I will be freed and I will free, Amen.
I will be wounded and I will wound, Amen.
I will be begotten and I will beget, Amen.
I will consume and I will be consumed, Amen.
I will hear and I will be heard, Amen.
I will be known, I who am all spirit, Amen.
I will be washed and I will wash, Amen.
Grace paces the round. I will blow the pipe. Dance the round all,
    Amen.
I will mourn: mourn all, Amen.
The one and only Eight sings praises with you, Amen.
The twelfth of the numbers paces the round aloft, Amen.
To each and all it is given to dance, Amen.
He who joins not in the dance mistakes the event, Amen.
I will flee and I will stay, Amen.
I will adorn and I will be adorned, Amen.
I will be understood and I will understand, Amen.
A mansion have I not and mansions have I, Amen.
A torch am I to thee who perceivest me, Amen.
A mirror am I to thee who discernest me, Amen.
A door am I to thee who knockest at me, Amen.
A way am I to thee who passest.

[96] And if thou givest ear to my round dance, behold thyself in me the speaker. And when thou seest what I do, keep my mysteries silent. If thou dancest, ponder what I do, for thine is this human suffering that I will suffer. For thou hadst been powerless to understand thy suffering, had not I been sent to thee as the Logos (inner spirit) by the Father. When thou sawest my suffering, thou sawest me as sufferer. And seeing it, thou stoodst not fast, but wert all shaken. In thy drive toward wisdom thou hast me for a pillow. Lean upon me. Thou wilt know who I am when I depart. I am not he for whom I am now taken. Thou wilt see when thou comest. If thou understoodest suffering thou wouldst have nonsuffering. See through suffering and thou wilt have nonsuffering. What thou knowest not, that will I myself teach thee. I am thy God, not the betrayer's God. I will bring the souls of the saints into harmony with myself. Understand the word of wisdom in me. Say to me once more:

Praise to thee, Father.
Praise to thee, Logos.
Praise to thee, Holy Ghost.

And if thou wouldst understand that which is me, know this: all that I have said, I have uttered playfully—and I was by no means ashamed of it. I danced, but as for thee, consider the whole, and having considered it, say:

Praise be to thee, Father, Amen.

[97] Dearly beloved, after the Lord had thus danced the round with us, he went out. And we fled like the lost or like nightwalkers, one this way, one that way. And when I saw him suffering, I dwelt not on his suffering, but fled to the Mount of Olives and mourned over what had befallen (the accident). And when he was hanged upon the thorn of the Cross, darkness descended on the whole earth at the sixth hour. And my Lord stood in the middle of the cave and illumined it and spake: John, for the multitude down in Jerusalem I am being crucified, and pierced with lances and staves; vinegar and gall are given me to drink. But to thee I speak, now hear me: I secretly caused thee to go up on this mountain, that thou mightest hear what the disciple must

[98] learn from his master and man from God. And with these words he showed me an implanted cross of light and round the cross a throng

that had not one (uniform) shape. And in that cross of light there was one form and one appearance. And upon the cross I saw the Lord himself, and he had no outline (no outward form) but only a voice. Yet it was not the voice that we knew, but a sweet and kindly and truly divine voice that spake to me: John, one man must hear this from me. I require one who shall hear it. For you (the disciples) I call this cross of light now logos, now spirit, now Jesus, now Christ, now door, now way, now bread, now seed, now resurrection, now Son, now Father, now divine spirit, now life, now truth, now faith, now grace. So it is for men. But according to its essence and selfhood, speaking to us, it is the delimitation of all things. And the vast elevation of the stable from the unstable, and the harmony of wisdom—of the wisdom that is in harmony.

But there are forces of the right and forces of the left, potencies, angelic powers and demons, efficacies, threats, upsurges of wrath, devils, Satan, and the lower root from which the nature of Becoming [99] issued. And so it is this cross which spiritually joined the universe, and which marked off the realm of change and the lower realm, and which caused all things to rise up.

It is not that cross, the wooden cross which thou wilt see when thou goest down thither. Nor am I he upon the stake, whom thou canst not see now, but whose voice alone thou perceivest. I passed for that which I am not, for what I was to the many others. What they will say of me is wretched and unworthy of me. Those who neither see nor [100] name the place of stillness will much less see the Lord. The uniform throng round the cross signifies the lower nature. And if those whom thou seest by the cross have as yet no single form, then all the parts of him who descended have not been gathered together. But when the nature of mankind has been taken up and a generation of men moved by my voice comes close to me, thou, who hearest me now, wilt have become the same and that which is will no longer be. For thou wilt stand then above the others, as I do now. For until thou callest thyself mine own, I shall not be what I am. But if thou understandest (hearest) me, thou wilt be an understander (hearer) like myself (next to myself).

For this thou art through me. Therefore have no concern for the many and despise the profane. Know that I am wholly with the Father

[101] and the Father wholly with me. None of what they will relate have I suffered. Even the passion that I revealed to thee and the others in the round dance, I would have it called a mystery. Behold, that which thou art, that have I shown thee. But that which I am, I alone know. No one else. Therefore let me have mine, but see thine through me. And see me in my essence, not as I have said I was, but as thou, being akin to me, knowest me.

> Thou hearest that I suffered, but I suffered not.
> An unsuffering one was I and I suffered.
> A transfixed one was I and yet not maltreated.
> Hanged was I and yet not hanged.
> Blood flowed from me and yet did not flow.

In brief, that which they say of me, that have I not suffered. But that which they do not say, that have I suffered. What it is, that do I intimate (in a riddle), for I know thou wilt understand. Know me then as the praise of the Logos, the transfixing of the Logos, the blood of the Logos, the wound of the Logos, the hanging of the Logos, the suffering of the Logos, the impaling of the Logos, the death of the Logos. And thus in my discourse have I distinguished the man from myself.

First therefore know the Logos (the inwardness, the meaning). Then thou wilt know the Lord; and thirdly the man and what he has [102] suffered. When he had spoken thus to me and still more which I cannot say as he did, he was caught up and none of the multitude saw him. And when I went thither, I laughed at them all, for he had told me what they had said concerning him. I only take to heart that the Lord carried out everything symbolically, for the conversion and salvation of men.

III

And now let us attempt to throw light on the basic meaning and mood of the whole, and clarify a few important passages in the text. Our introduction provides the groundwork for a general understanding.

The hymn begins with an eightfold formula of praise, in which the Father is named twice, the Logos once. Since Christ himself intones the hymn and in it praises the Logos, he himself cannot be the Logos. As I have shown in Part I, Christ is represented in Valentinian Gnosis, in the Hermetica, and in

182

Ignatius of Antioch as an emanation of God, standing between God and Logos. Here this seems to be again the case. The other predicates: Grace, Pneuma, Holy One, and Doxa (transfiguration) admit of a Christian interpretation, but they may equally well be understood on the basis of Gnosis and the Hermetic books. Compare, for example, the use of "Holy One" or "holy" in the *Poimandres:*

> Holy is God, Father of the Cosmos.
> Holy is God whose plan is carried out by his own powers.
> Holy is God, who will be known and is known by his own.
> Holy art Thou, who hast appointed Being by the Word.
> Holy art Thou in whose image all nature originated.
> Holy art Thou whom nature could not form.
> Holy art Thou who art mightier than all power.
> Holy art Thou who art more excellent than all excellence.
> Holy art Thou who art above all praises.[30]

Here we have nine predicates of holiness, parallel to the eight glorifications in our text, eight divine powers plus a ninth, the primordial godhead. In the hymn of the Acts of St. John, the Eight, the Egyptian *ogdoad*, is already announced in the eightfold *doxa*.

The eight glorifications of God are such as might also be found in non-Christian Hellenistic mysteries, beginning with the Father and going on to the above-mentioned Logos, who cannot be identical with Christ. And Charis, grace, also occurs in a related meaning in the Egyptian magic literature, as for example in the Mimaut Papyrus: "We give thanks to thee, lifting up our whole soul and heart to thee, ineffable name . . ."[31] And in the *Poimandres:* "Fill me with this grace."[32]

In the eighth prayer to Hermes—"Accomplish all charities"[33]—the Agathosdaimon is entreated by a magician who in another Hermetic book designates himself as the Charis of the Aeon.[34] The Aeon, or what is the same here, the Agathodaimon, is conceived as Pleroma Charitos, fullness

---

30 Sec. 31.
31 (χ)αριν σοι οιδαμεν ψυχη(ν) πασα(ν) και καρδιαν προς (σε) ανατεταμενην αφφαστον ονομα.—Reitzenstein, *Die Hellenistischen Mysterienreligionen* (Leipzig, 1927), p. 285.
32 (πλήρωσόν με) τῆς χάριτος ταύτης.—Ch. I, 32.
33 τέλει πάσας χάριτας.—Reitzenstein, *Poimandres*, p. 30.
34 ἐγώ εἰμι ἡ χάρις τοῦ Αἰῶνος.—Joannes Laurentius Lydus, *Liber de Mensibus*, ed. Richard Wünsch (Leipzig, 1898). [The author cited "IV 53, p. 109, 13," but the ref. is in error.—ED.]

of grace, herein recalling the Gospel (John 1 : 16): "And of his fullness have all we received, and grace for grace."

And pneuma, the other divine predicate, is anything but purely Christian. It occurs as "the pneuma" in the first eight lines of the hymn; in the following prose text, probably of later origin, we find "Praise be to thee, Holy Spirit"— πνεῦμα ἅγιον.

The pneuma of the first doxology is not unequivocal. We can best grasp its meaning by examining the linguistic usage of late Hellenism. Since it is an attribute of God, we may presumably identify it with the πνεῦμα θεῖον of the Hermetic writings. It is taken in a similar sense by the anti-Christian Celsus in Origen, when he quotes his Phoenician and Palestinian false prophets as saying: "I am God or the son of God or the divine spirit."[35] Living contemporaries in the second century make this assertion. But man becomes *pneuma theion* not only through rebirth, through palingenesis or anagenesis,[36] but also through his death.

The transference of the pneuma by blowing or breathing (πνοή) is described in John 20 : 22: "And when he had said this, he breathed [ἐνεφύση-σεν] on them, and saith unto them: Receive ye the Holy Ghost." Thus did the dead and risen Christ communicate the Holy Spirit to his disciples. Here the *dead* Christ imparts the pneuma to his living apostles.

The closer we come to the popular tradition, in the Magic Papyri for example, the more the "spirit" tends to become a ghost or even a skeleton. Though the literary documentation of these meanings is relatively late, in essence they are older than the spiritual concept of the pneuma. The later alchemical literature, for example, revives a concept of the pneuma originating in prehistoric times, as is proved by the excavations of the Necropolis of Negada.[37] This meaning relates to the so-called "secondary burial." The corpse is dismembered, the head removed, and in this moment a prophetic pneuma enters into the dead man. We are reminded of the visions of Zosimos: "He seized me and tore me asunder in accordance with the dictates of harmony."[38] This procedure occurs also in the Egyptian Book of the Dead;

35 ἐγὼ ὁ θεός εἰμι ἢ θεοῦ παῖς ἢ πνεῦμα θεῖον.—Origen, *Contra Celsum*, VII, 9 (Migne, PG, II, 1433).
36 In the sermon of the Naassenes, reworked under Christian influence. Recorded in Hippolytus, *Elenchos*, V, 5ff. (*Werke*, ed. Paul Wendland, Vol. III, Leipzig, 1916, pp. 77ff.).
37 Reitzenstein, *Poimandres*, p. 369.
38 ἔλων με καὶ διασπάσας κατὰ σύστασιν ἁρμονίας.—Marcellin Berthelot, *Collection des anciens alchimistes grecs* (Paris, 1887–88). Harmony usually signifies the astrological harmony of the Heimarmene, the fate governed by the stars.

the dead man is cut into his seven parts, the flesh is scraped off; then the bones are rearranged in the position of the embryo in the womb.[39]

In the liturgy of Mithras pneuma even occurs in the sense of "breath": "Take breath from the rays, breathing in three times."[40] In our text, pneuma may be presumed to have both the enthusiastic and the prophetic-mantic sense. This is as closely as we can define it here.

A word on the term *doxa*. *Doxa* means, first, "opinion"; then "appearance and illusion, sheen or radiance of light ($\delta\acute{o}\xi\alpha$ $\tau o\tilde{v}$ $\varphi\omega\tau\acute{o}s$), as of the sun and the moon"; finally, "glory, transfiguration, the aureole and glorification of the supreme God." That is why I have rendered the words $\delta\acute{o}\xi\alpha$ $\sigma o v$ $\tau\tilde{\eta}$ $\delta\acute{o}\xi\eta$ as "praise be to thee, transfiguration." In St. Paul as in the Gospel of St. John, but also in the papyrus literature, the noun $\delta\acute{o}\xi\alpha$ and the verb $\delta o\xi\acute{a}\zeta\omega$ usually mean "glory" and "glorify." "The prophet to whom it is granted by God to perform a miracle is thus glorified by God."[41]

In the hymn, the doxology is followed by the Johannine (I John 1 : 5) formula of thanksgiving to the "light in which there is no darkness." And after this transition begin the famous confessions of Christ the mystagogue, which would be unintelligible if we imputed them to the Christ of Church history:

I will be saved and I will save.
I will be freed and I will free.
I will be wounded and I will wound.
I will be begotten and I will beget.
I will hear and I will be heard.
I will be known, I who am all spirit.
I will be washed and I will wash.

But as soon as we replace Christ the Revealer by the Gnostic mystery god, the riddle solves itself.

These lines—as the introductory phrase "Wherefore we give thanks, that will I now utter" suggests—reveal or rather conceal the Gnostic eucharist. The Gnostic redeemer must himself be redeemed, he must collect the divine spermata that are dispersed in matter (hyle). He must be freed from this matter by a reascent and a return; he must be wounded in the mystery and he must wound his adept who must repeat the acts and sufferings of his

---

39 E. A. Wallis Budge, tr., *The Book of the Dead* (London, 2nd edn., 3 vols., 1909), ch. 43 and 90.
40 ἕλκε ἀπὸ τῶν ἀκτίνων πνεῦμα τρὶς ἀνασπῶν.—Albrecht Dieterich, *Eine Mithrasliturgie* (Leipzig, 1903), p. 6.
41 Reitzenstein, *Poimandres*, p. 22, n. 5.

god in the mystery action (dromenon) in order to achieve union with him, deification.

This Christ wishes to beget the Logos in the soul of his followers and he himself must be begotten by the Father, in order to issue from the pleroma and descend to fulfill his mission of collecting the divine spermata which are dispersed through matter. He has heard and followed the Logos (the creative Word) of God and demands that his followers likewise hear it. He wishes to be understood reflectively—"known," for only he who understands the meaning of his action can understand his essence, which is wholly intelligible. And he wishes to be washed in baptism, for through baptism the divine power is imparted. This baptism should probably be conceived as a baptism by fire (as in Matthew 3 : 11 and Luke 3 : 16, "with the Holy Ghost and with fire"); it recalls experiences during ecstasy, especially the primitive experience of rapture by the fiery spirit of God as it is recounted, for example, in the miracle of Pentecost (Acts 2 : 1–4).

Christ, having issued from the Father and his plenitude (pleroma) for the salvation of the world, sees himself as a torch. "He who is close to me is close to fire," wrote Didymus in his commentary on Psalm 88 : 8 [A. V., 89 : 7]. In baptism is death and the beginning of a new life. The Gnostic redeemer desires to be impregnated by the supreme godhead, in order to be enabled to carry out his mission; he desires to be washed, because he is inevitably tainted with matter while gathering the seeds of God in the sublunar world.

After these first confessions of Christ, Charis enters into the round, for it is the grace of the supreme godhead which sent the savior, and it is grace which permits the mystes to partake of initiation in this choral song. There follows the second series of Christ's confessions:

> I will blow the pipe. Dance the round all.
> I will mourn, mourn all (beat your breasts).

Here Christ appears plainly as the mystery god, piping the tune for the mystical round dance. For in the mystery the believer must incur the same sufferings as his god, and therefore he must mourn with him.

> The one and only Eight sings praises with you.
> The twelfth of the numbers paces the round aloft.

These two verses present a key to the understanding of the whole. The Eight and the number twelve derive from Egyptian conceptions related to Hermeticism but quite alien to true Christianity. It has been suggested above that the Eight refers to the eight divine powers. "The name of the Lord, that is, the name Eight," says the Leyden Papyrus.[42] Name is here identical with person.

In prophesying the ascent of the soul, the *Poimandres* says: "I desired, O Father, to know praise by the hymn that thou spakest, when I am come to hear the eightness of the divine powers."[43] For the Egyptians the eightness represented the body of the primordial god, it provided[44] the instrumentality for creation by the Word, or—archaically—by the emission of the sperm. This Egyptian conception was taken into various Gnostic systems, such as that of the Ophites or of Basilides, where the Eight is the eighth heaven, the sphere of the fixed stars above the seven planets. Sometimes the primordial god was distinguished from the eightfold powers that are his body; then, he is the archon of the Ogdoad, as in Basilides, who also knows two Christs, one in the Ogdoad, and a lower, solar Christ.

Best known are probably the ogdoads in the system of Valentinian Gnosis, where there is a pre-existent, original ogdoad and a second ogdoad: these two taken together and added to the heavenly luminaries yield the number thirty. Here the first ogdoad consists of Bythos, Pater, Anthropos, Logos, and their female partners with whom they form syzygies. The partners' names are Sige, Aletheia, Ecclesia, and Zoe.[45] In the writings of the Gnostic Ptolemaeus, Achamoth is called the Ogdoad and retains the number of the primordial and original ogdoad of the pleroma.[46] For the Gnostic Marcus the Eight becomes part of a play on numbers.

Thus this Eight that joins with the mystai in their hymns of praise occurs also in early Christianity wherever it discloses an Egyptian influence. Clement of Alexandria writes, for example: "He whom the mother bears will be led into death and into the world; but he whom Christ re-bears will be given over to life and the Eight."[47]

He who is given over to the Eight is released from the Heimarmene, the

---

42 Preisendanz, II, col. XVII, li. 742f., p. 121.
43 ἐβουλόμην, ὦ πάτερ, τὴν διὰ ὕμνου εὐλογίαν (μανθάνειν) ἣν ἔφης ἐπὶ τὴν Ὀγδοάδα γενομένου μου ἀκοῦσαι τῶν δυνάμεων.—*Corpus Hermeticum*, XIII, 15. (Cf. Scott, p. 249.)
44 Reitzenstein, *Poimandres*, p. 63, n. 3.
45 Epiphanius, *Panarion*, 31, 5–6 (Migne, *PG*, XLI, 481ff.).
46 Hans Leisegang, *Die Gnosis* (Leipzig, 1924), p. 317.
47 ὃν γεννᾷ ἡ μήτηρ, εἰς θάνατον ἄγεται καὶ εἰς κόσμον, ὃν δὲ ἀναγεννᾷ Χριστός, εἰς ζωὴν μετατίθεται (καὶ) εἰς Ὀγδοάδα.—*Excerpta ex Theodoto*, 80 (Migne, *PG*, IX, 696).

power of the stars. Thus the ogdoad is often the supreme realm: the divine pleroma itself. But not always; sometimes it is an intermediary realm to which the soul first returns in its reascent, where it finds the other souls[48] and joins them in praising God. Here then there is a realm beyond the ogdoad, where the *dynameis theou* praise God.[49] "And having become like unto the companions of this degree he (the mystes) hears certain powers above ogdoadic nature singing the praises of God with their own voices."[50] The *dynameis*, the divine potencies, are at the same time sacraments, that is to say, sacramental efficacies.

Now these powers above the ogdoad are probably the twelve divine potencies alluded to in the verse:

The twelfth of the numbers paces the round aloft.

To me it seems unlikely that this refers only to the twelve mansions of heaven, for these belong to the realm of astral fate, of Heimarmene, which is here equated with harmony, and not to the realm of promised freedom, to which initiation leads. For initiation promises precisely to liberate the mystes from the dictates of the stars and hence from the power of fate. The following verses again suggest that the secret is apprehended in the movement of the dance, in the ecstasy it releases.

To each and all it is given to dance.

This presumably means that the cosmos is magically transformed by this ritual dance, that it becomes God's dancing ground.

He who joins not in the dance mistakes the event.

And then, in the final phase of ecstasy, the confessions begin again:

I will flee and I will stay.
I will adorn and I will be adorned.
I will be understood and I will understand.

The Gnostic redeemer descends and rises again after gathering the seeds of God. He guides himself and his mystai back to the dignity of the primordial man, the Anthropos. This is the adorning and the being adorned; the

---

48 Reitzenstein, *Poimandres*, p. 53.
49 *Corpus Hermeticum*, I, 26. (Cf. Scott, p. 129.)
50 Ibid., XIII, 18: καὶ ὁμοιωθεὶς τοῖς συνοῦσιν ἀκούει καί τινων δυνάμεων ὑπὲρ τὴν ὀγδοαδικὴν φύσιν οὐσῶν φωνῇ τινι ἰδίᾳ ὑμνουσῶν τὸν θεόν. (Cf. Scott, p. 251.)

word "*cosmos*" means "ornament" and also the cosmos. He himself goes back into the essential world, taking his own with him. And this he can do only if man understands the meaning of his action, just as he desires to understand men in order to liberate them.

"I will be understood and I will understand" says the hymn. And in the *Corpus Hermeticum* we find virtually the same line with the same meaning: "He who would be known and is known (by his own)."[51] This "knowing" is a mystical union, a *henosis*, a *synousia*. It accomplishes the fusion of the mystes with his mystery god.

The next verse is: "A mansion have I not and mansions have I." The mystery Christ has no real body as his dwelling place, and yet he dwells in the bodies of those that belong to him, the mystai. The mansion —ὁ οἶκος (the house or dwelling), usually τὸ σκῆνος—is the body or corpse; in our introduction we quoted the line from the Hermetic books: "As is fitting, thou strivest for release from the body."[52] The mystes must do this, for his God, who is all spirit, has no mansion (no body) and consequently the mystes must temporarily or permanently—that is to say, in ecstasy or in death—leave his body in order to become like God. But the Lord of the mystery has mansions, the bodies of his initiates.

In the last four verses of the hymn Christ refers to himself as a torch, a mirror, a door, and a way. These are not only familiar symbols but also probably instruments of initiation. The mystery god is a light (λύχνος), candelabrum, or torch. In his first epistle to the Corinthians (XXI, 3), Clement of Alexandria wrote: "The spirit of the Lord is a light which searches the chambers of the body."[53] Thus if the mystery god is called a torch, it is because he penetrates and sees through his mystai, and not because he shines before them in an ethical sense. A parallel is assuredly provided by 21 : 23 of Revelation: "For the glory of God did lighten it [the city], and the Lamb is the light [λύχνος] thereof." But, above all, our line from the hymn seems to contain a reference to the torch as part of the paraphernalia of initiation, to point to the lychnomantic practice of the Magic Papyri.[54] Here the magician stares into a lamp or torch until he sees the god or until certain symbols appear in it. Examples of this may be

51 Ibid., I, 31: γνωσθῆναι βούλεται καὶ γινώσκεται (τοῖς ἰδίοις). (Cf. Scott, p. 131.) Acts of St. John: γνωθῆναι θέλω καὶ νῶσαι θέλω.
52 See n. 18, above.
53 φῶς κυρίου λύχνος ὃ ἐρευνᾷ ταμιεῖα κοιλίας.
54 Reitzenstein, *Poimandres*, p. 24, n. 3.

found in *Poimandres*, in the *Pistis Sophia*,[55] and in the previously cited passage from the liturgy of Mithras: "Take breath from the rays, breathing in three times as deeply as thou canst, and thou wilt see thyself crossing over to the heights. . . ."[56] The mystery Christ is the lamp in whose flames God appears to the gaze of the believer.

Similar is the meaning of the verse:

A mirror am I to thee who discernest me.

The suffering of the Gnostic mystery god reflects the suffering of man, left and right are transposed as in a mirror, the god seems to suffer bodily and yet does not suffer, but man as mystes suffers in reality as long as he remains a mere man and is not yet wholly an initiate. The relation between God and man thus seems reversed as in a mirror.

A similar idea is expressed in the Acts of St. Andrew: "Therefore I hold those blessed who have heard the prophecies through which as in a glass they behold the secrets of their own nature, for whose sake all things were created."[57] Or in Pseudo-Cyprian's *De montibus Sina et Sion* (ch. 13): "Behold me in yourselves as one of you beholds himself in water or in a mirror." And the thirteenth "Ode of Solomon"[58] bears the title "Our Mirror Is the Lord."

Thus when man looks into his magic mirror he sees not only himself but also the Lord or the Spirit. Here again we have a magical conception, a mirror magic. We are reminded of I Corinthians 13 : 12: "For now we see through a glass, darkly; but then face to face." Paul uses the mystery image, but he does not know or else does not acknowledge the transference of the suffering from God to man.

A door am I to thee who knockest at me.

This too is an ancient mystery image. In the liturgy of Mithras, for example: "Then open thine eyes and thou wilt see the doors opened and the world of the gods that is within the doors, so that thy spirit will be ravished by the joy of the sight and rise aloft."[59] And again, in another passage of the

55 Adolf Harnack, "Über das gnostische Buch 'Pistis-Sophia'," *Texte und Untersuchungen*, Vol. VII, part 2 (Leipzig, 1891), p. 91.
56 See n. 40, above.
57 Hennecke, p. 254 (Acts, ch. 15).
58 Ibid., p. 449.
59 εἶτα ἄνοιξον τοὺς ὀφθαλμοὺς καὶ ὄψει ἀνεῳγυίας τὰς θύρας καὶ τὸν κόσμον τῶν θεῶν, ὅς ἐστιν ἐντὸς τῶν θυρῶν. . . .—Dieterich, p. 10, li. 19.

liturgy, where the heavenly goddesses of fate emerge with the heads of serpents.[60]

In certain mysteries, such as these of Mithras, the door is a gate to the seven successive zones of paradise.[61] In response to Origen's remarks about Jacob's ladder (κλίμαξ), Celsus refers to Philo's De somniis, where the patriarch's vision is explained first as the realm of the air, then as the soul, thirdly as an image of the ascetic life, fourthly as a symbol of the things of this world. And then Celsus goes on to speak of the gates of heaven. Thus door and ladder often occur together in mystical vision. "This symbol is a ladder with seven gates, and above them an eighth gate."[62] The way of the soul in its ascent, or the way of the redeemer in his descent and reascent passes through this door and over this ladder or staircase. These gates have their demonic lords.[63] In our hymn the mystery Christ himself is the door between the realm of astral fate with its blind necessity, i.e., the realm of destiny, of tyche, and the realm of freedom from fate, the realm of providence, pronoia, that is promised to the initiate. Through this door leads the way spoken of in the last verse of the hymn:

A way am I to thee who passest.

Here again we are reminded of a passage in the fourth Gospel (14 : 6): "I am the way, the truth, and the life: no man cometh unto the Father, but by me." Through this door leads the mystagogue; he is the way for him who passes by, for the man, the wanderer, who, like his master himself, is a voyager bound for heaven. The mystagogue is the ὁδηγός, the guide to the upper world. Initiation is an act of decision before the entrance, and then it becomes a way, a long way—as is Gnosis also. With this the mystery hymn closes; it is an ἱερὸς λόγος, both initiation and Lord's Supper. There follows the injunction to silence: "When thou seest what I do, keep my mysteries silent."

The ensuing chapter 96 is probably later than the hymn. It explains the round dance, but by way of that strange dialectic which goes back from the known God to the known man, and from the man known by God back again to God. I have described this process in my lecture on "Gnostic Experience and Gnostic Life."[64] It corresponds to the circular movement of the round

60 Ibid., p. 13, li. 16.   61 Origen, Contra Celsum, VI, 22 (Migne, PG, II, 1523f.).
62 τοιόνδε τὸ σύμβολον κλίμαξ ἑπτάπυλος, ἐπὶ δὲ αὐτῇ πύλη ὀγδόη.
63 Ibid., VI, 30, 31 (Migne, PG, II, cols. 1338ff.).
64 "Gnostische Erfahrung und gnostisches Leben," EJ 1940–41.

dance. The explanations offered by chapter 96 are meditations, not really a search but a contemplation back and forth through a mirror. Lack of space prevents me from analyzing it or even from elucidating such interesting particulars as the sentence "I am thy God, not the betrayer's God," which should be compared with the opening words of chapter 94.

In the end the antitheses are resolved in the harmony of the holy souls with Christ, the Lord of the mysteries, and the doxology is repeated, this time with the Holy Ghost. Then the Gnostic meaning of all that has been said is disclosed. The initiate—and it is only to the initiate that Christ speaks—must understand that the mystagogue was playing with the mystes (as the Zen master plays with his pupil). This godhead (for in the modalistic belief, God and Christ are one) behaves like Aion (Time) in Heraclitus: "Time is a child playing a game of draughts; the kingship is in the hands of a child."[65] The god hops and jumps and we are expected to guess the meaning of his actions. A model of romantic irony sixteen hundred years before romanticism!

As far as the rest of our text is concerned, I should like only to stress Christ's double crucifixion: John, the sole initiate, first sees how Christ is seemingly crucified, and then he flees. Everything *seems* to happen as in the Synoptic Gospels—Matthew 26 : 56: "Then all the disciples forsook him and fled."[66] But after the crucifixion there is a sudden shift of scene: "And my Lord stood in the midst of the cave and illumined it and spake." There has been no previous mention of any such cave. It is called σπήλαιον, like the grotto of Mithras, which is the image of the cosmos, through which the mystes must pass. In this connection I should also like to mention Porphyry's *De antro nympharum*.[67]

Christ then says: "John, for the multitude down in Jerusalem I am being crucified." But to John, "to him who has received God's grace," he says the words that the disciple must learn from the master and the man from God. And he shows him the implanted cross of light and the formless throng around it. The sole form is in the luminous cross itself. The initiates have entered into the godhead, fused with it. And the mystery god has no longer any outward form but only a voice. His "own," his faithful, that is, make up his form: he is their voice. This voice imparts to them the symbols, the marks

65 Freeman, *Ancilla*, p. 28 (B 52).
66 Also Mark 15 : 33, Matthew 27 : 45, Luke 23 : 44, and John 19 : 14.
67 [The author cites "5 c II 39," but the ref. is apparently in error.—ED.]

of recognition and passwords extending from "Logos" to "Grace," which we already know from the hymn, except four (bread, seed, resurrection, faith). Then Christ speaks to John as the initiate and explains the Cross to him. It is the axis of the world, "the vast elevation of the stable from the unstable, and the harmony of wisdom," the balance of perfection. It binds the world together as opposed to the demonic powers (of the left); it determines the place and direction. In the presence of this Gnostic cross of light, the wooden cross on Golgotha pales. The mystes has become God's own, he lives in interchange with him, he apprehends His essence. "Not as I have said I was but as thou, being akin to me, knowest me."

And again the divine voice is raised in a hymn:

> Thou hearest that I suffered but I suffered not.
> An unsuffering one was I and I suffered.
> A transfixed one was I and yet not maltreated.
> Hanged was I and yet not hanged.
> Blood flowed from me and yet did not flow.
> Understand this riddle:
> Know me then as the praise of the Logos,
> The transfixing of the Logos, the Blood of the Logos,
> The wound of the Logos, the hanging of the Logos,
> The suffering of the Logos, the impaling of the Logos,
> The death of the Logos.

Apprehend the meaning, then you will know God—and thence you will know man.

Hans Leisegang

The Mystery of the Serpent

The alabaster bowl which is the starting point of the following inquiry and discussion belonged to a private collection in Leipzig at the time when I first saw it. Some eighty-seven years ago, the owner's grandfather had brought it back from his travels somewhere in the Mediterranean region. This is all that was known of its origin.

[Pl. I–II]   Dr. Ernst Bux put photographs of the well-preserved bowl at my disposal about 1929, as a basis for an inquiry into the meaning of its figures and the cult ritual which they obviously represent. In the course of time I managed to discover and collect considerable material which seemed to have a bearing on the subject; little by little it took form, casting the most surprising light on the ancient mystery cults and their echoes in the Christian world, and suggesting hitherto unsuspected connections.

In 1931, Hans Lamer called attention to this bowl in the *Philologische Wochenschrift;*[1] he gave a description of it but was unable to say anything of its meaning and purpose. He merely wrote: "Inside and outside it is abundantly ornamented with figures such as I have never encountered elsewhere; all others, including specialists, who have seen the piece have characterized it as absolutely unique."[2]

1 Berlin and Leipzig; no. 21 (May 23, 1931), pars. 653–56.
2 He added, however: "This was a mistake; later Ernst Bux was kind enough to show me a parallel in a bowl from the Pietroasa treasure, easily accessible in Ludwig Wolff's *Die Helden der Völkerwanderungszeit* (Jena, 1928); on the plate following p. 48 it is the bowl with the seated figure in the center. The similarity in the arrangement of the figures is striking. This parallel makes possible an approximate dating of our bowl, which is fully confirmed by the character of the letters in the inscription. This explodes most of the interpretations that more or less qualified persons have given the owner; although emanating from an authority, the notion that the bowl is Etruscan is the most absurd of all." The actual relation between our bowl and the sacrificial bowl from the Pietroasa treasure will be taken up in the last part of our inquiry. [Cf. PL. IX–XI.]

194

When my work was virtually complete and in large part committed to writing, I learned that meanwhile, shortly before the death of the owner, the bowl had been sold to Dr. J. Hirsch in Geneva, now in Paris,[3] and that the *Journal of Hellenic Studies*[4] had published an article on it, accompanied by excellent reproductions. Comparison of this article with my work revealed agreement on most points and disagreement on others. The description of the object, this "isolated phenomenon [that] defies classification,"[5] is excellent; I have only praise for the archaeological tests, employing mineralogical and chemical analysis and ultra-violet radiation, which provide new proofs of the bowl's authenticity, and I welcome the whole as a valuable complement to my own work.

But all this fails to throw light on the religious significance of this unique piece, and so far no satisfactory answer has been given to the essential questions: What do the figures adorning the bowl mean? What cult did it serve? And above all, in what religious atmosphere did it come into being? In seeking to answer these questions I had traveled other and longer roads, in the course of which I had gathered together the material which now presents itself as a unified picture. And it would indeed seem to be in keeping with the principle of collaboration among the sciences that after the archaeologists have spoken and laid the foundation, a student of religions, specializing in the Hellenistic mysteries, should make his contribution toward an explanation of this "unique representation of a cultic scene, a δρώμενον of the jealously hidden Orphic mysteries."[6]

The inside of the bowl, which first attracts our attention, has at the center [Pl. I] a winged snake—one wing is broken off—twined around an egg-shaped omphalos resting on a somewhat broader base. At its upper edge this base has radiate spikes and at its lower edge tongues of flame, so that the snake is surrounded by a double ring of rays. Delbrueck and Vollgraff[7] regard it as an open blossom with four interlocking rings of petals: the first is attached to the center and double, the second and third surround the center, and the fourth and outermost consists of long, pointed petals, visible only between the figures and extending almost to the rim of the bowl. But since the

3 [And now in New York, as is the bowl. Dr. Hirsch kindly furnished our photographs of it. —ED.]
4 R. Delbrueck and W. Vollgraff, in LIV (1934), 129–39 (London).
5 Ibid., 136.
6 Ibid.
7 Ibid., 131.

authors interpret the blossom as a sunflower and symbol of the sun[8] with the petals representing the rays of the sun, it is immaterial whether the wreath is composed of stylized tongues of flame or of petals. It signifies in either case the flaming light of the sun.

From the petals or flames surrounding the center, sixteen nude figures rise almost to the upper edge of the bowl. Seven are men and nine women. Four of the men wear beards. Men and women do not alternate regularly, but there are three pairs of women and one pair of men, in the following order: m-f-f-m-f-m-m-f-m-f-f-m-f-m-f-f.

All have their eyes turned toward the serpent. All hold one hand over the breast; as for the other hand, some of the women hold it over or near the pudendum; some of the figures hold it straight down, others raise it to head level, the palm turned toward the snake in supplication or worship.

On the physical type of these figures, Delbrueck and Vollgraff[9] remark that it seems un-Greek and none too spiritual. They have thin legs and stout torsos; the necks are invisible, the heads are oval with slanting, vulgar profiles, straight mouths, and weak chins. The breasts of the women are large and flat. The hair of the men resembles a flat cap, appearing to be cut at shoulder length, clipped around the edges. The old, bearded men have bare foreheads. The women have their hair parted, suggesting that it is done up in a knot behind. "The type is not Egyptian but is rather comparable to several ivory carvings attributable to Syria or central Asia Minor."[10]

[*Pl. II, above*] On the outside we find four winged figurines with little trumpets or shells, situated at regular intervals so as to mark corners; these Lamer inter-

8 Ibid., 136. From the earliest times the sun has been represented in Europe and the Orient in the form of an open blossom. Cf. further G. Contenau, *Manuel d'archéologie orientale* (Paris, 1927–47), Vol. II, 805, fig. 563; Sir Arthur Evans, *The Palace of Minos at Knossos* (London, 1921–36), Vol. I, p. 478, fig. 342b; p. 479, fig. 343; p. 514, fig. 371; D. G. Hogarth, *Journal of Hellenic Studies* (1902), p. 334 and pl. 12; E. Reisinger, *Kretische Vasenmalerei* (Berlin and Leipzig, 1912), Vol. II, p. 13, with incorrect interpretation. A particularly striking parallel is provided by the sunflower on the lintel of the temple of Sia in Hauran (Syria), dated between 37 and 32 B.C. An immediate parallel from the Dionysian mysteries is to be found in the Attic vase painting in Roscher, *Lexikon*, I, 2, 1998, reproduced and interpreted by Robert Eisler in *Orphisch-Dionysische Mysteriengedanken in der christlichen Antike* (Berlin and Leipzig, 1925), p. 372. Here the head of Helios appears in the same double wreath of petals as we see surrounding the snake on the bowl.

9 Loc. cit., 132.

10 Ibid., 136; e.g., the Andrews Diptych. R. Delbrueck, *Die Consulardiptychen und verwandte Denkmäler* (Berlin and Leipzig, 1929), N 70.

prets as wind gods, Delbrueck and Vollgraff as cupids. Since they are sculptured in the round and stand out from the rim of the bowl, they have been
damaged, and here and there an arm or leg is missing.

Between them, round the bowl, runs an arcade of twenty-four pillars
with semicircular arches in high relief; four more are hidden behind the
figures. Lamer points out a parallel to the bowl in Leonid Matzulewitsch,
Byzantinische Antike,[11] which has similar columns and dates from the year
343. Delbrueck and Vollgraff point out that beginning in the third century
the motif was commonly used in corners for mosaics both in architecture
and small pieces.

Around the outer edge runs an inscription in raised letters, divided into
four sections by the four figures; the style of the letters points to late
antiquity.[12] This inscription must be the starting point for our interpretation of the figures and of the pupose which this strange work of art was
meant to serve, for it is through the words that the stone speaks to us
most directly.

[Pl. II, below]

1. *The Inscription*

The text, beginning with one of the winged figures and reading round the
bowl, presents this picture:

[1] κεκλυθι τηλεπρου δινης ελικαυγεα κυκ
[2] ουρανος τε γαια τε ην μορφη μια
[3] θεοι ουνεκα δινει κατ απειρουα μακρον —
[4] Ολυμπον αγλαε Ζευ κοσμο γεννητο

Here we have verses in which

1. certain words are incomplete: κυκ[λον], δινει[ται], κοσμο[υ],
γεννητο[ρ];

2. others are written incorrectly: τηλεπρου instead of τηλεπορου,
απειρουα instead of απειρονα;

11 Leipzig, 1929; pl. 24.
12 Lamer, par. 654: size of the letters, 6 mm.; character of script definitely late, e.g., OY
joined, C for S; other elements cannot easily be rendered here in print. Delbrueck and
Vollgraff, p. 136: The shapes of the letters may theoretically offer a means of dating,
but this method must be applied with caution, because so few photographs or good
drawings of late inscriptions have been published. It may be an accident that similar
writing seems to appear most frequently in the northern and central Near East, where
similar uncial script with just such separate letters is common precisely between the
3rd and 6th cents.; e.g., *Princeton University Expeditions to Syria* (Leiden, 1908–22),
III, n. 763, 765 (Kanawat, Leathen); 813 (A.D. 605); 842 (A.D. 598/9), etc.

3. the last is incomplete; and

4. there is no mutual connection.

If we write the text so as to make each verse occupy a line, fill in the gaps, and correct the obvious mistakes, we obtain the following picture:

[1] κέκλυϑι τηλεπόρου δίνης ἑλικαύγεα κύκλον
[2] οὐρανός τε γαῖά τε ἦν μορφῇ μία ϑεοί
[3] οὕνεκα δινεῖται κατ' ἀπείρονα μακρὸν Ὄλυμπον
[4] ἀγλαὲ Ζεῦ, κόσμου γεννῆτορ – ◡ ◡ – ◡.

Damaged and destroyed letters cannot account for the mistakes and lacunae in this version. It represents the first of the riddles in which our bowl abounds. The false or incomplete shaping of certain letters might be explained by the theory that the artist, knowing no Greek, read his employer's copy incorrectly. Delbrueck and Vollgraff[1] explain the absence of the last letters in the sections—κυκ[λον] and γεννητο[ρ]—by the hypothesis that the bowl was a copy of a metal prototype composed of two separate parts, the inner bowl proper, the *phiale*, and a container consisting of the arcades with the four figures. The figures were soldered to the metal container, so that certain letters of the inscription were covered over; the stonecutter did not see them and consequently omitted them. The remaining errors are ascribed to lack of care in copying the inscription on the model. Thus in απειρουα, ου is written for ου, and in κοσμο conversely ο for ου. τηλεπρου instead of τηλεπόρου cannot be a mistake in hearing, for it is precisely the accented, stressed letter that is lacking. Perhaps in the model a small ο was written within the π.

But more important than these mistakes, which can be explained on the basis of technical deficiencies, is the lack of connection between the separate verses or sections of the inscription: even after the mistakes are corrected, the inscription is unintelligible. How shall we account for this? Lamer writes: "The idea of a forgery comes to mind; but it is not too likely. The bowl is not, to be sure, a work of art, but with its many figures in high relief, almost sculptured in the round, it represents a very painstaking effort. With such a work, a forger would not have aimed to take in an average purchaser, but only one who could pay extremely well. Even supposing that he could not read his text . . . on a memorandum (such as the abbreviation for δινεῖται), he would presumably have inquired and not discredited

1 Loc. cit., 134f. and 129.

a piece of work promising such good pay by chiseling so absurd an inscription into it. A work expected to sell for a high price is, after all, carefully examined. . . . Moreover, it is almost inconceivable that an ancient purchaser would have accepted such nonsense from a stonecutter."² We might also suppose that the sculptor worked from a model containing a number of connected verses, perhaps a whole poem, but that he did not find room for them on the bowl and consequently—perhaps on instructions from the purchaser himself—selected four verses and chiseled in as much of them as the space permitted. The users of the bowl were expected to have sufficient knowledge of poetry to fill in the gaps for themselves and restore the context. Surely a startling procedure and a bold hypothesis, but it is justified by the fact that we possess fragments of a poem in which two of these verses and two other words occur in a broader, meaningful context.

In his *Saturnalia*, Macrobius quotes two connected fragments of an Orphic hymn, each of which contains a line from our inscription. The first he quotes in seeking to prove that Dionysus meant, among other things, the "sun" and was a sun god:³

> And we hear that, also in Thrace, Sol [Helios] and Liber [Dionysus] are held to be the same whom they call Sabazius and worship with a magnificent cult, as Alexander writes: on the hill of Zilmissos there is a temple consecrated to this god; it is round in shape and its roof is open at the middle. The roundness is an allusion to the shape of the star, and through the top of the roof the light enters, by way of showing that the sun, shining from the uppermost summit, purifies all things with its light, and because when it rises the universe opens to view. Also Orpheus, when he wishes the sun to be understood [as Dionysus] says among other things:

> Melting the glittering ether that had previously been motionless, he appeared, a glorious sight to the gods,

2 Lamer, loc. cit., par. 655.
3 Macrobius, *Saturnalia*, Lib. I, cap. xviii, 12–15, and xxiii, 22:

Item in Thracia eundem haberi solem atque Liberum accipimus, quem illi Sebadium [Sabazium] nuncupantes magnifica religione celebrant, ut Alexander scribit: eique deo in colle Zilmisso aedes dicata est specie rotunda, cuius medium interpatet tectum. Rotunditas aedis monstrat huiusce sideris speciem, summoque tecto lumen admittitur, ut appareat solem cuncta vertice summo lustrare lucis inmissu, et quia oriente eo universa patefiunt. Orpheus quoque solem volens intellegi ait inter cetera:

Τήκων αἰθέρα δῖον, ἀκίνητον πρὶν ἐόντα,
ἐξανέφηνε θεοῖσιν ὁρᾶν κάλλιστον ἰδέσθαι,

199

he whom we now call Phanes and Dionysus,
Eubuleus the commander and Antauges the excellent.
Others among mortal men call him otherwise.
When he first came to light, he was called Dionysus,
because *he moves in a circle round the infinite broad Olympus.*
He has his name from the movement, and various designations
according to the hour in the passage of time.

He called the sun Phanes from φῶς and φανερός, that is, from,
"light" and "illumination," because it is visible to all and sees all;
Dionysus, as the Prophet himself says, from δινεῖσθαι and περιφέρεσθαι, because it moves in a circle. Whence Cleanthes writes
that he received this surname from διανύσαι ["accomplish," particularly a journey], because in daily circuit from east to west,
bringing forth night and day, it accomplishes the circuit of the
heavens. The physicists called Dionysus the spirit of Zeus because
the sun is the spirit of the cosmos, but the cosmos is named heaven,
which they call Jupiter.

These remarks of Macrobius are a part of his comprehensive demonstration that not only Saturn and the corresponding Cronus of the Greeks
signify the sun, but that the Roman Janus and likewise Liber and Dionysus,
Apollo, Asclepius, and Zeus are actually sun gods and are all connected with
one another. He concludes by saying that the sun is the supreme cosmic
divine power, and in support of this he cites the second fragment of the
Orphic poem, which contains another part of our inscription:[4]

The theologians in general believe that the power of the sun is
the summit of all forces, and they prove this in their sacred rites
by saying the short prayer: All-powerful Helios, spirit of the cos-

ὃν δὴ νῦν καλέουσι Φάνητά τε καὶ Διόνυσον
Εὐβουλῆά τ'ἄνακτα καὶ 'Ανταύγην ἀρίδηλον.
ἄλλοι δ'ἄλλο καλοῦσιν ἐπιχθονίων ἀνθρώπων.
Πρῶτος δ'ἐς φάος ἦλθε, Διόνυσος δ'ἐπεκλήθη,
οὕνεκα δινεῖται κατ' ἀπείρονα μακρὸν "Ολυμπον.
ἀλλαχθεὶς δ'ὄνομ' ἔσχε, προσωνυμίας πρὸς ἕκαστον
παντοδαπὰς κατὰ καιρὸν ἀμειβομένοιο χρόνοιο.

Φάνητα dixit solem ἀπὸ τοῦ φωτὸς καὶ φανεροῦ, id est a lumine atque inlumina-
tione, quia cunctis visitur cuncta conspiciens: Διόνυσον, ut ipse vates ait, ἀπὸ τοῦ
δινεῖσθαι καὶ περιφέρεσθαι, id est quod circumferatur in ambitum. Unde Cleanthes
ita cognominatum scribit ἀπὸ τοῦ διανύσαι quia cotidiano impetu ab oriente ad oc-
casum diem noctemque faciendo caeli conficit cursum. Physici Διόνυσον Διὸς νοῦν,
quia solem mundi mentem esse dixerunt: mundus autem vocatur caelum, quod appel-
lant Iovem.

4 Postremo potentiam solis ad omnium potestatum summitatem referri iudicant theologi,
qui in sacris hoc brevissima precatione demonstrant dicentes: "Ηλιε παντοκράτορ,

The alabaster "serpent bowl": interior

The alabaster "serpent bowl"

Above, one of the winged trumpeters;
below, part of the arcade and inscription (line 2)

Phanes in the egg. Relief, Modena

III

Helios as Aeon, with earth goddess. Mosaic, Sentinum

mos, force of the cosmos, light of the cosmos. And Orpheus too attests that the sun is all by the following verses:

*Hear, thou who turnest forever the radiant sphere
of distant motion* that runs round the celestial vortices,
glittering Zeus, Dionysus, father of the sea, father of the earth,
sun, all-engendering, all-moving, flaming with gold.

The passage in Macrobius tells us that our inscription consists of corrupt verses from an Orphic poem, probably one of the Βακχικά, among which Rohde and following him Kern[5] classify both fragments preserved in Macrobius. The parts of the inscription can consequently be explained by these Orphic fragments, and where these do not suffice, from other Orphic literature, since we may for the present assume that they originated in the same atmosphere.

I

The first line of the inscription

κεκλυϑι τηλεπρου δινης ελικαυγεα κυκ

contains an invocation. The verb to which ἐλικαύγεα κύκλον refers, and all the rest of the clause, can be filled in from the Orphic fragment, so that we obtain the following:

Κέκλυϑι τηλεπόρου δίνης ἑλικαύγεα κύκ[λον
οὐρανίαις στροφάλιγξι περίδρομον αἰὲν ἑλίσσων].

Hear, thou who [turnest forever] the radiant sphere
of distant motion [that runs round the celestial vortices].

This is an invocation of the celestial force which moves the outermost sphere encompassing all the other spheres of heaven. This celestial force, as the following verses cited by Macrobius indicate, is designated by the names of Zeus, Dionysus, and Helios. It follows from the text that this is

---

κόσμου πνεῦμα, κόσμου δύναμις, κόσμου φῶς. Solem esse omnia et Orpheus testatur his versibus:

Κέκλυϑι τηλεπόρου δίνης ἑλικαύγεα κύκλον
οὐρανίαις στροφάλιγξι περίδρομον αἰὲν ἑλίσσων,
ἀγλαὲ Ζεῦ Διόνυσε, πάτερ πόντου, πάτερ αἴης,
ἥλιε παγγενέτορ πανταίολε χρυσεοφεγγές.

5 Otto Kern, ed., *Orphicorum fragmenta* (Berlin, 1922), 236 and 237, p. 249. [Hereafter abbreviated *OF*.]

not the sun of scientific Greek astronomy, which is one of the seven planets, occupying the central position in the series: Moon, Mercury, Venus, Sun, Mars, Jupiter, Saturn; for the text speaks of the "distant" motion which embraces all the other heavenly spheres. This distant sphere, which encompasses the actual heavens with the planets and their orbits, is here the sphere of Helios and at the same time of Zeus-Dionysus who created and engendered all things out of himself. Thus we have to do with a cosmology different from the Ptolemaic system or its precursors. Side by side with the scientific cosmology of the Greeks there was another in which the sphere of the sun surrounded the whole starry firmament, as is perhaps most clearly attested by the Emperor Julian's great invocation of King Helios. Julian distinguished the hypotheses of the mystery theology from the theories based on observation of heavenly phenomena. According to ancient tradition, it was Orpheus who not only introduced the mysteries but also created a theology and physiology of the mysteries. Concerning the position of the sun in the cosmology of the mysteries, Julian wrote:

Some say then, even though all men are not ready to believe it, that the sun travels in the starless heavens far above the region of the fixed stars. And on this theory he will not be stationed midmost among the planets but midway between the three worlds: that is, according to the hypothesis of the mysteries, if indeed one ought to use the word "hypothesis" [κατὰ τὰς τελεστικὰς ὑποθέσεις] and not rather say "established truths" [δόγματα], using the word "hypothesis" for the study of the heavenly bodies. For the priests of the mysteries tell us what they have been taught by the gods or mighty daemons, whereas the astronomers make plausible hypotheses from the harmony that they observe in the visible spheres. It is proper, no doubt, to approve the astronomers as well, but where any man thinks it better to believe the priests of the mysteries, him I admire and revere, both in jest and earnest. And so much for that, as the saying is.

Now besides those whom I have mentioned, there is in the heavens a great multitude of gods who have been recognized as such by those who survey the heavens, not casually, nor like cattle. For as he divides the three spheres by four through the zodiac, which is associated with every one of the three, so he divides the zodiac also into twelve divine powers; and again he divides every one of these twelve by three, so as to make thirty-six gods in all. Hence, as I believe, there descends from above, from the heavens to us, a threefold gift of the Graces: I mean from the spheres, for this god, by thus dividing them by four, sends to us the fourfold glory of the seasons, which express the changes of time. And indeed on our earth the Graces imitate a circle [There is a play on the word κύκλος, which means both "sphere" and "circle"] in their statues. And it is Dionysus who is the giver of the Graces, and in this very connection he is said to reign with Helios.[6]

Here again we find the identification of Dionysus and Helios. But for Julian, Helios also coincides with Zeus,[7] so that we have here the same doctrine as in the fragments of the Orphic hymn preserved in Macrobius.[8] It is to this Helios-Zeus-Dionysus that the invocation in our inscription is addressed.

II

The second line

[Pl. II,
below]

ουρανος τε γαια τε ην μορφη μια
(Heaven and earth were one form)

is not connected by any chain of ideas with the first. It is a verse by itself and is not to be found in Macrobius' fragments of the Orphic poem. But I have discovered the same line word for word—except that the line is transformed into six iambi by the omission of one letter and the addition of a monosyllable—in a fragment from Euripides' tragedy *The Wise Melanippe*. Here it occurs in the following context:

κοὐκ ἐμὸς ὁ μῦθος, ἀλλ' ἐμῆς μητρὸς πάρα,
ὡς οὐρανός τε γαῖά τ'ἦν μορφὴ μία.
ἐπεὶ δ'ἐχωρίσθησαν ἀλλήλων δίχα,
τίκτουσι πάντα κἀνέδωκαν εἰς φάος,
δένδρα, πετεινά, θῆρας οὓς θ'ἅλμη τρέφει
γένος τε θνητῶν.

(And it is not my myth but that of my mother, that heaven and earth were one form; then they were separated from one another, they engendered and bore [both τίκτουσι in the Greek] all things and brought to light plants, birds, animals, and the creatures nourished by the sea water, and the race of mortals.)[9]

6 Julian the Apostate, *Oratio* IV, 148 A ff. (tr. Wilmer Cave Wright, LCL, 1913–23, Vol. I, pp. 405–7).

7 Ibid., 136 (p. 369) "Helios and Zeus have a joint or rather a single sovereignty." 144 C (p. 393): "equal and identical dominion of Helios and Zeus."

8 The above-quoted passages from Macrobius can likewise only be understood if the outermost sphere, the summit (*summitas*) of heaven, is assigned to the sun.

9 *Tragicorum Graecorum fragmenta*, ed. Nauck, 2nd edn., No. 484, p. 501.

203

Hermann Diels included these verses of Euripides among the fragments of the philosopher Anaxagoras.[10] What led him to do so was the remarks in which both Diodorus and the author of the *Ars rhetorica* (erroneously imputed to Dionysius of Halicarnassus) speak of them as quotations.[11]

Diodorus omits the first line—"And it is not my myth but that of my mother"—and uses the others as an effective conclusion to that chapter in his "Historical Library" which deals with the creation of the world and begins with the words:

> In the original state of the cosmos heaven and earth had one form since their essence was mixed; but then the bodies separated and the cosmos took on the whole order that is visible in it.[12]

The entire chapter, which is an elaboration of the teachings of Democritus,[13] consists in a detailed discussion of these ideas, from the separation of the elements out of the original mixture to the genesis of man. It concludes with these words:

> Concerning the nature of the universe the above does not appear to be contradicted by Euripides, who was a pupil of the physicist Anaxagoras; for in his Melanippe he espouses the view that heaven and earth were one form. . . .[14]

It should be plain to anyone familiar with the ideas and style of Democritus and Anaxagoras that what Euripides says in these verses about the generation of Uranus and Gaea[15] is not quite compatible with the purely physical concepts and ideas of those philosophers. The related tradition

10 Diels-Kranz, Anaxagoras fr. A 59 (Vol. II, p. 21).
11 Diodorus Siculus, *Historica bibliotheca*, I 7, 7; Dionysius of Halicarnassus, *Ars rhetorica*, IX, 10.
12 Κατὰ γὰρ τὴν ἐξ ἀρχῆς τῶν ὅλων σύστασιν μίαν ἔχειν ἰδέαν οὐρανόν τε καὶ γῆν, μεμιγμένης αὐτῶν τῆς φύσεως. μετὰ δὲ ταῦτα διαστάντων τῶν σωμάτων ἀπ'ἀλλήλων τὸν μὲν κόσμον περιλαβεῖν ἅπασαν τὴν ὁρωμένην ἐν αὐτῷ σύνταξιν.
13 On the basis of the research in Karl Reinhardt, "Hekataios von Abdera und Demokrit," *Hermes* (Berlin), XLVII (1912), 497ff., the whole chapter, with the exception of the allusion to the verses of Euripides and of the verses themselves, has now been included among the fragments of Democritus (Diels-Kranz, 68 B 5).
14 Ἔοικε δὲ περὶ τῆς τῶν ὅλων φύσεως οὐδ' Εὐριπίδης διαφωνεῖν τοῖς προειρημένοις, μαθητὴς ὢν Ἀναξαγόρου τοῦ φυσικοῦ, ἐν γὰρ τῇ Μελανίππῃ τίθησιν οὕτως, ὡς οὐρανός τε γαῖά τ'ἦν μορφὴ μία κτλ.
15 Concerning the marriage of heaven and earth as motif of mystery theology, see the abundance of material in R. Eisler, *Weltenmantel und Himmelszelt* (Munich, 1910), Vol. II, pp. 551ff., and my book *Die Gnosis* (Leipzig, 1924; 2nd edn., 1936), pp. 93ff.

shows that one cannot understand the verses by merely noting that Euripides was the pupil and friend of Anaxagoras.

The author of the *Ars rhetorica*, which was attributed to Dionysius of Halicarnassus, points out that these verses of the wise Melanippe open with the words "And it is not my myth but that of my mother."[16] He believed that Euripides put these words into the mouth of Melanippe to account for the extent of her philosophical education. He gives her a philosophical mother "lest her philosophy seem improbable." Moreover, he points out, one should consider that there are two philosophies set forth in this drama, that of the poet and that of his dramatic figure Melanippe. The two are not the same. Euripides associated with Anaxagoras. It is his doctrine (*logos*) that all things were together but were later differentiated.[17] Afterwards, the passage continues, he was with Socrates and carried on difficult investigations. Through the words of Melanippe he gave his support to the old doctrine (τὴν διδασκαλίαν τὴν ἀρχαίαν).

These remarks have been understood to imply that the ἀρχαία διδασκαλία was that of Anaxagoras and that the verses of Euripides, which he puts into the mouth of his wise Melanippe, contained the doctrine of Anaxagoras. According to this interpretation, Euripides had gone through a philosophical development taking him from the older philosophy of Anaxagoras to the newer doctrines of Socrates, but he had made Melanippe defend his earlier, his "old" standpoint. Not Euripides, but his Melanippe, would then be the spokesman for the philosophy of Anaxagoras.

But all this does not quite fit in with the verses of Euripides as they have come down to us. In the first place, Anaxagoras' doctrine that "all things were together" is different from what the verse expresses: "Heaven and earth were one form." Anaxagoras worked with abstract concepts, while here we have concrete entities: heaven, earth, form. Also, Melanippe explicitly in-

16 *Ars rhet.*, IX, 11: ἡ Μελανίππη σοφή, τὸ δρᾶμα Εὐριπίδου, ἐπιγέγραπται μὲν Σοφή, ὅτι φιλοσοφεῖ, καὶ διὰ τοῦτο τοιαύτης μητρός ἐστιν, ἵνα μὴ ἀπίθανος ᾖ ἡ φιλοσοφία. ἔχει δὲ διπλοῦν σχῆμα, τὸ μὲν τοῦ ποιητοῦ τοιόνδε, τὸ δὲ τοῦ προσώπου τοιόνδε. 'Αναξαγόρα προσεφοίτησεν Εὐριπίδης, 'Αναξαγόρου δὲ λόγος ἐστίν, ὅτι "Πάντα ἐν πᾶσιν εἶτα ὕστερον διεκρίθη," μετὰ ταῦτα ὡμίλησε καὶ Σωκράτε, καὶ ἐπὶ τὸ ἀπορώτερον ἤγαγε τὸν λόγον. ὁμολογεῖ οὖν τὴν διδασκαλίαν τὴν ἀρχαίαν διὰ τῆς Μελανίππης.

Καὶ οὐκ ἐμὸς ὁ μῦθος... κτλ.

17 Cf. Anaxagoras fr. B 12: "for in everything there is a portion of everything"; 6: "in everything there must be everything"; 4: "Before these things were separated off, all things were together." (Freeman, *Ancilla*, pp. 83–84.)

vokes the authority of her mother, from whom she received no scientific physical *logos*, but a *mythos*, and the content of the verses dealing with Uranus and Gaea, who engender and bear all living creatures, is entirely mythical and is related to the physical theory of mixture from which the elements are differentiated, only to the extent that in both cases a multiplicity issues from an original unity. If this myth embodied the doctrine of Anaxagoras, the wise Melanippe's mother, representing the older generation, must have been a pupil of Anaxagoras. Yet this can scarcely be what Euripides meant when he made Melanippe say that this was not her myth but one she had learned from her mother. It is possible, however, that Melanippe's mother was familiar with an Orphic myth, since women were admitted to the Orphic mysteries. The term ἀρχαία διδασκαλία would suggest the archaic wisdom of the mysteries. The passage in the *Ars rhetorica* may possibly go back to a more extensive source which the author hastily excerpted and failed to understand. It is also possible that Anaxagoras, like most of the pre-Socratic philosophers,[18] reinterpreted the old myths in terms of physics. Moreover, the Orphic theologians were themselves "physicists" or "physiologists," who transmuted the mythical gods into the elements and forces of the cosmos. It can be shown that the half-mythical, half-physical doctrine that heaven and earth were originally one form but were then separated from one another was part of the Orphic cosmogony and theogony. In his *Argonautica*, Apollonius Rhodius explicitly puts this conception, expressed in the same terms, into the mouth of Orpheus:

> . . . and Orpheus lifted his lyre in his left hand and made essay to sing. He sang how the earth, the heaven, and the sea, once mingled together in one form, after deadly strife were separated each from other. . . . [19]

It is true that, in the last line, strife (νεῖκος) is the cause of the separation and that this discloses the influence of Empedocles. But this does not argue

18 See my article, "Griechische Philosophie als Mysterion," *Philologische Wochenschrift* (Berlin), no. 35–38 (1932; Festschrift to F. Poland), 245ff.
19 I 494 = *OF* 29:

ἂν δὲ καὶ 'Ορφεὺς
λαιῇ ἀνασχόμενος κίθαριν πείραζεν ἀοιδῆς.
ἤειδεν δ' ὡς γαῖα καὶ οὐρανὸς ἠδὲ θάλασσα,
τὸ πρὶν ἐπ' ἀλλήλοισι μιῇ συναρηρότα μορφῇ,
νεῖκεος ἐξ ὀλοοῖο διέκριθεν ἀμφὶς ἕκαστα.

(Tr. R. C. Seaton, in Apollonius Rhodius, *Argonautica*, Vol. I, ll. 494ff., LCL, 1912, p. 36.)

against the Orphic origin of the first lines, or even of the last for that matter, since Empedocles himself took so much from Orphic sources.[20] The fact that these words attributed to Orpheus were quoted by so early a writer as Euripides is in any event a proof of their antiquity. The learned Tzetzes quotes these verses from Euripides' *Melanippe* with the remark: "As Orpheus the ancient says, and Hesiod, and with them Empedocles of Acragas, and Anaxagoras of Clazomenae, and Euripides, his pupil, who wrote the iambics I have just quoted."[21]

In view of all this, there can be no doubt that this line of our inscription is also an Orphic verse, presumably from the same Orphic hymn which is quoted by Macrobius and to which the other lines of the inscription belong. Since this verse was already known to Euripides, it must have been of ancient origin, an authentic fragment of the Orphic cosmogony. If we assume—and it is scarcely possible to do otherwise—that the verses of our inscription come from one and the same poem, the inscription itself proves that the two fragments quoted by Macrobius are actually, as his editors presume, parts of the same hymn and that this hymn, since it was known to Euripides himself, was an ancient and authentic Orphic work.

Now we are in a position to determine not only the source of this line in the inscription, but also its meaning and the school of thought to which it belonged. Among the many versions of the Orphic cosmogony, it is perhaps that transmitted by Athenagoras which best elucidates the conception to which it refers:

> For, according to him [Orpheus], water was the beginning of everything. From water mud was formed; and from these an animal was produced, a dragon that had on it a lion's head and a bull's head, and in between the face of a god. It was called Herakles and Chronos. This Herakles gave birth to an enormous egg, which through the power of its father got bigger and bigger and by friction was burst into two. The top part came to be the Heaven [Uranus]; the lower became Earth [Gaea].[22]

A biform god also came forth, who was Phanes, the Glittering One.

20 See the examples collected by Kern in *OF* 29, pp. 90 and 91.
21 *Exegesis in Iliad.* (ed. Hermann), 41, 21: Καθὰ φησὶν Ὀρφεύς τε ὁ παλαιὸς καὶ Ἡσίοδος, Ἐμπεδοκλῆς τε σὺν αὐτοῖς ὁ Ἀκραγαντῖνος καὶ Ἀναξαγόρας ὁ Κλαζομένιος καὶ ὁ τοῦ Ἀναξαγόρου τουτοῦ μαθητὴς Εὐριπίδης, οὕτινός εἰσιν ἔπη καὶ οἱ τανῦν ἐκτεθέντες μοι ἴαμβοι.
22 *Pro Christianis*, 18 = *OF* 57f. (Tr. C.C. Richardson, "A Plea Regarding Christians by Athenagoras the Philosopher," in *Early Christian Fathers*, Library of Christian Classics, Vol. I, ed. Richardson and others, London and New York, 1953, p. 316.)

And now let us consider a parallel passage in Damascius, omitting, however, the Neoplatonic schema of triads into which he tries to squeeze the Orphic theogony: "It is a serpent having the heads of a bull and a lion, with the face of a god in between; this god has wings; he is called Ageless Chronos or Unchanging Herakles. . . . This Chronos produced an egg." This egg contained male and female nature and all the many seeds; it contained also "an incorporeal [or, according to another reading, biform] god with golden wings on his shoulders and bulls' heads grown to his flanks. On his head he has a huge changing snake." In the Orphic theology he is celebrated as "Protogonos [first-born] and as Zeus the marshaler of all things and the whole cosmos, whence he is called Pan."[23]

"Heaven and earth were one form," says the inscription. This one form was the cosmic egg here described, which the serpent Chronos-Herakles had created around him and burst with his immense strength, so that it fell into two separate halves, the heavens above him and the earth beneath him, while at the same time a new god, Phanes, appeared.

[Pl. III]   We can form a picture of this conception from the Modena relief of Phanes.[24]

23 *De primis principiis*, 123 bis (ed. C. A. Ruelle, Paris, 1889, Vol. I, p. 317, ll. 15ff.) = *OF* 54.

24 First recognized as such by C. Cavedoni, "Dichiarazione di un bassorilievo Mitriaco," in *Atti e memorie delle RR. deputazioni di storia patria per le provincie Modenesi e Parmensi*, Vol. I (Modena, 1863) pp. 1ff., containing a lithographic reproduction of a drawing. It was described by F. Cumont, in his "Notice sur deux bas-reliefs Mithraiques" in *Revue archéologique* (Paris), 3rd series, XL (1902) pp. 1ff., who classified it as a representation of Mithras but expressly recognized its relation to Orphic cosmogony (large reproduction after a photograph at the end of the *Revue* vol., pl. 1). Finally, Eisler, in *Weltenmantel und Himmelszelt*, II, 399ff., interpreted it as purely Orphic. This work contains a smaller reproduction of Cumont's illustration, p. 400, repr. 47, which appears in still smaller format in Eisler's *Orphisch-dionysische Mysteriengedanken in der christlichen Antike*, Vol. II, Pl. IV, fig. 28. K. Ziegler expressed agreement with him in "Menschen- und Weltenwerden," *Neue Jahrbücher für das klassische Altertum, Geschichte und Deutsche Literatur*, 16th Jhg. (Leipzig and Berlin, 1913), p. 562, and in Roscher's *Lexikon*, V, col. 1535; F. M. Cornford in *Greek Religious Thought from Homer to the Age of Alexander* (London, 1923), p. 56. Nevertheless, it is given as a representation of Mithras in the 3rd German edn. of Cumont (tr. Gehrlich), *Die Mysterien des Mithra* (1923), pl. 13, bringing forth a protest from Eisler in *Orphisch-dionysische Mysteriengedanken*, Vol. II, 3. The still legible original inscription "Euphrosyne et Felix," which was later effaced and replaced by "P[ecunia] P[osuit] Felix Pater [scil. sacrorum]," points to the Orphic cult, in which women not only were admitted but played a significant role, while the mysteries of Mithras, for which this cult image was later used after the inscription was changed, were open only to men. The form of the letters and the whole character of the sculpture led Cumont (tr. Gehrlich), p. 9, to date the work from the 2nd cent. A.D.

The artist endeavored to state the whole Orphic cosmogony upon a stone slab about 28½ inches high and 19½ inches wide. Successive events are represented side by side or one inside the other. The oval as a whole shows us the original state of the world as a great egg. "Heaven and earth," as our inscription says, "were one form." This egg, with the four winds blowing round it (their heads are visible in the four corners of the relief),[25] encompasses—in a germinal state, as it were—the whole cosmic development, first of all the split of the egg's "one form" into two parts, the future heaven and earth, which are represented as two facing hemispheres over and under the central figure. From the two hemispheres flames shoot upward, so that the god himself stands between flames and is born from them: a luminous being, Phanes the Radiant, the sun of the nascent world. His face, as Cumont remarks,[26] discloses the features of Helios. He bears the golden wings mentioned in our text. But he is associated also with the moon, whose sickle appears over his left shoulder; and he is the whole glittering heaven, as is indicated by the zodiac surrounding him. He is also the lightning, represented by a thunderbolt which he holds in his right hand, and which, along with the scepter on which his raised left hand rests, identifies him as Zeus. His feet end in cloven hoofs, showing that he is also Pan with the goat's feet and twofold form, half man and half beast, of whom Plato,[27] speaking of Orphic etymologies, said that he is called αἰπόλος, because he is forever revolving the cosmos (ἀεὶ πολῶν) and that he is twofold in nature, smooth above but below rough and goatlike. In this relief, Phanes appears within the zodiac; there are also several representations of Pan within the zodiac,[28] at least one of which we shall reproduce here by way of comparison.[29]

This Orphic Phanes, who combined in himself all the gods and cosmic

---

25 Cf. the ὑπηνέμιον ᾠόν in Aristophanes, *Birds*, 695 (*OF* 1, p. 80).
26 "Notice," p. 3: "*Le type du visage, encadré par une abondante chevelure, est manifestement inspiré par celui d'Hlios; mais il a pris une expression sévère et presque menaçante, qui rappelle la puissance destructive du Temps.*"
27 *Cratylus*, 408 B ff.; cf. my article "Logos" in Pauly-Wissowa, XIII (1926), 1065f., in which I have traced the motif down to Hippolytus, *Elenchos* V, 8, 34. Here he also appears turning the cosmos, as son of the All-Father and as the Logos.
28 Roscher, *Lexikon*, Vol. III, pt. 1, s.v. "Pan," and his article, "Pan als Allgott," *Festschrift für Johannes Overbeck* (Leipzig, 1893), pp. 56–72.
29 From Roscher, "Pan als Allgott," p. 64. Cut stone. A description of two similar gems in E. H. Tölken, *Erklärendes Verzeichnis der antiken vertieft geschnittenen Steine der Kgl. Preussischen Gemmensammlung* (Berlin, 1835), no. 1113: Pan in human form sits beside a tree, playing a double flute in the center of the zodiac; and no. 1114: the same, with the addition of seven gods' chariots as symbols of the seven planets.

forces we have mentioned, was of both sexes. He had two faces, one in front and one behind; he had male sexual parts in front, female behind.[30] The latter could not, of course, be shown in a relief.

In the relief, however, his whole form is four times encircled by the great serpent which, having brought forth the now broken egg, still connects the two halves, holding them together from without, its head resting on the upper half of the shell. The head of a lion hangs down from the serpent upon the breast of Phanes, illustrating the words of Athenagoras: "... a dragon [or serpent] with the head of a lion growing to it; and between the two—the dragon and the lion's head—was the face of a god." To the right and left,

Fig. 1. *Pan in the Zodiac*

over Phanes' loins, the heads of a ram or bull and of an ibex,[31] in any case heads belonging to signs of the zodiac, hang down from the serpent. Damascius, on the other hand, speaks only of bulls' heads appended to the flanks of the gold-winged god, or of the heads of a bull and of a lion that grow out of the serpent. In this case, the stone is more worthy of credence than the later report, which is possibly based on false interpretations and on incomplete memories of similar reliefs.

This serpent surrounded by the signs of the zodiac is obviously intended to represent the sun and its path; in the written accounts it is called Herakles and Chronos. According to an Orphic etymology, *Herakles* means the coiling

---

30 *OF* 76 (p. 152): τετράσιν ὀφθαλμοῖσιν δρώμενος ἔνθα καὶ ἔνθα. 80 (p. 154): τὸν Φάνητα εἰσφέρει αἰδοῖον ἔχοντα ὀπίσω περὶ τὴν πυγήν.
31 Proclus mentions these same beasts' heads in his description of Phanes; see *On Plato's Timaeus*, 30 CD = *OF* 81: διὸ καὶ ὁλικώτατον ζῷον ὁ θεολόγος ἀναπλάττει κρίου καὶ ταύρου καὶ λέοντος καὶ δρεάκοντος αὐτῷ περιτιθεὶς κεφαλάς.

serpent: δράκων ἑλικτός.³² And Chronos, according to Orphic teachings, is the true form of the primal god Cronus (Kronos), father of Zeus; he is the god of time, creator of the Aeon.³³

According to mythical or mystery thinking, the gods and cosmic forces represented here are not conceived merely as existing successively or side by side: they act upon one another and within one another. All are manifestations of a single god and of one and the same cosmos, which is this god himself with all the powers which he discharges but still encompasses; and these forces are the whole world with all its creatures and forms.

Now let us consider the portion of this Phanes relief immediately over the head of the god. It discloses a wreath of flame, the upper half of an egg, and the snake coiled around it, its head resting on the top of the egg.

These are the precise components of the middle section of the bowl: wreath of flames, egg-shaped omphalos, snake twined round it with its head upward. Here we have unquestionably an Orphic motif, which is also contained in the Phanes relief: it is the upper half of the cosmos, the heavens, with the celestial fire and the celestial serpent. The four winds which blow round the cosmic egg in the relief are also present on the bowl, where they constitute the four outside figures.

The Modena Phanes relief and the Orphic alabaster bowl are directly related. The two reveal the same set of conceptions and the same religious symbolism. The bowl shows a section of the picture represented in the Phanes relief. In the relief we see the whole cosmos in its development, while the bowl represents only its upper part: the upper half of the burst cosmic egg, the heavens, surrounded by the fire of life bursting from the egg and by the coils of the sun serpent. Here dwell the mystai, looking down upon the sun at their feet; cloaked in flames rising from below, they stand in supercelestial space at the upper part of the vault of heaven, removed from the whole earthly cosmos. They see the head of the sun serpent towering over the heavens, round which the serpent coils, connecting them, as the Phanes relief shows, with the lower half of the cosmic egg, the earth; holding the two together both from without and within, encompassing them, filling them with its life and its light, which are the life and light of this world.

In the course of the mystery rite, the mystai have been led "the upper way" (ὁδὸς ἄνω); they have attained to the supercelestial region (ὑπερουράνιος τόπος), like Parmenides hastening away from all things earthly in

³² OF 58. ³³ Orphic Hymn XIII, 5: Αἰῶνος κρόνε παγγενέτορ.

the chariot of the sun; like the "immortal souls" in Plato's *Phaedrus* "standing on the outside of heaven [ἐπὶ τῷ τοῦ οὐρανοῦ νότῳ]; and the revolution of the spheres carries them round, and they behold the things beyond";[34] and like the souls in the inscriptions on the golden medallions of Thurii, which were put into the graves of the Orphic dead, who "enter the wreath of heaven," who "from mortals become gods,"[35] and who call themselves "sons of the earth and the starry heavens."[36]

And there are parallels which confirm our observation that the mystai represented on the bowl are situated outside the earthly world. The sixteen figures on the sacrificial bowl from the Pietroasa Treasure also represent [Pl. mystai with the form and attributes of gods; the sixteen male and female figures on the Etruscan lamp with the Gorgon's head (= the sun) in the cen- [Pl. ter, are similarly creatures halfway between gods and men, male sileni and female bird demons; and the sixteen figures on the Christian ciborium from [Pl. Mt. Athos are angels performing the celestial liturgy.

All these cult objects situate us in supracelestial space; the Phanes relief, however, represents not only the cosmos floating in this space, but also its genesis out of the cosmic egg—the Orphic cosmogony, to which the words on the alabaster bowl also point: "Heaven and earth were one form." The separation had not yet taken place; all the cosmic forces were embodied in the great egg, which the primal serpent had brought forth from within itself. The next verses, supplied by the mind of the beholder, dealt with what followed, the genesis of the world, the separation of heaven and earth, and the appearance of Phanes-Zeus-Dionysus.

Here, however, the question arises: What connection is there between the ideas and conceptions suggested by our explanation of the first line of the inscription and those following from our interpretation of the second line?

34 *Phaedrus*, 247 C: στάσας δὲ αὐτὰς περιάγει ἡ περιφορά, αἱ δὲ θεωροῦσι τὰ ἔξω τοῦ οὐρανοῦ.
35 Diels-Kranz, fr. 1 (66) B 18, (Vol. I, p. 16). *OF* 32, pp. 106ff. Eisler, in *Orphisch-dionysische Mysteriengedanken*, p. 365, presumes for good reason that this referred not only to the dead, but that there was also a cult which prepared "him who had been initiated into the future of his soul for this eschatological experience." The alabaster bowl is the clearest and most visible proof of the existence of such a cult. In the mystery of Isis, described by Apuleius, the mystes also goes through the gate of death, passes through all elements, rises from earth and water to the air and then to the ethereal fire, finally to behold and worship the gods face to face. At this point, he sees the sun shining with a white light at midnight.—Apuleius, *Metamorphoses*, 23. [Cf. tr. Robert Graves, *The Golden Ass*, London, 1954, p. 286.]
36 *OF* 32: Γᾶς υἱός εἰμι καὶ Ὠρανῶ ἀστερόεντος.

The words of the first line pointed to a Zeus-Dionysus, who eternally turns the "radiant distant cycle that runs round the celestial spheres," and who must therefore be presumed to dwell outside the starry heaven. This is the Helios of the mystery cosmology, which represents the sphere of the sun as a wreath of celestial fire surrounding the heaven of fixed stars. The second line, however, guides the reader's thoughts from the original unity of the cosmos to its separation into heaven and earth, between which the god Phanes-Zeus-Dionysus-Pan-Helios appears.

But can this Phanes, who is born from the cosmic egg and stands between heaven and earth, who reveals the characteristics of Helios and the symbols of Zeus, of the sun serpent and of the universal god Pan, be the same as the supracelestial Helios-Zeus-Dionysus, who encompasses heaven and earth, and to whom the invocation of the first line is addressed?

Here again the Orphic tradition, scanty and fragmentary as it is, comes to our help. The exact connecting link that we need is supplied by a homily of Clement of Rome,[37] in which he quotes verbatim a report of Apion concerning an Orphic cosmogony. Here we find that while the cosmos is taking form in the hollow between the two hemispheres, Phanes, still contained in the cosmic egg, "seats himself, as it were, on the summit of heaven, and from this ineffable region illumines the infinite Aeon."[38]

Phanes is no longer within the new cosmos. He now has his seat over the hemispheres, "on the summit of heaven," whence he "illumines" the ἄπειρος Αἰών, which corresponds to the ἄπειρος μακρὸς "Ολυμπος of our inscription. This is the supracelestial space, still unlimited by any celestial sphere, which extends into the infinite and ineffable, the empyrean of Dante and the Scholastics.

The invocation in the first line of the inscription is addressed to this Phanes-Zeus-Dionysus. The second line refers to his genesis, his birth from the cosmic egg, which is also the birth of the Aeon and of the whole cosmos.

III

From the third line of the inscription

ϑεοί ουνεκα δινει κατ απειρονα μακρον—

the word ϑεόί must first be removed. Metrically the verse begins with οὔνεκα and ends with the word "Ολυμπον, which must be taken from the

37 Clement of Rome, *Homilia* VI, 5–12 (Migne, *PG*, II, 200ff.) = *OF* 56.
38 Ibid. (*OF*, p. 134 middle.)

213

next line—as is suggested by the hyphen after μακρον in the inscription itself. The context to which the word θεόι belonged is no longer ascertainable. Delbrueck and Vollgraff interpret it as a formula of consecration and dedication to the gods, such as occurs over many ancient inscriptions,[39] and accordingly transfer it to the beginning of the inscription. The line then begins with "because thou movest in a circle," a dependent clause which makes no sense without the main clause to which it belongs. The inscription itself makes it clear that this dependent clause must refer to the name of Dionysus, since, as the Orphic verses cited by Macrobius show, it contains the etymological explanation of his name. The meaning of this line is, accordingly: "[First he—Phanes—came to light, he was called Dionysus], because he moves in a circle round the infinite, lofty Olympus."

The second line of the inscription, "Heaven and earth were one form," evokes the creation of the cosmic egg by the great serpent, since only in the cosmic egg can heaven and earth be said to have been one form, and thus brings us to the birth of Phanes. The third line takes up at this point, identifying Phanes with Dionysus and, by an etymological explanation of his name, stressing his aspect as the sphere of the sun which encompasses the whole of heaven.

IV

Of the fourth line

Ολυμπον αγλαε Ζευ κοσμο γεννητο

only the words ἀγλαὲ Ζεῦ, κόσμου γεννῆτορ remain to be explained. Their meaning follows from what has been said above and from the fragment cited by Macrobius, invoking the "glittering Zeus-Dionysus, father of the sea, father of the earth, sun, all-engendering, all-moving, flaming with gold." The identity of Zeus with Phanes-Dionysus is also shown by the Phanes relief. And an Orphic hymn that has come down to us shows us Phanes exactly as in the relief: both male and female, joining heaven and earth, embodying the elements of the cosmos. He is sun, moon, and lightning, king and ruler of the world. The verses are as follows:

> Zeus was first and last, Zeus radiant with lightning.
> Zeus is the head, Zeus the middle, Zeus is the completion of all things.

39 W. Larfeld, *Griechische Epigraphik* (3rd edn., Munich, 1914), pp. 306f.

Zeus is the foundation of the earth and the starry heavens.
Zeus was male; Zeus was a divine virgin.
Zeus is the breath of the universe, Zeus a flame of untiring fire.
Zeus the root of the sea, Zeus sun and moon.
Zeus is king, Zeus radiant with lightning, the ruler over all;
He concealed all things in himself and brought them back to the
  blessed light
Out of his holy heart, accomplishing terrible deeds.[40]

Let us sum up all the thoughts which this inscription was intended to arouse in readers whose knowledge of the Orphic poem, from which the verses were taken, enabled them to understand it. The inscription exhorts the reader to invoke the divine cosmic power, the sun which rules the infinite cosmic space over the heaven of fixed stars, which is the originator of the cosmos and of the motion of the heavens. This cosmic power is Zeus, Dionysus, and Helios at once. The inscription carries the reader's thoughts back to the primordial age before the birth of the cosmos, when heaven and earth were not yet separated from one another, when Chronos in the form of a great serpent bore the cosmic egg, which contained the whole cosmos and with it the god Phanes, who, when the world was completed, soared over it and took his place as Zeus at the summit of heaven, where as Helios he illumined the world, and as Dionysus and Pan maintained the rotation of the starry sphere. He is the life of the world, its Aeon, the life span[41] of this world which will endure as long as this Aeon itself. He is the great cosmic year which he orders into years, seasons, months, and days by the movements of the stars that take place in him and through him.

2. *The Serpent and the Four Winds*

Let us now turn our attention to the figures on the bowl. Our eye first falls [*Pl. I*] on the great serpent in the center.

The serpent is coiled about a round stone. This suggests an external, formal parallel to those altars adorned with snakes which were widespread

40 *OF* 21 a [tr. here from the German].
41 The word αἰών means first "vital force" and "life," then "life span," "χρόνος filled with content," "life destiny"; further, "era or eternity"; and finally it means the cosmic spheres which by their rotation determine the epochs and seasons. See the investigations and lexicographical collections of C. Lackeit, *Aion, Zeit und Ewigkeit in Sprache und Religion der Griechen*, Part I: Sprache (diss., Königsberg, 1916).

in Graeco-Roman antiquity, for the most part dedicated to the Lares.[1] The memory of these altars is still kept alive by the Serpent Stone in the park at Weimar, bearing the inscription *"Genio huius loci."*[2] There would seem to be no essential connection, however, between this snake as local genius or daemon and the motif on our bowl. For one thing the double wreath of rays, surrounding the snake on the bowl, identifies it as a sun god, as Helios himself. Furthermore, this snake has wings, which suggest that it is not a chthonian but a celestial being, or that it stands in some relation to the winds—we are reminded of Typhon, the hot wind that rises snake-footed from the bowels of the earth and is represented with two or three wings.[3] Finally, this snake is not coiled round a sacrificial altar but round the recognizable upper half of an egg.

Since the inscription on the bowl refers to the Orphic Helios-Zeus-Diony-sus-Phanes and since this Phanes is described in one fragment as having "the body and form of a serpent,"[4] the snake on the bowl is evidently the

---

1 See E. Küster, *Die Schlange in der griechischen Kunst und Religion* (Giessen, 1913), p. 66.
2 K. Walter, *Genius huius loci: eine Parkstudie* (Weimar, 1897), p. 43: "It [the Serpent Stone] was erected at the behest of the ruling Duke Carl August—as we are informed by a receipt for 40 thalers, dated May 5, 1787, still available in the Weimar archives—in the spring of that year, in other words while Goethe was in Italy. The court sculptor Martin Gottlieb Klauer was commissioned to execute it, and there is no doubt that he had as his model the snake altar preserved in *Le pitture antiche d'Ercolano*, Tom. I, Tav. XXXVIII, Napoli, 1757 [Vol. I of *Le Antichità di Ercolano esposte*, tr. Thomas Martyn and John Lettice, *The Antiquities of Herculaneum*, London, 1773, p. 158, pl. 38]. This altar also bears the inscription 'Genius huius loci montis.' A snake with yellow-ish-red belly and gray back with dark spots is twined up around it and is eating the fruits that lie upon it (figs and dates): beside it stands a youthful figure with wreathed head, holding an olive branch in his right hand." It does not seem to me so unquestionable that this was the precise model; for if it were, how would the Weimar artist have come to represent correctly the sacrificial cakes that lie on the altar, being consumed by the snake, according to the ancient pattern? Concerning these honey cakes sacrificed to the snake, cf. Küster, p. 66. The *genius loci* embodied in the snake was of course the earth spirit, the spirit of this bit of earth, the valley of the Ilm. It was this "ruler of the land in which he dwells" (Küster, p. 153) who was supposed to welcome Goethe on his return. The monument was not, as A. Mollberg (*Weimars klassische Kulturstätten*, Weimar, 1927, p. 31) supposed, "an altar dedicated to the poetic genius and for this reason inscribed with the words 'Genius huius loci.'" How W. Geese, in *Gottlieb Martin Klauer: Der Bildhauer Goethes* (Leipzig, 1935), pp. 194–95, comes to the conclusion that "Anna Amalia had the little monument built in memory of her recovery from a grave illness," he unfortunately does not tell us.
3 Küster, pp. 87ff.
4 Athenagoras, *Pro Christianis*, 20 (Richardson, p. 318) = *OF* 58: ἣ αὐτὸν τὸν Φάνητα δέξαιτο, θεὸν ὄντα πρωτόγονον — οὗτος γάρ ἐστι ὁ ἐκ τοῦ ὠιοῦ πρωχυθείς —, ἢ σῶμα ἢ σχῆμα ἔχειν δράκοντος.

216

Orphic Phanes. It has his golden wings, and the double crown of flames which we see in the Phanes relief and in many representations of Helios.

The cult of Sabazius, which was a Dionysian cult,[5] makes it clear that the Zeus-Dionysus of the bowl inscription, who is identical with Phanes, could take the form of a snake. And in the same passage where he quotes the Orphic verses from which our inscription is taken, Macrobius also mentions this Zeus-Dionysus-Sabazius, to whom the sun temple on the hill of Zilmissos in Thrace was dedicated.

Fig. 2 *Serpent Stone in the park at Weimar*

We have seen that the inscription is an invocation of Zeus-Dionysus, who, as the luminous, supracelestial sphere, encompasses the whole starry heavens. Now, Hellenistic astrology knew of a being which dominated the heavens and encompassed all the spheres of the cosmos: the great celestial serpent, *draco caelestis*,[6] the dragon of the Babylonians and Chaldaeans. This serpent, which coiled round the heavens, biting its tail, was the cause of solar and lunar eclipses.[7] In the Hellenistic cosmology, this serpent is assigned to the ninth, starless spheres of the planets and the zodiac.[8] This

5 See Eisele, s.v. "Sabazios," in Roscher's *Lexikon*.
6 Cumont, "De dracone caelesti," in *Catalogus codicum astrologorum Graecorum*, VIII, 1 (Brussels, 1929), pp. 194ff.
7 Ibid., VII (1908), Appendix, Cod. 7, p. 125 (Paris. 2506, f. 175 v): Τὴν μὲν σύστασιν ἔχουσιν ἐκ τῆς συμβλήσεως τῶν δύο παραλλήλων ἐκκέντρων κύκλων Ἡλίου τε καὶ Σελήνης᾽ αἱ δὴ κατὰ διάμετρον δύο συμβλήσεις ᾽Αναβιβάζων καὶ καταβιβάζων. τούτων τῶν [δύο] κύκλων ἡ περιφέρεια παρὰ τῶν Χαλδαίων Δράκων ὠνομάσθη καὶ αἱ τούτων συμβλήσεις ἡ μὲν κεφαλὴ τούτου ἡ δὲ οὐρά. λέγουσι δὲ τὸν ᾽Αναβιβάζοντα εἶναι τὴν κεφαλὴν τοῦ λεγομένου δράκοντος, τὸν δὲ Καταβιβάζοντα τὴν οὐρὰν τούτου καὶ αἱ σεληνιακαὶ καὶ αἱ ἡλιακαὶ ἐκλείψεις τότε γίνονται ὅτε πλησιάζουσιν εἰς τὰς συνόδους κτλ.
8 Ibid., X, p. 10 (Cod. Athen. 1265, f. 4 v), no. 9: Περὶ τοῦ δράκοντος ὅπου εἶναι εἰς τὸν ἔννατον οὐρανόν. p. 40 (Cod. 71, f. 229) no. 22: περὶ τῶν δώδεκα ζωδίων καὶ τὸν ἑπτὰ πλανητῶν καὶ περὶ τοῦ ἀνάστρου οὐ(ρα)νοῦ... Εἰς δὲ τὴν ἐννάτην σφέραν τοῦ οὐ(ρα)νοῦ ἐστι ὁ ἀστέρας ὁ δρακοντοειδὴς καὶ ὀφιομήμητος.

sphere goes round the heavens and the earth and also under the earth, and governs the winds.[9] It was usually represented in the familiar form of a circle formed by the snake biting its tail, but in an astrological codex preserved at Erlangen it takes the form of a spiral.

In Christian theology this serpent became the prince of this world, the adversary of the transcendental God, the dragon of outer darkness, who has barred off this world from above, so that it can be redeemed only by being annihilated. The twelfth chapter of the Revelation of St. John is devoted to it.[10] And in certain Gnostic writings, particularly the *Pistis Sophia*,[11] this snake plays an important role as the Antichrist and Satan, the Leviathan of the Old Testament.

The figure on the alabaster bowl cannot be this dragon of darkness; for the Orphic mystery theology, to which, as we have shown, the inscription points, has a different cosmology. Here the celestial serpent is not a dragon of outer darkness coiled around the glittering starry heaven; it is the sphere of the sun, Phanes-Helios, the "glittering Zeus," stretched like a radiant ribbon round the rim of the heaven of fixed stars; it is the universal god Pan, moving the whole cosmos in harmonious circles.

This follows from the old Orphic poem to which the inscription refers. This poem goes back to the age of Euripides, but the bowl itself, as we have shown, is more recent, dating from the first centuries of the Christian era. In this period we find a renaissance of Orphism, which is attested by the writings of the philosophers and the entire Christian literature down to the magic papyri. It was an age characterized by the revival of mystery cults, particularly Mithraism, but it was also the epoch of Christian gnosticism. It was the era of that Hellenistic universal religion, that "solar pantheism"

9 Ibid., X, p. 127 (Davidis et Salomonis Lunarium f. 29 v): τὸ αὐτὸ ἄστρον περιπατεῖ καὶ περιτρέπει τὸν οὐρανὸν καὶ τὴν γῆν καὶ ἐν τοῖς καταχθονίοις καὶ κυριεύει τοὺς ἢ ἀνέμους.

10 Cf. also the *Apocalypse of Baruch*, ed. M. R. James, *Apocrypha anecdota*, II (1897), 186 [R. H. Charles, *Apocrypha and Pseudepigrapha of the Old Testament*, Oxford, 1913, Vol. II, pp. 470ff.].

11 Tr. G. R. S. Mead (London, 1896), sec. 319, p. 320: "The outer darkness is a huge dragon, with its tail in its mouth; it is outside the world and surroundeth it completely." Other passages can easily be found with the help of the index in Carl Schmidt's *Koptisch-gnostische Schriften*, Vol. I (in *Die griechisch-christliche Schriftsteller der ersten drei Jahrhunderte*, 1905), s.v. "Drache." But the sun also appears here as a serpent, accompanied by the seven planets and with the four horses which in Greek mythology drew the sun chariot of Helios; ch. 136 (p. 262, 24): "But the disk of the sun was a great dragon with its tail in its mouth, which ascended to seven powers of the left and was drawn by four powers in the shape of white horses."

218

which Wendland, in his work on Hellenistic-Roman culture, refers to as the terminal form of the history of ancient religions.[12]

Philosophy also made its contribution to this trend. It was the Stoics who renewed the bond with the popular faith and, through the allegorical method of interpretation, brought the myths and theology of Orpheus, Musaeus, Hesiod, and Homer[13] into consonance with philosophy, so that all the gods became natural forces, which in turn became manifestations of a single universal godhead that was the cosmos permeated by divine forces. The older Stoics had already called the sun the ἡγεμονικόν of the cosmos.[14] Posidonius situated the ruler of the world in the ether which surrounds it,[15] but for him the sun was the center of the world, the demiurge of the universe, engendering and preserving all life, calling forth the seasons and ordering the year into months and days. In course of time this solar pantheism became enriched with other ideas from various sources, and Philo made it into a universal metaphysic and mystery of light,[16] in terms of which he even reinterpreted the Old Testament. From him this philosophy

12 Paul Wendland, *Die Hellenistisch-römische Kultur in ihren Beziehungen zu Judentum und Christentum* (Handbuch zum neuen Testament, Vol. I, pt. 2; 2nd edn., Tübingen, 1912), pp. 158ff.: "Astral religion, as was natural, culminated in the cult of the sun which leads the dance of the planets and is the supreme lord of the world. The history of ancient religion ends in a solar pantheism. The Chaldaean solar and astral theology, which became popular in the 2nd century B.C. with the advance of astronomical knowledge and the rise of Stoic philosophy, was combined in Posidonius with the current of Greek mysticism and with the idea of an essential unity between the soul and the world of the stars. . . . From the middle of the 1st century, we can follow the spread of this pantheism, which was furthered by the triumph of Mithraism; but the roots of the development extend back to the Hellenistic period. The attribute *Invictus* designates the universal power which succumbed only gradually to Christianity; under the Emperor Constantius the birthday of Jesus, the new sun, was fixed on the day of the birth festival of Sol Invictus, as an act of conscious juxtaposition. The significance of sun worship is also revealed by its close bond with the cult of the emperor, who was looked upon as the earthly image and epiphany of the sun god. This worship of Sol reinforced the trend of this age toward a monotheism, subordinating the separate divine powers and emanations to a principal comprehensive God."

13 J. von Arnim, *Stoicorum veterum fragmenta* (Leipzig, 1905–24), Vol. II, p. 315, fr. 1077ff.

14 Ibid., Vol. I, Cleanthes, p. 111, fr. 499ff.

15 I. Heinemann, *Poseidonios metaphysische Schriften* (Breslau, 1921–28), Vol. II, pp. 309f. and 396. See the chapter on "Helios Demiurgos" in K. Reinhardt, *Kosmos und Sympathie* (Munich, 1926), pp. 365ff., and his *Poseidonios* (Munich, 1921), pp. 205ff.

16 Cf. E. R. Goodenough, *By Light, Light: The Mystic Gospel of Hellenistic Judaism* (New Haven, 1935). Goodenough shows the core of Philo's theology to be a mystery of light that is closely related to the conceptions of Philo's Hellenistic environment.

of light passed into Neoplatonism and into Christian theology, continuously gathering new life from the Greco-Oriental *Zeitgeist*.

The old Orphic cosmology made its appearance everywhere: The sun is the supreme cosmic force; it is the highest god of this world and also, as the ultimate sphere encompassing the cosmos, the transcendent God, intermediary between the earthly heavens and the heavens beyond. It is not the evil dragon of darkness but the 'Αγαθὸs Δαίμων, the good spirit of light, which measures the seasons and controls the temporal destiny of the world, the Aeon.

This Aeon, as Helios and Agathodaimon, is represented in the religious writings and monuments of the period as the *great serpent* and, like the serpent on our bowl, is everywhere closely related to the four winds, the four quarters of the cosmos, and the four seasons.

In one of the magic papyri, Helios is invoked as "Thou who risest from the four winds, thou friendly good daemon, glittering Helios, shining over the whole earth, thou art the great serpent who leadest these gods."[17] This invocation corresponds exactly to the sun serpent surrounded by the four blowing figures on the bowl. The texts of the magic papyri are always authentic invocations and prayers, hallowed and made magically effective by their use in various cults. These are the texts underlying the commentaries of the literary authors. Macrobius,[18] for example, endeavors to explain why the sun is represented as a serpent. Like the snake, which sheds its skin and becomes young again, the sun grows old when it sets and rises again with new youth. The name of the snake also points to the sun; for δράκων was believed to derive from δέρκειν, "to see." Snakes were said to have particularly sharp eyesight,[19] so representing the all-seeing eye of the sun, for which reason they served as guardians of temples, *adyta*, oracles,

17 Pap. Bibl. Nat. suppl. gr. 574, in K. Preisendanz, *Papyri Graecae magicae* (Berlin and Leipzig, 1928–31), Vol. I, p. 124: ("Ηλιοs), ὁ ἀνατέλλων ἐκ τῶν τεσσάρων ἀνέμων, ὁ ἱλαρὸs 'Αγαθὸs Δαίμων, ... ὁ λαμπρὸs "Ηλιοs, αὐγάζων καθ' ὅλην τὴν οἰκουμένην. σὺ εἶ ὁ μέγαs "Οφιs, ἡγούμενοs τούτων τῶν θεῶν. Cf. IV, 2426 (p. 148): (Write) εἰs δὲ τὸν δράκοντα τὸ ὄνομα τοῦ 'Αγαθοῦ Δαίμονοs. IV, 395: ἐπικαλοῦμαί σειτὸν στην "Ωρον 'Αρποκράτην... τὸν πάντα φωτί-ζοντα καὶ διαυγάζοντα τῇ ἰδίᾳ δυνάμει τὸν σύμπαντα κόσμον, θεὲ θεῶν, εὐεργέτα, αο. 'Ιάω. εαψ. ὁ διέπων νύκτα καὶ ἡμέραν αἳ αω. ἡνιοχῶν καὶ κυβερνῶν ὁίακα, κατέχων δράκοντα, 'Αγαθὸν ἱερὸν Δαίμονα.
18 *Saturnalia*, I, 20, 3.
19 This is not true, as Küster, p. 57, points out, citing the authority of A. E. Brehm's *Tierleben* (3rd edn.), Vol. VII, pp. 187ff. Snakes actually have very poor eyesight.

and treasuries. And ὄφις, the other word for snake, was connected with ὀφθαλμός and interpreted in the same sense.[20] Philo of Byblos writes:

The nature of the dragon [δράκοντος] and of the snakes [τῶν ὄφεων] was called godlike by Taautos himself and after him by the Phoenicians and Egyptians. According to the doctrine which he handed down, this beast is the most pneumatic [πνευματικώτατον] of all beasts and of a fiery nature [πυρῶδες], so that by the force of the pneuma it achieves an unexcelled speed without the feet, hands, or other external organs, by which other animals accomplish their movements. It represents various kinds of figures, and advances at any desired speed by twisting and turning. It is the most long-lived of animals; not only can it cast off its age and rejuvenate itself, but in so doing actually adds to its growth.[21] And when it has completed the time span allotted to it, it devours itself, as Taautos himself recounted in the holy scriptures. And that is why this beast has been received into the temples and mysteries.[22]

Fire and the pneuma as wind, life breath, or spirit make the snake the beast of Helios. Its longevity, its power to rejuvenate itself and to grow at the same time, only to end by devouring itself, make it seem a fit symbol for the Aeon as life span of the cosmos, rejuvenating itself from spring to spring, only to consume itself inwardly in the end. The snake biting its tail signifies the cosmos itself. Macrobius[23] ascribes the invention of this symbol to the Phoenicians. As the snake devours itself, so does the world feed on itself and return to itself. Here we must recall the Heraclitean-Stoic doctrine of the development of the world from an original element, fire, to which the cosmos returns after the cosmic year has run its course.[24] Since this cosmic year is the Aeon, the life span allotted to the cosmos, the uroboros, the snake biting its tail, became the symbol of the Aeon, especially when bearing the

20 Examples in Küster, p. 57, 2.
21 Cf. Nonnus, *Dionysiaca*, Bk. 41, ll. 180ff.: ". . . and [the Aeon] casts off the burden of age like a snake which sheds its coils of worn-out scales, and it is rejuvenated by bathing in the waters of universal law." Viktor Stegemann, *Astrologie und Universalgeschichte: Studien und Interpretationen zu den Dionysiaka des Nonnos von Panopolis (Stoicheia,* Vol. IX; Leipzig and Berlin, 1930), pp. 20ff.
22 *Fragmenta Historicorum Graecorum* (ed. C. Müller, Paris, 1849), Vol. III, p. 572.
23 *Saturnalia*, I, 9, 12: "*Hinc et Phoenices in sacris imaginem eius exprimentes draconem finxerunt in orbem redactum caudamque suam devorantem, ut appareat mundum et ex se ipso ali et in se revolvi.*"
24 On this idea and its philosophical implications, see my book *Denkformen* (Berlin, 1928), pp. 60ff.

inscription ἓν τὸ πᾶν,[25] meaning that all things are one, to wit, that they arose from the One and will return to the One, so that the Aeon extends from the One to the One.

The magic papyri include a rule for the manufacture of a "ring conferring success and favor and victory" in which Helios as serpent fuses with this symbol of the Aeon:

> A sun is cut into a heliotrope stone as follows: let there be a fat snake with its tail in its mouth so as to form a wreath, and inside the snake a sacred scarab surrounded by rays.[26]

And a similar prescription runs:

> Ring for all success and happiness. [Much sought after by] kings. Very effective. Take a sky-blue jasper and etch on it a snake in the form of a circle with its tail in its mouth; in the middle of the snake make [a moon] with two stars on its two horns, and above them a sun on which is engraved "Abrasax" and on the reverse side of the stone the same name "Abrasax" and on the setting inscribe the great and sacred and all-powerful name "Iao Sabaoth."[27]

The magic word "Abrasax" or "Abraxas" signifies the Aeon. It was intended to express the numerical value 365 in one word. The association of this magic word with Sabaoth, one of the Jewish names for God, points to Christian-Gnostic sources, particularly the system of Basilides. According to St. Jerome, "Basilides designated his almighty god by the magic word Abraxas. By computing the numerical value of the Greek letters in this word, he [still according to St. Jerome] obtained the number of the circuits described each year by the sun; this was the same god whom the heathen called Mithras, for this name, although composed of other letters, yielded the same numerical value."[28] This identification of Helios, Mithras, and the Jewish

25 On the history of this formula, see E. Norden, *Agnostos Theos* (Leipzig, 1913), pp. 246ff.
26 Pap. Leiden, in Preisendanz, XII, 274: ἥλιος γλύφεται ἐπὶ λίθου ἡλιοτροπίου τὸν τρόπον τοῦτον· δράκων ἔστω ἐγκύμων, στεφάνου σχήματι οὐρὰν ἐν τῷ στόματι ἔχων. ἔστω δὲ ἐντὸς τοῦ δράκοντος κάνθαρος ἀκτινωτὸς ἱερός.
27 Pap. Leiden, in Preisendanz, XII, 202: Δακτυλίδιον πρὸς πᾶσαν πρᾶξιν καὶ ἐπιτυχίαν μ[ετίασιν] βασιλεῖς καὶ ἡγεμόνες. λίαν ἐνεργές. λαβὼν ἴασπιν ἀερίζοντα ἐπίγραψον δρά[κοντα, κυ]κλοτερῶς τὴν οὐρὰν ἔχοντα ἐν τῷ στόματι, καὶ ἔτι μέσον τοῦ δρ[άκ]οντο[ς Σελήνην] δύο ἀστέρας ἔχουσαν ἐπὶ τῶν δύο κεράτων καὶ ἐπάνω τούτων ἥλιον, ᾧ [ἐγγεγλύφθ]ω "'Αβρασάξ," καὶ ὄπισθεν τῆς γλυφῆς τοῦ λίθου τὸ αὐτὸ ὄνομα "'Αβρασάξ" καὶ κατὰ τοῦ π[εριζώμ]ατος ἐπιγράψεις τὸ μέγα καὶ ἅγιον καὶ κατὰ πάντων, τὸ ὄνομα 'Ιάω, Σαβαώθ.
28 Jerome, *on Amos*, Bk. I, ch. 3 (Migne, *PL*, XXV, col. 1018 D): *"Basileides, qui omnipotentem Deum portentoso nomine appellat Abraxas, et eumdem secundum graecas litteras, et annui cursus numerum dicit in solis circulo contineri, quem ethnici sub eodem numero aliarum litterarum vocant* Μείθραν."

THE MYSTERY OF THE SERPENT

God is accounted for by the solar pantheism of late antiquity, which made
Yahweh, like the leading gods of various other religions, a sun god.[29] An
invocation of this Helios-Aeon-Iao-Sabaoth runs:

> Draw close to me, thou who comest from the four winds, thou al-
> mighty god, who hast breathed the breath of life into man . . . thou
> good Daemon. Thou art the Lord, who bringest forth and nourish-
> est and increasest all things. . . . Who hath commanded the winds
> to perform their annual labors? What Aeon sustains the Aeon and
> ruleth over the Aeons? An immortal God.[30]

Helios appears repeatedly in association with the four winds. The magician apostrophizes him in the words: "Come to me. Come from the four
winds of the world—[I implore] thee, great god, god of the air."[31] And the
magnificent prayer (which Dieterich[32] identifies as part of a Mithraic liturgy)
contains the following passage, quite in the style of the Orphic hymn from
which the inscription on the alabaster bowl is taken:

> Thou who movest through the air in the winds, golden-haired
> Helios, ruling over the tireless flaming fire, revolving round the
> great pole in the circuits of the ether, all dissolving and all engender-
> ing—for, ever since the elements were ordered according to thy
> laws, they have nourished the whole cosmos throughout the four
> seasons of the year.[33]

And the magic papyri include a prayer to the Aeon of Aeons, which though
emanating from the brothers and sisters of a community calling themselves

29 See Th. Hopfner, "Orientalisch-religionsgeschichtliches aus den griechischen Zauber-
   papyri Ägyptens," *Archiv Orientalni* (Prague), VIII (1931), 340ff.
30 Pap. Leiden, in Preisendanz, XII, 239: δεῦρο μοι, ὁ ἐκ τῶν δ' ἀν[έ]μων, ὁ
   παντοκράτωρ θεός, ὁ ἐνφυσήσας πνεύματα ἀνθρώποις εἰς ζωήν... Ἀγαθὸς
   Δαίμων. σὺ εἶ κύριος ὁ γεννῶν καὶ τρέφων καὶ αὔξων τὰ πάντα... 245: τίς δὲ
   ἀνέμους ἐκέλευσεν ἔχειν ἐνιαύσια ἔργα; τίς δὲ Αἰὼν Αἰ[ῶ]να τρέφων Αἰῶσιν
   ἀνάσσει; εἷς θεὸς ἀθάνατος.
31 Pap. Louvre 2391, Mimaut, in Preisendanz, III, 495: Σύστασις πρὸς Ἥλιον...
   [δεῦ]ρο, δ[ε]ῦρό μοι ἐκ τῶν τεσσάρων ἀνέμων τοῦ κόσμου, ἀεροδρό[μον] μέγαν
   θεόν. Cf. J. 395, in Preisendanz, XIII, 782: δεῦρό μοι, ὁ ἐκ τῶν δ' ἀνέμων, ὁ παντοκράτωρ... ὁ Ἀγαθὸς Δαίμων.
32 A. Dieterich, *Eine Mithrasliturgie* (Leipzig, 1903), pp. 63ff.
33 Pap. Bibl. Nat. suppl. gr. 574, in Preisendanz, IV, 436; ibid., IV, 1955ff., and VIII,
   74ff.:   Ἀεροφοιτήτων ἀνέμων ἐποχούμενος αὔραις,
   Ἥλιε χρυσοκόμα, διέπων φλογὸς ἀκάματον πῦρ,
   αἰθερίαισι τριβαῖς μέγαν πόλον ἀμφιελίσσων,
   γεννῶν αὐτὸς ἅπαντα, ἅπερ πάλιν ἐξαναλύεις.
   ἐξ οὗ γὰρ στοιχεῖα πάντα τεταγμένα σοῖσι νομοῖσι,
   κόσμον ἅπαντα τρέφουσιν τετρά[τρο]πον εἰς ἐνιαυτόν.

223

the saints, might have been addressed to the great serpent by the men and women on the alabaster bowl. It calls to mind all the thoughts aroused by the inscription and by the sun serpent with the four winds:

> Hail, temple of the air spirit! Hail, spirit who reachest from heaven to earth and from the earth, which lies in the center of the cosmos, to the borders of the abyss! Hail, spirit who enterest into me and takest hold of me, and departest from me in lovingkindness as God wills! Hail, beginning and end of immutable nature! Hail, rotation of the elements full of untiring service! Hail, labor of the sunbeams, light of the world! Hail glittering nocturnal sphere of the changing moon! Hail, all ye spirits of the air daemons! Hail and be praised, ye brothers and sisters pious men and women: O great, spherical, unfathomable edifice of the world! Heavenly [spirit] which dwellest in heaven: ethereal spirit which dwellest in the ether: thou who takest the shape of water, of earth, of fire, of wind, of light: thou who art dark, thou who glitterest starlike: thou spirit humid, fiery and cold:—I praise thee, God of gods, who hast articulated the world, who hast gathered the depths on their firm invisible foundation; thou who hast separated heaven and earth, veiling the heavens with golden eternal wings, grounding the earth on eternal supports, dispersing the air by self-moved winds, laying water round about; thou who guidest the storm clouds, bringing thunder, lightning and rain; thou who engenderest living creatures, God of the Aeons, great art thou, lord, God, ruler of the universe.[34]

Helios and the Aeon, represented as a serpent, are also distinctly associated with the winds in the monuments of the cult of Mithras. Here Mithras, as Sol Invictus, takes the form of a winged lion-headed god entwined in a snake, resembling the Orphic Phanes. And several Mithraic reliefs represent the four winds in the corners, in the manner of the Phanes relief.[35]

There is, however, one possible objection to our interpretation of the four satellites of the serpent on the bowl. Delbrueck and Vollgraff[36] declared that these four winged figures are similar in physical type to the other figures on

34 In the great Paris Magic Papyrus (in Preisendanz, I, 111ff., IV, 1115–65) from Lower Egypt (Herakleopolis), believed to have been written shortly after A.D. 300. See R. Reitzenstein, *Poimandres* (Leipzig, 1913) pp. 277ff.

35 n. Dieterich, p. 63: "The winds are not infrequently represented in monuments of Mithras; usually as heads in the corners, sometimes four, sometimes only two (Cumont, I, 94; 95, 3). Often they are close to Helios (or to Selene—Cumont, *Mon.*, 273 b, 246 d, 267 a), and usually these heads are blowing into a tube, a kind of funnel, '*entonnoir*,' as Cumont often calls it (I, 95)."

36 Op. cit., p. 132.

the bowl, but have the stature of children and therefore cannot be wind gods, because wind gods are ordinarily represented as men. Moreover, these figures do not blow from the four corners of heaven, but are arranged in pairs, each member of which is blowing toward the other.

This last argument is easily disposed of; for in the Phanes relief, the Mithras relief, and other cosmological works which we shall have occasion to discuss, the winds face one another in pairs. It is true that they reveal the traits of men, but in later works they are represented as chubby-faced boys or youthful angels.

Since the Aeon is almost invariably associated with the four winds in the numerous texts that represent it as Helios and as a serpent, the four winged, blowing children on our bowl may be presumed to be winds. We need only ask how the adult wind gods came to be transformed into these little boys· The explanation is presumably that they are intended to represent something else besides winds. And it is the four seasons that we often find associated with the four winds in the texts and reliefs of the mystery religions with which we are here concerned.

Even in so early a writer as Philo, winds and seasons almost merge into one concept.[37] In the section we have quoted from the Emperor Julian's oration, Helios divides the spheres into four, so sending "us the fourfold glory of the seasons." Cumont[38] refers to a passage in Ptolemy,[39] assigning a wind to each season. There is a statue of Mithras as the Aeon,[40] in which he has four wings, symbolizing the four winds. On each wing is inscribed the symbol of a season: on the first, a dove and a swan; on the second, ears of grain; on the third, grapes; and on the fourth, palms and roses. The four winds and four seasons also appear side by side on the Mithras reliefs.[41]

We see, then, that while the trumpets and wings of the four figures on the alabaster bowl symbolize the winds, their childlike stature suggests the

37 Philo, in the tr. of F. H. Colson and G. H. Whitaker (LCL, 1929–41): *De specialibus legibus*, I, 322 (Vol. VII, p. 287): "The air so happily tempered by winds and breezes to make the yearly seasons." *De praemiis et poenis*, 41 (Vol. VIII, p. 337): "The air and breezes so happily tempered, the yearly seasons changing in harmonious order." *De congressu quaerendae eruditionis gratia*, 133 (Vol. IV, p. 527): "The shiftings of the winds and seasons."
38 *Textes et monuments figurés relatifs aux Mystères de Mithra*, Vol. I (Brussels, 1899), p. 94.
39 *Tetrabiblos*, I; cf. Proclus, *Paraphrasis in Ptolemaei Libros IV de Siderum Effectionibus*, Bk. I, cap. 12.
40 Cumont, *Textes et monuments*, Vol. I, fig. 68.
41 Ibid., p. 93: "*Ces dieux des saisons, à Cornutum comme à Heddernheim, sont joints à ceux des Vents.*"

seasons. It is not only in the cult of Mithras that the seasons were represented as little boys; wherever a reference to the Aeon and his satellites was
intended,[42] they appeared as male children, or else as adults of various ages
bearing the symbols of the seasons. The finest example of the representation
[Pl. IV] of the seasons as children is the Sentinum mosaic that Cumont classified
among the "doubtful monuments" of the cult of Mithras, because it has no
characteristic applicable only to this cult.[43]

The central figure is a youth, representing Helios as the Aeon. He has
wings in his hair, his hands touch the zodiac, which he swings round him.
In front of him is a group consisting of the earth goddess, her neck entwined
by a snake, and the four seasons. These are male children: at the lower
right, Winter wrapped in a cloak; at the right above him and behind the female figure, Autumn bearing fruit; beside him to the left, Summer with
ears of wheat in his hair; in the left-hand corner, Spring wreathed in flowers
and leaves. This mosaic fully shows the sympathy existing between the sun,
the starry heavens, the wind, the four seasons, and the earth, and brings us
back to the old cosmology, in which Helios turns the starry heavens. The
circuit of the stars; the circling sun; the resulting cycle of the seasons with
their changing winds; the earth that is rejuvenated in the seasons—all this
together is the Aeon, the god of time, who is manifested in all these cyclical
changes and is the cosmic law underlying them. The mystery of the Aeon,
arousing in man a sense of absolute dependence on a universe revolving in
itself according to great, eternal laws, is the most grandiose creation of dying
antiquity.

The ancient tradition of the four winds, which rise beyond the starry
heavens and blow upon the world from four sides, survives even in those
medieval pictures of the cosmos, which represent it as a sphere rather than
an egg. We have seen that the alabaster bowl is closely related to the Phanes
relief, which is a figuration of the genesis of the cosmos and of the whole
world. Our bowl then is descended from ancient representations of the cosmos,
and from it in turn a line runs to that medieval art in which the Christian
world is conceived according to models handed down from late antiquity,

42 Ibid., p. 92: *"Aux quatre coins d'un marbre de Sidon, quatre têtes d'enfants avec les at-
tributs divers (Bas-relief inédit de la collection de Clercq)"*; p. 93: *"L'art mithriaque n'a
donc fait que puiser dans une riche série de types depuis longtemps vulgarisés. On remarque
cependant que pour lui les Saisons sont toujours des dieux masculins et non, comme les
Heures en Grèce, des déesses."*
43 Ibid., pp. 419f. (no. 298).

and to the woodcuts illustrating the first printed books, which were copied from medieval manuscripts and drawings. Schedel's "World Chronicle"[44] contains a woodcut of the cosmos, in which the four winds in similar arrangement face one another in pairs, at the four corners of a world amplified by the crystal heavens, the Aristotelian *primum mobile*, and the nine angelic choirs of Dionysius.

In a woodcut of the creation from a Cologne Bible,[45] belonging to another type of medieval picture of the cosmos, four winds are represented in a purely decorative manner that shows no understanding of the tradition— blowing meaninglessly outwards. A much older map of the world, however, in a medieval manuscript,[46] shows them again in the same arrangement and [*Pl. V*] position, blowing the same conch horns as on the Orphic bowl, but riding on bellows. On another, thirteenth-century map,[47] the winds are represented as four beardless men, blowing horns.

In Christian art the four winds ultimately became four trumpet-blowing angels, facing one another in pairs as in the ancient models. Such angels occupy the four corners of the round map which Guillaume Filastre, dean of Reims Cathedral, in copying a manuscript by Pomponius Mela, drew inside the capital O of the first words: *"Orbis situm dicere aggredior."*[48] This fusion of the angels with the winds goes back to Matthew 24 : 31: "And he shall send his angels with a great sound of a trumpet, and they shall gather together his elect from the four winds, from one end of heaven to the other." In this way, Christian art, unknown to its authors, returned to the oldest pre-Christian motifs. On our Orphic bowl God's elect are like-

44 Woodcut from H. Schedel, *Liber Chronicarum*, printed by Anton Koberger (Nuremberg, 1493), leaf V, verso, at the end of the story of creation. A description and explanation is given by R. Bernoulli in "Das Weltall in Hartmann Schedels Weltchronik," in *Buch und Bucheinband* (Essays etc. for the 60th birthday of Hans Loubier; 1923), pp. 48–58. The same four winds, with similar characteristics and in similar arrangement, blow round the wheel of fortune in two woodcuts in a work of Petrarch: "Von der Artzney beyder Glück" (Augsburg, 1532), reproduced in A. Doren, "Fortuna im Mittelalter und in der Renaissance," *Vorträge der Bibliothek Warburg (1922–23)*, Part I (Leipzig and Berlin, 1924) after p. 144, Pl. IV, nos. 11 a and 11 b.
45 Printed by Heinrich Quentel in 1479. The same woodcut in colors and in part finished with gold is to be found in the *Kobergsche Deutsche Bibel* of 1483, reproduced in reduced size in Bernoulli, after p. 97, pl. 4; a similar woodcut, showing the winds in the same arrangement, position and form, in the *Biblia Saxonia*, printed in Lübeck in 1494.
46 From a 12th-century parchment codex of the *Apocalypse of Beatus* in the Turin Library (Cod. I, II, 1) described by Konrad Miller, *Mappaemundi: Die ältesten Weltkarten* (Stuttgart, 1895), Part I, 17, 26, 38.
47 Ibid., Part II, Pl. 2.
48 Ibid., Part III, 139. The copy was made in Constance in 1417.

wise gathered together from the four winds, from one end of heaven to the other. On a twelfth-century map of the world by Heinrich of Mainz,[49] preserved in Cambridge, the corners are occupied by angels without trumpets and not visibly characterized as winds, but facing one another in pairs according to the ancient pattern.

Thus a line of development can be traced from the Phanes relief and the corresponding bowl down to the late Middle Ages. The Christian cosmos can be shown to be directly related, both formally and conceptually, to the Orphic cosmos. Scholastic literature shows how the spherical cosmos of the Middle Ages developed from the Orphic cosmic egg. In her first visions, Hildegard of Bingen still saw the cosmos as a great egg,[50] in her later visions as a sphere. In his work on the allegorical cosmology of St. Hildegard,[51] Hans Liebeschutz compiled the passages showing the change from the Orphic to the Aristotelian cosmology, from the cosmic egg to the spherical cosmos of Ptolemy.[52]

But the relation of the Orphic bowl to Christianity is not limited to the outward forms and symbols. The content expressed by the figures on the Orphic bowl also played its part in Christianity. The whole conception of the Aeon was present in the Bible. In the Gospel of St. John, Christ was the "light of the world."[53] With him began the new Aeon, his birth was the birthday of the world, *natalis mundi,* and was set on the birthday of Sol Invictus.[54] In the New Testament, he already reveals the characteristics of the Aeon;

49 Ibid., Part II, Pl. 13, reconstructed in Pl. II.
50 *Scivias* I, vision 3 (Migne, *PL,* CXCVII, 405); 405 A, fol. 10, vb §2: "*Nam hoc maximum instrumentum quod vides, rotundum et umbrosum secundum similitudinem ovi superius arctum et in medio amplum ac inferius constrictum.*"
51 *Das allegorische Weltbild der heiligen Hildegard von Bingen* (Studien der Bibliothek Warburg, Vol. XVI; Leipzig, 1930).
52 Ibid., 66, 1, particularly the passage from William of Conches' *De imagine mundi,* I (Migne, *PL,* CLXXII, 121 A [where attrib. to Honorius of Autun—ED.]), in which it is expressly stated that the round figure actually signifies an egg: "*Huius figura est in modum pilae rotunda. Sed instar ovi elementis distincta.*"
53 Cf. the thorough researches of W. Bousset, *Kyrios Christos* (Göttingen, 1913), pp. 281ff., and especially p. 210: "But this designation [of Christ as the light] can be localized within a very definite milieu. . . . This mere observation that the symbolism of light can be shown to have been restricted to so limited a sphere, would suffice to indicate that the language of the Gospel of St. John was influenced by this milieu of Hellenistic mystery religion." Gillis Pyson Wetter, *Ich bin das Licht der Welt* (Beiträge zur Religionswissenschaft I, 2; Leipzig, 1914), pp. 171ff.
54 H. Usener, "Sol invictus" (*Rheinisches Museum,* LX, 465ff.), reprinted in the 2nd edition of his book *Das Weihnachtsfest* (Bonn, 1911). E. Norden, *Die Geburt des Kindes* (Studien der Bibliothek Warburg, Vol. II; Leipzig, 1924), p. 28.

228

he is the alpha and omega, the beginning and the end, the first and the last, he who is, who was, and who is to come.[55] The symbol of the serpent also appears in the Gospel of St. John (3 : 14): "And as Moses lifted up the serpent in the wilderness, even so must the Son of Man be lifted up." And in the *Epistle of Barnabas*, the serpent lifted up by Moses is designated (quite independently from the passage in St. John) as the type of Jesus and the counterpart of the Satanic serpent in paradise.[56] And the formula "I am the alpha and omega" leads also to the symbol of the serpent, for the serpent biting its tail was inscribed with the first and last letters of the alphabet as well as with $\dot{\epsilon}\nu$ $\tau\dot{o}$ $\pi\tilde{a}\nu$.[57] In one alchemistic test we read: "Thus did Agathodaimon place the beginning in the end and the end in the beginning. He wishes to be a snake biting its tail, but not to conceal this enviously as some of the profane suppose, for it is made perfectly evident, O Mystes, by a loudly proclaimed ΩA."[58]

Or else the two formulas of the Aeon, $\dot{\epsilon}\nu$ $\tau\dot{o}$ $\pi\tilde{a}\nu$ and $A\Omega$, are combined with the serpent, as in the figure of the serpent biting its tail with the inscription "$\dot{\epsilon}\nu$ $\tau\dot{o}$ $\pi\tilde{a}\nu$ $A\Omega$," which Berthelot borrowed from an alchemistic manuscript for the title page of his book on the origin of alchemy.[59]

55 Rev. 1:8; 21:6; 22:13. On the symbol $A\Omega$ as designation of the Aeon, see R. Reitzenstein, *Das iranische Erlösungsmysterium* (Bonn, 1921), pp. 244ff., where further material is given concerning Christ as the Aeon. Reitzenstein remarks: "It is in diametrical opposition to the Pauline conception which we have discussed, according to which the Aeon is the adversary of God, Belial, the antithesis of Christ. . . . But the conception of that eternal God was twofold (transcendent and immanent) and men had developed so strong a feeling for the Aeon as tutelary god, bestower of blessings, preserver of life, and intermediary, that the notion of the Aeon as Satan and death (a conception taken from the intense dualism of Judaism and related religions) could not thrive. Belief in the *divine* governance of the world won out; the characteristics of the Aeon were transferred to Christ as δεύτερος θεός and steward of God. This was one more triumph for the Greek love of the beauty of this world." Cf. also F. Dornseiff, *Das Alphabet in Mystik und Magie* (2nd edn., Leipzig and Berlin, 1925), pp. 122ff.

56 *Epistle of Barnabas*, XII, 5 (tr. Kirsopp Lake, *The Apostolic Fathers*, London and New York, 1914, Vol. I, p. 385); Christ as serpent becomes an unquestionable motif of Christian symbolism. Cf. J. B. Pitra, *Spicilegium Solesmense*, Vol. III (Paris, 1855): S. *Melitonis Clavis*, cap. ix, sec. lxiii, p. 88: "*Serpens, Christus, propter sapientiam*"; "*et sicut Moyses exaltavit serpentem in deserto*"; "*Estote prudentes sicut serpentes.*" Commentary of Petrus Cantor, p. 89: "*Per hunc serpentem aeneum in portica exaltatum, intelligimus Christum crucifixum*" etc.

57 The Aeon formula $\dot{\epsilon}\nu$ $\tau\dot{o}$ $\pi\tilde{a}\nu$ is transferred to Christ as the One, from whom and through whom and unto whom All is. E. Norden, *Agnostos Theos*, pp. 240ff., gives the entire history of this formula. On the meaning of the symbol and its use in St. Paul, cf. my book *Denkformen*, pp. 88ff.

58 In Marcellin Berthelot, *Collection des anciens alchimistes grecs* (Paris, 1888), text vol., p. 79, l. 24f.   59 Berthelot, *Origines de l'alchimie* (Paris, 1885), and Dornseiff, p. 125.

The conception of Christ as serpent was most fully developed in certain of the oldest Gnostic sects, which Hippolytus lumped together under the name of Ophites. Of the Naassenes, who took their name from the Hebrew word for snake (*nahash*), he said:

> They worship nothing other than the Naas [*nahash*], whence they are called Naassenes. Naas is the snake, wherefore all the naoi [temples] under the heavens are so called after the Naas. And to this Naas alone is every temple consecrated and every rite [τελετή] and every mystery [μυστήριον], and no mystery rite can be performed under the heavens without a naos [temple] and the Naas [serpent] in it, wherefore it [the temple] is called naos.[60]

In the doctrine of the Perates, the meaning of the serpent is fully revealed:

> The cosmos consists of Father, Son, and Matter. Each of these three principles contains infinitely many forces. Midway between the Father and Matter, the Son, the Logos, has his place, the Serpent that moves eternally toward the unmoved Father and moved Matter; now it turns to the Father and gathers up forces in its countenance; and now, after receiving the forces, it turns toward Matter, and upon Matter, which is without attribute and form, the Son imprints the ideas which had previously been imprinted upon the Son by the Father.[61]
>
> Now no one can be saved and rise up again without the Son, who is the serpent. For it was he who brought the paternal models down from above, and it is he who carries back up again those who have been awakened from sleep and have reassumed the features of the Father.[62]

A similar system was developed by the Sethites, and Hippolytus remarks explicitly that the symbol of the serpent in their system was derived from the ancient theologians, from Musaeus and Linus and Orpheus, particularly the latter's Βακχικά, whereas he ascribes the doctrine of the Naassenes to the Greek philosophers and to those who transmitted the mysteries; as for the doctrine of the Perates, he imputes it to the astrologers.[63] This is a

---

60 Hippolytus, *Elenchos* V, 9, 12.
61 Ibid., V, 17, 1–2; cf. my book *Die Gnosis* (2nd edn., Leipzig, 1936), pp. 145ff.
62 *Elenchos*, V, 17, 8.
63 Ibid., Book V, beginning, and V 20, 4 = *OF* 243: ὁ γὰρ περὶ τῆς μήτρας αὐτῶν καὶ τοῦ ὄφεως λόγος καὶ [ὁ] ὀμφαλός, ὅπερ ἐστὶν ανδρεία, διαρρήδην οὕτως ἐστὶν ἐν τοῖς Βακχικοῖς τοῦ Ὀρφέως.

surprisingly correct enumeration of the Hellenistic circles in which the speculations on Helios as Aeon and as Logos, symbolized by the serpent, had their origin. The alabaster bowl was obviously a ritual vessel. Our understanding of it is greatly enhanced by a passage in Epiphanius, relating that these Ophites worshiped the serpent as Logos-Christ and describing the mystery of the serpent:

> They have a snake which they keep in a certain chest—the *cista mystica*—and which at the hour of their mysteries they bring forth from its cave. They heap loaves upon the table and summon the serpent. Since the cave is open it comes out. It is a cunning beast, and knowing their foolish ways, it crawls up on the table and rolls in the loaves; this, they say, is the perfect sacrifice. Wherefore, as I have been told, they not only break the bread [the oldest symbol of the Lord's Supper] in which the snake has rolled and administer it to those present, but each one kisses the snake on the mouth, for the snake has been tamed by a spell, or has been made gentle for their fraud by some other diabolical method. And they fall down before it and call this the eucharist, consummated by the beast rolling in the loaves. And through it, as they say, they send forth a hymn to the Father on high, thus concluding their mysteries.[64]

If with this eucharistic ritual in mind, we look into the alabaster bowl with its worshiping mystai grouped around the serpent, we cannot but conclude that the bowl is related to a serpent cult of this sort. We know on good authority that in various mystery cults, particularly those of Sabazius-Dionysus, a snake was kept in a chest. We also know that the living snake was sometimes replaced by a golden snake, which served in the performance of the initiate's mystical marriage rite with the godhead.[65] It also seems possible that an artificial snake replaced the real one in the rite of the Ophites, just as, at a later date, the breaking of bread was replaced in the celebration of communion by consecrated wafers which merely suggested bread. Might not the alabaster bowl have served for the offering of such wafers in a eucharistic ritual such as that described by Epiphanius? The

---

64 *Panarion*, I, 37, 5 (272 A ff.). Cf. L. Fendt, *Gnostische Mysterien* (Munich, 1922), pp. 22ff.

65 Clement of Alexandria, *Protrepticus*, II, 16, 2: Σαβαζίων γοῦν μυστηρίων σύμβολον τοὺς μυομένους ὁ διὰ κόλπου θεός. δράκων δέ ἐστιν οὗτος διελκόμενος τοῦ κόλπου τῶν τελουμένων ἔλεγχος ἀκρασίας Διός.—Arnobius, *Adversus nationes*, V, 21: "aureus coluber in sinum demittitur consacratis et eximitur rursus ab inferioribus partibus atque imis." See Dieterich, *Eine Mithrasliturgie*, p. 123.

"loaves" would then have been laid in the bowl, around the serpent, who rolled in them as it were, while the gestures of the initiates gathered round the serpent would suggest the nature and original meaning of this eucharist.

What argues against this otherwise tempting explanation is that the bowl discloses no Christian features. The inscription is Orphic, and in it the name of Zeus appears beside an etymology of the name of another pagan god, Dionysus. This cannot be overlooked, close as the relations of the Gnostic sects to the Orphic and Dionysian mysteries may have been, and ready as the Christian Gnostics were to find their Christ in pagan gods such as Zeus, Dionysus, Helios, and particularly the Aeon. It is conceivable, however, that these Ophites, who were described by the early Christian Apologists as Christian heretics, were not real Christians at all, but pagans who invested their mystery god with the traits of the new Christ along with those of various Greek and oriental gods. This question can be settled only when we discover the meaning of the nude figures and their gestures. Meanwhile, this much seems definitely established on the basis of our investigations up to this point:

The serpent at the center of the alabaster bowl, taken in conjunction with the four wind gods on the rim, stands for Helios-Dionysus, who is known to us from Orphic theology and who, in the Hellenistic period, took on the more universal qualities of the god Aeon. This god has been described as a "combination of entirely different conceptions into one figure, who is the god of light, the god of time, the creator of the world, the ruler and god of the world, the god of revelation, and the redeemer, who assumes diverse names but remains always strangely indeterminate."[66] In the shape of the winged serpent, surrounded by rays and accompanied by the four winds, the Aeon is the celestial solar ether, encompassing the world and penetrating it with his rays; he is the light and life of this world, for according to Orphic doctrine, the winds engender life[67] and the soul is borne by the winds from the universe into man.[68]

66 Reitzenstein, *Das iranische Erlösungmysterium* (Bonn, 1921), p. 230.
67 *Orphic Hymn* XXXVIII, 3: ζωογόνοι πνοαί, κόσμου σωτῆρες, ἀγανοί.
68 *OF* 27; cf. the additional material in my book *Der heilige Geist* (Leipzig and Berlin, 1919), pp. 51f.

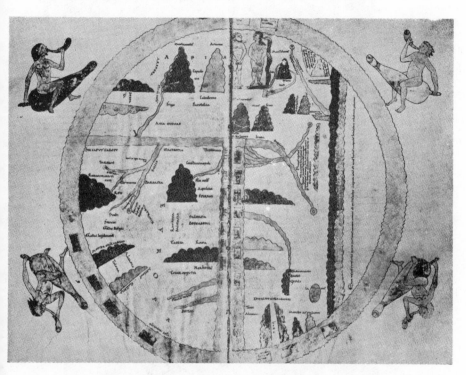

Map of the world. Codex, Turin Library, XII *century*

V

Tombstone of the Hecate Mysteries. Phrygia (?)

VI

Lamp with Gorgon's face. Etruscan,
  v *century* B.C.

With side view, showing position in
  which it is used

The Heavenly Liturgy. Eucharistic bowl, Mount Athos,
c. XIII *century*

3. The Worship of the Serpent

We have shown that the worship of the serpent represented on the bowl takes place in the supercelestial space beyond the starry heavens. This is confirmed by the winged serpent itself, the upper part of which is coiled around the upper half of the cosmic egg, which contains the starry heavens within it. And it is again confirmed by the inscription which informs us that this serpent is Helios-Dionysus-Phanes, who "turns forever the radiant sphere of distant motion that runs round the celestial vortices."

It is evident that the sixteen figures standing in this supercelestial space and forming a circle round the serpent are not gods but men: they lack all divine attributes, and moreover they stand in an attitude of worship suitable to men confronting the gods, but not to gods among gods. But how have men risen to this supercelestial space, to this "back" of heaven, as Plato calls it?

There are only two possibilities: Either they are souls who after departing from the body in death have risen up to heaven, have "fled from the mournful, terrible cycle to tread with nimble feet the lovely wreath,"[1] as the Orphics called the sphere forming the boundary of the starry heavens. Or else they are men who, having ascended to heaven and soared over the starry sphere in the ecstasy of their mystery cult, are re-enacting their experience in ritual. For all mystical experiences and the corresponding myths were either dramatically enacted before the initiates or represented in a ritual by the initiates themselves. Since nothing about the figures themselves indicates that they are disembodied souls (as might, for example, have been done by providing them with wings), but on the contrary their human corporeity is very much emphasized, we must decide for the second possibility: they are mystai, enacting that part of their religious experience which takes place in supercelestial space, where the God who encompasses the heavens and the whole cosmos appears to them in the form of the sun serpent. The flood of light which emanates from this God and envelops them with its rays is the seed and life of the world, as is unmistakably indicated by the attitude of the women's hands.[2]

1 OF 32 c:

κύκλου δ'ἐξέπταν βαρυπενθέος ἀργαλέοιο,
ἱμερτοῦ δ'ἐπέβαν στεφάνου ποσὶ καρπαλίμοισι.

2 Concerning the fertilization of women by a god in the form of the sun or of a sunbeam which penetrates the woman's body, see my book *Pneuma Hagion* (Leipzig, 1922), pp. 42ff.

Philo has given us a description of ecstasy in the terms and images of mystery theology: we can still perceive in it the fact that a cult served him as model:

> I . . . seemed always to be borne aloft into the heights with a soul possessed by some God-sent inspiration, a fellow-traveler with the sun and moon and the whole heaven and universe. Ah then I gazed down from the upper air, and straining the mind's eye beheld, as from some commanding peak, the multitudinous worldwide spectacles of earthly things, and blessed my lot in that I had escaped by main force from the plagues of mortal life.[3]

And in another passage this soaring of the soul to heaven and beyond it is described as follows:

> Again, when on soaring wing it has contemplated the atmosphere and all its phases, it is borne yet higher to the ether and the circuit of heaven, and is whirled round with the dances of planets and fixed stars, in accordance with the laws of perfect music, following that love of wisdom which guides its steps. And so, carrying its gaze beyond the confines of all substance discernible by sense, it comes to a point at which it reaches out after the intelligible world, and on descrying in that world sights of surpassing loveliness, even the patterns and the originals of the things of sense which it saw here, it is seized by a sober intoxication, like those filled with Corybantic frenzy, and is inspired, possessed by a longing far other than theirs and a nobler desire. Wafted by this to the topmost arch of the things perceptible to mind, it seems to be on its way to the Great King Himself; but, amid its longing to see Him, pure and untempered rays of concentrated light stream forth like a torrent, so that by its gleams the eye of the understanding is dazzled.[4]

Philo also repeatedly describes the experience of the soul in the super-celestial regions as a process of fertilization by the rays of the divine light.[5] He regards the Orphic-Dionysiac mystery as the symbolic expression of a process taking place in the soul. But through his image we can still discern the initiates rising above the earth and all things earthly, circling with

3 Philo, *De specialibus legibus*, III, 2f. (Tr. F. H. Colson, LCL, Vol. VII, 1941, pp. 475–77.)
4 *De opificio mundi*, 70f. (Tr. F. H. Colson and G. H. Whitaker, LCL, Vol. I, 1929, pp. 55–57.)
5 The passages are collected and explained in my book *Pneuma Hagion*, pp. 43ff. Also in J. Pascher, 'Η Βασιλικη 'Οδος, *Der Königsweg zu Wiedergeburt und Vergottung bei Philon von Alexandreia* (Paderborn, 1931), pp. 88ff.

the stars, and finally, at the summit of the heavenly vault, gazing into the infinite plenitude of light and beholding God at its center—just as, in Plato's *Phaedrus*, the soul ascends to the back of heaven, where it sees the circling stars and gazes into the spiritual world of ideas; or as Dante soars from the mount of Paradise to the starry spheres and is carried by them from one planet to another until at length he attains to the heaven of fixed stars and the outermost rim of this last heaven, upon which he stops and gazes into the celestial rose, in whose infinitely remote center shines the light of the triune God, source of all the light that here surrounds him. Whether we have to do with a cult ritual, with an actual ascension of the soul, or with the inward ascent of the soul to God—all three show the same structure.

If there are precisely sixteen mystai, it would seem to be because of the organization of the whole into fours, imposed by the four wind gods and the corresponding four quarters of heaven and earth; the four times four persons are merely a harmonious extension of these groups of four. Moreover, other bowls which we shall have occasion to discuss also disclose sixteen figures or sixteen heads grouped round the center, so that there would seem to have been a formal principle serving as a rule for such bowls and based on motifs of which we shall speak in the following pages. But since the center of our bowl is a representation of the sun and the figures form a continuation of the sun's rays, as though emanating from it, the whole stands in an obvious relation to the sixteen-rayed sun symbol, which is known to us from ancient oriental Greek and medieval art[6] and which has survived down to our own day in ornaments, particularly in the Japanese flag with its sixteen rays, on Japanese stamps with their sixteen sunflower leaves, and on the flag of Uruguay with its sixteen tongues of flame.

The number of initiates on the bowl may, however, have more than a

---

6 As, for example, the sixteen-rayed sun on the Cyprus Phoenician bowl in R. Dussaud, *Les Civilisations préhelléniques* (Paris, 1914), p. 307, fig. 220; in the *Liber Floridus* of Lambert of St. Omer, in Ghent Codex 2, fol. 225, reproduced in Miller, *Mappaemundi*, Part III, p. 125, fig. 60; cf. also the sun with the sixteen stars in a woodcut by Michael Ostendorfer in *Die Kunst im deutschen Buchdruck* (1915), pl. 53. Abundant material on the eight-rayed symbol of the sun and the year is to be found in Herman Wirth, *Die Ura Linda Chronik* (Leipzig, 1933), pp. 155ff., 183ff., and on the sixteen-rayed symbol, p. 185; see especially fig. 119, a golden disk (found in East Frisia) representing the solar year, divided into eight parts, each of which is in turn subdivided into eight parts; and fig. 120. Leo Frobenius gives an illustration of a sunflower divided into sixteen parts in the center of a wooden disk representing the universe and forming the centerpiece of a tent roof—see his *Kulturgeschichte Afrikas* (Frankfort on the Main, 1933), p. 171, fig. 120. Frobenius here calls sixteen a "templar" number.

purely formal significance. The Sabazius relief from Koloë[7] also discloses exactly sixteen worshipers, though here they are arranged in rows. The number occurs also in a magic papyrus, in which Helios-Aeon is invoked as "the mighty one of heaven, the airy one, who derives his power from himself, to whom all nature is subordinated, who inhabits the whole inhabited earth, [whose] spear-bearers are the sixteen giants."[8] But unfortunately we do not know the significance of these giants in the Aeon's train. This is all the material we have been able to gather concerning this number and its significance. And my inquiry into the asymmetrical and arbitrary order of men and women, of bearded and beardless men, has brought no positive result.

More illuminating is the circumstance that the sixteen figures on our bowl are totally nude. It is nowhere recorded, and it seems unthinkable, that men and women, participating in a public ritual at the time of the Roman emperors to which this bowl indubitably belongs, removed all their clothes. This is one more reason why the scene on the bowl can represent only a mystery cult, and only a mystery cult to which women were admitted. And this brings us again to the Orphic mysteries, in which, as in all Dionysian cults, women not only were admitted but played a leading part; for they were the vehicles and inciters of ecstasy.

In nearly all the mystery cults, the mystes undergoing initiation had to perform innumerable purifications and ablutions, in preparation for which he removed his clothing.[9] The representations, however, that have come down to us of initiations into the Eleusinian and other mysteries show us that not all the participants cast off their clothing, but only the mystes about to be initiated.

It was otherwise in the Orphic mysteries. In his *Clouds*, Aristophanes parodies an Orphic[10] initiation: "Here it is customary that they enter naked." After his initiation, the mystes is led into the holy of holies, which

7 "Sabazius led by the god Men," reproduced in Roscher's *Lexikon*, IV, s.v. "Sabazios," 244.
8 Papyrus Berolinensis, in Preisendanz, II, 101ff.
9 G. Anrich, *Das antike Mysterienwesen* (Göttingen, 1894), pp. 200ff.; J. Heckenbach, "De nuditate sacrisque vinculis," in *Religionsgeschichtliche Versuche und Vorarbeiten* (Giessen), IX (1911), pp. 12ff.
10 Cf. A. Dieterich's interpretation of the scene in *Clouds*, 498ff., as a parody of the Orphic rite, in *Rheinisches Museum*, XLVIII, (1893), and Heckenbach, p. 13: "*Strepsiades, qui lustratione purgatus ἐπόπτης factus est, in adytum intrat nudo corpore,* quo γυμνοὺς εἰσιέναι νομίζεται."

none may enter except naked; on his way, he says that he feels as though he were descending into the cave of Trophonius. And into this cave, as we know from other sources, the mystai entered naked.[11] There is also a passage in which Plotinus likens the ascent to the Good and Godly to the mysteries, by which the Neoplatonists always meant the Orphic version of the Eleusinian Mysteries:

> To attain it is for those that will take the upward path, who will set all their forces towards it, who will divest themselves of all that we have put on in our descent:—so, to those that approach the Holy Celebrations of the Mysteries, there are appointed purifications and the laying aside of the garments worn before, and the entry in nakedness.[12]

This accords with what Hippolytus says of the Eleusinian Mysteries, which the Naassenes, the Gnostic worshipers of the great serpent, appropriated and interpreted in their own way. He too knew that there was a descent and an ascent in these mysteries.[13] The descent belonged to the lesser mysteries of Persephone, the ascent to the great mysteries which were enacted by the hierophant "at night, by blazing firelight" and which culminated in the cry, "Queen Brimo has borne a holy child, Brimos!" According to the Gnostic interpretation, this "queen" signified the higher, celestial creation, to which the initiate ascended in order to be reborn in spirit: "This is the gate of heaven and this is the house of God, where the good God dwells alone, whither no profane person, no person of the soul or the flesh is admitted, but which is reserved solely for the spiritual men. On their arrival, they must cast off their clothes and all become bridegrooms, having been made male by the virgin Pneuma. For this is the virgin, who bears in her womb, conceives, and gives birth to a son, who is neither of the soul nor of the body, but is the blessed Aeon of Aeons."[14]

---

11 *Scholium on Aristophanes, Clouds*, l. 508, I: ἐκεῖ οὖν οἱ μυούμενοι καθέζονται ἐπὶ τοῦ στόματος γυμνόι.
12 Plotinus, *Enneads*, I, 6, 7 (tr. Stephen MacKenna, London, 1917, Vol. I, p. 86): τεῦξις δὲ αὐτοῦ ἀναβαίνουσι πρὸς τὸ ἄνω καὶ ἐπιστραφεῖσι καὶ ἀποδυομένοις, ἃ καταβαίνοντες ἠμφιέσμεθα. οἷον ἐπὶ τὰ ἄγια τῶν ἱερῶν τοῖς ἀνιοῦσι καθάρσεις τε καὶ ἱματίων ἀποθέσεις τῶν πρὶν καὶ τὸ γυμνοῖς ἀνιέναι.
13 Hippolytus, *Elenchos*, V, 8, 41ff.
14 ὅπου δεῖ γενομένους βαλεῖν τὰ ἐνδύματα καὶ πάντας γενέσθαι νυμφίους ἀπηρσενωμένους [cf. V, 7, 13] διὰ τοῦ παρθενικοῦ πνεύματος, αὕτη γάρ ἐστιν ἡ παρθένος ἡ ἐν γαστρὶ ὀχοῦσα καὶ συλλαμβάνουσα καὶ τίκτουσα υἱόν, οὐ ψυχικόν, οὐ σωματικόν, ἀλλὰ μακάριον αἰῶνα αἰώνων.

Here we are no longer in Eleusis, but in a mystery cult of the god Aeon, celebrated according to the Eleusinian model, with a descent and an ascent leading to the gate of heaven and the house of the "good God," Agathodaimon, in whose presence all must cast off their clothes. And here they behold the birth of the Aeon by the Virgin Pneuma of heaven. The circumstance that all the mystai become bridegrooms (νυμφίοι) recalls the shout heard in the Dionysian mysteries: "νυμφίε, χαῖρε, νέον φῶς."[15] Here Dionysus himself is hailed as the bridegroom and new light. But the mystai who have experienced spiritual rebirth also become νυμφίοι; for it lies in the nature of the mystery cult that the mystai undergo the same experience as their god, that, as St. Paul says, they die with him, are buried with him, are reborn with him, and are resurrected with him.

That there was such a festival celebrating the birthday of the Aeon is proved not only by the public birthday festival of Sol Invictus, but by a mystery which Epiphanius describes:

> In many places they celebrated a very great festival in the night of Epiphany. . . particularly in the so-called Koreion at Alexandria. There is an immense temple there, the *temenos* of Kore. After watching all night, singing and playing the flute in honor of the sacred image, and celebrating a *pannychis*, they go down after cock crow, bearing torches, into a kind of underground crypt, carrying a carved wooden idol, who sits naked on a bier and has a cruciform golden seal on his forehead, two more on his hands, and two more on his knees, altogether five gold seals. They carry the god seven times round the center of the temple amid loud playing of flutes and drums and singing of hymns, and then carry it to this underground place. When they are asked what mystery this is, they say that at this hour Kore—that is, the virgin—has given birth to the Aeon.[16]

It is not stated whom the sacred image represented. Most writers have thought it to be the Aeon. But there is nothing in the text to prove that it is not the Aeon's mother, Kore, the goddess of this cult, to whom the temple was dedicated. These mysteries of Kore still preserved a bond with the Eleusinian Mysteries after which, despite new interpretations and meanings, they were modeled. It is therefore interesting to note that in the mystery scene represented on the so-called Kerch vase, a goddess rises out of

15 Dieterich, *Eine Mithrasliturgie*, App. 214: "Reste antiker Liturgien VI."
16 *Panarion*, 51, 22, 8ff.; II, 285, 10ff.

the earth and hands Hermes a newborn child.[17] This rising of the goddess
out of the earth may very well have served as model for the ritual described
by Epiphanius, in which the image of the god is carried up out of the cave.

All this shows in any case that there were during the Hellenistic period
Gnostic mysteries of the birth of the Aeon, both Christian and non-Christian, which were celebrated either in the night of the winter solstice, December 24, or at Epiphany on the night of January 5.[18] And Laurentius Lydus[19]
tells us that the Roman god Janus was the father of the Aeon, if not the
Aeon himself, whose festival was celebrated by the ancients on the fifth day
of Januarius.

Hippolytus' account of the Naassene mystery of pneumatic rebirth shows
us that the initiates may well have cast off their clothing at the climax of
such a nocturnal mystery festival in honor of the Aeon's birthday. And a
passage in Epiphanius (which Kern includes in his *Orphicorum fragmenta*
because of the unquestionably Orphic implements and symbols mentioned
in it) shows that the Orphic mysteries were singled out for particular re-
proach because the women appeared in them naked.[20] Yet this nakedness
was not limited to the heathen mysteries; in the rites of the Barbelo Gnostics
the mystai were likewise "completely naked" when performing certain
rites.[21]

In the birthday festival of the Aeon at the Koreion in Alexandria, the
cult image itself was naked. But nothing is said as to whether the mystai
were clothed or not. However, their sevenfold march round the temple
with the naked image seems to suggest a possibility that has hitherto been
overlooked. Karl Holl cites a passage in Plutarch's treatise *On Isis and
Osiris*[22] in support of his theory that the procession was Egyptian[23] in origin

17 See A. Furtwängler, *Jahrbuch des Kaiserlich Deutschen Archäologischen Instituts*
(Berlin), VI (1891), 121ff.: "The woman rising up out of the earth is as usual Gaea;
the child wrapped in the deerskin is Iacchus, who was born to Persephone in the underworld. He is given first to Hermes. . . . The torchlight and the beating of the
tympanum are perfectly comprehensible in connection with Iacchus, of whose cult
these things form a part." Cf. Kern, *Die griechischen Mysterien der klassischen Zeit*
(Berlin, 1927), 67.
18 Cf. Karl Holl, "Der Ursprung des Epiphanienfestes," *Sitzungsberichte der Kgl. Preuss.
Akademie der Wissenschaften* (1917), 402ff.
19 *De mensibus*, IV, 1 (p. 64, ll. 6ff., Wünsch).
20 Epiphanius, *Catholicae et Apostolicae Ecclesiae fidei expositio*, 10 (p. 506, Oehl) = *OF*
34: τά τε ἐν Ἐλευσῖνι μυστήρια, Δηοῦς καὶ Φερεφάττης καὶ τῶν ἐκεῖσε ἀδύτων τὰ
αἰσχρουργήματα, γυναικῶν ἀπογυμνώσεις, ἵνα σεμνότερον εἴπω, τύμπανα τε
καὶ πόπανα κτλ.   21 Epiphanius, *Panarion*, 26, 5.
22 Ch. LII, 372 C.   23 Holl, pp. 426f.

and character. But since we are dealing with a birthday festival the Greek *amphidromia* comes equally to mind. On the name day, which was ordinarily celebrated five days after birth,[24] the child was carried round the altar, and those participating in the ceremony were naked.[25] The principal part in this rite was played by the mother. Now supposing that the cult image carried round the center of the temple in the Koreion was not the child, the newborn Aeon, whom the description does not fit, but its mother, Kore, to whom the shrine was dedicated, the ritual of the amphidromia would account for the idol's nakedness.

Since the Aeon was among other things the year, the celebration on the fifth day of the year suggests a name day rather than a birthday. True, Epiphanius states explicitly that those questioned as to the meaning of the festival had replied, *"At this hour,* Kore has given birth to the Aeon." But the procession round the temple recalls the name-day festival. Birthday and name-day festival seem to coincide, and in this connection it should be remembered that according to Hippolytus the *name* of the *newborn* god was proclaimed in a loud voice at the climax of the festival: "Brimo has given birth to Brimos!" And moreover, in the procession mentioned by Plutarch, a female image, Isis in the form of a cow, was carried round the shrine of Helios. All these rites were in some way related, though today the nature of the connection can only be surmised. In any case, it should be remembered that the mystai were naked in the Orphic mysteries and in various pagan and Gnostic cults of the Aeon as well; and this is the sphere to which our investigations of the bowl invariably lead.

It should further be considered that contact with sacred serpents seems to call for nakedness, and on the alabaster bowl the Aeon is manifested to the mystai as a serpent. Aelian[26] reports that the Epirots kept snakes in a grove sacred to Apollo, the sun god, and that these snakes were said to be descended from the Pythian dragon in Delphi. On the supreme festival of the year a naked virgin carrying food for the snakes had to enter this grove, which was surrounded by a high wall. If the beasts regarded her amicably

24 Plato, *Theaetetus*, 160 E; Aristophanes, *Lysistrata*, 757; Athenaeus, IX, 370; C. Becker, *Anecdota Graeca*, 207.
25 Hesychius, s.v. δρομιάμφιον ἦμαρ ἀμφιδρομία. ἔστι δὲ ἡμέρα ἐβδόμη [according to other traditions it was the fifth day] ἀπὸ τῆς γεννήσεως, ἐν ᾗ τὸ βρέφος βαστάζοντες περὶ τὴν ἑστίαν γυμνοὶ τρέχουσι.
26 *De natura animalium*, XI, 2: ἡ τοίνυν ἱέρεια, γυμνὴ παρθένος, πάρεισι μόνη καὶ τροφὴν τοῖς δράκουσι κομίζει.

240

and took the cakes which she carried, this betokened abundance and health for the coming year. Here again serpent, virginity, nakedness, and the sun god are related in some way which we can no longer exactly define. Further information is supplied by the gestures of the sixteen figures. All hold one hand, in most cases the right, before their breast, at varying heights. The other hand hangs down or, in the case of some of the women, is held before the pudendum. The men hold it at the level of their heads, with the palm facing the serpent, the godhead.

The gesture of the women holding one hand before their breast, the other before their pudendum, is easily explained. It is the attitude of the *Venus de' Medici*, the involuntary gesture of the nude woman, here particularly justified in the presence of the virile snake who contains within himself all fertility and all seed. And it should not astonish us that in this late work the women should lack the grace of Aphrodite.

The meaning of the raised hands likewise seems quite clear. It is the gesture of prayer, which can also be performed with *one* hand, particularly when the other hand is occupied, holding, for example, a shield in the case of the soldier, a sacrificial bowl or other ritual object[27] in the case of the priest. Since only the men raise their hands, we may assume that they are praying for the women or in their name.[28] That the other hand is not raised suggests that it is not free, but has another gesture to perform. It must be laid on the breast. And it was the right hand which belonged on the breast, since all with one exception raise their left hand in prayer, a gesture otherwise frowned upon and customary only in the cult of the gods of the underworld.[29]

It was not customary, in the Greek and Roman cults of the classical period, to lay the right hand on the breast. Only slaves laid their hand on their breast in token of submissiveness; then it was the left[30] hand, and this is true only of two figures on the bowl, who were perhaps thus characterized as slaves.

27 C. Sittl, *Die Gebärden der Griechen und Römer* (Leipzig, 1890), p. 188ff.
28 Delbrueck und Vollgraff, p. 132.   29 Sittl, p. 189, 1.
30 Ibid., p. 162: "Today one is scarcely aware of any servile implication in the gesture, now widespread in Greece, of laying the left hand on the breast (in a Campanian painting Deidamia petitions with this gesture [Helbig, 1300], at the same time raising her right hand). When the gesture is prolonged into a fixed attitude, it reveals the Greek slave awaiting his master's commands (Eustathius, *Makremb.*, 3, 1, 1: τὴν γάρ τοι λαιὰν περὶ τὸ στῆθος εἶχον δουλοπρεπῶς); in an Athenian funeral banquet (Sybel, 557) the servant is characterized by this attitude."

The custom of laying the right hand on the breast as a ritual gesture is found in a sect with which we have not yet concerned ourselves, and contemporary observers were unable to account for it. In his account of the curious sect of the Therapeutae, who had a settlement on Lake Mareotis, near Alexandria, Philo writes: "But every seventh day they meet together as for a general assembly [καθάπερ εἰς κοινὸν σύλλογον], and sit in order according to their age in the proper attitude, with their hands inside the robe, the right hand between the breast and the chin and the left withdrawn along the flank."[31] And in another passage he says that this is the customary attitude of the Jews going to synagogue to perform the customary *thiasos* "with your right hand tucked inside and the left held close to the flank under the cloak."[32]

In his commentary on Philo's *De vita contemplativa*, Conybeare says that this attitude is customary among the Jews and goes so far as to state that he has seen Polish Jews assume it on the Sabbath.[33] I wrote to an authority in these matters and received the following answer: "I have passed your inquiry on to a friend who was brought up in Poland and is throughly familiar with the local customs. He is of the opinion that Conybeare's statement must be based on a misunderstanding, since this attitude is not even customary on the street, much less at divine service. The Eastern Jew is far from sitting still when he prays; on the contrary, he moves violently. The passage in Philo cannot be explained on the basis of Eastern Jewish customs. It seems more likely that in this passage Philo is not imputing pagan customs to Jews, as he sometimes does, but that the Jews of the Diaspora actually were influenced by the manner of praying current among the people among whom they lived."

Philo's whole work is characterized by his endeavor to read a mystery theology into the Old Testament, and his account of the *thiasos* of the Therapeutae also contains elements drawn from the mysteries, which would seem to explain the attitude of prayer which he imputes to them.

31 *De vita contemplativa*, 30: εἴσω τὰς χεῖρας ἔχοντες, τὴν μὲν δεξιὰν μεταξὺ στέρνου καὶ γενείου, τὴν δὲ εὐώνυμον ὑπεσταλμένην παρὰ τῇ λαγόνι. (Tr. F. H. Colson, LCL, 1941, Vol. IX, p. 131.)
32 *De somniis*, II, 126: τὴν μὲν δεξιὰν εἴσω χεῖρα συναγάγοντες, τὴν δὲ ἑτέραν ὑπὸ τῆς ἀμπεχόνης παρὰ ταῖς λαγόσι πήξαντες. (Tr. Colson and Whitaker, Vol. V, p. 499.)
33 F. C. Conybeare, *Philo about the Contemplative Life* (Oxford, 1895), p. 214: "I have seen Polish Jews on a Sabbath day preserve the same attitude in walking."

In the Koloë Sabazius relief,[34] the worshipers coming from the left actually hold their right hand against their breast, though not quite so high as in Philo's account ("between the breast and the chin"), and the left hand is extended downward against their body, inside their garments. Those coming from the right, presumably for reasons of artistic symmetry, hold their hands in the reverse position, the left hand on their breast, the right hand extended downward.

Fig. 3. *Tombstone of the Attis Mysteries*

On a tombstone of the Roman period, ornamented with two figures of Attis suggesting that the family which had it made belonged to the mystery cult of Attis, we find, under the main group representing a family scene, a row of five busts, probably representing children or other relatives. All hold their right hand against their breast, while their left hand is pressed against their body under their garments.[35]

On another tombstone, probably from Phrygia,[36] a woman is shown entrusting her husband to the protection of Hecate; under the image of the goddess, we see husband and wife, both with their right hands on their [*Pl. VI*]

34 See p. 236, n. 7, above.
35 Laurenz Lersch, ed., *Centralmuseum rheinländischer Inschriften* (Bonn), II (1840), 63, no. 90. Also A. Haakh, *Attis-Bilder auf römischen Grabdenkmälern* (Vortrag der Philologentagung zu Stuttgart im Sept. 1856; 1857), 27.
36 Reproduced in C. Daremberg, E. Saglio, and E. Pottier, *Dictionnaire des antiquités*, Vol. III, 2 (Paris, 1904), p. 1395, with reference to S. Reinach, *Catalogue du Musée de Constantinople*, no. 244, p. 36; *Bulletin de correspondance hellénique* (Paris, 1896), Pl. XVI. According to J. H. Mordtmann, *Athenische Mittheilungen* (*AIDR*, 1885), p. 16, "the inscription suggests that the monument is from Cotyceum, in Phrygia."

breast and their left hands inside their garments, exactly as in Philo's account of the Therapeutae. The cult image discloses the triform Hecate as moon goddess, to her right Men with palm and crescent, to her left Herakles with the hound of hell, and above her Helios; the whole is surmounted by the eagle of Zeus and ornamented with ritual implements. This points to the mysteries of Hecate which in late antiquity merged with the Orphic-Dionysian mysteries and with those of Mithras.[37]

In the Eastern European territories dominated by the Greek Orthodox church, both the forms and the spirit of the ancient mysteries have been preserved down to our own day. In the Russian sect of the Men of God, to which, according to Fülöp-Miller,[38] Rasputin belonged, we find the same secrecy, the hymns, the round dances in the direction of the sun's course and in the contrary direction in imitation of the dances of the heavenly angels; the initiates cast off their clothes to don white shirts used solely for this purpose; they sing and dance to induce a state of ecstasy in which the Holy Ghost speaks through his prophets and prophetesses, and which culminates in a general sexual orgy, resulting in children begotten by the Holy Ghost.[39] Rasputin himself danced before his faithful and threw off his clothes at the climax. A well-known picture, reproduced in Fülöp-Miller, shows him in the very attitude assumed by the mystai on our bowl: one hand upon his breast, the other raised to the level of his head in blessing and adjuration.

All this makes it clear that the hand laid on the breast and the whole attitude described by Philo and represented on the bowl, on the Sabazius relief, and on the tombstones of the devotees of Attis and Hecate, were customary in mystery cults. Since it resembles the attitude of the slave, who lays his hand on his breast in token of his submissiveness and obedience, we may recall the familiar motif of the δοῦλος θεοῦ, the servant of God, who is a prisoner (κάτοχος), a bondsman (δέσμιος), and a servant (θεραπευτής) before God.[40] Thus Philo's Therapeutae merely disclose the attitude of the servant of God, which indeed is in keeping with their name.

---

37 Cf. Heckenbach's article on Hecate in Pauly-Wissowa, VII, 2781.
38 René Fülöp-Miller, Der heilige Teufel: Rasputin und die Frauen (1927). (Tr. F. S. Flint and D. F. Tait, Rasputin, the Holy Devil, London and New York, 1928.)
39 A description of the cults of this sect is given by A. Pfitzmaier in Die neuere Lehre der russischen Gottesmenschen (Vienna, 1883).
40 See the section "Στρατιῶται Θεοῦ, κάτοχοι, δέσμιοι," in Reitzenstein, Die hellenistischen Mysterienreligionen.

In short, the figures on our bowl represent a community of mystery worshipers who have risen to the supercelestial realm at the climax of their cult rite. Here the godhead appears to them in the form of the great serpent, whom they salute in the attitude of servants of the god, the women expecting to conceive by the god, the men praying for them.[41] We would seem to be dealing with a mystery similar to that of Sabazius-Dionysus, in which, it is related, the mystai drew a snake between their thighs in order to consummate a mystical union with the god.

4. The Parallels

As we have seen, the centerpiece of the alabaster bowl represents the cosmic egg entwined by the sun serpent and surrounded by sixteen mystai situated in the supracelestial region, with the four winds blowing round the whole. When we seek for parallels, our attention turns first of all to the oriental bowls and basins, found from Phoenicia to India, which show the cosmos, often with the sun in the middle, sometimes disclosing the serpent, and always divided into four, eight, or sixteen sections. The four quarters of heaven, sometimes represented as heads, play a prominent part in these figures.[1] But in none of them do we find sixteen fully elaborated figures with the feet turned inward and the head turned outward, which are so characteristic of our bowl.

A fifth-century Etruscan lamp bowl, however, now in the Museum of [Pl. VII] Cortona,[2] reveals sixteen full figures of just this type and in just this arrangement. The figures occupy the *lower* surface, since the whole hangs from the ceiling and is seen from below. Seen as a whole, it forms a cone, at the apex of which there is a considerable depression intended for the oil; at the base

---

41 Delbrueck and Vollgraff express the opinion (p. 132) that traces of the fibula are to be found on the sexual parts of the men. This would argue for the religious chastity of the men in deference to the god who is expected to fertilize the women. Similarly, in the myth of Plato's Apollonian parentage, Apollo, before entering into a union with Perictione, commands Ariston to leave his wife untouched until the divine child is born. See Olympiodorus, *Vita Platonis*, ch. 1, and Diogenes Laërtius, III, 2. This episode is repeated in the gospel story of the conception of Jesus. See also Eugen Fehrle, *Die kultische Keuschheit im Altertum* (Religionsgeschichtliche Versuche und Vorarbeiten, Vol. VI; Giessen, 1910), pp. 22ff.

1 Cf. The compilation and reproductions in Frobenius, *Kulturgeschichte Afrikas*, pp. 170ff.

2 P. Ducati and G. Q. Giglioli, *Arte Etrusca* (Rome and Milan, 1927), p. 84, and fig. 66.

of the cone there is a bowl with sixteen smaller depressions, in which burn wicks connected with the oil reservoir.

Looking at the lamp from below, we see in the middle the face of the Gorgon, the Gorgoneion, which, according to the investigations of Emperor William II,[3] signified in pre-Hellenic times the sun, and more particularly the nocturnal sun, that passes at night from west to east through the underworld. This nocturnal sun survived in the mystery cults, as is shown by the well-known passage in which Apuleius describes an initiation into the mysteries: "I approached the very gates of death and set one foot on Proserpine's threshold, yet was permitted to return, rapt through all the elements. At midnight I saw the sun shining as if it were noon; I entered the presence of the gods of the underworld and the gods of the upperworld, stood near and worshiped them."[4]

This passage cannot be understood without knowledge of the Gorgoneion as the nocturnal sun. For what the Etruscan lamp represents is the realm of the four elements, the whole cosmos in which the mystery is enacted. In the middle we see the nocturnal sun, which shines in the underworld into which descends the mystes who goes to the borders of death and passes Proserpine's threshold. Around it a circle with four groups of beasts, each consisting of a lion and a griffin, which are tearing an animal to pieces but would seem to signify life on earth, predestined to death. Around them lies a band of twenty-eight waves, four times seven (a number represented on our bowl by the twenty-eight arches supported by columns), with eight dolphins swimming upon them, so suggesting the element of water. After the water must come the air, and then the starry realm of fire and light. These two elements are represented by eight sirens with the wings of birds and human faces, squatting on a three-stepped base, covered with fine lines that I should interpret as rain falling from the clouds of the air. Beside each siren squats a flute-playing silenus with erect phallus; he symbolizes the rain that falls from heaven to fertilize the earth—an old motif which we find in Aeschylus:

> The holy heaven yearns to wound the earth, and yearning layeth hold on the earth to join in wedlock; the rain, fallen from the amorous heaven, impregnates the earth, and it bringeth forth for man-

3 Former Kaiser Wilhelm II, *Studien zur Gorgo* (Berlin, 1936), cf. particularly pp. 81 and 83, the Gorgon's head in the zodiac and the Gorgoneion with exactly sixteen rays or snakes darting in all directions.

4 *Metamorphoses*, XI, 23 (tr. Robert Graves, *The Golden Ass*, London, 1954, p. 286).

kind the food of flocks and herds and Demeter's gifts; and from that moist marriage-rite the woods put on their bloom. Of all these things I am the cause.[5]

According to Proclus, *"Hye, Kye,"* "Let there be rain, conceive!"[6] the old cry raised in the Eleusinian Mysteries, was an allusion to the marriage of heaven and earth.

Over the head of each of the sixteen figures we see a sun and ten stars, indicating the stellar realm, which extends to the real fire and light of the sixteen flames on the upper side of the bowl, directly over the heads of the sirens and sileni, presumably representing the luminous supercelestial realm to which the soul attains when it has passed the outermost sphere of heaven.

Ducati[7] has remarked that the whole work is archaistic rather than archaic, and it seems quite likely that its symbolism is closely related to the Orphic mystery religions which flourished in Greece and southern Italy in the fifth century. We find a curious reference to the eight sirens in Plato, who liked to associate the old Orphic myths and symbols with his philosophy and with the cosmology of his time. In the great myth at the end of his *Republic*, the souls descend after death to the underworld and then rise up through the air and the heavens, until they come to a place above the heaven of fixed stars, where the Milky Way surrounds the whole cosmos like the rainbow; it is the light which is the "band" holding heaven together. At its ends there is the spindle to which are fastened the eight celestial spheres, which move and are turned by it in circles of varying size. "The spindle," Plato writes, "turns on the knees of Necessity; and on the upper surface of each circle is a siren, who goes round with them, hymning a single tone or note. The eight together form one harmony."[8] It might be asked whether the eight sirens on the Etruscan lamp bowl, with a sun and stars over their heads, are not the starry spheres, while the sileni playing the flute, like the Pan with pipe whom we have encountered above,[9] are embodiments of the harmony emanating from the sphere.

5 Aeschylus, fr. 44 (Nauck). (Tr. H. Weir Smith, LCL, 1926, Vol. II, p. 395.)
6 Proclus on Plato, *Timaeus*, 40 E; cf. Dieterich, *Eine Mithrasliturgie*, 214, and my book *Die Gnosis* (2nd edn., 1936), pp. 93ff.
7 *Arte Etrusca*, p. 84.
8 *Republic*, 616 B ff. (*The Dialogues of Plato*, tr. Benjamin Jowett, New York, 1937, Vol. I, pp. 874ff.).
9 Cf. the article "Sirenen" in Pauly-Wissowa, 2nd series, III, 298, with a reference to Iamblichus, *Vita Pythagorae*, 18, regarding the Orphic allusions in the passage from Plato.

The Etruscan lamp is related to the Orphic bowl both by its outward form—the centerpiece in high relief, surrounded by sixteen figures with their feet turned inward—and by its symbolism derived from the mystery cults: in both cases the center represents the sun while the whole signifies the cosmos and the ascent of the soul through the elements to the supra-celestial realm.

[Pl. IX] Another parallel is to be found in the golden sacrificial bowl from the Pietroasa treasure, to which Ernst Bux drew attention years ago. It also has at its center an omphalos surmounted by a figure sculptured in the round. Here too the whole inner surface is ornamented with human forms in full figure which, just as in the alabaster bowl and the Etruscan lamp, stand with their feet on the centerpiece and radiate out to the rim. Here again we have exactly sixteen figures, and the whole is divided into four parts, indicated by the sections in the leafwork. The golden and the alabaster bowl have approximately the same diameter; but the female form in the center is much higher than the serpent.

But aside from the purely formal resemblance, do the figures with which they are ornamented suggest an inner relation between them? This is a difficult question, because it is no simple matter to state the significance of the figures on the golden bowl, especially as the interpretations offered so far are assuredly unsound in many respects.

The treasure has been discussed in a number of recent works devoted to the history of the Germanic tribes and their art. But these works mention the bowl only briefly and do not go into the meaning of the figures.[10] A detailed description and interpretation of the bowl is contained in the Romanian archaeologist Odobesco's monumental work, *Le Trésor de Pétrossa*.[11]

10 As for example L. Wolff, in *Die Helden der Völkerwanderungszeit* (Jena, 1928), p. 48, with an illustration of the treasure after a lithograph from C. C. Diculescu, *Die Wandalen und die Goten in Ungarn und Rumänien* (Mannus-Bibliothek, no. 34, Leipzig, 1923), p. 47, fig. 29. On p. 44, Diculescu writes: "There is also an antique or—as A. Goetze assures me—a barbaric-antique sacrificial bowl." And on p. 51: "Beside these works of oriental art, there is a round bowl ornamented with a circle of mythological deities grouped round a seated female figure, which seems rather to belong to a Greek-barbarian type of art, which may have had its home north of the Black Sea. De Linas has associated the female figure, presumably the Earth, with various Babylonian deities. It is characteristic of this bowl that the vine leaves forming the border hang down beyond it. This indicates an entirely new sense of space, quite alien to classical art." And though Herbert Kühn mentions the treasure in *Die vorgeschichtliche Kunst Deutschlands* (Berlin, 1935), p. 159, he tells us nothing about the bowl.
11 Alexander Odobesco (professor of archaeology, University of Bucharest): *Le Trésor de Pétrossa: historique-description; étude sur l'orfèvrerie antique* (3 vols., Paris and Leipzig,

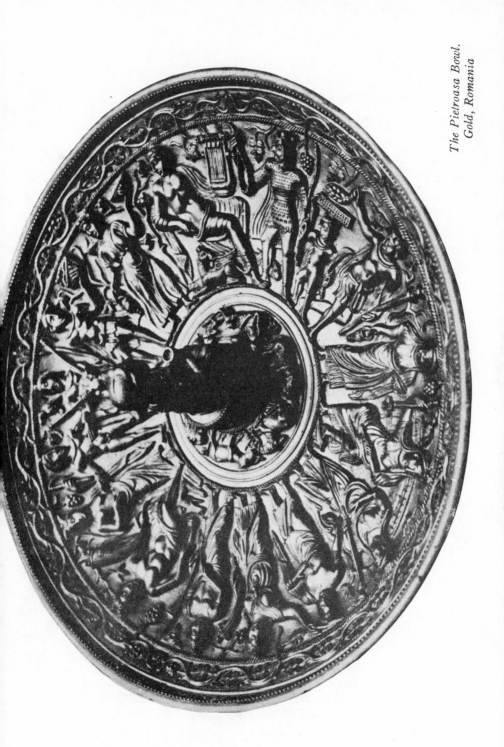

The Pietroasa Bowl.
Gold, Romania

IX

The Pietroasa Bowl, drawn without the center figure

First interpretation / Second interpretation

[1] Aegir / Orpheus the fisherman

[2] Fosite / Iacchus or Pluto

[3] Tyr / Mystes as torchbearer

[4] Urd, a Norn / Mystes as carrier of pail and bowl

[5] Verdandi, a Norn / Demeter

[6] Skuld, a Norn / Kore

[7] Saetor / The newly initiated mystes

[8] Freya / Tyche

[9] Odin / Agathodaimon

[10] Thor / Ptah

[11] Hela / Dionysius-Sabazius

[12, 13] The Alci / Castor and Triptolemus, or mystai

[14] Freyr / A mystes

[15] Ostara / A mystes (?)

[16] Baldur / Hyperborean Apollo

Center figure from the Pietroasa Bowl, drawn full face and in profile

The earth mother Herta / Magna Mater

This interpretation, however, is strongly influenced by associations with the place in which the treasure was found and by the first hypotheses concerning its origin. Whereas we do not know where the alabaster bowl originated or anything of its history, we have precise information about the treasure site, near Pietroasa, in the area of Buzau, in southeastern Romania, and about its adventurous history, which we cannot go into here.[12]

Of the twenty-two pieces of which the treasure originally consisted, only twelve were saved, most of them in a broken or bent condition; those which were recovered and taken to the National Museum in Bucharest weighed nineteen kilograms in all. The pieces consist of a large golden bowl, smooth both inside and outside; a single thick arm band; a still thicker arm band with runic writing scratched on it (the principal ground for associating the treasure with the Goths); a golden pitcher with handle and lid; the bowl under consideration, with mythological figures and the seated woman in the center; a necklace; one large clasp and three smaller ones; a golden, eight-cornered basket richly set with stones and a similar twelve-cornered basket.

At first the scientific world accorded little attention to the treasure. But after Odobesco exhibited it at the Paris Universal Exposition in 1867 and represented it as a product of "Gothic goldsmith's art," the French archaeologist Charles de Linas became interested and published the first scientific description of the pieces. De Linas' interpretation[13] of the golden bowl was embodied almost word for word by Odobesco in his large work on the "Trésor de Pétrossa,"[14] since it accorded perfectly with his own opinion that the treasure had once belonged to the Gothic king Athanaric, who supposedly hid it in Mount Istritza in 381 when he fled to the Emperor Theodosius in Byzantium, but was prevented from recovering it by his early death.

Charles de Linas begins his description of the bowl with the rim, sur- [Pls. IX, X] rounded by a band of pearls. Next to this, on the inside, is an ornament

---

1889–1900; "publié sous les auspices de sa Majesté le roi Charles Ier de Roumanie"). [Our reproductions of the bowl are from this source. It may be added that the treasure was discovered in 1837.—ED.]

12 The history of the treasure's discovery and subsequent vicissitudes was investigated and reported in detail by Odobesco. His findings were summarized in W. Krogmann, "Die Schicksale des Goldschatzes von Pietroasa," *Westermanns Monatshefte*, CLXII (1937), 2, 461–64, written on the occasion of the centenary of the discovery.

13 Charles de Linas, *Histoire du travail à l'Exposition universelle de 1867* (Arras and Paris, 1868), Vol. I, pp. 183–97, reprinted in *Revue archéologique de Paris*, N. S., IX (1868), pp. 46–56.

14 Vol. II, pp. 31ff.

consisting of four vines, from which leaves and bunches of grapes hang down into the interior of the bowl. The ornament is bounded on the inside by a raised cord.

The main surface is occupied by sixteen figures radiating from a center, the feet turned toward the centerpiece and resting on a second cordlike rim. Adjoining these are two parallel rings that delimit the center piece. The center piece consists of animals and a reclining human figure, grouped round a sitting female figure in high relief. The reclining figure is interpreted as a shepherd. At his feet lies a dog. The other beasts inside the circle are a recumbent ass, a running ass, another recumbent ass, a striding lion, and a running leopard. To the right and left of the running ass, a plant is to be seen.

[Pl. XI] The woman seated in the middle is dressed in a long sleeveless tunic that is fastened at the waist by a cord. Her hair, parted in the middle, is coiled round her head and gathered into a knot behind. The contours of her bosom and knees are visible beneath her garment. Her coarse features are those of a mature woman. She holds a conical goblet (*calathus*) in both hands in front of her breast. She seems to be sitting on a drum (*scamnum*). It is decorated with the same vine-leaf ornament as the rim of the bowl; and delimited above and below by the same cordlike line. The female figure is interpreted as the aged Jordh or Herta of the Germani, corresponding to the Mother Earth or Cybele of the Greeks and Romans. Odobesco gives reproductions of a few similar figures from antiquity, the most striking parallel being provided by a Babylonian goddess in exactly the same posture and holding the same goblet in her hand.[15]

Odobesco believed this figure and the others on the bowl to represent Gothic deities in the stylized form of late antiquity. He characterized it as a masterpiece produced by Gothic goldsmiths under Greek and Roman influence. He describes and interprets the figures occupying the principal surface of the bowl as follows:

[Pl. X] [1] A bearded man, standing beside a seated figure with a lyre. De Linas calls him Aegir, the Gothic Neptune. He has on a short tunic of skins with close-fitting sleeves (*chindota*), gathered at the waist by a belt. His headdress consists of the scalp of a wild animal, his feet are clad in low boots (*perones?*), his shoulders covered by a chlamys. In his right hand he holds a scarf

---

15 Odobesco, figs. 62 a and b. This piece, which is believed to have been found near Baghdad, is preserved in the Louvre. The illustration was taken from A. de Longpérier, *Musée Napoléon III* (Paris, n. d.), Pl. II.

(*strophium*) with its ends together, or else a sling (*funda*); and in his left hand he bears a bow with the string wound round it. A fat fish is to be seen between his legs.

[2] The figure of a standing child, naked except for a chlamys over his shoulders. He ostensibly represents the Gothic god Fosite. On his head he has a box resembling a chessboard (*arcula*) and in his left hand either an ear of grain or a palm branch.

[3] The god Tyr, the Gothic Mars, a beardless youth clad in a chlamys and a loincloth (*semicinctum*). A raven sits on his right shoulder. In his right hand he bears a cluster of grapes, in his left a torch.

[4] Urd, one of the three Norns, the Gothic Fates, standing, wearing a loose veil (*amictus*) and a garment resembling a judge's robe. In her right hand she holds a *situla*, or pail, in her left hand a *patera*, or bowl.

[5] The second Norn, Verdandi, dressed like the first, sitting in a chair on whose broad back a raven is perched. In her right hand she holds a short scepter, in her left a pair of open shears.

[6] Skuld, the third Norn, standing, with a torch in her left hand.

[7] Saetor, the Gothic Saturn, a bearded man with bare breast. The rest of his body is draped in a long cloak. In his right hand he holds a *strophium* twisted into a rope; his left hand rests on his breast.

[8] Freya, the Gothic Venus, wearing a gown like that of the Norns, with a cloak and a fringed *strophium* over her bosom. Her arms and breasts are bare; her hair is coiled in a wreath, and two braids fall down over her shoulders. With her right hand she holds a wreath over the god standing beside her, in her left hand she carries a cornucopia.

[9] Odin, whom Tacitus called the Mercury of the Germans, beardless, dressed like Saetor; he is wearing armlets and on his head he carries a grain measure (*modius*). In his right hand he holds a caduceus turned downward, in his left hand a large ear of grain or a palm branch.

[10] Sitting on either a walrus or crocodile, Thor, the Gothic Vulcan, wearing nothing but a loincloth (*semicinctum*). In his right hand he carries a round mallet or hammer, in his left a cornucopia.

[11] Hela, the goddess of death. The upper part of her body is bare; her long, wavy hair falls down over her shoulders. Over her head are two bird's wings; in her hands she holds a sacrificial bowl.

[12, 13] The two Alci, the German Dioscuri, each naked except for a chlamys, holding scourges in their hands. Between them is a raven.

[14] Freyr, the Gothic god of peace and abundance; he is a beardless youth, wearing only loincloth and chlamys. In his right hand he holds a staff, in his left a basket of fruit.

[15] Ostara, goddess of the spring, in a long dress with short sleeves and a plaited girdle. She carries a pail in her right hand and a sacrificial bowl in her left.

[16] Baldur, the Gothic Apollo, crowns the whole. He sits almost naked, draped in the ancient fashion in a wide mantle, and holds a lyre in his left hand and a plectrum in his right. A hippogriff[16] lies at his feet, and beside him rises a pomegranate branch.

No one familiar with classical antiquity will be able to read this description of a vineclad Gothic Olympus without indignation or at least amusement. And yet this interpretation has its historical value, for it drew attention to the treasure of Pietroasa and sustained public interest in it, even though Joseph Arneth,[17] the first scholar to give a brief interpretation of the bowl, had associated it with the cult of Dionysus, and although F. Matz in a brief article[18] had declared it to be a representation of the Eleusinian Mysteries and of the deities associated with the Mysteries in the Hellenistic period. Both men were on the right track, but no one listened to them.

After the Paris Exposition the treasure was taken to London, where it was exhibited for six months at the South Kensington Museum. Here the pieces were photographed and the pictures were published in a large album with detailed descriptions taken from Odobesco and de Linas.[19] Six of the pieces, among them our golden bowl, were galvanoplastically reproduced and the copies retained in the South Kensington (now the Victoria and Albert) Museum.

At about the same time Dr. Franz Bock drew attention to the treasure in Germany and Austria by his monograph on "the Treasure of Athanaric, king of the Visigoths, found in 1837 at Petreosa in Walachia,"[20] by which,

16 [Later identified as a griffin. See below p. 255, item no. 16—ED.]
17 *Sitzungsberichte der Kaiserlichen Akademie der Wissenschaften* (Vienna), 1848, Part II (historisch-philologischen Classe), p. 42.
18 "Goldschale von Pietraosa," *Archäologische Zeitung* (Berlin), IV (1872), pl. 4, 135ff.
19 *The Treasure of Petrossa and Other Goldsmith's Work from Roumania* (London, Arundel Society, 1869).
20 "Der Schatz des Westgotenkönigs Athanarich, gefunden im Jahre 1837 zu Petreosa in der Grossen Walachei," *Mitteilungen der K.K. Central-Commission zur Erforschung und Erhaltung der Baudenkmale* (Vienna), XIII (1868 : July-August), op. cit., 105–24, with nine woodcuts.

as Odobesco put it, "he made known to all Germany this admirable treasure and popularized it among the Germans by flattering their national pride with his evocation of Athanaric, one of the best-known chieftains of the Dacian Goths."[21] From this time on, the treasure was mentioned in histories of art, and scholars set out to determine how much of it was Gothic and how much Greco-Roman, Byzantine, or Oriental. The golden bowl with the figural ornamentation was usually numbered among the Greco-Roman or Byzantine works, but no one attempted to interpret the figures.

Meanwhile the treasure itself had disappeared from the Bucharest Museum. In the night of December 1, 1875, a young man broke in through the ceiling and stole it. When recovered, it was found to be damaged even more severely than after the rough handling of its original finders. In February, 1876, the wreckage was brought back to the Bucharest Museum, where it remained for years in this state, until a metal founder was sent from Berlin to make copies of the treasure.[22] The Romanian government commissioned this craftsman to fit the broken pieces together and restore the whole treasure, and he did so successfully with the help of photographs.

When Romania was threatened by the Germans in the first World War, the treasure was taken to Moscow, and it is unknown what became of it in the Russian Revolution and the ensuing years.[23]

As curious as the adventure of the treasure itself is the history of its interpretation, which alone concerns us here. While Odobesco, who clung to his "Gothic" interpretation, was still working on his compendious book Charles de Linas, to whom he owed his notion of a Gothic Olympus, revoked his opinion of 1868. For in the third volume of de Linas' work on the goldsmith's art,[24] which appeared posthumously, soon after his death in 1887, he put forward an entirely different interpretation, assigning the bowl to the milieu of the mystery cults of late antiquity and abandoning his former Gothic, Germanic hypothesis.[25] "Assuredly," he wrote, "these figures al-

21 Vol. I, p. 46.
22 One of these exact galvanoplastic copies was acquired by the Germanisches Museum in Nuremberg, which later ceded it to the Schloss-Museum in Berlin. [The author's original photographs were of this copy.—ED.]
23 [According to the Keeper of Metalwork, Victoria and Albert Museum, London, and also according to Romanian persons now resident abroad who are acquainted with official opinion on the subject, the Pietroasa treasure is now believed to have been melted down by order of the Russian authorities, as a consequence of a postwar dispute over reparations.—Ed.]
24 Charles de Linas, *Les Origines de l'orfèvrerie cloisonnée*, Vol. III (Paris, 1887).
25 Ibid., pp. 297–347.

lude to mysteries in which the sun is associated with the earth gods. The artist put Greco-Roman garb upon conceptions which were assuredly of oriental origin. What these mysteries were called I do not know."

The central figure was now the goddess of fertility, the Magna Mater, Nature, or Earth, conceived in accordance with a Babylonian model, and de Linas proved this by parallels drawn from all over the ancient world.[26] This was the universal goddess of late antiquity, who describes herself in Apuleius' *Golden Ass* as

> Nature, the universal Mother, mistress of all the elements, primordial child of time [*saeculorum progenies initialis*], sovereign of all things spiritual, queen of the dead, queen also of the immortals, the single manifestation of all gods and goddesses that are, whose nod governs the shining heights of Heaven, the wholesome sea breezes, the lamentable silences of the world below. She is worshiped in many aspects, known by countless names, and propitiated with all manner of different rites. She is the Phrygian Pessinuntia, mother of the gods; for the Athenians, she is Cecropian Artemis; for the islanders of Cyprus she is Paphian Aphrodite; for the Cretans she is Dictynna. She is Proserpine, Eleusinian Ceres, Juno, Bellona, Hecate, Rhamnusia. But the Egyptians call her by her true name, namely Queen Isis, who is represented with the rays of the rising sun god.[27]

Working with this passage from Apuleius, Charles de Linas takes the figure in the center of the bowl to be the Magna Mater, perhaps as she was worshiped in Pessinus, the principal shrine of Cybele, since here she was accompanied by lions and always associated with Attis, who is represented on the bowl by the shepherd lying at her feet.[28] The beasts to the right and left of the goddess are interpreted as the lion and lioness, who always appear in Cybele's train. The three asses belong to the cult of Hyperborean Apollo,[29] and the principal figure in the ring surrounding Cybele is Apollo.

The interpretation of the sixteen figures is again based on Apuleius;[30] this time on his description of the great procession in honor of Isis. The

---

26 These include, among many others, the limestone female figures, holding a chalice in both hands, from Yecla (Spain) on the Cerro de los Santos, now in the Madrid Museum. They are reproduced in Herman Wirth, ed., *Die Ura Linda Chronik* (Leipzig, 1933), pls. 163–70, text pp. 218ff.
27 *Metamorphoses*, XI, 5 (tr. Graves, p. 271, modified).
28 On Attis as shepherd, see the passages assembled in Roscher, *Lexikon*, I, i, 718.
29 Lucian, *De Dea Syria*, 31; Antoninus Liberalis, *Metamorphoses*, XX.
30 XI, 8ff. (Graves, pp. 274ff.).

procession opens with a throng of masked and costumed mystai. Next come white-clad women, bearing all sorts of implements for the worship of the goddess, and strewing the road with flowers. They are followed by men and women with lamps, torches, and candles. Behind these come singers and flute players and a group of initiates in white garments, the women with transparent veils on their heads, the men with shaven heads, all bearing sistra of bronze, silver, or gold. Then come priests bearing the symbols of the all-powerful goddess and others disguised as gods. Last comes the high priest carrying the sistrum of the goddess and a garland.

De Linas concluded that the figures on the golden bowl represent a similar assemblage of initiates and priests, some of them bearing the garments and symbols of gods. This is a highly plausible view, since all the Hellenistic mysteries, particularly those of the Great Mother, are in some way interrelated. The resulting interpretation of the sixteen figures is as follows:

[16] The figure face-to-face with the goddess, holding a lyre and sitting on a griffin—a winged lion with the head of an eagle—is Hyperborean Apollo. Here I should like to remark that particularly among the Orphics,[31] and consequently in all the mysteries descended from them, Apollo signified the sun. Hyperborean Apollo is the sun which in the dark winter dwells in the northland, where Delphic Apollo also had his garden,[32] and since the annual cycle was conceived as running parallel to the daily cycle,[33] he is likewise the sun which appears at night among the Hyperboreans at the other side of the earth.[34] In the song to Apollo which figures among the Orphic hymns, he is seen as the sun of day and night:

> For thou surveyest this boundless ether all,
> And every part of this terrestrial ball
> Abundant, blessed; and thy piercing sight
> Extends beneath the gloomy, silent night;
> Beyond the darkness, starry-eyed, profound,
> The world's wide bounds, all-flourishing, are thine,
> Thyself of all the source and end divine.[35]

31 OF 172ff.
32 U. von Wilamowitz-Moellendorff, Der Glaube der Hellenen (Berlin, 1931–32), Vol. I, p. 253.
33 O. Gilbert, Griechische Götterlehre (Leipzig, 1898), pp. 281ff.
34 Ibid., p. 20; cf. also OF 172ff.
35 Orphic Hymn XXXIV (tr. Thomas Taylor, Mystical Hymns of Orpheus, London, 1896, p. 77).

If the Apollo on the golden bowl, characterized by the lyre, the griffin, and the asses sacrificed in his cult, is Hyperborean Apollo, he is the nocturnal sun. This would relate the golden bowl to the Etruscan lamp, with the Gorgoneion signifying the nocturnal sun, and also to the passage in which Apuleius describes the journey of the initiate who passes through all the elements until he sees the sun shining at midnight and in its light worships the gods face to face. Thus the mystai on the golden bowl are situated at the summit of heaven or in the supercelestial region as on the alabaster bowl.

[1] Beside Apollo stands an initiate masked as a fisherman, holding in one hand a fishing pole with the line wound around it, and in the other hand a mesh bag (*funda*). Between his feet a fish is to be seen. This is all that Charles de Linas has to say of the strange fisherman. But if a fisherman stands beside Apollo with the lyre; if the whole is wreathed in vine leaves; if, as we shall see, Dionysus, Demeter, and Kore are present—must this man with the net and pole and fish not be Orpheus the Fisherman, whose features have been brought out so clearly by Eisler's investigations?[36]

It is evident that the artist who fashioned this bowl included plants, land animals, aquatic animals, and birds in order to indicate the elements earth, water, and air, and the creatures that inhabit them. This would account for the birds between the figures, which need no longer be interpreted as Odin's ravens.

[2] The child with the basket on his head, standing beside the "fisherman," then becomes Iacchus or Pluto, Demeter's son, whose part is enacted by an initiate. This figure, I should like to remark, is not necessarily a "child." Often in ancient reliefs, both of the classical and late periods, persons who are carrying something on their heads, who are being crowned with a wreath, or upon whose head a hand is laid in blessing, are made smaller than those beside them. What the naked mystes carries on his head is not a basket but the *cista mystica:* he is a *cistophoros*.[37] The object held above him is a pine cone; the pine cone occurs in the cults of Dionysus and of Cybele, and the pine tree was sacred to Attis.

[3, 4] The next figures—the torchbearer and the woman carrying the pail and sacrificial bowl, two ritual objects of frequent occurrence in the mystery reliefs—are also initiates.

36 Robert Eisler, *Orpheus the Fisher* (London, 1921).
37 Cf. the satyr in exactly the same attitude and with the same little box on his head in Roscher, *Lexikon*, II, 1, 1378, in the article entitled "Kora."

[5, 6] The two women, however, the one sitting on a throne and bearing a scepter, the other standing beside her with a torch in hand, are unquestionably Demeter and Kore, as is proved by countless familiar parallels.

[8, 7] The next two figures represent another inseparable pair: one is Tyche, with the cornucopia, touching the just-initiated mystes with her magic wand to raise his soul above the earthly world. We are reminded of Virgil's Hermes:

> Then he takes his wand; with this he calls pale ghosts from Orcus and sends others down to gloomy Tartarus, gives or takes away sleep, and unseals eyes in death.[38]

[9] Next to Tyche, turned toward her, is Agathodaimon. They appear together in Pliny,[39] who mentions their statues on the Capitol—*"Boni Eventus et Bonae Fortunae simulacra in Capitolio"*—and elsewhere describes[40] an image of Bonus Eventus (Agathodaemon), carrying a dish (*patera*) in his right hand and in his left hand an ear of grain (*spica*) and a poppy (*papaver*). On our bowl, to be sure, he has no *patera*, but he does have a poppy stalk in his right hand and in his left a large ear of grain.

[10] De Linas interprets the god sitting on a crocodile(?), holding the hammer and cornucopia, as the Egyptian Ptah, who was usually represented with a hammer and with crocodiles at his feet, and who in Abydos was replaced by Osiris, in Thebes by Ammon Ra. Ptah is the rising sun, the crocodile is chaos, the hammer is the instrument of the demiurge, the cornucopia expresses the fertility to which the god gives rise. According to Charles de Linas, there is nothing unusual about the appearance of an Egyptian god in this milieu, since the mysteries of Isis were related in more than one way to those of Cybele. I might add that as early a writer as Hecataeus declared the mysteries of Osiris to be the same as those of Dionysus, while those of Isis and Demeter were very similar; they differed really only in name.[41]

[11] Accordingly de Linas identifies the deity with the bowl, standing beside this Osiris, as Dionysus in the Thracian-Phrygian form of Sabazius. But there is nothing in the figure's appearance to substantiate his conjecture.

[12, 13, 14] "The three following figures," de Linas goes on, "are the most

38 *Aeneid*, IV, 242f. (tr. H. R. Fairclough, LCL, 1929, Vol. I, p. 413).
39 *Historia naturalis*, XXXVI, 4.
40 Ibid., XXXIV, 19.
41 Diodorus Siculus, *Bibliotheca*, I, 96, 5, in *OF*, 293.

puzzling of the whole group." The first two are "naked in the manner of heroes and wear the *stemma*, the wreath of the ancestral images." The third is "dressed like a common mortal, carries a basket of fruit, and holds a staff or scepter, forming a counterpart to the mystes [No. 7] beside the Kore, like whom he has a priestess at his side." He, de Linas, identifies the objects which the first two hold in their hands as a scourge, a hoe, and a plowshare, and interprets the two figures as Castor the horse tamer and Triptolemus. But this raises the difficulty that Castor, one of the inseparable Dioscuri, would be appearing without his twin brother. I prefer an earlier interpretation, according to which these two naked men are mystai, both holding scourges and one of them a torch. De Linas seems to have forgotten that flagellation was characteristic of the cult of Cybele.

[3, 5, 13] Finally,[42] he discusses at some length the three birds, interpreted as ravens, sitting variously on the arm of the torchbearer, on the back of Demeter's throne, and on the scourge of one of the initiates. He points out that ravens are not limited to Germanic mythology, but occur in India, where the raven Kaka-Busudha is an incarnation of Brahma, and in Egypt, where the raven was held sacred to the sun god. Two ravens accompanied Alexander on his way to the temple of Ammon.[43] Aelianus reports that a pair of ravens nested near Coptos in Egypt, because there was a temple of Apollo nearby.[44] Callimachus tells how the Theraeans saw Apollo in a raven who appeared to them on the march to the spring of Kyra.[45] Both in Greek and Roman literature the raven is often the companion of Phoebus Apollo.[46] Thus the ravens on the golden bowl are an adjunct of Apollo, who occupies the place of honor, facing Cybele.

This Apollo, sitting on a griffin and holding a lyre, appears in the same attitude and with the same symbols in a second-century mural painting in a crypt on the Hill of Mithridates, near Kerch (ancient Panticapaeum), in eastern Crimea,[47] and it is to this very region, which is rich in gold, that de Linas assigns the beautiful and precious bowl. It was probably fashioned

42 [The author unaccountably omits discussion of No. 15, a female figure carrying a pail and a bowl. Because of her similarity to No. 4, one may take her to be another initiate. —ED.]
43 Strabo, XVII, 1, 43. Ptolemaeus, *Fragmenta*, 7 (p. 83, ed. Didot).
44 *De natura animalium*, VII, 18.
45 Hyginus, *Fabulae*, CCII; *Astronomica*, Bk. II (ed. B. Bunte, Leipzig, 1875, p. 76); Albricus, *De deorum imaginibus, Apollo;* Plutarch, *De Iside et Osiride,* 71, 379 D.
46 Wilamowitz, *Der Glaube der Hellenen*, Vol. I (1931), pp. 145ff.
47 *Compte-rendu de la Commission Impériale archéologique pour l'année 1875* (St. Petersburg, 1878), p. xxiv; Ludolf Stephani, in ibid., *1876* (pub. 1879), p. 219.

258

in Panticapaeum; for there was a gold market in this city, and the chiseled gold vessels found near Kerch prove that this was a center of the goldsmith's art. Situated between Europe and Asia, known for its wealth, this city must have had mystery congregations which could afford such costly vessels, either for use in their festivals or as votive offerings in their shrines.

Comparison with the Etruscan lamp, the oriental bowls, and the alabaster [Pls, VI, 1] bowl bearing the snake enables us to enlarge considerably on de Linas' interpretation, and to add one important motif. All these bowls represent the cosmos with its four elements, or a certain region in it. The bowl of Pietroasa, be it noted, likewise represents the cosmos: in the center the earth with the earth goddess, around them the plants, the wild and tame beasts, and finally man, in the form of the shepherd, with his dog. The animal group consisting of the two asses with the two lions to the right and left of them recalls by its style the wild animals on the Etruscan lamp. The earth is surrounded by two sharply protruding rings, which separate the three spheres of earth, water, air. A third cordlike ring, on which the figures stand, separates the realm of the earthly elements from the celestial region in which the mystery rite is enacted and which the initiate reaches after passing through all the elements. Here he stands before the gods of the upper and lower world, and worships them face to face. The upper and the lower gods are distinctly characterized. One sees the separate scenes of the mystery rite: the torchlight procession through the darkness, the initiation, the bearing of the *cista mystica*, the rite of rebirth, the flagellation, the ecstatic vision (*epopteia*) of the gods, and particularly of the sun god, the midnight sun. The vine leaves in which the whole is entwined are a clear indication of its Dionysian origins.

Thus the Etruscan lamp, the alabaster bowl, and the golden bowl from the Pietroasa treasure are united by a common bond. They all bear witness to the mysteries, to the diverse yet always interrelated forms of the original Orphic-Dionysian cult. And the development whose beginnings can still be discerned in these magnificent pieces—which have come down to us but by a fortunate chance—extends beyond antiquity, deep into the Christian world. This I should like to demonstrate by one last example: the eucharistic bowl of Xeropotamu, on Mount Athos, Greece, which, since it cannot [Pl. VIII] have been fashioned before the thirteenth century, shows that the tradition was still alive in the late Middle Ages.[48]

48 Cf. Oskar Wulff, *Altchristliche und byzantinische Kunst* (Berlin, 1914), Vol. II, p. 616, fig. 536. [Our photograph is from Wulff's source: N. P. Kondakow's work in Russian on the Christian monuments on Athos (1902).—ED.]

The omphalos has disappeared from the center, since the vessel no longer serves the same purpose; but the centerpiece itself has remained, showing in place of the Magna Mater the Mother of God with the Child. The main surface is still divided into sixteen parts, fifteen of which are occupied by angels representing the heavenly congregation of mystai, the *Liturgia Caelestis;* above each angel an apostle kneels in prayer. The sixteenth section contains the Tabernacle. The gods, the men, and the mystery itself have changed in form. Yet it is evident that this has been no arbitrary change, but rather the transformation of one form and one archetype, the "eternally One, manifesting itself in diverse ways."

Julius Baum

Symbolic Representations of the Eucharist

1. The Symbolic Character of Early Christian Art

The early Christians looked upon the supernatural foundations of their faith—the Nativity, the Last Supper, the Crucifixion, the Resurrection and Ascension—with a sacred awe. The *disciplina arcani*[1] which was introduced in the third century to safeguard the content and ritual of the Christian mysteries against the profane and which remained in force even after the Edict of Milan, in 313, and up to the abolition of the catechumenate, applied not only to the liturgy but to its artistic representation as well. This discipline of the secret required that the Christian paintings and sculptures in the congregation rooms and catacombs be kept hidden from profane eyes, and in any event that their inner meaning be inaccessible to the uninitiate. What in this art mystified outsiders was its symbolic character, which was rooted in the very nature of Christianity.

What for pagan antiquity was tangible reality existed for the Christian only as a metaphor referring to the hereafter. Material, earthly existence had lost its own value and become an intimation of the life to come. All sensuous existence became symbolic. Similarly in art, the emphasis was no longer on the visible, but on the deeper meaning expressed by the outward form. Not that all this art can only be understood symbolically. But behind certain representations of reality—one need only think of the *ichthys*—the believer found a deeper significance. He was able, through complex symbolic relations, to situate them within the history of redemption. And if this is true of simple, realistic pictures, how much richer in symbolic relations we may assume the representations of the actual Christian mysteries to have been.[2]

---

1 The term is no older than the 17th-century theologian Jean Daillé (Johannes Dallaeus). See Johann Peter Kirsch, in Michael Buchberger, *Lexikon für Theologie und Kirche* (2nd edn., Freiburg i. B., 1930–38), Vol. I, col. 652.

2 Adolf Hasenclever, in *Der altchristliche Gräberschmuck* (Brunswick, 1886), denies to early Christian art any symbolic character whatever. This work, characteristic of the materialist view of history, requires no refutation.

Among all the episodes in the story of salvation, it is the Lord's Supper whose representation was most shunned down to the fifth century. No other event is more mysterious and miraculous in its effect, none occupies the thoughts and feelings of the believer more powerfully and persistently. In place of the Last Supper, the early Christian artists represented the Eucharistic rite.

The Eucharist derives directly from Christ's sermon of promise (John 6 : 26–51), and from the words with which he instituted the Last Supper (Matthew 26 : 26ff., Mark 19 : 22ff., Luke 22 : 19ff., I Cor. 11 : 23ff.). These words were taken literally by the Church from its earliest beginnings, as is attested by the early and late Church Fathers,[3] and also by liturgical usage. At the time when the secular supper, whose sometimes undignified conduct St. Paul attacks in I Corinthians 11 : 21, was discontinued, the Eucharistic ritual already consisted in the parts listed by Justin in his first Apology, addressed to the young Antoninus Pius in 138 or 139: reading from the Old and New Testament, sermon by the head of the congregation, general intercessory prayer, kiss of peace, offering of bread and wine, Eucharistic prayer with consecration of the offering, communion of the faithful.[4] These are still the main elements in the Mass. Its sacramental form was set by the words with which Christ instituted the Lord's Supper, stating that his body and his blood which he shed for the remission of sins are present. "The Christian offering of the Eucharist is a true mystery, divine

---

3 Theophil Spáčil, in Buchberger, Vol. III, col. 822. Early Church Fathers: Ignatius of Antioch, *Ad Smyrnaeos*, c. 7; *Ad Ephesios*, c. 20; *Ad Philippenses*, c. 4. Justin, *Apologia*, I, c. 66. Irenaeus, *Contra haereses*, IV, 17, 5; IV, 18, 4; V, 2, 2. Tertullian, *De carnis resurrectione*, 8, *De pudicitia*, 9, *De oratione*, 19, *De idolatria*, 7, *De baptismo*, 16. Cyprian, *De oratione dominica*, 18, *De lapsis*, 16. Late Church Fathers: Gregory of Nyssa, *Oratio catechetica*, 37. Cyril of Jerusalem, *Catecheses mystagogicae*, 4, 2ff. John Chrysostomus, *Homilia 82 (83) in Matth.*, n. 1ff.; *Hom. 46 in Johannem*, n. 2ff.; *Hom. 24 in I Cor.*, n. 1ff.; *Hom. 9 de poenitentia*, n. 1. Hilary, *De trinitate*, VIII, 13. Ambrose, *De mysteriis*, VIII, 49; IX, 51ff. Augustine, *In Ps. 33 enarratio*, I, 10; *Epistola*, 54, 7, 8; *Sermo* 272.

4 The description of the ritual is followed by a warning that no unbelievers, unbaptized, or heretics may take part in it. For the bread and wine they receive are the flesh and blood of the Lord. The passage that follows is one of the foundations of the Patristic theology: "Οὐ γὰρ ὡς κοινὸν ἄρτον, οὐδὲ κοινὸν πόμα ταῦτα λαμβάνομεν · ἀλλ' ὃν τρόπον διὰ λόγου Θεοῦ σαρκοποιηθεὶς 'Ιησοῦς Χριστὸς ὁ σωτὴρ ἡμῶν, καὶ σάρκα καὶ αἷμα ὑπὲρ σωτηρίας ἡμῶν ἔσχεν, οὕτως καὶ τὴν δι' εὐχῆς λόγου τοῦ παρ' αὐτοῦ εὐχαριστηθεῖσαν τροφήν, ἐξ ἧς αἷμα καὶ σάρκες κατὰ μεταβολὴν τρέφονται ἡμῶν, ἐκείνου τοῦ σαρκοποιηθέντος 'Ιησοῦ καὶ σάρκα καὶ αἷμα ἐδιδάχθημεν εἶναι."—Justin, *Apologia*, I, 66 (Migne, *PG*, VI, 428). Cf. also Peters, "Eucharistie," in Kraus, *Realencyclopädie*, Vol. I, p. 436.

action in earthly symbols—the congregation feels the horror of death, the intimation of eternity, and the victorious power of the unfathomable miracle which Christ bestows on his own."[5]

Even Leonardo does not venture to express the full spiritual import of the Last Supper, but contents himself with the more dramatic and consequently more thankful representation of the announcement of Judas' betrayal. The mural painters of the Roman Empire did not approach Leonardo's creative achievement. With their modest talents they strove to paint the sacrament of the Eucharist in symbolic terms compatible with early Christian feeling. Neither the Consecration nor the Communion is directly shown. Instead, the Eucharistic rite is represented through symbolic acts of Christ considered as prototypes of its main elements. The miraculous multiplication of the loaves and fishes and the transformation of water into wine at the marriage at Cana typify the Consecration, while the feeding of the multitude and perhaps occasionally the supper of the seven disciples typify Communion. Usually these scenes are fused into a unit. The following study deals principally with these representations. In conclusion we shall devote a few words to representations of the Heavenly Banquet and of Feasts of the Dead.

The monuments available for our study belong almost exclusively to the province of mortuary art, outside of which only a very few pieces have come down to us. The publication of this art is incomplete. The most important publications, on whose illustrations this study is largely based and to which we shall repeatedly refer, are, for sculpture, Wilpert's *I Sarcofagi cristiani antichi;* for painting, his *Die Malereien der Katakomben Roms* and Rossi's *La Roma sotterranea cristiana.*[6] Both the nonmortuary art and the painting found in tombs outside Rome have likewise been only partially published. This circumstance has stood in the way of any conclusive iconographical study of this art, and moreover the scientific basis for a reliable dating is lacking. Rossi's dating of Roman cemeterial painting, emended and thoroughly documented by Styger,[7] has remained for the most part uncontested. However, Fritz Wirth, in his *Römische Wandmalerei vom Untergang Pompejis*

5 Hans Lietzmann, *A History of the Early Church*, tr. B. L. Woolf, Vol. III (London, 1950), pp. 288ff., in a detailed account of the 4th-century liturgy.
6 Josef Wilpert, *I Sarcofagi cristiani antichi* (3 vols., Rome, 1929-36) and [*Roma Sotterranea*], *Die Malereien der Katakomben Roms* (2 vols., Freiburg, 1903); Giovanni B. de Rossi, *La Roma sotterranea cristiana* (3 vols., Rome, 1864-77).
7 Paul Styger, "Die altchristliche Kunst, grundlegende Erörterungen über die Methode der Datierung und Auslegung," *ZKT*, LIII (1929), 545ff.

bis ans Ende des dritten Jahrhunderts (Berlin, 1934), has, on the basis of comparison with the surviving monuments of pagan antiquity, attempted a later dating of the oldest Christian monuments in Rome.[8] The first, but still not superseded, attempt at an iconographical summary of early Christian representations of the Last Supper is Eduard Dobbert's article "Das Abendmahl Christi in der bildenden Kunst," to which we shall also refer in the following.[9]

2. Representations of the Consecration

The Gospels mention two miraculous multiplications of bread and fishes for the feeding of the multitude. Matthew 14 : 17ff., Mark 6 : 38ff., Luke 9 : 13ff., and John 6 : 5ff. all relate that five loaves and two fishes were multiplied and that after the feeding of the five thousand there remained twelve baskets full of fragments. Matthew 15 : 32ff. and Mark 8 : 1ff. speak of a second occasion on which four thousand are fed on seven loaves and a few fishes. In Mark 8 : 18ff., the Lord speaks of both feedings. Origen[10] already regarded the loaves blessed by Jesus, with which he fed the multitude, as prototypes of the Eucharistic bread which is given the believer in Communion. For Prudentius,[11] the feeding of the multitude is the prototype of the Eucharist; the twelve baskets are filled with Christ's mysterious gifts. When Marcellina, sister of St. Ambrose, took the veil, Pope Liberius spoke of the miracle of the bread and wine, and went on to say: "He has invited more guests to thy marriage, to feed them not on barley bread, but on the bread of heaven, His body."[12] In the multiplication of the loaves, the divinity of Christ, who performed this miracle and who repeats it continu-

8 On the basis of his stylistic investigations, Wirth insists that no cemeterial paintings have come down to us from the 1st or 2nd century. In his opinion, the earliest paintings preserved are those from the tomb of Lucina in the catacomb of San Callisto, which he dates from 220. Next he lists those of the Flavian gallery of the catacomb of Domitilla, which previously had been placed in the 1st century and regarded as the earliest of extant Christian paintings. Wirth assigns the important murals of the Cappella Greca in the catacomb of Priscilla to the Constantinian period. These opinions have a bearing on iconography, for the hitherto accepted dating of the first appearance of several artistic themes is upset. Although a critical discussion is here impossible, we may permit ourselves to ask what has become of those monuments of Christian painting which originated before 220.
9 In *Repertorium der Kunstwissenschaft* (Berlin and Stuttgart), XIII–XIV (1890–91).
10 *In Matthaeum*, 10, 25 (Migne, *PG*, XIII, 902ff.).
11 *Apotheosis*, 736ff. (Migne, *PL*, LIX, 980ff.).
12 Ambrose, *De virginitate*, 3, 1 (Migne, *PL*, XVI, 219ff.).

a. *The Multiplication of the Loaves. Sarcophagus, Velletri Museum*

b. *The Multiplication of the Loaves. Catacomb of Santi Pietro e Marcellino, Cripta della Madonna, Rome*

I

a. *The Marriage at Cana. Catacomb of Santi Pietro e Marcellino, Rome*

b. *Communion scene. Catacomb of San Callisto, Cappella del Sacramento A 3, Rome*

c. *Fractio panis. Catacomb of Santa Priscilla, Cappella Greca, Rome*

a. *Communion scene. Sarcophagus lid, III century, Museo delle Terme, Rome*

b. *Feeding the Multitude. Sarcophagus lid, Museo delle Terme, Rome*

c. *The Induction of Vibia. Tomb of Vincentius, Rome*

III

a. *The Heavenly Banquet. Catacomb of Santi Pietro e Marcellino, Rome*

b. *Feast of the Dead. Tomb of Vincentius, Rome*

IV

ously in the Eucharist, is even more evident than in the feeding of the multitude. However, representations of the feeding predominate in the early period. After the fourth century, pictures of the multiplication of the loaves became more frequent, often juxtaposed to representations of the wine miracle, also symbolizing the Consecration.

We shall first take up the examples of the multiplication of the loaves. In sarcophagus sculpture a terse three-figure composition develops in the course of time. Christ stands between two apostles who hold out bread and fish for him to bless. At the Lord's feet are bread baskets. The fine sarcophagus in the museum of Velletri (Wilpert, *Sarcofagi*, pl. 4, 3; Pl. I*a* in the present volume), showing only the multiplication of the loaves and representing the Lord with hands upraised as if in prayer, belongs to the period before the type was definitely established. By far the greater number of the sarcophagi follow the normal type.[13] In the later representations, the Lord touches the bread baskets as in the miracle of the wine he touches the waterpots. Wilpert counts twenty-eight Roman mortuary paintings of this kind, the oldest from the third century in the Cripta della Madonna at the catacomb of Santi Pietro e Marcellino (Pl. I*b*).[14] The Consecration in the Cripta delle Pecorelle at the catacomb of San Callisto[15] is an exception, following the usual sarcophagus scheme. Three figures are arranged symmetrically. In the middle stands Christ, his hands extended in blessing over the bread and fishes held out by two apostles. In most of the paintings, the Lord stands alone amid the baskets, which he touches with his staff.

Two paintings in a more abstract manner, belonging to the earliest ornaments of San Callisto, which according to Wirth were completed in about 230, and according to Wilpert in the second century, are to be found in sacramental chapels A 3 and A 2.[16] In the first, Christ approaches an altar

13 Examples, in Wilpert, *Sarcofagi:* pl. 9, 2, Capua, S. Marcello; 86, a, Lateran Museum; 98, 2, Vigna near the Baths of Caracalla; 106, 1, Narbonne, SS. Serge et Paul; 106, 2, Campli (Teramo); 127, 2, Rome, Museo nazionale delle Terme; 128, 1, cemetery of SS. Marco e Marcelliano; 129, 1, 2, S. Damaso; 203, 2, Terni Duomo; 212, 2, Museo delle Terme; 214, 8, and 218, 1, Lateran Museum; 219, 2, Toledo; 220, 1, Museo delle Terme; 226, 2, cemetery of S. Lorenzo; 227, 1, Arles, Musée; 236, 6, Lateran Museum; 236, 11, Arles, Musée.
14 Examples, in Wilpert, *Malereien:* pl. 45, 1; 68, 1; 71, 1; 105, 2; 158, 2; 165; 186, 1, all in SS. Pietro e Marcellino; 74, 2, Nunziatella; 115, S. Ermete; 120, 1; 212, Vigna Massimo; 54, 2; 139, 1; 142, 2; 196; 199; 226, 3; 228, 1, 3; 240, 1, all in S. Domitilla; 143, 1, S. Callisto; 216, 1, SS. Marco e Marcelliano.
15 Pl. 237, 1; p. 300.
16 Pl. 41, 1, 3; Wirth, p. 185. Cf. also the divergent interpretation in Peters, "Eucharistie" (Kraus, *Realencyklopädie*, Vol. I, pp. 441ff.).

in order to bless the bread and fish lying upon it. Across from him stands a veiled orant, the soul of the deceased living in the bliss acquired through Communion. Beside this picture is a representation of the feeding of the multitude, to which we shall return. Still more succinct is the painting on the ceiling of sacramental chapel A 2. A three-legged table stands in the midst of seven loaves; on it lie a fish and two loaves.[17] Similarly, a marble tombstone from Sant' Ermete, now in the Museo delle Terme, shows five loaves and among them two fishes;[18] and the Syntrophion tombstone in Modena discloses five loaves between two fishes.[19]

Of the three gilded glasses with representations of the multiplication of the loaves, preserved in the Christian Museum of the Vatican Library and in the museum of Verona, two show the Lord performing the miracle alone, and in the other he is accompanied by an apostle but staffless.[20]

The transformation of water into wine at the marriage of Cana was first interpreted by Cyprian and by Cyril of Jerusalem as a prototype of the transformation of wine into the blood of Christ in the Consecration.[21] If the Lord could perform the miracle of the wine at Cana, says Cyril, shall we not believe that His blood can be transformed into wine? In the same sense, the celebrant in the Epiphany mass of the *Missale Gothicum* prays that the Lord may transform the wine of the offering into His blood, as He transformed water into wine.[22]

Wilpert has counted representations of the miracle of the wine on fifty-nine sarcophagi, mostly with the Lord standing and touching one of the hydrias at his feet with his staff. The number of the hydrias varies from one to six. Often the multiplication of the loaves is the subject of a companion piece. On two earlier sarcophagi, in Saint Trophime at Arles and, from Cività Castellana, in the Lateran Museum,[23] Jesus performs the miracle not with his staff, but with upraised hands. In the Lateran sarcophagus a servant pours water from an amphora into a hydria. The filling of the waterpots is also to be found on one of the pillars of the tabernacle of San Marco

17 Wilpert, *Malereien*, pl. 38.
18 Kraus, *Realencyklopädie*, Vol. I, fig. 177. Dobbert, p. 363.
19 Charles Rohault de Fleury, *La Messe*, Vol. IV (Paris, 1886), pl. 266.
20 Hermann Vopel, *Die altchristlichen Goldgläser* (Freiburg i. B., 1889), p. 104, nos. 253–55.
21 Cyprian, *Epistola*, 63, 12 (Migne, *PL*, IV, 383). Cyril of Jerusalem, *Catechetical Lectures*, XXII, 12 (Migne, *PG*, XXXIII, 1098).
22 Migne, *PL*, LXXII, 242.
23 Wilpert, *Sarcofagi*, pl. 125, 2; 143, 1.

at Venice, and also on the architrave embedded in the northwest portal of San Marco: two servants approaching the Lord each fill three hydrias.[24] On another early sarcophagus in Marseilles[25] Jesus touches one of the hydrias with his hand. A monument in the Lateran Museum (no. 175) shows an apostle presenting a sick boy during the miracle.[26] In Spain, finally, sarcophagi in Gerona and Castiliscar[27] show an apostle holding out a fish to the Lord as he performs his miracle.

In the field of cemeterial painting, an example in the catacombs of Santi Pietro e Marcellino,[28] which Wilpert assigns to the third century but which stylistic considerations seem to place later, represents the marriage at Cana in detail (Pl. IIa). Four men and three women are seated at a three-legged table. A servant presents a bowl to the guest seated at the right corner, while on the other side, the Lord touches one of the six hydrias with his staff. A later picture in the *regione delle agapi* of the same cemetery shows a heavenly supper in the lunette, and in the arcosolium Noah between the miracle of the loaves and the miracle of the wine.[29]

Six gilded glasses with this representation have been preserved in the Vatican and in the Museo Olivieri at Pesaro; an additional piece was formerly in the Fould collection in Paris.[30] Jesus standing performs the miracle by holding out his hand over the hydrias that are visible at his feet.

The most complete symbolic expression of the Consecration is provided by two paintings, frequently reproduced, of large fishes, over the central tomb on the rear wall of the crypt of Lucina in San Callisto. They are symmetrically arranged, and each has before it a basket containing the two Eucharistic substances, bread and wine. Wilpert dates these fine paintings in the early second century, Wirth at about 220.[31] Despite the silence of the Gospels, there can be no doubt that the fish, like the bread, sufficed to symbolize the body of the Lord as administered in the Eucharist.[32] The designation of Christ as fish was familiar by the second century. Before Tertullian the acrostic Ἰησοῦς Χριστὸς Θεοῦ Ὑιὸς Σωτήρ for ΙΧΘΥΣ was generally known. In *De baptismo*, Tertullian wrote: "But we poor

---

24 Hans von der Gabelentz, *Mittelalterliche Plastik in Venedig* (Leipzig, 1903), p. 34.
25 Wilpert, *Sarcofagi*, pl. 17, 2.   26 Pl. 218, 1.   27 Pl. 111, 1; 219, 3.
28 Wilpert, *Malereien*, pl. 57.   29 Pl. 186, 1; p. 303.
30 Vopel, p. 104, nos. 246–52.
31 Wilpert, *Malereien*, pl. 27, 1; p. 288; Wirth, pp. 168, 184.
32 F. J. Dölger, *Der heilige Fisch in den antiken Religionen und im Christentum* (ΙΧΘΥΣ: das Fischsymbol in frühchristlicher Zeit, II; Münster, 1922), pp. 448ff.

fishes, following after our IXΘΥΣ, Jesus Christ, are born in water, nor are we saved, except by abiding in the water."[33] And in his commentary on Matthew[34] Origen calls the Lord "he who is figuratively [by a trope] called a fish." Tertullian's conception of the "birth in water" goes back to the baptism in Jordan, through which Jesus was manifested as the son of God. The Gospel passage on the Saviour standing in the water provided further support of the fish symbol. In the third-century "Book of the three fruits of Christian life," preserved in a ninth-century copy from the Würzburg Cathedral library,[35] the fish is called a symbol of Christ and so equated with the Eucharist. Also the Aberkios inscription from Hierapolis in Syria speaks of the "fish caught by a pure virgin" as blessed nourishment.[36]

3. Representations of Communion

The Communion directly symbolizes the Lord's Supper. Particularly in cemeterial painting, representations of it begin at an early date and usually occupy a favored position. These works do not exactly reproduce the rite of Communion, but rather symbolize it in the feeding of the multitude, so that elements of the gospel story and the Sacrament are fused into a new ideal unity. The iconographical details are different in painting and in sculpture.

In the paintings, seven men are sitting on the stibadium. The number seven is sacred to all peoples (e.g., at the feast of the dead in the hypogeum of Vincentius, priest of Sabazius, to which we shall refer later, *septem pii sacerdotes* are also assembled); here it need not refer to the disciples gathered round Jesus by the Sea of Tiberias (John 21 : 12ff.). These men may equally well represent the miraculously fed multitude or the faithful gathered in Communion. In accordance with the Gospel passage on the feeding of the multitude, bread and fish are laid out before the company.[37] On the ground are baskets with the loaves left over from the feeding, usually seven, but

33 Tr. C. Dodgson, *Tertullian*, Vol. I (Library of Fathers of the Holy Catholic Church; Oxford, 1842), p. 256. Cf. Hans Achelis, *Das Symbol des Fisches und die Fischdenkmäler der römischen Katakomben* (Marburg, 1888); Dölger, op. cit.
34 Achelis, p. 19.
35 Würzburg, University Library, Codex Wirceburgensis Theol. f. 33. Richard Reitzenstein, "Eine frühchristliche Schrift von den dreierlei Früchten des christlichen Lebens," *Zeitschrift für neutestamentliche Wissenschaft*, XV (Giessen), (1914), 60ff.
36 Dölger, p. 458ff.
37 Edgar Hennecke, *Altchristliche Malerei und altkirchliche Literatur* (Leipzig, 1896), p. 262.

sometimes two, eight, or twelve. The earliest and finest paintings, which Wilpert dates in the second century, Wirth at about 220,[38] are in the sacramental chapels of San Callisto. In chapel A 6, two dishes stand on a table, each bearing a fish. Between them the remnants of a dish holding bread are recognizable. Six bread baskets stand at either side of the table.[39] The Communion scene in chapel A 3 (Pl. IIb) has been mentioned above in connection with the Consecration beside it. On the table are two fishes on two plates, on the ground eight bread baskets.[40] In chapel A 5, two fishes and three loaves are on a plate, and members of the multitude hold out their hands toward them; on the ground stand seven bread baskets.[41] A similar painting in the cemetery of Vigna Massimo has been destroyed.

In connection with these paintings, the Communion scene in sacramental chapel A 2 of San Callisto should be mentioned. Seven men are reclining on the stibadium; before them stand two plates, each bearing one fish. The baskets are missing. For this reason, Wilpert interprets the scene as the repast of the seven disciples by the Sea of Tiberias (John 21 : 12ff.).[42] This repast can also be regarded as a prototype of the Communion. But we find no literary reference before St. Augustine's commentary on the passage: "The roasted fish is Christ in His Passion. He also is the Bread which descended from heaven."[43] The late literary parallel argues against an early artistic treatment of the theme.

A painting in the Cappella Greca of the catacomb of Priscilla, which, according to Wilpert's method,[44] has been designated as a *Fractio panis* and dated at the early second century, comes closest to an objective representation of the Communion. "The picture represents the moment in which the bishop breaks the sacred bread in order to present it, along with the consecrated wine, to the faithful partaking of the Communion."[45] However, this picture is not purely realistic, for it also includes the seven bread baskets of the miracle (Pl. IIc). On the stibadium recline six of the faithful, five men

38 Wilpert, *Malereien*, pp. 290ff.; Wirth, pp. 166ff.
39 Wilpert, *Malereien*, pl. 15, 2.
40 Pl. 41, 3.   41 Pl. 41, 4.   42 Pl. 27, 2; p. 290.
43 *"Piscis assus Christus est passus,"* etc.—*In Johannem Tractatus*, 123 (Migne, *PL*, XXXV, 1966). Tr. anon., *Homilies on the Gospel according to St. John*, Vol. II (Library of Fathers of the Holy Catholic Church; Oxford, 1849), p. 1071.
44 Wilpert, *Fractio panis; die älteste Darstellung des eucharistischen Opfers in der "Cappella greca"* (Freiburg i. B., 1895); Wirth, p. 215, dates the ornamentation of the Cappella Greca in the period of the Constantinian Renaissance, after 320.
45 Wilpert, *Malereien*, pl. 15, 1; p. 287.

and one woman, who is clearly recognizable by her covered hair. To the side, separate from the others, the celebrant sits on a chair, breaking the bread. Before him on the table stand a liturgical chalice, a dish bearing two fishes, and a dish bearing five loaves.

Sarcophagus sculpture knows three types of Communion. They differ from the type of the paintings in two ways. Fewer persons (one of them is usually shown drinking from a goblet) are reclining on the stibadium and a servant is added. A fine example of the oldest type is an early third-century sarcophagus in the Lateran Museum.[46] Five men are reclining on the stibadium. Before them lies a fish on a plate, surrounded by eight bread baskets. A servant coming from the side bears an additional loaf and a fish. Related with this are fragments of sarcophagi in the Bishop's Palace at Ostia and in the Lateran Museum.[47] A second type is attested by the fragment of a third-century sarcophagus lid in the Museo delle Terme (Pl. IIIa),[48] long erroneously regarded as a representation (not yet common in this period) of the disciples at Emmaus; it is also exemplified by the lid of the sarcophagus of Baebia Hertofile from the Cimitero dei Giordani, by a sarcophagus in the Palazzetto Corsetti, and two others in the Museo delle Terme.[49] This type shows three to five persons at table, one holding a goblet to his lips. Before them lie three to five loaves with cruciform notches but no fish. A servant is raising a loaf from a basket lying to one side, beside which in the three last examples a second servant is to be seen. A third type is characterized by a large table on lions' feet, and upon it a plate with a fish; on either side are two loaves with cruciform notches. On the stibadium recline four men, one turned toward a servant who is bringing bread, the other drinking. Examples are to be found in the Lateran Museum (no. 172), in the Bishop's Palace at Ostia, and in the Camposanto Teutonico, and formerly there was one in the Palazzo Castellani.[50] A special position is occupied by a painted sarcophagus lid of unknown origin in the Museo delle Terme (Pl. IIIb);[51] its broad representation of the Sermon on the Mount reveals it to be the product of a later period. Above, a group of three figures suggests the multiplication of the loaves as a symbol of the Consecration. Below, the feeding of the multitude is depicted more as a historical episode than symbolically. Before four men

46 Wilpert, *Sarcofagi*, pl. 8, 2.
48 Pl. 27, 1; pp. 103, 345.
50 Pl. 2, 1; 255, 5, 1; fig. 216.
51 Wilpert, "Due frammenti di sculture policrome," *Römische Quartalschrift*, 1927, 729ff.; *Sarcofagi*, pl. 220, 1; p. 343.

47 Pl. 255, 1; 254, 7.
49 Pl. 53, 1, 3; 163, 1, 3.

reclining on the stibadium lie six baskets of loaves, some of them marked with the *crux monogrammatica*. One man is drinking from a goblet. The others are eating. The Lord, standing behind them with three apostles, lays his hand on one man's head. This narrative bursts the limits of the symbolic treatment usual in the early period, and with it we approach a historical representation.

4. The Heavenly Banquet and Feasts of the Dead

In addition to the symbolic representations of the Lord's Supper, there are representations of repasts which can only indirectly be related to the Eucharist. This is particularly true of the Heavenly Banquet of the Blessed, the conception of which is based on Luke 22 : 29ff.: "And I appoint unto you a kingdom, as my Father hath appointed unto me; that ye may eat and drink at my table in my kingdom." The symbolism of the heavenly banquet is deeply rooted in the Christian faith, as is amply shown both by the acts of the martyrs and by the liturgy. Agathonike, who was present at the martyrdom of Saints Carpus and Papylus under Marcus Aurelius, cried out at the sight of their sufferings: "For me too this preliminary banquet is prepared, I too must take part in the banquet of glory."[52] The deacon James, who in 259 witnessed the martyrdom of Bishop Agapius and his companion Marianus in Cirta, wrote in similar terms: "*Et bene ad Agapium caeterorumque martyrum beatorum pergo convivium. Nam ista nocte Agapium nostrum videbam, inter omnes alios laetiorem, quos una nobiscum Cirtensis carcer incluserat, sollemne quoddam et laetitiae plenum celebrare convivium.*"[53] Among the Church Fathers, Irenaeus gives a particularly vivid picture of the heavenly banquet, the "triclinium on which will lie those who sup after they have been called to the wedding feast."[54] This symbolism was universally disseminated by the liturgical prayers for the dead.[55] Thence this

52 *Martyrium SS. Carpi et Sociorum*, par. 42, in *Acta Martyrum Selecta* (*Ausgewählte Martyrakten*), ed. Oscar von Gebhardt (Berlin, 1902), p. 16. Leonhard Atzberger, *Geschichte der christlichen Eschatologie innerhalb der vornicänischen Zeit* (Freiburg i. B., 1896), p. 168.
53 *Passio SS. Mariani et Jacobi*, ed. Pio Franchi de Cavalieri (Studi e testi, 3; Rome, 1900), p. 60.
54 Irenaeus, *Contra haereses*, V, 36, 2; Hennecke, pp. 198ff.
55 Eusèbe Renaudot, *Liturgiarum orientalium collectio* (Paris, 1716), Vol. II, p. 138: "*ad convivium beatum regni tui nos et illos pervenire fac*"; p. 195: "*da illis spiritum gaudii ... in ea regione ... ubi vocati ad convivium, ut ascendant, praestolantur*"; p. 482: "*Deus pater, fac, ut corpora et spiritus servorum tuorum ... ad bona coelestia perveniant, ad convivium indesinens.*"

271

conception of the heavenly banquet was taken into the inscriptions in which the survivors besought heavenly refreshment for their dead and into the works of art immortalizing the dead as guests at the heavenly banquet. The subject matter of these Christian banquet scenes is by no means new; they rather gave new content to a pagan conception. By way of comparison, we shall cite certain contemporary pagan examples. Wilpert has collected a group of pagan sarcophagi, all disclosing the same scene.[56] A youth, accompanied by a dog, has reached the goal of his last journey, where he is received by a second young man. In another part of the picture we see a banquet of four soldiers, one of whom is reaching out after a fish lying on the table, while the others hold goblets in their hands. The outermost soldier is turned toward a servant standing in the corner and warming water in a bowl (wine was mixed with warm water in this period). Similar representations are found in the Chiaramonti Museum of the Vatican, in the Villa Guicciardini at Sesto Fiorentino, and at the museum of San Callisto. The heavenly banquets painted in the tomb of Vincentius, priest of Sabazius, and his wife Vibia (near a Jewish catacomb on the Via Appia) are not Christian. The sequence shows Vibia being snatched away by Hades, appearing before the judges of the underworld in the presence of the three Fates, and finally being led to the heavenly banquet by her good angel, a personage doubtless borrowed from Christian conceptions (Pl. IIIc). Beside this painting is a representation of the feast in her memory held by her husband Vincentius, with six other *pii sacerdotes*.[57]

Christian representations of the heavenly banquet are to be found in the catacomb of Santi Pietro e Marcellino, in a section laid out in the fourth century. Four similar paintings have been preserved.[58] The deceased buried in the vault are shown reclining at the banquet, and for this reason the number and sex of the persons vary. The wine is not prepared by servants as in the pagan pictures, but by two female figures, identified by inscriptions as Agape and Irene, Love and Peace, two essential qualities of life in the hereafter. The guests ask them to pass the wine mixed with warm water, as is made clear by the inscriptions *"Agape da calda"* and *"Irene misce mi."*

56 Wilpert, *L'ultimo viaggio nell' arte sepolcrale* (Rendiconti della ponteficia Accademia romana; Rome, 1925), p. 61; *Sarcofagi*, p. 340, pl. 254.
57 Wilpert, *Malereien*, pl. 132, 1; 133, 1; p. 506. Karl Prümm, *Religionsgeschichtliches Handbuch für den Raum der altchristlichen Umwelt* (1944), p. 248.
58 Wilpert, *Malereien*, pl. 157, 1; 133, 2; 184; 157, 2; p. 471.

The food is the fish, the symbol of the Lord, in whom and with whom the Blessed live. In the earliest picture (Pl. IV*a*) three men are reclining on the stibadium. In front sits Irene beside a crater. Opposite her are Agape and a cupbearer extending a goblet. In the other picture three adults and two children are reclining on the stibadium. In front stand Agape, presenting a goblet, and Irene with a pitcher in her hand. The other representations are similar.

Nor is the pagan custom of the feast of the dead shunned by the Christians, who could invoke Tobias 4 : 18 (D.V.): "Lay out thy bread and thy wine upon the burial of a just man." However, the feast is not celebrated at the grave itself, but on triclinia over it. In Africa, stone tables were set up for it, whose inscriptions leave no doubt as to their purpose. One inscription from the year 299 informs us that on this table *"cibi ponuntur calicesque,"* another from the year 324 that Varia, servant of Christ, *"fecit sibi ipsa sana sanctorum mensam."*[59] These feasts of the dead, which originally served for feeding the poor, were discontinued toward the end of the fourth century.

As an example of a pagan feast of the dead, we have already mentioned that of Vincentius, priest of Sabazius, in memory of his wife Vibia (Pl. IV*b*). The related Christian representations are for the most part to be found in the catacomb of Santi Pietro e Marcellino. In a mural in the vestibule of room 6, a husband and wife are reclining on the stibadium, before which stands a three-legged table. A servant holds out a goblet to the man; the woman is accompanied by a maidservant. This scene is preceded by another, showing the woman shopping with her maidservant.[60] In a painting on the rear wall of room 7, six guests are reclining on the stibadium, some of them holding goblets. Similar representations are to be found in room 10, and, as far as one can still ascertain, on the rear wall of the Flavian gallery in Santa Domitilla.[61]

A survey of the early Christian banquet scenes prior to the fifth century shows that the Eucharistic Communion is treated quite differently from the heavenly banquet and the feast of the dead. Although there was no need for keeping the Christian mysteries secret after the Edict of Milan, in 313, more than a century passed before the first historical representation of the Coena Domini.

59 P. 510.   60 Pl. 65, 3.   61 Pl. 167; 7, 4.

C. G. Jung

Transformation Symbolism in the Mass[1]

The Mass is a still-living mystery, the origins of which go back to early Christian times. It is hardly necessary to point out that it owes its vitality partly to its undoubted psychological efficacy, and is therefore a fit subject for psychological study. But it should be equally obvious that psychology can only approach the subject from the phenomenological angle, for the realities of faith lie outside the realm of psychology.

My exposition falls into four parts: in the introduction I indicate some of the New Testament sources of the Mass, with notes on its structure and significance. In section 2, I recapitulate the sequence of events in the rite. In 3, I cite a parallel from pagan antiquity to the Christian symbolism of sacrifice and transformation: the visions of Zosimos. Finally, in 4, I attempt a psychological discussion of the sacrifice and transformation.

1. Introduction

The oldest account of the sacrament of the Mass is to be found in I Corinthians 11 : 23ff.:

> For the tradition which I have received of the Lord and handed down to you is that the Lord Jesus, on the night he was betrayed,

[1] The following account and examination of the principal symbol in the Mass is not concerned either with the Mass as a whole, or with its liturgy in particular, but solely with the ritual actions and texts which relate to the transformation process in the strict sense. In order to give the reader an adequate account of this, I had to seek professional help. I am especially indebted to the theologian Dr. Gallus Jud for reading through and correcting the first two sections.

[First published as two lectures in *EJ 1941;* later published in revised and expanded form in *Von den Wurzeln des Bewusstseins* (Zurich, 1954). The present translation is made from the original version, with minor textual alterations and some additional illustrative material from the 1954 version. I would like to acknowledge with thanks the help derived from Monica Curtis's very perceptive translation of extensive portions of the original essay, published as Guild Lecture No. 69 by the Guild of Pastoral Psychology, London. Certain passages are incorporated here almost verbatim. — TRANS.]

274

took bread, gave thanks, broke it, and said: *This is my body for you; do this in remembrance of me. And after he had supped, he took the chalice also, and said: This chalice is the new testament in my blood.* As often as you drink, do this in remembrance of me. For as often as you eat this bread and drink the chalice, you declare the death of the Lord, until he comes.[2]

Similar accounts are to be found in Matthew, Mark, and Luke. In John the corresponding passage speaks of a "supper,"[3] but there it is connected with the washing of the disciples' feet. At this supper Christ utters the words which characterize the meaning and substance of the Mass (John 15 : 1, 4, 5): "I am the true vine." "Abide in me, and I in you." "I am the vine, ye are the branches." The correspondence between the liturgical accounts points to a traditional source outside the Bible.

The Mass is a Eucharistic feast with an elaborately developed liturgy. It has the following structure:

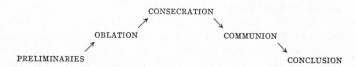

In the sacrifice of the Mass two distinct ideas are blended together: the ideas of *deipnon* and *thysia*. *Thysia* comes from the verb θύειν, "to sacrifice" or "to slaughter"; but it also has the meaning of "blazing" or "flaring up." This refers to the leaping sacrificial fire by which the gift offered to the gods was consumed. Originally the food-offering was intended for the nourishment of the gods; the smoke of the burnt sacrifice carried the food up to their heavenly abode. At a later stage the smoke was conceived as a spiritualized form of food-offering; indeed, all through the Christian era up to the

---

2 [This is a translation of the Karl von Weizsäcker version (1875) used here by Professor Jung. Elsewhere the Biblical quotations are taken from the Authorized Version. Following are the Greek and Latin (Vulgate) versions of the italicized portion of this passage.—TRANS.]

". . . τοῦτό μού ἐστιν τὸ σῶμα τὸ ὑπὲρ ὑμῶν· τοῦτο ποιεῖτε εἰς τὴν ἐμὴν ἀνάμνησιν· ὡσαύτως καὶ τὸ ποτήριον μετὰ τὸ δειπνῆσαι λέγων· τοῦτο τὸ ποτήριον ἡ καινὴ διαθήκη ἐστὶν ἐν τῷ ἐμῷ αἵματι."

". . . hoc est corpus meum, quod pro vobis tradetur: hoc facite in meam commemorationem. Similiter et calicem, postquam coenavit, dicens: Hic calix novum testamentum est in meo sanguine."

3 δεῖπνον, "coena."

time of the Middle Ages, spirit (or *pneuma*) continued to be thought of as a fine, vaporous substance.[4]

Deipnon means "meal." In the first place it is a meal shared by those taking part in the sacrifice, at which the god was believed to be present. It is also a "sacred" meal at which "consecrated" food is eaten, and hence a *sacrifice* (from *sacrificare*, "to make sacred," "to consecrate").

The dual meaning of *deipnon* and *thysia* is implicitly contained in the words of the sacrament: "the body (which was given) for you."[5] This may mean either "which was given to you to eat" or, indirectly, "which was given for you to God." The idea of a meal immediately invests the word "body" with the meaning of $\sigma \acute{a} \rho \xi$, "flesh" (as an edible substance). In Paul, $\sigma \hat{\omega} \mu a$ and $\sigma \acute{a} \rho \xi$ are practically identical.[6]

Besides the authentic accounts of the institution of the sacrament, we must also consider Hebrews 13 : 10–15 as a possible source for the Mass:

> We have an altar, whereof they have no right to eat which serve the tabernacle. For the bodies of those beasts, whose blood is brought into the sanctuary by the high priest for sin, are burned without the camp. Wherefore Jesus also, that he might sanctify the people with his own blood, suffered without the gate. Let us go forth therefore unto him without the camp, bearing his reproach. For here have we no continuing city, but we seek one to come. By him therefore let us offer the sacrifice of praise to God continually. . . .

As a further source we might mention Hebrews 7 : 17: "Thou art a priest for ever after the order of Melchisedec."[7] The idea of perpetual sacrifice and of an eternal priesthood is an essential component of the Mass. (Melchisedec, who according to Hebrews 7 : 3 was "without father, without mother, without descent, having neither beginning of days, nor end of life, but made like unto the Son of God," was believed to be a pre-Christian incarnation of the Logos.)

The idea of an eternal priesthood and of a sacrifice offered to God "con-

4 This of course has nothing to do with the official conception of spirit by the Church.
5 "$\tau \grave{o} \ \sigma \hat{\omega} \mu a \ \tau \grave{o} \ \grave{v} \pi \grave{e} \rho \ \grave{v} \mu \hat{\omega} \nu$."
6 Ernst Käsemann, *Leib und Leib Christi* (Beiträge zur historischen Theologie, 9; Tübingen, 1933), p. 120.
7 Dr. Jud kindly drew my attention to the equally relevant passage in Malachi 1 : 10–11: "Who is there even among you that would shut the doors for nought? neither do ye kindle fire on mine altar for nought. . . . And in every place incense shall be offered unto my name, and a pure offering. . . ."

tinually" brings us to the true *mysterium fidei*, the transformation of the substances, which is the third aspect of the Mass. The ideas of *deipnon* and *thysia* do not in themselves imply or contain a mystery, although, in the burnt offering which is reduced to smoke and ashes by the fire, there is a primitive allusion to a transformation of substance in the sense of a spiritualization. But this aspect is of no practical importance in the Mass, where it only appears in subsidiary form in the censing, as an incense-offering. The *mysterium*, on the other hand, manifests itself clearly enough in the eternal priest "after the order of Melchisedec" and in the sacrifice which he offers to God "continually." The manifestation of an order outside time involves the idea of a *miracle* which takes place *"vere, realiter, substantialiter"* at the moment of transubstantiation, for the substances offered are no different from natural objects, and must in fact be definite commodities whose nature is known to everybody, namely pure wheaten bread and wine. Furthermore, the officiating priest is an ordinary human being who, although he bears the indelible mark of the priesthood upon him and is thus empowered to offer sacrifice, is nevertheless not yet in a position to be the instrument of the divine self-sacrifice enacted in the Mass.[8] Nor is the congregation standing behind him yet purged from sin, consecrated, and itself transformed into a sacrificial gift. The ritual of the Mass takes this situation and transforms it step by step until the climax is reached—the Consecration, when Christ himself, as sacrificer and sacrificed, speaks the decisive words through the mouth of the priest. At that moment Christ is present in time and space. Yet his presence is not a reappearance, and therefore the inner meaning of the consecration is not a repetition of an event which occurred once in history, but the revelation of something existing in eternity, a rending of the veil of temporal and spatial limitations which separates the human spirit from the sight of the eternal. This event is necessarily a mystery, because it is beyond the power of man to conceive or imagine. In other words, the rite is necessarily and in every one of its parts a

---

8 That is to say, not before he has accomplished the preparatory part of the service. In offering these gifts the priest is not the "master" of the sacrifice. "Rather that which causes them to be sacrificed in the first place is sanctifying grace. For that is what their sacrifice means: their sanctification. The man who each time performs the sacred act is the servant of grace, and that is why the gifts and their sacrifice are always pleasing to God. The fact that the servant may be bad does not affect them in any way. The priest is only the servant, and even this he has from grace, not from himself." Joseph Kramp, S.J., *Die Opferanschauungen der römischen Messliturgie* (Regensburg, 1924), p. 148.

symbol. Now a symbol is not an arbitrary or intentional sign standing for a known and conceivable fact, but an admittedly anthropomorphic—hence limited and only partly valid—expression for something suprahuman and only partly conceivable. It may be the best expression possible, yet it ranks below the level of the mystery it seeks to describe. The Mass is a symbol in this sense. Here I would like to quote the words of Father Kramp: "It is generally admitted that the sacrifice is a *symbolic* act, by which I mean that the offering of a material gift to God has no purpose in itself, but merely serves as a means to express an idea. And the choice of this means of expression brings a wide range of anthropomorphism into play: man confronts God as he confronts his own kind, almost as if God were a human being. We offer a gift to God as we offer it to a good friend or to an earthly ruler."[9]

In so far, then, as the Mass is an anthropomorphic symbol standing for something otherworldly and beyond our power to conceive, its symbolism is a legitimate subject for comparative psychology and analytical research. My psychological explanations are, of course, exclusively concerned with the symbolical expression.

2. *The Sequence of the Rite of Transformation*

The rite of transformation may be said to begin with the Offertory, an antiphon recited during the offering of the sacrificial gifts. Here we encounter the first ritual act relating to the transformation.[1]

I. OBLATION OF THE BREAD

The Host is lifted up towards the cross on the altar, and the priest makes the sign of the cross over it with the paten. The bread is thus brought into relation with Christ and his death on the cross; it is marked as a "sacrifice" and thereby becomes sacred. The elevation exalts it into the realm of the spiritual: it is a preliminary act of spiritualization. Justin makes the interesting remark that the presentation of the cleansed lepers in the temple was an image of the Eucharistic bread.[2] This links up with the later alchemical idea of the imperfect or "leprous" substance which is made perfect by the *opus. (Quod natura relinquit imperfectum, arte perficitur.)*

9 Kramp, p. 17.

1 In the account that follows I have made extensive use of Johannes Brinktrine, *Die Heilige Messe in ihrem Werden und Wesen* (2nd edn., Paderborn, 1934).
2 "Τύπος τοῦ ἄρτου τῆς εὐχαριστίας."

2. PREPARATION OF THE CHALICE

This is still more solemn than that of the bread, corresponding to the "spiritual" nature of the wine, which is reserved for the priest.[3] Some water is mingled with the wine.

The mixing of water with the wine originally referred to the ancient custom of not drinking wine unless mixed with water. A drunkard was therefore called *akratopotes*, an "unmixed drinker." In modern Greek, wine is still called κρασι (mixture). From the custom of the Monophysite Armenians, who did not add any water to the Eucharistic wine (so as to preserve the exclusively divine nature of Christ), it may be inferred that water has a hylical, or physical, significance and represents man's material nature. The mixing of water and wine in the Roman rite would accordingly signify that divinity is mingled with humanity as indivisibly as the wine with the water.[4] St. Cyprian (bishop of Carthage, d. 258) says that the wine refers to Christ, and the water to the congregation as the body of Christ. The significance of the water is explained by an allusion to the Book of Revelation 17 : 15: "The waters which thou sawest, where the whore sitteth, are peoples, and multitudes, and nations, and tongues." (In alchemy, *meretrix* the whore is a synonym for the *prima materia*, the *corpus imperfectum* which is sunk in darkness, like the man who wanders in the darkness unconscious and unredeemed. This idea is foreshadowed in the Gnostic image of Physis, who with passionate arms draws the Nous down from heaven and wraps him in her dark embrace.) As the water is an imperfect or even leprous substance, it has to be blessed and consecrated before being mixed, so that only a purified body may be joined to the wine of the spirit, just as Christ is to be united only with a pure and sanctified congregation. Thus this part of the rite has the special significance of preparing a perfect body—the glorified body of resurrection.

At the time of St. Cyprian the communion was generally celebrated with water.[5] And, still later, St. Ambrose (bishop of Milan, d. 397) says: "In the shadow there was water from the rock, as if it were the blood of Christ."[6] The water communion is prefigured in John 7 : 37–39: "If any

---

3 That is, in the Roman rite. In the Greek Uniate rites, communion is received in bread *and* wine.
4 This is the interpretation of Yves, bishop of Chartres (d. 1116).
5 Cyprian attacks this heretical custom in his letter to Caecilius.
6 "*In umbra erat aqua de petra quasi sanguis ex Christo.*" The *umbra*, "shadow," refers to the foreshadowing in the Old Testament, in accordance with the saying: "*Umbra*

man thirst, let him come unto me, and drink. He that believeth on me, as the scripture hath said, out of his belly shall flow rivers of living water. (But this he spake of the Spirit, which they that believe on him should receive: for the Holy Ghost was not yet given, because that Jesus was not yet glorified.)" And also in John 4 : 14: "But whosoever drinketh of the water that I shall give him shall never thirst; but the water that I shall give him shall be in him a well of water springing up into everlasting life." The words "as the scripture hath said, out of his belly shall flow rivers of living water" do not occur anywhere in the Old Testament. They must therefore come from a writing which the author of the Johannine gospel obviously regarded as holy, but which is not known to us. It is just possible that they are based on Isaiah 58 : 11: "And the Lord shall guide thee continually, and satisfy thy soul in drought, and make fat thy bones: and thou shalt be like a watered garden, and like a spring of water, whose waters fail not." Another possibility is Ezekiel 47 : 1: "Afterward he brought me again unto the door of the house; and, behold, waters issued out from under the threshold of the house eastward . . . and the waters came down from under the right side of the house, at the south side of the altar." In the liturgy of Hippolytus (d. *ca.* 235) the water chalice is associated with the baptismal font, where the inner man is renewed as well as the body.[7] This interpretation comes very close to the baptismal *krater* of Poimandres[8] and to the Hermetic basin filled with *nous* which God gave to those seeking ἔννοια.[9] Here the water signifies the *pneuma*, i.e., the spirit of prophecy, and also the doctrine which a man receives and passes on to others.[10] The same image of the spiritual water occurs in the "Odes of Solomon":[11]

---

in lege, imago in evangelio, veritas in coelestibus." Note that this remark of Ambrose does not refer to the Eucharist but to the water symbolism of early Christianity in general; and the same is true of the passages from John. St. Augustine himself says: "There the rock was Christ; for to us that is Christ which is placed on the altar of God" (*Tractatus in Johannem*, XLV, 9; tr. James Innes in *Works*, ed. Marcus Dods, Vol. XI, Edinburgh, 1874).

7 Edgar Hennecke, ed., *Neutestamentliche Apokryphen* (2nd edn., Tübingen, 1924), p. 580.

8 Marcellin Berthelot, *Collection des anciens alchimistes grecs* (Paris, 1887–88), III, li, 8.

9 *Corpus Hermeticum*, Lib. IV, 4, in *Hermetica*, ed. Walter Scott (Oxford, 1924–36), Vol. I, p. 151.

10 H. L. Strack and Paul Billerbeck, *Kommentar zum Neuen Testament aus Talmud und Midrasch*, Vol. II (Munich, 1924), p. 492.

11 A collection of Gnostic hymns from the 2nd century, in Hennecke, p. 441.

For there went forth a stream, and became a river great and broad; ... and all the thirsty upon earth were given to drink of it; and thirst was relieved and quenched; for from the Most High the draught was given. Blessed then are the ministers of that draught who are entrusted with that water of His; they have assuaged the dry lips, and the will that had fainted they have raised up; and souls that were near departing they have caught back from death; and limbs that had fallen they straightened and set up; they gave strength for their feebleness and light to their eyes. For everyone knew them in the Lord, and they lived by the water of life for ever.[12]

The fact that the Eucharist was also celebrated with water shows that the early Christians were mainly interested in the symbolism of the mysteries and not in the literal observance of the sacrament. (There were several other variants—"galactophagy," for instance—which all bear out this view.)

Another, very graphic, interpretation of the wine and water is the reference to John 19 : 34: "And forthwith came there out blood and water." Deserving of special emphasis is the remark of St. John Chrysostom (patriarch of Constantinople, d. 407), that in drinking the wine Christ drank his own blood. (See below, p. 299.)

In this section of the Mass we meet the important prayer:

O God, who in creating human nature, didst wonderfully dignify it, and hast still more wonderfully renewed it; grant that, by the mystery of this water and wine, we may be made partakers of his divinity who vouchsafed to become partaker of our humanity, Jesus Christ. . . .[13]

3. ELEVATION OF THE CHALICE

The lifting up of the chalice in the air prepares the spiritualization (i.e., volatilization) of the wine.[14] This is confirmed by the invocation to the

---

12 Ode VI in *The Odes of Solomon*, ed. J. H. Bernard (Texts and Studies, VIII, 3; Cambridge, 1912), p. 55, after the J. Rendel Harris version. Cf. the ὕδωρ θεῖον, the *aqua permanens* of early alchemy, also the treatise of Komarios (Berthelot, IV, xx).

13 "Deus, qui humanae substantiae dignitatem mirabiliter condidisti, et mirabilius reformasti; da nobis per huius aquae et vini mysterium, eius divinitatis esse consortes, qui humanitatis nostrae fieri dignatus est particeps, Jesus Christus . . ." [Here and throughout this essay the English translation is taken from *The Small Missal*, London, 1924(?).—TRANS.]

14 This is *my* interpretation and not that of the Church, which sees in this only an act of devotion.

Holy Ghost which immediately follows (*Veni sanctificator*), and it is even more evident in the Mozarabic[15] liturgy, which has "*Veni spiritus sancti-ficator.*" The invocation serves to infuse the wine with holy spirit, for it is the Holy Ghost who begets, fulfills, and transforms (cf. the "Obumbratio Mariae," Pentecostal fire). After the elevation, the chalice was, in former times, set down to the right of the Host, to correspond with the blood that flowed from the right side of Christ.

4. CENSING OF THE SUBSTANCES AND THE ALTAR

The priest makes the sign of the cross three times over the substances with the thurible, twice from right to left and once from left to right.[16] The counterclockwise movement (from right to left) corresponds psychologically to a circumambulation downwards, in the direction of the unconscious, while the clockwise (left-to-right) movement goes in the direction of consciousness. There is also a complicated censing of the altar.[17]

The censing has the significance of an incense offering and is therefore a relic of the original *thysia*. At the same time it signifies a transformation of the sacrificial gifts and of the altar, a spiritualization of all the physical substances subserving the rite. Finally, it is an apotropaic ceremony to drive away any demonic forces that may be present, for it fills the air with the fragrance of the *pneuma* and renders it uninhabitable for evil spirits. The vapor also suggests the sublimated body, the *corpus volatile sive spiri-tuale*, or wraithlike "subtle body." Rising up as a "spiritual" substance, the incense implements and represents the ascent of prayer—hence the *Di-rigatur, Domine, oratio mea, sicut incensum, in conspectu tuo* ("Let my prayer, O Lord, ascend like incense in thy sight").

The censing brings the preparatory, spiritualizing rites to an end. The gifts have been sanctified and prepared for the actual transubstantiation. Priest and congregation are likewise purified by the prayers *Accendat in nobis Dominus ignem sui amoris* ("May the Lord enkindle in us the fire of his love") and *Lavabo inter innocentes* ("I will wash my hands among the innocent"), and are made ready to enter into the mystic union of the sacrificial act which now follows.

15 From Arabic *musta'rib*, "Arabianized," with reference to the Visigothic-Spanish form of ritual.
16 The circumambulation from left to right is strictly observed in Buddhism.
17 The censing is only performed at High Mass.

5. THE EPICLESIS

The *Suscipe, sancta Trinitas*, like the *Orate, fratres*, the *Sanctus*, and the *Te igitur*, is a propitiatory prayer which seeks to insure the acceptance of the sacrifice. Hence the Preface that comes after the Secret is called *Illatio* in the Mozarabic rite (the equivalent of the Greek ἀναφορά), and in the old Gallican liturgy is known as *Immolatio* (in the sense of *oblatio*), with reference to the presentation of the gifts. The words of the *Sanctus: "Benedictus qui venit in nomine Domini,"* point to the expected appearance of the Lord which has already been prepared, on the ancient principle that a "naming" has the force of a "summons." After the Canon there follows the "Commemoration of the Living," together with the prayers *Hanc igitur* and *Quam oblationem*. In the Mozarabic Mass these are followed by the Epiclesis (invocation): *"Adesto, adesto Jesu, bone Pontifex, in medio nostri: sicut fuisti in medio discipulorum tuorum."* This naming likewise has the original force of a summons. It is an intensification of the *Benedictus qui venit*, and it may be, and sometimes was, regarded as the actual manifestation of the Lord, and hence as the culminating point of the Mass.

6. THE CONSECRATION

This, in the Roman Mass, is the climax, the transubstantiation of the bread and wine into the body and blood of Christ. The formula for the consecration of the bread runs:[18]

> Qui pridie quam pateretur, accepit panem in sanctas ac venerabiles manus suas, et elevatis oculis in caelum ad te Deum, Patrem suum omnipotentem, tibi gratias agens, benedixit, fregit, deditque discipulis suis, dicens: Accipite, et manducate ex hoc omnes. Hoc est enim Corpus meum.

And for the consecration of the chalice:

> Simili modo postquam coenatum est, accipiens et hunc praeclarum Calicem in sanctas ac venerabiles manus suas, item tibi gratias agens, benedixit, deditque discipulis suis, dicens: Accipite, et bibite ex eo omnes. Hic est enim Calix Sanguinis mei, novi et aeterni testamenti: mysterium fidei: qui pro vobis et pro multis effundetur in remissionem peccatorum. Haec quotiescumque feceritis, in mei memoriam facietis.

18 According to the edict of the Church these words ought not, on account of their sacredness, to be translated into any profane tongue. Although there are missals that sin against this wise edict, I would prefer the Latin text to stand untranslated.

The priest and congregation, as well as the substances and the altar, have now been progressively purified, consecrated, exalted, and spiritualized by means of the prayers and rites which began with the Preliminaries and ended with the Canon, and are thus prepared as a mystical unity for the divine epiphany. Hence the uttering of the words of the consecration signifies Christ himself speaking in the first person, his living presence in the *corpus mysticum* of priest, congregation, bread, wine, and incense, which together form the mystical unity offered for sacrifice. At this moment the eternal character of the one divine sacrifice is made evident: it is experienced at a particular time and a particular place, as if a window or a door had been opened upon that which lies beyond space and time. It is in this sense that we have to understand the words of St. Chrysostom: "And this word once uttered in any church, at any altar, makes perfect the sacrifice from that day to this, and till his Second Coming."[19] It is clear that only by our Lord's presence in his words, and by their virtue, is the imperfect body of the sacrifice made perfect, and not by the preparatory action of the priest. Were this the efficient cause, the rite would be no different from common magic. The priest is only the *causa ministerialis* of the transubstantiation. The real cause is the living presence of Christ which operates spontaneously, as an act of divine grace.

Accordingly John of Damascus (d. 754) says that the words have a consecrating effect no matter by what priest they be spoken, as if Christ were present and uttering them himself.[20] And Duns Scotus (d. 1308) remarks that in the sacrament of the Last Supper Christ, by an act of will, offers himself as a sacrifice in every Mass, through the agency of the priest.[21] This tells us plainly enough that the sacrificial act is not performed by the priest, but by Christ himself. The agent of transformation is nothing less than the divine will working through Christ. The Council of Trent declared that in the sacrifice of the Mass "the selfsame Christ is contained and bloodlessly sacrificed,"[22] although it is not a repetition of the historical sacrifice but a bloodless renewal of it. As the sacramental words have the

19 "Et vox haec semel prolata in ecclesiis ad unamquamque mensam ab illo ad hodiernum usque tempus et usque ad adventum eius sacrificium perfectum efficit."
20 "Haec verba virtutem consecrativam sunt consecuta, a quocumque sacerdote dicantur, ac si Christus ea praesentialiter proferret."
21 Ignaz Klug in *Theologie und Glaube* (Paderborn), XVIII (1926), 335f. Cited by Brinktrine, p. 192.
22 "idem ille Christus continetur et incruente immolatur."

power to accomplish the sacrifice, being an expression of God's will, they can be described metaphorically as the sacrificial knife or sword which, guided by his will, consummates the *thysia*. This comparison was first drawn by the Jesuit father Lessius (d. 1623), and has since gained acceptance as an ecclesiastical figure of speech. It is based on Hebrews 4 : 12: "For the word of God is quick, and powerful, and sharper than any two-edged sword," and perhaps even more on the Book of Revelation 1 : 16: "And out of his mouth went a sharp two-edged sword." The "mactation theory" first appeared in the sixteenth century. Its originator, Cuesta, bishop of Leon (d. 1560), declared that Christ was slaughtered by the priest.[23] So the sword metaphor followed quite naturally.[24] Nicholas Cabasilas, archbishop of Thessalonica (d. *ca.* 1363), gives a vivid description of the corresponding rite in the Greek Orthodox Church:

> The priest cuts a piece of bread from the loaf, reciting the text: "As a lamb he was led to the slaughter." Laying it on the table he says: "The lamb of God is slain." Then a sign of the cross is imprinted on the bread and a small lance is stabbed into its side, to the text: "And one of the soldiers with a spear pierced his side, and forthwith came there out blood and water." With these words water and wine are mixed in the chalice, which is placed beside the bread.[25]

The δῶρον (gift) also represents the giver; that is to say Christ is both the sacrificer and the sacrificed.

Kramp writes: "Sometimes the *fractio* and sometimes the *elevatio* which precedes the Pater noster was taken as symbolizing the death of Christ, sometimes the sign of the cross at the end of the *Supplices*, and sometimes the *consecratio;* but no one ever thought of taking a symbol like the 'mystical slaughter' as a sacrifice which constitutes the essence of the Mass. So it is not surprising that there is no mention of any 'slaughter' in the liturgy."[26]

7. THE GREATER ELEVATION

The consecrated substances are lifted up and shown to the congregation. The Host in particular represents a beatific vision of heaven, in fulfillment

23 "Missa est sacrificium hac ratione quia Christus aliquo modo moritur et a sacerdote mactatur" (The Mass is a sacrifice because Christ after a certain fashion dies and is slaughtered by the priest).

24 The sword as a sacrificial instrument also occurs in the Zosimos visions (see below, pp. 295, 301ff.).

25 Kramp, p. 114.   26 Ibid., p. 56.

of Psalm 27 : 8: "Thy face, Lord, will I seek," for in it the Divine Man is present.

8. POST–CONSECRATION

There now follows the significant prayer *Unde et memores*, which I give in full together with the *Supra quae* and *Supplices:*

> Wherefore, O Lord, we thy servants, as also thy holy people, calling to mind the blessed passion of the same Christ thy Son our Lord, his resurrection from hell, and glorious ascension into heaven, offer unto thy most excellent majesty, of thy gifts and grants, a pure Host, a holy Host, an immaculate Host, the holy bread of eternal life, and the chalice of everlasting salvation.
>
> Upon which vouchsafe to look down with a propitious and serene countenance, and to accept them, as thou wert graciously pleased to accept the gifts of thy just servant Abel, and the sacrifice of our patriarch Abraham, and that which thy high priest Melchisedec offered to thee, a holy sacrifice, an immaculate Host.
>
> We most humbly beseech thee, almighty God, command these things to be carried by the hands of thy holy angel to thy altar on high, in the sight of thy divine majesty, that as many of us as, by participation at this altar, shall receive the most sacred body and blood of thy Son, may be filled with all heavenly benediction and grace. Through the same Christ, our Lord. Amen.[27]

The first prayer shows that the transformed substances contain an allusion to the resurrection and glorification of our Lord, and the second prayer calls to mind the prefigurations in the Old Testament. Abel sacrificed a lamb; Abraham was to sacrifice his son, but a ram was substituted at the last moment. Melchisedec offers no sacrifice, but comes to meet Abraham with bread and wine. This sequence is probably not accidental and is a sort

---

27 "Unde et memores, Domine, nos servi tui, sed et plebs tua sancta, eiusdem Christi Filii tui, Domini nostri, tam beatae passionis, nec non et ab inferis resurrectionis, sed et in caelos gloriosae ascensionis: offerimus praeclarae majestati tuae de tuis donis ac datis, hostiam puram, hostiam sanctam, hostiam immaculatam, Panem sanctum vitae aeternae, et Calicem salutis perpetuae.

"Supra quae propitio ac sereno vultu respicere digneris: et accepta habere, sicuti accepta habere dignatus es munera pueri tui justi Abel, et sacrificium Patriarchae nostri Abrahae: et quod tibi obtulit summus sacerdos tuus Melchisedech, sanctum sacrificium, immaculatam hostiam.

"Supplices te rogamus, omnipotens Deus: jube haec perferri per manus sancti Angeli tui in sublime altare tuum, in conspectu divinae majestatis tuae: ut, quotquot ex hac altaris participatione sacrosanctum Filii tui corpus, et sanguinem sumpserimus, omni benedictione caelesti et gratia repleamur. Per eundem Christum, Dominum nostrum. Amen."

of crescendo. Abel is essentially the son, and sacrifices an animal; Abraham is essentially the father—indeed, the "tribal father"—and therefore on a higher level. He does not offer a choice possession merely, but is ready to sacrifice the best and dearest thing he has—his only son. Melchisedec ("teacher of righteousness"), is, according to Hebrews 7 : 1, king of Salem and "priest of the most high God," El 'Elyon. Philo Byblius mentions a Ἐλιοῦν ὁ ὕψιστος as a Canaanite deity,[28] but he cannot be identical with Jehovah. Abraham nevertheless acknowledges the priesthood of Melchisedec[29] by paying him "a tenth part of all." Sir Leonard Woolley gives a very interesting explanation of this in his report on the excavations at Ur.[30] By virtue of his priesthood, Melchisedec stands above the patriarch, and his feasting of Abraham has the significance of a priestly act. We must therefore attach a symbolical meaning to it, as is in fact suggested by the bread and wine. Consequently the symbolical offering ranks even higher than the sacrifice of a son, which is still the sacrifice of somebody else. Melchisedec's offering is thus a prefiguration of Christ's sacrifice of himself.

In the prayer *Supplices te rogamus* we beseech God to bring the gifts "by the hands of thy holy angel to thy altar on high." This singular request derives from the apocryphal *Epistolae Apostolorum*, where there is a legend that Christ, before he became incarnate, bade the archangels take his place at God's altar during his absence.[31] This brings out the idea of the eternal priesthood which links Christ with Melchisedec.

9. END OF THE CANON

Taking up the Host, the priest makes the sign of the cross three times over the chalice, and says: "Through Him, and with Him, and in Him." Then he makes the sign of the cross twice between himself and the chalice. This establishes a relation of identity among Host, chalice, and priest, thus affirming once more the unity of all parts of the sacrifice. The union of Host and chalice signifies the union of the body and blood, i.e., the quickening of the body with a soul, for blood is equivalent to soul. Then follows the *Pater noster*.

---

28 Eusebius, *Evangelica praeparatio*, I, 10, 11.
29 "Sidik" is a Phoenician name for God.
30 *Abraham: Recent Discoveries and Hebrew Origins* (London, 1936).
31 Kramp, p. 98.

10. BREAKING OF THE HOST ("FRACTIO")

The prayer "Deliver us, O Lord, we beseech thee, from all evils, past, present, and to come" lays renewed emphasis on the petition made in the preceding *Pater noster:* "but deliver us from evil." The connection between this and the sacrificial death of Christ lies in the descent into hell and the breaking of the infernal power. The breaking of the bread that now follows is symbolic of Christ's death. The Host is broken in two over the chalice. A small piece, the *particula*, is broken off from the left half and used for the rite of *consignatio* and *commixtio*. In the Byzantine rite the bread is divided into four, the four pieces being marked with letters as follows:

$$IΣ$$
$$NI \qquad KA$$
$$XΣ$$

This means "Ἰησοῦς Χριστὸς νικᾷ"—"Jesus Christ is victorious." The peculiar arrangement of the letters obviously represents a quaternity, which as we know always has the character of wholeness. This quaternity, as the letters show, refers to Christ glorified, king of glory and Pantokrator.

Still more complicated is the Mozarabic *fractio:* the Host is first broken into two, then the left half into five parts, and the right into four. The five are named *corporatio* (*incarnatio*), *nativitas, circumcisio, apparatio,* and *passio;* and the four *mors, resurrectio, gloria, regnum*. The first group refers exclusively to the human life of our Lord, the second to his existence beyond this world. According to the old view, five is the number of the natural ("hylical") man, whose outstretched arms and legs form, with the head, a pentagram. Four, on the other hand, signifies eternity and totality (as shown for instance by the Gnostic name "Barbelo," which is translated as "fourness is God"). This symbol, I would add in passing, seems to indicate that extension in space signifies God's suffering (on the cross) and, on the other hand, his dominion over the universe.

11. CONSIGNATIO

The sign of the cross is made over the chalice with the *particula*, and then the priest drops it into the wine.

12. COMMIXTIO

This is the mingling of bread and wine, as explained by Theodore of Mopsuestia (d. 428?): ". . . he combines them into one, whereby it is made manifest to everybody that although they are two they are virtually one." The text at this point says: "May this mixture and consecration [*commixtio et consecratio*] of the body and blood of our Lord help us," etc. The word "consecration" may be an allusion to an original consecration by contact, though that would not clear up the contradiction since a consecration of both substances has already taken place. Attention has therefore been drawn to the old custom of holding over the sacrament from one Mass to another, the Host being dipped in wine and then preserved in softened, or mixed, form. There are numerous rites that end with minglings of this kind. Here I would only mention the consecration by water, or the mixed drink of honey and milk which the neophytes were given after communion in the liturgy of Hippolytus.

The *Leonine Sacramentary* (seventh century) interprets the *commixtio* as a mingling of the heavenly and earthly nature of Christ. The later view was that it symbolizes the resurrection, since in it the blood (or soul) of our Lord is reunited with the body lying in the sepulcher. There is a significant reversal here of the original rite of baptism. In baptism, the body is immersed in water for the purpose of transformation; in the *commixtio*, on the other hand, the body, or *particula*, is steeped in wine, symbolizing spirit, and this amounts to a glorification of the body. Hence the justification for regarding the *commixtio* as a symbol of the resurrection.

13. CONCLUSION

On careful examination we find that the sequence of ritual actions in the Mass contains, sometimes clearly and sometimes by subtle allusions, a representation in condensed form of the life and sufferings of Christ. Certain phases overlap or are so close together that there can be no question of conscious and deliberate condensation. It is more likely that the historical evolution of the Mass gradually led to its becoming a concrete picture of the most important aspects of Christ's life. First of all (in the *Benedictus qui venit* and *Supra quae*) we have an anticipation and prefiguration of his coming. The uttering of the words of consecration corresponds to the incarnation of the Logos, and also to Christ's passion and sacrificial death, which appears again in the *fractio*. In the *Libera nos* there is an allusion to the descent into hell, while the *consignatio* and *commixtio* hint at resurrection.

In so far as the offered gift is the sacrificer himself, in so far as the priest and congregation offer themselves in the sacrificial gift, and in so far as Christ is both sacrificer and sacrificed, there is a mystical unity in all parts of the sacrificial act. The combination of offering and offerer in the single figure of Christ is implicit in the doctrine that just as bread is composed of many grains of wheat, and wine of many grapes, so the mystical body of the Church is made up of a multitude of believers. The mystical body, moreover, includes both sexes, represented by the bread and wine.[32] Thus the two substances—the masculine wine and the feminine bread—also signify the androgynous nature of the mystical Christ.

The Mass thus contains, as its essential core, the mystery and miracle of God's transformation taking place in the human sphere, his becoming Man, and his return to his absolute existence in and for himself. Man, too, by his devotion and self-sacrifice as a ministering instrument, is included in the mysterious process. God's offering of himself is a voluntary act of love, but the actual sacrifice was an agonizing and bloody death brought about by men *instrumentaliter et ministerialiter*. (The words *incruente immolatur*— "bloodlessly sacrificed"—refer only to the rite, not to the thing symbolized.) The terrors of death on the cross are an indispensable condition for transformation. This is in the first place a bringing to life of substances which are in themselves lifeless, and, in the second, a substantial alteration of them, a spiritualization, in accordance with the ancient conception of *pneuma* as a subtle material entity (the *corpus glorificationis*). This idea is expressed in the concrete participation in the body and blood of Christ in the Communion.

3. A Parallel from Pagan Antiquity

I. THE AZTEC "TEOQUALO"

Although the Mass itself is a unique phenomenon in the history of comparative religion, its symbolic content would be profoundly alien to man were it not rooted in the human psyche. But if it is so rooted, then we may expect to find similar patterns of symbolism both in the earlier history of mankind and in the world of pagan thought contemporary with it. As the prayer *Supra quae* shows, the liturgy of the Mass contains allusions to the "prefigurations" in the Old Testament, and thus indirectly to ancient

32 Kramp, p. 55.

sacrificial symbolism in general. It is clear, then, that in Christ's sacrifice and the Communion one of the deepest chords in the human psyche is struck: human sacrifice and ritual anthropophagy. Unfortunately I cannot enter into the wealth of ethnological material in question here, so must content myself with mentioning the ritual slaying of the king to promote the fertility of the land and the prosperity of his people, the renewal and revivification of the gods through human sacrifice, and the totem meal, the purpose of which was to reunite the participants with the life of their ancestors. These hints will suffice to show how the symbols of the Mass penetrate into the deepest layers of the psyche and its history. They are evidently among the most ancient and most central of religious conceptions. Now with regard to these conceptions there is still a widespread prejudice, not only among laymen, but in scientific circles too, that beliefs and customs of this kind must have been "invented" at some time or other, and were then handed down and imitated, so that they would not exist at all in most places unless they had got there in the manner suggested. It is, however, always a risky business to draw conclusions from our modern, "civilized" mentality about the primitive state of mind. Primitive consciousness differs from that of the present-day white man in several very important respects. Thus, in primitive societies, "inventing" is a very different thing from what it is with us, where one novelty follows another. With primitives, life goes on in the same way for generations; nothing alters, except perhaps the language. But that does not mean that a new one is "invented." Their language is "alive" and can therefore change, a fact that has been an unpleasant discovery for many lexicographers of primitive languages. Similarly, no one "invents" the picturesque slang spoken in America; it just springs up in inexhaustible abundance from the fertile soil of colloquial speech. Religious rites and their stock of symbols must have developed in much the same way from beginnings now lost to us, and not just in one place only, but in many places at once, and also at different periods. They have grown spontaneously out of the basic conditions of human nature, which are never invented but are everywhere the same.

So it is not surprising that we find religious rites which come very close to Christian practices in a field quite untouched by classical culture. I mean the rites of the Aztecs, and in particular that of *teoqualo*, the "god-eating," as recorded by Fray Bernardino de Sahagún, who began his missionary work among the Aztecs in 1529, eight years after the conquest of Mexico. In this rite, a doughlike paste was made out of the crushed and pounded seeds of the prickly poppy (*Argemone mexicana*) and molded into the figure of the god Huitzilopochtli:

> And upon the next day the body of Huitzilopochtli died.
> And he who slew him was the priest known as Quetzalcoatl. And that with which he slew him was a dart, pointed with flint, which he shot into his heart.
> He died in the presence of Moctezuma and of the keeper of the god, who verily spoke to Huitzilopochtli—who verily appeared before him, who indeed could make him offerings; and of four masters of the youths, front rank leaders. Before all of them died Huitzilopochtli.
> And when he had died, thereupon they broke up his body of . . . dough. His heart was apportioned to Moctezuma.
> And as for the rest of his members, which were made, as it were, to be his bones, they were distributed and divided up among all. . . . Each year . . . they ate it. . . . And when they divided up among themselves his body made of . . . dough, it was broken up exceeding small, very fine, as small as seeds. The youths ate it.
> And of this which they ate, it was said: "The god is eaten." And of those who ate it, it was said: "They guard the god."[1]

The idea of a divine body, its sacrifice in the presence of the high priest to whom the god appears and with whom he speaks, the piercing with the spear, the god's death followed by ritual dismemberment, and the eating (*communio*) of a small piece of his body, are all parallels which cannot be overlooked and which caused much consternation among the worthy Spanish Fathers at the time.

In Mithraism, a religion that sprang up not long before Christianity, we find a special set of sacrificial symbols and, it would seem, a corresponding ritual which unfortunately is known to us only from dumb monuments. There is a *transitus*, with Mithras carrying the bull; a bull sacrifice for seasonal fertility; a stereotyped representation of the sacrificial act, flanked on either side by dadophores carrying raised and lowered torches; and a meal at which pieces of bread marked with crosses were laid on the table. They have even found small bells, and these probably have some connection

1 Bernardino de Sahagún, *General History of the Things of New Spain (Florentine Codex)*, Book 3: *The Origin of the Gods*, tr. Arthur J. O. Anderson and Charles E. Dibble (Monographs of the School of American Research, 14, Part IV; Santa Fe, 1952), pp. 5f. (slightly modified).

with the bell which is sounded at Mass. The Mithraic sacrifice is essentially a self-sacrifice, since the bull is a world bull which was originally identical with Mithras himself. This may account for the singularly agonized expression on the face of the *tauroktonos*,[2] which bears comparison with Guido Reni's *Crucifixion*. The Mithraic *transitus* is a motif that corresponds to Christ carrying the cross, just as the transformation of the beast of sacrifice corresponds to the resurrection of the Christian God in the form of food and drink. The representations of the sacrificial act, the tauroctony (bull-slaying), recall the crucifixion between two thieves, one of whom is raised up to paradise while the other goes down to hell.

These few references to the Mithras cult are but one example of the wealth of parallels offered by the legends and rites of the various Near Eastern gods who die young, are mourned, and rise again. For anyone who knows these religions at all, there can be no doubt as to the basic affinity of the symbolic types and ideas.[3] At the time of primitive Christianity and in the early days of the Church the pagan world was saturated with conceptions of this kind and with philosophical speculations based upon them, and it was against this background that the visionary ideas of the Gnostic philosophers were unfolded.

II. THE VISION OF ZOSIMOS

A characteristic representative of this school of thought was Zosimos of Panopolis, a natural philosopher and alchemist of the third century A.D., whose works have been preserved, though in corrupt state, in the famous alchemical Codex Marcianus, and were published in 1887 by Berthelot in his *Collection des anciens alchimistes grecs*. In various portions of his treatises[4] Zosimos relates a number of dream visions, all of which appear to go back to one and the same dream.[5] He was clearly a non-Christian Gnostic, and in particular—so one gathers from the famous passage about the *krater*[6]— an adherent of the Poimandres sect, and therefore a follower of Hermes. Although alchemical literature abounds in parables, I would hesitate to class these dream visions among them. Anyone acquainted with the language

2 Franz Cumont, *Textes et monuments figurés relatifs aux mystères de Mithra* (Brussels, 1894–99), Vol. I, p. 182.
3 Cf. Frazer's *The Golden Bough*, Part III: "The Dying God."
4 *Alchimistes*, III, i, 2, 3; III, v; III, vi.
5 Cf. my paper "Einige Bemerkungen zu den Visionen des Zosimos," which gives a translation of the relevant passages.   6 Berthelot, III, li, 8.

of the alchemists will recognize that their parables are mere allegories of ideas that were common knowledge. In the allegorical figures and actions, one can usually see at once what substances and what procedures are being referred to under a deliberately theatrical disguise. There is nothing of this sort in the Zosimos visions. Indeed, it comes almost as a surprise to find the alchemical interpretation, namely that the dream and its impressive machinery are simply an illustration of the means for producing the "divine water," the famed solvent or tincture. Moreover a parable is a self-contained whole, whereas our vision varies and amplifies the theme just as a dream does. So far as one can assess the nature of these visions at all, I should say that the contents of an imaginative meditation have grouped themselves round the kernel of an actual dream and been woven into it. That there really was such a meditation is evident from the fragments of it that accompany the visions in the form of a commentary. As we know, meditations of this kind are often vividly pictorial, as if the dream were being continued on a level nearer to consciousness. In his *Lexicon alchemiae*, Martin Ruland, writing in Frankfort in 1612, defines the meditation that plays such an important part in alchemy as an "internal colloquy with someone else, who is nevertheless not seen, it may be with God, with oneself, or with one's good angel." The latter is a milder and less obnoxious form of the *paredros*, the familiar spirit of ancient alchemy, who was generally a planetary demon conjured up by magic. It can hardly be doubted that real visionary experiences originally lay at the root of these practices, and a vision is in the last resort nothing less than a dream which has broken through into the waking state. We know from numerous witnesses all through the ages that the alchemist, in the course of his imaginative work, was beset by visions of all kinds,[7] and was sometimes even threatened with madness.[8] So the visions of Zosimos are not something unusual or unknown in alchemical experience, though they are perhaps the most important self-revelations ever bequeathed to us by an alchemist.

I cannot reproduce here the text of the visions in full, but will give as an example the first vision, in Zosimos' own words:

> And while I said this I fell asleep, and I saw a sacrificial priest standing before me, high up on an altar, which was in the shape of a

7 Cf. the examples given in *Psychology and Alchemy* (New York and London, 1953), pars. 347f.
8 Olympiodorus says this is particularly the effect of lead. Cf. Berthelot, II, iv, 43.

shallow bowl. There were fifteen steps leading up to the altar. And the priest stood there, and I heard a voice from above say to me: "Behold, I have completed the descent down the fifteen steps of darkness and I have completed the ascent up the steps of light. And he who renews me is the priest, for he cast away the density of the body, and by compulsive necessity I am sanctified and now stand in perfection as a spirit [*pneuma*]." And I perceived the voice of him who stood upon the altar, and I inquired of him who he was. And he answered me in a fine voice, saying: "I am Ion, priest of the innermost hidden sanctuary, and I submit myself to an unendurable torment. For there came one in haste at early morning, who overpowered me and pierced me through with the sword and cut me in pieces, yet in such a way that the order of my limbs was preserved. And he drew off the scalp of my head with the sword, which he wielded with strength, and he put the bones and the pieces of flesh together and with his own hand burned them in the fire, until I perceived that I was transformed and had become spirit. And that is my unendurable torment." And even as he spoke this, and I held him by force to converse with me, his eyes became as blood. And he spewed out all his own flesh. And I saw how he changed into a manikin [ἀνθρωπάριον: i.e., an homunculus] who has lost a part of himself. And he tore his flesh with his own teeth, and sank into himself.

In the course of the visions the Hiereus (priest) appears in various forms. At first he is split into the figures of the Hiereus and the Hierourgon, who is charged with the performance of the sacrifice. But these figures blend into one in so far as both suffer the same fate. The sacrificial priest submits voluntarily to the torture by which he is transformed. But he is also the sacrificer who is sacrificed, since he is pierced through with the sword and ritually dismembered.[9] The *deipnon* consists in his tearing himself to pieces with his own teeth and eating himself; the *thysia*, in his flesh being sacrificially burned on the altar.

He is the Hiereus in so far as he rules over the sacrificial rite as a whole, and over the human beings who are transformed during the *thysia*. He calls himself a guardian of spirits. He is also known as the "Brazen Man" and as Xyrourgos, the barber. The brazen or leaden man is an allusion to the

9 The dismemberment motif belongs in the wider context of rebirth symbolism. Consequently it plays an important part in the initiation experiences of shamans and medicine men, who are dismembered and then put together again. For details, see Mircea Eliade, *Le Chamanisme* (Paris, 1951), pp. 47ff.

spirits of the metals, or planetary demons, as protagonists of the sacrificial drama. In all probability they are *paredroi* who were conjured up by magic, as may be deduced from Zosimos' remark that he "held the priest by force" to converse with him. The planetary demons are none other than the old gods of Olympus who finally expired only in the eighteenth century, as the "souls of the metals"—or rather, assumed a new shape, since it was in this same century that paganism openly arose for the first time (in the French Revolution).

Somewhat more curious is the term "barber," for there is no mention of cutting the hair or shaving. There is, however, a scalping, which in our context is closely connected with the ancient rites of flaying and their magical significance.[10] I need hardly mention the flaying of Marsyas, who is an unmistakable parallel to the son-lover of Cybele, namely Attis, the dying god who rises again. In one of the old Attic fertility rites an ox was flayed, stuffed, and set up on its feet. Herodotus reports a number of flaying ceremonies among the Scythians, and especially scalpings.[11] In general, flaying signifies transformation from a worse state to a better, and hence renewal and rebirth. The best examples are to be found in the religion of ancient Mexico.[12] Thus, in order to renew the moon-goddess a young woman was decapitated and skinned, and a youth then put the skin round him to represent the risen goddess. The prototype of this renewal is the snake casting its skin every year, a phenomenon round which primitive fantasy has always played. In our vision the skinning is restricted to the head, and this can probably be explained by the underlying idea of spiritual transformation. Since olden times shaving the head has been associated with consecration, that is, with spiritual transformation or initiation. The priests of Isis had their heads shaved quite bald, and the tonsure, as we know, is still in use at the present day. This "symptom" of transformation goes back to the old idea that the transformed one becomes like a new-born babe

---

10 Cf. Frazer's *The Golden Bough*, Part IV: *Adonis, Attis, Osiris* (2nd edn., London, 1907), pp. 242ff. and p. 405, and my *Symbols of Transformation* (New York and London, 1956), pars. 594 f. Cf. also Colin Campbell, *The Miraculous Birth of King Amon-Hotep III* (London, 1912), p. 142, concerning the presentation of the dead man, Sen-nezem, before Osiris, Lord of Amentet: "In this scene the god is usually represented enthroned. Before and behind him, hanging from a pole, is the dripping skin of a slain bull that was slaughtered to yield up the soul of Osiris at his reconstruction, with the vase underneath to catch the blood."

11 Book IV, 60.

12 Cf. Eduard Seler's account in Hastings, *ERE*, Vol. VIII, pp. 615f.

(neophyte, *quasimodogenitus*) with a hairless head. In the myth of the night sea journey the hero loses all his hair during his incubation in the belly of the monster, because of the terrific heat.[13] The custom of tonsure, which is derived from these primitive ideas, naturally presupposes the presence of a ritual barber. Curiously enough, we come across the barber in that old alchemical "mystery," the *Chymical Wedding* of 1616.[14] There the hero, on entering the mysterious castle, is pounced on by invisible barbers, who give him something very like a tonsure.[15] Here again the initiation and transformation process is accompanied by a shaving.[16]

In one variant of these visions there is a dragon who is killed and sacrificed in the same manner as the priest, and therefore seems to be identical with him. This makes one think of those far from uncommon medieval pictures, not necessarily alchemical, in which a serpent is shown hanging on the Cross in place of Christ. (Note the comparison of Christ with the serpent of Moses in John 3 : 14.)

We have already mentioned the leaden homunculus as one of the names of the priest, and this is none other than the leaden spirit or planetary demon Saturn. In Zosimos' day Saturn was regarded as a Hebrew god, presumably on account of the keeping holy of the Sabbath—Saturday means "Saturn's Day"[17]—and also on account of the Gnostic parallel with the supreme

13 Leo Frobenius, *Das Zeitalter des Sonnengottes* (Berlin, 1904), p. 30.
14 [The *Chymische Hochzeit*, dated 1459, actually published at Strasbourg, 1616. Signed "Christian Rosencreutz," but actually written by Johann Valentin Andreae, Professor Jung states elsewhere. The 1616 edn. was reprinted under the editorship of F. Maack, Berlin, 1913. Tr. by E. Foxcroft, *The Hermetick Romance; or, The Chymical Wedding* (London, 1690).—Ed.]
15 As Andreae, the author of the *Chymical Wedding*, must have been a learned alchemist, he might very well have got hold of a copy of the Codex Marcianus and seen the writings of Zosimos. Manuscript copies exist in Gotha, Leipzig, Munich, and Weimar. I know of only one printed edition, published in Italy in the 16th century, which is very rare.
16 Hence the "shaving of a man" and the "plucking of a fowl," mentioned further on among the magical sacrificial recipes. A similar motif is suggested by the "changing of wigs" at the Egyptian judgment of the dead. Cf. the picture in the tomb of Sennezem (Campbell, p. 143). When the dead man is led before Osiris his wig is black; immediately afterwards (at the sacrifice in the Papyrus of Ani) it is white.
17 Plutarch, *Quaestiones convivales*, IV, 5, and Diogenes Laertius, II, §112; Richard Reitzenstein, *Poimandres* (Leipzig, 1904), pp. 75f. and 112. In a text named "Ghâya al-hakîm," ascribed to Maslama al-Madjrîtî, the following instructions are given when invoking Saturn: "Arrive vêtu à la manière des Juifs, car il est leur patron." Reinhart Dozy and M. J. de Goeje, "Nouveaux documents pour l'étude de la religion des Harraniens," *Actes du Sixième Congrès international des Orientalistes*, 1883 (Leyden, 1885), p. 350.

archon Ialdabaoth ("child of chaos") who, as λεοντοειδής,[18] may be grouped together with Baal, Kronos, and Saturn.[19] The later Arabic designation of Zosimos as al-'Ibrî (the Hebrew) does not of course prove that he himself was a Jew, but it is clear from his writings that he was acquainted with Jewish traditions.[20] The parallel between the Hebrew god and Saturn is of considerable importance as regards the alchemical idea of the transformation of the God of the Old Testament into the God of the New. The alchemists naturally attached great significance to Saturn, for, besides being the outermost planet, the supreme archon (the Harranites named him "Primas"), and the demiurge Ialdabaoth, he was also the *spiritus niger* who lies captive in the darkness of matter, the deity or that part of the deity which has been swallowed up in his own creation. He is the dark god who reverts to his original luminous state in the mystery of alchemical transmutation. As the *Aurora consurgens* (Part I) says: "Blessed is he who has discovered this science and on whom the providence of Saturn flows."[21]

The later alchemists were familiar not only with the ritual slaying of a dragon but also with the slaying of a lion, which took the form of his having all four paws cut off.[22] Like the dragon, the lion devours himself,[23] and so is probably only a variant.

The vision itself indicates that the main purpose of the transformation process is the spiritualization of the sacrificing priest: he is to be changed into *pneuma*. We are also told that he would "change the bodies into blood, make the eyes to see and the dead to rise again." Later in the visions he appears in glorified form, shining white like the midday sun.

Throughout the visions it is clear that sacrificer and sacrificed are one and the same. This idea of the unity of the *prima* and *ultima materia*, of that which redeems and that which is to be redeemed, pervades the whole of alchemy from beginning to end. "Unus est lapis, una medicina, unum vas, unum regimen, unaque dispositio" is the key formula to its enigmatic

18 Origen, *Contra Celsum*, V, 31. *Pistis Sophia*, ch. 31. Wilhelm Bousset, *Hauptprobleme der Gnosis* (Göttingen, 1907), pp. 351ff.
19 Roscher, *Lexikon*, s.v. Kronos, 1496. The dragon and Kronos are often confused.
20 E. O. von Lippmann, *Entstehung und Ausbreitung der Alchemie* (Berlin, 1919–31), Vol. II, p. 229.
21 "Beatus homo qui invenerit hanc scientiam et cui affluit providentia Saturni."
22 See the illustration in Béroalde de Verville's *Pandora* (1588) and the frontispiece of his *Poliphile* (1600).
23 Generally the pictures show two lions eating one another. The uroboros, too, is often pictured in the form of two dragons engaged in the same process (*Viridarium chymicum*, 1624).

language.[24] Greek alchemy expresses the same idea in the formula ἓν τὸ πᾶν. Its symbol is the uroboros, the tail-eating serpent. In our vision it is the priest as sacrificer who devours himself as the sacrifice. This recalls the saying of St. John Chrysostom that in the Eucharist Christ drinks his own blood. By the same token, one might add, he eats his own flesh. The grisly repast in the dream of Zosimos reminds us of the orgiastic meals in the Dionysus cult, when sacrificial animals were torn to pieces and eaten. They represent Dionysus Zagreus being torn to pieces by the Titans, from whose mangled remains the νέος Διόνυσος arises.[25]

Zosimos tells us that the vision represents or explains the "production of the waters." The visions themselves only show the transformation into *pneuma*. In the language of the alchemists, however, spirit and water are synonymous,[26] as they are in the language of the early Christians, for whom water meant the *spiritus veritatis*. In the "Book of Krates" we read: "You make the bodies to liquefy, so that they mingle and become an homogeneous

24 Cf. the "Rosarium philosophorum," in the *Artis auriferae* (Basel, 1593), Vol. II, p. 206.

25 Cf. the Cretan fragment of Euripides (Albrecht Dieterich, *Eine Mithrasliturgie*, Leipzig, 1910, p. 105):

"ἁγνὸν δὲ βίον τείνων ἐξ οὗ
Διὸς Ἰδαίου μύστης γενόμην
καὶ νυκτιπόλου Ζαγρέως βούτας
τοὺς ὠμοφάγους δαῖτας τελέσας"

(living a holy life, since I have been initiated into the mysteries of the Idaean Zeus, and eaten raw the flesh of Zagreus, the night-wandering shepherd).

26 "Est et coelestis aqua sive potius divina Chymistarum . . . pneuma, ex aetheris natura et essentia rerum quinta" (There is also the celestial, or rather the divine, water of the alchemists . . . the pneuma, having the nature of the pneuma and the quintessence of things).—Hermolaus Barbarus, *Coroll. in Dioscoridem*, cited in M. Maier, *Symbola aureae mensae* (Frankfort, 1617), p. 174.

"Spiritus autem in hac arte nihil aliud quam aquam indicari . . ." (In this art, spirit means nothing else but water).—Theobaldus de Hoghelande, in the *Theatrum chemicum*, Vol. I (Ursel, 1602), p. 196. Water is a "spiritus extractus," or a "spiritus qui in ventre (corporis) occultus est et fiet aqua et corpus absque spiritu: qui est spiritualis naturae" (spirit which is hidden in the belly [of the substance], and water will be produced and a substance without spirit, which is of a spiritual nature).— J. D. Mylius, *Philosophia reformata* (Frankfort, 1622), p. 150. This quotation shows how closely spirit and water were associated in the mind of the alchemist.

"Sed aqua coelestis gloriosa *scil.* aes nostrum ac argentum nostrum, sericum nostrum, totaque oratio nostra, quod est unum et idem *scil.* sapientia, quam Deus obtulit, quibus voluit" (But the glorious celestial water, namely our copper and our silver, our silk, and everything we talk about, is one and the same thing, namely the Wisdom, which God has given to whomsoever he wished).—"Consilium coniugii," in the *Ars chemica* (Strasbourg, 1566), p. 120.

liquid; this is then named 'divine water.' "[27] The passage corresponds to the Zosimos text, which says that the priest would "change the bodies into blood." For the alchemists, water and blood are identical. This transformation is the same as the *solutio* or *liquefactio*, which is a synonym for the *sublimatio*, for "water" is also "fire": "Item ignis . . . est aqua et ignis noster est ignis et non ignis" (For fire . . . is water and our fire is the fire that is no fire). "Aqua nostra" is said to be "ignea" (fiery).[28]

The "secret fire of our philosophy" is said to be "our mystical water,"[29] and the "permanent water" is the "fiery form of the true water."[30] The permanent water (the ὕδωρ θεῖον of the Greeks) also signifies "spiritualis sanguis,"[31] and is identified with the blood and water that flowed from Christ's side. Heinrich Khunrath says of this water: "So there will open for thee an healing flood which issues from the heart of the son of the great world." It is a water "which the son of the great world pours forth from his body and heart, to be for us a true and natural Aqua Vitae."[32] Just as a spiritual water of grace and truth flows from Christ's sacrifice, so the "divine water" is produced by a sacrificial act in the Zosimos vision. It is mentioned in the ancient treatise entitled "Isis to Horus,"[33] where the angel Amnael brings it to the prophetess in a drinking vessel. As Zosimos was probably an adherent of the Poimandres sect, another thing to be considered here is the *krater* which God filled with *nous* for all those seeking ἔννοια.[34] *Nous* is identical with the alchemical Mercurius. This is quite clear from the Ostanes quotation in Zosimos, which says: "Go to the streams of the Nile and there thou wilt find a stone which hath a spirit. Take and divide it, thrust in thy hand and draw out its heart, for its soul is in its heart." Commenting on this, Zosimos remarks that "having a spirit" is a metaphorical expression for the *exhydrargyrosis*, the expulsion of the quicksilver.[35]

During the first centuries after Christ the words *nous* and *pneuma* were used indiscriminately, and the one could easily stand for the other. Moreover the relation of Mercurius to "spirit" is an extremely ancient astrological

27 M. Berthelot, *La Chimie au moyen âge* (Paris, 1893), Vol. III, p. 53.
28 Mylius, pp. 121 and 123. For the blood–water–fire equation see George Ripley, *Opera omnia chemica* (Kassel, 1649), pp. 162, 197, 295, 427.
29 Ripley, *Opera*, p. 62.   30 "Rosarium," p. 264.   31 Mylius, p. 42.
32 H. C. Khunrath, *Von hylealischen . . . Chaos* (Magdeburg, 1597), pp. 274f.
33 Berthelot, *Alchimistes*, I, xiii.
34 Ibid., III, li, 8, and *Hermetica*, ed. Scott, Vol. I, p. 151.
35 Berthelot, *Alchimistes*, III, vi, 5.

fact. Like Hermes, Mercurius (or the planetary spirit Mercury) was a god of revelation, who discloses the secret of the art to the adepts. The *Liber quartorum*, which being of Harranite origin cannot be dated later than the tenth century, says of Mercurius: *"Ipse enim aperit clausiones operum cum ingenio et intellectu suo"* (For he opens with his genius and understanding the locked [insoluble] problems of the work).[36] He is also the "soul of the bodies," the *"anima vitalis,"*[37] and Ruland defines him as "spirit which has become earth."[38] He is a spirit that penetrates into the depths of the material world and transforms it. Like the *nous*, he is symbolized by the serpent. In Michael Maier he points the way to the earthly paradise.[39] Besides being identified with Hermes Trismegistus,[40] he is also called the "mediator"[41] and, as the Original Man, the "Hermaphroditic Adam."[42] From numerous passages it is clear that Mercurius is as much a fire as a water, both of which aptly characterize the nature of spirit.

Killing with the sword is a recurrent theme in alchemical literature. The "philosophical egg" is divided with the sword, and with it the "King" is transfixed and the dragon or "corpus" dismembered, the latter being represented as the body of a man whose head and limbs are cut off.[43] The lion's paws are likewise cut off with the sword. For the alchemical sword brings about the *solutio* or *separatio* of the elements, thereby restoring the original condition of chaos, so that a new and more perfect body can be produced by a new *impressio formae*, or by a "new imagination." The sword is therefore that which "kills and vivifies," and the same is said of the permanent water or mercurial water. Mercurius is the giver of life as well as the destroyer of the old form. In ecclesiastical symbolism the sword which comes out of the mouth of the Son of Man in the Book of Revelation is, according to Hebrews 4 : 12, the Logos, the Word of God, and hence Christ himself. This analogy did not escape the notice of the alchemists, who were

---

36 Of the later authors I will mention only Joannes Christophorus Steeb, *Coelum sephiroticum* (Mainz, 1679): *"Omnis intellectus acuminis auctor . . . a coelesti mercurio omnem ingeniorum vim provenire"* (The author of all deeper understanding . . . all the power of genius comes from the celestial Mercurius). For the astrological connection see Auguste Bouché-Leclercq, *L'Astrologie grecque* (Paris, 1899), pp. 312, 321–23.

37 *Aurora consurgens*. In Mylius (p. 533) he is a giver of life.

38 *Lexicon*.   39 *Symbola*, p. 592.   40 P. 600.

41 Ripley, *Opera*, Foreword, and in Khunrath's *Chaos*. In Plutarch, Mercurius acts as a kind of world soul.

42 Gerhard Dorn, "Congeries Paracelsicae chemicae . . .," in the *Theatrum chemicum*, Vol. I, p. 589.

43 Illustration in "Splendor solis," *Aureum vellus* (Rorschach, 1598).

always struggling to give expression to their fantasies. Mercurius was their mediator and savior, their *filius macrocosmi* (contrasted with Christ the *filius microcosmi*),[44] the solver and separator. So he too is a sword, for he is a "penetrating spirit" ("more piercing than a two-edged sword"!). Gerhard Dorn, an alchemist of the sixteenth century, says that in our world the sword was changed into Christ our Saviour. He comments as follows:

> After a long interval of time the Deus Optimus Maximus immersed himself in the innermost of his secrets, and he decided, out of the compassion of his love as well as for the demands of justice, to take the sword of wrath from the hand of the angel. And having hung the sword on the tree, he substituted for it a golden trident, and thus was the wrath of God changed into love. . . . When peace and justice were united, the water of Grace flowed more abundantly from above, and now it bathes the whole world.[45]

44 Cf. Khunrath, *Chaos*, and *Amphitheatrum sapientiae aeternae* . . . (Hanau, 1604).
45 Dorn, "Speculativae philosophiae," in the *Theatrum chemicum*, Vol. I, pp. 284ff. The whole passage runs as follows:

Post primam hominis inobedientiam, Dominus viam hanc amplissimam in callem strictissimam difficillimamque (ut videtis) restrinxit, in cuius ostio collocavit Cherubin angelum, ancipitem gladium manu tenentem, quo quidem arceret omnes ab introitu felicis patriae: hinc deflectentes Adae filii propter peccatum primi sui parentis, in sinistram latam sibimet viam construxerunt, quam evitastis. Longo postea temporis intervallo D. O. M. secreta secretorum suorum introivit, in quibus amore miserente, accusanteque iustitia, conclusit angelo gladium irae suae de manibus eripere, cuius loco tridentem hamum substituit aureum, gladio ad arborem suspenso: & sic mutata est ira Dei in amorem, servata iustitia: quod antequam fieret, fluvius iste non erat, ut iam, in se collectus, sed ante lapsum per totum orbem terrarum roris instar expansus aequaliter: post vero rediit unde processerat tandem ut pax & iustitia sunt osculatae se, descendit affluentius ab alto manans aqua gratiae, totum nunc mundum alluens. In sinistram partem qui deflectunt, partim suspensum in arbore gladium videntes, eiusque noscentes historiam, quia mundo nimium sunt insiti, praetereunt: nonnulli videntes eius efficaciam perquirere negligunt, alii nec vident, nec vidisse voluissent: hi recta peregrinationem suam ad vallem dirigunt omnes, nisi per hamos resipiscentiae, vel poenitentiae nonnulli retrahantur ad montem Sion. Nostro iam saeculo (quod gratiae est) mutatus est gladius in Christum salvatorem nostrum qui crucis arborem pro peccatis nostris ascendit.

(After man's first disobedience the Lord straitened this wide road into a very narrow and difficult path, as you see. At its entrance he placed an angel of the Cherubim, holding in his hand a double-edged sword with which he was to keep all from entering into Paradise. Turning from thence on account of the sin of their first parents, the sons of Adam built for themselves a broad left-hand path: this you have shunned. After a long interval of time the Deus Optimus Maximus immersed himself in the innermost of his secrets, and he decided, out of the compassion of his love as well as for the demands of justice, to take the sword of wrath from the hand of the angel. And having hung the sword on the tree, he substituted for it a golden trident, and thus was the wrath of God changed into love, and justice remained unimpaired. Previous to this, however, the river was not collected into one as it is now, but before the Fall

302

This passage, which might well have occurred in an author like Rabanus Maurus or Honorius of Autun without doing them discredit, actually occurs in a context which throws light on certain esoteric alchemical doctrines, namely in a colloquy between Animus, Anima, and Corpus. There we are told that it is Sophia, the Sapientia, Scientia, or Philosophia of the alchemists, *"de cuius fonte scaturiunt aquae"* (from whose fount the waters gush forth). This Wisdom is the *nous* that lies hidden and bound in matter, the *"serpens mercurialis"* or *"humidum radicale"* that manifests itself in the *"viventis aquae fluvius de montis apice"* (stream of living water from the summit of the mountain).[46] That is the water of grace, the "permanent" and "divine" water which "now bathes the whole world." The apparent transformation of the God of the Old Testament into the God of the New is in reality the transformation of the *deus absconditus* (i.e., the *natura abscondita*) into the *Medicina catholica* of alchemical wisdom.[47]

The divisive and separative function of the sword, which is of such importance in alchemy, is prefigured in the flaming sword of the angel that separated our first parents from paradise. Separation by a sword is a theme that can also be found in the Gnosis of the Ophites: the earthly cosmos is surrounded by a ring of fire which at the same time encloses paradise. But paradise and the ring of fire are separated by the "flaming sword."[48] An important interpretation of this flaming sword is given in Simon Magus:[49] there is an incorruptible essence potentially present in every human being, the divine *pneuma* "which is stationed above and below in the stream of

---

it was spread equally over the whole world, like dew. But later it returned to the place of its origin. When peace and justice were united, the water of grace flowed more abundantly from above, and now it bathes the whole world. Some of those who take the left-hand path, on seeing the sword suspended from the tree, and knowing its history, pass it by, because they are too entangled in the affairs of this world; some, on seeing it, do not choose to inquire into its efficacy; others never see it and would not wish to see it. All these continue their pilgrimage into the valley, except for those who are drawn back to Mount Zion by the hook of repentance. Now in our age, which is an age of grace, the sword has become Christ our Saviour, who ascended the tree of the Cross for our sins.)

46 Another remark of Dorn's points in the same direction: "The sword was suspended from a tree over the bank of the river" (p. 288).

47 A few pages later Dorn himself remarks: *"Scitote, fratres, omnia quae superius dicta sunt et dicentur in posterum, intelligi posse de praeparationibus alchemicis"* (Know, brothers, that everything which has been said above and everything which will be said in what follows can also be understood of the alchemical preparations).

48 Hans Leisegang, *Die Gnosis* (Leipzig, 1924), pp. 171f.

49 The passage which follows occurs in Hippolytus, *Elenchos* (in *Werke*, ed. Paul Wendland, Vol. III; Leipzig, 1916), vi, pp. 4f.

water." Simon says of this *pneuma:* "I and thou, thou before me. I, who am after thee." It is a force "that generates itself, that causes itself to grow; it is its own mother, sister, bride, daughter; its own son, mother, father; a unity, a root of the whole." It is the very ground of existence, the procreative urge, which is of fiery origin. Fire is related to blood, which "is fashioned warm and ruddy like fire." Blood turns into semen in men, and in women into milk. This "turning" is interpreted as "the flaming sword which turned every way, to keep the way of the tree of life."[50] The operative principle in semen and milk turns into mother and father. The tree of life is guarded by the turning (i.e., transforming) sword, and this is the "seventh power" which begets itself. "For if the flaming sword turned not, then would that fair Tree be destroyed, and perish utterly; but if it turneth into semen and milk, and there be added the Logos and the place of the Lord where the Logos is begotten, he who dwelleth potentially in the semen and milk shall grow to full stature from the littlest spark, and shall increase and become a power boundless and immutable, like to an unchanging Aeon, which suffereth no more change until measureless eternity."[51] It is clear from these remarkable statements of Hippolytus concerning the teachings of Simon Magus that the sword is very much more than an instrument which divides; it is itself the force which "turns" from something infinitesimally small into the infinitely great: from water, fire, and blood it becomes the limitless aeon. What it means is the transformation of the vital spirit in man into the Divine. The natural being becomes the divine *pneuma*, as in the vision of Zosimos. Simon's description of the creative *pneuma*, the true arcane substance, corresponds in every detail to the uroboros or *serpens mercurialis* of the Latinists. It too is its own father, mother, son, daughter, brother, and sister from the earliest beginnings of alchemy right down to the end.[52] It begets and sacrifices itself and is its own instrument of sacrifice, for it is a symbol of the deadly and life-giving water.[53]

Simon's ideas also throw a significant light on the above-quoted passage from Dorn, where the sword of wrath is transformed into Christ. Were it not that the philosophemes of Hippolytus were first discovered in the nineteenth century, on Mount Athos, one might almost suppose that Dorn had made use of them. There are numerous other symbols in alchemy whose

---

50 Genesis 3 : 24.   51 Leisegang, p. 80.
52 That is why it is called "Hermaphroditus."
53 One of its symbols is the scorpion, which stings itself to death.

origin is so doubtful that one does not know whether to attribute them to tradition, or to a study of the heresiologists, or to spontaneous revival.[54]

The sword as the "proper" instrument of sacrifice occurs again in the old treatise entitled "Consilium coniugii de massa solis et lunae." This says: "Both must be killed with their own sword" ("both" referring to Sol and Luna).[55] In the still older "Tractatus Micreris,"[56] dating perhaps from the twelfth century, we find the "fiery sword" in a quotation from Ostanes: "The great Astanus [Ostanes] saith: Take an egg, pierce it with the fiery sword, and separate its soul from its body."[57] Here the sword is something that divides body and soul, corresponding to the division between heaven and earth, the ring of fire and paradise, or paradise and the first parents. In an equally old treatise, the "Allegoriae sapientum . . . supra librum Turbae," there is even mention of a sacrificial rite: "Take a fowl [*volatile*], cut off its head with the fiery sword, then pluck out its feathers, separate the limbs, and cook over a charcoal fire till it becomes of one color."[58] Here we have a decapitation with the fiery sword, then a "clipping," or more accurately a "plucking," and finally a "cooking." The cock, which is probably what is meant here, is simply called "volatile," a fowl or winged creature, and this is a common term for spirit, but a spirit still nature-bound and imperfect, and in need of improvement. In another old treatise, with the very similar title "Allegoriae super librum Turbae,"[59] we find the following supplementary variants: "Kill the mother [the *prima materia*], tearing off her hands and feet." "Take a viper . . . cut off its head and tail." "Take a cock . . . and pluck it alive." "Take a man, shave him, and drag him over a [hot] stone till his body dies." "Take the glass vessel containing bridegroom and bride, throw them into the furnace, and roast them for three days, and they will be two in one flesh." "Take the white man from the vessel."[60]

---

54 So far I have come across only two authors who admit to having read any heresiologists. The silence of the alchemists in this matter is nothing to wonder at, since the mere proximity to heresy would have put them in danger of their lives. Thus even 90 years after the death of Trithemius of Spanheim, who was supposed to have been the teacher of Paracelsus, the abbot Sigismund of Sion had to compose a moving defense in which he endeavored to acquit Trithemius of the charge of heresy. Cf. *Trithemius sui-ipsius vindex* (Ingolstadt, 1616).

55 *Ars chemica*, p. 256. Printed in J. J. Manget, *Bibliotheca chemica curiosa* (Geneva, 1702), Vol. II, p. 235.

56 "Micreris" is probably a corruption of "Mercurius."

57 *Theatrum chemicum*, Vol. V (1622), p. 103.   58 P. 68.

59 *Artis auriferae*, Vol. I, pp. 139f.   60 Pp. 151, 140, 140, 139, 151, 151, resp.

One is probably right in assuming that these recipes are instructions for magical sacrifices, not unlike the Greek magic papyri.[61] As an example of the latter I will give the recipe from the Mimaut Papyrus (li. 2ff.): "Take a tomcat and make an Osiris of him[62] [by immersing] his body in water. And when you proceed to suffocate him, talk into his back." Another example from the same papyrus (li. 425): "Take a hoopoe, tear out its heart, pierce it with a reed, then cut it up and throw it into Attic honey."

Such sacrifices really were made for the purpose of summoning up the *paredros*, the familiar spirit. That this sort of thing was practiced, or at any rate recommended, by the alchemists is clear from the "Liber Platonis quartorum," where it speaks of the *"oblationes et sacrificia"* offered to the planetary demon. A deeper and more somber note is struck in the following passage, which I give in the original (and generally very corrupt) text:[63]

> Vas . . . oportet esse rotundae figurae: Ut sit artifex huius mutator firmamenti et testae capitis, ut cum sit res, qua indigemus, res simplex, habens partes similes, necesse est ipsius generationem, et in corpore habente similes partibus . . . proiicies ex testa capitis, videlicet capitis elementi hominis et massetur totum cum urina. . . .

> (The vessel . . . must be round in shape. Thus the artifex must be the transformer of this firmament and of the brain-pan, just as the thing for which we seek is a simple thing having uniform parts. It is therefore necessary that you should generate it in a body [i.e., a vessel] of uniform parts . . . from the brain-pan, that is, from the head of the element Man, and that the whole should be macerated with urine. . . .)

One asks oneself how literally this recipe, with its implied human sacrifice,[64] is to be taken. The following story from the "Ghâya al-hakîm" is exceedingly enlightening in this connection:

The Jacobite patriarch Dionysius I set it on record that in the year 765, a man who was destined for the sacrifice, on beholding the bloody head of his predecessor, was so terrified that he took flight and lodged a complaint with Abbas, the prefect of Mesopotamia, against the priests of Harran, who were afterwards severely punished. The story goes on to say that in 830

---

61 *Papyri Graecae Magicae*, tr. and ed. Karl Preisendanz (Leipzig, Berlin, 1928–31, 2 vols.).
62 ἀποθέωσις = "sacrifice."
63 *Theatrum chemicum*, Vol. V, p. 153.
64 See also pp. 127, 128, 130, and 149 of the same work. The preparation known in medieval alchemy as *mumia* had to be compounded of *fresh* human bones.

the Caliph Mamun told the Harranite envoys: "You are without doubt the people of the head, who were dealt with by my father Rashid." We learn from the "Ghâya" that a fair-haired man with dark-blue eyes was lured into a chamber of the temple, where he was immersed in a great jar filled with sesame oil. Only his head was left sticking out. There he remained for forty days, and during this time was fed on nothing but figs soaked in sesame oil. He was not given a drop of water to drink. As a result of this treatment his body became as soft as wax. The prisoner was repeatedly fumigated with incense, and magical formulae were pronounced over him. Eventually his head was torn off at the neck, the body remaining in the oil. The head was then placed in a niche on the ashes of burnt olives, and was packed round with cotton wool. More incense was burned before it, and the head would thereupon predict famines or good harvests, changes of dynasty, and other future events. Its eyes could see, though the lids did not move. It also revealed to people their inmost thoughts, and scientific and technical questions were likewise addressed to it.[65]

Even though it is possible that the real head was, in later times, replaced by a dummy, the whole idea of this ceremony, particularly when taken in conjunction with the above passage from the "Liber quartorum," seems to point to an original human sacrifice. The idea of a mysterious head is, however, considerably older than the school of Harran. As far back as Zosimos we find the philosophers described as "children of the golden head," and we also encounter the *"rotundum,"* which Zosimos says is the letter omega (Ω). This symbol may well be interpreted as the head, since the "Liber quartorum" also associates the round vessel with the head. Zosimos, moreover, refers on several occasions to the "whitest stone, which is in the head."[66] Probably all these ideas go back to the severed head of Osiris, which crossed the sea and was therefore associated with the idea of resurrection. The "head of Osiris" also plays an important part in medieval alchemy.

In this connection we might mention the legend that was current about Gerbert of Reims, afterwards Pope Sylvester II (d. 1003). He was believed to have possessed a golden head which spoke to him in oracles. Gerbert was one of the greatest savants of his time, and well known as the trans-

---

65 Dozy and de Goeje, p. 365.
66 "Τὸν πάνυ λευκότατον λίθον τὸν ἐγκέφαλον."—The importance of the cerebrum was also stressed by the medieval alchemists.

mitter of Arabic science.[67] Can it be that the translation of the "Liber quartorum," which is of Harranite origin, goes back to this author? Unfortunately there is little prospect of our being able to prove this.

It has been conjectured that the Harranite oracle head may be connected with the ancient Hebrew teraphim. Rabbinic tradition considers the teraphim to have been originally either the decapitated head or skull of a human being, or else a dummy head.[68] The Jews had teraphim about the house as a sort of lares and penates (who were plural spirits, like the Cabiri). The idea that they were heads goes back to I Samuel 19 : 13f., which describes how Michal, David's wife, put the teraphim in David's bed in order to deceive the messengers of Saul, who wanted to kill him. "Then Michal took an image and laid it on the bed and put a pillow of goats' hair at its head, and covered it with the clothes." The "pillow of goats' hair" is linguistically obscure and has even been interpreted as meaning that the teraphim were goats. But it may also mean something woven or plaited out of goats' hair, like a wig, and this would fit in better with the picture of a man lying in bed. Further evidence for this comes from a legend in a collection of midrashim from the twelfth century, printed in Bin Gorion's *Die Sagen der Juden*. There it is said:

> The teraphim were idols, and they were made in the following way. The head of a man, who had to be a first-born, was cut off and the hair plucked out. The head was then sprinkled with salt and anointed with oil. Afterwards a little plaque, of copper or gold, was inscribed with the name of an idol and placed under the tongue of the decapitated head. The head was set up in a room, candles were lit before it, and the people made obeisance. And if any man fell down before it, the head began to speak, and answered all questions that were addressed to it.[69]

This is an obvious parallel to the Harranite ritual with the head. The tearing out of the hair seems significant, since it is an equivalent of scalping or shearing, and is thus a rebirth mystery. It is conceivable that in later times the bald skull was covered with a wig for a rite of renewal, as is also reported from Egypt.

67 Lynn Thorndike, *A History of Magic and Experimental Science*, Vol. I (New York, 1923), p. 705. [Here begins a passage added in the 1954 version of Professor Jung's paper.—ED.]
68 *Jewish Encyclopaedia* (New York, 1901–1906), Vol. XII, s.v. "Teraphim."
69 Micha Josef Bin Gorion, pseud., *Die Sagen der Juden* (Frankfort, 1935), p. 325. I am indebted to Dr. Riwkah Schärf for drawing my attention to this passage.

It seems probable that this magical procedure is of primitive origin. I have to thank the South African writer, Laurens van der Post, for the following report from a lecture which he gave in Zurich in 1951:

> The tribe in question was an offshoot of the great Swazi nation—a Bantu people. When, some years ago, the old chief died, he was succeeded by his son, a young man of weak character. He soon proved to be so unsatisfactory a chief that his uncles called a meeting of the tribal elders. They decided that something must be done to strengthen their chief, so they consulted the witch doctors. The witch doctors treated him with a medicine which proved ineffective. Another meeting was held and the witch doctors were asked to use the strongest medicine of all on the chief because the situation was becoming desperate. A half brother of the chief, a boy of twelve, was chosen to provide the material for the medicine.
>
> One afternoon a sorcerer went up to the boy, who was tending cattle, and engaged him in conversation. Then, emptying some powder from a horn into his hand, he took a reed and blew the powder into the ears and nostrils of the boy. A witness told me that the lad thereupon began to sway like a drunken person and sank to the ground shivering. He was then taken to the river bed and tied to the roots of a tree. More powder was sprinkled round about, the sorcerer saying: "This person will no longer eat food but only earth and roots."
>
> The boy was kept in the river bed for nine months. Some people say a cage was made and put into the stream, with the boy inside it, for hours on end, so that the water should flow over him and make his skin white. Others reported seeing him crawling about in the river bed on his hands and knees. But all were so frightened that, although there was a mission school only one hundred yards away, no one except those directly concerned in the ritual would go near him. All are agreed that at the end of nine months this fat, normal, healthy boy was like an animal and quite white-skinned. One woman said, "His eyes were white and the whole of his body was white as white paper."
>
> On the evening that the boy was to be killed a veteran witch doctor was summoned to the chief's kraal and asked to consult the tribal spirits. This he did in the cattle kraal, and after selecting an animal for slaughter he retired to the chief's hut. There the witch doctor was handed parts of the dead boy's body: first the head in a sack, then a thumb and a toe. He cut off the nose and ears and lips, mixed them with medicine, and cooked them over a fire in a broken clay pot. He stuck two spears on either side of the pot. Then those

present—twelve in all including the weak chief—leaned over the pot and deeply inhaled the steam. All save the boy's mother dipped their fingers in the pot and licked them. She inhaled but refused to dip her fingers in the pot. The rest of the body the witch doctor mixed into a kind of bread for doctoring the tribe's crops.

Although this magical rite is not actually a "head mystery," it has several things in common with the practices previously mentioned. The body is macerated or transformed by long immersion in water. The victim is killed, and the salient portions of the head form the main ingredient of the "strengthening" medicine which was concocted for the chief and his immediate circle. The body is kneaded into a sort of bread, and this is obviously thought of as a strengthening medicine for the tribe's crops as well. The rite is a transformation process, a sort of rebirth after nine months of incubation in the water. Laurens van der Post thinks that the purpose of the "whitening"[70] was to assimilate the mana of the white man, who has the political power. I agree with this view, and would add that painting with white clay often signifies transformation into ancestral spirits, in the same way as the neophytes are made invisible in the Nandi territory, in Kenya, where they walk about in portable, cone-shaped grass huts and demonstrate their invisibility to everyone.

Skull worship is widespread among primitives. In Melanesia and Polynesia it is chiefly the skulls of the ancestors that are worshiped, because they establish connections with the spirits or serve as tutelary deities, like the head of Osiris in Egypt. Skulls also play a considerable role as sacred relics. It would lead us too far to go into this primitive skull worship, so I must refer the reader to the literature.[71] I would only like to point out that the cut-off ears, nose, and mouth can represent the head as parts that stand for the whole. There are numerous examples of this. Equally, the head or its parts (brain, etc.) can act as magical food or as a means for increasing the fertility of the land.

It is of special significance for the alchemical tradition that the oracle head was also known in Greece. Aelian [72] reports that Cleomenes of Sparta had the head of his friend Archonides preserved in a jar of honey, and that he consulted it as an oracle. The same was said of the head of Orpheus. Onians [73] rightly emphasizes the fact that the ψυχή, whose seat was in the

70 Cf. the alchemical *albedo* and *homo albus*.
71 Hastings, *ERE*, Vol. VI, pp. 535f.   72 *Varia Historia*, XII, 8.
73 R. B. Onians, *The Origins of European Thought* (Cambridge, 1951), pp. 101ff.

head, corresponds to the modern "unconscious," and that at that stage of development consciousness was identified with θυμός (heart) and φρένες (diaphragm), and was localized in the chest or heart region. Hence Pindar's expression for the soul—αἰῶνος εἴδωλον (image of Aion)—is extraordinarily apt, for the collective unconscious not only imparts "oracles" but forever represents the microcosm (i.e., the form of a physical man mirroring the Cosmos).[74]

There is no evidence to show that any of the parallels we have drawn are historically connected with the Zosimos visions. It seems rather to be a case partly of parallel traditions (transmitted, perhaps, chiefly through the Harran school), and partly of spontaneous fantasies arising from the same archetypal background from which the traditions were derived in the first place. As my examples have shown, the imagery of the Zosimos visions, however strange it may be, is by no means isolated, but is interwoven with older ideas some of which were certainly, and others quite possibly, known to Zosimos, as well as with parallels of uncertain date which continued to mold the speculations of the alchemists for many centuries to come. Religious thought in the early Christian era was not completely cut off from all contact with these conceptions;[75] it was in fact influenced by them, and in turn it fertilized the minds of the natural philosophers to an increasing degree during the next centuries. Towards the end of the sixteenth century the alchemical *opus* was even represented in the form of a Mass. The author of this tour de force was the Hungarian alchemist, Melchior Cibinensis. I have elaborated this parallel in my book *Psychology and Alchemy*.[76]

In conclusion, I would like to quote Zosimos' own commentary on his visions. He says:

> Beautiful it is to speak and beautiful to hear, beautiful to give and beautiful to take, beautiful to be poor and beautiful to be rich. How does nature teach giving and taking? The brazen man gives, and the moist stone receives; the metal gives, and the plant receives; the stars give, and the flowers receive; the sky gives, and the earth receives; the thunderclaps give darting fire. And all things are woven together and all things are undone again, and all things are mingled with one another, and all things are composed, and all

74 [End of inserted passage.—ED.]
75 Cf. my paper "Einige Bemerkungen zu den Visionen des Zosimos," *EJ 1937*, pp. 45ff.
76 Pars. 480–89.

things are permeated with one another, and all things are decomposed again. And everything will be moistened and become desiccated again, and everything puts forth blossoms and everything withers again in the bowl of the altar. For each thing comes to pass with method and in fixed measure and according to the weighing of the four elements. The weaving together of all things and the undoing of all things and the whole fabric of things cannot come to pass without method. The method is natural, preserving due order in its inhaling and its exhaling; it brings increase and it brings stagnation. And to sum up: through the harmonies of separating and combining, and if nothing of the method be neglected, all things bring forth nature. For nature applied to nature transforms nature. Such is the order of natural law throughout the whole cosmos, and thus all things hang together.

This commentary is a general philosophical conclusion drawn from the character of the visions, showing that the Hiereus who is transformed into *pneuma* represents the transformative principle at work in nature and the harmony of opposing forces. Chinese philosophy formulated this process as the enantiodromian interplay of Yin and Yang.[77] But the curious personifications which characterize not only these visions but alchemical literature in general show in the plainest possible terms that we are dealing with a psychic process that takes place mainly in the unconscious and therefore can come into consciousness only in the form of a dream or vision. At that time and until very much later no one had any idea of the unconscious; consequently all unconscious contents were projected into the object, or rather were found in nature as apparent objects or properties of matter and were not understood as purely internal psychic events. There is some evidence that Zosimos was well aware of the spiritual or mystical side of his art, but he believed that what he was concerned with was a spirit that dwelt in natural objects, and not something that came from the human psyche. It remained for modern science to despiritualize nature through its so-called objective knowledge of matter. All anthropomorphic projections were withdrawn from the object one after another, with a twofold result: firstly man's mystical identity with nature[78] was curtailed as never before, and secondly the projections falling back into the human soul caused such

---

77 The classical example being *The I Ching, or Book of Changes* (tr. Richard Wilhelm, English tr. Cary F. Baynes; London and New York, 1950).

78 Mystical or *unconscious* identity occurs in every case of projection, because the content projected upon the extraneous object creates an apparent relationship between it and the subject. [Note from 1954 version.]

a terrific activation of the unconscious that in modern times man was compelled to postulate the existence of an unconscious psyche. The first beginnings of this can be seen in Leibniz and Kant, and then, with mounting intensity, in Schelling, Carus, and von Hartmann, until finally modern psychology discarded the last metaphysical claims of the philosopher-psychologists and restricted the idea of the psyche's existence to the psychological statement, in other words, to its phenomenology.[79] The gods of Olympus were lost, but in exchange we have discovered the inner wealth of the psyche that lies buried in the heart of every man.

4. The Psychology of the Mass

I. GENERAL REMARKS ON THE SACRIFICE

While discussing the transformation rite in section 2, I kept as far as possible to the ecclesiastical point of view; but in the present section I shall treat the Church's interpretation as a purely psychological statement. This method of procedure is simply a *modus considerandi* and does not imply any evaluation of the content of religious belief. It has nothing to do with that side of the question. Critical science is of course bound to adhere to the view that when something is held as an opinion, thought to be true, or believed, it does not posit the existence of any real fact other than a psychological one; but we must also bear in mind the legitimate criticism that in using the term "psychological" we are alluding to a "reality" about whose nature science knows little or nothing. At best—or at worst—we cannot know whether anything is "posited" or not by the fact that something is held to be true. We just cannot know how much stands or falls with the so-called "reality" of the psyche.

The ritual event that takes place in the Mass has a dual aspect, human and divine. From the human point of view, gifts are offered to God at the

79 [Concluding sentence in 1954 version:] So far as the dramatic course of the Mass represents the death, sacrifice and resurrection of a god and the inclusion and active participation of the priest and congregation, its phenomenology may legitimately be brought into line with other fundamentally similar, though more primitive, religious customs. This always involves the risk that sensitive people will find it unpleasant when "small things are compared with great." In fairness to the primitive psyche, however, I would like to emphasize that the "holy dread" of civilized man differs but little from the awe of the primitive, and that the God who is present and active in the mystery is a mystery for both. No matter how crass the outward differences, the similarity or equivalence of meaning should not be overlooked.

altar, signifying at the same time the self-oblation of the priest and the congregation. The ritual act consecrates both the gifts and the givers. It commemorates and represents the Last Supper which our Lord took with his disciples, the whole Incarnation, Passion, death, and resurrection of Christ. But from the point of view of the divine, this anthropomorphic action is only the outer shell or husk in which what is really happening is not a human action at all but a divine event. For an instant the life of Christ, eternally existent outside time, becomes visible and is unfolded in temporal succession, but in condensed form, in the sacred action: Christ incarnates as a man under the aspect of the offered substances, he suffers, is killed, is laid in the sepulcher, breaks the power of the underworld, and rises again in glory. In the utterance of the words of consecration the God-head intervenes, Itself acting and truly present, and thus proclaims that the central event in the Mass is Its act of grace, in which the priest has only the significance of a minister. The same applies to the congregation and the offered substances: they are all ministering causes of the sacred event. The presence of Godhead binds all parts of the sacrificial act into a mystical unity, so that it is God himself who offers himself as a sacrifice in the substances, in the priest, and in the congregation, and who, in the human form of the Son, offers himself as an atonement to the Father.

Although this act is an eternal happening taking place within the divinity, man is nevertheless included in it as an essential component, firstly because God clothes himself in our human nature, and secondly because he needs the ministering co-operation of the priest and congregation, and even the material substances of bread and wine which have a special significance for man. Although God the Father is of one nature with God the Son, he appears in time on the one hand as the eternal Father and on the other hand as the Son of Man in a human body of limited duration. Mankind as a whole is included in God's human nature, which is why man is also included in the sacrificial act. Just as, in the sacrificial act, God is both *agens* and *patiens*, so too is man according to his limited capacity. The *causa efficiens* of the transubstantiation is a spontaneous act of God's grace. Ecclesiastical doctrine insists on this view and even tends to attribute the preparatory action of the priest, indeed the very existence of the rite, to divine prompting,[1] rather than to slothful human nature with its load of original sin. This

---

1 John 6 : 44: "No man can come to me, except the Father which hath sent me draw him."

view is of the utmost importance for a psychological understanding of the Mass. Wherever the magical aspect of a rite tends to prevail, it brings the rite nearer to satisfying the individual ego's blind greed for power, and thus breaks up the mystical body of the Church into separate units. Where, on the other hand, the rite is conceived as the action of God himself, the human participants have only an instrumental or "ministering" significance. The Church's view therefore presupposes the following psychological situation: human consciousness (represented by the priest and congregation) is confronted with an autonomous event which, taking place on a "divine" and "timeless" plane transcending consciousness, is in no way dependent on human action, but which impels man to act by seizing upon him as an instrument and making him the exponent of a "divine" happening. In the ritual action man places himself at the disposal of an autonomous and "eternal" agency operating outside the categories of human consciousness—*si parva licet componere magnis*—in much the same way that a good actor does not merely represent the drama, but allows himself to be overpowered by the genius of the dramatist. The beauty of the ritual action is one of its essential properties, for man has not served God rightly unless he has also served him in beauty. Therefore the rite has no practical utility, for that would be making it serve a purpose—a purely human category. But everything divine is an end-in-itself, perhaps the only legitimate end-in-itself we know. How something eternal can "act" at all is a question we had better not touch, for it is simply unanswerable. Since man, in the action of the Mass, is a tool (though a tool of his own free will), he is not in a position to know anything about the hand which guides him. The hammer cannot discover within itself the power which makes it strike. It is something outside, something autonomous, which seizes and moves man. What happens in the consecration is essentially a miracle, and is meant to be so, for otherwise we should have to consider whether we were not conjuring up God by magic, or else lose ourselves in philosophical wonder how anything eternal can act at all, since action is a process in time with a beginning, a middle, and an end. It is necessary that the transubstantiation should be a cause of wonder and a miracle which man can in no wise comprehend. It is a *mysterium fidei*, a "mystery" in the sense of a δρώμενον and δεικνύμενον, a secret that is acted and displayed. The ordinary man cannot find anything in himself that would cause him to perform a "mystery." He can only do so if and when *it* seizes upon *him*. This seizure, or rather the sensed or presumed existence of a power outside consciousness which seizes him, is the miracle par excellence, really and truly a miracle when one considers *what* is being represented. What is it that induces us to represent an absolute impossibility? What is it that for thousands of years has wrung from man the greatest spiritual effort, the loveliest works of art, the profoundest devotion, the most heroic self-sacrifice, and the most exacting service? What else but a miracle? It is a miracle which is not man's to command; for as soon as he tries to work it himself, or as soon as he philosophizes about it and tries to comprehend it intellectually, the bird is flown. A miracle is something that arouses man's wonder precisely because it seems inexplicable. And indeed, from what we know of human nature we could never explain why men are constrained to such statements and to such beliefs. (I am thinking here of the impossible statements made by all religions.) There must be some compelling reason for this, even though it is not to be found in ordinary experience. The very absurdity and impossibility of the statements proves the existence of this reason. That is the real ground for belief, as was formulated most brilliantly in Tertullian's *"prorsus credibile, quia ineptum."*[2] An improbable opinion has to submit sooner or later to correction. But the statements of religion are the most improbable of all and yet they persist for thousands of years.[3] Their wholly unexpected vitality proves the existence of a sufficient cause which has so far eluded scientific investigation. I can, as a psychologist, only draw attention to this fact and emphasize my belief that there are no facile "nothing but" explanations for psychic phenomena of this kind.

The dual aspect of the Mass finds expression not only in the contrast between human and divine action, but also in the dual aspect of God and the God-man, who, although they are by nature a unity, nevertheless represent a duality in the ritual drama. Without this "dichotomy of God," if I may use such a term, the whole act of sacrifice would be inconceivable and would lack actuality. According to the Christian view God has never ceased to be God, not even when he appeared in human form in the temporal order. The Christ of the Johannine gospel declares: "I and my Father are one.

---

2 *"Et mortuus est Dei filius, prorsus credibile est, quia ineptum est. Et sepultus resurrexit; certum est, quia impossibile est"* (And the Son of God is dead, which is to be believed because it is absurd. And buried He rose again, which is certain because it is impossible).

3 The audacity of Tertullian's argument is undeniable, and so is its danger, but that does not militate against its psychological truth.

He that hath seen me hath seen the Father" (John 10 : 30, 14 : 9). And yet on the Cross Christ cries out: "My God, my God, why hast thou forsaken me?" This contradiction must exist if the formula "very God and very man" is psychologically true. And if it is true, then the different sayings of Christ are in no sense a contradiction. Being "very man" means being at an extreme remove and utterly different from God. "*De profundis clamavi ad te, Domine*"—this cry demonstrates both, the remoteness and the nearness, the outermost darkness and the dazzling spark of the Divine. God in his humanity is presumably so far from himself that he has to seek himself through absolute self-surrender. And where would God's wholeness be if he could not be the "wholly other"? Accordingly it is with some psychological justification, so it seems to me, that when the Gnostic Nous fell into the power of Physis he assumed the dark chthonic form of the serpent, and the Manichaean "Original Man" in the same situation actually took on the qualities of the Evil One. In Tibetan Buddhism all gods without exception have a peaceful and a wrathful aspect, for they reign over all the realms of being. The dichotomy of God into divinity and humanity and his return to himself in the sacrificial act hold out the comforting doctrine that in man's own darkness there is hidden a light that shall once again return to its source, and that this light actually *wanted* to descend into the darkness in order to deliver the Enchained One who languishes there, and lead him to light everlasting. All this belongs to the stock of pre-Christian ideas, being none other than the doctrine of the Anthropos, the "Man of Light," which the sayings of Christ in the gospels assume to be common knowledge.

II. THE PSYCHOLOGICAL MEANING OF SACRIFICE

(a) The Sacrificial Gifts

Kramp, in his book on the Roman liturgy, makes the following observations about the substances that symbolize the sacrifice:

> Now bread and wine are not only the ordinary means of subsistence for a large portion of humanity, they are also to be had all over the earth (which is of the greatest significance as regards the worldwide spread of Christianity). Further, the two together constitute the perfect food of man, who needs both solid and liquid sustenance. Because they can be so regarded as the typical food of man, they

are best fitted to serve as a symbol of human life and human personality, a fact which throws significant light on the gift-symbol.[4]

It is not immediately apparent why precisely bread and wine should be a "symbol of human life and human personality." This interpretation seems very likely a conclusion *a posteriori* from the special meaning which attaches to these substances in the Mass. In that case the meaning would be due to the liturgy and not to the substances themselves, for no one could imagine that bread and wine, in themselves, signify human life or human personality. But, in so far as bread and wine are important products of culture, they do express a vital human striving. They represent a definite cultural achievement which is the fruit of attention, patience, industry, devotion, and laborious toil. The words "our daily bread" express man's anxious care for his existence. By producing bread he makes his life secure. But in so far as he "does not live by bread alone," bread is fittingly accompanied by wine, whose cultivation has always demanded a special degree of attention and much painstaking work. Wine, therefore, is equally an expression of cultural achievement. Where wheat and the vine are cultivated, civilized life prevails. But where agriculture and vine-growing do not exist, there is only the uncivilized life of nomads and hunters.

So in offering bread and wine man is in the first instance offering up the products of his culture, the best, as it were, that human industry produces. But the "best" can be produced only by the best in man, by his conscientiousness and devotion. Cultural products can therefore easily stand for the psychological conditions of their production, that is, for those human virtues which alone make man capable of civilization.[5]

As to the special nature of these substances, bread is undoubtedly a food. There is a popular saying that wine "fortifies," though not in the same sense as food "sustains." It stimulates and "makes glad the heart of man" by virtue of a certain volatile substance which has always been called "spirit." It is thus, unlike innocuous water, an "inspiriting" drink, for a spirit or god dwells within it and produces the ecstasy of intoxication. The wine miracle

4 *Die Opferanschauungen*, p. 55.
5 My reason for saying this is that every symbol has an objective and a subjective—or psychic—origin, so that it can be interpreted on the "objective level" as well as on the "subjective level." This is a consideration of some importance in dream analysis. Cf. *Psychological Types* (New York and London, 1923), defs. 38 and 50.

at Cana was the same as the miracle in the temple of Dionysus, and it is profoundly significant that, on the Damascus Chalice, Christ is enthroned among vine tendrils like Dionysus himself.[6] Bread therefore represents the physical means of subsistence, and wine the spiritual. The offering up of bread and wine is the offering of both the physical and the spiritual fruits of civilization.

But, however sensible he was of the care and labor lavished upon them, man could hardly fail to observe that these cultivated plants grew and flourished according to an inner law of their own, and that there was a power at work in them which he compared to his own life breath or vital spirit. Frazer has called this principle, not unjustly, the "corn spirit." Human initiative and toil are certainly necessary, but even more necessary, in the eyes of primitive man, is the correct and careful performance of the ceremonies which sustain, strengthen, and propitiate the vegetation numen.[7] Grain and wine therefore have something in the nature of a soul, a specific life principle which makes them appropriate symbols not only of man's cultural achievements, but also of the seasonally dying and resurgent god who is their life spirit. Symbols are never simple—only signs and allegories are simple. The symbol always covers a complicated situation which is so far beyond the grasp of language that it cannot be expressed at all in any unambiguous manner.[8] Thus the grain and wine symbols have a fourfold layer of meaning:

1. as agricultural products;

2. as products requiring special processing (bread from grain, wine from grapes);

3. as expressions of psychological achievement (work, industry, patience, devotion, etc.) and of human vitality in general;

4. as manifestations of mana or of the vegetation daemon.

From this list it can easily be seen that a symbol is needed to sum up such a complicated physical and psychic situation. The simplest symbolical formula for this is "bread and wine," giving these words the original complex significance which they have always had for tillers of the soil.

---

6 Further material in Robert Eisler, *Orpheus—the Fisher* (London, 1921), pp. 280f.
7 Similarly, in hunting, the *rites d'entrée* are more important than the hunt itself, for on these rites the success of the hunt depends.
8 Cf. *Psychological Types*, def. 51.

(b) The Sacrifice

It is clear from the foregoing that the sacrificial gift is symbolic, and that it embraces everything which is expressed by the symbol, namely the physical product, the processed substance, the psychological achievement, and the autonomous, daemonic life principle of cultivated plants. The value of the gift is enhanced when it is the best or the first fruits. Since bread and wine are the best that agriculture can offer, they are by the same token man's best endeavor. In addition, bread symbolizes the visible manifestation of the divine numen which dies and rises again, and wine the presence of a pneuma which promises intoxication and ecstasy.[9] The classical world thought of this pneuma as Dionysus, particularly the suffering Dionysus Zagreus, whose divine substance is distributed throughout the whole of nature. In short, what is sacrificed under the forms of bread and wine is nature, man, and God, all combined in the unity of the symbolic gift.

The offering of so significant a gift at once raises the question: Does it lie within man's power to offer such a gift at all? Is he psychologically competent to do so? The Church says no, since she maintains that the sacrificing priest is Christ himself. But, since man is included in the gift—included, as we have seen, twice over—the Church also says yes, though with qualifications. On the side of the sacrificer there is an equally complicated, symbolic state of affairs, for the symbol is Christ himself, who is both the sacrificer and the sacrificed. This symbol likewise has several layers of meaning which I shall proceed to sort out in what follows.

The act of making a sacrifice consists in the first place in giving something which belongs to me. Everything which belongs to me bears the stamp of "mineness," that is, it has a subtle identity with my ego. This is vividly expressed in certain primitive languages, where the suffix of animation is added to an object—a canoe, for instance—when it belongs to me, but not when it belongs to somebody else. The affinity which all the things bearing the stamp of "mineness" have with my personality is aptly characterized by Lévy-Bruhl as *participation mystique*. It is an irrational, unconscious identity, arising from the fact that anything which comes into contact with me is not only itself, but also a symbol. This symbolization comes about firstly because every human being has unconscious contents, and secondly because every object has an unknown side. Your watch, for instance. Unless

9 Hans Leisegang, *Pneuma Hagion* (Leipzig, 1922), pp. 248ff.

you are a watchmaker, you would hardly presume to say that you know how it works. Even if you do, you wouldn't know anything about the molecular structure of the steel unless you happened to be a mineralogist or a physicist. And have you ever heard of a scientist who knew how to repair his pocket watch? But where two unknowns come together, it is impossible to distinguish between them. The unknown in man and the unknown in the thing fall together into one. So there arises an unconscious identity which sometimes borders on the grotesque. No one is permitted to touch what is "mine," much less use it. One is affronted if "my" things are not treated with sufficient respect. I remember seeing two Chinese rickshaw boys engaged in furious argument. Just as they were about to come to blows, one of them gave the other's rickshaw a violent kick, thus putting an end to the quarrel. So long as they are unconscious our unconscious contents are always projected, and the projection fixes upon everything "ours," inanimate objects as well as animals and people. And to the extent that "our" possessions are projection carriers, they are *more* than what they are in themselves, and function as such. They have acquired several layers of meaning and are therefore symbolical, though this fact seldom or never reaches consciousness. In reality, our psyche spreads far beyond the confines of the conscious mind, as was apparently known long ago to the old alchemist who said that the soul was for the greater part outside the body.[10]

When, therefore, I give away something that is "mine," what I am giving is essentially a symbol, a thing of many meanings; but, owing to my unconsciousness of its symbolic character, it adheres to my ego, because it is part of my personality. Hence there is, explicitly or implicitly, a personal claim bound up with every gift. There is always an unspoken "give that thou mayest receive." Consequently the gift always carries with it a personal intention, for the mere giving of it is not a sacrifice. It only becomes a sacrifice if I give up the implied intention of receiving something in return. If it is to be a true sacrifice, the gift must be given as if it were being destroyed.[11] Only then is it possible for the egoistic claim to be given up. Were the bread and wine simply given without any consciousness of an

---

10 Michael Sendivogius, "Tractatus de sulphure" (16th cent.), in the *Musaeum hermeticum* (Frankfort, 1678), p. 617: "[Anima] quae extra corpus multa profundissima imaginatur" ([The soul] which imagines many things of the utmost profundity outside the body).

11 The parallel to this is total destruction of the sacrificial gift by burning, or by throwing it into water or into a pit.

egoistic claim, the fact that it was unconscious would be no excuse, but would on the contrary be sure proof of the existence of a *secret* claim. Because of its egoistic nature, the offering would then inevitably have the character of a magical act of propitiation, with the unavowed purpose and tacit expectation of purchasing the good will of the Deity. That is an ethically worthless simulacrum of sacrifice, and in order to avoid it the giver must at least make himself sufficiently conscious of his identity with the gift to recognize how far he is *giving himself up* in giving the gift. In other words, out of the natural state of identity with what is "mine" there grows the ethical task of sacrificing oneself, or at any rate that part of oneself which is identical with the gift. One ought to realize that when one gives or surrenders oneself there are corresponding claims attached, the more so the less one knows of them. The conscious realization of this alone guarantees that the giving is a real sacrifice. For if I know and admit that I am giving myself, forgoing myself, and do not want to be repaid for it, then I have sacrificed my claim, and thus a part of myself. Consequently, all absolute giving, a giving which is a total loss from the start, is a self-sacrifice. Ordinary giving for which no return is received is felt as a loss; but a sacrifice is meant to be like a loss, so that one may be sure that the egoistic claim no longer exists. Therefore the gift should be given as if it were being destroyed. But since the gift represents myself, I have in that case destroyed myself, given myself away without expectation of return. Yet, looked at in another way, this intentional loss is also a gain, for if you can give yourself it proves that you possess yourself. Nobody can give what he has not got. So anyone who can sacrifice himself and forgo his claim must have had it; in other words, he must have been conscious of the claim. This presupposes an act of considerable self-knowledge, lacking which one remains permanently unconscious of such claims. It is therefore quite logical that the confession of sin should come before the rite of transformation in the Mass. The self-examination is intended to make one conscious of the selfish claim bound up with every gift, so that it may be consciously given up; otherwise the gift is no sacrifice. The sacrifice proves that you possess yourself, for it does not mean just letting yourself be passively taken: it is a conscious and deliberate self-surrender, which proves that you have full control of yourself, that is, of your ego. The ego thus becomes the object of a moral act, for "I" am making a decision on behalf of an authority which is superordinate to my ego nature. I am, as it were, deciding against my ego and renouncing my claim. The possibility of self-renunciation is an established psychological fact whose philosophical implications I do not propose to discuss. Psychologically, it means that the ego is a relative quantity which can be subsumed under various superordinate authorities. What are these authorities? They are not to be equated outright with collective moral consciousness, as Freud wanted to do with his superego, but rather with certain psychic conditions which existed in man from the beginning and are not acquired by experience. Behind a man's actions there stands neither public opinion nor the moral code,[12] but the personality of which he is still unconscious. Just as a man still is what he always was, so he already is what he will become. The conscious mind does not embrace the totality of a man, for this totality consists only partly of his conscious contents, but for the other and far greater part, of his unconscious, which is of indefinite extent with no assignable limits. In this totality the conscious mind is contained like a smaller circle within a larger one. Hence it is quite possible for the ego to be made into an object, that is to say, for a more compendious personality to emerge in the course of development and take the ego into its service. Since this growth of personality comes out of the unconscious, which is by definition unlimited, the extent of the personality now gradually realizing itself cannot in practice be limited either. But, unlike the Freudian superego, it is still individual. It is in fact individuality in the highest sense, and therefore theoretically limited, since no individual can possibly display *every* quality. (I have called this process of realization the "individuation process.") So far as the personality is still potential, it can be called transcendent, and so far as it is unconscious, it is indistinguishable from all those things that carry its projections—in other words, the unconscious personality merges with our environment. This fact is of the greatest practical importance because it renders intelligible the peculiar symbols through which this projected entity expresses itself in dreams. By this I mean the symbols of the outside world and the cosmic symbols. These form the psychological basis for the conception of man as a microcosm,

---

12 If there were really nothing behind him but collective standards of value on the one hand and natural instincts on the other, every breach of morality would be simply a rebellion of instinct. In that case valuable and meaningful innovations would be impossible, for the instincts are the oldest and most conservative element in man and beast alike. Such a view forgets the creative instinct which, although it can behave like an instinct, is seldom found in nature and is confined almost exclusively to Homo sapiens.

whose fate, as we know, is bound up with the macrocosm through the astrological components of his character.

The term "self" seemed to me a suitable one for this unconscious substrate, whose actual exponent in consciousness is the ego. The ego stands to the self as the moved to the mover, or as object to subject, because the determining factors which radiate out from the self surround the ego on all sides and are therefore superordinate to it. The self, like the unconscious, is an a priori existent out of which the ego evolves. It is an unconscious prefiguration of the ego. It is not I who create myself, rather I happen to myself. This realization is of fundamental importance for the psychology of religious phenomena, which is why Ignatius Loyola started off his spiritual exercises with *"Homo creatus est"* as their *"fundamentum."* But, fundamental as it is, it can be only half the psychological truth. If it were the whole truth it would be tantamount to determinism, for if man were merely a creature that came into being as a result of something already existing unconsciously, he would have no freedom and there would be no point in consciousness. Psychology must reckon with the fact that despite the causal nexus man does enjoy a feeling of freedom, which is identical with autonomy of consciousness. However much the ego can be proved to be dependent and preconditioned, it cannot be convinced that it has no freedom. An absolutely preformed consciousness and a totally dependent ego would be a pointless farce, since everything would proceed just as well or even better unconsciously. The existence of ego consciousness has meaning only if it is free and autonomous. By stating these facts we have, it is true, established an antinomy, but we have at the same time given a picture of things as they are. There are temporal, local, and individual differences in the degree of dependence and freedom. In reality both are always present: the supremacy of the self and the hybris of consciousness. If ego consciousness follows its own road exclusively, it is trying to become like a god or a superman. But exclusive recognition of its dependence only leads to a childish fatalism and to a world-negating and misanthropic spiritual arrogance.

This conflict between conscious and unconscious is at least brought nearer to a solution through our becoming aware of it. Such an act of realization is presupposed in the act of self-sacrifice. The ego must make itself conscious of its claim, and the self must cause the ego to renounce it. This can happen in two ways:

    1. I renounce my claim in consideration of a general moral principle,

324

namely that one must not expect repayment for a gift. In this case the "self" coincides with public opinion and the moral code. It is then identical with Freud's superego because it is projected, and therefore essentially unconscious and identical with environmental circumstances.

2. I renounce my claim because I feel impelled to do so for painful inner reasons which are not altogether clear to me. These reasons give me no particular moral satisfaction; on the contrary, I even feel some resistance to them. But I must yield to the power which suppresses my egoistic claim. Here the self is integrated; it is withdrawn from projection and has become perceptible as a determining psychic factor. The objection that in this case the moral code is simply unconscious must be ruled out, because I am perfectly well aware of the moral criticism against which I would have to assert my egoism. Where the ego wish clashes with the moral standard, it is not easy to show that the tendency which suppresses it is individual and not collective. But where it is a case of conflicting loyalties, or we find ourselves in a situation of which the classical example is Hosea's marriage with the harlot, then the ego wish coincides with the collective moral standard, and Hosea would have been bound to accuse Jehovah of immorality. Similarly, the unjust steward would have had to admit his guilt.[13] Experiences of this kind make it clear that the self cannot be equated either with collective morality or with natural instinct, but must be conceived as a determining factor whose nature is individual and unique. The superego is a necessary and unavoidable substitute for the experience of the self.

These two ways of renouncing one's egoistic claim reveal not only a difference of attitude, but also a difference of situation. In the first case the situation need not affect me personally and directly; in the second, the gift must necessarily be a very personal one which seriously affects the giver and forces him to overcome himself. In the one case it is merely a question, say, of going to Mass; in the other it is more like Abraham's sacrifice of his son or Christ's decision in Gethsemane. The one may be felt very earnestly and experienced with all piety, but the other is the real thing.[14]

---

13 Jesus took a different view. To the defiler of the Sabbath he said:"Man, if indeed thou knowest what thou doest, thou art blessed; but if thou knowest not, thou art cursed, and a transgressor of the law." M. R. James, *The Apocryphal New Testament* (Oxford, 1924), p. 33.
14 In order to avoid misunderstandings, I must emphasize that I am speaking only of the personal experience of the Mass, and not of the mysterious reality which it has for the believer.

So long as the self is unconscious, it corresponds to Freud's superego and is a source of perpetual moral conflict. If, however, it is withdrawn from projection and is no longer identical with public opinion, then one is truly one's own yea and nay. The self then functions as a union of opposites and thus constitutes the most immediate experience of the Divine which it is psychologically possible to imagine.[15]

(c) The Sacrificer

What I sacrifice is my own selfish claim, and by doing this I give up myself. Every sacrifice is therefore, to a greater or lesser degree, a self-sacrifice. The degree to which it is so depends on the significance of the gift. If it is of great value to me and touches my most personal feelings, I can be sure that in giving up my egoistic claim I shall challenge my ego personality to revolt. I can also be sure that the power which suppresses this claim, and thus suppresses me, must be the self. Hence it is the self that causes me to make the sacrifice; nay more, it compels me to make it.[16] The self is the sacrificer, and I am the sacrificed gift, the human sacrifice. Let us try for a moment to look into Abraham's soul when he was commanded to sacrifice his only son. Quite apart from the compassion he felt for his child, would not a father in such a position feel himself as the victim, and feel that he was plunging the knife into his own breast? He would be at the same time the sacrificer and the sacrificed.

Now, since the relation of the ego to the self is like that of the son to the father, we can say that when the self calls on us to sacrifice ourselves, it is really carrying out the sacrificial act on itself. We know more or less what this act means to us, but what it means to the self is not so clear. As the self can only be comprehended by us in particular acts, but remains concealed from us as a whole because it is more comprehensive than we are, all we can do is to draw conclusions from the little of the self that we can experience. We have seen that a sacrifice only takes place when we feel the self actually carrying it out on ourselves. We may also venture to surmise that in so far as the self stands to us in the relation of father to son, the self in some sort feels our sacrifice as a sacrifice of itself. From that sacrifice we

---

15 Cf. the "uniting symbol" in *Psychological Types*, def. 51.
16 In Indian philosophy we find a parallel in Prajapati and Purusha Narayana. Purusha sacrifices himself at the command of Prajapati, but at bottom the two are identical. Cf. the Shatapatha-Brahmana (*SBE*, Vol. XLIV, pp. 172ff.); also the Rig-Veda, X, 90.

gain ourselves—our "self"—for we only have what we give. But what does the self gain? We see it entering into manifestation, freeing itself from unconscious projection, and, as it grips us, entering into our lives and so passing from unconsciousness into consciousness, from potentiality into actuality. What it is in the diffuse unconscious state we do not know; we only know that in becoming ourself it has become man.

This process of becoming human is represented in dreams and inner images as the putting together of many scattered units, and sometimes as the gradual emergence and clarification of something that was always there.[17] The speculations of alchemy, and also of some Gnostics, revolve round this process. It is likewise expressed in Christian dogma, and more particularly in the transformation mystery in the Mass. The psychology of this process makes it easier to understand why, in the Mass, man appears as both the sacrificer and the sacrificed gift, and why it is not man who is these things, but God who is both; why God becomes the suffering and dying man, and why man, through partaking of the Glorified Body, gains the assurance of resurrection and becomes aware of his participation in Godhead.

As I have already suggested, the integration or humanization of the self is initiated from the conscious side by our making ourselves aware of our egoistic aims; we examine our motives and try to form as complete and objective a picture as possible of our own nature. It is an act of self-recollection, a gathering together of what is scattered, of all the things in us that have never been properly related, and a coming to terms with oneself with a view to achieving full consciousness. (Unconscious self-sacrifice is merely an accident, not a moral act.) Self-recollection, however, is about the hardest and most repellent thing there is for man, who is predominantly unconscious. Human nature has an invincible dread of becoming more conscious of itself. What nevertheless drives us to it is the self, which demands sacrifice

17 This contradiction is unavoidable because the concept of the self allows only of antinomial statements. The self is by definition conceived as an entity which is more comprehensive than the conscious personality. Consequently the latter cannot pass any comprehensive judgment on the self; any judgment and any statement about it is incomplete and has to be supplemented (but not nullified) by a conditioned negative. If I assert, "The self exists," I must supplement this by saying, "But it seems not to exist." For the sake of completeness I must also invert the proposition and say, "The self does not exist, but yet seems to exist." Actually, this inversion is superfluous in view of the fact that the self is not a philosophical concept like Kant's "thing-in-itself," but an empirical concept of psychology, and can therefore be hypostatized if the above precautions are taken.

by sacrificing itself to us. Conscious realization or the bringing together of the scattered parts is in one sense an act of the ego's will, but in another sense it is a spontaneous manifestation of the self,[18] which was always there. Individuation appears, on the one hand, as the synthesis of a new unity which previously consisted of scattered particles, and on the other hand, as the revelation of something which existed before the ego and is in fact its father or creator and also its totality. Up to a point we create the self by making ourselves conscious of our unconscious contents, and to that extent it is our son. This is why the alchemists called their incorruptible substance— which means precisely the self—the *filius philosophorum*.[19] But we are forced to make this effort by the unconscious presence of the self, which is all the time urging us to overcome our unconsciousness. From that point of view the self is the father. This accounts for certain alchemical terms, such as Mercurius Senex (Hermes Trismegistus) and Saturnus, who in Gnosticism was regarded as a graybeard and a youth, just as Mercurius was in alchemy. These psychological connections are seen most clearly in the ancient conceptions of the Original Man, the Protanthropos, and the Son of Man. Christ as the Logos is from all eternity, but in his human form he is the "Son of Man."[20] As the Logos, he is the world-creating principle. This corresponds with the relation of the self to consciousness, without which no world could be perceived at all. The Logos is the real *principium individuationis*, because everything proceeds from it, and because everything which is, from crystal to man, exists only in individual form. In the infinite variety and differentiation of the phenomenal world is expressed the essence of the *auctor rerum*. As a correspondence we have, on the one hand, the indefiniteness and unlimited extent of the unconscious self (despite its individuality and uniqueness), its creative relation to individual consciousness, and, on the other hand, the individual human being as a mode of its manifestation. Ancient philosophy paralleled this idea with the legend of the dismembered Dionysus, who, as creator, is the ἀμέριστος (undivided) νοῦς, and, as the creature, the μεμερισμένος (divided) νοῦς.[21] Dionysus is distributed through-

---

13 In so far as it is the self that actuates the ego's self-recollection.
19 Cf. *Psychology and Alchemy*, index, s.v.
20 If I use the unhistorical term "self" for the corresponding processes in the psyche, I do so out of a conscious desire not to trespass on other preserves, but to confine myself exclusively to the field of empirical psychology.
21 Firmicus Maternus, *De errore profanarum religionum* (Corpus scriptorum ecclesiasticorum latinorum, Vol. II; Vienna, 1867), 7, 8.

out the whole of nature, and just as Zeus once devoured the throbbing heart of the god, so his worshipers tore wild animals to pieces in order to reintegrate his dismembered spirit. The gathering together of the light-substance in Barbelognosis and in Manichaeism points in the same direction. The psychological equivalent of this is the integration of the self through conscious assimilation of the split-off contents. Self-recollection is a gathering together of the self. It is in this sense that we have to understand the instructions which Monoimos gives to Theophrastus:

> Seek him [God] from out yourself, and learn who it is that takes possession of everything in you, saying: *my* god, *my* spirit [νοῦς], *my* understanding, *my* soul, *my* body; and learn whence come sorrow and gladness, and hate and love, and the unwished-for wakefulness and the unwished-for drowsiness, and the unwished-for anger and the unwished-for love. And when you examine all this closely, you will find him within yourself, the One and the Many, like that little speck, for it is from you that he has his origin.[22]

Self-recollection or—what comes to the same thing—the urge to individuation gathers together what is scattered and multifarious, and exalts it to the original form of the One, the Primordial Man. In this way our existence as separate beings, our former ego nature, is abolished, the circle of consciousness is widened, and because the paradoxes have been made conscious the sources of conflict are dried up. This approximation to the self is a kind of repristination or apocatastasis, in so far as the self has an "incorruptible" or "eternal" character on account of its being pre-existent to consciousness.[23] This feeling is expressed in the words from the *Benedictio fontis: "Et quos aut sexus in corpore aut aetas discernit in tempore, omnes in unam pariat gratia mater infantiam"* (And may Mother Grace bring forth into one infancy all those whom sex has separated in the body, or age in time).

The figure of the divine sacrificer corresponds feature for feature to the empirical modes of manifestation of the archetype that lies at the root of almost all known conceptions of God. This archetype is not merely a static

---

22 Hippolytus, *Elenchos*, VIII, 15.
23 And also on account of the fact that the unconscious is only conditionally bound by space and time. The comparative frequency of telepathic phenomena proves that space and time have only a relative validity for the psyche. Evidence for this is furnished by Rhine's experiments. Cf. my paper on "synchronicity," in *The Interpretation of Nature and the Psyche* (London and New York, 1955), by W. Pauli and me.

image, but dynamic, full of movement. It is always a drama, whether in heaven, on earth, or in hell.[24]

(d) The Archetype of Sacrifice

Comparing the basic ideas of the Mass with the imagery of the Zosimos visions, we find that, despite considerable differences, there is a remarkable degree of similarity. For the sake of clearness I give the similarities and differences in tabular form.

Zosimos	Mass
SIMILARITIES	
1. The chief actors are two priests.	1. There is the priest, and Christ the eternal priest.
2. One priest slays the other.	2. The *Mactatio Christi* takes place as the priest pronounces the words of consecration.
3. Other human beings are sacrificed as well.	3. The congregation itself is a sacrificial gift.
4. The sacrifice is a voluntary self-sacrifice.	4. Christ offers himself freely as a sacrifice.
5. It is a painful death.	5. He suffers in the sacrificial act.
6. The victim is dismembered.	6. Breaking of the Bread.
7. There is a *thysia*.	7. Offering up of incense.
8. The priest eats his own flesh.	8. Christ drinks his own blood (St. Chrysostom).
9. He is transformed into spirit.	9. The substances are transformed into the body and blood of Christ.
10. A shining white figure appears, like the midday sun.	10. The Host is shown as the Beatific Vision ("*Quaesivi vultum tuum, Domine*") in the greater elevation.
11. Production of the "divine water."	11. The Grace conferred by the Mass; similarity of water chalice and font; water a symbol of grace.

24 The word "hell" may strike the reader as odd in this connection. I would, however, recommend him to study the brothel scene in James Joyce's *Ulysses*, or James Hogg's *The Private Memoirs and Confessions of a Justified Sinner* (London, 1824; edn. with intro. by André Gide, London, 1947). [Note added.]

DIFFERENCES

1. The whole sacrificial process is an individual dream vision, a fragment of the unconscious depicting itself in dream consciousness.
2. The dreamer is only a spectator of the symbolic action.
3. The action is a bloody and gruesome human sacrifice.

4. The sacrifice is accompanied by a scalping.
5. It is also performed on a dragon, and is therefore an animal sacrifice.
6. The flesh is roasted.

7. The meaning of the sacrifice is the production of the divine water, used for the transmutation of metals and, mystically, for the birth of the self.
8. What is transformed in the vision is presumably the planetary demon Saturn, the supreme Archon (who is related to the God of the Hebrews). It is the dark, heavy, material principle in man—*hyle* —which is transformed into pneuma.

1. The Mass is a conscious artifact, the product of many centuries and many minds.

2. Priest and congregation both participate in the mystery.
3. Nothing obnoxious; the *mactatio* itself is not mentioned. There is only the bloodless sacrifice of bread and wine (*incruente immolatur!*).
4. Nothing comparable.

5. Symbolic sacrifice of the Lamb.

6. The substances are spiritually transformed.

7. The meaning of the Mass is the communion of the living Christ with his flock.

8. What is transformed in the Mass is God, who as Father begat the Son in human form, suffered and died in that form, and rose up again to His origin.

The gross concretism of the vision is so striking that one might easily feel tempted, for aesthetic and other reasons, to drop the comparison with the Mass altogether. If I nevertheless venture to bring out certain analogies, I do so not with the rationalistic intention of devaluing the sacred ceremony by putting it on a level with a piece of pagan nature worship. If I have any aim at all apart from scientific truth, it is to show that the most important mystery of the Catholic Church rests, among other things, on psychic conditions which are deeply rooted in the human soul.

The vision, which in all probability has the character of a dream, must be

331

regarded as a spontaneous psychic product which was never consciously aimed at. Like all dreams, it is a product of nature. The Mass, on the other hand, is a product of man's mind or spirit, and is a definitely conscious proceeding. To use an old but not antiquated nomenclature, we can call the vision *psychic*, and the Mass *pneumatic*. The vision is undifferentiated raw material, while the Mass is a highly differentiated artifact. That is why the one is gruesome and the other beautiful. If the Mass is antique, it is antique in the best sense of the word, and its liturgy is therefore satisfying to the highest requirements of the present day. In contrast to this, the vision is archaic and primitive, but its symbolism points directly to the fundamental alchemical idea of the incorruptible substance, namely to the self, which is beyond change. The vision is a piece of unalloyed naturalism, banal, grotesque, squalid, horrifying, and profound as nature herself. Its meaning is not clear, but it allows itself to be divined with the abysmal uncertainty and ambiguity that pertains to all things nonhuman, suprahuman, and subhuman. The Mass, on the other hand, represents and clearly expresses the Deity itself, and clothes it in the garment of the most beautiful humanity.

From all this it is evident that the vision and the Mass are two different things, so different as to be almost incommensurable. But if we could succeed in reconstructing the natural process in the unconscious on which the Mass is psychically based, we should probably obtain a picture which would be rather more commensurable with the vision of Zosimos. According to the view of the Church, the Mass is based on the historical events in the life of Jesus. From this "real" life we can single out certain details that add a few concretistic touches to our picture and thus bring it closer to the vision. For instance, I would mention the scourging, the crowning with thorns, and the clothing in a purple robe, which show Jesus as the archaic sacrificed king. This is further emphasized by the Barabbas episode (the name means "son of the father") which leads to the sacrifice of the king. Then there is the agony of death by crucifixion, a shameful and horrifying spectacle, far indeed from any *"incruente immolatur"*! The right pleural cavity and probably the right ventricle of the heart were cut open by the spear, so that blood clots and serum flowed out. If we add these details to the process which underlies the Mass, we shall see that they form a striking equivalent to certain archaic and barbarous features of the vision. There are also the fundamental dogmatic ideas to be considered. As is shown by the reference to the sacrifice of Isaac in the prayer *Unde et memores*, the sacrifice has the character not only of a human sacrifice, but the sacrifice of a son—and an *only* son. That is the cruellest and most horrible kind of sacrifice we can imagine, so horrible that, as we know, Abraham was not required to carry it out.[25] And even if he had carried it out, a stab in the heart with a knife would have been a quick and relatively painless death for the victim. Even the bloody Aztec ceremony of cutting out the heart was a swift death. But the sacrifice of the son which forms the essential feature of the Mass began with scourging and mockery, and culminated in six hours of suspension on a cross to which the victim was nailed hand and foot—not exactly a quick death, but a slow and exquisite form of torture. As if that were not enough, crucifixion was regarded as a disgraceful death for slaves, so that the physical horror is balanced by the moral horror.

Leaving aside for the moment the unity of nature of Father and Son— which it is possible to do because they are two distinct Persons who are not to be confused with one another—let us try to imagine the feelings of a father who saw his son suffering such a death, knowing that it was he himself who had sent him into the enemy's country and deliberately exposed him to this danger. Executions of this kind were generally carried out as an act of revenge or as punishment for a crime, with the idea that both father and son should suffer. The idea of punishment can be seen particularly clearly in the crucifixion between two thieves. The punishment is carried out on God himself, and the model for this execution is the ritual slaying of the king. The king is killed when he shows signs of impotence, or when failure of the crops arouses doubts as to his efficacy. He is thus killed in order to improve the condition of his people, just as God is sacrificed for the salvation of mankind.

What is the reason for this "punishment" of God? Despite the almost blasphemous nature of this question—my arguments here are not for chil-

25 How Jewish piety reacted to this sacrifice can be seen from the following Talmudic legend: " 'And I,' cried Abraham, 'swear that I will not go down from the altar until you have heard me. When you commanded me to sacrifice my son Isaac you offended against your word, "in Isaac shall your descendants be named." So if ever my descendants offend against you, and you wish to punish them, then remember that you too are not without fault, and forgive them.' 'Very well, then,' replied the Lord, 'there behind you is a ram caught in the thicket with his horns. Offer up that instead of your son Isaac. And if ever your descendants sin against me, and I sit in judgment over them on New Year's Day, let them blow the horn of a ram, that I may remember my words, and temper justice with mercy.' " Jakob Frommer and Manuel Schnitzer, *Legenden aus dem Talmud* (Berlin, 1922), pp. 34f. [Note added.]

dren—we must nevertheless ask it in view of the obviously punitive character of the sacrifice. The usual explanation is that Christ was punished for our sins.[26] The dogmatic validity of this answer is not in question here. As I am in no way concerned with the Church's explanation, but only wish to reconstruct the underlying psychic process, we must logically assume the existence of a guilt proportionate to the punishment. If mankind is the guilty party, logic surely demands that mankind should be punished. But if God takes the punishment on himself, he exculpates mankind, and we must then conjecture that it is not mankind who is guilty, but God (which would logically explain why he took the guilt on himself). For reasons that can readily be understood, a satisfactory answer is not to be expected from orthodox Christianity. But such an answer may be found in the Old Testament, in Gnosticism, and in late Catholic speculation. From the Old Testament we know that though Yahweh was a guardian of the law he was not just, and that he suffered from fits of rage which he had every occasion to regret.[27] And from certain Gnostic systems it is clear that the *auctor rerum* was a lower archon who falsely imagined that he had created a perfect world, whereas in fact it was woefully imperfect. On account of his Saturnine disposition this demiurgic archon has affinities with the Jewish Yahweh, who was likewise a world creator. His work was imperfect and did not prosper, but the blame cannot be placed on the creature any more than one can curse the pots for being badly turned out by the potter! This argument led to the Marcionite Reformation and to purging the New Testament of elements derived from the Old. Even as late as the seventeenth century the learned Jesuit, Nicolas Caussin, declared that the unicorn was a fitting symbol for the God of the Old Testament, because in his wrath he reduced the world to confusion like an angry rhinoceros (unicorn), until, overcome by the love of a pure virgin, he was changed in her lap into a God of Love.[28]

26 Isaiah 53 : 5: "But he was wounded for our transgressions, he was bruised for our iniquities: the chastisement of our peace was upon him; and with his stripes we are healed."
27 See my *Answer to Job* (London, 1954).
28 Caussin, *De symbolica Aegyptiorum sapientia. Polyhistor symbolicus, Electorum symbolorum, et Parabolarum historicarum stromata* (Paris, 1618 and 1623), p. 348. Cf. also Philippus Picinelli, *Mundus symbolicus* (Cologne, 1680–81), Vol. I, p. 419: "Of a truth God, terrible beyond measure, appeared before the world peaceful and wholly tamed after dwelling in the womb of the most blessed Virgin. St. Bonaventura said that Christ was tamed and pacified by the most kindly Mary, so that he should not punish the sinner with eternal death."

In these explanations we find the natural logic we missed in the answer of the Church. God's guilt consisted in the fact that, as creator of the world and king of his creatures, he was inadequate and therefore had to submit to the ritual slaying. For primitive man the concrete king was perfectly suited to this purpose, but not for a higher level of civilization with a more spiritual conception of God. Earlier ages could still dethrone their gods by destroying their images or putting them in chains. At a higher level, however, one god could be dethroned only by another god, and when monotheism developed, God could only transform himself.

The psychic basis for this transformation is the process of transformation in the unconscious. One of the finest examples of this is the vision of Zosimos, which contains a whole series of archetypal transformation symbols expressed in the Gnostic-alchemical language of his time. A rich harvest of transformation symbols is to be found in alchemy generally, whether influenced by Christianity or not, in the initiation rites of all primitive peoples, and—last but not least—in the dreams of modern men and women. It would lead us too far to cite examples from any of these fields, which each demand a separate study. But I ought at least to mention Christian Rosencreutz's *Chymical Wedding*, which reads almost like a first draft of *Faust*, Part II, and the transformation symbol of the uroboros which I dealt with in my earlier paper on Zosimos.

Taken in this wider sense, the archetypal image of sacrifice is always one of transformation as well. The simplest and most striking example of this is the whale-dragon myth of Leo Frobenius. The archetype of transformation always appears when a psychologically unsatisfactory situation has to be replaced by a satisfactory one, no matter how great or small the issue may be. If only a minor change of attitude is involved, the dream does not use any obviously mythological language. For instance, instead of a dragon it is an automobile, instead of the dragon's belly a spooky cellar, instead of spiritualization an elevator, instead of the sacrificial knife a hypodermic syringe, instead of torture a tight squeeze or a difficult climb, instead of the dismemberment of a man a horse whose hooves are cut off, instead of the bleeding sacrificial wound a leaking gasoline tank, and so on.

If, however, it is a question of a fundamental change of personality or of one's general attitude, as was obviously the case with Zosimos (witness his advice to Theosebeia[29]), then mythological motifs appear, sometimes bor-

29 Berthelot, *Alchimistes*, III, li, 8.

rowed, sometimes spontaneously produced, which do not fail to suggest the most intense suffering, even at a time when the conscious mind is not aware of anything painful, except perhaps a vague sense of oppression or uneasiness. It is true that the onset of conscious suffering is not as a rule very long delayed. If the inner transformation enters more or less completely into consciousness, it becomes one of the vividest and most decisive experiences a man can have of his individual fate. The saying *"extra ecclesiam nulla salus"*—there is no salvation outside the Church—is no doubt a profound truth; but the grace of God, it seems to me, is profounder still.

Hugo Rahner

The Christian Mystery and the Pagan Mysteries

> Come, I shall show you the Logos, and
> the mysteries of the Logos, and I shall
> explain them to you in images that are
> know to you.[1]

These words from the *Protrepticus* of Clement of Alexandria may well serve as our leitmotiv, for in them the whole problem before us is formulated. We shall here attempt to draw a comparison between the pagan mysteries as they have passed before our eyes in the preceding lectures[2] and the inner essence as well as the outward forms of ancient Christianity. The Incarnate Logos also has his mysteries; indeed, his whole work of salvation is the "mystery which hath been hidden from ages and generations, but now is manifested to his saints" (Col. 1 : 26). But is it permissible, from a religious and historical point of view, to draw a comparison between the Christian mystery and the mystery cults that surrounded the origins of Christianity? Or are we at least justified in speaking of the Christian mystery in images drawn from the world of the Hellenistic mysteries? Did not St. Paul himself do as much? Is it not, in any event, true that from the second to the fifth century a broad stream of Greek mystery religion entered into the Church and transformed simple Biblical Christianity into the mystical sacramentalism that survived in the Byzantine-Russian, and to somewhat less degree in the Roman, Church? These questions have occupied historians of religion for more than half a century, in the course of which impassioned study has

---

1 *Protrepticus*, XII, 119, 1. [Cf.tr. G. W. Butterworth, *Clement of Alexandria*, LCL, 1919, p. 255.]
2 [Father Rahner's lecture concluded the 1944 Eranos meeting and was preceded by a number of the lectures contained in the present selection; see the appendix of "Contents of the *Eranos-Jahrbücher*" in this volume for a full list of the 1944 lectures. The Biblical quotations in this paper are DV, unless otherwise noted.—ED.]

brought about complex shifts of opinion. And today we are still far from seeing an end to all the questions and answers.

My first task (Part 1) will be to acquaint you with the present state of scholarship in these questions. And once this exposition—which is bound to be of a rather theoretical character—has disclosed the dividing lines as well as the points of contact between the ancient mysteries and the Christian mystery, we shall be in a position to turn our attention to two aspects of the Christian mystery that reveal with particular clarity wherein the two phenomena under comparison are distinguished and wherein they have influenced one another: (2) the mysteries of the Cross and (3) the mystery of baptism. Here we shall proceed in the manner of that great Christian and Greek, Gregory of Nazianzus. In his magnificent sermon on the mystery of baptism,[3] he passed in review all the chaotic splendor of the ancient mysteries, and then began to speak of the Christian mystery "with trembling tongue and quaking heart and spirit, as always when I speak of God."

1. The History and Significance of the Comparison between the Christian Mystery and the Ancient Mysteries

The mysteries of the Hellenistic world in which Christianity was born are indubitably the "chief factor in the spiritual life of the ancient world," and they were also the final utterance of "the pagan religions."[1] This in itself has led any number of modern scholars, oriented as they are toward comparative religion, to seek parallels with Christianity. The preceding papers have acquainted you with the vast scope of the religious experience that we subsume under the general concept of "mysteries": from the primordial beginnings of the prehistoric mother cults to the sublime transfigurations of the Hermetic "literary mysteries" and Plotinus, and from here to the Islamic and Oriental Christian mysticism of prayer; from the Cabiri to the Ka'ba; from the inchoate depths of Shaktism and Barbelo-Gnosticism[2] (the description of which fills us with horror, because in spirit all of us remain Greeks) to the venerable nocturnal rites of Eleusis. What a world

---

3 *Oratio* 39, 11 (*PG*, XXXVI, 345 c).

1 Georges Lafaye, *Histoire du culte des divinités d'Alexandrie* (Paris, 1884), p. 108; Eduard Bratke, *Die Stellung des Clemens Alexandrinus zum antiken Mysterienwesen* (Theologische Studien und Kritiken, 1887), p. 654.

2 [Cf. the lectures by Koppers and by Pulver in *EJ 1944*, which are not in the present volume.—ED.]

of contrasts, what a vast mixture of lunar-maternal darkness and clear, solar awareness we express in this word *mystery!*

This in itself must incline us to caution in attempting comparisons between the ancient mysteries and the Christianity that suddenly burgeoned among them. And, moreover, Christianity itself has a history in the truest sense; it is a living thing; it cannot be comprehended in any static concept or written formula. My first task (section I), therefore, will be to outline the history of this comparison in order to suggest the difficulty of the problems arising out of any attempt at a conceptual, not to mention a genetic, comparison of the two phenomena. Next (II), we shall have to follow the complex and highly differentiated development of our terms of comparison, with a view to showing at what stage in their historical growth they entered into a demonstrable contact. Only then (III) shall we be able to establish, on a solid historical groundwork, the essential differences between and mutual influences of the ancient mysteries and the Christian religion.

I

One thing is certain when we survey the considerable history of the comparison between the ancient mysteries and the ancient Church: it was this urgent question of a comparison which in almost every case led scholars to discover the mystery religions of late antiquity, the knowledge of which had been totally lost to the Middle Ages and to the Humanistic period as well. The very first work to concern itself seriously with the Greek mystery religions, the *Exercitationes de rebus sacris* of Isaac Casaubon (Geneva, 1655), was an attempt by a Calvinistic Christian to represent the sacramentalism of the Catholic Church as an outgrowth of the ancient mysteries. And at the beginning of the nineteenth century, when Christian Lobeck's famous *Aglaophamus* put an end to the shallow Enlightenment of the Hellenizing eighteenth century, a number of writers eagerly ascribed essential elements of the Catholic religion to the influence of the ancient mystery cults. The most extraordinary work of this sort, a book totally forgotten today, is perhaps Father Nork's *Der Mystagog*, an "interpretation of the secret doctrines and festivals of the Christian Church."[3] Meanwhile classical philology (impelled, no doubt, by a sound distrust of this obscure, mysticizing science)

---

3 *Der Mystagog, oder Deutung der Geheimlehren und Feste der christlichen Kirche* (Leipzig, 1838). ["Nork" was pseud. of Felix Korn.—ED.]

had once again turned away from the mysteries—its most celebrated victim, as we all know, was J. J. Bachofen, who quotes his adversaries as saying: "We want no theology and least of all the mystical-symbolic half-darkness of a physical doctrine of immortality. This 'higher idiocy' fails to take into account the freshness and clarity of the classical mind, sustained even at the grave of loved ones."[4] It was reserved to our own century to lay solid foundations for scientific research (we need only think of Cumont, Hepding, Frazer, Wilamowitz, and Kern, to mention at random a few of the most important names). But at the same time there arose the school of comparative religion, searching with unparalleled zeal for relations between the ancient and Christian mysteries, with a view to revealing the essential contribution of the mysteries to the genesis or at least the development of ecclesiastical Christianity. Yet here too the first enthusiasm has given way to sober research, and accordingly we can break down these scholarly efforts into three successive groups, the last of which represents the present state of opinion on the question.

The first group insisted on an actual relation of dependency between the ancient mysteries and nascent Christianity, particularly the theology of St. Paul. Above all, the concept of "rebirth" was found to be common to the two. Hermann Usener, the pioneer in this trend, was followed by Albrecht Dieterich and Richard Reitzenstein. Reitzenstein's great work on the Hellenistic mysteries[5] attained broad influence. He thought he had found the sources of Christian doctrine, first in a newly discovered "Iranian mystery of redemption," later in the allegedly pre-Christian cult of the Mandaeans.[6] Since then, sober research has rejected both theories. Even before the Mandaean and Iranian theories had actually been disproved, Carl Clemen expressed his well-founded doubts in a book that is still well worth reading, on the influence of the mystery religions on earliest Christianity.[7] In it he pronounces the sharp but quite justified verdict: "Simply to assume that every conceivable mystery regardless of locality already existed in the first Christian century is scientific nonsense." Next, a more fruitful basis of comparison was thought to have been found in the "imitation of the cult

4 J. J. Bachofen, *Die Unsterblichkeitslehre der orphischen Theologie* (Basel, 1867), p. 47.
5 *Die hellenistischen Mysterienreligionen nach ihren Grundgedanken und Wirkungen* (Leipzig, 1910; 3rd edn., 1927).
6 Reitzenstein, *Das iranische Erlösungsmysterium* (Leipzig and Bonn, 1921) and *Die Vorgeschichte der christlichen Taufe* (Leipzig and Berlin, 1929).
7 *Die Einfluss der Mysterienreligionen auf das älteste Christentum* (Giessen, 1913).

hero." The liturgical-mystical dromenon in which the members of the cult re-enacted the death and resurrection of the cult god with a view to participating in his transcendent powers was held to be a motif common to all the mysteries of late antiquity, and also to constitute the basic structure of the Christian doctrine of redemption and the sacrament. The leader of this school of thought was Wilhelm Bousset, with his *Kyrios Christos*.[8] Though exercising the utmost circumspection in his particular deductions, Bousset found that the cultic imitation of the death and resurrection of the god provided "the spiritual atmosphere within which is situated the Pauline participation in the death and resurrection of Christ" (p. 139). According to Bousset, this was no crude borrowing, however, but more in the nature of an unconscious adaptation to a basic form of religious experience that enjoyed wide currency in late antiquity. One need only read Wilhelm Leipoldt's otherwise so learned book on dying and resurrected gods[9] in order to realize the profound influence still exerted by Bousset's conception. The most radical position is taken by the French writer Alfred Loisy in his brilliantly written *Les Mystères payens et le mystère chrétien*.[10] For him the essence both of the Greek mysteries and of Christianity (as shaped by St. Paul) is the cultic-ritual enactment of the death and resurrection of the cult hero: *"mythe et rite"* correspond. In Christianity the myth is the great drama of the world's redemption by Christ, which St. Paul, under the influence of the hero myths of his time, read into the simple narrative of the Gospels. And the rite is the lesser drama of the mystical initiation of the individual. "St. Paul's belief in the resurrection of Christ through baptism and faith contains no more and no fewer contradictions than that of the initiates of Eleusis, who looked upon their participation in the anguish and joy of Demeter as a pledge of the joys of immortality; than that of Lucius, who obtained the same assurance from his participation in the death, burial, and resurrection of Osiris; than that of the believers in Cybele, whose faith brought eternal rebirth through the instrumentality of the bloody taurobolium which united them with the dead and resurrected god."[11] More cautious as to particulars, but adhering to the same fundamental position, is Samuel Angus, in his *The Mystery-Religions and Christianity*.[12]

8 2nd edn., Göttingen, 1921.
9 *Sterbende und auferstehende Götter* (Leipzig, 1923).   10 Paris, 1930.
11 Loisy, p. 267. Cf. the excellent summary of the subject in Karl Prümm, *Der christliche Glaube und die altheidnische Welt* (Leipzig, 1935), Vol. II, p. 472.
12 3rd edn., New York and London, 1928.

Today a number of scholars still take the possibility, or even the proved fact, of a genetic dependence of early Christianity on the ancient mysteries as the point of departure for specialized studies. Nevertheless, a more precise application to the problem is generally evident, and its conclusions can no longer be held in doubt: the hypothesis of a strictly genetic, historical dependence of essential Christian positions on the Hellenistic mysteries is simply untenable. This is the opinion of Clemen; and, most recently, Karl Prümm has shown in a number of works that all attempts to explain the origin of Christianity solely on the basis of comparative religion have been unsuccessful.[13] Yet this detracts in no way from the value of the special insights into the ancient mysteries that have been achieved through comparisons in this field.

As to the second group of studies on the same problem, I can mention it only in passing: a more detailed exposition (involving a partly negative evaluation) belongs rather to the sphere of specialized Catholic theology. I am referring to the so-called *Mysterienlehre* (mystery theory) developed chiefly by the monks of Maria Laach, under the guidance of Odo Casel.[14] With ample historical knowledge, these writers reject the theories of genetic dependence. But they do find a common factor in the "cult *eidos*" that in the ancient mysteries took a shadowy, incomplete, yet somehow prototypical form (as a kind of guidance toward Christ by the all-pervading Logos) and then in the Christian mystery found its God-given completion. This *eidos*, in the light of which Hellenistic mysteries and Christian mystery are examined and indeed compared, is the "cultic presence of the act of redemption" as it is forever re-enacted in the mystery: in the re-enactment of the mystery rite, transcending space and time, the redeeming efficacy of the dying and resurrected god becomes a new reality for the consecrated community. In his work on symbol and reality in the cult mystery,[15] Gottlieb Söhngen has attempted to clarify the theological problems resulting from

13 The work, in two volumes, has just been cited. A second work is *Christentum als Neuheitserlebnis, Durchblick durch die christlich-antike Begegnung* (Freiburg i. B., 1939). A third: *Religionsgeschichtliches Handbuch für den Raum der altchristlichen Welt* (Freiburg i. B., 1943; new edn., Rome, 1954). Cf. also B. Heigl, *Antike Mysterienreligionen und Urchristentum* (Münster, 1932). And the still informative work of Gustav Anrich, *Das antike Mysterienwesen in seinem Einfluss auf das Christentum* (Göttingen, 1894).
14 Other main works include *Das Christliche Kultmysterium* (2nd edn., Regensburg, 1935); "Antike und christliche Mysterien," *Bayrische Blätter für das Gymnasialschulwesen*, LIII (1927), 329. Cf. also *Mysterium: Gesammelte Arbeiten Laacher Mönche* (Münster, 1926).
15 *Symbol und Wirklichkeit im Kultmysterium* (Bonn, 1937).

342

such a view. To what degree this theory may prove sound in its application to a later period in the sacramental development of the Christian mystery (viz., the fourth and fifth centuries) is a question that cannot be discussed here; for the era of early Christianity and the Pauline mystery theology, it must probably be rejected in view of the most recent philological studies regarding the word μυστήριον.[16] The matter still is very much under discussion.

There remains the third group. It is characterized by the most scrupulous method. First of all, it distinguishes far more accurately than the other groups between the genesis of the fundamental Christian positions, as we find them in St. Paul and the early Christian writers, and the impact upon later, fully developed Christianity of the Hellenistic mysteries, which likewise did not achieve their full development until a later period (i.e., beginning in the second century A.D.). Furthermore, this group of scholars draws a clear distinction between dependence in the genetic sense and the dependence of "adaptation": when St. Paul—or even the Church Fathers of the third and fourth centuries, who gave form to the cult—borrowed words, images, and gestures from the mysteries, they did so not as seekers but as possessors of a religious substance; what they borrowed was not the substance but a dress wherein to display it—or, as Clement of Alexandria couched it in our motto: "I shall explain the mysteries of the Logos in images that are known to you." Accordingly, this group of scholars has done greater justice than the others to the essence of both terms of the comparison: they do not reduce Christianity to a common level in order to prove that it is a genetic or at least a phenomenological outgrowth of the mysteries; but neither do they fall into the trap of implicitly Christianizing the ancient mysteries— in the manner of the early Church Fathers, who thus combated the "diabolical" borrowing of Christian elements by the mystery cults, and of modern scholars, who so frequently "have pictured these cults in Christian colors."[17] As early a writer as Adolf von Harnack came out clearly against such amalgamation as a basis for genetic dependence.

16 The most recent exhaustive summary of the ancient, New Testament, and early Christian history of the word μυστήριον is by Heinrich Bornkamm, in Gerhard Kittel, ed., *Theologisches Wörterbuch zum Neuen Testament*, Vol. IV (Stuttgart, 1942), pp. 809–34. Cf. also E. Marsh, "The Use of μυστήριον in the Writings of Clement of Alexandria," *Journal of Theological Studies* (London), XXXVII (1936), 64–80; Prümm, "Mysterion von Paulus bis Origenes," *ZKT*, LXI (1937), 391–425; J. de Ghellinck, *Pour l'histoire du mot sacramentum* (Louvain, 1924).

17 Prümm, *Handbuch*, p. 308.

We must reject the comparative mythology which finds a causal connection between everything and everything else, which tears down solid barriers, bridges chasms as though it were child's play, and spins combination from superficial similarities. . . . By such methods one can turn Christ into a sun god in the twinkling of an eye, or transform the Apostles into the twelve months; in connection with Christ's nativity one can bring up the legends attending the birth of every conceivable god, or one can catch all sorts of mythological doves to keep company with the baptismal dove; and find any number of celebrated asses to follow the ass on which Jesus rode into Jerusalem; and thus, with the magic wand of "comparative religion," triumphantly eliminate every spontaneous trait in any religion.[18]

Exercising a fortunate circumspection, the most recent scholars tend rather to stress the essential differences between the two religious forms under comparison—and are thus in a better position to evaluate any dependencies that may occur. In his Uppsala lectures on the history of religions and early Christianity, the Protestant theologian Gerhard Kittel declared:

It is not a sign of scientific distinction but of banal dilettantism when work in the history of religions exhausts itself in revealing analogies and similarities. We are not impelled by any motive of apologetics but solely by the desire for intellectual insight, when we say that research in comparative religion has its aim, not in a leveling process, but in bringing out, through comparison, the contours of that which is peculiar to each religion. To recognize the nature of things, and specifically the true nature of the particular religions, hence also of Christianity, is the profoundest purpose of the theologian's work in comparative religion.[19]

Proceeding along these lines, Franz Josef Dölger and his students have worked out excellent methods and arrived at new answers to a number of questions. And much valuable material, hitherto scattered through scientific periodicals, has been collected with infinite pains by Prümm in his most recent work, on ancient paganism according to its basic trends.[20]

Today the opponents of the liberal-historical amalgams of ancient mysteries and nascent Christianity may even be said to have overshot the mark and fallen into the opposite error, declaring the two to be utterly incom-

18 *Wissenschaft und Leben*, Vol. II (Giessen, 1911), p. 191.
19 *Die Religionsgeschichte und das Urchristentum* (Gütersloh, 1932), p. 9.
20 *Das antike Heidentum nach seinen Grundströmungen: Ein Handbuch zur biblischen und altchristlichen Umweltkunde.* [See n. 13, above.—ED.]

mensurable. It was only to be expected that the dialectical school of theology, having newly discovered the concepts of "revelation" and "word of God," after the liberals had so thoroughly vaporized the whole substance of Christianity, would instinctively reject any notion remotely connected with comparative religion. Such an attitude is evident in every chapter of Karl Barth's dogmatics. At first sight this insight into the ultimately incomparable nature of Christianity can only be welcomed. How far this school, overjoyed at its new-found independence, has gone in its rejection of the formerly so beloved "comparative religion" is shown by an eloquent passage in Erich Fascher's work on understanding the New Testament:[21] "We have gone far afield, in our comparative religion we have searched the whole world over for parallels; but we are on our way home, and perhaps it will be given to us, as to the prodigal son, to see how pleasant it is at home." At first sight, as I say, this seems all very well; but it is to be feared that those who go too far in this direction may, for the sake of supernaturalism, turn Christianity into an "inhuman," purely transcendent religion of words.

Contrary to this tendency, those scholars whom we have placed in our third group, while making the sharpest distinctions, stress the theoretical possibility and historical reality of influences, though not in fundamentals. The Church is no ready-made structure existing in a vacuum, but a continuous incarnation of God: that is to say, it must address the revelation with which it was entrusted by Christ to men, and in its beginnings this meant to the men of the Greco-Roman world with their language and their culture. Its history is therefore the history of the embodiments of revelation. The soul of this body which we call the Church is of heaven— but its blood is of the Greeks and its language is of Rome. And the points whence the soul received the blood in its constant fresh flow—that is to say, the manner in which the ancient mysteries could, despite the essential cleft between them, influence Christianity—are threefold.

First (in a manner of speaking), from *below:* Christian revelation turns essentially to man, i.e., to a creature of spirit and flesh, who can express the most transcendent truths only in the sensuous language of word and image and gesture, and must, therefore, precisely in religious expression, always have recourse to symbols. But man's symbols are handed down to him, he does not arbitrarily construct them; in their basic forms they are present in

21 *Von Verstehen des Neuen Testaments* (Giessen, 1930), p. 2.

every religion, they are among the archetypes of all human searching for God. This, I might say in passing, is the theological justification for saying that the studies of C. G. Jung do not, as has sometimes been supposed, represent a repristination of the old liberal "history of religion" with its superficial theories of derivation, but penetrate into a far deeper stratum common to all religious life, namely the mysterious world of the human archetypes—Catholic theology would say into the God-oriented nature common to all men, a "religiosity" manifesting itself always in the same primal forms and receptive to a possible revelation of the speaking God, who can speak only in "human" words if He is to be understood by men. Demonstration of these common archetypal elements, therefore, does not (even though the specific documentation may be open to discussion) signify a leveling of nature and revelation, of purely human piety and supernatural faith.

Second, there is a possible contact from the *middle:* that is to say, in the strictly historical sphere of influences—on this point we shall have occasion to speak in detail. But once we have clearly apprehended the nature of Christian revelation, this borrowing reduces itself to nonessentials.

Third, finally, the Catholic theology of religious history has never forgotten that there may also be contact from *above:* a God-given purpose runs through the religious development of mankind, and most particularly of the peoples of late antiquity. This development is not only a *"krisis,"* as in St. Paul's Epistle to the Romans, but also a pedagogy oriented toward Christ. "Nevertheless He left not himself without testimony," says the same St. Paul (Acts 14 : 16). The ancient mysteries are an altar bearing the inscription "To the Unknown God."

II

Here we shall inquire into the concrete nature of the contact between the mysteries and Christianity—and our inquiry will essentially be based on the principles of the "third group," as set forth above. But first we shall require a survey of the history and character of the ancient mysteries. Only if we bear in mind their rich *differentiation* shall we be able to compare them with so clearly differentiated a phenomenon as Christianity. The "mysteries" of the early Eleusinian or Cabirian period were something quite different from those of the third century A.D., despite the great similarity in their basic structure. And despite its unchanging divine basis, Christianity discloses a very different outward form in the simple baptismal rites of the Book of Acts and in the rich and splendid ceremonial of the Pseudo-Areopagite. And yet the old school of comparative religion showed no compunction about confounding primitive with highly developed forms, and displayed a veritable juggler's art in comparing evidence situated centuries apart or originating in religious heights and depths that never had anything in common.

Thus, we must briefly inquire into the history of the mysteries in order to ascertain at what stage they entered into contact with Christianity.

Today we know, on the basis of significant ethnological studies,[22] that the mysteries that rose up so overwhelmingly out of the depths of Greek life were a religious heritage of the "world into which the Greeks entered," to use the words of Fritz Kern:[23] the final dark outgrowths of pre-Aryan Great Mother religions, transfigured by the Hellenic spirit and yet essentially pre-Greek. They enter into our historical ken at the moment they begin to conflict with the Ionic worldliness of the Homeric religion, which, as late as the fifth century, brought forth the Apollonian splendor of Greek statuary, but was powerless to quell the dark "Orphic anguish" that assails the religious spirit. For "beautiful statues of the gods of death cannot put an end to his gloomy riddle."[24] And as the spirit of the Attic comedy and, later, the rationalism of the Stoa disintegrated the traditional religion, more and more Greeks took refuge in the mystery cults. Their piety became warmer but also more frenzied; to express the new, they went back to what was believed to be age-old, to Orpheus and Pythagoras. Kurt Latte has characterized this turning of religious feeling from the classical to the Hellenistic in the words: "A new life rhythm, a loud, stormy emphasis on the individual, replaced the self-restraint in word and feeling that had hitherto passed as the characteristics of the cultivated man. Now men sought, even in the gods,

---

22 Cf. particularly K. H. E. de Jong, *Das antike Mysterienwesen in religionsgeschichtlicher, ethnologischer und psychologischer Beleuchtung* (2nd edn., Leiden, 1919); Prümm, "Materialnachweise zur völkerkundlichen Beleuchtung des antiken Mysterienwesens," *Anthropos* (Salzburg), XXVIII (1933), 759ff.; *Das antike Heidentum*, p. 219.

23 "Die Welt, worein die Griechen traten," *Anthropos*, XXIV (1929), 167–219, XXV (1930), 195ff., 793ff.; N. M. P. Nilsson, *The Minoan-Mycenaean Religion and Its Survival in Greek Religion* (Oxford and Lund, 1927); Prümm, "Neue Wege einer Ursprungsdeutung antiker Mysterien," *ZKT*, LVII (1933), 89ff., 254ff.; Prümm, "An Quellen griechischen Glaubens," *Biblica* (Rome), XI (1930), 266ff.

24 Prümm, *Handbuch*, p. 300, n. 1. Cf. Ulrich von Wilamowitz-Moellendorff, *Der Glaube der Hellenen*, Vol. II (Berlin, 1932), p. 260.

the baroque, the pathetic, as opposed to the Olympian calm of the classical period."[25] At the same time the un-Greek mystery cults of the East invaded the Greek mind, whose outward defenses, breached in the days of Alexander, were fast crumbling; the black fetish stone of the Magna Mater was carried from Pessinus to Rome, followed by the gentle Isis of the Ptolemies, and everywhere pious women wept for the dead Adonis. In vain did thoughtful Greeks and the sober Romans of the Republic resist the current. For all these foreign cults (which we must not necessarily equate with actual mysteries) expressed the religious needs of man better than the official cults of the national gods. Cumont is assuredly right when he says: "Even though the triumph of the Oriental cults sometimes has the appearance of a resurgent barbarism, they nevertheless represent a more advanced type than the old national religion. They are less primitive, less simple, more versatile than the old Greek-Italic idolatry."[26]

This "mysterization" of Hellenistic religious experience, however—and this is a fundamental conclusion increasingly documented by research—was by no means completed at the dawn of the Christian era; in fact, it had not yet gathered its full impetus. In the first century we find what may be characterized as a "mystery" atmosphere. We need only think of the systems of philosophy that in this period grew out of the work of Posidonius, all of them tending to become a substitute for religion, a consolation for this life, promising a life beyond the grave: theosophy and Neopythagorean theurgy, *somnium Scipionis*. The actual mysteries of this period, however, were still limited to particular circles and localities.

Beginning in the second century of the Christian era, a great change took place. Philosophy crystallized more and more into a Neoplatonic henotheism, and in religious feeling an attitude took form that has been well named the "dogmatic *koinè* of late antiquity":[27] it was a solar pantheism, centering round the ascent of the salvation-hungry soul by lunar ways to a blissful hereafter, which is no longer conceived as a subterranean Hades, but as an astral-celestial heaven. It was this attitude which now entered into all the countless forms of mystery religion (which up to this time were of little more than local importance), not only into the frenzied Corybantic cults of the

25 Latte, "Religiöse Strömungen in der Frühzeit des Hellenismus," *Die Antike* (Berlin), I (1925), 153ff.
26 Franz Cumont, *Les Religions orientales dans le paganisme romain* (4th edn., Paris, 1929), p. 23.
27 Prümm, *Das antike Heidentum*, pp. 306f.

East (whose un-Greek savagery it ennobled with theosophical symbolisms) but even into the sober Eleusinian rites, in which it found what Cicero, as he wrote in a famous passage, had already sought: "We have learned from [these rites] the beginnings of life, and have gained the power not only to live happily, but also to die with better hope."[28] The mysteries now achieved a popular influence throughout the Empire, but a smelting process occurred in which the particular cults lost their original character: strange mixtures came into being, mysteries were now a dish at which everyone could nibble; this was the epoch of what Festugière has aptly called the "literary mysteries": classic examples are the Hermetic books, the so-called Mithras liturgy reconstructed by Dieterich, or the *Royal Road* of Philo.[29] It is in the third century—and not before—that we find the Hellenistic mysteries in a fully developed form that we can reconstruct from an abundance of Greek and Christian sources. And anyone who undertakes the difficult task of disentangling the original localized indigenous cults from these cosmopolitan mysteries must take care not to be misled by the accounts of writers ranging from Plutarch to Iamblichus.

We must say a few words more of these late mysteries, for it is with them that early Christianity had to deal. Let us attempt to delineate the basic traits that are common to all of them.

All the mysteries retained one element from their early phase: they are cults of a Mother religion, centered round the goddess and her male consort.[30] A primordial fertility rite crystallized into a cult legend and this in turn into a mystery rite, the enactment of which endowed the initiate with the powers of the godhead. Originally, these mysteries were all fertility rites, and the Great Mother is the embodiment of the forever resurgent, all-generating force of nature. And this brings us to the peculiar, "mystical" feature of the mysteries: behind the annual revival and death of nature, the growth and generation and death of living creatures, the man of the mystery cults perceived something else; the "symbol" of the natural process was for him only half of the σύμβολον: the other half jutted into the beyond,

---

28 *De legibus*, II, 14, 36 (tr. C. W. Keyes, New York and London, 1928, p. 414).
29 A. M. J. Festugière, *L'Idéal religieux des Grecs et l'Évangile* (Paris, 1932), ch. 3. For Philo: Josef Pascher, *Der Königsweg zur Wiedergeburt und Vergottung bei Philon von Alexandreia* (Paderborn, 1931).
30 Cf. Prümm, *Der christliche Glaube und die altheidnische Welt*, Vol. I, pp. 290ff.: "Die Vorstufe griechischer mütterlicher Gottgestalten"; and his "Die Endgestalt des orientalischen Vegetationsheros in der hellenistisch-römischen Zeit," *ZKT*, LVIII (1934), 463.

349

transcending death. We know definitely that, at a very early date, hopes of afterlife became associated with the mystical rites of these vegetation cults, and the gods of growth are in large part also gods of the dead. And so the primordial mystery, after its purification by the Greek spirit, became a symbol of the whole mystery of life, a consecration of the chain of the generations forever engendering new life (Jung has called it the apocatastasis of ancestral life), a consecration, perceived and experienced in the familiar guise of dying and resurrected nature, of the sexual power that generates the future. All living things arise from the womb of the earth and to it all return, and the grave in turn is a womb sheltering new life. "Earth bears all things and takes them back again," as a fine fragment of Euripides has expressed it. And through all the mysteries murmurs the age-old prayer to the Earth Mother, which Aeschylus has preserved: "Mother Earth, Mother Earth, avert his fearful cries!"[31] What is most profound in these mysteries remains enclosed in the unbroken circle of natural life: that is, the "natural mystery" of which we have heard in earlier lectures.[32]

Closely related to this is a second peculiarity of the mysteries. They are a religion of feeling. They do not address themselves to the perplexed intellect of man, they are no "doctrine" or "dogma," and the cult legend with its thousands of variations has no bearing upon religious action. Hugo Hepding has brilliantly elucidated this in connection with the mysteries of Attis. This mystery cult is "free from all dogmatism," he says, and the same is true of nearly all the ancient cults, and he continues: "Essentially it consists rather in the performance of certain old traditional rites. These are the fixed, enduring element; he who venerates the gods by exactly executing these prescriptions is $\epsilon\dot{v}\sigma\epsilon\beta\dot{\eta}s$, according to the conception of the ancients."[33] Thus the mystery rite appeals essentially to obscure religious emotions, and in certain forms it may be said to act directly upon the nerves. "Common to all mysteries is a ritual that speaks to the feelings through powerful external techniques, through glaring light and sound effects and a polyvalent symbolism that sublimates the elementary actions into images

31 Ἅπαντα τίκτει χθών πάλιν τε λαμβάνει.—Μᾶ γᾶ, μᾶ γᾶ, βοὰν φοβερὸν ἀπό-τρεπε.—Both quotations after A. Dieterich, *Mutter Erde* (2nd edn., Leipzig, 1913), pp. 37ff. [the first in fr. 195, in Aug. Nauck, *Euripidis Tragoediae* (Leipzig, 1895), Vol. I, p. 47; the second, from *Suppliants*, ll. 890–91, tr. H. Weir Smyth, *Aeschylus* (LCL, 1922), Vol. I, p. 86.—ED.]

32 [See above, the lectures of Professor Kerényi, pp. 32–59, and of Father de Menasce, pp. 135–48.—ED.]

33 *Attis, seine Mythen und sein Kult* (Giessen, 1903), p. 98.

350

of supersensory secrets. The godhead is thus brought much closer to the believers than in the old cults. . . . Everything is calculated to compel an inner concentration for which the bustle of life otherwise leaves no room . . . and this also accounts for the preference given to ecstatic cults for whose unrestrained frenzy the Hellenic soul had formerly felt nothing but horror."[34] Now it is certainly true (as Professor Kerényi has astutely called to my attention in the course of this meeting) that we must evaluate such descriptions of emotional mystery rites with caution: for we probably tend to be too much influenced by ancient accounts, which doubtless contain a large element of literary elaboration and belong properly to the category of "literary mysteries." The classical example is Apuleius' account of the rite of Isis. And to the same category belongs Plutarch's famous record of his impressions of a mystery festival:

> First labyrinthine turnings and arduous gropings, various unsuccessful and perilous passages in the darkness. Then, before the rite itself, all manner of terrors, shuddering and trembling, silence and terrified amazement. After this a wonderful light bursts forth, friendly landscapes and meadows receive us, voices and dances and the splendor of sacred songs are disclosed to us.[35]

But with all due caution, we are entitled to say that the mystery cult was entirely a religion of feeling. "The mystai are not intended to learn anything, but to suffer something and thus be made worthy"[36] runs a fragment from Aristotle. The aim of the initiation is οὐ μαθεῖν ἀλλὰ παθεῖν—"not to learn but to suffer."

There is still a third trait, of which we shall here speak briefly, and it applies particularly to the mysteries in their final stage of extreme popularity and approaching disintegration. I should like to call the religious mood of late antiquity, from which the mysteries drew their tenacious vitality, a "nervous uncertainty of salvation," the oscillation of the waning impulse of a dying religious form. Amid the weariness of decay, the mysteries assimilated to themselves everything that was borne in on them from outside—including Christian elements. And at the same time a strange thing happened: their decomposed elements were taken up by fresh blood—in

34 Latte, "Religiöse Strömungen," pp. 154f.
35 Stobaeus, *Anthologia*, IV, 107 (cf. N. Turchi, *Fontes historiae mysteriorum aevi hellenistici*, Rome, 1923, no. 118).
36 Preserved in Synesius, *Dion*, c. 7 (*PG*, LXVI, 1136 A).

Byzantium, among the Arabs, and in Christianity. The religious life of the time was characterized by an intense yearning for salvation, a sublimely aloof, world-weary philosophy, and a confused medley of mysteries promising salvation. In A.D. 376 the Roman Sextilius Agesilaus Aedesius erected a marble altar to the Great Mother and her consort Attis; on it he listed the mysteries in which he had been initiated and which promised him "eternal rebirth":

> Pater patrum dei Solis invicti Mithrae, hierofanta Hecatarum, dei Liberi archibucolus, taurobolio criobolioque in aeternum renatus."

And according to her epitaph, the Roman patrician Paulina was

> sacrata apud Eleusinam deo Baccho Cereri et Corae, sacrata apud Laernam deo Libero et Cereri et Corae, sacrata apud Aegynam deabus, taurobolita, Isiaca, hierophantria deae Hecatae.[37]

This was truly the end. And we must bear in mind this decomposed state of the mystery cults when we attempt to decide whether and how they exerted an influence on Christianity.

This survey of the historical development and typical traits of the mysteries must be accompanied by a similar survey of the nature and development of Christianity in the same period. For though in the first five centuries the doctrine and life of Christianity retained a strict unity imposed by Apostolic tradition, it is equally true that in the same period the visible form of the Church, as manifested in explicit doctrine, in ritual and religious ideal, underwent an immense transformation. Any comparison between mysteries and Christianity must take this period of transformation into account. The theologies of Paul and Origen and Augustine: what worlds of change in the living unity of the same truth! The early Christian Lord's Supper in Corinth—and the mystery hidden by the gold iconostasis of the Byzantine rite: what a transformation in the living unity of the same faith! We must differentiate with the utmost caution, in order to leave the centuries in their place, as it were. We cannot, to cite an example, prove that the mimesis of the dead and resurrected Christ, as enacted in baptism according to St. Paul in the Epistle to the Romans, partook of the character of a mystery by quoting from Cyril of Jerusalem; and we cannot transfer the Pseudo-Areopagite with his mystery language back to the Areopagus of

---

37 *CIL*, VI, 510 and 1779; Hepding, *Attis*, pp. 89, 205. Other records of this accumulation of mystery initiations are cited in Anrich, *Das antike Mysterienwesen*, p. 55.

St. Paul. We must bear in mind three distinct periods in this segment of Christian history: the early period (first and second centuries); the period of theological, ritual formation (third century); and the final period, in which the ancient Church achieved its full development (fourth and fifth centuries.)

To these periods correspond the three periods of the late mysteries, and only now are we in a position to survey what we may call the contrapuntal attraction and repulsion between the two religious forms.

Early Christianity, formed primarily by the Pauline theology, found itself situated in that world which we have found filled with the "mystery" atmosphere. Thus it is an absurdity to attempt to show exactly which "mystery" Paul was attacking in Colossians, or which mystery was the ultimate "source" of the doctrines set forth in Romans or in the First Epistle of Peter. Let us again consult the astute Clemen concerning these questions, which are the most important in the whole complex of the relations between the mysteries and Christianity:

> Christianity was distinguished from the mystery religions by its historical character and the entirely different significance it imputed to the coming and death of the Christian redeemer . . . and thus we may say with Heinrici: an inquiry into the general character of early Christianity shows it to be more in the nature of an anti-mystery religion than of a mystery religion![38]

Nevertheless, we cannot deny that St. Paul and even such later writers as Ignatius adapted a subdued sort of mystery language to their needs.

Quite different is the situation in the second period. The third century saw a "mysterization" of all Hellenistic thought, the mysteries were incorporated into Neoplatonic philosophy and mysticism: and it was in this same period that the theology and cult of the Church took on a set form. It was then (and not before) that the immediate encounter between mysteries and Christianity began. The Apologists, above all Tertullian, combated the mysteries as a "diabolical aping "of Christian truth; Gnosis was thriving and its opponents showed how the theurgists of the new doctrines mixed Christian elements with the myths and rites of the mysteries; the theologians, led by Clement of Alexandria, set out to show the Greeks the mystery of the Logos in images familiar to them. And their theology, expressed in these terms, gave to Greek Christianity its enduring form. As much as fifty years

38 Clemen, *Der Einfluss der Mysterienreligionen auf das älteste Christentum*, pp. 81ff.

ago, Gustav Anrich [39] learnedly and circumspectly described this process as it developed slowly from its beginnings in Alexandria, and showed how a certain mystery terminology entered into the linguistic usage of the Church; and recent studies on the history of the words μυστήριον and sacramentum [40] reveal even more clearly how in this period the writing of polemics against the mysteries as well as a spirit of adaptation tended to carry certain ideas and linguistic usages from the mysteries into the language of Christianity.

Different again are the relations between mysteries and Christianity in the days when ancient paganism was drawing to an end and the cosmopolitan mysteries were in full process of decay. Despite the reaction of the Emperor Julian, they were no longer a living adversary, despite the reappearance in certain circles (for, at the very end, strange to say, the mystery cults retreated again to such aristocratically withdrawn, secret groups) of a Neoplatonic anti-Christianism in the spirit of Porphyry, and despite the Alexandrian praise of Julian's work as a "Hellenic bastion against the glory of Christ." [41] Yet the spirit of this dying adversary imposed on victorious Christianity what might almost be called a mannered mystery terminology, a secret discipline, and certain liturgical acts. The most classic example of this is the Pseudo-Areopagite, whose style was to exert so powerful an influence on the Byzantine Church. But even earlier, Chrysostom had spoken in his sermons of the mysteries that make men "freeze with awe." And the significant transformation of liturgical forms that we find in the Apostolic Constitutions or in Basilius shows us Hellenism gradually turning to Byzantinism. It was in this process that the last faded remnants of the mysteries passed into Christianity, there to take on an entirely new meaning and radiance.

These three stages in the development of Christianity and the mysteries must therefore be as painstakingly distinguished as the layers of a palimpsest. Only then may we venture to state and evaluate the differences and the similarities between the mysteries and Christianity. This will now be our task: we shall endeavor to show how Christianity, as revealed by God in Christ, has in neither its genesis nor its growth anything fundamental in common with the ancient mysteries—and we shall clearly show the basic

39 *Das antike Mysterienwesen*, pp. 130–54.
40 Cf. above, p. 343, n. 16. Also Hermann von Soden, "Mysterion und Sacramentum in den ersten zwei Jahrhunderten der Kirche," *ZNW*, XII (1911), 188–227.
41 Cyril of Alexandria, *Contra Julianum* (*PG*, LXXVI, 508 D).

differences between the two. But then we shall also be obliged to show how beginning in the third century the Church adapted itself to the Hellenistic world with its enthusiasm for mysteries and interpreted its own mysteries in the old, familiar images and words. Here, Clement of Alexandria was the leader. In the famous chapter on mysteries in his *Protrepticus* he addresses Hellenistic man as follows:

> Come, thou frenzy-stricken one, not resting on thy wand, not wreathed with ivy! Cast off thy headdress; cast off thy fawnskin; return to soberness! I shall show you the Logos, and the mysteries of the Logos, and I shall explain them to you in images that are known to you. This is the mountain beloved of God, no longer the scene for tragedies, like Cithaeron, but devoted to the dramas of truth. . . . O truly sacred mysteries! O pure light! . . . I become holy by initiation. The Lord reveals the sacred signs, for He Himself is the hierophant. . . . And thou shalt dance with angels around the unbegotten and imperishable and only true God, and God's Logos shall join with us in our hymns of praise.[42]

III

In a metaphorical sense, the Christological tessera of the Council of Chalcedon—ἀσυγχύτως καὶ ἀδιαιρέτως, "unmingled, but undivided"—sums up the profound relation between Greek and Christian mystery. For in approaching this problem we must endeavor to observe a mean between an all-too-human mingling in the sense of a genetic or ideal dependency and an inhuman division implying that the essence of Christianity is in every respect incommensurable with any work of man.

It will be therefore my first duty to demonstrate to you, by means of the scientifically irreproachable method delineated above, the ἀσυγχύτως: the essential difference between Christianity as a revealed religion and the Greek mysteries; between the "hidden mystery" (μυστήριον ἀποκεκρυμμένον: Eph. 3 : 9) of the Christians and the μυστήρια of the Hellenistic world; between the "natural mystery" of the Greek mystery symbolism and the "supernatural mystery" of the New Testament doctrine of salvation. And this in no merely apologetic sense but according to the dictates of actual history.

42 *Protrepticus* ("Exhortation to the Greeks"), XII, 119, 1–120, 2 (*GCS*, I, p. 84, ll. 4–29; cf. Butterworth, pp. 255–57).

The same Clement of Alexandria, whom we have heard speaking to the Greeks "in images familiar to you," defines with unparalleled sharpness the essential difference between the ancient mysteries and the Christian mystery:

> And shall I recount the mysteries for you? I will not give away their secrets, as Alcibiades is said to have done. But I will thoroughly lay bare, led by the Logos of truth, the swindle they conceal.

And then, after describing the most important of their cult rites in a chapter that is of fundamental importance for the study of the ancient mysteries, he continues:

> These are the mysteries of the atheists. And I am right in branding as atheists men who are ignorant of the true God. . . . But I wish to display to you at close quarters the gods themselves . . . in order that at last you may cease from error and run back again to heaven. "For we too were once children of wrath, as also the rest; but God being rich in mercy, through His great love wherewith He loved us, when we were already dead in trespasses, made us alive together with Christ." For the Word is living, and he who has been buried with Christ is exalted together with God. . . . We . . . are no longer creatures of wrath, for we have been torn away from error and are hastening towards the truth.[43]

Here the Alexandrian Greek and Christian, who cannot be suspected of hostility to the mysteries, expresses in Pauline terms and with Pauline sharpness the unbridgeable distinction between our two terms of comparison. The μυστήριον of New Testament revelation, as we find it primarily in St. Paul (Romans 16 : 25ff.; I Cor. 2 : 7–10; Col. 1 : 26ff.; Eph. 1 : 8–10 and 3 : 3–12), can be summed up as follows: *mysterion* is the free decision of God, taken in eternity and hidden in the depths of the godhead, to save man, who in his sinfulness has been separated from God; this hidden decision is revealed in Christ the man-God, who by his death gives "life" to all men, that is, calls them to participate in his own divine life, which through the ethical will is comprehended in faith and sacrament and transcends earthly death in the beatific vision of perfect union with God.

Mysterion is therefore, at least in St. Paul, the epitome of the decision of salvation revealed in Christ and of its workings.[44] *Mysterion* is the

---

43 *Protrepticus*, II, 12, 1; 27, 1, 2 (*GCS*, I, p. 11; 17; 20; tr. Butterworth, pp. 29, 47, 55).
44 Cf. D. Deden, "Le Mystère Paulinien," *Ephemerides Theolog. Lovanienses*, XIII (1936), 405–42.

stupendous drama of human redemption, which issues from the depths of God, is manifested in Christ and the Church, and returns to the depths of God, the "drama of truth,"[45] as Clement of Alexandria states in a subsequent passage. Hence *mysterion* is always both a manifesting and a concealment of the divine act of salvation: manifest in the communication of the truth through the promised Christ; concealed in the unfathomable nature of the divine utterance, which even after its communication cannot be fully understood but is apprehended only by faith. For this *mysterion* is a supernatural drama transcending all human nature and all human thought, the drama of man's acceptance as the son of God. The Christian *mysterion* is always a "secret revelation": secret, because here on earth it appeals only to faith and once taken in faith permits only a slow ascent to understanding, to a holy gnosis; revealed, because it is "proclaimed from the rooftops," addressed to all mankind, free from all esotericism and occultism.

This in itself makes it clear that both the words and doctrine of St. Paul are sharply differentiated from what were known to Hellenistic thought as μυστήρια. And philological considerations carry us even farther. Where did St. Paul derive his terminology? We must indeed (in line with the principles set forth above) acknowledge the possibility that he consciously made use of such words at Colossae, at Ephesus, and at Corinth in order to combat what we have described as the "mystery" atmosphere. But along with such suppositions, we have facts: even before St. Paul, there was a "linguistic usage based on the mysteries"—Christ himself brought tidings of the "mysteries of the kingdom of heaven" (μυστήρια τῆς βασιλείας τῶν οὐρανῶν: Matth. 13 : 11; Mark 4 : 11; Luke 8 : 10). True, we do not know exactly how this was said in the original Aramaic of Jesus, but in any case the term was assuredly used before St. Paul by Mark and by the Greek, Matthew. And in what sense? The mysteries of the kingdom are the "secret revelation" of Jesus, his royal messages, which are hidden beneath the cloak of parables "in order that they may see and yet not see, hear and yet not hear"[46] (Matth. 13 : 13): Christ himself gives this interpretation of his mystery. And this usage goes back to the Old Testament, particularly to the so-called deuterocanonical books: here *mysterion* is the "*sacramentum regis*" (Tobit 12 : 7), the "secret of a king" that he confides only to trusted councilors, the

45 *Protrepticus*, XII, 119, 1 (*GCS*, I, p. 84, li. 8ff.; tr. Butterworth, p. 255).
46 [Tr. from the German because neither AV nor DV gives the sense desired by author.— TR.]

all-powerful ruler's plan of campaign that he condescends to communicate to his council (Judith 2 : 2), the stratagem that the renegade betrays to the enemy. This is the meaning that the translators of the Septuagint associated with the word μυστήριον. Jesus and St. Paul after him extended it to the divine plan that was hidden and that is "manifested to his saints" (Col. 1 : 26). How far removed we are here from the meaning that Hellenistic thought attached to the term μυστήρια (always used in the plural)! Recent research has indeed shown that the New Testament *mysterion* cannot be interpreted in the cultic sense that it possesses in the pagan religions of antiquity.

Far into the second century, in Ignatius and Justin and Irenaeus, even in Clement of Alexandria, the word *mysterion* remained far closer to this Pauline meaning than to that of the ancient cult mystery.[47] The great drama of the revelation of God in Christ, and in particular the whole Old Testament story of salvation conceived as a single parable finding its key and explanation in Christ; Christ's acts, particularly his death on the Cross; the Church, and within the Church the sacraments and formulations of the truths embodied in the symbol of faith—all these are called *mysterion*, because they are acts and rites and words that flow from God's unfathomable plan and that themselves in turn, in their visible, modest, unpretentious cloak, conceal and intimate and communicate God's unfathomable depths. They are a "drama of truth." An unknown Greek of the fourth century formulated this essence of the Christian mystery in the words: "Our testimony concerning Christ is not a mere speaking in words but a mystery of piety. Christ's whole work of salvation is called a mystery because the mystery is not manifested merely in the letter, but proclaimed through an act [ἐν τῷ πράγματι κηρύττεται]."[48]

We must now compare this Christian mystery more closely with the ancient mysteries in order to make clear the difference between them. The difference may be summed up in three points: Christianity is a mystery of revelation; it is a mystery of ethical law; it is a mystery of salvation by grace. And in these three points it contrasts sharply with Hellenistic mystery religion.

As a *mystery of revelation* of the one God in the historical person of Christ,

47 Cf. Prümm, "Mysterium und Verwandtes bei Hippolyt und bei Athanasius," *ZKT*, LXIII (1939), 207ff., 350ff.
48 Pseudo-Chrysostom, *Christmas Homily* (*PG*, LIX, 687).

Christianity is based on the strictest monotheism, it accepts an exactly defined dogmatic doctrine, and it testifies to Jesus Christ, crucified under Pontius Pilate. And now let us cast a glance at the Greek mysteries as they were at the dawn of the Christian era: there is no trace of the solar henotheism painstakingly constructed by the theosophical, symbolistic thinkers of the third century; the heterogeneous, confused cult legends are utterly irrelevant to the doctrine; and we find a purely emotional longing for a salvation that is conceived in naturalistic terms. It is and remains a riddle how in the period of unrestricted "comparative religion" scholars should even have ventured a comparison, not to speak of trying to derive the basic doctrines of Christ from the mystery religions. "Without being a prophet, we can predict that a coming generation will simply fail to understand that the idea of an inner kinship between mysteries and Christianity in so many basic concepts could ever have been put forward with so much seriousness."[49] Christian revelation is not myth but history, and its deposit is the visible Church, the concrete language of the New Testament, the precisely ascertainable Apostolic tradition, the set form of the sacraments. The God of the Christian mystery is no intellectual construction or embodiment of yearning, however sublime, such as grew from the religious searchings of Hellenistic man, not the God of the learned, not even the God of the mystic, but the God of whom Pascal said in his famous creed: "God of Abraham, Isaac, and Jacob, not of the philosophers and scholars, God who is found only in the ways taught by the Gospel." That is why the Christian mystery is "foolishness" to every mere Greek (I Cor. 1 : 23). For it is the incarnation and human death of God.

"The gospel of Christ crucified is utterly unmythical," said Kittel in his lectures at the University of Uppsala:

> It is not a song and not a strain of music, and not an idea, and not a myth or a symbol. It does not speak of a remote legend, but of an immediately near, realistic, brutal, wretched, and terrible episode in history. . . . The terrible realism of the Cross is softened by no patina of age and by no aesthetics. We can understand why this message was looked upon as "foolishness" and a "stumbling block." And yet the two things are closely related: this same realism, in which is concentrated the contempt and sense of outrage inspired by Christianity at the time of its entrance into the world, is at the same time the ultimate and profoundest root of its

49 Prümm, *Handbuch*, p. 308.

power. . . . Beautiful and profound ideas, secret magic, mystery
—all this was as well or better known to other religions than
to early Christianity. If their believers gave heed to the message of
Christ, they did so solely because it was a perfectly realistic
message."[50]

And thus for the Christian, who had risen from the soft enchantment of the
Hellenistic atmosphere of mysteries into the redeeming clarity of faith in
Christ, the whole of this mystery cult vanished like an evil specter.

Mystery of ethical law: in order to elucidate the fundamental difference
between Christianity and the mysteries in this sphere, we shall have to give
some attention to what so competent a scholar as Leipoldt called a "question
of vast implications,"[51] namely the relation between the ancient mystery
religions and an ethical law. Originating as they did in fertility rites with
their sexual implications, the ancient mysteries can scarcely be expected
to have exerted an ethical influence; however, let us not be skeptical in the
manner of Erwin Rohde[52] some years ago, and of Gerhard Kittel[53] more
recently; but let us rather follow the learned and discerning Johann Leipoldt
in differentiating between the ethical content of the old Greek mysteries
and the almost total lack of ethics in the mystery cults imported from the
non-Greek East; furthermore, let us distinguish carefully between the ethical status of the mysteries at the dawn of the Christian era and in the third
century, when solar henotheism strove to mold them into a religion of
consolation. Yet at no stage do the mysteries bear comparison with the
ethical commandments of the New Testament and their realization in
early Christianity. The two terms are truly incommensurable—and this is
not the foregone conclusion of apologists but results from an unbiased
examination of the sources by scholars who cannot be accused of denomina-
tional commitment.[54] No, measured by the standard of ethical content,
Christianity and the mysteries are worlds apart. Mystery religion at best
is man's earthbound, tragic attempt to purge and raise himself morally
(and sometimes only ritually) by his own resources—while in Christianity

---

50 *Die Religionsgeschichte und das Urchristentum*, pp. 124ff.
51 "Der Sieg des Christentums über die Religionen der alten Welt," in *Das Erbe Martin
Luthers und die gegenwärtige theologische Forschung* (Festgabe for L. Ihmels, Leipzig,
1928), p. 66.
52 *Psyche*, tr. W. B. Hillis (London, 1925), p. 228.
53 *Die Religionsgeschichte*, pp. 116ff.
54 Cf. also Latte, "Schuld und Sünde in der griechischen Religion," *Archiv für Religionswissenschaft* (Freiburg i. B.), XX (1920–21), 254ff.

it is not man who raises himself up but *God* who descends, conferring upon man the divine grace that makes possible his moral regeneration in the love of Christ.

Closely related is the third difference: Christianity is a *mystery of redemption by grace*. Much has been written about the Hellenistic "religions of redemption"—and here we find the classic example of the ruinous mania for painting the Greek mysteries in Christian colors. Recent scholars of all camps have come to more sober conclusions. The Hellenistic world at the dawn of the Christian era was indeed characterized by a universal, though vague, yearning for a redeeming God and for a golden age of peace, but it must be recognized that the "redemption" promised in the mysteries was utterly naturalistic in character and merely transposed into the other world. "The conception that the god dies and is resurrected in order to lead his faithful to eternal life is represented in no Hellenistic mystery religion," writes the learned critic André Boulanger.[55] The salvation proclaimed by Christ lies on an entirely different plane. It presupposes the ethical fall from grace, and is therefore a redemption from guilt, from ethical and theological evil, but not a liberation from the substance of the flesh somehow conceived as ungodly or evil. Christian redemption is the remission of sins through Christ's death on the Cross, and even a scholar so convinced of the genetic dependence of Christianity on the mysteries as Reitzenstein sees here an essential distinction: "The new element in Christianity is redemption as remission of sins. The terrible seriousness of the doctrine of guilt and atonement is lacking in Hellenism."[56] And like sin, the newly bestowed life in the Christian mystery transcends the merely natural: it is "eternal life," "rebirth," and "vision" in a sense nowhere attested in the mysteries. Albrecht Oepke sums up this fundamental difference as follows: "On the one hand a timeless, naturalistic individualism of rebirth, on the other a spiritual bond with history, a recreation of the totality, conceived in an eschatological sense."[57] And A. J. Festugière, one of the most unbiased students of the Hellenistic mind, says the union with the god in the mysteries is always within the sensuous sphere, while the purely spiritual pneuma of the Christian mystery removes it from any bond with nature.[58] And F. J. Dölger: "In the

55 *Orphée: Rapports de l'orphisme et du christianisme* (Paris, 1925), p. 102; cf. Prümm, *Christentum als Neuheitserlebnis*, pp. 142ff.
56 *Poimandres* (Leipzig, 1904), p. 180, n. 1.
57 In his dissertation on the "Heilsbedeutung der Taufe auf Christus," in Kittel, I, p. 539.   58 *L'Idéal religieux des Grecs*, p. 219.

mystery deities, the god is equated with nature. The rite of resurrection . . . does not commemorate a historical event, but an occurrence that is repeated each year."[59] The Christian mystery of redemption is intelligible only in the light of the conception that man was originally the son of God, that he lost this supernatural kinship with God by the first sin and regained it through the Cross; and the mystery of grace can be understood only through the eschatological conception that in the hereafter man will see God face to face. These are basic dogmas of Christianity as proclaimed by Jesus and formulated by St. Paul. In this respect the Christian mystery is distinctly new and quite different from the ancient mysteries, and researches in the direction of comparative religion will never yield any other result than a more profound knowledge of the incomparable nature of Christianity. The Protestant theologian Kittel concluded his Uppsala lectures with words that I should like to cite as a summation of my own remarks concerning the ἀσυγχύτως, the impossibility of a comparison between Hellenic and Christian mystery:

> The creed of early Christianity runs: "Being justified therefore by faith, let us have peace with God, through our Lord Jesus Christ. . . . For I am sure that neither death, nor life . . . nor any other creature, shall be able to separate us from the love of God which is in Christ Jesus our Lord" (Rom. 5 : 1 and 8 : 38–39). Anyone who has understood these verses knows wherein lay the specific and different character of early Christianity, and also wherein lay its profound strength as opposed to all other religions and philosophies of its time.[60]

And now that we have distinguished between the two terms of our comparison, we are in a position to reintegrate them, for they are also ἀδιαιρέτως, joined together through Him who is both the God of the Hellenes and the Father of Jesus Christ. We are in a position to evaluate the mutual influences of the mysteries and ancient Christianity. And here we shall go back to the three points of contact where, as we stated above, an exchange can have taken place.

A vast number of ideas, words, rites, which formerly were designated off-

---

59 *Ichthys*, Vol. I (new edn., Münster, 1928), p. 7 *; cf. also Dölger's basic articles: "Mysterienwesen und Urchristentum" and "Zur Methode der Forschung," in *Theologische Revue* (Münster), XV (1916), 385ff., 433ff.

60 *Die Religionsgeschichte*, p. 132.

hand as "borrowings" of Christianity from the mysteries, grew to life in the early Church from a root that has indeed no bearing on a historical-genetic dependence, but that did spring from the universal depths of man, from the psychophysical nature common to heathen and Christian alike—"from below," as we have said. Every religion forms sensory images of spiritual truths: we call them symbols. The revealed religion of the God-man could speak only in images intelligible to man: "And without parable he did not speak unto them" (Mark 4 : 34). And the transcendent content of his message was cloaked in primordial human images of the father, the king, of light and darkness, of the living water and the burning fire, of the pearl and the seed of grain. The same is true of the cult rites that he instituted with a view to intimating and inducing transcendent grace: the cleansing, the supper, the anointing, the judgment. If after careful reading and evaluation of the source texts, we find similar intimations and symbols in the mystery religions, it is in keeping with the law that Prümm[61] called the law of the relation between matter and form: in order to express a higher, transcendent idea, religious man must always make use of the primal symbols provided by nature. The common factor is therefore to be found in the human need for symbolism. In another work and in another connection the same scholar aptly characterized the theology of the symbol:

> It is no wonder that the old Church symbolism has in a sense been rediscovered today. All epochs in which the existence of a spiritual realm is freshly experienced, perhaps after a period of banalizing orientation toward the outward and visible, toward matter and its manifestations, take pleasure in the symbol. In it the split between the sensuous and the spiritual world is resolved, the tension between the two realms in which man is situated is bridged over. . . . It is because the young Church was free from the weariness of age, because it thought and felt with the freshness of youth, that it so quickly and willingly took up the symbol set forth by Scripture, by the words and acts of the Lord, and elaborated upon it. In the fifth book of his *Stromateis*, Clement of Alexandria has a highly learned digression in which he justifies the use of symbols by a wealth of philosophical arguments. Among the pagan examples of symbolism, he particularly stresses the secret cults. And here indeed lies, it seems to me, the only noteworthy contact between the ancient mysteries and the Christian cult.[62]

61 *Handbuch*, p. 331.
62 *Christentum als Neuheitserlebnis*, pp. 415–17.

This leads us to the second possibility of exchange between Greek life and Christianity—the historically demonstrable current, which we have described as flowing "from the middle." Many elements that were formerly declared to be direct borrowings from the mystery cults entered into Christian life through the cultural heritage held in common with the Greeks. It was the same with the cultic words and usages with which the Greeks fashioned their mysteries: here, too, symbols were formed of elements taken from everyday life. For it is a fundamental law of religious development that "the concepts and expressions for the higher realms of religion all have their ultimate origin in a lower sphere."[63] Accordingly, the use of identical and similar words, gestures, rites in the Christian and the Hellenistic cults does not imply derivation of one from the other but a common source in domestic and civil life. The mystagogue kisses the altar and the Christian priest does likewise; both set their right foot first across the threshold of the sanctuary; in both the mysteries and the early Christian ritual of baptism, the novice is given milk and honey: but these are not "influences" of the mysteries on Christianity; they are simply usages that the various cults drew quite independently from daily life, and fashioned into symbols for very different contents. Dölger has performed a lasting service in stressing this point in his studies on Antiquity and Christianity, which compose a work of impressive learning and unexceptionable method. And it is to be hoped that his *Reallexikon für Antike und Christentum*, begun so hopefully, will go further in the same direction.[63a]

A third point in which Christianity may seem to have been influenced by the Hellenistic mysteries may be sought in what might be called the sociological law of concealment, a law applying to all religious thought. The deeper and more fervent religious experience becomes, the more men tend to safeguard it from the profane. And this is particularly true in times when the masses threaten to invade the temple. The fine dissertation of Odo Casel[64] has acquainted us with this "mystical silence" among the Greeks. There is an old Orphic saying that applies to all Greek religious feeling: "I shall speak to those to whom it is right to do so; shut your ears, profane ones" (φθέγξομαι οἷς θέμις ἐστί, θυρὰς ἐπίθεσθε βέβηλοι).[65] In the *Hermetica* it is written: "To expose this treatise imbued with all the majesty of

---

63 Prümm, *Handbuch*, p. 328, n. 3.   63a [Leipzig, 1941– . ED.]
64 *De philosophorum graecorum silentio mystico* (Giessen, 1919).
65 Preserved in Eusebius, *Praeparatio evangelica*, III, 7 (*PG*, XXI, 180 B).

God to the knowledge of the many would be to betoken a godless mind."[66] And a late Pythagorean wrote: "The goods of knowledge must not be communicated to him whose soul is not cleansed. For it is not fitting to expose that which has been achieved with so much pains to the first comer, nor to reveal the mysteries of the Eleusinian goddesses to the profane."[67] This law began to operate in Christianity as soon as the circumstances favored it. True, the Christian message was public, "preached from the rooftops," addressed to all men; yet, beginning in the third century, Christianity had to defend itself against the incursion of the masses: it was then and only then that the so-called arcane discipline came into being, and it was not fully formed until the fourth century. In this connection it is understandable that the Church Fathers who had come to Christianity from Neoplatonism should have coined a language that undoubtedly does derive from the dying mysteries. The mysteries of baptism and of the sacrificial altar were surrounded with a ritual of awe and secrecy, and soon the iconostasis concealed the holy of holies from the eyes of the noninitiate: these became φρικτὰ καὶ φοβερὰ μυστήρια—"mysteries that make men freeze with awe."[68] "This is known to the initiates" is a phrase running through all the Greek sermons,[69] and as late a writer as the Pseudo-Areopagite warns the Christian initiate who has experienced the divine mystagogy to keep silence: "Take care that you do not reveal the holy of holies, preserve the mysteries of the hidden God so that the profane may not partake of them and in your sacred illuminations speak of the sacred only to saints."[70]

Going still more deeply, we can indicate a fourth point at which the language of the ancient mysteries exerted an influence on Christian thought. It lies in the very nature of the symbolic word and the symbolic action that a spiritual meaning can never be fully and exhaustively expressed in sensuous terms. The symbol always retains its mysterious background; it is a garment that reveals and at the same time masks the form of the body. Indeed, this quality of the symbol is needed to conceal the radiance of the transcendent and divulge it only to those who have eyes for it. The Hellenistic sym-

---

66 *Corpus Hermeticum*, II, 1; II, 11. Cf. Anrich, *Das antike Mysterienwesen*, p. 70.
67 Iamblichus, *Vita Pythagorae*, 17, 35 (cf. Anrich, p. 69).
68 This is amply attested in the literature. Cf. Anrich, p. 157.
69 Cf. ibid., p. 158.
70 *Ecclesiastica hierarchia*, I, 1 (*PG*, III, 372 A). Cf. Hugo Koch, *Pseudo-Dionysius Areopagita in seinen Beziehungen zum Neuplatonismus und Mysterienwesen* (Mainz, 1900), pp. 108ff.

bologists made this the basis for their sublime reinterpretations of the mystery rites. In their heavenly concealment, says Macrobius in his *Commentary on Scipio's Dream*, the divine truths are inaccessible to the human eye, and the initiate know that the truth is not susceptible of naked representation. For this reason, he tells us, the mysteries are wrapped about with the protective covering of symbols: *"ipsa mysteria figurarum cuniculis opperiuntur."*[71] Thus Clement of Alexandria is stating a common Hellenic truth when he writes: "Dreams and signs are all more or less obscure to men, not because of God's grudge (for it is wrong to conceive of God as subject to such a feeling), but in order that research should try to penetrate to the meaning of enigmas and thus ascend to the discovery of truth."[72] And by way of illustration he cites the profound words of Sophocles:

> And such is the nature of God, that I know for certain:
> For wise men his divine word is always full of riddles,
> For the weak it is simple and teaches much with few words.[73]

And this, says Macrobius, was known also to St. Paul, when he wrote: "But we speak the wisdom of God in a mystery" (I Cor. 2 : 7). Indeed, this Greek mysticism of the symbolic word was the basis for the allegorical exegesis developed in Alexandria. The divine word of Scripture is a mystery, and behind the audible meaning of its words and images, of its whole historical narrative, are concealed unknown realms of the spirit and unsuspected possibilities of ascent to the imageless truth. For those endowed with an eye for this, that which is perceptible to the senses is only a kind of extension, jutting into this dark world, of a more real, transcendent realm, a miniature sketch of the vast divine ideas that are the source and ultimate goal of all created thought. The man endowed with this eye is the true "gnostic," who is "initiated" into the mystery of the divine word. But despite the mystery terminology in which these ideas are cloaked, the Christian gnostic and non-Christian gnostic are far apart. Christian gnosis (we might say Christian mysticism) remains always within the limits of the faith, of the historical purpose implicit in God's word, of the visible Ecclesia. Non-Christian gnosis strives to redeem through knowledge, detaches itself from the written word, and isolates itself in solitude or conventicles. In this innermost sphere of

---

71 *Commentarii in Somnium Scipionis*, I, 2, 17; *Saturnalia*, V, 13, 40.
72 *Stromata*, V, 4, 24, 2 (*GCS*, II, p. 341; cf. tr. Wm. Wilson, *Writings of Clement of Alexandria*, Edinburgh, 1867–69, Vol. II, p. 234).
73 Sophocles, *Fragmentum incertum*, 704 (*GCS*, II, p. 341, li. 6–8).

ancient thought, where the "mystical" springs from Christian idea and Greek word, we must again distinguish between substance and expression. We shall then be free to recognize how in this domain what was best in ancient mysteries flowed into Christianity. Chrysostom profoundly characterized this mystical theology of symbols: "This is all mystery, although it is everywhere proclaimed. For it remains unfathomable to those who have not the right understanding for it. And it is revealed not by human wisdom, but by the Holy Ghost in such measure as it is possible for us to receive the spirit."[74] This is the feeling of the ancient mysteries, but assimilated to Christianity: it is no longer σοφία but πνεῦμα ἅγιον that breaks through the veil of the symbol. The Latin writer Chrysologus sees this as the reason that Christ cloaked his doctrine in parables: *"hinc est quod doctrinam suam Christus parabolis velat, tegit figuris, sacramentis opperit, reddit obscuram mysteriis."*[75] Christianity is never a religion of the naked word, of mere reason and ethical law, but of the veiled word, of loving wisdom, of grace concealed in sacramental symbols—and hence also the religion of mysticism, in which the infinite depths of God are disclosed hidden behind simple words and rituals. But (and this is the specifically Christian element) God alone is the mystagogue and hierophant of these mysteries: only when His spirit confers the power of vision does man become an epoptes of the Christian mystery. Clement writes:

> He who is still blind and dumb, not having understanding or the undazzled and keen vision of the contemplative soul which the Saviour confers, must, like the uninitiated at the mysteries, or the unmusical at dances, not being yet pure and worthy of the pure truth, stand outside of the divine choir.[76]

And now to the last source of so many similarities between the Hellenistic and the Christian mysteries. As modern scholars have become more objective in this field, they have turned with increasing interest to another aspect, namely the possible influence of Christianity on the Greek mysteries. We have seen above how greatly the relation between mysteries and Christianity changed between the century of St. Paul and Clement and the late period when a victorious Christianity confronted a weary and decaying but still rich world of mysteries. But it is precisely from this fourth century

74 Homily VII, 2, on I Corinthians (*PG*, LXI, 56 C).
75 *Sermo* 96, 1 (*PL*, LII, 469 D).
76 *Stromateis*, V, 4, 19, 2 (*GCS*, II, p. 338, li. 22–26; tr. Wilson, Vol. II, p. 234, modified).

that we have the most abundant documents concerning the mystery cults. Is it not possible that Christian elements should have exerted an influence on the decaying mysteries and that consequently a number of mystery documents, formerly accepted uncritically, were colored by the influence of Christianity? Here, to be sure, we must proceed with the utmost caution. But so competent a scholar as Franz Cumont does not hesitate to say: "Christianity influenced even its enemies once it had become a moral force in the world. The Phrygian priests of the Great Mother opposed their festival of the vernal equinox to the Christian Easter celebration and attributed to the blood shed in the taurobolium the redeeming power belonging to the Lamb of God."[77] It is known that the priests of this same cult complained that it was the Christians and not themselves who imitated the blood mystery of atonement on the *"dies sanguinis"* (March 24),[78] and St. Augustine once expressed his indignation at a priest of Attis who asserted that "the god in the Phrygian cap is also a Christian."[79] This makes it clear that the dying mysteries were at all events open to Christian influences. In his work on Attis, Hepding wrote: "In the late period, the allegorical interpretation of myths, theosophical speculations deriving from the dominant philosophy and perhaps here and there an idea based on Christian influence, may have contributed to a deepening of the religious content of the mysteries."[80] Speaking of the taurobolium in the mystery of Attis, he says: "Actually it is not impossible that the Christian doctrine of redemption through the blood of Christ, of atonement through the blood of the Lamb, contributed to the conception of this blood baptism."[81] Such an influence seems more than probable if we recall the considerable influence of Jewish monotheism on the mysteries, and particularly on the practices described in the Magic Papyri.[82] And as late a Christian as St. Augustine still felt it necessary to warn his flock against the mystery priests who injected the name of Christ into their magic spells.[83] If we consider in this light the inscription of A.D. 376 in which the Roman aristocrat Aedesius records the numerous mysteries in which he has been initiated and boasts of having thereby been *"in aeternum renatus,"* it

77 Les Religions orientales, preface, p. ix.
78 Ibid., pp. 54, 66.
79 Tractatus in Ioannem, VII, 6 (PL, XXXV, 1440 C).
80 Attis, seine Mythen und sein Kult, p. 179.
81 Ibid., p. 200, n. 7.
82 Documented in Cumont, pp. 59–60, p. 208, n. 9, p. 232, n. 4.
83 Miscent praecantationibus suis nomen Christi (PL, XXXV, 1440).

inevitably loses much of the value so often ascribed to it as proof (the only one put forward in this connection) that the doctrine of rebirth came to Christianity from the mysteries. This record dates from a time when the Church in Rome already enjoyed official recognition, when the Phrygian mystery grotto of the Vatican was already covered over by the Basilica of St. Peter, built by Constantine, when the Christian mystery of eternal rebirth from the baptismal font was really preached from the rooftops, and when, not the dead pine bough of the Phrygian mystery was carried through the streets of Rome, but the Cross of the new mystery whose praises were sung by Firmicus Maternus. We shall have more to say of these two mysteries of the Cross and of baptism. It was in them that Christianity triumphed over the ancient mysteries. The Church gathered Greek man to its bosom, addressing him in the words of Clement of Alexandria:

> Come to me, old man, come thou too! Quit Thebes; fling away thy prophecy and Bacchic revelry and be led by the hand to truth. Behold, I give thee the wood of the Cross to lean upon. Hasten, Tiresias, believe! Thou shalt have sight. Christ, by whom the eyes of the blind see again, shineth upon thee more brightly than the sun. . . . Thou shalt see heaven, old man, though thou canst not see Thebes.
> O truly sacred mysteries! O pure light! In the blaze of the torches I have a vision of heaven and of God. I become holy by initiation.[84]

2. The Mystery of the Cross

Fulget crucis mysterium.

The wood on which Tiresias leans is the Cross. And the mystery of light that opens his blind eyes is baptism.

The foregoing remarks have perhaps been too theoretical or even (the impression might easily arise) too apologetic. But if we distinguished so sharply between the Christian and the Greek mystery, and exerted so much caution in relating them to one another, it was solely in the interest of a sound method, which, it is hoped, will now bear fruit as we prepare to experience the mysteries of the Cross and of baptism in all the depth of their Christian content and all the beauty of their Greek form. "The mystery

84 *Protrepticus*, XII, 119, 3; 120, 1 (*GCS*, I, p. 84, li. 17ff.; tr. Butterworth, p. 257).

of the Cross shines resplendent," sang Venantius Fortunatus,[1] and his hymn still re-echoes in the liturgy.

To gain a deeper understanding of what the ancient Christian meant by his mystery of the Cross, we must once again return briefly to our theoretical findings. The Christian mystery is the "drama of truth": the plan of salvation hidden in God is revealed in Christ crucified, and beneath the cloak of his human life is concealed the unfathomable "mystery of godliness" (μυστήριον τῆς εὐσεβείας: I Tim. 3 : 16). Everything that happens in the historical unfolding of His plan of salvation—that is to say, in the Church —partakes of this character of mystery: everything is both revealed and hidden, and beneath the simple visible cloak is hidden the unfathomable wisdom of God that will be manifest only at the end of days, the "wisdom. . . in a mystery" (σοφία ἐν μυστηρίῳ: I Cor. 2 : 7). Thus the Church itself is a "great sacrament" (μυστήριον μέγα: Eph. 5 : 32), because its now manifest presence is the revelation of the secret intimated to Adam and Eve (Gen. 2 : 24), but for this very reason the Church itself in its historically tangible form is also a cloak for a secret to be revealed only eschatologically, namely the secret of its innermost bond with Christ (cf. Col. 1 : 27), from which one day the δόξα, which now works in secret, will burst forth.

This quality of the Christian mystery is discernible primarily in the principal episode of salvation: Christ's death on the Cross. In this event, the early Christians, beginning with St. Paul, saw the mystery of all creation. For all its inexorable historical fact, Christ's death on the Cross is also a mystery encompassing the whole history of the world before and after it. Christian mystery (to quote a recent scholar) is

the plan of God, preceding the world and hidden from the world but disclosed to those imbued with the spirit, a plan fulfilled on the Cross of the Κύριος τῆς δόξης and including the glorification of those who believe. In this form the concept shows its clear dependence on the late Jewish apocalyptic concept and its distance from the mystery cults and Gnosis. As μυστήριον τοῦ θεοῦ, the history of the crucifixion and transfiguration of Christ is beyond worldly wisdom, a history planned and enacted in the sphere of God. . . . When God's μυστήριον is fulfilled in Christ, creation and fulfillment, beginning and end of the world, are encompassed in it and removed from their own sphere of action and cognition.

1 Carmen II, 6 ("Vexilla Regis prodeunt"), in *Analecta hymnica*, Vol. L (Leipzig, 1907), p. 74.

In the revelation of the divine mystery, time comes to an end (Eph. 1 : 10). But the concept of μυστήριον implies not only a history removed from the laws of earthly action and cognition, fulfilled in accordance with the hidden plan of God; it also implies a history enacted *in the world*. In the mystery, a divine reality breaks into the old aeon: the Κύριος τῆς δόξης dies on the Cross erected by the princes of this world. In the Cross the radical conflict between the hitherto hidden wisdom of God and the wisdom of the powers is made manifest—a conflict devastating for the rulers of this world, bringing salvation to those who believe in the kerygma.[2]

It is of the utmost importance for the understanding of this mystery of the Cross that we recall the fundamental structure of all mysteries—and even for an understanding of the "natural mystery" of antiquity, this seems to us more important than the strictly cultic, ritual element. "Is it not, perhaps, the secret of every true and great mystery that it is simple?" C. Kerényi has aptly asked.[3] The ear of grain, the sprouting tree, the bath, the life-giving union of the sexes, light and darkness, moon and sun, all these, precisely because they are so simple and human, provided, even in the natural mystery, the most suitable expression for the profoundest ἄρρητον and ἀνεκλάλητον. This fundamental structure is retained, though on an entirely different plane and with a new divine content, in the mystery of the Cross. The agony, the blood, the bleeding heart; the primordial, simple form of the Cross; all the humbly and simply narrated historical details of the Lord's death and resurrection: these are the base and foolish things, the weak and despised things (I Cor. 1 : 24, 25), in the crucifixion of the "Lord of glory" (I Cor. 2 : 8). But in these very things is the μυστήριον cloaked, and through the lowly visible symbolon we behold the glory that embraces the whole world. Justin the Philosopher once said that the heathen accuse us Christians of foolishness because we dare to set a crucified human being beside the creator of the universe, but that they speak in this way only because "they do not discern the mystery" inherent in this crucified human being.[4] And one of the oldest early Christian hymns, preserved in a fragment of Melito of Sardis, contains the lines:

2 Bornkamm, in Kittel, IV, p. 826.
3 With C. G. Jung, *Essays on* (or *Introduction to*) *a Science of Mythology* (New York, 1949; London, 1950), p. 256.
4 *Apologia*, I, 13 (J. C. T. von Otto, *Corpus apologetarum Christianorum*, Jena, 1876, Vol. I, p. 42).

371

The earth shook. . . the whole creation was amazed,
marveling and saying, "What new mystery, then, is this? . . .
The Invisible One is seen, and is not ashamed;
the Incomprehensible is laid hold upon, and is not indignant . . .
The Impassible suffereth, and doth not avenge;
the Immortal dieth, and answereth not a word. . . .
What new mystery is this?"[5]

In speaking of the "mystery of the Cross," we shall cautiously attempt to enter into the sublime thoughts of the early Christians who, at the sight of the despised, base, foolish Cross, beheld the radiance concealed in it, the δόξα that encompasses all the aeons, concentrating the Creation and God's whole work of salvation in its glittering focus. All the copious early Christian writings on the Cross can be summed up under two heads: (1) the Cross as cosmic mystery, and (2) the Cross as Biblical mystery.

I

The vision of the Christian mystic, illumined by faith, mounts upward from the Cross on which the Creator and Logos died to the starry firmament of Helios and Selene, penetrates the profoundest structure of the cosmos, the structure of the human body, and even the forms of the everyday things that serve him: and wherever he looks he sees the form of the Cross imprinted on all things. It is as though the Cross of his Lord had enchanted the whole world.

For him the form of the Cross is, first of all, the fundamental schema imprinted on the cosmos by God (who from the very beginning looked secretly toward the coming Cross of his Son); it is the structural law of the universe; in Christian eyes the two great celestial circles, the equator and ecliptic, which intersect one another in the form of a horizontal X, and around which the whole vault of the starry firmament moves in miraculous rhythm, are the celestial cross. Adapting an old Pythagorean notion, Plato had written in the Timaeus[6] of the world soul revealed in the celestial X; to the early Christian this was a pagan intimation of the world-building crucified Logos who encompasses the cosmos and causes it to revolve around the mystery of the Cross. Bousset has discussed this speculation on the Cross in his fine article on Plato's world soul and the Cross of Christ.[7]

5 Melito of Sardis, fr. 13 (Otto, IX, p. 419).
6 Timaeus, 36 BC. Cf. the commentary in Otto Apelt, Platons Dialoge Timaios und Kritias (Leipzig, 1922), pp. 159ff.
7 "Platons Weltseele und das Kreuz Christi," ZNW, XIV (1913), 273–85.

As early a writer as Justin related this passage in Plato to the Son of God, and although he suggests it only briefly, there can be no doubt that he was already familiar with the conception of the celestial X as a symbol foreshadowing the Cross.[8] Irenaeus incorporates the idea in his conception of the Cross as a recapitulation of all cosmic and Biblical history:

> So then by the obedience wherewith He obeyed *even unto death*, hanging on the tree, He put away the old disobedience which was wrought in the tree. Now seeing that He is the Word of God Almighty, who in unseen wise in our midst is universally extended in all the world, and encompasses its length and breadth and height and depth—for by the Word of God the whole universe is ordered and disposed—in it is crucified the Son of God, inscribed crosswise upon it all: for it is right that He, being made visible, should set upon all things visible the sharing of His Cross, that He might show His operation on visible things through a visible form. For He it is who illuminates the height that is the heavens; and encompasses the deep that is beneath the earth; and stretches and spreads out the length from east to west; and steers across the breadth of north and south; summoning all that are scattered in every quarter to the knowledge of the Father.[9]

This is one of the most classical of early Christian texts on the mystery of the Cross. The lowly sign of the cross is the epitome and manifestation of the whole cosmic process, for all things in nature are included in the drama of the world's redemption on the Cross, and in the four dimensions of the Cross the ancient Christian, by a bold extension of the words of St. Paul (Eph. 3 : 18), saw the four dimensions of the cosmos suggested as in a mystical symbol. The Cross is the "recapitulation" of the work of Creation, it is the epitome, the simple sign, the sensuous symbol of something vast and unknown—in short, it is a mystery. In his work against the Gnostics, Irenaeus summed this up briefly in the words:

> For the Creator of the world is truly the Word of God: and this is our Lord, who in the last times was made man, existing in this world, and who in an invisible manner contains all things created, and is inherent in the entire creation, since the Word of God governs and arranges all things; and therefore He came to His own in

8 *Apologia*, I, 60, 1 (Otto, I, p. 160).
9 *Epideixis*, I, 34, text transmitted only in Armenian (tr. J. Armitage Robinson, *The Demonstration of the Apostolic Preaching*, London, 1920, pp. 101–2).

a visible manner, and was made flesh, and hung upon the tree, that He might sum up all things in Himself.[10]

Through the whole of early Christian literature there runs a never-ending hymn to the cosmic mystery of the Cross and to the outstretched hands of the Logos who from the Cross embraces the whole world and gathers it home to the Father. So numerous are these wonderful hymns of praise[11] that there is not space here to quote even the most beautiful of them. Golgotha becomes the center of the cosmos, around which everything turns in a divine rhythm. "God has held out his arms to embrace the limits of the Oikoumene, and therefore this hill of Golgotha is the cardinal point of the world," said Cyril of Jerusalem to his candidates for baptism at the historic site of the crucifixion.[12] Gregory of Nyssa praised the Cross as the cosmic seal, impressed on the heavens and on the depths of the earth.[13] It was most of all among the Byzantines that the cosmic understanding of the mystery of the Cross endured. "O Cross, thou atonement of the cosmos," runs one of these panegyrics, "thou limit of the world, thou height of heaven, thou depth of earth, thou bond of creation, thou width of all that is visible, thou breadth of the Oikoumene."[14] But also for the Latin Christians of Rome and northern Africa, this was an old theological heritage. At the beginning of the third century (when the Syrian emperors were spreading the mystery religions throughout the West), Pseudo-Chrysostom lauds the cosmic mystery of the Cross in ecstatic words—which we shall recite at the end of this lecture.[15] Lactantius, the Christian Cicero, wrote: "And so God in his suffering stretched out His arms and embraced the earth, in order to intimate that from the rising to the setting sun a new people would gather beneath His wings."[16] In a famous chapter, Firmicus Maternus compared the symbolic bough of the ancient mysteries to the wood of the Cross, in which he beheld a cosmic mystery: "The sign of the cross holds together the heavenly mecha-

10 *Adversus haereses*, V, 18, 3 (W. W. Harvey edn., Cambridge, 1857, Vol. II, pp. 374f.; tr. A. Roberts and W. H. Rambaut, Ante-Nicene Christian Library, Edinburgh, 1869, pp. 105–6).
11 They are almost all collected in the three folio volumes of Jacob Gretser, *De sancta Cruce* (Regensburg, 1734). Cf. also Otto Zoeckler, *The Cross of Christ*, tr. M. J. Evans (London, 1877).
12 *Catechesis*, 13, 28 (*PG*, XXXIII, 805 B).
13 *Oratio I de resurrectione* (*PG*, XLVI, 621–25). *Catechesis magna* 32 (*PG*, XLV, 81 C).
14 Andrew of Crete, *In Exaltationem sanctae Crucis* (*PG*, XCVII, 1021 C).
15 Cf. also *De Antichristo*, 61 (*GCS*, I, 2, p. 42, li. 14–16).
16 *Divinae institutiones*, IV, 26, 36 (*CSEL*, XIX, p. 383, li. 7–11).

nism, strengthens the foundation of the earth, leads those who hold it in their hearts to life."[17] And such praises of the cosmic cross were sung by the Latin mystics until far into the Middle Ages.[18]

We are now in a position to understand certain ideas and images that enrich the cosmic mystery of the Cross. Since the Cross is the epitome of the structural law of the universe, it will shine in the heavens at the end of the earth's visible history to foreshadow the coming of the transfigured Christ. We may interpret in this sense a highly controversial passage in so early a work as the *Didache*.[19] At the end of days, "the signs of truth will appear: first the sign of extension [$\dot{\epsilon}\kappa\pi\epsilon\tau\dot{\alpha}\sigma\epsilon\omega\varsigma$] in the heavens, then the sign of the trumpet blast, and then the resurrection of the dead." This $\sigma\eta\mu\epsilon\hat{\iota}o\nu$ $\dot{\epsilon}\kappa\pi\epsilon\tau\dot{\alpha}\sigma\epsilon\omega\varsigma$ $\dot{\epsilon}\nu$ $o\dot{\upsilon}\rho\alpha\nu\hat{\omega}$ is the Cross, on which Christ has extended his arms that embrace the cosmos. And Ephraim the Syrian says in one of his sermons: "When Christ shall appear from the East, the Cross will go before him as a standard before the king."[20] And even today, in the Latin liturgy for the feast of the Exaltation of the Cross, the eschatological cosmic mystery is celebrated in the words "*Hoc signum crucis erit in caelo, cum Dominus ad iudicandum venerit.*" For the mystery of the Cross will be fully revealed only by the radiance that will dawn at the end of days. "*In te universa perficis mysteria,*" Leo the Great says of the Cross.[21] But the eschatological mystery of the transfigured Cross is already reflected in this temporal world; for in the festival of Exaltatio Crucis, the early Christians gave liturgical form to the mystical paradox of "joy in the Cross" and "victory in death." The content of this festival is the anticipated rejoicing at the final triumph of the Cross[22]—and in this it has remained genuinely Greek down to our own day. "*Car tout* $\mu\upsilon\sigma\tau\dot{\eta}\rho\iota o\nu$ *pour le Grec*

---

17 *De errore profanarum religionum*, 27 (*CSEL*, II, p. 121, li. 6–8).
18 Under the influence of St. Augustine, who often speaks of the cosmic dimensions of the Cross (*Tract. 19 in Evang. S. Joannis*, *PL*, XXXV, 1949ff.; *Sermo* 54, *PL*, XXXVIII, 371ff.; *Sermo* 165, Ibid., 903ff.). Cf. Richard of St. Victor (*PL*, CXCVI, 524ff.); Honorius of Autun, *Speculum ecclesiae* (*PL*, CLXXII, 946); Thiofrid of Echternach, *Flores epitaphii sanctorum* (*PL*, CLVII, 385ff.).
19 *Didache*, 16, 6 (F. X. Funk, *Opera patrum apostolicum*, Tübingen, 1881, Vol. I, p. 36, li. 12).
20 T. J. Lamy, *S. Ephraem Syri Hymni et Sermones*, Vol. II (Mechlin, 1886), col. 407, li. 3–6. Cyril of Jerusalem, *Catechesis*, 13, 41 (*PG*, XXXIII, 821 A): "The Cross will come again from heaven with Jesus, for the *tropaion* will go before the *basileus*." Cf. also Wilhelm Bousset, *The Antichrist Legend*, tr. A. H. Keane (London, 1896), pp. 233ff.
21 *Sermo* 59, 7 (*PL*, LIV, 341 C).
22 Cf. Odo Casel, *Das christliche Festmysterium* (Paderborn, 1941), pp. 102–8, 206–14.

c'est l'éternité dans le temps," writes a discerning Russian author.[23] The
mystery of the Cross shines resplendent—and through the Byzantine and
the Roman liturgies for the Exaltation of the Cross runs a note recalling the
verses of the Christian sibyl:

> O blessed wood on which God was crucified,
> the earth will not retain thee,
> no, thou wilt see the house of heaven,
> when thy fiery eye will gleam, O God [24]

The beginning and the end of the world come together in the Cross;
and accordingly the mystery of the Cross is reflected in all the things and
proportions of this earthly phenomenal world. In the apocryphal Acts of
Andrew, the apostle, on his way to the Cross, utters these sublime words in
praise of the cosmic mystery hidden behind the symbol of the Cross:

> I know thy mystery, for the which thou art set up; for thou art
> planted in the world to establish the things that are unstable . . .
> and another part of thee is spread out to the right hand and the
> left that it may put to flight the envious and adverse power of the
> evil one, and gather into one the things that are scattered abroad
> (*or,* the world): And another part of thee is planted in the earth,
> and securely set in the depth, that thou mayest join the things
> that are in the earth and that are under the earth unto the heavenly
> things. O Cross, device of the salvation of the Most High! O Cross,
> trophy of the victory [of Christ] over the enemies! O Cross, planted
> upon the earth and having thy fruit in the heavens! O name of the
> Cross, filled with all things! Well done, O Cross, that hast bound
> down the mobility of the world (*or,* the circumference)! Well done,
> O shape of understanding that hast shaped the shapeless (earth?)![25]

In the so-called *Actus Vercellenses,* dealing with the martyrdom of the
apostle Peter, and showing considerable Gnostic influence, the cosmic mystery of the Cross is related to the manner of the crucified apostle's death:
the apostle is nailed head downward to the Cross, and therein the narrator
sees a symbol of the first man's fall into sin, which to the Gnostics meant
corporeal existence. Here Platonic conceptions are mingled with the myths
of the original man known to us from *Poimandres* and Hippolytus' Sermon
to the Naassenes;[26] but there is also a suggestion of the Christian doctrine of

23 M. Lot-Borodine, "La Grâce déifiante des sacrements d'après Nicolas Cabasilas,"
Revue des sciences philosophiques et théologiques (Paris), XXV (1936), 315.
24 *Oracula sibyllina,* VI, 26–28 (*GCS,* p. 132).
25 *Martyrium Andreae,* 19 (tr. M. R. James, *The Apocryphal New Testament,* Oxford,
1924, p. 359).   26 Cf. Reitzenstein, *Poimandres,* pp. 242ff.

Adam's original sin that is atoned for on the Cross—for in the mystery of the Cross man is halted in his fall and begins to move heavenward. As he hangs on the Cross the apostle prays:

> O name of the Cross, thou hidden mystery! O grace ineffable that is pronounced in the name of the Cross! O nature of man, that cannot be separated from God! . . . Learn ye the mystery of all nature, and the beginning of all things, what it was. For the first man, whose race I bear in mine appearance (*or*, of the race of whom I bear the likeness), fell (was borne) head downwards.[27]

For the whole cosmos the Cross is the "μηχανή" (as Ignatius of Antioch once called it[28]) of the return to heaven, and its mystical sign can be seen in the whole cosmos. This seeking and listing of symbols of the Cross in inanimate nature, in man, and even in the implements of daily life is typical of the earliest Christian symbolism; we can understand it only if we understand the fundamental conception of the mystery of the Cross. The Cross is everywhere: in the figure of the human body when a man holds out his arms in prayer; in the flight of birds; in agricultural implements; in the masts of ships, crossed by their yards. All things are implicitly a μυστήριον τοῦ σταυροῦ. As early as the second century, Justin reveals this symbolism in its finished form.

> Reflect on all things in the universe [and consider] whether they could be governed or held together in fellowship without this figure [the cross]. For the sea cannot be traversed unless the sign of victory, which is called a sail, remain fast in the ship; the land is not plowed without it; similarly diggers and mechanics do not do their work except with tools of this form. The human figure differs from the irrational animals precisely in this, that man stands erect and can stretch out his hands. . . . Even your own symbols display the power of this figure—on the standards and trophies, with which you [heathen] make all your solemn processions.[29]

Similar passages in Tertullian[30] and in Minucius Felix[31] show how prevalent this symbolism was in the early Church. And, as late as the fifth century

27 *Actus Vercellenses*, 37, 38 (tr. James, p. 334).
28 *Epistle to the Ephesians*, 9, 1 (Funk, p. 220, li. 12). [In *The Apostolic Fathers*, tr. Kirsopp Lake, Vol. I (London and New York, 1914), pp. 182–83, translated "engine."—ED.]
29 *Apologia*, I, 55 (tr. E. R. Hardy, Library of Christian Classics, Vol. I, ed. C. C. Richardson and others, London and New York, 1953, p. 278).
30 *Apologeticum*, 16, 6–8 (*CSEL*, LXIX, pp. 42ff.).
31 *Octavius*, 29, 6, 7 (*CSEL*, II, p. 43).

(to pass over a vast number of documents that we have discussed more thoroughly in another connection), Maximus of Turin preached to his flock:

> Magnificent is this mystery of the Cross! For in this sign the whole earth is saved. A symbol of this mystery is the sail that hangs on the mast of the ship as though it were Christ raised on the Cross. And when the good countryman prepares to plow the soil of his field: see, he too can accomplish his task only with the figure of the Cross. Even the vault of heaven is shaped in the form of the Cross. And man, when he walks along, when he raises his arms: he describes a Cross, and for this reason we should pray with outstretched arms, in order that we ourselves with the posture of our limbs may imitate the suffering of our Lord.[32]

The vision and thought and prayer of the ancient Christian were wholly imbued with this beloved mystery of the Cross, and this is essential for understanding of early Christian art and its symbols. The seemingly awkward simplicity of the painted and scribbled crosses in the catacombs, the simple posture of prayer: these are a mystery precisely because they are so simple. Ancient man retained a strong feeling of the almost dialectical antithesis between the pitifully small symbol of a design or a gesture and the stupendous content hidden in it, a feeling for this "mystery tension," as it were. The mystery of the Cross demands a choice of symbols in which this tension is perceptible. The Cross is that paltry bit of wood to which men trust their souls (cf. Wisdom 14 : 5), it is the frail ship that alone carries men over the wild sea, the tiny wooden rudder that guides the whole ship—"saving the cosmos with pitiful wood," says Gregory of Nazianzus.[33] Gregory of Nyssa,[34] with his truly Greek feeling for the divine paradoxes inherent in the mystery of salvation, expresses the same fundamental idea when he says that the miracle of it is that such a mystery should have been enacted in "the infinitesimal time" of three days. For the mystery of the Cross is God's great wisdom, discernible in the foolish little symbol.

And this finally is the profoundest reason why the mystery of the Cross triumphed over all the pagan mysteries. We have noted the chapter in which Firmicus Maternus contrasts the Cross with the cult symbols of the mysteries. "The life of man should be fastened to the Cross and thus woven

32 *Homilia* 50: *De cruce Domini* (*PL*, LVII, 341ff.).
33 *Oratio* 4, 18 (*PG*, XXXV, 545 C). *Oratio* 43, 70 (*PG*, XXXVI, 592 B).
34 *Catechesis magna*, 36 (*PG*, XLV, 92 D).

into the texture of eternal immortality."[35] And this is accomplished by the *mysterium crucis*. An unknown Greek of the fourth century compares the Cross to Helios, who in the late period was the supreme god of all the mysteries. But now, the writer exults, Helios has been conquered by the Cross, "and man whom the created sun in heaven could not enlighten, behold, now he is enlightened by the sunlight of the Cross and illumined [in baptism]." And then the speaker bursts into sublime praise of the mystery of the Cross:

> O this truly divine wisdom! O Cross, thou celestial lever [μηχανὴ οὐράνιος]! The Cross was implanted, and behold, idolatry was destroyed. It is no common wood, but the wood that served God for his victory. Wood and lance and nails and death: these are the cradle of eternal life, here the second man was born. O paradoxical wonder![36]

It is no longer the mourning for the dead Adonis or rejoicing for the rising of Venus' lover that fills the cities—as Origen[37] and Cyril of Alexandria[38] tell us—but the lamentation of the Cross and the Easter rejoicing of the new mystery. "In the single sign of the Cross the magic spells of the Cabiri came to an end, and, by the force of this humble, simple word that passed over the whole earth, men came to despise death and began to think immortal thoughts," says Athanasius.[39] Christ crucified is the "true Orpheus," who carried home mankind as his bride from the depths of dark Hades—the "'Ορφεὺς βακχικός," as he is called in a famous early Christian representation of the Crucifixion.[40] And the Middle Ages retain a last echo of this notion in a hymn to the mystery of the Cross:

> As of old the serpent brazen
> Unto Israel brought salvation
>   Lest in Pharaoh's bonds they die,
> So his bride our Orpheus raises
> From the nether deep, and places
>   In his royal seat on high.[41]

35 *De errore prof. rel.*, 27, 1 (*CSEL*, II, p. 120, li. 12ff.).
36 Pseudo-Athanasius, *De passione Domini* (*PG*, XXVIII, 1056 B).
37 *Selecta in Ezechielem* (*PG*, XIII, 800 A).
38 *Commentarium in Isaiam* II. iii (*PG*, LXX, 441 B).
39 *Oratio de incarnatione Verbi*, 47 (*PG*, XXV, 180ff.), here somewhat condensed.
40 Cf. Fernand Cabrol and Henri Leclercq, eds., *Dictionnaire d'archéologie chrétienne*, Vol. XII (Paris, 1936), cols. 2735–55; its reproduction of the Orpheus Cross, fig. 9249. Also cf. Boulanger, *Orphée: Rapports de l'orphisme et du christianisme*, p. 7. [In the inscription, actually "ΟΡΦΕΟC ΒΑΚΚΙΚΟC."—ED.]
41 Tr. A. S. B. Glover from: "Israelem in Aegypto/Pharaone circumscripto/Serpens salvat

II

This cosmic mystery of the Cross reveals the whole essence of the early Christian conception of mystery: the Cross is a mystery because it expresses all the basic laws of cosmic events—but in a form so simple as to be almost contemptible. The mystery resides in this paradox, in this astounding contradiction between what is said and what is meant, between the visible and invisible.

The Cross is at the same time the center of the story of salvation, the climax of the drama of revelation played by God for the salvation of man. This "vain mystery of the Cross, full of every shame" (as an early Christian put it[42]), is also a Biblical mystery, because in it are expressed all the fundamental laws of God's hidden will to salvation.

It is one of the fundamental doctrines of the early Christian symbol theology that everything that God revealed in the Old Testament, from the "tree of life" (Gen. 2 : 9) up to His own personified wisdom in whom this tree of life is embodied (Prov. 3 : 18), was uttered only with a view to the future act of salvation in which this incarnate Wisdom would be crucified. The entire Old Testament is seen as one vast parable in which the future is veiled but at the same time revealed to those gifted with insight. The old covenant contains the "mystery of the Logos."[43] According to Justin,[44] it contains the "mystery of the Cross," and in his dialogue with the Jew Trypho we can see how subtle a form this theology of the Biblical mystery of the Cross had assumed as early as the first part of the second century. And in the so-called *Epistle of Barnabas* a special chapter, almost artificial in its interpretations, is devoted to citing all the Old Testament prototypes of the Cross.[45] Today we may smile at this childish exegesis in which the first traces of the Alexandrian school are discernible. But the fundamental doctrine from which it emanates is the Pauline theology: "Now all these things happened to them in figure: and they are written for our correction, upon whom the ends of the world are come" (I Cor. 10 : 11). The early

---

aeneus./Sponsam suam ab inferno/Regno locans in superno/Noster traxit Orpheus."—
Unknown author (12th cent.) of the Easter sequence "Morte Christi celebrata." Text in A. Mai, *Nova patrum bibliotheca*, Vol. I, 2 (Rome, 1852), p. 208.
42 Justin, *Dialogue*, 131 (Otto, Vol. II, p. 466).
43 Hippolytus, *De Antichristo*, 2 (*GCS*, I, pt. 2, p. 4, li. 17).
44 *Dialogue*, 91 (Otto, II, p. 330).
45 *Epistola Barnabae*, 12 (Lake, *Apostolic Fathers*, Vol. I, pp. 383ff.).

Christian's mystic belief in the significance of the Cross was so profound that it elucidated the Old Testament and the cosmos alike as by a stroke of magic: the veil of the temple was rent, and the mystery of God revealed—only to cover itself once more with the bloody veil of the Crucifixion, which will be raised only when the end of days is at hand. Biblical exegesis became an enthralling mystery drama. St. Augustine felt this with all the genius of his Christian and classical soul. "In order that everything that was cloaked in the Old Testament might be revealed in the mystery of the Cross: for that was the veil of the temple rent," he once wrote.[46] And Tertullian expressed the same thought in more dialectical terms:

> Yes, in the old revelation this mystery of the Cross had to be cloaked in images. For if it had been divulged naked and without images, the outrage would have been even greater. And the more grandiose this mystery of the Cross was to become, the more it had to remain in the shadow of images, in order that the difficulty of understanding should forever impel men to seek the grace of God.[47]

Within the space at my disposal, I can give scarcely an intimation of the wealth of profound dogma, of lyrical and fascinating ideas and images, that this mystery of the Cross opened up to the early Christians. Every mention of wood in the Old Testament became for the New Testament mystes an ὑπόδειγμα (Hebr. 9 : 23); in it he saw the "power that God put into the mystery of the Cross":[48] the wood of Noah's ark, Moses' wooden staff with its power to give water, the wooden scaffolding on which the brass serpent hung, the tree planted beside the flowing brook. I have elsewhere[49] shown in greater detail the development of this "mystery of the wood" from the image of Noah's ark, and any one of these symbols of the Cross might form the subject of a similar study, which could not but prove significant both for the history of mysticism and the history of art—for scholarship has not penetrated deeply enough into this early Christian feeling for mystery, which remained alive in Romanesque and Gothic art. But we must limit ourselves, so I shall speak of only one of these Old Testament images considered in the light of the Cross: the Latin writers called it *sacramentum*

---

46 *Sermo* 300, 4 (*PL*, XXXVIII, 1378 D).
47 *Adversus Marcionem*, III, 18 (*CSEL*, XLVII, p. 406, li. 7–11).
48 Justin, *Dialogue*, 91, 1 (Otto, II, p. 330).
49 My "Das Schiff aus Holz," *ZKT*, LXVII (1943), 1–21.

ligni vitae, the Greek μυστήριον τοῦ ξύλου. It is the wood of the tree of life in paradise, interpreted as the cross of Christ.[50]

For the Jewish prophets the tree of life in the center of paradise watered by the four rivers (Gen. 2 : 9–10) was already a symbol of Messianic salvation (cf. Ezech. 47 : 12),[51] indeed, this tree was God's wisdom itself (Prov. 3 : 18). In the same image, the author of the New Testament Apocalypse saw the fulfillment of redemption (2 : 7; 22 : 2). But here a decisive new element is added: only those who have washed their raiment in the blood of the Lamb have "right to the tree of life" (Apoc. 22 : 14). Between the tree of life in paradise and the tree of life in the heaven to come, the early Christian beheld a tree of life on which the fate of the race of Adam was decided: the Cross. And with his feeling for mystery, he saw these trees as in a single image. The tree of paradise is only a prefiguration of the Cross, and the Cross is the center of the world and of the human drama of salvation. It rises from Golgotha to heaven, embracing the cosmos, it is erected in the same place where Adam was once created, where he lies buried, where at the same day and hour the second Adam was to die. And round it surge the four rivers of paradise, the mystery of baptism, through which the descendants of Adam gain a new right to the eternally flowering tree of life.[52] An early Christian poem of the third century begins with the words:

> There is a spot that we believe the whole world's midpoint:
> The Jews in their mother tongue call it Golgotha.[53]

It goes on to describe how this tree of life grows up to fabulous heights, spreads forth its arms to encompass the earth: how at its foot the baptismal spring issues from the earth and all the peoples hasten to it to drink of immortality. The final verse runs:

50 Cf. Ferdinand Piper, *Der Baum des Lebens* (Berlin, 1863); August Wünsche, "Die Sagen vom Lebensbaum und Lebenswasser: Altorientalische Mythen," in H. Winckler, *Ex Oriente Lux*, I, 2 (Leipzig, 1905); F. Kampers, *Mittelalterliche Sagen vom Paradiese und vom Holze des Kreuzes Christi* (Cologne, 1897); Ludwig von Sybel, "ξύλον ζωῆς," *ZNT*, XIX (1920), 85–91; XX (1921), 93ff.; R. Bauerreiss, *Arbor Vitae: Der Lebensbaum und seine Verwendung in Liturgie, Kunst und Brauchtum des Abendlandes* (Munich, 1938).

51 Cf. also Book of Enoch 24 : 3–6; 25 : 1–7 (R. H. Charles, ed., *Apocrypha and Pseudepigrapha of the Old Testament*, Vol. II, Oxford, 1913, p. 204).

52 Cf. R. E. Schlee, *Ikonographie der Paradiesesflüsse* (Leipzig, 1937); W. von Reybekiel, "Der Fons Vitae in der christlichen Kunst," *Niederdeutsche Zeitschrift für Volkskunde* (Hamburg), XII (1934), 87–136.

53 Pseudo-Cyprian, *Carmen de Pascha vel de ligno vitae* (*CSEL*, III, pt. 3, pp. 305–8).

382

By the branches of that lofty tree is the road to heaven.
It is the tree of life to all believers. Amen.

This is the early Christian mystery of the "Cross in the spring of water"—
and who is not reminded of the wonderful mosaics with which the early
Christians of Rome decorated their baptisteries?[54] There is an old Hebrew
tradition that associates the tree of paradise and the creation of Adam with
Messianic salvation. To this tradition the Christians gave their own interpretation, which is most clearly expressed in the so-called *Syrian Cave of
Treasures*, a work emanating from the circle of Ephraim the Syrian.[55] It
tells how from the four elements God made the first man, a glorious, sunlike
creature:

> God formed Adam with His holy hands, in His own Image and
> Likeness, and when the angels saw Adam's glorious appearance
> they were greatly moved by the beauty thereof. For they saw the
> image of his face burning with glorious splendor like the orb of the
> sun, and the light of his eyes was like the light of the sun, and the
> image of his body was like unto the sparkling of crystal. And when
> he rose at full length and stood upright in the center of the earth,
> he planted his two feet on that spot whereon was set up the Cross
> of our Redeemer.[56]

This was at the foot of the tree of life, which stood in the midst of paradise.
And a little later it is expressly stated:

> That Tree of Life which was in the midst of Paradise prefigured
> the Redeeming Cross, which is the veritable Tree of Life, and this
> it was that was fixed in the middle of the earth.[57]

The same prefiguring mystery is found in the death of Adam, who through
sin has lost his solar nature, to regain it again only through the death of the
coming Saviour:

> And the departure of Adam from this world took place . . . on the
> fourteenth day of the moon, on the sixth day of the month of Nisan
> [April], at the ninth hour, on the day of the Eve of the Sabbath
> [i.e., Friday]. At the same hour in which the Son of Man delivered
> up his soul to His Father on the Cross did our father Adam deliver
> up his soul to Him that fashioned him.[58]

54 Josef Wilpert, *Die römischen Mosaiken und Malereien*, Text Vol. I (Freiburg i. B.,
1916), pp. 193, 223, 227.
55 *The Book of the Cave of Treasures*, tr. E. A. Wallis Budge (London, 1927).
56 Ibid., pp. 52–53.   57 Ibid., p. 63.   58 Ibid., p. 73.

Here, to be sure, we find ourselves in the realm of poetic fantasy. But the foundation of all these legends of the tree of life, often full of a delightful poetry, is the theological mystery of the Cross; and what can one understand of ancient or medieval Christian art without a knowledge of this ancient symbolism? In the Ethiopic version of the so-called *Book of Adam and Eve*,[59] the connection between Adam and the Cross is made even clearer. The dying Adam commands his son Seth to bury him in the earth after the flood.

> For the place where my body shall be laid is the middle of the earth, and God shall come from thence and shall save our kindred.[60]

And, after the flood, when the coffin is carried out of the ark, Adam's voice is heard:

> Upon the land whither we are going shall the Word of God come down, and suffer and be crucified on the place in which my body is laid. My skull shall be baptized with His blood. . . .[61]

The representation of Adam's skull at the foot of the Cross is familiar to us all from medieval art, and now we know the early Christian sources of this powerful symbol. Indeed, the *sacramentum ligni* gave rise to a thousand images and phrases whose meaning evades us, because we have lost the ancient Christian understanding for the mystery of the Cross.

Here we must mention a wonderful legend cycle based on the tree of life: On his deathbed Adam sent his son Seth to paradise to bring him the fruit of immortality from the tree of life. But the angel who guarded paradise gave him only three seeds, and from them sprang the threefold tree, of cedar, pine, and cypress, growing out of the dead Adam's mouth. The story of this tree and its wood is then pursued throughout the Old Testament, and finally the soldiers make Christ's cross from it. These legends were elaborated throughout the Middle Ages—and they are nothing other than popular, naïve images of what we know as the early Christian mystery of the Cross.[62] In the background of all these myths stands the theological

59 German text of the Ethiopic version in Ernst Trumpp, *Der Kampf Adams oder das christliche Adambuch des Morgenlandes* (Abhandlung der bayrischen Akademie der Wissenschaften. Philos.-philolog. Klasse, XV, 3, 1880); excerpts in Kampers, *Mittelalterliche Sagen*, pp. 16–25. Cf. also Piper, "Adams Grab auf Golgotha," *Evangelisches Jahrbuch* (Berlin), 1861, 17ff.
60 *The Book of Adam and Eve*, tr. S. C. Malan (London and Edinburgh, 1882), p. 115.
61 Ibid., p. 169 (modified).
62 Cf. also A. Mussafia, *Sulla legenda del legno della Croce* (Sitzungsbericht der Wiener Akademie der Wissenschaften, 1869), pp. 165–216; and my "Das Schiff aus Holz," 10ff.

conviction of the profound bond between Adam and Christ, between the earthly and the pneumatic man (cf. I Cor. 15 : 45–49). Beginning with the earliest Christian theology, this clearly defined dogma, this classical antithesis between the tree of paradise and the wood of the Cross, runs parallel to the stream of images and legends. It is a primary heritage of Christian theology. As early a writer as Irenaeus speaks of it as a tradition transmitted by the presbyters of Asia Minor:

> For as we lost [the Logos] by means of a tree, by means of a tree again was it made manifest to all, showing the height, the length, the breadth, the depth in itself, and as a certain man among our predecessors observed, "through the extension of the hands of a divine person, gathering together the two peoples to one God."[63]

The two nations are the Jews and the Greeks, who are made one through the wood of the Cross (cf. Eph. 2 : 13–14). The cosmos of the Greeks and the Bible of the Hebrews converge in the mystery of the Cross. Ephraim the Syrian therefore declared: "The Lord of all men fulfilled three mysteries in his crucifixion ... and he embraced two worlds when he embraced his cross."[64] Consequently, the Greek and Byzantine theologians gave profound thought to this conception and devoted eloquent panegyrics to the life-giving wood of the Cross. Consider, for example, the dogma of the tree of life in Gregory of Nyssa[65] or the hymn to the Biblical mystery of the Cross by the Byzantine Theophanes Kerameus.[66] And in a Good Friday sermon, an unknown Greek celebrated this day as the fulfillment and reiteration of the original creation of Adam:

> Today, on the sixth day of the week, Adam was formed; today he received his form and his godlike nature; today he, the microcosm, was placed in the macrocosm. O what a day of vicissitudes! O sad and grievous day! O thou morning [of Creation] that barest sorrow, O thou evening [the death on the Cross] that gavest us joy![67]

The thought expressed in this hymn became theological dogma for all time in the clear formulation of John of Damascus.[68]

63 *Adversus haereses*, V, 17, 4 (Harvey, Vol. II, p. 372).
64 *Sermo 6 in Hebdomadam Sanctam*, 17 (Lamy, Vol. I, col. 502).
65 *Oratio 4 in resurrectionem Domini* (*PG*, XLVI, 684 AB).
66 *Homilia 4 in exaltationem Crucis* (*PG*, CXXXII, 183–204).
67 Pseudo-Chrysostom, *In magnam Parasceve* (*PG*, L, 812).
68 *De fide orthodoxa*, IV, 11 (*PG*, XCIV, 1132f.).

In the West, the mystery of the Cross developed along similar lines. St. Augustine gave it philosophical form and enriched it with the beauty of his dialectical style. The *sacramentum ligni* was one of his profoundest ideas.[69] And his spiritual heirs fed on it: it is echoed in the Roman liturgy and the hymns of Venantius Fortunatus. *"Per arborem mortui, per arborem vivificati,"* preached a post-Augustinian, and exclaimed, *"O sacramentorum immane mysterium!"*[70]—astounding, superhuman mystery! In this connection, Thomas Aquinas merely continues in the spirit of St. Augustine,[71] and without these conceptions implicit in the early Christian mystery of the Cross we can understand neither Dante's *Purgatorio* (XXIII, 73–75) nor the sublime dialogue with "Old Father Adam" in the *Paradiso* (XXVI). The charming Salzburg miniature of Berthold Furtmayr[72] (done in the year 1481) may be regarded as the last word on this mystery of the tree of life: Eve in her disgraced nakedness deals out the death-giving fruit from the tree of paradise, but on the same tree hangs Christ crucified, and from him the Ecclesia breaks off the *pharmakon* of immortality.

At the beginning of the third century, Pseudo-Chrysostom sang a wonderful paean of praise to the cosmic and Biblical mystery of the Cross in an Easter sermon. We shall conclude our remarks on the Mystery of the Cross with his words:

> This tree as broad as the heavens has grown up from earth to heaven. Immortal tree, it extends from heaven to earth. It is the fixed pivot of the universe, the fulcrum of all things, the foundation of the world, the cardinal point of the cosmos. It binds together all the multiplicity of human nature. It is held together by invisible nails of the spirit in order to retain its bond with the godhead. It touches the highest summits of heaven and with its feet holds fast the earth, and it encompasses the vast middle atmosphere in between with its immeasurable arms.
>
> O crucified one, thou leader of the mystical dance! O spiritual marriage feast! O divine Pascha, passing from the heavens to the earth and rising again to the heavens! O new feast of all things, O cosmic festive gathering, O joy of the universe, O honor, O joy,

---

69 *De Genesi ad litteram VIII*, 4, 5 (*PL*, XXXIV, 375ff.); *De Genesi contra Manichaeos*, II, 22 (*PL*, XXXIV, 213ff.); *De catechizandis rudibus*, 20 (*PL*, XL, 335ff.).
70 Pseudo-Augustine, *Sermo de Adam et Eva et Sancta Maria* (A. Mai, Nova Patrum Bibliotheca, I, 1, Rome, 1852, p. 3).
71 *Summa theologica*, III, q. 46, a. 4.
72 Color reproduction in G. Leidinger, *Meisterwerke der Buchmalerei aus Handschriften der bayrischen Staatsbibliothek München* (Munich, 1921), pl. 38.

O delight, through which dark death is destroyed, life is given to the universe, the gates of heaven are opened! God appeared as man, and man rose up as God, for he shattered the gates of hell and burst the brass bolts asunder. And the people which was in the depths arises from the dead and proclaims to the hosts above: the chorus of the earth returns![73]

3. The Mystery of Baptism

Felix sacramentum aquae nostrae.

"Blessed mystery of our water": with those words Tertullian begins his work on baptism.[1] And almost a century earlier the author of the *Epistle of Barnabas* sang: "Blessed are those who hoped on the Cross and descended into the water."[2] The mystery of baptism can only be understood in connection with the mystery of the Cross—the water of life springs up at the foot of the tree of life. For only through the redeeming power of God's death on the Cross has the water gained the power to give life. God died "that by himself submitting [*or*, by his suffering] he might purify the water," said Ignatius of Antioch.[3] This bond between the two mysteries is already found in the theology of St. Paul: "Know you not that all we who are baptized in Christ Jesus are baptized in his death? For we are buried together with him by baptism into death: that, as Christ is risen from the dead by the glory of the Father, so we also may walk in newness of life." (Rom. 6 : 3–4.) Thus the baptismal bath works in two ways. It redeems from sins, and it bestows a new, Christlike life—both solely through the efficacy of Christ's death on the Cross.

Thus baptism is the fundamental mystery of Christianity, the true initiation into participation in the divine life of the dead and resurrected Christ: later it was actually called the μυστήριον τῆς τελειώσεως.[4] It is no wonder that the comparative religionists should have dealt extensively with this

---

73 *De Pascha Homilia* 6 (*PG*, LIX, 743–46). [Rendered from a German tr. in Henri de Lubac, *Katholizismus als Gemeinschaft* (Einsiedeln, 1943), pp. 420–24. Cf. the English edn., *Catholicism, a Study of Dogma*, London, 1950, pp. 282f., where the passage differs somewhat.—ED.]
1 *De baptismo*, 1 (*CSEL*, XX, p. 201, li. 3).
2 *Epistola Barnabae*, 11, 8 (tr. Lake, Vol. I, p. 381).
3 *Epistle to the Ephesians*, 18, 2 (tr. Lake, p. 193).
4 Gregory of Nazianzus, *Oratio* 40, 28 (*PG*, XXXVI, 400 B).

particular mystery.[5] For they believed that they could show how the "syncretistic mystery of baptism"[6] resulted from the grafting of Hellenistic hopes of deification on the original lustral rite taken over by the Christians from Judaism. This seemed all the more easily done since considerable material regarding the lustral rites of the ancient mysteries was available. We know of an ablution in the ritual of Eleusis; the laurel-wreath oration of Demosthenes speaks of purificatory ablutions in the mystery of Sabazius; the cult of Attis had its taurobolium, and the mystery of Isis knew a sanctifying baptismal bath, as did the mysteries of Dionysus and of Mithras.[7] Upon mature consideration modern scholarship has rejected the idea that such rites exerted an influence on the baptismal doctrine of the New Testament, more especially of the Epistle to the Romans. But this does not prevent the comparative religionists from putting forward the thesis that beginning in the second century the sacrament of baptism underwent a process of Hellenization, and that this "old Catholic" mystery had lost all connection with the message proclaimed by Jesus and correctly understood by St. Paul. This attempt is always based on the ineradicable notion that sacramentalism contains a "magical element." Even Oepke, who elsewhere distinguishes so aptly between Christian baptism and the "purely ritual, magical-natural, and not at all ethical purification and renewal" of the Hellenistic baptismal usages, succumbs to the unwarranted idea that an exaggerated sacramentalism colored by magic had become grafted on the Pauline theology under the influence—it goes without saying—of the mystery religions that had taken possession of Christianity. It would exceed the scope of these lectures to confute all this on the basis of the sources; the task has in large part been performed by other scholars. We wish only to make two points: first, as we have shown in our first two lectures, a distinction must be made between

5 Cf. Paul Gennrich, *Die Lehre von der Wiedergeburt, die christliche Zentrallehre in dogmengeschichtlicher und religionsgeschichtlicher Beleuchtung* (Berlin, 1907); Richard Perdelwitz, *Die Mysterienreligion und das Problem des ersten Petrusbriefs* (Giessen, 1911); Johann Leipoldt, *Die urchristliche Taufe im Licht der Religionsgeschichte* (Leipzig, 1928); Richard Reitzenstein, *Die Vorgeschichte der christlichen Taufe* (Berlin and Leipzig, 1929). Critical studies: Joseph Dey, Παλιγγενεσία: *Ein Beitrag zur Klärung der religionsgeschichtlichen Bedeutung von Titus 3, 5* (Münster, 1937); Karl Prümm, *Der christliche Glaube und die altheidnische Welt*, Vol. II, pp. 273ff.: "Paulinische Tauflehre und Christusmystik in ihrem Verhältnis zum hellenistischen Mysterienkult."
6 Albrecht Oepke, in Kittel, I, pp. 541–43: "Die Taufe als synkretistisches Mysterium."
7 Cf. Johann Steinbeck, "Kultische Waschungen und Bäder im Heidentum und Judentum und ihr Verhältnis zur christlichen Taufe," *Neue kirchliche Zeitschrift* (Erlangen), XXI (1910), 778ff. For a complete bibliography, see Oepke, in Kittel, I, pp. 528–33.

the essence of the Christian mystery, which remained Christian, and the mystery terminology that gradually grew up around it; Christians never lost their basic conviction that the efficacy of the sacrament as established by Christ himself—here the simple bath of water and the simple words that went with it (Matt. 28 : 19)—proceeded from Christ crucified and resurrected, from the free, personal will of the God-man, so that "magical efficacy" is out of the question—provided we use "magic" in the sense normally accepted by students of religious psychology.[8] The rites and images and words that in the course of time clustered round this sacramental core, i.e., "exorcism and unction, the rituals of consecration and investiture, the burning of candles," are another matter. They are not, indeed, "remnants of the mystery religions,"[9] but, as we have suggested above, they may be examined for a substratum in common with the mysteries.

All this by way of theoretical clarification of the concept "mystery of baptism." In the following we shall cite a few of the most precious fragments from the treasure house of this ancient Christian mystery. We shall see that the mystery of baptism underwent a process of organic growth extending over the first four centuries of our era; and yet in its almost confusing richness, it remained and must remain forever the simple symbol of water and word (Eph. 5 : 26) that takes its life-giving power from the death of Christ. This is the basic concept from which the sacrament grew; this, in a manner of speaking, is the soul, which enabled the early Christian mind to fashion the mystery of baptism not only from the cosmic and Biblical mystery of the Cross, but also from what was purest and most profound in the thoughts and words of the mysteries. That the Christian mystery in all its fullness could develop from the simple baptismal rite of the New Testament lies in the nature of the rite itself—for was not this humble, trivial action of water and word a symbol appointed by Christ himself for the most stupendous meaning? At this point the ancient sense of the mystery took hold, the ancient feeling for the symbolic tension between what is said and what is meant, between the simplicity of the visible and the might of the invisible. Tertullian states this admirably in his treatise on baptism, where he contrasts the two polarities: *"simplicitas divinorum operum quae in actu videtur et magnificentia quae in effectu promittitur."*[10] "Simple but mag-

---

8 Cf. Prümm, *Christlicher Glaube*, Vol. II, pp. 270ff.: "Christliche Taufe und Zauber-handlung."   9 Oepke, in Kittel, I, p. 542, li. 15–17.
10 *De baptismo*, 2 (*CSEL*, XX, p. 201, li. 20ff.).

nificent"—this is indeed an apt formula for the essence of mystery. And if in the course of four centuries the Church surrounded the simple core of baptism with a rich mystery ritual, this was merely an attempt to make humanly visible the divine magnificence suggested and effected by the simple original symbol. Gregory of Nyssa gives expression to the same sense of mystery when he says that baptism is "a trifling thing, and yet the foundation of great riches."[11] In the Gallican liturgy[12] the baptistery is called "a modest place but full of grace," and in his poem to the baptismal church, St. Ambrose set down words that express his wonder at the paradoxical contrast between the "infinitesimal point" of the visible and the invisible divine efficacy that bursts from it—words that capture the essence of the mystery of baptism:

> For what can be more sublime
> Than that the guilt of the people should be annulled in so mean a place?[13]

Here I shall mention certain aspects of the early Christian mystery of baptism, which may give us an idea of how it follows from the mystery of the Cross, and how the materials for the building of this most fundamental mystery flowed in upon the early Christian from all sides.

Baptism is first of all the "mystery of eternal life." It is this ζωὴ αἰώνιος (St. John) which creates the basic distinction between the Christian mystery and the ancient mysteries with their naturalistic yearnings for rebirth. St. Paul describes it as participation in the transfigured life of the resurrected Lord. It is a supernatural kinship with the divine nature, fulfilled at the end of days in the immediate vision of God, but ordained and inaugurated in baptism (II Peter 1 : 4).[14]

To express this gift of grace (so far exceeding any heathen yearning) "in familiar images" and to signify what he believed, in common with St. Paul, about this approximation to the transfigured life of the resurrected Saviour, the ancient Christian took from his religious environment a symbol that in

---

11 *Catechesis magna*, 36 (*PG*, XLV, 92 D).
12 *Missale Gothicum, Collectio ad fontes benedicendos* (*PL*, LXXII, 274 B).
13 "Nam quid divinius isto ut puncto exiguo culpa cadat populi?"—*Carmina latina epigraphica*, ed. F. Bücheler et al., Vol. II, p. 420, no. 908.
14 Cf. Prümm, *Das Christentum als Neuheitserlebnis*, pp. 167ff.: "Das Mysterium der christlichen Taufe."

its Christian adaptation was to know a rich and varied history: the "mystery of the Ogdoad," the symbol of the number eight.[15]

Christ arose from the dead on the eighth day, the day of Helios; this had been the first day of the Creation and for the Christians it became again the first day. We have previously spoken of the mystery of this "sun day."[16] According to an ancient Pythagorean conception, the number eight was the symbol of perfection, of eternal, absolute repose. Eight is the number of the cube, the figure that presents the same area on all sides; eight is the number of the spheres moving around the earth—πάντα ὀκτώ, says an old proverb.[17] The ancient Christian was familiar with all these notions. His fundamental belief in the efficacy of baptism led him to find this mystical symbol everywhere and imbue it with a Christian meaning. The Lord rose on the eighth day: on an Easter Sunday, the liturgical eighth day, the Christian received baptism; and this is the day on which the "Spirit moved upon the face of the waters." Eight persons rode the ark over the waters, and this wooden structure by which man was saved is a symbol of the Cross. Everything is full of secret signs and symbols. In the second Epistle of Peter (2 : 5) we read: "And [God] spared not the original world, but preserved Noah the eighth person [ὄγδοον Νῶε], the preacher of justice." This was a prefiguration of baptism, and the first Epistle of Peter declares (3 : 20–21): ". . . wherein a few, that is, eight souls, were saved by water. Whereunto baptism, being of the like form [ἀντίτυπον], now saveth you also . . . by the resurrection of Jesus Christ."

By the second century, we find this mystery of the number eight fully developed in Justin. "By this which God said was meant," he says in the dialogue with Trypho,

> that the mystery of saved men appeared in the deluge. For righteous Noah, along with the other mortals at the deluge, i.e., with his own wife, his three sons, and their wives, being eight in number, were a symbol of the eighth day wherein Christ appeared when he rose from the dead, forever the first in power. For Christ, being the first-born of every creature, became again the chief of another

15 The following is based on F. J. Dölger, "Zur Symbolik des altchristlichen Taufhauses: Das Oktogon und die Symbolik der Achtzahl," *Antike und Christentum*, IV (1934), 153–87.
16 [Father Rahner's lecture on the Christian mystery of sun and moon; see *EJ 1943.*—ED.]
17 Theon of Smyrna, *Expositio rerum mathematicarum* (ed. E. Hiller, p. 105, li. 12).

race regenerated by himself through water, and faith, and wood, containing the mystery of the Cross.[18]

Thus baptism is rebirth to eternal life, to that eternal peace which is symbolized in the age-old image of the Ogdoad, the antithesis of earthly birth. In the excerpts from Theodotus prepared by Clement of Alexandria, we read:

> He whom the Mother generates is led into death and into the world, but whom Christ regenerates is transferred to life into the Ogdoad. And they die to the world but live to God, that death may be loosed by death, and corruption by resurrection.[19]

The baptismal font is the grave of transitory life and the womb of the new life of the heavenly Ogdoad—like Mother Earth it is grave and womb, but in an entirely different, higher sense.[20] One of Origen's finest hymns is dedicated to this μυστήριον τῆς ὀγδοάδος; it is a praise of Sunday as the eighth day:

> This is the day which the Lord hath made. To what shall we liken this day? On it God was reconciled with men. On it the war of temporality was ended and the earth became worthy of heaven. It is the day when men who were unworthy of the earth were manifested worthy of the kingdom of heaven, when the first-born of our nature was exalted over the heavens, and paradise was opened, when we received our old home back again, when the curse was taken away and sin was annulled. Even though God made all days—He made this day in a special way. For on this day He brought the highest of our mysteries to fulfillment.[21]

The understanding of this mystery lived on in Alexandria. Cyril retained it:

> For us this eighth day designates the time of the resurrection, when Christ, who suffered death for our sake, returned to life. And in

18 *Dialogue with Trypho*, 138, 1, 2 (Otto, II, p. 486). Cf. also *Dialogue* 41, 4 (Otto, II, pp. 138ff.).
19 *Excerpta ex Theodoto*, 80, 1 (*GCS*, III, p. 131, li. 24ff.; tr. R. P. Casey, London, 1934).
20 Clement of Alexandria, *Stromata*, IV, 25, 160 (*GCS*, II, p. 319, li. 12; tr. Wilson, Vol. II, p. 214). Baptismal font as womb and grave also occurs in Cyril of Jerusalem, *Mystagog. Catech.*, 2, 4 (*PG*, XXXIII, 1080 C), in Pseudo-Dionysius Areopagita, *Eccl. hier.*, II, 2, 7 (*PG*, III, 396 C), and in St. Augustine, *Sermo* 119, 4 (*PL*, XXXVIII, 674 D): *"vulva matris aqua baptismatis."* Cf. also Dieterich, *Mutter Erde*, p. 114.
21 *Selecta in Psalmos* (*Opera*, ed. C. H. E. Lommatzsch, Berlin, 1831–48, Vol. XI, pp. 358ff.). Cf. my "Taufe und geistliches Leben bei Origenes," *Zeitschrift für Askese und Mystik* (Innsbruck), VII (1932), 205–23.

spirit we are made like him, since through holy baptism we die, in order that we too may partake of the resurrection. And the time that seems best suited to such a rite of consecration [τελείωσις] is the *mysterion Christi*, which is symbolized by the Ogdoad.[22]

The Latin writers also knew this symbol, the *"sacramentum ogdoadis,"* as Hilary called it, the *"sacramentum octavi"* of which Augustine so frequently speaks:[23] the number eight is the symbol of rebirth through baptism, and at the same time of the eternal life that finds its mystical beginning in the water and its fulfillment in the bliss and eternal peace of the divine vision. Between baptism and divine vision lies the spiritual ascent of the Christian gnostic, his gradual deification through the power of baptism. And it too is a mystery of the number eight. Clement of Alexandria described it:

> Such, according to David, "rest in the holy hill of God" in the Church far on high, in which are gathered the philosophers of God, "who are Israelites indeed, who are pure in heart, in whom there is no guile"; who do not remain in the seventh seat, the place of rest, but are promoted, through the active beneficence of the divine likeness, to the heritage of beneficence that is the eighth grade; devoting themselves to the pure vision of insatiable contemplation.[24]

The early Christians conceived the earthly abode of the mystery, that "humble site full of all grace," in accordance with the mystical symbolism of the number eight. They tended to build their baptisteries in octagonal form and surrounded the basin of life-giving water by an eight-cornered rail. The inscription Ambrose wrote for the baptistery of St. Thecla at Milan has come down to us in an ancient copy:

> The holy temple has eight niches,
> octagonal is the font, worthy of its sacred work.
> The house of our baptism must be built in the mystical eight,
> for in it eternal salvation is given to all peoples
> through the light of Christ resurrected who burst the bars of death
> and freed all the dead from their dungeon,
> who redeems repentant sinners from the stain of guilt,
> when he cleanses them in the bath of this crystal source.[25]

22 *Glaphyra in Exodum* 2 (*PG*, LXIX, 441 BC).
23 Hilary, *Instructio Psalmorum* 14 (*CSEL*, XXII, p. 12, li. 24); Augustine, *Epistula* 55, 9, 13, 15 (*CSEL*, XXXIV, pp. 188, 194ff., 201); numerous other texts in Dölger, pp. 165ff.
24 *Stromata*, VI, 13, 107ff. (*GCS*, II, pp. 485ff.).
25 Latin text in Dölger, p. 155, with a literal tr. into German [here rendered].

And in the final verse, which is already known to us, Ambrose utters those words which suggest the profoundest essence of the mystical paradox that is enacted in the mystery of baptism: *"Nam quid divinius isto ut puncto exiguo culpa cadat populi?"*

This takes us a step further toward the understanding of the ancient mystery of baptism. Baptism is a "mystery of eternal life," a *"sacramentum octavi,"* only because the power of God's death on the Cross is effective in it. "What is water without the Cross of Christ? A common element," says Ambrose to his neophytes.[26] And Augustine: "The water of the baptismal font is consecrated by the sign of the Cross."[27] Only through the generative power of the Cross is the womb of the Church made fertile. *"Per signum crucis in utero sanctae Matris Ecclesiae concepti estis,"* says a post-Augustinian baptismal sermon.[28] In a word, this mystery is the form taken by the Pauline theology, stated in Romans, which sees baptism and the Cross of Christ as a single mystery. Baptism, "the mystery of wood and water,"[29] is but a partial aspect of the mystery as a whole. And without an understanding of this larger mystery, the mysticism and liturgy of early Christianity, as well as Christian art down through the Middle Ages, would remain unintelligible.

For a fuller insight into this mystery, we must go back to the baptism of Jesus in the Jordan, which the early Christian theologians already regarded as the true paradigm of the mystery of baptism. "Jesus the Christ was born and was baptized, that by himself submitting (*or*, by his suffering) he might purify the water," runs a famous text from Ignatius of Antioch.[30] That God himself in human form should have stood in earthly water, and that in this moment God should have spoken to say, This is my son: for the ancient Christian this was a paradox, a mystery, a moment foreshadowing the decision between light and darkness, the irruption of the transcendent principle to be realized through Christ's suffering on the Cross. This belief in the mystical nature of Jesus' baptism soon found expression in images. A fiery flame issued from the waters of Jordan, the waters receded

26 *De mysteriis*, 4, 20 (*PL*, XVI, 394 C).
27 *Contra Julianum*, VI, 19, 62 (*PL*, XLIV, 861 A). Cf. also *De catechizandis rudibus*, 20 (*PL*, XL, 325).
28 Pseudo-Augustinus, *De symbolo ad catechumenos* (*PL*, XL, 659 D).
29 The following is based on the highly learned work of Per Lundberg, *La Typologie baptismale dans l'ancienne église* (Acta Seminarii neotestamentici Upsaliensis, X, Uppsala and Leipzig, 1942), pp. 167ff.: "La croix dans le fleuve."
30 *Epistle to the Ephesians* 18, 2 (tr. Lake, Vol. I, pp. 191–93).

in fright, the angels came flying to bring the Son of God the white raiment of his luminous divine essence. Here we cannot concern ourselves with all the questions that this mystical conception of the baptism in Jordan raises for the history of religion.[31] We shall merely point out that this baptism symbolizes what became reality in the Crucifixion and was transmitted to men through the mystery of baptism. Jesus immersed in the Jordan is the symbol of that divine humility with which he would later immerse himself in death, in order to be resurrected as the transfigured Son of God. Baptism and Cross converge in a single image. Baptism, Cross, and descent into the darkness of the underworld constitute the mystery of the divine destruction from which new life surges, the night from which the new day dawns. I have dealt previously with the magnificent text in which Melito of Sardis compared this descent of God into the baptismal water and the world of the dead with the immersion of the sun in the Western Ocean.[32] And a Syrian baptismal liturgy contains this prayer:

> And so, O Father, Jesus lived, through thy will and the will of the Holy Ghost, in three earthly dwellings: in the womb of the flesh, in the womb of the baptismal water, and in the somber caverns of the underworld. Make us thereby worthy to be exalted from the deep abyss to the glorious dwellings of the sublime Trinity.[33]

The immersion of God in baptism is the source and prototype of our ascent through baptism. St. Ambrose expresses this eloquently as follows: *"Unus enim mersit, sed elevavit omnes. Unus descendit, ut ascenderemus omnes."*[34] The baptism of Jesus became efficacious through the death of Jesus.

This twofold mystical vision was expressed in art by a cross placed in the middle of the river Jordan. In part, this cross was the tree of life at the source of the rivers of paradise. But more than that it was the symbol of the crucified Saviour, who fructified the baptismal water with his blood. We know from the *Itinerarium* of the so-called Antoninus of Piacenza that a wooden cross actually was set up at the traditional baptismal site in the Jordan, in that place where according to legend the Jordan receded in terror: *"et in loco ubi redundat aqua in alveum suum, posita est crux lignea intus in*

---

31 Cf. Johann Kosnetter, *Die Taufe Jesu: Exegetische und religionsgeschichtliche Studien* (Vienna, 1936), pp. 223ff.
32 Cf. *EJ 1943*, pp. 335ff.
33 James of Sarug, *Consecration of the Baptismal Water* (Heinrich Denzinger, *Ritus Orientalium*, Vol. I, Würzburg, 1863, p. 244).
34 *Commentary on St. Luke* II, 91 (*CSEL*, XXXII, pt. 4, p. 94, li. 14ff.).

aquam ex utraque parte marmoris."[35] This cross, known throughout the world through the reports of pilgrims, but symbolizing a far older mystical idea, is represented in many works of art. We find it on the portal of St. Paul's in Rome, in St. Mark's in Venice, in an ivory at Salerno and in the British Museum, in the Khludov Psalter in Russia, and even so late as the baptismal picture in the *Hortus deliciarum* of Herrad of Landsberg.[36] This cross signifies that the baptismal water became life-giving through the death of Jesus; the cross is the tree of life. In many Eastern liturgies the baptismal font is simply called "Jordan." And in consecrating the baptismal water, the priest immerses a cross in it, by way of suggesting the same idea as the early Christians meant to express with their wooden cross in Jordan. A prayer from the Greek liturgy, the Proöimion Hymn for the feast of Epiphany, runs:

> Come and see how the radiant Helios
> Is baptized in the waters of a wretched river.
> A mighty Cross appeared over the baptismal font.
> The servants of sin descend,
> And the children of immortality rise up.
> Come then and receive the light![37]

Wretched river and mighty Cross: and from them arises immortal light. This is the *mysterion*, both Christian and Greek. But here we encounter a new element: the wooden cross as symbol of the humble crucified Jesus gives light, it is alive with the fire that since the earliest period has been identified with the baptism of Jesus in Jordan. The Cross is a bringer of light. The liturgy expresses this mystery by the dipping of a lighted candle into the baptismal font; this symbolism suggests that through the power of Christ crucified the water gives the perpetual light of eternal life. In a word: the Cross is tree of life and bearer of light in one, and both symbols stand for Christ himself, who "hallowed the water, by his suffering," endowing it

---

35 *Itinerarium*, c. 11 (*CSEL*, XXXIX, p. 200, li. 14–16).
36 Cf. Guillaume de Jerphanion, *La Voix des monuments* (Paris, 1930), p. 183ff.; Karl Künstle, *Ikonographie der christlichen Kunst* (Freiburg i. B, 1928), Vol. I, pp. 377ff.; Wilpert, *Die römischen Mosaiken und Malereien*, Text Vol. II, pp. 777–80; A. Straub and G. Keller, eds., *Herrade de Landsberg: Hortus deliciarum* (Strasbourg, 1901), Pl. XXXVIII.
37 Text in F. C. Conybeare, *Rituale Armenorum* (Oxford, 1905), p. 427. Also in Lundberg, pp. 170ff. On the whole subject, cf. Adolf Franz, *Die kirchlichen Benediktionen im Mittelalter*, Vol. I (Freiburg i. B., 1909), pp. 70–75.

with the δόξα that he earned on the Cross, the power of the Holy Ghost. When in the Roman baptismal liturgy the priest breathes upon the water in the figure of a Greek Ψ, this has nothing to do with a misunderstood Hellenistic symbol of life, but is (as the most recent research makes clear)[38] simply a sign for the tree of life, the Cross. And when the priest dips the candle into the water with the words *"Descendat in hanc plenitudinem fontis virtus Spiritus Sancti,"* this gesture (introduced only in the ninth century, be it said in passing[39]) reveals no phallic symbolism left over from the ancient mysteries, as has been asserted with inconceivable disregard of historical contexts,[40] but once again a symbol of the crucified Christ, imbuing the water with the luminous power of the spirit. It seems incredible that anyone should interpret this candle as a phallic symbol, when the Roman liturgy like all others refers to the baptismal font as an *immaculatus uterus* and states that the Church, like Mary, bears its children purely through the power of the spirit.[41] No, the immersed candle of the baptismal ritual is the same as the immersed cross in the Greek liturgy. In fact, we have works of Christian art in which the wooden cross in Jordan is replaced by a large candle—as, for example, in the representation of the baptism in the Cloister of the Archangel, at Djemil, in central Turkey.[42] The Easter candle is a symbol of Christ crucified, the five grains of incense inserted into it are five wounds; it is the Cross as the tree of life, and that is why it is adorned with flowers, as we see in pictures from the southern Italian exultet rolls. Cross and tree of life give the life of light—and that is why the candle is immersed in the water of the baptismal font. The wonderful Easter candelabrum at St. Paul's in Rome carries the inscription:

> Other trees bear fruit, but I bear light.
> Christ is risen! Of this boon I am surety.[43]

38 Bauerreiss, *Arbor Vitae*, pp. 48–50.
39 Cf. Franz, *Die kirchlichen Benediktionen*, Vol. I, pp. 549–51.
40 Hermann Usener, in *Archiv für Religionswissenschaft* (Freiburg i. B.), VII (1904), 294ff.; Dieterich, *Mutter Erde*, p. 114. C. G. Jung, "Mind and the Earth," *Contributions to Analytical Psychology* (London and New York, 1928), p. 129.
41 Cf. H. Scheidt, *Die Taufwasserweihegebete im Sinne vergleichender Liturgiegeschichte* (Münster, 1935).
42 Reproduction in Michael Buchberger, ed., *Lexikon für Theologie und Kirche*, Vol. IX (2nd edn., Freiburg i. B., 1937), pl. after col. 1020. In an ivory in the British Museum, two candelabra in the river Jordan: reproduction in Cabrol et al., eds., *Dictionnaire d'archéologie chrétienne*, Vol. II (Paris, 1910), p. 363, fig. 1297.
43 "Arbor poma gerit, arbor ego lumina gesto./Surrexit Christus. Nam talia munera praesto." Cf. Bauerreiss, pp. 50–57: "Symbolik der Osterkerze als Lebensbaum und Kreuzsymbol."

We have gone into this matter in some detail because the phallic interpretation of the Easter candle, put forward by Usener and Dieterich, still enjoys a certain currency; we have tried to show how the Christian mystery of baptism should and should not be explained. Baptism and Cross cannot be separated, and behind all the wealth of mystical and liturgical forms, there remains the basic theology of the Epistle to the Romans. In an Easter baptismal sermon an unknown Greek once expressed this thought. His words are those of the Hellenistic mysteries but his ideas are those of St. Paul:

> Thou newly illumined one, a share in the resurrection has fallen to thee, through this initiation into the mysteries of grace. Thou hast imitated the descent of thy Lord into the tomb. But thou hast arisen once more and now beholdest the works of resurrection. May what thou hast beheld in symbol now become thine in reality.[44]

III

In the two aspects of the mystery of baptism discussed so far we have recognized the aim and the source of the Christian mystery: the aim is the Ogdoad of eternal life—the source is the redeeming power of the Cross. In between lies the earthly life span of the mystes: here the divine power of the initiation received in baptism is at work, but has not yet achieved its own "fulfillment": for the end and goal ($\tau\acute{\epsilon}\lambda$os) of Christian teleiosis is the eschatological vision of God in the transfiguration of the flesh. In this earthly life, he who has received the initiation of baptism is indeed possessed of life everlasting (he has entered into the Ogdoad but he cannot yet behold it: "it hath not yet appeared what we shall be, [but] we know that when he shall appear, we shall be like to him; because we shall see him as he is"—I John 3 : 2), but his possession of it is not secure. The mystery of baptism is a lifelong decision between light and darkness, between Christ and Belial, life and death. Or else, to use another early Christian image: the mystes has already reached the harbor of the transcendent world, and yet his perilous voyage continues; he bears in his soul the seal that opens all gates on his heavenward journey, but his ascent is still threatened by demons and spirits. This is the paradox of the mystery. It would be highly profitable to adduce all the profound ideas and precious images with which the early Christians adorned this "mystery of the interim." It would be

44 Pseudo-Athanasius, *De Pascha* (*PG*, XXVIII, 1081ff.).

profitable to show how the mystery of decision is expressed in the ritual of baptism: how the mystes turns away from Satan, the "black one," and toward Christ the king of light, who comes from the East like the sun and brings him the illumination (φωτισμός) of baptism. Such a study would be particularly significant because the ritual of this mystery of the fundamental Christian decision contains much Greek material, emanating largely from that common sphere which also forms the background of the symbolic usages of the mysteries. To this category belong the image of Satan dwelling in the dark West; the breathing and spitting upon the evil one; milk and honey as the food of the mystes; and the symbolism of the salt. But here we must content ourselves with a passing mention of these matters. Dölger has given us a work concerning this whole mystery of light and darkness. It bears the title *Die Sonne der Gerechtigkeit und der Schwarze: eine religionsgeschichtliche Studie zum Taufgelöbnis.*[45] We should likewise speak of the mystery of the ascension, which begins in baptism, but here again we already have fine studies, to which I can refer only in passing.[46] The same paradox finds expression in the wealth of images based on the ancient conception of baptism as a mystical voyage to the haven of peace. In the primeval ship, the ark built of the wood of the Cross, the mystes traverses the black bitter sea of the world; he is in deadly peril, yet he has already reached the haven, and his ship is safe from harm, as long as the mast that is the Cross remains in its place. Again the "mystery of the wood" and the "mystery of decision" are enacted: Christ on the Cross has gained the final victory, he has achieved peace, and so the mystes, who like Odysseus in his mystical voyage has himself tied to the mast—in this case, the Cross—is already certain of his home-coming. An Eastern liturgy of baptism contains the lines:

> In the dark vale of earth thou journeyest as upon a sea. O thou who hast not yet been baptized, make haste to enter the glorious ship of baptism. It will carry thee safely home, for this is the glorious resurrection of Christ our Saviour.[47]

45 *Liturgiegeschichtliche Forschungen* II (Münster, 1918).
46 Cf. Bousset, "Die Himmelsreise der Seele," *Archiv für Religionswissenschaft*, IV (1901) 136ff., 229ff.; Reitzenstein, "Himmelswanderung und Drachenkampf in der alchemistischen und frühchristlichen Literatur," *Festschrift für Friedrich Carl Andreas* (Leipzig, 1916), pp. 33–50; *Über die Vorstellungen von der Himmelsreise der Seele* (Vorträge der Bibliothek Warburg, ed. F. Saxl, 1928–29; Berlin and Leipzig, 1930).
47 Text in Conybeare, p. 335.

Per Lundberg[48] has examined this symbolism of the mystical voyage of baptism in detail; I myself, in my articles on the *"antenna crucis,"* have discussed a few of the countless images that the early Christians conceived in this connection.[49] Here I cannot go into particulars. But all of these mystical symbols of baptism have an inner orientation that despite their diversity remains the same: they are all oriented toward the profoundest content of the Christian mystery of baptism, the resurrection of the incarnate God, and hence toward man's deification through his share in the transfigured Lord. "Ταῦτα χριστιανῶν τὰ μυστήρια," says a Greek Christian; "these are the mysteries of the Christians: we celebrate the panegyris because of the resurrection of the dead and because of eternal life."[50]

*

This brings us to the end of our attempt to characterize the early Christian conception of mystery through the mysteries of the Cross and of baptism. When the Church of the Greeks and Romans celebrated its mystery in the holy vigil of Easter, when the faithful beheld the tree of the Cross, immersed in the life-giving water amid the candlelight and the resplendent white raiment: then they may have realized that in this new mystery the old mysteries were ended and fulfilled. They may have felt what Gregory of Nazianzus said at the beginning of his splendid sermon of the lights: "Jesus is here again and a mystery is here again. But no longer the mystery of Hellenic drunkenness, but a mystery from above, a divine mystery."[51] And in his ode to Easter night, Drepanius passes the ancient mysteries in review:

Behold, how in radiant throngs the people hasten to our mystery. Not like the Idaean Gauls, who imitate Dindyma, not like the

48 *La typologie baptismale,* pp. 73ff. Cf. also the prayers in C. R. C. Allberry, *A Manichean Psalm-Book* (Stuttgart, 1938), pp. 132 and 166; Adolf Rücker, "Die 'Ankunft im Hafen' des syrisch-jakobitischen Festrituals und verwandte Riten," *Jahrbuch für Liturgiewissenschaft* (Münster), III (1923), pp. 78–92; Tomas Arvedson, *Das Mysterium Christi* (Leipzig and Uppsala, 1937), pp. 204ff.
49 "Odysseus am Mastbaum," *ZKT,* LXV (1941), 123–52; "Das Meer der Welt," ibid., LXVI (1942), 89–118; "Das Schiff aus Holz," ibid., LXVI (1942), 196–227, and LXVII (1943), 1–21. ["Navicula Petri," LXIX (1947), 1–35; "Das Kreuz als Mastbaum und Antenne," LXXV (1953), 129–73; "Das mystische Tau," LXXV (1953), 385–410.—H. R. (1955).]
50 Pseudo-Chrysostom, *In triduanam resurrectionem Domini* (*PG,* L, 824).
51 *Oratio* 39, 1 (*PG,* XXXVI, 336 A).

vigils of Eleusis in honor of the Attic mother, not like the sacred orgies on the Theban Cithaeron, are our mysteries. Here there is no vapor of incense, no flow of blood, here all is pure prayer and simple action.[52]

From the mystery of Easter night, when the Cross bears new life in the water, the gaze of the Christian mystes rises to the land of light, and joyously he cries: "χαῖρε νέον φῶς!"[53] What on earth was cloaked in the symbolic signs of the Cross and of baptism will be revealed in heaven, in that beatific realm of the Ogdoad, of peace and perfection. Christ has opened it up to us with his Cross, he has "crucified death unto life." The baptized mystes will in a Christian sense reveal what Plato foreshadowed when he spoke of the blessed realm from which the souls come and to which the good return.[54]

And now we shall let Clement of Alexandria, who is without equal in interpreting the Christian mystery in Greek images, say the last word:

> Away then, away with our forgetfulness of the truth! Let us remove the ignorance and darkness that spreads like a mist over our sight; and let us get a vision of the true God, first raising to Him this voice of praise, "Hail, O Light." Upon us who lay buried in darkness and shut up in the shadow of death a light shone forth from heaven, purer than the sun and sweeter than the life of earth. That light is life eternal, and whatsoever things partake of it live. . . . The universe has become sleepless light and the setting has turned into a rising. This is what was meant by "the new creation." For He who rides over the universe, "the sun of righteousness," . . . changed the setting into a rising and crucified death into life; who having snatched man out of the jaws of destruction raised him to the sky, transplanting corruption to the soil of incorruption, and transforming earth into heaven.[55]

Ταῦτα Χριστιανῶν τὰ μυστήρια: These are the mysteries of the Christians.

52 Based on: Non sicut Idaeis simulatur Dindyma Gallis,
Attica nec Grais nuribus vigilatur Eleusis,
Orgia Thebanus vel agit nocturna Cithaeron.
Nil habet insanum strepitu, nil thure vaporum,
Sanguine nil madidum, nil cursibus immoderatum
Nox sacris operanda tuis. Tantum prece pura
Simplicibus votis manibusque ad celsa supinis
Te colimus natumque tuum.
—De cereo paschali, vv. 17–26 (Analecta hymnica, Vol. L, Leipzig, 1907, p. 217).
53 Cf. Dölger, "Lumen Christi," Antike und Christentum, V (1936), 1–43.
54 Phaedrus, 250 B.
55 Protrepticus, XI, 11, 114 (GCS, I, p. 80, li. 13–29; tr. Butterworth, p. 243).

APPENDICES

Biographical Notes

JULIUS BAUM, Ph.D. Born 1882, Wiesbaden. Director, Württemberg State Museum, Stuttgart. Before the war, a curator there; also director of the Ulm Museum and professor of art history at the Technical Institute in Stuttgart. Ousted from his posts by the Hitler regime and imprisoned in a concentration camp; later, through the intervention of Swiss friends, enabled to leave and enter Switzerland. During the war years, catalogued the medieval art collection of the Bern Historical Museum. 1945, recalled at the invitation of the Allied occupation forces, reinstated at the Institute, and entrusted with re-establishing the Württemberg Museum, of which he became director. Main publications: *Romanische Baukunst in Frankreich* and *Italienische Baukunst der Frührenaissance* (Vols. III and IX, Bauformen Bibliothek; 2nd edns., Stuttgart, 1928, 1926); *Die Plastik und Malerei des Mittelalters in Deutschland, Frankreich und Britannien* (Potsdam, 1933); *La Sculpture figurale en Europe à l'époque mérovingienne* (Paris, 1937). (Full bibliography in *Neue Beiträge zur Archäologie und Kunstgeschichte Schwabens, Julius Baum zum 70. Geburtstag gewidmet*, Stuttgart, 1952.) Professor Baum lectured at the 1944 and 1949 Eranos meetings.

C. G. JUNG, M.D., Litt.D. (hon., Clark), Sc.D. (hon., Harvard), Litt.D. (hon., Benares), Litt.D. (hon., Allahabad), Sc.D. (hon., Oxford), Sc.D. (hon., Calcutta). Born 1875, Kesswil, Canton Thurgau, Switzerland. 1905–1909, privatdocent, University of Zurich. 1907–13, associated with Bleuler and Freud in experimental research. 1933–42, taught at the Federal Polytechnic Institute, Zurich. He was called to the University of Basel in 1944 to occupy the chair of medical psychology, established for him, but was forced to resign owing to illness after only a year. His principal works, among more than 150 publications, include (in English translation): *Psychology of the Unconscious* (New York, 1916; now superseded by a revision, *Symbols of Transformation*, Collected Works, Vol. 5, in press); *Psychological Types* (London and New York, 1923); *Two Essays on Analytical Psychology* (London, 1928; published in the Collected Works, Vol. 7, New York and London, 1953); with Richard Wilhelm, *The Secret of the Golden Flower* (London and New York, 1931); *Psychology and Religion* (Terry Lectures, New Haven, 1938); *Psychology and Alchemy* (Collected Works, Vol. 12, New

405

York and London, 1953); *Answer to Job* (London, 1954). Jung has lectured at thirteen Eranos meetings, beginning with the first, in 1933. The 1955 meeting was dedicated to him, on the occasion of his eightieth year.

C. KERÉNYI, Ph.D. Born 1897, Temesvár, (then) Hungary. Formerly professor of classical studies and the history of religion, Universities of Szeged and Pécs, Hungary. Resident of Switzerland since 1943. Lecturer, C. G. Jung Institute, Zurich. Founder and editor of the Albae Vigiliae series (Zurich) on mythology, art, and related subjects. Principal works: *Apollon* (2nd edn., Amsterdam, 1940); *Die antike Religion* (3rd edn., Düsseldorf, 1951); with C. G. Jung, *Essays on a Science of Mythology* (New York, 1949; London, 1950, as *Introduction to a Science of Mythology*); *Niobe* (Zurich, 1949); *The Gods of the Greeks* (New York and London, 1951). Dr. Kerényi lectured frequently at Eranos meetings in the 1940's.

HANS LEISEGANG, Ph.D. Born 1890, Blankenburg, Germany; died 1951. The work of this eminent German philosopher was interrupted in 1934, when he was removed from his chair at the University of Jena owing to his opposition to the Nazi movement. He was confined in a concentration camp for a number of years. From 1945, he was professor of philosophy at the Free University, Berlin. Principal works include: *Der heilige Geist* (Leipzig, 1919); *Pneuma Hagion* (Leipzig, 1922); *Die Gnosis* (Leipzig, 1924); *Denkformen* (Leipzig, 1928); *Luther als Deutscher Christ* (Leipzig, 1934). Professor Leisegang never actually lectured at an Eranos meeting. The paper in this volume was written in response to an invitation, in the early 1930's, which his situation in Germany prevented his accepting; the paper was nevertheless published in the 1939 *Jahrbuch*. In 1950, he contributed a paper to the volume in honor of C. G. Jung's seventy-fifth birthday.

PAUL MASSON-OURSEL, Ph.D. Born 1882, Paris. Directeur d'études, École des Hautes-Études, Sorbonne. Special field, the comparative study of Western and Eastern philosophy. Principal publications: *Philosophie comparée* (Paris, 1923); *Esquisse d'une histoire de la philosophie indienne* (Paris, 1923); *L'Inde antique* (Paris, 1933); *La Philosophie en Orient* (Histoire de philosophie de Brehier, final vol.; Paris, 1937); *Le Fait métaphysique* (Paris, 1941); *La Pensée en Orient* (Paris 1943). Dr. Masson-Oursel lectured at the Eranos meetings of 1936 and 1937.

FRITZ MEIER, Ph.D. Born 1912, Basel. Since 1949, professor of Oriental philology, University of Basel. Philological research in the mosque libraries of Istanbul (1936) and Iran (1937). 1946–48, maître de conférences, University of Farouk I, Alexandria. His special field is Islamic religion and mysticism. Principal publications: *Vom Wesen der islamischen Mystik* (Basel, 1943); *Die Vita des Scheich*

Abū Ishāq al-Kāzarūnī (Bibliotheca Islamica, vol. 14; Leipzig, 1948); *Die 'Fawā'iḥ al-ǧamāl wa fawātiḥ al-ǧalāl' des Naǧm ad-dīn al-Kubrā* (a study of Islamic mysticism from A.D. 1200; Basel, 1953). He has lectured at the Eranos meetings of 1944, 1945, 1946, and 1954.

JEAN DE MENASCE, O.P., D.S.T., B.A., B.Litt. (Oxon.). Born 1902, Alexandria, Egypt. Since 1949, professor of ancient Iranian religion, École des Hautes-Études, Sorbonne. 1938–48, professor of comparative religion, University of Fribourg, Switzerland. 1951 and 1953, Temporary Member, Institute for Advanced Study, Princeton. Chief publications: *Quand Israel aime Dieu* (Paris, 1932); *Shkand-Gumānīk Vicār* (Fribourg, 1945); articles in *Journal asiatique* (Paris), *Revue de l'histoire des religions* (Paris), *Anthropos* (Fribourg). Father de Menasce lectured at the 1944 and 1945 Eranos meetings.

GEORGES NAGEL, Th.D. Born 1899, Verrières, Neuchâtel, Switzerland. Since 1937, professor of Hebrew, exegesis, and Old Testament history, Protestant Theological School of the University of Geneva; since 1944, has also taught Egyptology. 1927–30, at the Institute français d'archéologie orientale, Cairo. 1931–37, pastor, La Chaux du Milieu, Neuchâtel. 1938–39, again at the Institut, with a French governmental mission. Principal publications: *Un Papyrus funéraire de la fin du Nouvel Empire* (Cairo, 1929); *Fouilles de Deir el Médineh (nord)* (Rapports préliminaires des fouilles de l'Institut, VI, 3; Cairo, 1929); *La Céramique du Nouvel Empire à Deir el Médineh* (Documents des fouilles, X; Cairo, 1938). Professor Nagel lectured at the Eranos meetings of 1942, 1943, and 1944.

WALTER F. OTTO, Ph.D. Born 1874, Hechingen, Württemberg, Germany. Since 1946, guest professor of classical philology, University of Tübingen. Between 1910 and 1946, professor at the universities of Munich, Vienna, Basel, Frankfort, Königsberg, and Göttingen. Principal works: *Der Geist der Antike und die christliche Welt* (Bonn, 1923); *Die Götter Griechenlands* (Bonn, 1929; tr. Moses Hadas, *The Homeric Gods*, New York, 1954); *Dionysos: Mythos und Kultus* (Frankfort, 1933); *Der griechische Göttermythos bei Goethe und Hölderlin* (Berlin, 1939); *Der Dichter und die alten Götter* (Frankfort, 1942); *Das Vorbild der Griechen* (Stuttgart, 1949); *Gesetzt, Urbild und Mythos* (Stuttgart, 1951). Professor Otto lectured at the 1939 Eranos meeting.

MAX PULVER, Ph.D. Born 1889, Bern; died 1952. Writer and poet. In his later years, an internationally known graphologist, working in Zurich. He had a special interest in Gnosticism, and lectured on this and related subjects at several Eranos meetings. Principal works: *Symbolik der Handschrift* (Zurich, 1931); *Trieb und Verbrechen* (Zurich, 1934); *Person, Charakter, Schicksal* (Zurich, 1944); *Intelligenz im Schriftausdruck* (Zurich, 1949); and several volumes of belles-lettres, drama, and poetry.

HUGO RAHNER, S.J., Ph.D., D.S.T. Born 1900. Since 1937, professor of Church history, University of Innsbruck. His special field of historical research is that of early Christianity. Principal works: *Abendländische Kirchenfreiheit* (Einsiedeln, 1943); *Griechische Mythen in christlicher Deutung* (Zurich, 1945); *Der spielende Mensch* (Einsiedeln, 1952). He has lectured at a number of Eranos meetings since 1943.

PAUL SCHMITT, Ph.D. Born 1900, Basel; died 1953. His doctorate was awarded in economics and political science by the University of Munich. Early in his career in Munich: partner, Schneider and Münzing Bank; director, Knorr and Hirth, publishers; editor and business manager, *Münchner Neueste Nachrichten, Süddeutsche Monatshefte*, and other periodicals. Actively opposed the rise of Nazism; after official threats and arrest, escaped from Germany, March, 1934. 1934–38, student of patristic theology at the Vatican and Rome representative of various Swiss and Austrian newspapers. In 1938, found political asylum in Switzerland, whose citizenship he received in 1953. Dr. Schmitt's special interests were philosophy, history, and politics. He contributed more than two hundred essays and reviews to periodicals; under the pseudonym Paolo Agostino Sebastiani, he wrote *Vier philosophische Erzählungen* (Bern, 1950). Lectured at the Eranos meetings of 1943, 1944, 1945, and 1946, and contributed to the two Festschrift volumes for C. G. Jung.

WALTER WILI, Ph.D. Born 1900, Lucerne. Since 1932, professor of classical philology, University of Bern. Special fields of interest, Roman literature and culture and the Latin literature of the Middle Ages and the Renaissance. Principal publications: *Vergil* (Munich, 1930); *Europäisches Tagebuch* (Bern and Hamburg, 1939); *Tibulls 10. Elegie* (Basel, 1942); *Horaz und die augusteische Kultur* (Basel, 1948). He is president of Thesaurus Mundi, a scholarly society whose purpose is to publish critical editions of important medieval and Renaissance texts. Dr. Wili has lectured at the Eranos meetings of 1943, 1944, and 1945.

Contents of the *Eranos-Jahrbücher*

The contents of the *Eranos-Jahrbücher*, consisting up to the present time of twenty-three volumes, are here listed in translation as a reference aid and an indication of the scope of the Eranos meetings. The lectures were originally delivered in German, with a few exceptions in French, English, and Italian. In the first eight *Jahrbücher*, all of the papers were published in German; in the later volumes, the papers were published respectively in the original language. An index of contributors is on pp. 417–18.

I: 1933: Yoga and Meditation in the East and the West
HEINRICH ZIMMER: On the Meaning of the Indian Tantric Yoga
Mrs. RHYS DAVIDS: Religious Exercises in India and the Religious Man
ERWIN ROUSSELLE: Spiritual Guidance in Living Taoism
C. G. JUNG: A Study in the Process of Individuation
G. R. HEYER: The Meaning of Eastern Wisdom for Western Spiritual Guidance
FRIEDRICH HEILER: Contemplation in Christian Mysticism
ERNESTO BUONAIUTI: Meditation and Contemplation in the Roman Catholic Church

II: 1934: Symbolism and Spiritual Guidance in the East and the West
ERWIN ROUSSELLE: Dragon and Mare, Figures of Primordial Chinese Mythology
J. W. HAUER: Symbols and Experience of the Self in Indo-Aryan Mysticism
HEINRICH ZIMMER: Indian Myths as Symbols
Mrs. RHYS DAVIDS: On the History of the Symbol of the Wheel
C. G. JUNG: The Archetypes of the Collective Unconscious
G. R. HEYER: The Symbolism of Dürer's Melancholia
FRIEDRICH HEILER: The Madonna as a Religious Symbol
ERNESTO BUONAIUTI: Symbols and Rites in the Religious Life of Various Monastic Orders
MARTIN BUBER: Symbolic and Sacramental Existence in Judaism
RUDOLF BERNOULLI: On the Symbolism of Geometrical Figures and of Numbers
SIGRID STRAUSS-KLOEBE: On the Psychological Significance of the Astrological Symbol

C. M. VON CAMMERLOHER: The Position of Art in the Psychology of Our Time

Swami YATISWARANANDA: A Brief Survey of Hindu Religious Symbolism in Its Relation to Spiritual Exercises and Higher Development

III: 1935: Spiritual Guidance in the East and the West

C. G. JUNG: Dream Symbols of the Individuation Process

G. R. HEYER: On Getting Along with Oneself

ERWIN ROUSELLE: Lao-tse's Journey through Soul, History, and World

Mrs. RHYS DAVIDS: Man, the Search, and Nirvana

RUDOLF BERNOULLI: Psychic Development in the Mirror of Alchemy and Related Disciplines

ERNESTO BUONAIUTI: I. Gnostic Initiation and Early Christianity. II. The Exercises of St. Ignatius Loyola

ROBERT EISLER: The Riddle of the Gospel of St. John

J. B. LANG: Pauline and Analytical Spiritual Guidance

IV: 1936: The Shaping of the Idea of Redemption in the East and the West

C. G. JUNG: The Idea of Redemption in Alchemy

PAUL MASSON-OURSEL: I. The Indian Theories of Redemption in the Frame of the Religions of Salvation. II. The Doctrine of Grace in the Religious Thought of India [2]

Mrs. RHYS DAVIDS: Redemption in India's Past and in Our Present

ERNESTO BUONAIUTI: Redemption in the Orphic Mysteries

HEINRI-CHARLES PUECH: The Concept of Redemption in Manichaeism

BORIS VYSHESLAWZEFF: Two Ways of Redemption: Redemption as a Solution of the Tragic Contradiction

V: 1937: The Shaping of the Idea of Redemption in the East and the West

C. G. JUNG: Some Observations on the Visions of Zosimos

LOUIS MASSIGNON: The Origins and Significance of Gnosticism in Islam

PAUL MASSON-OURSEL: I. The Indian Conception of Psychology. II. Indian Techniques of Salvation [1]

JEAN PRZYLUSKI: I. Redemption after Death in the Upanishads and in Early Buddhism. II. Redemption in This Lifetime, in Advanced Buddhism

ANDREAS SPEISER: The Concept of Redemption in Plotinus

CHARLOTTE A. BAYNES: The Idea of Redemption in Christian Gnosticism

THEODOR-WILHELM DANZEL: On the Psychology of Aztec Symbolism

JOHN LAYARD: The Myth of the Journey of the Dead in Malekula

ERNESTO BUONAIUTI: Ecclesia Spiritualis [1]

[1] In *Spirit and Nature* (Papers from the Eranos Yearbooks, 1, 1954).
[2] In *The Mysteries* (Papers from the Eranos Yearbooks, 2, 1955).

2 In *The Mysteries* (Papers from the Eranos Yearbooks, 2, 1955).

GEORGES NAGEL: The God Thoth according to the Egyptian Texts
MAX PULVER: Jesus' Round Dance and Crucifixion according to the Acts of St. John [2]
C. G. JUNG: The Spirit Mercurius
J. B. LANG: The Demiurge of the Priests' Codex (Gen. 1 to 2 : 4a) and His Significance for Gnosticism

X: 1943: Ancient Sun Cults and Light Symbolism in Gnosticism and Early Christianity

GEORGES NAGEL: The Cult of the Sun in Early Egypt
CHARLES VIROLLEAUD: The God Shamash in Ancient Mesopotamia
C. KERÉNYI: Father Helios
WALTER WILI: The Roman Sun-Gods and Mithras
PAUL SCHMITT: Sol Invictus: Reflections on Late Roman Religion and Politics
MAX PULVER: The Experience of Light in the Gospel of St. John, in the Corpus Hermeticum, in Gnosticism, and in the Eastern Church
LOUIS MASSIGNON: Astrological Infiltration in Islamic Religious Thought
HUGO RAHNER: The Christian Mystery of Sun and Moon

XI: 1944: The Mysteries

C. KERÉNYI: The Mysteries of the Kabeiroi (Appendix: The Castello di Tegna) [2]
WALTER WILI: The Orphic Mysteries and the Greek Spirit [2]
PAUL SCHMITT: The Ancient Mysteries in the Society of Their Time, Their Transformation and Most Recent Echoes [2]
GEORGES NAGEL: The "Mysteries" of Osiris in Ancient Egypt [2]
JEAN DE MENASCE: The Mysteries and the Religion of Iran [2]
FRITZ MEIER: The Mystery of the Ka'ba: Symbol and Reality in Islamic Mysticism [2]
WILHELM KOPPERS: On the Origin of the Mysteries in the Light of Ethnology and Indology
MAX PULVER: On the Scope of the Gnostic Mysteries
JULIUS BAUM: Symbolic Representations of the Eucharist [2]
HUGO RAHNER: The Christian Mystery and the Pagan Mysteries [2]

XII: 1945: Studies on the Problem of the Archetypal (For C. G. Jung on His Seventieth Birthday, July 26, 1945)

ANDREAS SPEISER: Plato's Theory of Ideas
C. KERÉNYI: Heros Iatros: On the Transformations and Symbols of the Genius of Medicine in Greece
WALTER WILI: Problems Connected with the Aristotelian Theory of the Soul
PAUL SCHMITT: The Archetypal in St. Augustine and Goethe

[2] In *The Mysteries* (Papers from the Eranos Yearbooks, 2, 1955).

[1] In Spirit and Nature (Papers from the Eranos Yearbooks, 1, 1954).
[*] Title changed in Spirit and Nature to "The Phenomenology of the Spirit in Fairy Tales."

413

VICTOR WHITE: Anthropologia rationalis: The Aristotelian-Thomist Conception of Man
LEO BAECK: Individuum ineffabile

XVI: 1948: Man

HUGO RAHNER: Man as Player
GILLES QUISPEL: Gnostic Man: The Doctrine of Basilides
GERARDUS VAN DER LEEUW: Man and Civilization: The Implications of the Term "Evolution of Man"
C. KERÉNYI: Man and Mask
JOHN LAYARD: The Making of Man in Malekula
C. G. JUNG: On the Self
ERICH NEUMANN: Mystical Man
HERMANN WEYL: Science as Symbolic Construction of Man
MARKUS FIERZ: On Physical Knowledge
ADOLF PORTMANN: Man as Student of Nature

XVII: 1949: Man and the Mythical World

GERARDUS VAN DER LEEUW: Primordial Time and Final Time
C. KERÉNYI: The Orphic Cosmogony and the Origin of Orphism
E. O. JAMES: Myth and Ritual
HENRY CORBIN: The "Narrative of Initiation" and Hermeticism in Iran
ERICH NEUMANN: The Mythical World and the Individual
LOUIS BEIRNAERT: The Mythical Dimension in Christian Sacramentalism
GERSHOM G. SCHOLEM: Cabala and Myth
JULIUS BAUM: Representations of the Germanic Saga of Gods and Heroes in Nordic Art
PAUL RADIN: The Basic Myth of the North American Indians
ADOLF E. JENSEN: The Mythical World View of the Ancient Agricultural Peoples
ADOLF PORTMANN: Mythical Elements in Science

XVIII: 1950: From the World of the Archetypes (Special Volume for C. G. Jung on His Seventy-fifth Birthday, July 26, 1950)

HANS LEISEGANG: The God-Man as Archetype
HENRY CORBIN: Jābir ibn Hayyān's "Book of the Glorious"
FRITZ MEIER: The World of Archetypes in Ali Hamadani (d. 1385)
GILLES QUISPEL: Anima naturaliter christiana
GERARDUS VAN DER LEEUW: Immortality
KARL LUDWIG SCHMIDT: Jerusalem as Archetype and Image
PAUL RADIN: The Religious Experiences of an American Indian
PAUL SCHMITT: The Archetype in the Philosophy of Nicholas of Cusa
ERICH NEUMANN: On the Moon and the Matriarchal Consciousness
HANS BÄNZIGER: Faith as an Archetypal Attitude
ADOLF PORTMANN: The Problem of Archetypes from the Biological Standpoint

* With certain changes, in preparation as Papers from the Eranos Yearbooks, 3.

415

MAX KNOLL: Quantum Conceptions of Energy in Physics and Psychology
LANCELOT LAW WHYTE: A Scientific View of the "Creative Energy" of Man

XXII: 1953: Man and Earth

ERICH NEUMANN: The Significance of the Earth Archetype for Modern Times
MIRCEA ELIADE: Terra Mater and Cosmic Hierogamies
GILLES QUISPEL: Gnosis and Earth
HENRY CORBIN: Celestial Earth and the Body of the Resurrection according to Various Iranian Traditions: I. Mazdean Imago Terrae. II. Hurqalya's Mystical Earth (Shaikhism)
GERSHOM G. SCHOLEM: The Conception of the Golem and Its Tellurian and Magical Contexts
GIUSEPPE TUCCI: Earth as Conceived of in Indian and Tibetan Religion, with Special Regard to the Tantras
DAISETZ SUZUKI: The Role of Nature in Zen
JEAN DANIÉLOU: Earth and Paradise in Greek Mysticism and Theology
ERNST BENZ: I. The Sacred Cave in Eastern Christianity. II. The Charismatic Type of the Russian Saints
ADOLF PORTMANN: The Earth as the Home of Life

XXIII: 1954: Man and Transformation

MIRCEA ELIADE: Mysteries and Spiritual Regeneration in Non-European Religions
FRITZ MEIER: The Transformation of Man in Mystical Islam
HENRI CORBIN: Divine Epiphany and Initiatic Birth in Shiite Gnosis
ERICH NEUMANN: The Creative Principle in Psychic Transformation
PAUL TILLICH: New Being as the Central Concept of a Christian Theology
DAISETZ SUZUKI: The Awakening of a New Consciousness in Zen
LANCELOT LAW WHYTE: The Growth of Ideas, Illustrated by Man's Changing Conception of Himself
ERNST BENZ: Theogony and the Transformation of Man in Schelling
JEAN DANIÉLOU: The Transfiguration of Man in Early Byzantine Mysticism
ADOLF PORTMANN: Metamorphosis in Animals

Index of Contributors

References are to volumes in the foregoing list. Places of residence at the time of speaking or writing are noted in parentheses.

417

Radin, Paul (Berkeley), XVII–XIX
Rahner, Hugo (Sion; 1945, Innsbruck),
X–XIII, XV, XVI
Read, Herbert (London), XXI
Rhys Davids, Mrs. (London), I–IV
Rousselle, Erwin (Frankfort on the Main), I–III

Schmidt, Karl Ludwig (Basel), XIII–XV, XVIII
Schmitt, Paul (Lucerne), X–XIV, XVIII
Scholem, Gershom G. (Jerusalem), XVII, XIX, XXI, XXII
Schrödinger, Erwin (Dublin), XIV
Speiser, Andreas (Zurich; 1945, Basel), V, VIII, XII–XIV
Strauss-Kloebe, Sigrid (Munich), II
Suzuki, Daisetz (Enkakuji, Kamakura, Japan; 1954, New York), XXII, XXIII

Thurnwald, Richard (Berlin), VII
Tillich, Paul (New York), XXIII
Tucci, Giuseppe (Rome), XXII

Virolleaud, Charles (Paris), VI, VII, X
Vysheslawzeff, Boris (Paris), IV

Weyl, Hermann (Princeton), XVI
White, Victor (Oxford), XV
Whyte, Lancelot Law (London), XX, XXI, XXIII
Wilhelm, Hellmut (Seattle), XX
Wili, Walter (Bern), X–XIII

Yatiswarananda, Swami (Ramakrishna-Vivekenanda Mission), II

Zimmer, Heinrich (Heidelberg; 1939, Oxford), I, II, VI, VII

ABBREVIATIONS

AIDR	Archaeologisches Institut des Deutschen Reiches.
AV	Authorized (King James) Version.
CIL	*Corpus Inscriptionum Latinarum.* Berlin, 1893–.
CSEL	*Corpus Scriptorum Ecclesiasticorum Latinorum.* Vienna, 1866–.
Diels-Kranz	Diels, Hermann, tr. *Die Fragmente der Vorsokratiker.* 5th edn., ed. by Walther Kranz. Berlin, 1934–37. 3 vols.
DV	Douay Version.
EJ	*Eranos-Jahrbuch.* Zurich.
Enc. of Islam	*The Encyclopedia of Islam.* Leiden and London, 1908–36.
Freeman, *Ancilla*	Kathleen Freeman, tr. *Ancilla to the Pre-Socratic Philosophers.* Oxford and Cambridge, Mass., 1948.
GCS	*Die griechischen christlichen Schriftsteller,* ed. O. Stählin. Berlin, 1905–36. 4 vols.
Hastings, *ERE*	James Hastings, ed. *Encyclopedia of Religion and Ethics.* Edinburgh and New York, 1908–27.
Kabirenheiligtum	Paul H. A. Wolters and Gerda Bruns. *Das Kabirenheiligtum bei Theben,* I. (Archaeologisches Institut des Deutschen Reiches.) Berlin, 1940.

Kittel	Gerhard Kittel. *Theologisches Wörterbuch zum Neuen Testament*. Stuttgart, 1932–38.
Kraus, *Realencykl*	F. X. Kraus. *Realencyklopädie der Christlichen Alterthümer*. Freiburg i.B., 1882–86.
LCL	Loeb Classical Library. Cambridge, Mass. (orig. New York) and London.
Migne, *PL* and *PG*	J. P. Migne, ed. *Patrologiae cursus completus*. *PL* = Latin Series. Paris, 1844–64. 221 vols. *PG* = Greek Series. Paris, 1857–66. 166 vols.
OF	*Orphicorum fragmenta*, ed. Otto Kern. Berlin, 1922.
Otto	J. C. T. von Otto. *Corpus apologetarum Christianorum saeculi secundi*. Jena, 1876.
Pauly-Wissowa	*Paulys Real-Encyclopädie der Classischen Altertumswissenschaft*. Begun by Georg Wissowa, ed. by Wilhelm Kroll. Stuttgart, 1894–. Refs. are to columns.
Preller-Robert	Ludwig Preller. *Griechische Mythologie*, 4th edn., revised by Carl Robert. Berlin, 1894–1928. 2 vols.
PW	See Pauly-Wissowa.
Roscher, *Lexikon*	W. H. Roscher. *Ausführliches Lexikon der griechischen und römischen Mythologie*. Leipzig, 1884–1936. 6 vols. Refs. are to columns.
SBE	*Sacred Books of the East*, ed. by Friedrich Max Müller. Oxford, 1879–1910. 50 vols.
ZKT	*Zeitschrift für katholische Theologie*. Innsbruck.
ZNW	*Zeitschrift für die neutestamentliche Wissenschaft*. Giessen.

INDEX

INDEX

Reference to a text figure is indicated by an asterisk after the page number. With a plate reference, the page it follows is indicated in parentheses, preceded by *f*.

INDEX

Cumont, Franz, 67, 142&*n*, 208*n*, 209, 217*n*, 224*n*, 225, 226, 293*n*, 340, 368*n;* quoted, 109*n*, 110*n*, 114, 209*n*, 225*n*, 226*n*, 348, 368
cupids, 197
cure, striving for, 7
Curtis, Monica, 274*n*
custom, forces of, 153; "invention" of, 291
Cybele, 16, 109, 110*n*, 250, 254, 256, 257, 258, 296, 341
Cyprian, Pseudo-, quoted, 190, 382, 383
Cyprian, St., 262*n*, 266, 279&*n*
Cyprus, 235*n*, 254
Cyril of Alexandria, St., 379; quoted, 354, 392–93
Cyril of Jerusalem, St., 262*n*, 266, 352, 392*n;* quoted, 374, 375*n*
Cyrus the Great, king of Persia, 170
Cyzicus, 34*n*

D

Dacia, 253
dadophores, 292
daduchos, 104
daemons, 72, 88, 89, 111, 202, 216&*n*, 224; good, 220; vegetation, 319, 320
daēnā, 159*n*
Daillé, Jean, 261*n*
Daktyloi, 48
Damascius, 208, 210
Damascus Chalice, 319
damnation, 23
Danäus, 132
dance, 10, 27, 33, 38, 78, 101, 102, 127, 175, 244; round, of Christ, 169, 174–76, 179, 180, 182, 186, 188, 191–92; sun, 28
Dante Alighieri, 213, 235; *Paradiso,* 386; *Purgatorio,* 386
Danube River, 61
Daremberg, C., 243*n*
darkness, 34, 41, 43, 65, 98, 99, 102, 111, 259, 279; creatures of, 144; and death, 99; and light, 23, 26, 27, 38, 39–40, 71, 81, 95, 167*n*, 179, 185,

295, 298, 317, 363, 371, 394, 398, 399, "outer," 111, 218&*n;* Spirit of, 148
Darmesteter, James, 140&*n*
dating, of mysteries, 100
daughter, and mother, 16, 18, 29, 54, 81
David, 308, 393
dawn, 47, 58
day(s), 98, 215, 219; holy, 29; lucky and unlucky, 122
dea, earth as, 113
dead, the, ashes of, 95, 113&*n;* burial of, 80; and Demeter, 16, 20, 21; feasts of, 263, 268, 271–73; Pl. IVb (*f265*); funeral rites of, 27, 120–21, 129–31, 133; gods of, 350; judges of, 76; judgment of, 86, 88, 89, 90, 111, 147, 297*n;* medallions for, 212; Orphic, 212&*n;* Osiris and, 121; Persephone and, 17, 19, 20, 21, 29–30; prayers for, 271–72; and Zagreus, 74
Dea Syria, 109
death, 15, 16, 30, 65, 80, 99, 101*n*, 137, 212*n*, 246, 263; Aeon as, 229*n;* of beloved, 16; birth and, 20, 99; and darkness, 99; dealing, 59; fear of, 6; and fertility, 20, 29; and generation, 20; and godhead, 113; and growth of grain, 20, 350; happiness after, 21, 23; as illusion, 177; life after, 4, 5, 21, 23, 88, 95, 123, 129–31, 138, 158–59, 272, 348, 350, 401; life and, 20, 29, 65, 76, 95, 350; and man, 5–6, 20–21, 30, 95; and marriage, 40–41; and primordial mother, 113*n*–14*n*, 314; and procreation, 20–21, 82; and resurrection, 16, 17, 24–25, 27, 123, 341, 342, 350, 371, 392, 400; and striking of gongs, 27; terrors of, 23, 290; victory in, 5–6, 375
decision, mystery of, 399
decisions, man and his, 65
Deden, D., 356*n*
deed, sacred, 47
definitions, importance of, 32
Defrémery, C., 162*n*
Deidamia, 241*n*
deification, and suffering, 176, 185–86
deipnon, 275, 276, 277, 295

434

INDEX

life (*continued*)
58–59, 83; spirits, 59; spiritual, 11, 137; as suffering, 80; supernatural, 5; transition from animal to human, 14; tree of, 304, 380, 381–87, 395, 396; "true," 153; vegetative, 139; virtue in, 88; and water, 102*n;* and winds, 232
light, 47, 69*n*, 71, 111, 189, 200, 211, 224, 233, 246, 247, 350, 396, 399; Christ as, 228&*n;* cross of, 180–81, 192, 193; and darkness, 23, 26, 27, 38, 39–40, 71, 81, 95, 167*n*, 179, 185, 295, 298, 317, 363, 371, 394, 398, 399; ecstasy and, 234; God and, 148, 234–35, 401; Man of, 317; and Mazdaism, 144, 148; mystery of, 112, 219&*n*–20, 396, 401; soul and, 112; spirit of, 220; torch-, *see* torch
light-substance, 329
lightning, 73, 209, 214, 215
Ligurians, 61&*n*, 62*n*
like and unlikeness, 150
lime, in Orphic rites, 77
Linas, Charles de, 248*n*, 249&*n*, 250, 252, 253–58, 259; quoted, 253–54, 257–58
Linus, 230
lion, 207, 208, 210, 246, 250, 254, 255, 259, 298&*n*, 301
Lion of Corfu, 72*n*
Lippmann, E. O., 298*n*
Lipsius, R. A., 169*n*, 173, 178*n*
liquefactio, 300
"literary" mysteries, 338, 349, 351
literature, alchemical, 293, 312; early Christian, 374; Greek, 170–71; mystical, 111
Liturgia Caelestis, 260; Pl. VIII (*f*227)
liturgy (ies), 126, 127, 139, 140, 283; Byzantine, 288, 337, 352, 354, 376; Christian, 261, 271, 275, 290, 332; celestial, 212; Gallican, 283, 390; Greek, 396, 397; Mazdean, 140; Mithras, 349; Mozarabic, 282&*n*, 283, 288; Roman, 376, 386, 397; sacrificial, 140, 143; Syrian, 395; Yasna, 140

Livadia, 46
loaves, and eucharist, 231–32; multiplication of, 263, 264–66, 267, 268, 269, 271; Pl. I (*f*265)
Lobeck, Christian August, 339; *Aglaophamus*, 48*n*, 339
local genius, 216
Locarno, 60*n*
logic, 90
logike thysia, 174, 176
logos/Logos, 71, 205, 206, 353; and Christ, 177, 179, 180, 182–83, 186, 193, 231, 289, 301, 304, 328, 342, 343, 372, 374, 385; in Gnosticism, 174, 177, 179, 180, 181, 230, 231; and God, 177, 182–83, 186, 193, 301; Incarnate, 289, 337; Melchisedec and, 276; "mystery of the," 380; and *mythos*, 87, 206; Phanes as, 209*n;* and soul, 186; spirit and, 177, 181
loincloth, 251, 252
Loisy, Alfred, 341; *Les Mystères payens et le mystère chrétien*, 341, quoted, 341
Lommatzsch, C. H. E., 392*n*
Lommel, Herman, 141&*n*
London, 252
Longpérier, A. de, 250*n*
Lord's Supper, 174, 176, 177, 191, 231, 262, 268, 271, 275, 352, 363
loss, and sacrifice, 322
Lot-Borodine, M., quoted, 375–76
Louvre, 250*n*
Lovatelli Urn, 38*n*
love, 11, 13, 16, 90–91, 136, 140, 152, 290, 329; Christ and, 139, 302, 361; God of, 334; play, 43; secret, 101, 114
Loyola, St. Ignatius of, *see* Ignatius
loyalties, conflicting, 325
Lubac, Henri de, 387*n*
Lucian, Greek satirist, 52*n*, 100, 254*n*
Lucian the Martyr, 96
Lucina, tomb of, 264*n*, 267
luck, 122
Luke, St., Gospel According to, *see* Bible s.v. New Testament
luminosity, 5, 82, 153, 167*n*
Luna, 101*n*, 305
Lundberg, Per, 394*n*, 400

450

religion(s) (*continued*)
14–31, 93–104; and Gnosis, 145; of
grace, 8–13; Greek and Hellenistic-
Roman, 93, 114; Hellenistic universal,
218–19; hereditary, 104&*n*–5; Hesiodic, 66; history of, 32; Homeric,
64–66; of Iran, 135, 140–48; Islamic,
149–68; Mazdean, 4, 140, 141, 143–48;
mysterization of, 348; and mysticism,
32–33; and natural science, 108; of
nature, 37; pagan and Christian,
337–401; and philosophy, 106, 348;
and poetry, 138; psychology and, 5;
and reason, 4, 151; of redemption, 33,
74, 105, 361; repression of, 97; of
salvation, 3–8, 9, 11, 106, 112, 135,
143–44, 336, 337, 358; secrecy of, 37–
38; state, 109; and structure of society, 136–37; universal, 104–5
remembrance, thought as, 89–90
Renaudot, Eusèbe, quoted, 271*n*
renewal, by changing wigs, 297*n*, 308;
by flaying, 296
Reni, Guido, *Crucifixion*, 293
renunciation, 7, 324–25
repentance, 76, 83, 145, 303*n*
repression, of religion, 97
repristination, 329
resignation, 24
restoration, of myths, 139
resurrectio, 288
resurrection, 56, 130, 178, 193, 279, 286,
289, 293, 307, 327, 362, 398; death
and, 16, 17, 24–25, 27, 123, 313, 341,
342, 350, 371, 392, 400; transcending
intellect as, 153; and true life, 153
Resurrection, 261
retribution, 76, 77, 78, 83, 84, 85, 86,
88, 89, 90
Revelation, *see* Bible s.v. New Testament
revelation, 4, 5, 6, 9–10, 25, 66, 97, 138,
139–40, 148, 160*n*, 277, 301, 345–46;
and cognition, 24, 136; God and, 346;
of gods, 10, 11; and grace, 10–11;
man and, 345–46; mystery of, 358–60,
371, 380–87; and the practical, 136;
"secret," 357–58

revolution, Dionysian, 66–67, 80, 105*n*
Reybekiel, W. von, 382*n*
Rhadamanthus, 86
Rhamnusia, 254
rhapsodists, Ionian, 65
Rharus, 15, 25
rheitoi, 81
Rhine, Joseph Banks, 329*n*
rhinoceros, 334
rhomboi, 59
Richard of St. Victor, 375*n*
Richardson, C. C., 207*n*, 377*n*
riches, of Christ, 97, 103, 104; of Pluto,
17, 81, 99, 103
Rig-Veda, 326*n*
ring, magic, 222
Ripley, George, 300*n*, 301*n*
rishis, 9
rites, 136, 233, 236, 259; of amphidromia, 240; of Aztecs, 291–92; baptismal, 347, 387–400; bathing, 40, 81,
101&*n*–2&*n*, 371, 388; beauty of, 315;
Brahman, 8–9, 13; Christian, 140,
173, 174, 188, 261, 262&*n*, 263, 341,
363, 364; of closing the eye, 39, 40,
94; Eleusinian, 14–15, 21–31, 45, 52,
81–82, 94–95&*n*, 101–3; eucharistic,
231–32; and feeling, 350–51; fertility,
296, 349; funeral, 27, 120–21, 129–31,
133; of Haloa, 100–101; hunting,
319*n*; "invention" of, 291; Kabeiroi,
45, 47; of Kore mysteries, 238–40;
lustral, 388; magical aspect of, 315;
of Mithraism, 142, 143, 292–93; of
mystery of the Ka'ba, 161&*n*, 166,
167; and myth, 341; of ordeal, 146,
147; Orphic, 76, 77–78, 82, 211–12;
of Osiris, 124–31, 132–33, 240; of
primitive peoples, 22, 25, 30, 95, 114,
319, 335; of protection, 41; of sea
bath, 40, 81, 101&*n*–2&*n*; secret, 98–
100; of Serapis, 108; of serpent bowl,
231–32; solemnity of, 95*n*, 96*n*; of
soul and, 102*n*; sound and, 350; and
spirit, 167–68; of transformation, in
the Mass, 278–90, 322
Ritter, Hellmut, 152*n*, 155*n*
ritual, cults, 4, 21, 138, 139; of the Mass,

INDEX

séances, shaman's, 146, 147
seasons, 203, 215, 219, 220, 223, 225;
and winds, 225&n–26
Seaton, R. C., 206n
Second Coming, 284, 289
secrecy, and Christianity, 140, 173, 261,
357–58, 370; in mysteries, 30, 37–38,
41–42, 47, 48, 55, 77, 94, 95&n, 96n,
98, 103, 111, 114, 117, 125n, 136,
138, 148, 351
secret, discipline of the, 261, 354, 365;
of king, 357–58
seed, 17, 19, 22, 71, 193, 208; cross as,
181; of God, 11, 186, 188, 233; as
word of God, 96
seeing, 152
Seeliger, K., 72n, 78n
seemly, devotion to the, 85
seer, 81, 91, 94
Selene, 100, 102, 116, 224n, 372
Seler, Eduard, 296n
Seleucia, 107
self, 5, 324, 327n, 332; and atman, 10;
birth of, 331; and collective morality,
325; and consciousness, 164, 166, 328,
329; of cosmos, 162–63; and Divine,
326; and ego, 324, 326–27; "event"
in, 115; expansion of, 7; human and
cosmic, 164–65; integration of, 325,
327–28, 329; manifestation of, 327,
328; and public opinion, 325; renunciation of, 5; supremacy of, 324;
transcendent, 156–57&n, 158; and
unconscious, 324, 325, 326, 328; as
union of opposites, 326
self-consciousness, 152–53
self-encounter, 74, 156–58, 162, 166, 168
self-examination, 322
self-knowledge, 156, 157n, 322
self-oblation, 314
self-recollection, 327, 328n, 329
self-renunciation, 323
self-restraint, 347
self-sacrifice, 277, 290, 293, 316, 322,
324, 326, 330; unconscious, 327
self-surrender, 322
Selincourt, Aubrey de, 126n
Semele, 75

semen, 304; *Dei*, 11
semicinctum, 251
Semites, 48
Sendivogius, Michael, quoted, 321n
Sen-nezem, 296n, 297n
senses, closing of, in mysteries, 94, 153
sensibility, 139
Sentinum mosaic, of Helios as Aeon,
226; Pl. IV (*f*194)
separating and combining, 312
separatio, 301
Septeria, 34n
Septerion, 34n
Septuagint, 93, 96&n, 141, 358
Serapeion, 108
Serapis, cult of, 104, 106–8
Sermon on the Mount, 270–71
sermons, 262
serpens mercurialis, 303, 304
serpent, 208, 210, 211, 212, 213, 214,
215–24, 229, 230, 231, 232, 301, 317,
379, 381; celestial, 217–18, 220, 224,
233; Christ as, 229n, 230, 231, 297;
on Cross, 297; and fate, 191; God as
sun, 233; as godhead, 245; mystery
of the, 194–260; worship, 233–45
serpent bowl, alabaster, 194–260; Pls. I &
II (*f*194); inscription on, 197–215;
ritual of, 231–32; serpent and four
winds on, 215–32
Serpent Stone (Weimar), 216&n, 217*
servant of God, 244–45
service, divine, 93–94
servitude, of action, 7; and birth, 6–7
Servius Marius Honoratus, quoted,
102n
Sesostris III, king of Egypt, 124&n
Sesto Fiorentino, 272
Set, *see* Seth
Seth (Adam's son), 384
Seth (Egyptian god), 120&n, 121&n,
122–23, 127, 128, 129
Sethe, Kurt, 121n, 124n, 127n
Sethites, 230
seven, number, 268
Severus, house of, 110
sexes, union of, 371
sexuality, and shame, 138

467

INDEX

470

X

Y

Z